# A BIBLIOGRAPHY OF BRITISH COLUMBIA

# A BIBLIOGRAPHY OF BRITISH COLUMBIA

## LAYING THE FOUNDATIONS 1849-1899

by Barbara J. Lowther B.A. B.L.S.

*with the assistance of* Muriel Laing B.A. B.L.S.

Prepared Under the Auspices of the Social Sciences Research Centre, University of Victoria

Published by the University of Victoria, Victoria, British Columbia

# FOREWORD

In 1965 the Centennial Committee of the University of Victoria agreed to sponsor the preparation and publication of a bibliography of British Columbia. The need for it was obvious and long standing. Further, the University has had a long and fruitful association with the major source of British Columbiana at the Provincial Library and Archives located only a few miles away.

The production of the work was placed under the supervision and administration of a group formed at the University in 1964 to encourage research and writing in the social sciences of British Columbia, i.e., the Social Sciences Research Committee. Initially the services and funds available to the committee served to get the bibliography well launched, but it soon became apparent that additional funds must be found to carry the project through. The committee wishes to express its sincere appreciation to The Canada Council for two grants totalling $7,500 which it made in 1966-67, and to the Leon and Thea Koerner Foundation for $1,500 in 1965-66. Without this financial assistance this volume would have been far more difficult to produce despite the assistance and encouragement from the University.

Shortly after the project was approved a meeting was held to consider and define the scope of the bibliography. Mr. D. W. Halliwell, Mr. W. E. Ireland, Dr. Samuel Rothstein, Mr. R. D. Hilton-Smith, Dr. R. H. Roy and the bibliographer, Mrs. Barbara Lowther discussed the work to be done. It was apparent that the number of items to be included were far greater than at first expected. As a result it was suggested that the bibliography should consist of three volumes. One would cover the period from the early discoveries to 1848, one would deal with the 1849-1899 era and the third would include those works relating to this century.

The committee has been most fortunate in securing the services of Mrs. Barbara Lowther to undertake the task of completing the first volume. The form of the bibliographic entry has been her responsibility, and indeed the committee has drawn heavily on her past editorial experience in each stage of the preparation of the book. Her professional ability speaks for itself.

Reginald H. Roy, Ph.D.
Associate Professor of History and Chairman, Social Sciences Research Centre

University of Victoria, Victoria, British Columbia, December 1967

# PREFACE

Work on this volume of *A bibliography of British Columbia* was begun in June of 1965 when I was employed by the Social Sciences Research Centre of the University of Victoria to undertake its compilation. A Bibliographic Committee under the chairmanship of the University Librarian, Mr. Dean Halliwell, was already in existence. During the first two months of the project the form that the bibliography was to take was established.

The committee decided that the first volume should have as its subject commencement date the year 1849, the beginning of settlement on Vancouver Island, and should cover the first fifty years of the province's history. It was decided that the bibliography should list published material relating to the province from 1849 to 1899 in chronological order by imprint date, and should include works published up to the year 1964 that were concerned with the period of coverage. It was the committee's opinion that the entries in the bibliography should be more informative than those found in a card catalogue; that it should include significant general books, books with relevant chapters or sections, and serials; and that it should be annotated, particularly in cases where the titles of the entries were not descriptive of their content. Although librarians, book dealers, and private collectors undoubtedly will make use of the bibliography, it was envisaged as being primarily for the use of the student doing research at the independent level.

Under the broad term "published material" are included mimeographed works, microforms, and materials to do with trials. Though the latter were printed for expediency rather than for public distribution, they are of interest because they are the product of the province's presses. Every effort was made to list catalogued British Columbia imprints from the beginning of printing in the province in 1858 to the end of 1899. Although they have undoubted historical value, it was not practical to list uncatalogued material — single issues of printed programmes, play bills, menus, and the like. Before starting the bibliography, I saw a proclamation by Governor James Douglas in pamphlet form which may be earlier than the one described by Douglas McMurtrie in his *The earliest British Columbia imprint* (Chicago, 1931). Unfortunately it has not been entered in this bibliography, but it is worthy of mention because it emphasizes that in the field of bibliography there are always new discoveries to be made, and that within certain set limits completeness, though it may be the aim, is an almost impossible goal.

Every effort was made to include the government publications of the two colonies of Vancouver Island and British Columbia and, after their union in 1866, of the united colony of British Columbia to 1871, the year of British Columbia's union with Canada. Government publications after this date are to be found in Marjorie Holmes' *Publications of the government of British Columbia, 1871-1947* (Victoria, 1950), or in her *Royal commissions and commissions of inquiry . . . in British Columbia; a checklist* (Victoria, 1945), both indispensable works to the student doing historical research. If a British Columbia government document was noticed as being accessioned by the Provincial Archives after 1950, it was entered in the bibliography, but not every document found was checked in *Publications of the government of British Columbia, 1871-1947* for its inclusion therein. A few important publications listed by Miss Holmes, such as the relevant Provincial Archives memoirs, are listed in the bibliography for two reasons: their exclusion would leave a gap in completeness, and the student might not at first be aware that this type of material could be found in her work.

Fiction, poetry, and drama, especially when contemporary, are obvious sources for anyone trying to recapture the atmosphere of the earlier days of settlement in British Columbia. In this field of selection, the Social Sciences Research Centre was fortunate to have the services of Miss Muriel Laing to sort through hundreds of books and pamphlets classified as literature in the Dewey classification. Although Miss Laing visited the Victoria Public Library, the bulk of her work was undertaken in the Provincial Archives under circumstances that may be moderately described as difficult. If the volume was not a British Columbia imprint published before 1900, the selection was made on the basis of the text's relevancy to British Columbia during the period. No attempt was made to list works of "British Columbia writers," so that poetry, therefore, written by someone living in British Columbia between 1859-1899, but published in England and not offering a description of British Columbia, would be excluded.

Offprints of periodical articles are entered in the bibliography. When there was doubt as to whether or not a particular article was separately issued or was an author's edition it was also included. The transactions of the Royal Society of Canada were listed only if they were found separately catalogued. Its *Proceeding and transactions,* which first appeared in 1883, are therefore a further source of information on such topics as annexation, boundary disputes, and British Columbia's Indian population.

The publications of the Geological Survey of Canada were excluded because such a large number deal wholly or in part with British Columbia, and because they are well indexed. The student is referred to its *Report of progress,* published from 1845 to 1885, and its *Report,* published from 1886 to 1907, containing reports which describe not only the province's geography, geology, climate, and resources, but also its animal life, native population, and economic activity. Studies on British Columbia fossils appear in *Contributions to Canadian palaeontology,* published from 1885 to 1911. A useful bibliography by A. G. Johnston, which also lists indexes, appeared in 1961 as *Index of publications of the Geological Survey of Canada (1845-1958).*

The serials included in the bibliography are mainly those published in the province before 1900, and comprise the main entries for journals, annual reports, yearbooks, and directories. As the Provincial Archives planned to publish its own list, no attempt was made to include newspapers, except for those government gazettes which began in the colonial period. An exception to the imprint-before-1900 criterion was made for scholarly periodicals on Pacific Northwest history and for reports of the Columbia Mission. It was originally planned to list other serials — more general ones having occasional articles on British Columbia. The length of the serial entries, their number, and their complexity weighed against their inclusion in this volume.

The annual reports of various Canadian government departments contain a wealth of information on early British Columbia. They appear, or are reprinted in, the *Sessional papers of the Parliament of Canada* from 1867 to 1925. Many annual reports were also issued separately. The Department of the Interior issued reports from 1874 to 1936. At various times before 1900, this department included important branches of the government that were concerned with affairs in the West. The Department of Militia and Defence issued annual reports for the years 1868 to 1922. The reports of the Department of Public Works were usually issued separately and before 1900 included information on railways which, in 1880 and subsequently, appeared in the reports of the Department of Railways and Canals. This latter department also published annual *Railway statistics* to 1920. The Department of Marine and Fisheries, which was separated into two departments for the period 1885 to 1891, issued annual reports from 1868. Early reports from the Department of Agriculture include information on immigration, the census, and health; later reports also have information on the development of the province's agriculture. The Dominion Bureau of Statistics publishes the decennial *Census of Canada,* which contains many types of subject statistics in addition to demographic information. Indian affairs were under the administration of the Department of Crown Lands from 1860 to 1867, the Department of the Secretary of State from 1868 to 1872, and the Department of the Interior from 1873 to 1879. The independent Department of Indian Affairs, organized in 1880, lasted until 1936. Other annual reports the student might examine include those of the Departments of Trade and Commerce, Public Printing and Stationery, Justice, the Secretary of State, and the Post Office.

Contemporary accounts by missionaries not only outline their activities, but describe gold rushes, Indians, and many other aspects of life in early British Columbia. To mention but a few periodicals which contain reports and letters from British Columbia missionaries, there are the Church of England Church Missionary Society's publication, *Church missionary intelligencer,* the *Missionary notices* of the Methodist Church of Canada, the *Baptist year book, Les missions catholiques,* and *Missions de la congregation des missionaires Oblats de Marie Immaculée.*

Many anthropological, geographical, and geological associations published reports of work undertaken in British Columbia in their journals and proceedings. Of particular interest, especially for the colonial period, are the descriptions of Vancouver Island, the Queen Charlotte Islands, and the mainland to be found in the publications of the Royal Geographical Society, London, notably in its *Journal* (1831-1880), the *Proceedings of the Royal Geographical Society* (1855-1878), and the *Proceedings of the Royal Geographical Society and monthly record of geography* (1879-1892). The reports of explorations made by Robert Brown, William Downie, Richard Mayne, and Henry Palmer, and a description of Vancouver Island in 1857 by its first colonist, Walter C. Grant, along with many other accounts, may be found in these sources. Contemporary Canadian scientific and technical publications also reflect interest in the province. For example, substantial articles on the development of mining can be found in the *Canadian mining review* (which later became the *Canadian mining journal*).

As can be seen from the examples of publications listed above, contemporary serials are numerous. This can also be said of the periodicals which publish retrospective, historical articles. A thorough search for information on the province between 1849 and 1899 should include consideration of the varied serial sources.

Selection on the basis of subject offered few problems. As far as the Klondike gold rush is concerned, only those publications which either describe passage through portions of the province, or which promoted it, are included. Publications dealing with that small portion of the province entered by way of the Chilkoot Pass and offering no further description of British Columbia, were found to be too numerous to list.* Books and pamphlets concerned with the Canadian Pacific Railway are included if they relate to its construction in British Columbia, or to federal government policy regarding construction. The Alaskan boundary dispute is treated in its entirety, although it was not settled until the award of 1903. Works in the various Indian languages spoken within the province, and publications dealing with anthropology, are entered if they were published prior to 1900.**

As has already been stated, the arrangement of the bibliography is chronological by date of imprint. Within the division by year, the arrangement is alphabetical by main entry. In the few cases where the date of publication was not found, or closely approximated, the work is listed in the most likely year of publication, determined by the subject content and the clues offered by typography, book design, the name of the press, etc. With few exceptions, all entries are for first editions, with a note being made for subsequent appearances. Edition or reprint notes are varied and not always exhaustive. No attempt was made to list editions beyond those found in the libraries visited and the bibliographies consulted. The cut-off date for listing edition imprints is 1964.

When the details for an entry were obtained from bibliographies, the information given has been as full as these sources would allow. Occasionally it was possible to combine the information obtained from card catalogues, bibliographies, and research in the Provincial Archives to give a more complete entry. The last line of the entry designates the location of the publication or the source from which the entry was made. Although a publication may be in various libraries, only the library at which the publication was first examined, or from which the most complete information was obtained, is given as a location.

In the author entry that part of the author's name not appearing in the book is enclosed in brackets. Brackets in all other cases enclose letters, words, and dates not appearing on the title page.

The bibliography was compiled in several stages. I spent the first fourteen months selecting publications from approximately 34,000 books and pamphlets in the Provincial Archives and making bibliographic entries for them. The collection in the Archives is not limited to works on British Columbia, but extends to those relating to California, Oregon, Washington, Alaska, and western Canada, which makes it a rich source for this type of bibliography, particularly as the card catalogue lists analytics, including important chapters. After the bulk of entries had been obtained in this way, I visited the National Library to use a bibliography entitled "Canadiana 1867-1900" which was being compiled for publication. At the time of my visit in the fall of 1966, cards for

---

* The bibliography of Pierre Berton's *Klondike . . .* (Toronto, 1958) is a good source for further information on various aspects of the gold rush.

** This bibliography has accepted the names for Indian ethnic divisions, languages, and dialects used by Wilson Duff in the first volume of *The Indian History of British Columbia* (Victoria, 1964).

some 25,000 entries had been obtained from numerous sources, including the Library of Parliament, the Public Archives of Canada, the union catalogue in the National Library, and *A catalog of books represented by Library of Congress printed cards* (New York, 1958-60) and its first supplement. "Canadiana 1867-1900" yielded five hundred books and pamphlets for possible inclusion, nearly all of which were eventually located in Canadian libraries that I visited or were obtained on interlibrary loan. After examination, about half these publications warranted inclusion in the bibliography. I next examined relevant material in the University of British Columbia Library and the Vancouver Public Library. In the spring of 1967 I returned to the University of British Columbia Library to search through the G. K. Hall & Co. reproductions of various library card catalogues, and then visited the University of Washington Library and the Oregon Historical Society Library. During the last stage of the book's compilation I frequently returned to the Provincial Archives and Provincial Library to clarify and and extend entries for which further research was needed.

I should like to thank the members of the Bibliographic Committee for their support and advice throughout the project. Mr. Willard Ireland, Provincial Librarian and Archivist, gave willingly of his time to discuss various bibliographic problems that arose during the time I was examining the Archives' collection. My thanks are also due him for reading the bibliography, partly in manuscript and partly in galley form. Dr. R. H. Roy, whose original idea it was to publish the bibliographies, was involved with this volume more as the chairman of the Social Sciences Research Centre than as a member of the Bibliographic Committee. As chairman of the Centre he was responsible for providing the required facilities, staff, and travelling expenses for the compilation and publication of this volume. Without his successful endeavours to meet the continual demands I put on him in this regard, the bibliography would not have been published.

The obligations which I incurred while working on this volume are too numerous to list in detail. By their helpfulness many librarians in the libraries I visited contributed to its compilation. It will have to suffice if I mention those to whom I am especially indebted.

The librarians and staff of the British Columbia Provincial Archives and Provincial Library frequently assisted Miss Laing and myself. Mr. Dave Mason, Miss Inez Mitchell, Assistant Provincial Archivist, and Dr. Dorothy Blakey Smith were particularly helpful. I owe a special debt of gratitude to Dr. Smith for often lending her research talents in tracking down information that I would have been unable to find unaided. Mrs. Anne Yandle of the Special Collections Division, University of British Columbia Library, offered many suggestions as to various bibliographic sources of value. As can be gathered from this Preface, "Canadiana 1867-1900" played an important part in the volume's compilation. My thanks are due to Mr. Bruce Peel, University Librarian, University of Alberta, Calgary, for guiding me to this source and to Dr. William Kaye Lamb, National Librarian, for allowing me to consult the work while it was still in card form.

As has been previously mentioned, Miss Muriel Laing contributed her professional experience to the selection of publications classified as literature. Her contribution went far beyond these entries, which number nearly one hundred. She had the difficult task of completing the authors' names and finding or verifying their birth and death dates. She also was responsible for gathering the biographical information on the authors which is given in the Index, along with the biographical sources that she consulted. I wish to thank her, not only for her work, but for her devotion to it since September 1965. I should also like to thank Mr. Lance Irvine for his summer's work completing the serial entries and Mr. Nicholas Koerner for his help during the initial stages of compilation.

B. J. L.

University of Victoria Library
December 1967

Libraries, collections, and bibliographies cited after each entry
and referred to in bibliographic description

BANCROFT LIBRARY CATALOGUE

California. University. Bancroft Library. Catalogue of printed books. Boston, G. K. Hall, 1964. 22 v.

BIBLIOTHÈQUE SAINT-SULPICE

Bibliothèque Saint-Sulpice, Montreal. Now called the Province of Quebec's Bibliothèque Nationale.

B.C. ARCHIVES

Provincial Archives of British Columbia, Victoria.

B.C. PROVINCIAL LIBRARY

Provincial Library of British Columbia, Victoria.

BRITISH MUSEUM CATALOGUE

British Museum, London. Department of Printed Books. General catalogue of printed books. 1931-66. Supplements.

CANADIAN ARCHIVES

Public Archives of Canada, Ottawa.

COMMONWEALTH OFFICE, LONDON

Colonial Office, Commonwealth Relations Office and Ministry of Overseas Development Joint Library. Entries located in: Great Britain. Colonial Office. Library. Library Catalogue of the Colonial Office Library, London. Boston, G. K. Hall, 1964. 15 v.

DEPARTMENT OF FISHERIES LIBRARY

Department of Fisheries Library, Ottawa.

DEPARTMENT OF NATIONAL DEFENCE LIBRARY

Department of National Defence Library, Ottawa.

EBERSTADT

Eberstadt (Edward) and Sons, New York. The annotated Eberstadt catalogs of americana, numbers 103-138; 1939-1956. Introduction by Archibald Hanna, jr. Index by Karl Brown. New York, Argosy-Antiquarian, 1965. 4 v.

GLENBOW FOUNDATION LIBRARY

Glenbow Foundation Library and Archives, Calgary.

HOLMES

Holmes, Marjorie Colquhoun. Publications of the government of British Columbia, 1871-1947; being a complete revision and enlargement of Publications of the government of British Columbia, 1871-1937, by Sydney Weston. Victoria, King's printer, 1950. 254 p.

LIBRARY, GEOLOGICAL SURVEY OF CANADA

Library, Geological Survey of Canada, Ottawa.

LIBRARY OF CONGRESS

Library of Congress. A catalog of books. Ann Arbor, 1942. Supplements.

LIBRARY OF PARLIAMENT

Library of Parliament, Ottawa. The publications examined were bound as "Canadian pamphlets."

LONDON LIBRARY CATALOGUE

London Library. Catalogue of the London Library, St. James's Square, London, by C. T. Hagberg Wright. London, Williams & Norgate, 1903. xiii, 1626 p. Supplement 1-8, 1904-11 in 8 v.

MCGILL UNIVERSITY. LANDE COLLECTION

McGill University, Montreal. Listed in: McGill University, Montreal. Library. The Lawrence Lande Collection of canadiana . . . a bibliography. Montreal, 1965. xxxv, 301 p.

MCGILL UNIVERSITY LIBRARY

McGill University Library, Montreal.

MANITOBA PROVINCIAL LIBRARY

Manitoba Provincial Library, Winnipeg.

MORICE

Morice, Adrian Gabriel. Dans le champ des lettres canadiennes. Winnipeg, 1936. 109 p.

NATIONAL LIBRARY

National Library of Canada, Ottawa.

NATIONAL LIBRARY BIBLIOGRAPHY

A bibliography compiled by the National Library which has the title "Canadiana 1867-1900." When the bibliographer used it in the fall of 1966, it was in card form and numbered approximately 25,000 entries.

NEWBERRY LIBRARY

Newberry Library, Chicago. Edward E. Ayer Collection. Catalog of the Edward E. Ayer Collection of Americana and American Indians. Boston, G. K. Hall, 1961. 8 v. Vols. 2-8 have title: Dictionary catalog.

NOVA SCOTIA PUBLIC ARCHIVES

Public Archives of Nova Scotia, Halifax.

OREGON HISTORICAL SOCIETY

Oregon Historical Society Library, Portland, Oregon.

PEEL

Peel, Bruce Braden. A bibliography of the prairie provinces to 1953. Toronto, University of Toronto Press, 1956. xix, 680 p. Supplement.

PILLING'S ATHAPASCAN BIBLIOGRAPHY

Pilling, James Constantine. Bibliography of the Athapascan languages. Washington, Government Printing Office, 1892. xii, 125 p. (United States. Bureau of American Ethnology. Bulletin, no. 14)

PILLING'S CHINOOKAN BIBLIOGRAPHY

Pilling, James Constantine. Bibliography of the Chinookan languages (including Chinook jargon). Washington, Government Printing Office, 1893. xiii, 81 p. (United States. Bureau of American Ethnology. Bulletin, no. 15)

PILLING'S SALISHAN BIBLIOGRAPHY

Pilling, James Constantine. Bibliography of the Salishan languages. Washington, Government Printing Office, 1893. xi, 86 p. (United States. Bureau of American Ethnology. Bulletin, no. 16)

QUEEN'S UNIVERSITY LIBRARY

Queen's University Library, Kingston.

SHORTT COLLECTION

Shortt Collection of Canadiana, University of Saskatchewan Library, Saskatoon.

SMITH

Smith, Charles Wesley (compiler). Pacific Northwest americana; a check list of books and pamphlets relating to the history of the Pacific Northwest. Edition 3, revised and extended by Isabel Mayhew. Portland, Ore., Oregon Historical Society, 1950. 381 p.

SOLIDAY

Soliday, George. A descriptive check list, together with short title index, describing almost 7,500 items of western americana; comprising books, maps, and pamphlets of the important library (in four parts) formed by George W. Soliday, Seattle, Wash. Compiled with notes by Peter Decker, 1940-45. New York, Antiquarian Press, 1960. 4 pts. in 1 v. A reprint with corrections. "Peter Decker" is a pseudonym.

TORONTO PUBLIC LIBRARY

Toronto Public Library, Toronto.

UNION CATALOGUE

A catalogue of the holdings of numerous Canadian libraries, kept by the National Library of Canada, Ottawa. Entries given with this location were obtained from the National Library bibliography.

UNITED CHURCH ARCHIVES

United Church of Canada Archives, Toronto.

UNIVERSITY OF TORONTO LIBRARY

University of Toronto Library, Toronto.

U.B.C. SPECIAL COLLECTIONS

Special Collections, University of British Columbia Library, Vancouver.

UNIVERSITY OF VICTORIA LIBRARY

University of Victoria Library, Victoria.

UNIVERSITY OF WASHINGTON LIBRARY

University of Washington Library, Seattle. Most of the publications examined were in Special Collections.

VANCOUVER CITY ARCHIVES

Vancouver City Archives, Vancouver.

VANCOUVER PUBLIC LIBRARY

Vancouver Public Library, Vancouver.

VICTORIA PUBLIC LIBRARY

Victoria Public Library, Victoria.

YALE WESTERN AMERICANA CATALOGUE

Yale University. Library. Catalog of the Yale Collection of Western Americana. Boston, G. K. Hall, 1961. 4 v.

**1 Great Britain. Parliament**

Imperial blue books on affairs relating to Canada. Reports, returns and other papers presented to the Imperial Houses of Parliament of Great Britain and Ireland relating to Canada. London, Arranged and bound by P. S. King & Son [1803-98]

50 v. maps, diagrs. 25, 33, 41 cm. Contents in part: v. 39. British Columbia. — v. 41-42. Hudson's Bay Company, 1819-1857. — v. 45. Boundaries, 1851-1876. — v. 46-48. Behring Sea, 1892-1898.

Volume 39 includes documents relating to British Columbia and Vancouver Island from 1848 to 1889. Some documents in other volumes not mentioned above also relate in part to British Columbia.

B.C. ARCHIVES

**2 Great Britain. Treaties, etc.**

Convention between His Majesty and the Emperor of Russia; signed at St. Petersburgh, February $\frac{28}{16}$, 1825. Presented to both Houses of Parliament by His Majesty's command, May 1825. London, Printed by R. G. Clarke [1825]

6 p. 34 cm. Text in French and English.

Articles III and IV of the treaty set the demarcation line between Russian and British territory in the Pacific Northwest. Their lack of perspicuity led to different interpretations by Great Britain and the United States as to where the boundary line between Canada and Alaska should be drawn.

B.C. ARCHIVES

**3 Bonnycastle, Sir Richard Henry**
1791-1847

Canada and the Canadians in 1846. London, Henry Colburn, 1846.

2 v. 21 cm.

Volume 1, page 138, contains an early reference to the desirability of a railway to the Pacific.

New edition: London, Henry Colburn, 1849. 2 v.

B.C. PROVINCIAL LIBRARY

**4 Fitzgerald, James Edward**
1818-1896

Proposal for the formation of a colony in Vancouver's Island on the west coast of North America (for private circulation) [London, 1847]

4 p. 19 cm. Caption title.

A prospectus calling for capital to establish a company that would colonize the Island.

B.C. ARCHIVES

**5 Fitzgerald, James Edward**
1818-1896

Vancouver's Island, the Hudson's Bay, and the government. London, Simmonds & Co., Colonial publishers, 1848.

30 p. 21 cm. Reprinted from the *Colonial magazine* for September 1848.

Discusses House of Commons paper 619 of 1848 which requested a return for "Copy of correspondence between the chairman of the Hudson's Bay Company and the Secretary of State for the Colonies relative to the colonization of Vancouver's Island" (entry 7). Fitzgerald was a staunch critic of the Colonial Office policy of entrusting colonization to the company.

OREGON HISTORICAL SOCIETY

**6 Fitzgerald, James Edward**
1818-1896

Vancouver's Island, the new colony. Reprinted from the "Colonial magazine" for August 1848. London, Simmonds & Co., 1848.

16 p. 22 cm.

The author voiced the opinion that Vancouver Island's strategic location made it too important a possession to be left to the Hudson's Bay Company's colonization method.

B.C. ARCHIVES

**7 Great Britain. Colonial Office**

Vancouver's Island. Return . . . "Copy of correspondence between the chairman of the Hudson's Bay Company and the Secretary of State for the Colonies, relative to the colonization of Vancouver's Island." Ordered by the House of Commons to be printed, 10 August 1848. [London, 1848]

17 p. 33 cm. ([Great Britain. Parliament, 1848. House of Commons papers] 619)

B.C. ARCHIVES

**8 [Martin, Robert Montgomery]**
1803?-1868

The Hudson's Bay territories and Vancouver's Island, with an exposition of the chartered rights, conduct, & policy of the Hon$^{ble}$ Hudson's Bay Corporation. London [Printed by T. Brettell] 1848.

vii, 172 p. 1 illus. 22 cm.

In support of the company's policy. Written in part: "To inquire into the qualifications of the Hudson's Bay Company for the colonization of Vancouver's Island."—p. iv. In a letter to William Gladstone, dated 27 November 1848, James Fitzgerald made the comment: "The whole turn of the book is sufficient evidence that the Company's purse has stimulated the authors [sic] brains."—*British Columbia historical quarterly*, v. 13, p. 11. Also see entry 12.

Another edition of this work was published in 1849 by T. W. Boone, London (printed by T. Brettell). The 1849 edition of 175 pages has folding map, errata and addenda, and additional material on the Red River Settlement following Appendix D.

B.C. ARCHIVES

## 9     Monteagle [of Brandon, Thomas Spring Rice]
### 1ST BARON   1790-1866

Colonization of Vancouver's Island; substance of the speech of the Lord Monteagle, in the House of Lords, Thursday, August 24, 1848. Extracted from Hansard's parliamentary debates. [London, George Woodfall and Son] 1848.

15 p.   18 cm.

A censure of government policy with respect to the granting of Vancouver Island to the Hudson's Bay Company.

B.C. ARCHIVES

## 10     Synge, Millington Henry
### 1823-1907

Canada in 1848; being an examination of the existing resources of British North America, with considerations for their further and more perfect development, as a practical remedy, by means of colonisation, for the prevailing distress in the united empire, and for the defence of the colony. London, Effingham Wilson [1848?]

32, vii p.   21 cm.

In order that British North America be secured, Synge advocated a railway to the Pacific.

U.B.C. SPECIAL COLLECTIONS

## 11     Colonization ...

Colonization of Vancouver's Island.   London, Printed for Burrup and Son, 1849.

28 p.   22 cm.   Cover title.

Written to encourage emigrants to obtain land from the Hudson's Bay Company for settlement, the work outlines conditions of land purchase and quotes published sources as to the suitability of Vancouver Island for colonization.

B.C. ARCHIVES

## 12     Fitzgerald, James Edward
### 1818-1896

An examination of the charter and proceedings of the Hudson's Bay Company, with reference to the grant of Vancouver's Island.   London, Trelawney Saunders, 1849.

xv, 293 p.   double map.   18 cm.

A reply to Robert Martin's *The Hudson's Bay territories and Vancouver's Island* (entry 8) in which Fitzgerald vigorously attacked the policies of the Hudson's Bay Company.

B.C. ARCHIVES

## 13     Great Britain. Colonial Office

Vancouver's Island. Copies and extracts of despatches and other papers relating to Vancouver's Island; also, copies of charter of grant of that island to the Hudson's Bay Company, with correspondence thereon; and report of committee of Privy Council for trade on the grant. Ordered by the House of Commons to be printed, 7 March 1849.   [London, 1849]

20, [2] p.   34 cm.   ([Great Britain. Parliament, 1849. House of Commons papers] 103 )   Title from p. [22] Returns to three addresses of the House of Commons, dated respectively, 16 August 1848, 6 February 1849, and 1 March 1849. Census of the Indian tribes in the Oregon Territory, from latitude 42° to latitude 54°: p. 9-10.

B.C. ARCHIVES

## 14     Great Britain. Foreign Office

Vancouver's Island. Warrant to prepare letters patent under the great seal for appointing Richard Blanshard, Esq., to be governor and commander-in-chief in and over the island of Vancouver and its dependencies.   [London] Printed at the Foreign Office, 1849.

8 p.   33 cm.

B.C. ARCHIVES

## 15     Perils ...

Perils, pastimes, and pleasures of an emigrant in Australia, Vancouver's Island and California. [Edited by J. W.]   London, Thomas Cautley Newby, 1849.

404 p.   21 cm.

A book of letters by an anonymous correspondent in which five pages describe a Vancouver Island visit. In Soliday (pt. 4, item 126) the copy described is called an "Author's autographed copy," and is attributed to "Baywater, J. W."

B.C. ARCHIVES

## 16     Smyth, Robert [Stewart] Carmichael
### 1800?-1888

The employment of the people and the capital of Great Britain in her own colonies, at the same time assisting emigration and penal arrangements by undertaking a great national work; and thus opening the shortest road to the most extensive regions of wealth ever before at the command of any nation in the world (not regions of gold, but for commerce and industry) so that at no future period (within at least the imagination of man) will Great Britain have to complain either of too great a population on her soil, or too small a market for her labour. All this is fully explained in a letter from Major Robert Carmichael-Smyth to his friend the author of "The Clockmaker," containing thoughts on the subject of a British colonial railway communication between the Atlantic and the Pacific, from the magnificent harbour of Halifax, in Nova Scotia (north-eastern America) to the mouth of Frazer's River in New Caledonia (north-western America) or such other port as he may be determined upon.   London, W. P. Metchim, 1849.

vii, 68 p.   fold. map.   22 cm.   Title carries over from p. [i] to p. [iii]; p. [iii] begins: A letter from Major Robert Charmichael-Smyth . . .

Peel lists another issue in 1849 which appeared under title: *A letter to the author of the Clockmaker . . .* In 59 pages, without the author's name.   Second edition: London, Frome, W. C. & J. Penny, 1885. viii, 70 p. In the second edition the preliminary pages with title are reversed; title begins: *A letter from Major Robert Carmichael-Smyth . . .*

B.C. ARCHIVES

## 17   Smyth, Robert [Stewart] Carmichael
### 1800?-1888

The employment of the people and the capital of Great Britain in her own colonies, at the same time assisting emigration, colonization and penal arrangements, by undertaking the construction of a great national railway between the Atlantic and the Pacific, from Halifax harbour, Nova Scotia, to Frazer's River, New Caledonia.   London, W. P. Metchim, 1849.

vii, 75 p.   2 fold. maps, diagr.   22 cm.

B.C. ARCHIVES

## 18   Canadian Land and Railway Association

Report & outline of a plan by which an extensive railway may be constructed in the British North American colonies, combining its execution with an enlarged scheme of colonization and reclamation of waste land, and executing the works so that the company and the emigrants shall be mutually benefited. With a map and plan. London, Printed by J. Bradley, 1850.

52 p.   fold. map, fold. plan.   22 cm.

Comprised of letters from Alexander Doull to the *Morning Chronicle* and to the secretary of the association. One letter has the heading "Continuation of the railway from Quebec to near Vancouver's Island, in the Pacific."

B.C. ARCHIVES

## 19   Smyth, Robert [Stewart] Carmichael
### 1800?-1888

A letter to the Right Honourable Earl Grey, on the subject of transportation and emigration, as connected with an Imperial railway communication between the Atlantic and Pacific.   London, W. P. Metchim, 1850.

27 p.   21 cm.

B.C. ARCHIVES

## 20   Wilson, F. A.

Britain redeemed and Canada preserved, by F. A. Wilson and Alfred B. Richards.   London, Longman, Brown, Green, and Longmans, 1850.

xxx, 556 p.   plates (1 fold.) fold. map.   23 cm.

Proposes elaborate details for the construction of a railway to the Pacific as part of a scheme to decrease the criminal population of the United Kingdom and relieve pauperism.

B.C. ARCHIVES

## 21   . . . Atlantic and Pacific railroad

Imperial Atlantic and Pacific railway. [Advocating as the best line of route "a railway from the Atlantic to the Pacific through the British territory in North America."]   London, Trelawny Saunders, 1851.

4 p.   Not seen.

BRITISH MUSEUM CATALOGUE

## 22   Doull, Alexander

Employment and colonization for the million, based upon a proposed railway communication with the Atlantic to the Pacific in the territories of B.N.A. . . . Read before the British Association for the Advancement of Science at Ipswich, on the 7th July 1851.   London, Canada Land and Railway Association, 1851.

15 p.   Not seen.   A copy is in the Nova Scotia Archives.

PEEL

## 23   Findlay, Alexander G[eorge]
### 1812-1875

A directory for the navigation of the Pacific Ocean; with descriptions of its coasts, islands, etc., from the Strait of Magalhaens to the Arctic Sea, and those of Asia and Australia; its winds, currents and other phenomena. In two parts. Part I: The coasts of the Pacific Ocean.   London, Printed for R. H. Laurie, 1851.

xlvi, 650 p.   fold. map, tables.   25 cm.

B.C. ARCHIVES

**24**    Latham, R[obert] G[ordon]
*1812-1888*

The ethnology of the British colonies and dependencies.    London, John van Voorst, 1851.

vi, 264 p.    17 cm.

Has several pages on Pacific Northwest Indians.

B.C. ARCHIVES

**25**    MacDonell, Allan

A railroad from Lake Superior to the Pacific; the shortest, cheapest and safest communication for Europe with all Asia. Toronto, Printed by Hugh Scobie, 1851.

16 p.    21 cm.    Xerox copy examined. Original in McGill University Library.

Reprinted in *The North-west Transportation, Navigation and Railway Company,* pages [31]-54 (entry 74).

UNIVERSITY OF VICTORIA LIBRARY

**26**    Oregon (Territory)    Legislative Assembly

Memorial of the legislature of Oregon, praying for the extinguishment of the Indian title and the removal of the Indians from certain portions of that Territory; payment of the debt growing out of the recent Indian war . . . purchase of the land held by the Puget Sound Agricultural Society . . . January 6, 1851; referred to the Committee on Territories, January 10, 1851. Bill S. no. 405. Washington, 1851.

6 p.    23 cm.    ([United States] 31st Cong., 2d sess. Senate. Misc. no. 5)    Caption title.

B.C. ARCHIVES

**27**    Broun, Sir Richard
BARONET    *1801-1858*

British and American intercourse; letter to the Rt. Hon. the Earl of Derby, on the Imperial Halifax and Quebec railway and Anglo-Asian steam transit project.    London, Trelawny Saunders, 1852.

30 p.    21 cm.

A request for support from Lord Derby with regard to the incorporation of a company empowered to construct a railway from Halifax to Quebec and to extend communication to the Pacific.

B.C. ARCHIVES

**28**    Doull, Alexander

A project for opening a north-west passage between the Atlantic and Pacific oceans, by means of a railway on British territory; also, outlines of a plan proposed by the Canadian Land & Railway Association, for an extensive system of employment & colonization, in connexion with the railways of British North America.    London, Canadian Land and Railway Association, 1852.

32 p.    21 cm.

B.C. ARCHIVES

**29**    Project . . .

Project for the construction of a railroad to the Pacific through British territories, with report of the committee of the Legislative Assembly of Canada, thereupon, 30th August 1851; to whom was referred after its 2nd reading on the 2nd day of July 1851, the bill authorizing the incorporation of a company with power to construct such road.    Toronto, Printed by Lovell and Gibson, 1852.

36 p.    19 cm.    Not seen. Copy in the Toronto Public Library.

Also published in: Canada. Legislative Assembly. *Journals,* 1851. Appendix UU.

PEEL

**30**    Synge, Millington Henry
*1823-1907*

Great Britain one empire. On the union of the dominions of Great Britain by intercommunication with the Pacific and the East via British North America, with suggestions for the profitable colonization of that wealthy territory. London, John W. Parker and Son, 1852.

124 p.    fold. map.    20 cm.

B.C. ARCHIVES

**31**    Synge, M[illington] H[enry]
*1823-1907*

Proposal for a rapid communication with the Pacific and the East, via British North America. [Read before the Geographical Society of London on January 12 and 26, 1852.    London, Printed by W. Clowes and Son, 1852]

28 p.    fold. map.    23 cm.    Reprinted from: Royal Geographical Society. *Journal.* v. 22, 1852, p. 174-200.

A project involving a transcontinental canal, river, and railroad system. The proposed route in British Columbia was via the Peace River, along part of the Fraser, then westward to what appears to be the head of Dean Channel above Rivers Inlet.

B.C. ARCHIVES

**32**    [Blanchet, Francis Norbert]
*1795-1883*

A comprehensive, explanatory, correct pronouncing dictionary, and jargon vocabulary, to which is added numerous conversations enabling any person to speak the Chinook jargon. Second edition.  Portland, O.T., Published by S. J. M'Cormick, 1853 [c1852]

39 p.   13 cm.   Introduction: p. [5]-23.

The first edition appeared in 1852. Titles of editions vary. The seventh edition was issued in 1879. J. K. Gill compiled the editions subsequent to the seventh (see entry 655). The B.C. Provincial Archives holds the fifth edition which has title: *Dictionary of the Chinook jargon, to which is added numerous conversations, thereby enabling any person to speak Chinook correctly.*

OREGON HISTORICAL SOCIETY

## 33      Great Britain. Colonial Office

Queen Charlotte's Island. Further return . . . "Copies or extracts of correspondence relative to the discovery of gold at Queen Charlotte's Island." Ordered by the House of Commons to be printed, 9 August 1853.  [London, 1853]

12 p.   32 cm.   ([Great Britain. Parliament, 1853. House of Commons papers] 788-1)

B.C. ARCHIVES

## 34      Great Britain. Colonial Office

Queen Charlotte's Island. Return . . . "Copies or extracts of correspondence relative to the discovery of gold at Queen Charlotte's Island." Ordered by the House of Commons to be printed, 19 July 1853.  [London, 1853]

iv, 15 p.   32 cm.   ([Great Britain. Parliament, 1853. House of Commons papers] 788)

B.C. ARCHIVES

## 35      Great Britain. Colonial Office

Vancouver's Island. Return made since 1849 by the Hudson's Bay Company to the Secretary of State for the Colonies, relating to Vancouver's Island. Ordered by the House of Commons to be printed, 23 December 1852. [London, 1853?]

4 p.   33 cm.   ([Great Britain. Parliament, 1852-3. House of Commons papers] 83)   Title from p. 4.

B.C. ARCHIVES

## 36      [Imray, James Frederick]
### 1829?-1891

Sailing directions for the west coast of North America, embracing the coast of Central America, California, Oregon, Fuca Strait, Puget Sound, Vancouver Island, and the islands and rocks off the coasts of Central America and California. With an appendix containing various remarks on the winds, tides, currents, &c.  London, James Imray, 1853.

iv (i.e. vi), 232 p.   illus., tables.   23 cm. Also see entry 310.

B.C. ARCHIVES

## 37      [Lionnet, Jean]

Vocabulary of the jargon or trade language of Oregon.  Washington, Published by the Smithsonian Institution, 1853.

22 p.   Caption title. French, English, and jargon vocabulary, alphabetically arranged by French words.  Not seen. From Pilling's *Chinookan languages,* p. 53.

Pilling attributed this work to a Catholic priest, Père Lionnet, and cited the source of his information as the Preface of George Gibbs' *A Dictionary of the Chinook jargon.*

PILLING'S CHINOOKAN BIBLIOGRAPHY

## 38      Nicolay, Charles Grenfell

A proposal to establish a missionary college on the north-west coast of British America, in a letter to the Right Honourable William Ewart Gladstone . . .  London, Saunders and Stanford, 1853.

28 p.   21 cm.

The college's proposed location was Vancouver Island.

B.C. ARCHIVES

## 39      Anglo-Asian . . .

Anglo-Asian intercourse via Great Britain in the western hemisphere; further exposition of Sir Richard Broun's great scheme for direct Anglo-Asian intercourse by route of British North America, and the monarchical settlement of the vacant territory between the Atlantic and Pacific oceans.  London, Edward Stanford, 1854.

14 p.   20 cm.   At head of text on p. [3]: Anglo-Asian intercourse and monarchical settlement of British North America. Photographed copy examined. Original in the London Library, London.

B.C. ARCHIVES

## 40      Further exposition . . .

Further exposition of Sir Richard Broun's great scheme for direct Anglo-Asian intercourse. London, Ed. Stanford, 1854.

78 p.   Not seen.

LONDON LIBRARY CATALOGUE

## 41      United States. Department of State

Letter from the Secretary of State to the chairman of the Committee on Foreign Relations, communicating the report of Governor Stevens of Washington Territory to the Department of State, of June 21, 1854, relative to the property of the Hudson's Bay and Puget's Sound Company in that Territory.   [Washington, 1855]

22 p.   23 cm.   ([United States] 33d Cong., 2d sess. Senate. Ex. doc. no. 37)   Caption title. Report of Isaac I. Stevens; report of Isaac N. Ebey to Governor Stevens.

B.C. ARCHIVES

## 42   Aborigines' Protection Society

Canada West and the Hudson's Bay Company: a political and humane question of vital importance to the honour of Great Britain, to the prosperity of Canada, and to the existence of the native tribes; being an address to the Right Honourable Henry Labouchere, Her Majesty's principal Secretary of State for the Colonies. With an appendix.   [London] Published for the Society by W. Tweedie, 1856.

19 p.   21 cm.

Relates in part to territory west of the Rocky Mountains.

B.C. ARCHIVES

## 43   Buschmann, Johann Karl Eduard
1805-1880

Die Pima-Sprache und die Sprache der Koloschen, dargestellt von Hrn. Buschmann. [Berlin, 1856]

[321]-432 p.   29 cm.   Caption title. "Gelesen in der Akademie der Wissenschaften [Berlin] am 26 April 1855." Reprinted from its: Philosophisch-historische Klasse. Abhandlungen. 1856.   Not seen.

Relates to the Tlingit Indian language.

BANCROFT LIBRARY CATALOGUE

## 44   Commission of Claims under the Convention of February 8, 1853, between the United States and Great Britain

Report of decisions of the commission . . . transmitted to the Senate by the President of the United States, August 11, 1856.   Washington, A.O.P. Nicholson, 1856.

viii, 478 p.   24 cm.   N. G. Upham, American commissioner; Edmund Hornby, British commissioner.

Contains references to the Hudson's Bay Company claim for expenditures incurred in coming to the relief of Americans who were captured by Indians (1847, 1851), and to the seizing of the "Albion." (1850).

Also issued as: United States. 34th Cong., 1st sess. Senate. Ex. doc. 103.

B.C. ARCHIVES

## 45   Commission of Claims under the Convention of February 8, 1853, between the United States and Great Britain

Report of the proceedings of the mixed commission on private claims, established under the convention between Great Britain and the United States of America of the 8th February 1853. With the judgements of the commissioners and umpire. Compiled from the original by Edmund Hornby.   London, Printed by Harrison and Sons, 1856.

ix, 485 p.   21 cm.   N. G. Upham, American commissioner; Edmund Hornby, British commissioner.

Contains references to various Hudson's Bay Company claims.

B.C. ARCHIVES

## 46   United States. Congress. Senate. Committee on Foreign Relations

In the Senate of the United States Mr. Mason submitted the following report (to accompany Bill S. 405) . . .   [Washington, 1856]

7 p.   23 cm.   ([United States] 34th Cong., 1st sess. Senate. Rep. com. no. 251)   Caption title.

Concerns appropriation for marking the boundary of Washington Territory with reference to the difficulties on San Juan Island.

B.C. ARCHIVES

## 47   Canada. Governor-General
1854-1861   (HEAD)

Return to an address of the Honorable Legislative Assembly, dated 16th March 1857, requiring copies of any charters, leases, or other documents, under which the Honorable Hudson's Bay Company claim title to the Hudson's Bay Territory, or any maps relating thereto in the possession of the government. [Toronto, Printed by Stewart Derbishire & George Desbarats, 1857]

75 p.   25 cm.   Appendix E: Vancouver's Island; royal grant. Appendix F includes: An Act to Provide for the Administration of Justice in Vancouver's Island (28th July 1849)

Mentions the desirability of Canada acquiring Vancouver Island (p. 40-41).

B.C. ARCHIVES

## 48   Canada. Governor-General
1854-1861   (HEAD)

Return to an address, with correspondence, &c., relating to the Hudson's Bay Territory. Ordered, by the Legislative Assembly to be printed, 7th March 1857.   Toronto, Printed by John Lovell, 1857.

5 p.   24 cm.   Caption title: Return to an address from the Legislative Assembly to His Excellency the Governor General, dated the 2nd instant, praying His Excellency to cause to be laid before the House "copies of all correspondence between the government and Mr. Justice Draper, relative to his appointment as agent to England on the subject of the Hudson's Bay Territory, of the Commission and instructions given to Mr. Draper, and of all correspondence between the Imperial and provincial governments on the subject of the said Territory."

Concerns the renewal of the Hudson's Bay Company's license of occupation which was due to expire. This document refers to the question of the limits of Canada in the direction of the territory over which the Hudson's Bay Company had control, and to whether or not the boundaries of Canada extended to the Pacific.

B.C. ARCHIVES

## 49   Financial Reform Association (Liverpool)

The Hudson's Bay Company versus Magna Charta and the British people.   Liverpool, P. S. King [1857]

36 p.   fold. col. map.   22 cm.   (Financial Reform tracts, new ser., no. 21)

Calls for the end of Hudson's Bay Company jurisdiction over North American territory.

UNIVERSITY OF TORONTO LIBRARY

## 50   Freeport, Andrew
PSEUDONYM

The case of the Hudson's Bay Company, in a letter to Lord Palmerston.   London, Edward Stanford, 1857.

18 p.   22 cm.   Cover title.

Written to protest the possible renewal of the Hudson's Bay Company charter.

GLENBOW FOUNDATION LIBRARY

## 51   Great Britain. Colonial Office

Vancouver's Island. Return . . . "Copies or extracts of any despatches that have been received by Her Majesty's Secretary of State for the Colonies, on the subject of the establishment of a representative assembly at Vancouver's Island." Ordered by the House of Commons to be printed, 3 August, 1857.   [London, 1857]

20 p.   33 cm.   ([Great Britain. Parliament, 1857, 2d. sess. House of Commons papers] 229)

B.C. ARCHIVES

## 52   Great Britain. Parliament. House of Commons. Select Committee on the Hudson's Bay Company

Report from the Select Committee on the Hudson's Bay Company; together with the proceedings of the committee, minutes of evidence, appendix, and index. Ordered to be printed 17th August 1857.   [London, 1857]

xviii, 547 p.   fold. maps.   34 cm.   ([Great Britain. Parliament, 1857. House of Commons papers] 224, 260)

Concerns in part the administration of Vancouver Island. The committee recommended that the Hudson's Bay Company's connection with Vancouver Island be terminated and that the colony be extended to encompass the mainland west of the Rocky Mountains.

Also appeared as Great Britain. Parliament, 1857. House of Lords papers, 197.

B.C. ARCHIVES

## 53   The Hudson's Bay . . .

The Hudson's Bay question . . .   London, W. Tweedie, 1857.

28 p.   fold. col. map.   20 cm.   Reprinted from the *Colonial intelligencer.* Preface signed in print: F.W.C. Memorial signed in print on p. [25]: F. W. Chesson.

A collection of excerpts which were republished to emphasize the position of the Indians in the territories controlled by the Hudson's Bay Company.

TORONTO UNIVERSITY LIBRARY

## 54   Swan, James G[ilchrist]
1818-1900

The Northwest Coast; or, Three years' residence in Washington Territory.   New York, Harper & Brothers, 1857.

435 p.   illus., plates, fold. map.   20 cm.

One chapter contains remarks on the Chinook jargon and includes a Chinook jargon vocabulary of two hundred and fifty words.

Also: London, Sampson Low, Son & Co., 1857.

B.C. ARCHIVES

## 55   Alta California (San Francisco)

Extra. Daily Alta California . . . June 19, 1858. Later from the North. Arrival of the Republic! News from Frazer River. More confirmation! Confiscation of goods by the Hudson Bay Company!   San Francisco, 1858.

sheet.   58 x 40 cm.   Xerox copy examined. Original in the Yale University Library.

UNIVERSITY OF VICTORIA LIBRARY

## 56   Anderson, Alexander C[aulfield]
1814-1884

Hand-book and map to the gold region of Frazer's and Thompson's rivers. With table of distance, to which is appended Chinook jargon—language used, etc., etc.   San Francisco, J. J. Le Count, c1858.

31 p.   col. fold. map.   15 cm.   Cover title. Chinook jargon: p. [25]-31. Manuscript note on presentation copy to H. H. Bancroft in Bancroft Library: N.B. This vocabulary procured by the publisher from some one in S.F., is a miserable affair and was appended without my knowledge. A.C.A.

B.C. ARCHIVES

### 57   Ballantyne, Robert Michael
EDITOR   1825-1894

Handbook to the new gold fields; a full account of the richness and extent of the Fraser and Thompson River gold mines, with a geographical and physical account of the country and its inhabitants, routes, etc., etc.   Edinburgh, Alex. Strahan, 1858.

iv, 116 p.   fold. map.   17 cm.

B.C. ARCHIVES

### 58   British Columbia. Laws, statutes, etc.

[Proclamations and ordinances, 1858-1864. Victoria, New Westminster, 1858-64]

1 v. (various paging)   28 cm.   At head of text of first printed page: British Columbia; list of proclamations [and ordinances] for 1858 . . . 1864. Includes proclamations made for British Columbia by James Douglas when he was acting in the capacity of governor of Vancouver Island only. Also see entry 223.

For a partial table of proclamations and ordinances before 1871 see *The laws of British Columbia, consisting of the acts, ordinances & proclamations of the formerly separate colonies of Vancouver Island and British Columbia, and of the united colony of British Columbia* (Victoria, Government Printing Office, 1871).

B.C. ARCHIVES

### 59   British Columbia . . .

British Columbia and Vancouver's Island; a complete hand-book replete with the latest information concerning the newly-discovered gold fields. With a map.   [London, Effingham Wilson, 1858]

67 p.   fold. map.   22 cm.   Cover title: The new government colony; British Columbia and Vancouver's Island . . .   On cover: Printed by William Penny.

Contains a reference to the possibility of a railway to the Pacific through British territory.

B.C. ARCHIVES

### 60   Coffin, Charles Carleton
1823-1896

Great commercial prize; addressed to every American who values the prosperity of his country.   Boston, A. Williams, 1858.

23 p.   Not seen.   Copy in the Spokane Public Library.

"An account of the Puget Sound region, Frazer River and Oregon; exposing the attempt of Great Britain to gain control of the Northwest and an impassioned appeal to all Americans to 'wake up'."

SMITH

### 61   Cornwallis, Kinahan
1839-1917

The new El Dorado; or British Columbia. London, Thomas Cautley Newby, publisher, 1858.

xxviii, 405 p.   plate, fold. map.   21 cm.   Chapter 8: Overland railway and other communication between Canada, the United States, and British Columbia.

A glowing description of British Columbia and its settlement possibilities, written by an Englishman who arrived in Victoria from San Francisco in June 1858 to prospect for Fraser River gold.

Second edition: 1858.

B.C. ARCHIVES

### 62   Dower, John
FLOURISHED   1838-1858

New British gold fields; a guide to British Columbia and Vancouver Island. With a coloured map, showing the gold and coal fields, constructed from authentic sources. By John Domer [*sic*]   London, William Henry Angel [1858]

52 p.   fold. col. map.   19 cm.   Xerox copy seen. Original in the Yale University Library.

UNIVERSITY OF VICTORIA LIBRARY

### 63   Ermatinger, Edward
1797-1876

The Hudson's Bay Territories; a series of letters on this important question.   Toronto, Maclear, Thomas & Co., 1858.

32 p.   25 cm.

A criticism of the Liverpool Financial Reform Association's hostile attitude towards the Hudson's Bay Company.

SHORTT COLLECTION

### 64   European and Asiatic . . .

European and Asiatic intercourse via British Columbia by means of a main through trunk railway from the Atlantic to the Pacific; containing: I—Correspondence with ministers and other proceedings on the subject since 1845. II—Memorandum placed in the hands of the Colonial Minister [by Sir Richard Broun] III—Extracts from the evidence taken by the committee on the Hudson's Bay Territory, 1857. IV—Appendix containing notes, extracts, statistics, &c. V—Map of the railway.   London, Robert Hardwicke, 1858.

58 p.   fold. map.   21 cm.   On map: Map of the Atlantic & Pacific Junction Railway and Land Company.

A publication on the subject of Sir Richard Broun's railway and colonization project.

B.C. ARCHIVES

## 65    Financial Reform Association (Liverpool)

Constitution, objects, and proceedings of the Financial Reform Association. The Hudson's Bay monopoly.   Liverpool, Published by the Association [1858]

32 p.   21 cm.   (Financial Reform tracts, new ser., no. 24)   The Hudson's Bay Company and the late government: p. [24]-32.

The section from page 24 comments upon the 1857 report of the British parliamentary select committee on the Hudson's Bay Company, and calls for either the transfer to Canada of company lands or for the establishment of separate colonies.

B.C. ARCHIVES

## 66    The Frazer River thermometer ...

The Frazer River thermometer ...   San Francisco, Published by Sterett & Butler, 1858.

2 sheets.   illus.   43 x 28 cm.   Contents: [No. 1] Great gold discoveries of 1858; the Frazer River gold mines and their history.—No. 2. The bubble bursted!! [a poem]   Xerox copy examined. Original in the Yale University Library.

UNIVERSITY OF VICTORIA LIBRARY

## 67    Great Britain. Colonial Office

Copies or extracts of correspondence relative to the discovery of gold in the Fraser's River district, in British North America. Presented to both Houses of Parliament by command of Her Majesty, July 2, 1858.   London, Printed by George Edward Eyre and William Spottiswoode, 1858.

18 p.   fold. map.   32 cm.   ([Great Britain. Parliament. Command papers] 2398)

A xerox copy of another printing, a draft or proof copy, is in Special Collections, University of British Columbia Library. It has manuscript corrections and deletions and lacks the Appendix.

B.C. ARCHIVES

## 68    Great Britain. Colonial Office

Hudson's Bay Company. Copies of correspondence that has taken place between the Colonial Office and the Hudson's Bay Company, or the government of Canada, in consequence of the report of the select committee on the affairs of the company, which sat in the last session of Parliament. Ordered by the House of Commons to be printed, 26 February 1858.   [London, 1858]

7 p.   34 cm.   ([Great Britain. Parliament, 1858. House of Commons papers] 99)

B.C. ARCHIVES

## 69    Great Britain. Colonial Office

Vancouver's Island. Return . . . "Return of lands in Vancouver's Island sold to any individual or company, with the names of the persons or company to whom such lands have been sold, and the localities in which they are situated." Ordered by the House of Commons to be printed, 2 August 1858.   [London, 1858]

3 p.   33 cm.   ([Great Britain. Parliament, 1858. House of Commons papers] 524)

B.C. ARCHIVES

## 70    Great Britain. Laws, statutes, etc.

Government of New Caledonia. A bill to provide, until the thirty-first day of December (one thousand eight hundred and sixty-two) for the government of New Caledonia. Prepared and brought in by Sir Bulwer Lytton and Mr. Hamilton. Ordered by the House of Commons to be printed, 1 July 1858.   [London, 1858]

4 p.   43 cm.   ([Great Britain. Parliament. House of Commons] Bill no. 170)

B.C. ARCHIVES

## 71    Great Britain. Privy Council

[Order in council constituting the Supreme Court of Civil Justice of Vancouver Island and rules of practice and forms to be used therein.   Victoria, Victoria Gazette, 1858]

vii, 74, v p.   tables.   36 cm.   Wanting covers and t. p. Signed in print on p. 23: David Cameron, C.J. Contents: Rules and manner of proceeding of the Supreme Court of Civil Justice for Vancouver's Island: p. [1]-23. — [Schedules of forms, etc.]: p. [25]-46. — Rules of practice for the Inferior Court of Civil Justice: p. [47]-65. — [Schedules of Fees, etc.]: p. 67-74. — Index: p. [i]-v.

The advertisement in the Victoria *Gazette* for 13 November 1858, gives the title as *The Rules of practice and the forms to be used in the Superior and Inferior Courts of Civil Justice of Vancouver Island*, but no copy of this first edition, complete with title page and cover, has been found. This publication has the distinction of being the first book printed in the colony of Vancouver Island, coming off the press ahead of Waddington's *Fraser mines vindicated* (see entry 1716).

Another edition with additional material: Victoria, Vancouver Printing and Publishing Company, 1865. vi, 90, v p.

B.C. ARCHIVES

## 72 Guide-book . . .

Guide-book to the gold regions of Frazer River, with a map of the different routes, &c. New York, 1858.

55 p. Not seen.

Has a vocabulary of the Chinook jargon (p. 45-55).

PILLING'S CHINOOKAN BIBLIOGRAPHY

## 73 Hazlitt, William Carew
### 1834-1913

British Columbia and Vancouver Island; comprising a historical sketch of the British settlements in the north-west coast of America; and a survey of the physical character, capabilities, climate, topography, natural history, geology and ethnology of that region. Compiled from official and other authentic sources. London, New York, G. Routledge & Co., 1858.

viii, 247 p. fold. map. 17 cm.

Includes a vocabulary of the Chinook jargon (p. 241-243).

B.C. ARCHIVES

## 74 MacDonell, Allan

The North-west Transportation, Navigation and Railway Company; its objects. Toronto, Printed by order of the Board by Lovell and Gibson, 1858.

55 p. 21 cm. Observations upon the construction of a railroad from Lake Superior to the Pacific: p. [31]-54. See note, entry 25.

B.C. ARCHIVES

## 75 Minnesota. Legislature. House. Select Committee on Overland Route to British Oregon.

Report from a select committee of the House of Representatives on the overland emigration route from Minnesota to British Oregon. With appendix. Printed by order of the H. of R. Saint Paul, Earle S. Goodrich, 1858.

100 p. 24 cm. Report: p. [3]-6. Appendix 1: Proceedings of public meetings held at St. Paul, Minnesota . . . July, A.D. 1858 [p. 9-38] Appendix 2: Particulars of the gold discovery on Frazer and Thompson rivers, and of emigration thither [p. 39-47]

The report of the committee was in response to resolutions of certain citizens of St. Paul on the subject

of emigration to British Columbia. Some of the eight appendices form testimony as to the superiority of a route to the gold fields via the Red River and Saskatchewan valleys.

The report also appeared as an appendix to the Minnesota *Journals* of the Senate and House for the session 1857-8.

B.C. ARCHIVES

## 76 North-west Transportation, Navigation, and Railway Company

Prospectus. Chief office: Toronto, Canada. Toronto, Globe Book and Job Office, 1858.

12 p. 22 cm.

One of the objects of the company was the construction of a railway to the Pacific.

What is possibly another edition is listed in: **Toronto. Public Library.** *A bibliography of Canadiana,* item 3834.

B.C. ARCHIVES

## 77 Snow, W[illiam] Parker
### 1817-1895

British Columbia; emigration and our colonies, considered practically, socially and politically. London, Piper, Stephenson, and Spence, 1858.

xii, 108 p. 17 cm.

The author advocated the emigration of the British working classes.

B.C. ARCHIVES

## 78 Stevens, Isaac I[ngalls]
### 1818-1862

Address on the Northwest before the American Geographical and Statistical Society, delivered at New York, December 2, 1858. Washington, G. S. Gideon, printer, 1858.

56 p. tables. 21 cm.

A discussion of east to west communication, including the possibility of a railway route following the Thompson and Fraser rivers.

B.C. ARCHIVES

## 79 Table of distances . . .

Table of distances [to forks of Thompson River] Fort Langly route . . . Columbia River via the Dalles . . . Overland route from Cal'a . . . Vocabulary of the Chinook jargon . . . [n.p., 1858?]

sheet. 25 x 19 cm. The vocabulary of the 350 Chinook jargon words and phrases printed in four columns. Xerox copy examined. Original in the Yale University Library.

UNIVERSITY OF VICTORIA LIBRARY

## 80     Vancouver Island. Governor
### 1851-1864    (DOUGLAS)

Proclamation by His Excellency, James Douglas, governor of Vancouver's Island, and its dependencies, vice admiral of the same, etc., etc., etc. [with regard to harbour rules and regulations observed in the ports of Victoria and Esquimalt, and all other ports in Vancouver's Island and its dependencies]    Victoria, Printed at the Vancouver Island Gazette Office, 1858.

8 p.   21 cm.   Dated 25 August 1858.

This publication was the subject of Douglas McMurtrie's *The earliest British Columbia imprint* (entry 1729).

B.C. ARCHIVES

## 81     Waddington, Alfred [Penderill]
### 1801?-1872

The Fraser mines vindicated; or, The history of four months. [Second issue]    Victoria, Printed by P. de Garro, 1858.

49 p.   22 cm.   Cover title.

During the summer of 1858 the Fraser River was so high that gold could not be obtained easily from its bars. As a result, many miners left the gold fields. Waddington wrote this pamphlet to re-establish faith in the wealth of the deposits.

*The Fraser mines vindicated* has the distinction of being the first non-government book printed in the colony of Vancouver Island. There were two issues: the first, had two corrections in the errata notice; the second issue, one.

The first issue was reprinted in Vancouver in 1949 with an introduction by William Kaye Lamb on the private press of Robert R. Reid. In xvi, 93 pages.

B.C. ARCHIVES

## 82     Blakiston, T[homas] W[right]
### 1832-1891

Report of the exploration of two passes through the Rocky Mountains in 1858, by Captain T. W. Blakiston, Royal Artillery.    Woolwich [Eng.] Printed at the Royal Artillery Institution, 1859.

18 p.   fold. map.   23 cm.   Cover title. At head of report: Report on the exploration of the Kootanie and Boundary passes of the Rocky Mountains in 1858.

The day after renouncing his connection with the Palliser expedition, Blakiston set off to survey and explore the Kootenay passes.

B.C. ARCHIVES

## 83     Blakiston, Thomas Wright
### 1832-1891

Report on the exploration of two passes (the Kootanie and Boundary passes) of the Rocky Mountains in 1858.    [New Haven, 1859]

320-345 p.   fold. map.   23 cm.   Reprinted from the *American journal of science*, v. 78, 1859. Not seen.

YALE WESTERN AMERICANA CATALOGUE

## 84     Campbell, Archibald
### BISHOP OF LONDON

A sermon preached in Westminster Abbey on St. Matthias' Day 1859, at the consecration of the first Bishop of British Columbia.    London, Rivingtons, 1859.

20 p.   21 cm.

U.B.C. SPECIAL COLLECTIONS

## 85     De Groot, Henry
### 1815-1893

British Columbia; its condition and prospects, soil, climate, and mineral resources considered. San Francisco, Printed at the Alta California Job Office, 1859.

24 p.   23 cm.   In pref.: ... originally published in the columns of the *Daily Alta California,* where they appeared in a series of articles prepared for that paper.

The author, a newspaper correspondent, spent seven months travelling in the Interior.

B.C. ARCHIVES

## 86     Great Britain. Colonial Office

British Columbia. Papers relative to the affairs of British Columbia ... Presented to both Houses of Parliament by command of Her Majesty ... London, Printed by George Edward Eyre and William Spottiswoode, 1859-62.

4 v.   fold. map.   32 cm.   ([Great Britain. Parliament. Command papers] 2476, 2578, 2724, 2952)   Parts 3-4 have title: British Columbia. Further papers ...   Contents: pt. 1. Copies of despatches from the Secretary of State for the Colonies to the Governor of British Columbia, and from the Governor to the Secretary of State relative to the government of the colony; also, copies of the act of Parliament to provide for the government of British Columbia; Governor's commission and instructions; order in council to provide for the administration of justice; and instrument revoking so much of the crown grant of 30th May 1838 to the Hudson's Bay Company for exclusive trading with the Indians as relates to the territories comprised within the colony of British Columbia. — pts. 2-4. Copies of despatches ... relative to the government of the colony.

B.C. ARCHIVES

## 87     Great Britain. Colonial Office

British Columbia. Returns of all appointments, civil, military, and ecclesiastical, made or authorised by the home government, to the colony of British Columbia; stating the names of persons appointed, the dates of their appointments, and the salaries in each case; and, of any other charges connected with the colony authorised by the home government. Ordered by the House of Commons to be printed, 21 March 1859.   [London, 1859]

3, [1] p.   32 cm.   ([Great Britain. Parliament, 1859. House of Commons papers] 146)    Title from p. [4]

B.C. ARCHIVES

## 88       Great Britain. Colonial Office

Papers relative to the Hudson's Bay Company's charter and licence of trade. Presented to both Houses of Parliament by command of Her Majesty, April 1859.   London, Printed by George Edward Eyre and William Spottiswoode, 1859.

v, 26 p.   33 cm.   ([Great Britain. Parliament. Command papers] 2507)

B.C. ARCHIVES

## 89       Great Britain. Commissioners for Emigration

Vancouver's Island; survey of the districts of Nanaimo and Cowichan Valley.   London, Groombridge and Sons, 1859.

14 p.   22 cm.   Contents: Survey at Nanaimo, report of engineer in charge of survey [B. W. Pearse to Joseph Pemberton] — General report of the survey of the districts Shawnigan, Cowichan, Comiaken, Quamichan, and Somenos [by Oliver Wells to Joseph Pemberton]

B.C. ARCHIVES

## 90       Great Britain. Foreign Office

Correspondence relative to the occupation of the Island of San Juan by United States' troops. [Part I] August to October 1859.   Part II: October 1859 to July 1860.   [London] Printed for the use of the Foreign Office, 1859-60.

2 v.   32 cm.   At head of title: Confidential.

B.C. ARCHIVES

## 91       Great Britain. Foreign Office

Memorandum respecting the Island of San Juan. [London] Printed at the Foreign Office, 1859.

39 p.   32 cm.   Cover title. At head of title: Confidential.

A résumé of government instructions.

B.C. ARCHIVES

## 92       Harney, [William Selby]
### 1800-1889

Correspondence between Gen. Harney and Gov. Douglas.   [Victoria? 1859]

[1] p. (folder)   26 cm.

Consists of a letter from General Harney to Governor Douglas, dated 6 August 1859, concerning the occupation of San Juan Island and the treatment of American citizens, together with Governor Douglas' reply of 13 August 1859.

B.C. ARCHIVES

## 93       Hills, George
### BISHOP OF COLUMBIA   1816-1895

A sermon preached at the farewell service celebrated in St. James's Church, Piccadilly, on Wednesday, Nov. 16, 1859, the day previous to his departure for his diocese by George Hills, D.D., Bishop of Columbia. With an account of the meeting held on the same day at the Mansion House of the city of London, in aid of the Columbia Mission.   London, Rivingtons, 1859.

55 p.   21 cm.   Columbia mission; report of proceedings at a public meeting . . . : p. [13]-55.

B.C. ARCHIVES

## 94       Morris, Alexander
### 1826-1889

The Hudson's Bay and Pacific territories; a lecture.   Montreal, John Lovell, 1859.

57 p.   23 cm.

Also appeared as the second lecture in his *Nova Britannia* (entry 665).

B.C. ARCHIVES

## 95       North America

North America.   [n.p., 1859?]

[14] p.   7 plates.   25 cm.   Caption title.

Apparently reprinted from a missionary periodical, this collection of seven short articles includes one on the Indians near Fort Simpson.

B.C. ARCHIVES

## 96       Palliser, John
### 1807-1887

Exploration—British North America. Papers relative to the exploration by Captain Palliser of that portion of British North America which lies between the northern branch of the river Saskatchewan and the frontier of the United States, and between the Red River and Rocky Mountains. Presented to both Houses of Parliament by command of Her Majesty, June 1859.   London, Printed by George Edward Eyre and William Spottiswoode, 1859.

64 p.   maps (1 fold.) diagr., tables.   34 cm.

B.C. ARCHIVES

**97** St. Pancras Foreign Affairs Committee

The boundary between the British and the Russian empires on the north-west coast of America. Memoir by the St. Pancras Foreign Affairs Committee. [London, Office of the "Diplomatic Review," 1859]

sheet (2 p.) 37 x 23 cm.

B.C. ARCHIVES

**98** United States. President
1857-1861 (BUCHANAN)

Claim of Governor Douglas of Vancouver's Island. Message from the President of the United States, transmitting documents relative to advances made by Governor Douglas of Vancouver's Island to Governor Stevens of Washington Territory, and recommending the payment of same. [Washington, 1859]

11 p. 23 cm. ([United States] House. 35th Cong., 2d sess. Ex. doc. no. 72) Caption title.

Relates to the aid, both financial and otherwise, given to Washington Territory by Douglas during Stevens' Indian campaigns of 1856.

VANCOUVER PUBLIC LIBRARY

**99** United States. President
1857-1861 (BUCHANAN)

Vancouver's Island and British Columbia. Message from the President of the United States, communicating the report of the special agent of the United States recently sent to Vancouver's Island and British Columbia. [Washington 1859]

30 p. 23 cm. ([United States] 35th Cong., 2d sess. House Ex. doc. no. 111) Caption title. Special agent: John Nugent.

According to his instructions, the purpose of Nugent's mission was to infuse a spirit of subordination to British law among the American citizens in British Columbia and to inform the government about American emigration to the Fraser River mines.

B.C. ARCHIVES

**100** Vancouver Island

Government gazette for the colonies of Vancouver Island and British Columbia. no. 1-51; 10 September 1859—28 August 1860. Victoria, 1859-60.

1 v. 30 cm. weekly. Suspended August 1860—October 1863. Official notices between 1860 and 1863 appeared in New Westminster *Times* and the *British Columbian* on the mainland, and the *Colonist* and Victoria *Press* on Vancouver Island (see Madge Wolfenden, "The early government gazettes," *British Columbia historical quarterly*, v. 7, 1943, p. 171-190)

B.C. ARCHIVES

**101** [Waddington, Alfred Penderill]
1801?-1872

The necessity of reform; a tract for the times, addressed to the colonists of Vancouver Island by one of the people. Victoria, Printed at the British Colonist Office, 1859.

12 p. 30 cm. Photostat copy seen. Original in the library of Acadia University. The work was attributed to Waddington by Hubert Bancroft in *History of British Columbia* (San Francisco, 1887) p. 769.

Bancroft describes the work as "a tirade against the restricted franchise, and the petty infelicities of the day."

B.C. ARCHIVES

**102** Archibald, C. D.

Two letters to His Grace the Duke of Newcastle . . . on the importance and necessity of carrying out the Intercolonial and Atlantic and Pacific railways continuously through the British North-American possessions. London, William Penny [1860?]

16 p. fold. map. 22 cm. Cover title. At head of title: Colonial agenda.

B.C. ARCHIVES

**103** Aylmer, Fenton
EDITOR

A cruise in the Pacific; from the log of a naval officer. London, Hurst and Blackett, 1860.

2 v. fronts. 20 cm.

Much of Volume 2 is about Vancouver Island and the B.C. mainland. The writer of the book, probably a midshipman, travelled about the colonies while on leave and while awaiting a ship transfer.

B.C. ARCHIVES

**104** [Batterton, J. H.]

Facts and acts: what has been done and what is going on in British Columbia; a letter to the people of British Columbia, by one of themselves. Victoria, Printed at the British Colonist Office, 1860.

16 p. 18 cm.

An appeal for a governor and legislature for the colony of British Columbia.

B.C. ARCHIVES

**105** British Columbia. Laws, statutes, etc.

Act of Incorporation of the British Columbia and Victoria Steam Navigation Company, Limited, incorporated February 1860. Victoria, Printed at the British Colonist Office, 1860.

11 p.  22 cm.

One of the promoters of the company was William Irving. Because of a troublesome Vancouver Island House of Assembly, the company was incorporated in British Columbia (N. Hacking, "Steam boating on the Fraser . . . ," p. 5-6).

There is no record of the "act" having been printed by the government printer, and it probably was originally only in manuscript form.

B.C. ARCHIVES

## 106  Church of England. Liturgy and ritual

Form of consecration of a new church in the Diocese of Columbia and Vancouver, 1860. Victoria, Printed by George E. Nias & Co. [n. d.]

12 p.  20 cm.

The name of the diocese was not the "Diocese of Columbia and Vancouver," but the "Diocese of British Columbia."

B.C. ARCHIVES

## 107  Church of England. Liturgy and ritual

Office to be used in laying the corner-stone of a church.  [Victoria? 1860]

7 p.  18 cm.  Cover title.

B.C. ARCHIVES

## 108  Columbia Mission

An occasional paper on the Columbia Mission, with letters from the Bishop. June 1860. Published for the benefit of the mission. London, Rivingtons [1860]

50 p.  plate, fold. maps.  22 cm.  Cover title. Compiled by John Garrett, commissary to the Bishop of Columbia, from the letters of Bishop George Hills. Appendix 1-5: p. [37]-50.

An interesting account of Bishop Hills' first impressions of his large diocese.

For the repercussions of this publication, see entries 117 and 123.

B.C. ARCHIVES

## 109  Columbia Mission

Special fund obtained during a ten months' appeal by the Bishop of Columbia, since his consecration in Westminster Abbey, on the twenty-fourth of February 1859; with a statement of the urgent need which exists for sympathy and support in aid of the Columbia Mission.  London, Printed by R. Clay, 1860.

xiv, 33 p.  21 cm.  At head of title: Columbia Mission. Subscription list: p [1]-33.

B.C. ARCHIVES

## 110  The Dashaway Association No. 15 (Victoria)

Constitution and by-laws.  Victoria, Printed by Amor de Cosmos at the Colonist Office [1860 or 1861]

8 p.  17 cm.

The association was a temperance organization.

B.C. ARCHIVES

## 111  First Victoria directory

First Victoria directory; comprising a general directory of citizens, also, an official list, list of voters, postal arrangements and notices of trades and professions, preceded by a synopsis of the commercial progress of the colonies of Vancouver Island and British Columbia. By Edward Mallandaine, architect.  1860-74.  Victoria, E. Mallandaine & Co.

5 v.  24 cm.  First to fifth issues in 1860, 1868, 1869, 1871, 1874. Subtitle varies.

B.C. ARCHIVES

## 112  Freemasons. Victoria

Order of proceedings at the dedication of the new masonic hall, Victoria, V.I., Monday, 25th June 1860.  [Victoria, 1860]

4 p. (folder)  21 cm.  Caption title.

B.C. ARCHIVES

## 113  Freemasons. Victoria. Victoria Lodge No. 1085

By-laws of Victoria Lodge No. 1085, English Registry, F. and A.M.; instituted August 20, 1860. Victoria, Printed at the British Colonist Office, 1860.

14 p.  14 cm.

Also see entry 283.

B.C. ARCHIVES

## 114  [Gosset, William Driscoll]

Elementary rules for the guidance of officers entrusted with the expenditure of public money. [n.p., 1860?]

6, [6] p.  23 cm.  Cover title.

Rules and regulations for the keeping of accounts for the colony of British Columbia. It is probable that this publication was from the Royal Engineers' press in New Westminster which was requisitioned in 1860 for some of the government printing of the colony of British Columbia.

B.C. ARCHIVES

**115    Great Britain. Foreign Office**

Correspondence respecting the Island of San Juan. Presented to both Houses of Parliament by command of Her Majesty, 1860.    London, Printed by Harrison and Sons [1860]

4 p.    34 cm.    ([Great Britain. Parliament. Command papers, 2709])

Correspondence with enclosures from Lord Lyons in Washington to Lord Russell.

B.C. ARCHIVES

**116    Great Britain. Privy Council**

Order in council, bearing date the 22nd day of November 1860, establishing rules and regulations and table of fees for the Vice-Admiralty Court at Vancouver Island.    London, Printed by George E. Eyre and William Spottiswoode, 1860.

1v. (various paging)    27 cm.

B.C. ARCHIVES

**117    [Hills, George]**
BISHOP OF COLUMBIA   1816-1895

The "Occasional paper"; two letters from the Bishop of Columbia to the Rev. E. Cridge and Bishop Demers.    Victoria, Printed at the British Colonist Office, 1860.

8 p.    19 cm.

The reference in the title is to *An occasional paper on the Columbia Mission . . .* (entry 108) in which Bishop Hills made comments on the political designs of the Americans in the election of 1860 and disparaging remarks about the Roman Catholic Bishop. In these two letters Bishop Hills offers his explanations.

B.C. ARCHIVES

**118    Mackenzie, Henry**

Occupy till I come; a sermon preached at the first annual service of the Columbia Mission, in the church of St. Martin's-in-the-Fields on Wednesday, June 6, 1860. Published by request for the benefit of the mission.    London, Rivingtons, 1860.

24 p.    20 cm.

B.C. ARCHIVES

**119    New Westminster (city)**

By-laws of the municipal council of the city of New Westminster.    [New Westminster, Printed at the office of the "New Westminster Times," 1860]

4 p.    16 cm.    Caption title.

B.C. ARCHIVES

**120    Palliser, John**
1807-1887

Exploration—British North America. Further papers relative to the exploration by the expedition under Captain Palliser of that portion of British North America which lies between the northern branch of the river Saskatchewan and the frontier of the United States; and between the Red River and the Rocky Mountains, and thence to the Pacific Ocean. Presented to both Houses of Parliament by command of Her Majesty, 1860.    London, Printed by George Edward Eyre and William Spottiswoode, 1860.

75 p.    fold. maps, diagr., tables.    34 cm.    Reports of T. W. Blakiston, magnetic observer: p. 29-75.

B.C. ARCHIVES

**121    Pearse. B[enjamin] W[illiam]**
1832-1902

General report on the country round Nanaimo. [Victoria? 1860?]

2 p.    30 cm.    Caption title. Copy not found for examination. Also in Yale University Library.

B.C. ARCHIVES

**122    Pemberton, J[oseph] Despard**
1821-1893

Facts and figures relating to Vancouver Island and British Columbia, showing what to expect and how to get there.    London, Longman, Green, Longman and Roberts, 1860.

ix, 171 p.    4 fold. maps.    23 cm.

B.C. ARCHIVES

**123    Skewton, Lady Lavinia**
PSEUDONYM

The "Occasional paper"; one letter from the Honorable Lady Lavinia Skewton, London, to the Lord Bishop of Colombia [*sic*] Second edition.    Victoria, Printed at the British Colonist Office, 1860.

7 p.    18 cm.

This satirical letter comments on *An occasional paper . . .* (entry 108), which contained letters written by Bishop George Hills to the Columbia Mission.

B.C. ARCHIVES

**124    Taylor, James W[ickes]**
1819-1893

Legislature of Minnesota. Northwest British America and its relations to the state of Minnesota. [Reliable information relative to the overland route from Pembina via the Red River Settlement and the Saskatchewan Valley to Fraser

River, etc.] Printed as a supplement to the Journal of the House of Representatives, session 1859-60. St. Paul, Newton & Foster Print, 1860.

53 p.   map.   23 cm.   Not seen.

"Taylor was commissioned by Governor Sibley to explore and report on the country westward from St. Paul and the Selkirk Settlement to the Rocky Mountains and beyond. Appended to his reports are the following appendices: A. Central British America: the Hudson's Bay Company, its charter: Fraser River Gold Discovery, etc. . . . G. British Columbia and the Cascade Country, the gold discoveries, routes to the mines, etc." — Eberstadt, cat. 104, item 281.

LIBRARY OF CONGRESS

## 125    Union Hook and Ladder Co. No. 1 (Victoria)

Constitution and by-laws of the Union Hook and Ladder Co. No. 1, Victoria, Vancouver's Island.   San Francisco, Towne & Bacon, 1860.

11 p.   15 cm.

B.C. ARCHIVES

## 126    United States. President
### 1857-1861 (BUCHANAN)

Message of the President of the United States, communicating, in compliance with a resolution of the Senate of the 9th instant, the correspondence of Lieutenant General Scott, in reference to the Island of San Juan, and of Brigadier General Harney, in command of the department of Oregon.   [Washington, 1860]

75 p.   23 cm.   ([United States] 36th Cong., 1st sess. Senate. Ex. doc. no. 10)   Caption title.

Also in: United States. 36th Cong., 1st sess. House. Doc. 65.

B.C. ARCHIVES

## 127    United States. Department of State

Island of San Juan. Letter from the Secretary of State transmitting a report relative to the occupation of the Island of San Juan. [Washington, 1860]

16 p.   26 cm.   ([United States] 36th Cong., 1st sess. House. Ex. doc. no. 77)   Caption title. Report of Henry R. Crosbie.

B.C. ARCHIVES

## 128    United States. War Department

Affairs in Oregon. Letter from the Secretary of War, communicating in compliance with a resolution of the House of Representatives, correspondence with General Harney, relating to affairs in the department of Oregon. April 12, 1860—laid upon the table, and ordered to be printed.   [Washington, 1860]

269 p.   23 cm.   ([United States] 36th Cong., 1st sess. House. Ex. doc. no. 65)   Caption title.

Relates to the San Juan Island dispute and general military affairs. Most of the material is dated in the years 1858, 1859, and 1860.

U.B.C. SPECIAL COLLECTIONS

## 129    United States. War Department

Correspondence with General Harney. Letter of the Secretary of War, communicating copies of correspondence with General Harney, not heretofore published, in reference to his administration in Oregon.   [Washington, 1860]

29 p.   25 cm.   ([United States] 36th Cong., 1st sess. House. Ex. doc. no. 98)

Concerns the San Juan boundary dispute.

B.C. ARCHIVES

## 130    Vancouver Island. Supreme Court of Civil Justice

Order of court; in the Supreme Court of Civil Justice of the colony of Vancouver Island, Tuesday, the third day of April, in the twenty-third year of Her Majesty's reign, A.D. 1860. [Victoria, 1860]

20 p.   36 cm.   Caption title. Orders signed by David Cameron.

Schedules of various fees, costs, and charges.

B.C. ARCHIVES

## 131    Victoria. Collegiate School

[Prospectus]   Victoria, 1860.

sheet.   25 x 20 cm.   The Rev. Charles T. Woods, principal. Dated: Victoria, V.I., Sept. 1860.

B.C. ARCHIVES

## 132    Victoria. Select School

Private educational institute, established 1858; prospectus [Edward Mallandaine, headmaster. Victoria, 1860]

[2] p. (folder)   26 cm.   Caption title.

Mallandaine purchased the school from Julius Silversmith in 1860.

B.C. ARCHIVES

## 133    Vocabulary . . .

Vocabulary of the Chinook jargon; the complete language used by the Indians of Oregon, Washington Territory and British possessions. San Francisco, Published by Hutchings & Rosenfield, 1860.

8 p.   15 cm.   Cover title. Table of disances: p. [7]-8.

B.C. ARCHIVES

**134  Waddington, Alfred [Penderill]**
1801?-1872

Judicial murder.  [Victoria, 1860]

3 p. (folder)  26 cm.  Caption title.

Written to protest the iniquity of an Indian's execution for murder.

B.C. ARCHIVES

**135  Wells, Oliver**

General report on the Cowichan Valley. [Victoria? 1860]

2 p. (folder)  28 cm.  Caption title. Published by command of His Excellency William A. G. Young, acting colonial secretary.

B.C. ARCHIVES

**136  Ainsworth, W[illiam] F[rancis]**
EDITOR  1807-1896

All round the world; an illustrated record of voyages, travels and adventures in all parts of the globe.  London, W. Kent & Co. [1861-62?]

4 v.  illus., ports., maps.  30 cm.

Volume 1 has a section on Vancouver Island and information on the Palliser expedition.

Also: London, William Collins, 1871-72. 2 v.  Also: New York, Selmar Hess, n.d. 4 v.

B.C. ARCHIVES

**137  British Columbia Agricultural Association (Victoria)**

Provincial exhibition prize list.  1861-1941? Victoria.

v.  16, 22 cm.  annual.  Cover title. Various printers. Title varies: 1861-1907 as *British Columbia exhibition* or *British Columbia agricultural, mining, industrial exhibition.*

Gives surveys of climate, resources, communications, and agricultural history; includes constitution, contest rules, and prize lists.

B.C. ARCHIVES

**138  Columbia Mission**

Report.  1860-1880/81.  London, Rivingtons, 1861-62.

21 v.?  illus., maps (part fold.)  21 cm.  annual (irregular)  Title varies. Table of contents only. On microfilm.

On the missionary activity of the Church of England in British Columbia. Of particular value are the various extracts from the journals of George Hills, Bishop of Columbia, which, because of his journeys to the Cariboo mines, the missions of the Northwest Coast, etc., offer a wealth of detail on a wide range of subjects.

B.C. ARCHIVES

**139  Downall, John**

"The voice of Him that crieth in the wilderness"; a sermon, preached in St. James's Church, Piccadilly, at the annual service of the Columbia Mission . . .  London, Rivingtons [1861]

15 p.  22 cm.  Not seen.

YALE WESTERN AMERICANA CATALOGUE

**140  Gosset, W[illiam] Driscoll**

Industrial exhibition; circular respectfully addressed to the inhabitants of British Columbia, by Captain W. Driscoll Gosset, and J. Vernon Seddall.  New Westminster, Printed at the R.E. Camp by Corporal R. Wolfenden, 1861.

20 p.  21 cm.

An outline of proposed contributions to the London International Exhibition of 1862, with remarks and suggestions for the preparation of specimens.

B.C. ARCHIVES

**141  Great Britain. Hydrographic Office**

Vancouver Island pilot. Part I: sailing directions for the coasts of Vancouver Island and British Columbia, from the entrance of Juan de Fuca Strait to Burrard Inlet and Nanaimo Harbour, by Captain George Henry Richards.  London, Printed for the Hydrographic Office, 1861.

vii, 120 p.  24 cm.

Valuable for early description; includes coastal place names.

Supplement: London, George E. B. Eyre and William Spottiswoode, 1864. vii, 172 p.  Also see entries 229 and 284.

B.C. ARCHIVES

**142  [Hills, George]**
BISHOP OF COLUMBIA  1816-1895

A tour in British Columbia, &c.  London [Clay Printers] 1861.

74 p.  21 cm.  Cover title.

Mainly comprised of excerpts from Bishop Hills' journal for the period from 19 May to 8 August 1860.

B.C. ARCHIVES

**143  London International Exhibition, 1862. Executive Committee for Vancouver Island and British Columbia**

Industrial exhibition.  [Victoria? 1861]

[3] p. (folder)  32 cm.  Caption title.

Relates to the articles that were being considered for exhibition.

B.C. ARCHIVES

144    London International Exhibition, 1862. General Committee of Vancouver Island and British Columbia.

[An open letter dated February 13th, 1861, with resolutions adopted at a public meeting. Victoria, 1861]

[2] p. (folder)   23 cm.   Letters signed by Chas. B. Wood and Joseph W. Trutch.

B.C. ARCHIVES

145    Mayne, Richard C[harles]
1835-1892

Report on a journey in British Columbia in the districts bordering on the Thompson, Fraser, and Harrison rivers. Communicated by the Admiralty. London, Printed by W. Clowes and Sons [n.d.]

10 p.   fold. map, tables.   22 cm.   Cover title. On cover: Read before the Royal Geographical Society of London on the 12th of March 1859.

Also in: Royal Geographical Society. *Journal.* v. 31, 1861, p. 213-223.

B.C. ARCHIVES

146    Mayne, Richard C[harles]
1835-1892

Sketch of the country between Jervis Inlet and Port Pemberton, on the Lilloet River, a branch of the Fraser River, British Columbia. Communicated by the Lords Commissioners of the Admiralty.   London, Printed by W. Clowes and Sons [n.d.]

6 p.   fold. map.   22 cm.   Cover title. On cover: Read before the Royal Geographical Society of London on the 10th of June 1861.

The object of Mayne's expedition was to find out if a road could be built from the head of Jervis Inlet to the gold fields.

Also in: Royal Geographical Society. *Journal.* v. 31, 1861, p. 297-302.

B.C. ARCHIVES

147    Queen Charlotte Mining Company, Limited

Memorandum of association [and articles of association.   Victoria, 1861?]

3 p. (folder)   23 cm.   Caption title.

B.C. ARCHIVES

148    Sparshott, E[dward] C[harles]
COMPILER   D. 1867

A military manual of infantry drill, including the manual and platoon exercises, designed for the use of the officers, non-commissioned officers, and privates of the volunteer forces of Vancouver Island and British Columbia. [New Westminster?] Printed for the compiler, 1861.

viii, 103 p.   19 cm.

B.C. ARCHIVES

149    Synge, M[illington] H[enry]
1823-1907

The country v. the company; or, Why British North America may be peopled, and how it may be done, with suggestions towards a plan for doing so to the best advantage.   London, Edward Stanford, 1861.

22 p.   21 cm.

Advocates a colonization policy involving the termination of Hudson's Bay Company territorial control and the construction of a railway to the Pacific.

B.C. ARCHIVES

150    Victoria. Tiger Engine Company No. 2

Constitution and by-laws.   Victoria, Printed for the Company, 1861.

20 p.   15 cm.

B.C. ARCHIVES

151    Victoria Jockey Club

[Rules and regulations of the] Victoria, V.I., Jockey Club.   Victoria, Printed at the British Colonist Office, 1861.

7 p.   16 cm.

B.C. ARCHIVES

152    Victoria Literary Institute

Constitution of the Victoria Literary Institute, adopted at a public meeting, 26th October 1861.   Victoria, Printed at the office of the "Daily Press," 1861.

7 p.   21 cm.

B.C. ARCHIVES

153    Victoria Market Company, Limited

[Announcement of opening of the New Market on Fort and Broughton.   Victoria, 1861]

[1] p. (folder)   25 cm.   Signed in print by the secretary, J. J. Cochrane.

The New Market operated from September until November 1861.

B.C. ARCHIVES

**154    Victoria Market Company, Limited**

Report on the affairs of the Victoria Market Company, Limited, by the directors, to the General Meeting of the shareholders, 21st October 1861.   [Victoria, 1861]

[2] p. (folder)   26 cm.   Caption title. Signed in print by the chairman, K. McKenzie.

B.C. ARCHIVES

**155    Antler Bed-Rock Flume Company, Limited**

[Prospectus of] Antler Bed-Rock Flume Company, Limited, duly incorporated and registered under the Joint Stock Company's Act, 1860.   [n.p., n.d.]

sheet.   25 x 19 cm.   Signed in print: J. J. Cochrane, secretary. Probably printed in 1862.

B.C. ARCHIVES

**156    The Bank of British Columbia**

Charter of incorporation and deed of settlement. London, Printed by Rixon & Arnold, 1862.

90 p.   24 cm.

For supplemental charter see entry 222.

B.C. ARCHIVES

**157    Barrett-Lennard, C[harles] E[dward]**

Travels in British Columbia, with the narrative of a yacht voyage round Vancouver's Island. London, Hurst and Blackett, 1862.

xii, 307 p.   front.   22 cm.

Meant for the intended emigrant; includes discussions of various Indian tribes.

B.C. ARCHIVES

**158    Benjamin, Israel Joseph**
1818-1864

Drei Jahre in Amerika, 1859-1862, von J. J. Benjamin II.   Hannover, Selbstverlag des Verfassers, 1862.

3 pts. in 2 v.   port.   22 cm.

Part 3 of the work, "Reise in den Norwestgegenden Nord-Amerika's," includes the author's impressions of conditions on Vancouver Island in 1861. One chapter relates to Indian life.

An English translation by Charles Reznikoff, with an introduction by Oscar Handlin, was published by the Jewish Publication Society of America in 1956 in the "Jacob R. Schiff library of Jewish contributions to American democracy" series. The two chapters in Part 3 not pertaining to Indians were translated by Martin Wolff and appeared in

mimeographed form under title: *Benjamin II on British Columbia* (Montreal Archives Committee of the Canadian Jewish Congress, 1940).

B.C. ARCHIVES

**159    Bentinck Arm and Fraser River Road Company, Limited**

Prospectus [and report]   Victoria, Printed at the British Colonist Office, 1862.

7 p.   26 cm.   On t.p.: This company was organized under the Joint Stock Company's Limited Liability Act, 1860. The report is by Ranald McDonald and John G. Barnston.

The object of the company was to construct a wagon road from North Bentinck Arm to the Fraser River.

An appendix to the report was separately published as a folder (2 p.) under title: *Coast route to the northern mines, from Victoria to Bentinck Arm, thence to Cariboo* (Victoria, Colonist Print, 1862).

B.C. ARCHIVES

**160    Cariboo . . .**

Cariboo, the newly discovered gold fields of British Columbia, fully described by a returned digger, who has made his own fortune there, and advises others to go and do likewise.   London, Darton & Co., 1862.

iv, 76 p.   tables.   18 cm.   Pilling attributes this publication to William Carew Hazlitt (see *Chinookan languages*, p. 41)

There were at least six editions of this work published in 1862.

B.C. ARCHIVES

**161    Colonial Bank of British Columbia (Limited)**

[Prospectus.   n.p., 1862?]

2 l.   32 cm.   Signed in print: Henry Holbrook; John Cooper; F. G. Claudet.

The attempt to establish this bank (with head offices at New Westminster) was unsuccessful.

B.C. ARCHIVES

**162    Dictionary of Indian tongues . . .**

Dictionary of Indian tongues, containing most of the words and terms used in the Tshimpsean, Hydah, & Chinook, with their meaning or equivalent in the English language.   Victoria, Published by Hibben & Carswell, 1862.

15 p.   20 cm.   Cover title. Colophon: Printed at the office of the Daily Chronicle.

A rearrangement of material appeared in 1865 under the same title (in 14 p.).

B.C. ARCHIVES

**163**   Epner, Gustavus
COMPILER

Map of the gold regions in British Columbia.
Compiled from sketches and information
given by His Excellency James Douglas, C.B.,
governor of British Columbia and Vancouver
Island, and from data obtained from the most
intelligent and reliable miners.   Victoria, Hibben
& Carswell, 1862.

map.   49 x 39 cm.   Cover title. Scale: 1 inch to 20
miles. Title on map: Map of gold regions of British
Columbia, compiled from sketches and informations
by His Excellency James Douglas ...   Lithographed
by Britton & Co., San Francisco.

B.C. ARCHIVES

**164**   Féry, Jules H.
B. 1812

Map and guide to the Cariboo gold mines of
British Columbia, by Jules H. Féry. With
notes, observations, directions, and information
gathered from official and other authentic
sources, by G. J. Wight.   San Francisco,
Published by F. Truette & Co., 1862 [c1861]

24 p.   2 fold. maps, tables.   17 cm.   Reader-printer
copy examined. Original in the Bancroft Library.

A second edition appeared in 1862 under title: *Map
& Guide to Cariboo and Frazer River gold mines,
British Columbia.*

UNIVERSITY OF VICTORIA LIBRARY

**165**   Fleming, [Sir] Sandford
1827-1915

Suggestions on the inter-colonial railway, and the
construction of a highway and telegraph line
between the Atlantic and Pacific oceans, within
British territory, respectfully submitted to the
government of Canada by Sandford Fleming.
Toronto, August 5th, 1862.   [Toronto] W. C.
Chewett & Co., 1862.

[77]-134 p.   16 cm.   Cover title. Includes: Practical
observations on the construction of a continuous line
of railway from Canada to the Pacific Ocean on
British territory.

CANADIAN ARCHIVES

**166**   Forbes, Charles

Prize essay; Vancouver Island, its resources and
capabilities as a new colony.   [Victoria] The
Colonial Government, 1862.

63, 18 p.   tables.   22 cm.

B.C. ARCHIVES

**167**   The Gold fields ...

The gold fields of British Columbia, by the
correspondent of The Times.   London, Rixon &
Arnold, 1862.

24 p.   Not seen.

BRITISH MUSEUM CATALOGUE

**168**   Guide book ...

Guide book for British Columbia, &c., by a
successful digger; containing practical
information for the emigrant, and other useful
matter.   [London, Dean & Son, 1862]

31 p.   fold. map.   18 cm.   Cover title: Guide book
for British Columbia; the wonders of the gold diggings
of British Columbia, by a successful digger, who has
made his fortune there, and advises others to go and
make theirs.   Xerox copy seen. Original in the Yale
University Library.

The pamphlet could have been written without
the author ever having left England.

UNIVERSITY OF VICTORIA LIBRARY

**169**   The Handbook of British
Columbia ...

The handbook of British Columbia, and
emigrant's guide to the gold fields. With map
and two illustrations from photographs by
M. Claudet.   London, W. Oliver [1862?]

82 p.   2 plates (1 double) fold. map.   19 cm.

"This book is compiled from the most recent and
trustworthy authorities it has been possible to find.
The chief amongst these are the Parliamentary papers
relative to the affairs of British Columbia (1858-
1861), the Colonization Circular (1862), *The Times*
newspaper (1858-1862), the reports of Mr. W.
Downie, a gentleman in Government employ, and the
printed information by Mr. McLean, an officer of the
Hudson's Bay Company."—pref.

B.C. ARCHIVES

**170**   Hazlitt, William Carew
1834-1913

The great gold fields of Cariboo, with an authentic
description, brought down to the latest period, of
British Columbia and Vancouver Island. With an
accurate map.   London, New York, Routledge,
Warne and Routledge, 1862.

viii, 184 p.   map.   17 cm.

B.C. ARCHIVES

**171**   Hind, Henry Youle
1823-1908

A sketch of an overland route to British
Columbia.   Toronto, W. C. Chewett & Co.,
printers, 1862.

128 p. fold. map. 17 cm. Practical observations on the construction of a continuous line of railway from Canada to the Pacific Ocean on British territory, by Sandford Fleming: p. 81-117. Appendix 1: The gold diggings of British Columbia [p. 119-126]

B.C. ARCHIVES

172　James, Sir Henry
EDITOR　1803-1877

Abstracts from the meteorological observations taken in the years 1860-61, at the Royal Engineer Office, New Westminster, British Columbia.　London, Printed by Edward Eyre and George Spottiswoode, 1862.

9 p. tables. 31 cm.

B.C. ARCHIVES

173　Langley, A[lfred] J[ohn]
1820-1896

A glance at British Columbia and Vancouver's Island in 1861.　London, Robert Hardwicke, 1862.

44 p. 18 cm. Xerox copy examined. Original in the British Museum.

Succinct, interesting comments upon business activity, social life, living conditions, and the attitudes of the colonists, particularly those in Victoria. The pamphlet also deals with various aspects of the Cariboo gold finds.

UNIVERSITY OF VICTORIA LIBRARY

174　Lindley, Jo.

Three years in Cariboo, by Jo. Lindley; being the experience and observations of a packer: what I saw and know of the country, its traveled routes, distances, villages, mines, trade and prospects. With distances, notes and facts relative to the Salmon River and Nez Perces gold fields, by T. R. Olney.　San Francisco, Published by A. Rosenfield, 1862.

36 p. 14 cm. Towne & Bacon, printers. On cover: Guide and history of Salmon River & Cariboo mining districts, containing valuable information, with correct tables of modes and prices of traveling; also giving the distances from point to point, of all routes. Vocabulary of the Chinook jargon: p. 32-36.

An itinerary of the routes from Victoria to the Cariboo is given in pages 3-14.

U.B.C. SPECIAL COLLECTIONS

175　London. Citizens

Speeches delivered by the Lord Bishop of Oxford, the Lord Bishop of London, the Hon. Arthur Kinnaird, M.P., Sir J. K. Shuttleworth, and other influential friends of the Columbia Mission, at the public meeting held in the London Tavern, on

Thursday, 27th February 1862.　London, Rivingtons [1862]

32 p. 20 cm. Not seen.

YALE WESTERN AMERICANA CATALOGUE

176　London International Exhibition, 1862

Catalogue of the Vancouver contribution, with a short account of Vancouver Island and British Columbia.　London, 1862.

8, 8 p. 21 cm.

B.C. ARCHIVES

177　Macdonald, Duncan George Forbes
1823?-1884

British Columbia and Vancouver's Island, comprising a description of these dependencies: their physical character, climate, capabilities, population, trade, natural history, geology, ethnology, gold-fields, and future prospects; also, an account of the manners and customs of the native Indians.　London, Longman, Green, Longman, Roberts, & Green, 1862.

xiii, 524 p. fold. map. 23 cm. Chinook jargon and English equivalent terms: p. 394-398.

Written to expound the author's view that opportunities for settlers in the two colonies had been exaggerated and that it was highly unjust to promote emigration to them.

Second edition: London, 1862.　Third edition: London, 1863.

B.C. ARCHIVES

178　Mayne, R[ichard] C[harles]
1835-1892

Four years in British Columbia and Vancouver Island; an account of their forests, rivers, coasts, gold fields and resources for colonisation.　London, John Murray, 1862.

xi, 468 p. plates, maps (1 fold.) 23 cm.

B.C. ARCHIVES

179　Mayne, Richard C[harles]
1835-1892

Route in exploring a road from Albernie Canal to Nanaimo, in Vancouver Island, in May 1861. With a track chart. Communicated by the Lords Commissioners of the Admiralty.　London, Printed by W. Clowes and Sons [n.d.]

7 p. map. 22 cm. Cover title. On cover: From the Journal of the Royal Geographical Society of London for 1862.

Also in: Royal Geographical Society. *Journal.* v. 32, 1862, p. 529-535.

B.C. ARCHIVES

**180   The New gold fields . . .**

The new gold fields of British Columbia and Vancouver's Island.   London, Printed by P. Grant & Co., 1862.

23 p.   18 cm.   On cover: The new gold fields of British Columbia and Vancouver's Island; a complete handbook for intending emigrants; those who ought and those who ought not to go; your outfit, the voyage, diet; description of the country, climate, where the gold lies, and how to get it; etc., etc., etc. London, Published at Plummer's Library.   Xerox copy examined. Original in the British Museum.

UNIVERSITY OF VICTORIA LIBRARY

**181   New Westminster. Royal Columbian Hospital**

Report.   1862/63 +   New Westminster.

v.   22, 28 cm.   annual.   Title of 1863 report: *Report of the Board of Management for the year ending February 12, 1863.* On t.p., 1902-1903: First annual report since amalgamation of Women's and Royal Columbian Hospital, June 30, 1903. Current reports mimeographed.

Report for 1862/63 contains a brief history of the formation and early operation of the newly-established hospital.

B.C. ARCHIVES

**182   Oregon Association (Edinburgh)**

Expedition to Vancouver's Island and British Columbia.   [Edinburgh, 1862]

2, [1] p. (folder)   27 cm.   Caption title.

Includes a resolution of the association to form the British Columbia Botanical Association for the purpose of sending Robert Brown to the two colonies to collect botanical specimens for its subscribers.

B.C. ARCHIVES

**183   Parsons, R[obert] M[ann]**

Abstract of meteorological observations, taken at the Royal Engineer Camp during the year 1861, by order of Col. R. C. Moody, R.E., commanding the troops.   New Westminster, Printed at the Royal Engineer Press [1862?]

[3] p. (folder)   map.   24 cm.   Caption title. At head of title: New Westminster, British Columbia.

B.C. ARCHIVES

**184   [Parsons, Robert Mann]**

[Report of a journey from New Westminster to Lake La Hache.   New Westminster, Printed at the Royal Engineer Press, 1862]

8 p.   2 maps, fold. diagr.   25 cm.   Dated: 16th September 1862. Addressed to Colonel R. C. Moody. Report begins: Sir, In obedience to your instructions I have the honor to offer a few general observations . . .

B.C. ARCHIVES

**185   Rattray, Alexander**

Vancouver Island and British Columbia; where they are, what they are, and what they may become; a sketch of their history, topography, climate, resources, capabilities, and advantages, especially as colonies for settlement.   London, Smith, Elder & Co., 1862.

viii, 182 p.   col. plates, 2 fold. maps, tables (1 fold.) 21 cm.

B.C. ARCHIVES

**186   Victoria Fire Department (Victoria)**

Regulations of the Victoria Fire Department; rules and orders of the Board of Delegates, and an act to extend and amend the provisions of the "Fireman's Protection Act, 1860." San Francisco, Towne & Bacon, 1862.

35p.   15 cm.

The Victoria Fire Department was organized under legislative enactments passed in 1861, 1864, and 1873. It functioned independently of Victoria's administration, and its business was carried out by delegates from the volunteer fire companies. Also see entry 446.

B.C. ARCHIVES

**187   British Columbia**

British Columbia gazette.   v. 1, no. 1+ 3 January 1863+   New Westminster, Victoria.

v.   34, 40 cm.   weekly.   Title varies: 3 January 1863—14 November 1871 as *Government gazette— British Columbia* (published by authority). Published in New Westminster 1863-68; in Victoria, 30 May 1868 to date. Government regulations published separately 1958 to date.

B.C. ARCHIVES

**188   British Columbia. Governor, 1858-1864   (DOUGLAS)**

Rules and regulations issued in conformity with the Gold Field Act, 1859.   Victoria, Printed at the British Colonist Office, 1860 [i.e. 1863?]

12 p.   13 cm.   On p. 12: Issued . . . this 24th day of February, A.D. 1863, and in the twenty-sixth year of Her Majesty's reign.

A commercial printing of a government document with numerous explanatory headings added. As rules and regulations were also issued by Governor Douglas in 1860, the title page may have been printed for an earlier edition.

B.C. ARCHIVES

**189   The British Columbian and Victoria guide . . .**

The British Columbian and Victoria guide and directory for 1863, under the patronage of His

Excellency Governor Douglas, C.B., and the executive of both colonies. Compiled and published by Frederick P. Howard and George Barnett. First year of publication. Victoria, Office of the British Columbian and Victoria Directory, 1863.

216 p. (incl. advertisements) 24 cm. On verso of t.p.: Towne & Bacon, printers, Excelsior Office . . . San Francisco.

B.C. ARCHIVES

## 190 Brown, R[obert] C[hristopher] Lundin
D. 1876

British Columbia; an essay. New Westminster, Printed at the Royal Engineer Press, 1863.

64, xxxiii p. 20 cm.

A prize-winning essay describing the advantages of the new crown colony, written by one of the early missionaries.

B.C. ARCHIVES

## 191 Bute Inlet Wagon Road Company, Limited.

[Prospectus. Victoria, 1863?]

3 p. (folder) 25 cm.

A report on the company by Alfred Waddington, dated 7 December 1863, offering unallotted shares to the public.

B.C. ARCHIVES

## 192 Canada. Governor-General
1861-1868 (MONCK)

Copies of all communications made to any members of the government—of any report or reports made by any member of His Excellency in Council—of any communication to or from the Imperial government, and all orders in council passed in relation to the opening of a route to Red River, or to British Columbia and the Pacific, since the last session of Parliament. Quebec, Hunter, Rose & Lemieux, 1863.

19 p. 24 cm. Not seen. Missing from Shortt collection.

PEEL

## 193 Deluge Engine Company No. 1 (Victoria)

Constitution and by-laws of Deluge Company No. 1, Victoria, Vancouver Island. Victoria, Printed at the British Colonist Office, 1863.

18 p. 13 cm.

B.C. ARCHIVES

## 194 Emigrant soldiers' gazette . . .

The emigrant soldiers' gazette, and Cape Horn chronicle. Published originally on manuscript forms . . . during the voyage, from Gravesend to Vancouver Island, of the detachment of Royal Engineers selected for service in British Columbia, between the 10th November 1858 and the 12th April 1859. Edited by Second-Corporal Charles Sinnett, R.E., assisted by Lieut. H. S. Palmer, R.E. New Westminster, Printed by John Robson at the office of the "British Columbian," 1863.

68 p. illus. 29 cm.

The *Gazette* ran to 17 numbers. The original manuscript is preserved in the British Columbia Provincial Archives.

Reprinted in 1907, with addenda, by Richard Wolfenden.

B.C. ARCHIVES

## 195 Fleming, [Sir] Sandford
1827-1915

A great territorial road to British Columbia. Quebec, 1863.

57 p. Not seen. From: L. J. Burpee, *Sandford Fleming*, p. 279.

PEEL

## 196 Freemasons. Victoria. Vancouver Lodge No. 421

[Letter of the secretary transmitting a list of officers for the ensuing masonic year. A.D. 5863, 5866, 5867; i.e. 1863, 1866, 1867. Victoria, 1863, 1866, 1867]

3 sheets. 25 x 19 cm.; 26 x 21 cm.; 26 x 21 cm.

B.C. ARCHIVES

## 197 Gibbs, George
1815-1873

A dictionary of the Chinook jargon; or, Trade language of Oregon. New York, Cramoisy Press, 1863.

xiv, 43 p. 24 cm. (Shea's library of American linguistics, no. 12) Bibliography of the Chinook jargon: p. [xiii]-xiv.

Includes a short discussion on the jargon and its derivation. James Pilling considered this work the standard authority for Chinook jargon words.

Also appeared as Smithsonian miscellaneous collection, no. 161 (Washington, Smithsonian Institution, 1863).

B.C. ARCHIVES

## 198 Great Britain. Admiralty

Station regulations and port orders for the squadron in the Pacific, 1863.   Victoria, Printed at the British Colonist Office, 1863.

73 p.   23 cm.

The regulations and orders were issued by Rear-Admiral John Kingcome, commander-in-chief, Pacific Station.

B.C. ARCHIVES

## 199 Great Britain. Colonial Office

Canada and British Columbia. Return . . . "Copy of all correspondence from the 1st day of January 1862 to the present time, between the Colonial Office and the Hudson's Bay Company or other parties, relative to a road and telegraph from Canada to British Columbia, and the transfer of the property and rights of the Hudson's Bay Company to other parties." Ordered by the House of Commons to be printed, 15 July 1863.   [London, 1863]

21 p.   34 cm.   ([Great Britain. Parliament, 1863. House of Commons papers] 438)

B.C. ARCHIVES

## 200 Great Britain. Colonial Office

Vancouver Island. Return . . . "Copies or extracts of correspondence between Mr. Langford and the Colonial Department, relative to alleged abuses in the government of Vancouver Island; of correspondence between the Colonial Department and Governor Douglas, referring to Mr. Langford's charges; and, of correspondence with the governor of Vancouver Island relative to the appointment of Chief Justice Cameron, and remonstrances against such an appointment." Ordered by House of Commons to be printed, 25 July 1863.   [London, 1863]

52, [2] p.   32 cm.   ([Great Britain. Parliament, 1863. House of Commons papers] 507)   Title from p. [54]

B.C. ARCHIVES

## 201 Great Britain. Laws, statutes, etc.

British Columbia boundaries. A bill intituled: An act to define the boundaries of the colony of British Columbia, and to continue an act to provide for the government of the said colony. Brought from the Lords 13 July 1863. Ordered by the House of Commons to be printed, 14 July 1863.   [London, 1863]

2, [2] p. (folder)   33 cm.   ([Great Britain. Parliament, 1863. House of Commons] Bill 187) Title from p. [4]

B.C. ARCHIVES

## 202 Hills, George
### BISHOP OF COLUMBIA   1816-1895

Pastoral address of George Hills, D.D., Bishop of Columbia, to the clergy and laity of the Diocese of Columbia. March 26, 1863.   Victoria, Printed at the British Colonist Office, 1863.

10 p.   24 cm.

B.C. ARCHIVES

## 203 Husdell, G. Davison
### COMPILER

Extracts relating to Vancouver Island and British Columbia, compiled by G. Davison Husdell and J. D. Churchill.   London, Ward Brothers [pref. 1863]

52 p.   23 cm.   Xerox copy examined. Original in the library of the Commonwealth Office, London.

UNIVERSITY OF VICTORIA LIBRARY

## 204 Knight, William H[enry]
### EDITOR   1835-1925

Hand-book almanac for the Pacific states; an official register and business directory of the states of California and Oregon, the territories of Washington, Nevada and Utah, and the colonies of British Columbia and Vancouver Island, for the year 1863.   San Francisco, H. H. Bancroft & Company [1863]

420 p.   tables.   17 cm.   Cover title: Bancroft's hand-book almanac . . .

Has five pages on the two colonies.

An edition for the year 1862 listed in Smith does not contain information on British Columbia. Two subsequent editions were published for the years 1864 and 1865.

UNIVERSITY OF WASHINGTON LIBRARY

## 205 Macdonald, D[uncan] G[eorge] F[orbes]
### 1823?-1884

Lecture on British Columbia and Vancouver's Island, delivered at the Royal United Services Institute on March 27, 1863.   London, Longman, Green, Longman, Roberts, & Green, 1863.

59 p.   22 cm.

A comment written on the lining paper of the copy examined reads: "This man was a gross fabricator, ignorant of his subject and malignant, yet a cunning distorter of the truth about B.C. and V.I."

B.C. ARCHIVES

## 206 Mark, W[illia]m

Cariboo; a true and correct narrative, by Wm. Mark, containing an account of his travel over ten thousand miles, by sea, rivers, lakes, and land, to the Cariboo gold diggings, British Columbia. Stockton [Eng.] Printed by W. M. Wright, 1863.

34 p.   18 cm.   Xerox copy seen.   Original in the Yale University Library.

Pages 18-34 give an interesting, detailed account of travel to the Cariboo from Victoria in 1862 and of conditions at the gold fields.

UNIVERSITY OF VICTORIA LIBRARY

### 207     Newcastle, [Henry Pelham Fiennes Pelham Clinton]
5TH DUKE OF   1811-1864

Correspondence respecting certain officials in the colonies of British Columbia and Vancouver Island, between His Grace the Duke of Newcastle, Secretary of State for the Colonies, and Mr. Edward E. Langford.   London, Edward West, 1863.

11 p.   22 cm.

Because he lacked evidence of property qualifications, Edward Langford was not allowed to sit in Vancouver Island's first Legislative Assembly. He hoped to be re-elected in 1860, but an attempt was made to discredit him in an anonymous public notice. Langford sued the alleged author, lost his case, and was himself sued for contempt. In his letters to the Duke of Newcastle, written in England, he aired his grievances against the colonies' officials.

B.C. ARCHIVES

### 208     Palliser, John
1807-1887

Exploration—British North America. The journals, detailed reports, and observations relative to the exploration, by Captain Palliser, of that portion of British North America, which, in latitude, lies between the British boundary line and the height of land or watershed of the Northern or Frozen Ocean respectively, and in longitude, between the western shore of Lake Superior and the Pacific Ocean during the years 1857, 1858, 1859, and 1860. Presented to both Houses of Parliament by command of Her Majesty, 19th May 1863.   London, Printed by George Edward Eyre and William Spottiswoode, 1863.

325 p.   diagrs., tables.   *and* atlas of 5 fold. maps. 33 cm.   Atlas has date 1865 and cover title: Index and maps to Captain Palliser's reports.

B.C. ARCHIVES

### 209     Palmer, H[enry] Spencer
1838-1893

British Columbia: Williams Lake and Cariboo; report on portions of the Williams Lake and Cariboo districts, and on the Fraser River from Fort Alexander to Fort George.   New Westminster, Printed at the Royal Engineer Press, 1863.

[iv], 25 p.   3 maps (2 fold.) fold. diagr., tables. 25 cm.

Another edition appeared in 1863. It is smaller (22 cm.) and has on page [iv]: "N.B. — The three first [maps] only have been lithographed." The larger edition has "N.B. — the two first . . ." The collation is the same.

B.C. ARCHIVES

### 210     Palmer, H[enry] Spencer
1838-1893

Report of a journey of survey from Victoria to Fort Alexander, via North Bentinck Arm.   New Westminster, Printed at the Royal Engineer Press, 1863.

30 p.   3 tables, 2 fold. maps.   25 cm.   Cover title: North Bentinck Arm route; report of journey of survey . . .   At head of cover title: British Columbia.

Lieutenant Palmer's report made it clear that the road then being constructed by way of the Fraser River was the best route to the Cariboo.

*The Catalog of the Yale Collection of Western Americana* notes two issues. Another issue has one folding map.

B.C. ARCHIVES

### 211     Parsons, R[obert] M[ann]

Abstract of meteorological observations, taken at the Royal Engineer Camp, during the year 1862, by order of Col. R. C. Moody, R.E., commanding the troops.   New Westminster, Printed at the Royal Engineer Press [1863?]

[3] p. (folder)   map.   24 cm.   Caption title. At head of title: New Westminster, British Columbia. Map drawn by J. Launders, R.E. Printed on blue lettersheet paper.

Also printed in larger format of 27 cm. on white paper. The map, which is drawn by C. Sinnett, R.E., shows the location of gold fields.

B.C. ARCHIVES

### 212     Red River Settlement. Citizens

Memorial of the people of Red River to the British and Canadian governments, with remarks on the colonization of central British North America, and the establishment of a great territorial road from Canada to British Columbia. Submitted to the Canadian Government by Sandford Fleming. Printed by order of the Leglislative Assembly.   Quebec, Printed for the contractors by Hunter, Rose & Co., 1863.

57 p.   25 cm.   Not seen. Copy in Shortt Collection.

PEEL

**213    Rossi, L[ouis]**

Six ans en Amérique (Californie et Orégon) par l'abbé L. Rossi, missionnaire.    Paris, Perisse Frères, 1863.

322 (i.e. 298) p.    2 fold. maps.    21 cm.

Includes a chapter on the San Juan Island dispute and references to the author's visits to Victoria.

Second edition: Paris, Dentu, 1863. 322 p.    A Paris edition of 1864 was published under title: *Souvenirs d'un voyage en Orégon et en Californie.*

B.C. ARCHIVES

**214    Sansum Copper Mining Company, Limited**

Prospectus.    [Victoria, 1863]

[2] p. (folder)    25 cm.    Caption title. Signed in print: Charles Bedford Young and Charles McKeivers Smith.

B.C. ARCHIVES

**215    United States. Treaties, etc.**

A convention between the United States and Her Britannic Majesty, for the final adjustment of claims of the Hudson's Bay and Puget's Sound Agricultural companies, concluded at Washington the 1st day of July 1863. Washington, 1863.

3, [1] p.    ([United States] 38th Cong., 1st sess. Ex. G) At head of title: confidential.    On microfilm.

B.C. ARCHIVES

**216    Vancouver Island. Governor**
1849-1851    (BLANSHARD)

Vancouver Island, despatches; Governor Blanshard to the Secretary of State, 26th December 1849 to 30th August 1851. New Westminster, Printed at the Government Printing Office [1863]

15 p.    33 cm.

B.C. ARCHIVES

**217    Vancouver Island. Governor**
1851-1864    (DOUGLAS)

Despatches and correspondences transmitted to the House of Assembly in Governor Douglas' message of 3rd September 1863.    Victoria, Printed at the "Daily Chronicle" Office, 1863.

3 pts. in 1 v.    27 cm.    Part 3 has title: Correspondence upon the conveyance to the crown of certain lands by the Hudson's Bay Company . . .

Reprinted in 1881 with additional material: British Columbia. Legislative Assembly. *Papers in connection with crown lands in British Columbia and title of the Hudson's Bay Company.*

B.C. ARCHIVES

**218    Vancouver Island. Laws, statutes, etc.**

A collection of the public general statutes of the colony of Vancouver Island, 1859, 1860, 1861, 1862 and 1863 [and proclamations of Governor James Douglas, 1860-62]    Victoria, Printed at the "Daily Evening Express" Office, 1863-[66?]

3 v.    25 cm.    Contents: p. [3]-[4] Vols. 2-3 lack title pages.

For a partial table of proclamations and acts see: *The laws of British Columbia, consisting of the acts, ordinances & proclamations of the formerly separate colonies of Vancouver Island and British Columbia, and of the united colony of British Columbia* (Victoria, Government Printing Office, 1871).

Two other collections in the B.C. Provincial Archives have title pages with imprints: Victoria, Printed at the British Colonist Office, 1866;    Victoria, Printed at the "Evening Express" Office, 1864. Vols. 2-3 lack title pages.

B.C. ARCHIVES

**219    Victoria Typographical Union**

Constitution and by-laws of the Victoria Typographical Union, including the scale of prices and list of members.    Victoria, Printed at the British Colonist Office, 1863.

30 p.    14 cm.

B.C. ARCHIVES

**220    Addresses and memorials . . .**

Addresses and memorials, together with articles, reports, &c., &c., from the public journals, upon the occasion of the retirement of Sir James Douglas, K.C.B., from the governorship of the colonies of Vancouver's Island, and British Columbia.    Deal [England?] Edward Hayward, Victoria Printing Office, 1864.

74 p.    22 cm.

B.C. ARCHIVES

**221    Addresses presented to . . .**

Addresses presented to His Excellency A. E. Kennedy, C.B., on assuming the government of Vancouver Island.    [Victoria? 1864]

30 p.    25 cm.

B.C. ARCHIVES

**222    The Bank of British Columbia**

Supplemental charter.    London, Printed by Rixon & Arnold, 1864.

12 p.    24 cm.

Supplemental charters were also printed in 1884 and 1894.

B.C. ARCHIVES

**223    British Columbia. Laws,**
              **statutes, etc.**

Ordinances passed by the Legislative Council
during the session from February 1864—March
1871.    New Westminster, Victoria, Government
Printing Office, 1864-71.

8 v.    29, 34 cm.    Vol. [1] in B.C. Archives has no
t.p. For session from 5 January to 28 March 1871,
t.p. has title: *Acts passed by the Legislative Council*.
Includes ordinances 1-18 (1 February 1864 to 21
December 1864), 1-28 (January to April 1865), 1-17
(January to April 1866), 1-40 (January to April
1867), 1-12 (March to May 1868), 1-26 (December
1868 to March 1869), 1-18 (February to April
1870), 1-24 (January to March 1871) Each volume
has a list of ordinances, with short titles, at the front.

For a partial table of ordinances before 1871 see *The
laws of British Columbia, consisting of the acts,
ordinances & proclamations of the formerly separate
colonies of Vancouver Island and British Columbia,
and of the united colony of British Columbia*
(Victoria, Government Printing Office, 1871).

Also see entry 58.

B.C. ARCHIVES

**224    British Columbia. Legislative**
              **Council**

Journals. 1st-8th session; 1864-71.    New
Westminster, Victoria, Government Printing
Office, 1864-71.

8 v. in 1.    34 cm.    1868/69-1871 printed
in Victoria. Includes sessional papers and colonial
estimates for 1866-71. Table of contents, index.

Contains minutes, speeches, schedule of bills,
departmental estimates, reports, and rolls of the
legislative councillors. When British Columbia
entered Canada in 1871, the Legislative Council was
succeeded by the Legislative Assembly.

B.C. ARCHIVES

**225    British North America . . .**

British North America; comprising Canada,
British central North America, British Columbia,
Vancouver's Island, Nova Scotia and Cape
Breton, New Brunswick, Prince Edward's
Island, Newfoundland and Labrador.    London,
The Religious Tract Society [1864]

viii, 370 p.    2 maps (1 fold.)    18 cm.

Written to present the history, condition, and
prospects of British North America.

B.C. ARCHIVES

**226    Catholic Church. Liturgy and**
              **ritual**

Consecration of the Right Rev. Dr. D'Herbomez,
O.M.I., which has taken place in the Cathedral
of St. Andrews, Victoria, V.I., October 9th,
1864 (21st Sunday after Pentecost)    [n. p., n. d.]

10 p.    22 cm.    Caption title. At head of title: Ad
majorem Dei-gloriam et Beatœ Marioe
semper Virginis.

B.C. ARCHIVES

**227    Great Britain. Colonial Land and**
              **Emigration Commissioners**

No. 23, colonization circular . . . 1864.    London,
Printed by George E. Eyre and William
Spottiswoode [1864]

125 p.    tables.    19 cm.

Information on British Columbia and Vancouver
Island is scattered.

UNIVERSITY OF WASHINGTON LIBRARY

**228    Great Britain. Colonial Office**

Canada and Pacific telegraph. Return . . .
"Copy or extracts of any correspondence
between the Colonial Office and the authorities
in Canada and British Columbia on the subject
of the proposed telegraphic communication
between Canada and the Pacific (in continuation
of Parliamentary paper, no. 438 of session
1863)" Ordered by the House of Commons to
be printed, 17 June 1864.    [London, 1864]

16 p.    34 cm.    ([Great Britain. Parliament, 1864.
House of Commons papers] 402)

B.C. ARCHIVES

**229    Great Britain. Hydrographic**
              **Office**

The Vancouver Island pilot, containing sailing
directions for the coasts of Vancouver Island,
and part of British Columbia. Compiled
from the surveys made by Captain George
Henry Richards, R.N., in H.M. ships Plumper
and Hecate, between the years 1858 and 1864.
London [Printed by George E. B. Eyre and
William Spottiswoode] 1864.

ix, 270 p.    24 cm.

Valuable for early description; includes coastal
place names. Also see entries 141 and 284.

B.C. ARCHIVES

**230    Great Britain. Treaties, etc.**

Treaty between Her Majesty and the United States
of America, for the settlement of the claims of
the Hudson's Bay Company and Puget's Sound
Agricultural companies. Signed at Washington,
July 1, 1863. Presented to both Houses of
Parliament by command of Her Majesty, 1864.
London, Printed by Harrison and Sons [1864]

2 p.    35 cm.    ([Great Britain. Parliament.
Command papers] 3310)

B.C. ARCHIVES

**231    Hyack Engine Company No. 1 (New Westminster)**

Constitution, bye-laws, and rules of order.   New Westminster, Printed at the office of the "British Columbian," 1864.

14 p.   13 cm.

B.C. ARCHIVES

**232    Morison, John H[opkins]**
**1808-1896**

Dying for our country; a sermon on the death of Capt. J. Sewall Reed and Rev. Thomas Starr King, preached in the First Congregational Church in Milton, March 13, 1864.   Boston, Printed by J. Wilson and Son, 1864.

28 p.   24 cm.   Not seen.

"Gives a first-hand account of Capt. Reed's activities in the California Vigilance Committee, and his gold-hunting tour to the Fraser River Mines in 1858, with experiences at Fort Langley and Fort Yale."—Eberstadt, cat. 133, item 846.

LIBRARY OF CONGRESS

**233    [Nelson, Joseph]**

The Hudson's Bay Company; what is it? London, A. H. Baily & Co., 1864.

v, 81 p.   22 cm.   Cover title.

The author, hostile to the Hudson's Bay Company, advocated the termination of its charter.

B.C. ARCHIVES

**234    New Westminster. Public Library**

List of works in the New Westminster Public Library.   [New Westminster, n.d.]

8 p.   22 cm.

B.C. ARCHIVES

**235    New Westminster. Public Library**

Rules and regulations for the management of the Public Library, New Westminster.   [New Westminster, 1864?]

[2] p. (folder)   25 cm.   Caption title.

B.C. ARCHIVES

**236    Park, Joseph**
**1828-1877**

A practical view of the mining laws of British Columbia.   Victoria, Printed at the British Colonist Office, 1864.

xii, 64, 1xv-1xx p. (incl. advertisements)   17 cm.

A miner's handbook.

B.C. ARCHIVES

**237    Rawlings, Thomas**

Emigration, with special reference to Minnesota, U.S., and British Columbia.   London, Clayton & Co. [1864]

24 p.   fold. map.   24 cm.

A German edition, translated by Eduard Pelz, with an introduction and added material on Minnesota by Pelz, has title: *Die Auswanderung mit besonderer Beziehung auf Minnesota und Britisch Columbia* (Hamburg, Hoffmann & Campe, 1866). In 63 pages; lacking map.

B.C. ARCHIVES

**238    Reece, William S[heldon]**

"Education"; a sermon preached at Christ's Church, Victoria, V.I., on Sunday, October 9th, 1864.   Victoria, V.I., Printed at the "Evening Express" Office, 1864.

10 p.   21 cm.   Cover title.

B.C. ARCHIVES

**239    Rowe, G[eorge]**

The colonial empire of Great Britain, considered chiefly with reference to its physical geography and industrial productions. The American colonies.   London, Society for Promoting Christian Knowledge [1864?]

165 p.   maps.   17 cm.

Includes one chapter on British Columbia and Vancouver Island.

B.C. ARCHIVES

**240    United States. Congress. Senate. Committee on Foreign Relations**

Mr. Sumner, for the Committee on Foreign Relations, reported the following bill . . . A bill to carry into effect a treaty between the United States and Her Britannic Majesty, for the final settlement of the claims of the Hudson's Bay and Puget's Sound Agricultural companies. Washington, 1864.

2 p.   ([United States] 38th Cong., 1st sess. Senate. S. 187)   On microfilm.

B.C. ARCHIVES

**241    Vancouver Club (Victoria)**

By-laws.   Victoria, Printed by Harries & Co., British Colonist Office, 1864.

13 p.   18 cm.

B.C. ARCHIVES

**242    Vancouver Island**

The government gazette.  v. 1, no. 1—v. 3, no. 38; 17 May 1864—6 November 1866.  Victoria.

3 v.  33 cm.  weekly.  Full title: *Government gazette, Vancouver Island.* With added phrase: Published by authority. Publisher varies. Published on Vancouver Island simultaneously with the publication of the *British Columbia gazette* at New Westminster. Terminated with the union of the colonies of Vancouver Island and British Columbia. Superseded by the latter.

B.C. ARCHIVES

**243    Vancouver Island. House of Assembly. Select Committee on Crown Lands**

Minutes of proceedings of a select committee of the House of Assembly, appointed to inquire into the present condition of the crown lands of the colony, with reference to the proposal of Her Majesty's Secretary of State for the Colonies, dated 15th June 1863, to hand over the crown lands to the Legislature.  Victoria, Printed by Harries and Company, 1864.

66, xv p.  tables.  33 cm.  At head of title: Vancouver Island.

B.C. ARCHIVES

**244    Vancouver Island. House of Assembly. Select Committee on Crown Lands**

Report of the committee on crown lands, Vancouver Island; June 14th, 1864; House of Assembly, Third Parliament, first session, 1863-64.  [Victoria, 1864]

15, 12 p.  tables.  25 cm.  Cover title. Chairman: James Trimble.

U.B.C. SPECIAL COLLECTIONS

**245    British and American Joint Commission for the Final Settlement of the Claims of the Hudson's Bay and Puget's Sound Agricultural Companies**

[Memorial and statement of claims of the Hudson's Bay Company upon the United States. London, 1865]

11 p.  32 cm.  Dated: 8 April 1865. Text addressed to the commissioners.

CANADIAN ARCHIVES

**246    British and American Joint Commission for the Final Settlement of the Claims of the Hudson's Bay and Puget's Sound Agricultural Companies**

[Memorial and statement of claims of the Puget Sound Agricultural Company upon the United States.  London, 1865]

4 p.  32 cm.  Dated: 10 April 1865. Text addressed to the commissioners.

CANADIAN ARCHIVES

**247    British and American Joint Commission for the Final Settlement of the Claims of the Hudson's Bay and Puget's Sound Agricultural Companies**

[Papers]  Washington, Government Printing Office; Montreal, Printed by J. Lovell, 1865-69.

14 v.  21-25 cm.  No general t.p. Volume numbers cited below are supplied by the Library of Congress. Caleb Cusing, counsel for the United States; Charles D. Day, counsel for Hudson's Bay Company and Puget Sound Agricultural Company. Contents: [v. 1] Memorials presented to the commissioners [by the Hudson's Bay Company and the Puget Sound Agricultural Company] April 17, 1865 (Washington, 1865) 30 p. — [v. 2] Evidence on the part of the Hudson's Bay Company (Montreal, 1868) 490 p. — [v. 3] Evidence on the part of the Puget's Sound Agricultural Company (Montreal, 1868) 188 p. — [v. 4] Memorial and argument on the part of the Hudson's Bay Company (Montreal, 1868) xiv, 239, 22 p. — [v. 5] In the matter of the claim of the Hudson's Bay Company, closing argument of the claimants, in reply to the responsive argument of the United States (Montreal, 1869) 39, 8 p. — [v. 6] Memorial and argument on the part of the Puget's Sound Agricultural Company (Montreal, 1868) vii, 177 p. — [v. 7] In the matter of the claim of the Puget Sound Agricultural Company, closing arguments of the claimants, in reply to the responsive argument for the United States (Montreal, 1869) 11 p. — [v. 8-9] Evidence for the United States in the matter of the claim of the Hudson's Bay Company (Washington, 1867) 399, 562 p. — [v. 10] Evidence for the United States in the matter of the claim of the Puget Sound Agricultural Company (Washington, 1867) 350 p. — [v. 11] Evidence for the United States in the matter of the claims of the Hudson's Bay Company and the Puget's Sound Agricultural companies; miscellaneous (Washington, 1867) 397 p. — [v. 12] Indexes to the evidence [for the claimants and for the United States] (Washington, 186-?) 15, 8, 20, 27, 9, 11, 4, 1 p. — [v. 13] Arguments in behalf of the United States, with supplement and appendix; C. Cushing, counsel (Washington, 1868) 24, 156, 74 p. — [v. 14] Opinions and award of the commissioners . . . pronounced September 10, 1869 (Montreal, 1869) 31 p.  Not seen.

The microfilm copy of the papers in the B.C. Archives was obtained from the Hudson's Bay Company archives in London.

LIBRARY OF CONGRESS

248    [Brown, Robert]
       1842-1895

Vancouver Island; exploration, 1864. Victoria, Printed by authority of the government by Harries and Company [1865]

ii, 27 p.   25 cm.

The expedition was sponsored by Governor Kennedy and a group of businessmen with the hope of discovering gold and suitable farmland. It led to the development of coal and copper mines, and to the discovery of gold in the Leech River.

The first appearance of a map based on Brown's survey — and also on information by the British Admiralty — may be found with Robert Brown's "Das Innere der Vancouver Insel" in *Mittheilungen aus Justus Perthes' geographischer Anstalt* for January, and March, 1869, p. 1-10, 85-95. The map was compiled by August Heinrich Petermann. The map also appears in: Royal Geographical Society. *Journal.* v. 39, 1869, facing p. 121.

B.C. ARCHIVES

249    Cameron, Malcolm [Colin]
       1832-1898

Lecture delivered . . . to Young Men's Mutual Improvement Association; the Lord Bishop of the diocese in the chair. Published by request and sold for the benefit of the association.   Quebec, Printed by G. E. Desbarats, 1865.

23 p.   20 cm.

Describes a journey made in 1862 from Montreal to British Columbia via the Isthmus of Panama, and a visit to Vancouver Island and British Columbia.

B.C. ARCHIVES

250    Cridge, E[dward]
       BISHOP   1817-1913

Pastoral address on the occasion of the consecration of Christ Church, Victoria, December 7th, 1865, by the Rev. E. Cridge, Rector. With statement of facts respecting the church reserve.   Victoria, Printed at the Daily Chronicle Office [1865]

7 p.   23 cm.

B.C. ARCHIVES

251    Emmerson, John

British Columbia and Vancouver Island; voyages, travels, & adventures.   Durham [Eng.] Printed and published for the author by Wm. Ainsley, 1865.

154 p.   19 cm.

The author tells of his journey to the Cariboo gold fields in 1862 and of conditions at the mines.

B.C. ARCHIVES

252    Female Aid Association
       (Victoria)

Report of annual meeting held in 1865. [Victoria, 1865]

Not seen.   Signed in print: E. Cridge, Hon. Secretary. Dated: Decr. 31, 1865. Reprinted in Patience Day's *Pioneer days; Provincial Royal Jubilee Hospital*, p. 14.

B.C. ARCHIVES

253    Hudson's Bay Company

The memorials of the Hudson Bay Company and the Puget Sound Agricultural Company to the commissioners (under the treaty of July 1, 1863) between Great Britain and the United States for the final settlement of the claims of the Hudson's Bay and Puget Sound Agricultural companies.   Washington, Government Printing Office, 1865.

21 p.   34 cm.   Cover title.

Contains two memorials addressed to the commissioners by Charles D. Day, counsel for the Hudson's Bay Company, which are dated 8 April and 10 April 1865.

OREGON HISTORICAL SOCIETY

254    Janion, Green & Rhodes
       (Liverpool)

[Prospectus of British Columbia Steam Traction Engine Company.   n.p., 1865]

13 p.   35 cm.   The promoters of the proposed company were Janion, Green & Rhodes, Joseph W. Trutch, and Anthony Bower.

The aim of the promoters was to form a company to haul freight from Yale to the Cariboo.

B.C. ARCHIVES

255    Macfie, Matthew

Vancouver Island and British Columbia; their history, resources, and prospects.   London, Longman, Green, Longman, Roberts & Green, 1865.

xxi, 574 p.   illus., fold. maps.   23 cm.

Written "chiefly for the perusal of merchants, statesmen, and intending emigrants."—pref.

B.C. ARCHIVES

256    Milton, [William Wentworth
       Fitzwilliam]
       VISCOUNT   1839-1877

An expedition across the Rocky Mountains into British Columbia, by the Yellow Head or Leather Pass, by Viscount Milton and W. B. Cheadle. London, Printed by Petter and Galpin, Belle Sauvage Works [1865]

37 p.   22 cm.   On title page: Read before the British Association at Bath, Sept. 17, 1864; the Royal Geographical Society of London, Nov. 18, 1864; the Literary and Philosophical Society of Leeds, Jan. 3, 1864; and the Literary and Philosophical Society of Sheffield, Jan. 19, 1865. Printed for private circulation.

The text is not the same as in the author's paper of the same title in: Royal Geographical Society. *Proceedings.* v. 9, 1864-65, p. 17-21.

B.C. ARCHIVES

## 257   Milton, [William Wentworth Fitzwilliam]
VISCOUNT   1839-1877

The North-west Passage by land; being the narrative of an expedition from the Atlantic to the Pacific, undertaken with the view of exploring a route across the continent to British Columbia through British territory by one of the northern passes in the Rocky Mountains, by Viscount Milton and W. B. Cheadle.   London, Cassell, Petter, and Galpin [1865]

xviii, 397 p.   plates, 2 fold. maps (1 in pocket) 23 cm.

Despite the two names on the title page, a comparison with Cheadle's *Journal* (entry 1726) makes it fairly evident that this work was written by Walter Butler Cheadle. Milton and Cheadle arrived in Quebec in the spring of 1862. They made their way to Edmonton where they formed a party to cross the Rockies via Yellow Head Pass. After weeks of hardships and privations in the mountains they finally reached Kamloops. From Kamloops they journeyed to Westminster and Victoria, but they returned to the mainland to visit the Cariboo gold diggings before sailing for England via the Isthmus of Panama.

Within the first ten years the book had run through eight editions. The fact that the book attracted immediate attention may be attributed in part to its literary merit.

B.C. ARCHIVES

## 258   Queen Charlotte Coal Mining Company, Limited

Memorandum of association [and regulations for the management of the company.   New Westminster, 1865?]

12 p.   22 cm.   Caption title. The registered office of the company is given as being in New Westminster.

B.C. ARCHIVES

## 259   Queen Charlotte Coal Mining Company, Limited

Prospectus and report, with articles of association [and memorandum of association]   Victoria, Printed at the British Colonist Office [1865]

14 p.   22 cm.   Report by George Robinson read at a general meeting, 14 August 1865.

B.C. ARCHIVES

## 260   Rawlings, Thomas

The confederation of the British North American provinces; their past history and future prospects; including also British Columbia & Hudson's Bay Territory; with a map, and suggestions in reference to the true and only practicable route from the Atlantic to the Pacific Ocean.   London, Sampson Low, Son, and Marston, 1865.

ix, 244 p.   plates, fold. map, tables.   24 cm.

B.C. ARCHIVES

## 261   Vancouver Island. Governor
1863-1867   (KENNEDY)

Despatches. [A letter dated 12 December 1865 from Governor Kennedy to the Legislative Assembly enclosing despatches concerning crown lands.   Victoria, 1865?]

4 p.   27 cm.   Caption title.

In part concerns the question of title to certain lands claimed by the Hudson's Bay Company.

B.C. ARCHIVES

## 262   Vancouver Island. Governor
1863-1867   (KENNEDY)

Message from His Excellency Governor Kennedy, C.B., to the Legislative Assembly, 27th November, 1865, enclosing despatch no. 39, 14th August 1865, from the Rt. Hon. Secretary of State for the Colonies upon the crown lands of the colony.   Victoria, Printed at Daily Chronicle Office [1865?]

8 p. (incl. cover)   27 cm.   Cover title.

In part concerns the question of title to certain lands claimed by the Hudson's Bay Company.

B.C. ARCHIVES

## 263   Victoria. Chamber of Commerce

Progress of British commerce under free trade showing the effects of the free trade policy recently inaugurated in England as indicated by its practical results; a memorandum of the Board of Trade respecting British commerce, navigation and finance before and since the adoption of free trade and repeal of the navigation laws; a statement showing the effect of a diminution in import duties on certain articles upon the amount of revenue received on those articles. Published for distribution by order of the Victoria, V.I., Chamber of Commerce.   Victoria, Printed at the Vancouver Times Office, 1865.

16 p.   18 cm.

B.C. ARCHIVES

**264    Work in the colonies . . .**

Work in the colonies; some account of the missionary operations of the Church of England in connexion with the propagation of the Gospel in foreign parts.    London, Griffith and Farran, 1865.

vi, 374 p.    plates, fold. map.    16 cm.

Includes several pages on missionary work in the Diocese of Columbia.

B.C. ARCHIVES

**265    Almanack . . .**

Almanack and list.    Victoria, J. H. Turner & Co.

v.    16 cm.    Printed by John King and Company, Ltd., London, England. Only copies for 1866 and 1868 examined. On t.p.: London Firm, J. P. Tunstall & Co.

Lists imported drygoods for sale, including silks, shawls, hosiery, haberdashery, gifts, toiletries, and furniture coverings. The 1868 almanac has section "British Columbia tariff."

B.C. ARCHIVES

**266    British Columbia. Lands and Works Department**

Columbia River exploration, 1865. Instructions, reports and journals relating to the government exploration of country lying between the Shuswap and Okanagan lakes and the Rocky Mountains. New Westminster, Printed at the Government Printing Office, 1866.

36 p.    fold. maps.    32 cm.    Cover title. At head of title: British Columbia.

Includes the reports and journals of Walter Moberly, Ashdown H. Green, and James Turnbull.

Another report for the exploration undertaken in 1866 was issued in 1869 (entry 322). Both reports were reissued together in 1869 with new title page and table of contents under title: *Columbia River exploration, 1865-6* (Victoria, Printed at the Government Printing Office).

B.C. ARCHIVES

**267    British Columbia. Lands and Works Department**

Report of the operations of the Lands and Works Department of British Columbia in the year 1865.    New Westminster, Printed at the Government Printing Office, 1866.

7 p.    23 cm.    Report signed in print: Joseph W. Trutch, chief commissioner of Lands and Works and surveyor general. Dated: 29th October 1865. Reader-printer copy examined. Original in the Bancroft Library.

UNIVERSITY OF VICTORIA LIBRARY

**268    British Columbia Botanical Association (Edinburgh)**

[An abstract of a catalogue of a fourth box of seeds, etc., collected by Robert Brown in 1865. Edinburgh, 1866?]

3 p. (folder)    35 cm.    At head of text: From *The Farmer* of May 16, 1866.

B.C. ARCHIVES

**269    British Columbia Botanical Association (Edinburgh)**

Sir, I am instructed by the committee of the association to transmit a copy of resolutions adopted at a meeting held on 14th May current. [Edinburgh, 1866]

[2] p. (folder)    27 cm.    Title from letter signed in print: I. Anderson-Henry, secretary. At head of title: British Columbia Botanical Association.

One of the resolutions called for Robert Brown's services as a collector to be discontinued.

U.B.C. SPECIAL COLLECTIONS

**270    Churchill, J. D.**

British Columbia and Vancouver Island, considered as a field for commercial enterprise & emigration, by J. D. Churchill and J. Cooper. London, Rees and Collin, "Lombard Steam Press," 1866.

15 p.    tables.    17 cm.    Cover title.

B.C. ARCHIVES

**271    Demers, [Modeste]**
BISHOP    1809-1871

Letter on the founding of the Diocese of Vancouver Island.    [n.p., 1866?]

4 p.    21 cm.    Title used is written on cover supplied with photostat copy. At head of text: Letter from Mgr. Demers; mission of Vancouver Island, founded in 1846. Photostat copy examined.

An appeal for funds written in New York at the Convent of the Most Holy Redeemer, 6 December 1866.

B.C. ARCHIVES

**272    Great Britain. Laws, statutes, etc.**

British Columbia. A bill for the union of the colony of Vancouver Island with the colony of British Columbia. Prepared and brought in by Mr. William Edward Forster and Mr. Secretary Cardwell. Ordered by the House of Commons to be printed, 11 June 1866.    [London, 1866]

3, [1] p.    33 cm.    ([Great Britain. Parliament, 1866. House of Commons] Bill 186)

SHORTT COLLECTION

**273    Great Britain. Parliament**

A further despatch relative to the proposed
union of British Columbia and Vancouver Island.
(In continuation of papers presented 31st May
1866) Presented to both Houses of Parliament
by command of Her Majesty, 25th June 1866.
London, Printed by George Edward Eyre and
William Spottiswoode, 1866.

2 p.    32 cm.    ([Great Britain. Parliament.
Command papers 3694])

B.C. ARCHIVES

**274    Great Britain. Parliament**

Papers relative to the proposed union of British
Columbia and Vancouver Island. Presented
to both Houses of Parliament by command
of Her Majesty, 31st May 1866.    London,
Printed by George Edward Eyre and William
Spottiswoode, 1866.

44 p.    34 cm.    ([Great Britain. Parliament.
Command papers 3667])

B.C. ARCHIVES

**275    Lord, John Keast**
          1818-1872

The naturalist in Vancouver Island and British
Columbia.    London, Richard Bentley, 1866.

2 v.    plates.    21 cm.    A list of mammals, birds,
insects, reptiles, fishes, shells, annelides, and
diatomaceæ, collected by myself . . . with notes on
their habits: v. 2, p. 289-375.

Written for the general reader from the author's
observations and experiences while he was the
naturalist for the British North American Boundary
Commission. It contains extensive general descriptive
information, and offers some information about the
work of the commission.

B.C. ARCHIVES

**276    New Westminster Home Guards**

Rules and regulations of the New Westminster
Home Guards (enrolled 14th June, 1866)    New
Westminster, Printed at the Government Printing
Office, 1866.

8 p.    14 cm.

B.C. ARCHIVES

**277    Somerville, Thomas**
          D. 1915

Oration delivered at the inauguration of the new
Masonic Hall on Government Street, Victoria,
Vancouver Island, on Monday, 25th June A.L.
5866.    [Victoria] Colonist and Chronicle Print
[1866]

9 p.    24 cm.    Cover title.

B.C. ARCHIVES

**278    Victoria. Chamber of Commerce**

Reply of the Victoria, V.I. Chamber of
Commerce to His Excellency Frederick Seymour,
governor of British Columbia, forwarded to the
Secretary of State for the Colonies, October 1st,
1866.    [Victoria] Daily Colonist and Chronicle
Print [1866]

47 p.    tables.    23 cm.    Cover title: Contents: First
report of the Victoria, V.I. Chamber of Commerce,
and H. E. Governor Seymour's despatch respecting
it. — Reply of the Victoria, V.I. Chamber of
Commerce to H. E. Governor Seymour's despatch. —
Appendix.

Concerns the union of the two colonies of Vancouver
Island and British Columbia and the creation of New
Westminster as the seat of government.

B.C. ARCHIVES

**279    Victoria. First Presbyterian
          Church**

Trust deeds of the First Presbyterian Church
of Vancouver Island.    [Victoria? 1866]

4 p. (folder)    31 cm.    Caption title.

A conveyance.

B.C. ARCHIVES

**280    British Columbia. Governor**
          1864-1869    (SEYMOUR)

Correspondence between the Governor of
British Columbia and the Treasurer of Vancouver
Island, on the subject of the abolition of the
office of Treasurer, 1866-1867.    [n.p. 1867?]

4 p. (folder)    26 cm.    Caption title.

B.C. ARCHIVES

**281    British Columbia. Governor**
          1864-1869    (SEYMOUR)

Message no. 1. [Enclosing a copy of such portions
of Her Majesty's instruction to the Governor as
refer to the constitution of the colony and the
construction of the Legislative Council.    n.p.,
1867]

sheet.    33 x 21 cm.

B.C. ARCHIVES

**282    Freemasons. British Columbia.
          Grand Lodge**

[Report of a special meeting of Provincial
Grand Lodge of Free and Accepted Masons of
British Columbia, R. S., held in Victoria
24 December 1867.    Victoria, 1867]

sheet (2 p.)    26 x 20 cm.    Signed in print:
A. G. Richardson, provincial grand secretary.

B.C. ARCHIVES

## 283 Freemasons. Victoria. Victoria Lodge No. 783

Bye-Laws of Victoria Lodge No. 783 (late 1085) F. and A.M., held under the jurisdiction of the Grand Lodge of England; instituted August 20th, 1860. Victoria, Higgins, Long & Co., printers, 1867.

35 p. 12 cm.

Also see entry 113.

B.C. ARCHIVES

## 284 Great Britain. Hydrographic Office

Pilote de l'île Vancouver; routes à suivre sur les côtes de l'île Vancouver et de la Colombie-Anglaise, depuis le golfe Burrard et le havre Nanaimo, jusqu'au cap Scott et sur la côte ouest de l'île, par le capitaine George-Henry Richards de la marine anglaise. Traduit de l'anglais par M. Hocquart. Deuxième partie, suive d'un appendice á la première partie. Paris, 1867.

2 v. 23 cm. Vol. 1 examined. It begins with Chapter 5.

This is the French edition of entry 229.

U.B.C. SPECIAL COLLECTIONS

## 285 Great Britain. Parliament

Further papers relative to the union of British Columbia and Vancouver Island. (In continuation of papers presented 25th June 1866) Presented to both Houses of Parliament by command of Her Majesty, May 1867. London, Printed by George Edward Eyre and William Spottiswoode, 1867.

iv, 47 p. 33 cm. ([Great Britain. Parliament. Command papers] 3852)

B.C. ARCHIVES

## 286 Harvey, Arthur
COMPILER 1834-1905

A statistical account of British Columbia. Ottawa, Printed by G. E. Desbarats, 1867.

41 p. map, tables. 21 cm.

Designed as a companion to the *Year book of Canada* for 1868.

Also: 1870.

B.C. ARCHIVES

## 287 Hughes, Thomas
1818-1883

The gold-seeker's handbook and practical assayist, intended to be used in the detection of gold, silver, copper, and other metals found in the Dominion of Canada, United States, and British Columbia; so simplified as to be understood by any man of ordinary capacity. Napanee, Published by S. Vivian, 1867.

60 p. 17 cm.

TORONTO PUBLIC LIBRARY

## 288 Klaucke, M. F.

Prospectus of a joint stock company to be formed under the name and style of the British North-west American Emigrants' Settlement Association (Limited) . . . [Ottawa? 1867?]

23 p. 20 cm. Caption title. Signed in print on p. 16: M. F. Klaucke. Reader-printer copy examined. Original in the Bancroft Library.

The object of the association was to acquire large blocks of land in British Columbia for settlement purposes.

UNIVERSITY OF VICTORIA LIBRARY

## 289 [Lord, John Keast]
1818-1872

At home in the wilderness; being full instructions how to get along, and to surmount all difficulties by the way, by "The Wanderer" [pseud.] London, Robert Hardwicke, 1867.

xvi, 323 p. illus., port. 20 cm.

Based mainly on the author's experiences as naturalist to the British North American Boundary Commission. It contains a number of references to British Columbia.

Second edition: London, Robert Hardwicke, 1867. Third edition: London, Hardwicke & Bogue, 1876.

B.C. ARCHIVES

## 290 McKenney's Pacific coast directory

McKenney's Pacific coast directory . . . of business and professional men of California, Oregon, Washington, British Columbia, Nevada, Utah, Idaho and Montana . . . 1867-? San Francisco, L. M. McKenney & Co.

v. 23 cm. Title varies: 1867 as *Pacific coast business directory*. Subtitle varies slightly. Publisher varies.

B.C. ARCHIVES

## 291 Naval Club (Esquimalt)

Rules of the Naval Club, Esquimalt, V.I., established 1867. Victoria, Higgins, Long & Co., printers, 1867.

10 p. 17 cm.

B.C. ARCHIVES

**292    Saint Ann's journal**

Saint Ann's journal.    v. 1+ 1867?+ Victoria, Sisters of St. Ann.

v. illus.  22 cm.  quarterly.  B.C. Provincial Archives has holdings from v. 78 (1944) to date.

Includes short, popularly-written articles on historical missionary work in British Columbia.

B.C. ARCHIVES

**293    United States. Department of State**

Island of San Juan. Message from the President of the United States in answer to a resolution of the House of the 19th instant relative to the Island of San Juan in Washington Territory. January 7, 1867—referred to the Committee on Foreign Affairs and ordered to be printed.  [Washington, 1867]

1 1.  23 cm.  ([United States] 39th Cong., 2d sess. House. Ex. doc. no. 24)

Statement from William H. Seward advising that certain correspondence on the joint occupancy of San Juan should not be made public.

U.B.C. SPECIAL COLLECTIONS

**294    Victoria. Citizens**

Proceedings of a public meeting, held Thursday evening, 28th Nov., 1867, at Victoria, British Columbia. From the "Daily British Colonist" of Nov. 29th.  [Victoria, 1867]

4 p. (folder)  25 cm.  Caption title. Chairman: Mayor James Trimble.

Concerns the making of Victoria as the capital city of the united colonies of Vancouver Island and British Columbia.

B.C. ARCHIVES

**295    Victoria. Citizens**

Resolutions passed at a public meeting held at Victoria, British Columbia, Nov. 28, 1867. [Victoria? 1867?]

sheet.  31 x 9 cm.

Relates to the relocation of the capital of British Columbia at Victoria.

B.C. ARCHIVES

**296    Waddington, Alfred [Penderill]**
1801?-1872

Overland communication by land and water through British North America; June, 1867. Victoria, Higgins, Long & Co., printers, 1867.

22 p.  tables.  22 cm.  Cover title.

Mainly an exposition of Waddington's proposed railway route in British Columbia, which was by way of Yellow Head Pass, along 280 miles of the upper Fraser, then westerly to a terminal at the head of Bute Inlet.

B.C. ARCHIVES

**297    Anderson, James**
1839?-1923?

Sawney's letters; or, Cariboo rhymes from 1864-1868.  [Barkerville, Cariboo Sentinel, 1868]

[4] p. (folder)  25 cm.  Caption title. Rhymed letters and songs printed in three columns. Dated 22 June 1868.

This is the second edition. It was printed in the office of the *Cariboo Sentinel* on the first press brought into British Columbia. Anderson's verses give many sidelights on the life in a mining town in the mid-1860's. For more information on the poet, etc., see William Kaye Lamb, *Sawney's letters, or Cariboo rhymes* (entry 2094).

No copy of the first edition exists. It was advertised in an issue of the *Cariboo Sentinel* dated 30 July 1866, and described as being printed on a sheet of letter paper. The third and considerably enlarged edition was published in 1869 under title: *Sawney's letters and Cariboo songs* (Barkerville, Printed at the Cariboo Sentinel Office). In 28, 24 pages. Another edition was published in 1895 in 49 pages by W. S. Johnston & Co'y, Toronto. The 1868 edition was printed in mimeographed form in 1950 with an introduction by William Kaye Lamb under title: *Sawney's letters* (Toronto, Bibliographical Society of Canada). In 26 pages. The verses appeared in 1962 in 64 pages with an introduction by Willard E. Ireland under title: *Sawney's letters and Cariboo rhymes* (Victoria, Published by the Barkerville Restoration Advisory Committee of the Province of British Columbia).

B.C. ARCHIVES

**298    Blake, William P[hipps]**
1826-1910

Geographical notes upon Russian America and the Stickeen River; being a report addressed to the Hon. W. H. Seward, Secretary of State. With a map of the Stickeen River.  Washington, Government Printing Office, 1868.

19 p.  fold. map, diagrs., tables.  23 cm. ([United States] 40th Cong., 2d sess. House. Ex. doc. 177, pt. 2)  Cover title. Includes: Journal of an exploration of the Stickeen River — 1863 [p. 9-17]

The survey of the Stikine was a Russian venture under the command of Lieutenant Bassarguine. William Blake participated as a guest for scientific purposes.

B.C. ARCHIVES

**299    British Columbia. Lands and Works Department**

Overland coach road. Minute of the Chief Commissioner of Lands and Works, 1868.  New

Westminster, Printed at the Government Printing Office, 1868.

6 p. tables. 35 cm. At head of title: British Columbia. At head of text: Minute of the Chief Commissioner of Lands and Works [Joseph W. Trutch] on the subject of an overland coach road through British territory, between the Pacific coast and Canada, comparing the merits of the various passes through the Rocky Mountains, and showing the extent of this road already built in British Columbia, and what remains to be done to complete it beyond the eastern boundary of the colony to the head of steamboat navigation on the Saskatchewan.

This minute was reprinted in 1871 in 7 pages.

B.C. ARCHIVES

### 300 Brown, Robert
#### 1842-1895

Observations on the medicinal and economic value of the oulachan (*Osmerus pacificus,* rich.) a fish belonging to the family Salmonidæ, found on the north-west coast of America. [n.p., 1868]

[3]-7 p. 21 cm. Reprinted from the *Pharmaceutical journal,* June 1868.

B.C. ARCHIVES

### 301 Brown, Robert
#### 1842-1895

Synopsis of the birds of Vancouver Island. [n.p., 1868]

[414]-428 p. 22 cm. On t.p.: From 'The Iris' for November 1868.

B.C. ARCHIVES

### 302 Canada. Department of the Secretary of State

Correspondence respecting the North-west Territory, including British Columbia. Ottawa, Printed by Hunter, Rose & Company, 1868.

14 p. 25 cm. Half title: Return to an address of the House of Commons, dated 17th March 1868, for copy of a correspondence had with the government respecting the North-west Territory, including British Columbia since 5th December 1867 . . .

Relates in part to the union of British Columbia with Canada.

TORONTO PUBLIC LIBRARY

### 303 Coleman, E[dmund] T[homas]
#### D. 1892?

Prize essay and poem of the Literary Institute, Victoria, V.I., on the beauties of the scenery surveyed from Beacon Hill. Victoria, J. E. McMillan, printer, Morning News Office, 1868.

15 p. 22 cm. The poem is by W. H. Parsons.

B.C. ARCHIVES

### 304 Confederate League

[Declaration, constitution, list of officers] Victoria, 1868.

sheet. 40 x 18 cm. Begins: Officers, Confederate League; President, James Trimble, Esq., mayor Victoria. Xerox copy seen. Original in the Yale University Library.

The organization was a political association formed to promote confederation with Canada and representative government.

UNIVERSITY OF VICTORIA LIBRARY

### 305 Confederate League. Yale Convention

Minutes of a preliminary meeting of the delegates, elected by the various districts of British Columbia, convened at Yale, pursuant to the following call: "Yale Convention." [New Westminster, British Columbian Print, 1868]

12 p. 21 cm. Caption title.

Forty-two resolutions were passed, including those concerned with equitable terms of admission into the Dominion and representative and responsible government. For an interesting comment on the status of the delegates see the Victoria *Colonist,* 2 October 1868, p. 3.

B.C. ARCHIVES

### 306 Cridge, Edward
#### BISHOP 1817-1913

Sketch of the rise and progress of Metlahkatlah, in the Diocese of British Columbia. London, Church Missionary House, 1868.

16 p. 20 cm.

Written after a seven-week visit to Metlahkatla.

UNITED CHURCH ARCHIVES, TORONTO

### 307 Freemasons. British Columbia. Grand Lodge

St. John's Day, December 27th; special meeting of the Provincial Grand Lodge. [Victoria, 1868]

sheet. 26 x 20 cm. Signed in print: A. G. Richardson, provincial grand secretary.

B.C. ARCHIVES

### 308 Great Britain. Colonial Office

British Columbia. Return . . . "Copy or extracts of correspondence between Governor Kennedy of Vancouver Island, Governor Seymour of British Columbia, and the Colonial Office, on the subject of a site for the capital of British Columbia." Ordered by the House of Commons to be printed, 28 July 1868. [London, 1868]

14 p. 33 cm. ([Great Britain. Parliament, 1868. House of Commons papers] 483)

B.C. ARCHIVES

**309     Harnett, Legh**

Two lectures on British Columbia.    Victoria, Higgins & Long, 1868.

50 p.    24 cm.

The first lecture deals with gold mining; the second, with the colony's advantageous natural resources and geographical position.

B.C. ARCHIVES

**310     Imray, James F[rederick]**
         1829?-1891

Sailing directions for the west coast of North America, between Panama and Queen Charlotte Islands. Second edition.    London, J. Imray & Son, 1868.

xi, 380 p.    front., fold. maps.    22 cm.    [North Pacific pilot, pt. 1]    Not seen.

Also: 1870.    Part 1 of the third and fourth editions of the *North Pacific pilot* has title: "The west coast of North America, between Panama and Queen Charlotte Islands, including Port Simpson and Sitka Sound" (London, 1881, 1885). See entry 36 for what appears to be the first edition.

BANCROFT LIBRARY CATALOGUE

**311     [Knipe, C.]**

Some account of the Tahkaht language, as spoken by several tribes on the western coast of Vancouver Island.    London, Hatchard and Co., 1868.

80 p.    20 cm.

Nootka grammar and vocabulary (Tahkaht-English; English-Tahkaht), preceded by an introduction which contains an account of some Indian customs.

TORONTO PUBLIC LIBRARY

**312     Rouhard, Hippolyte**

Les régions nouvelles; histoire du commerce et de la civilisation au nord de l'océan Pacifique. Paris, E. Dentu, 1868.

vi, 404 p.    24 cm.

Briefly discusses the advantageous location of British Columbia as far as British interests in the Pacific are concerned.

B.C. ARCHIVES

**313     Sproat, Gilbert Malcolm**
         1834-1913

Scenes and studies of savage life.    London, Smith, Elder and Co., 1868.

xii, 317 p.    front.    20 cm.

An interesting account of Indian life on the west coast of Vancouver Island, where Malcolm Sproat was a justice of the peace and magistrate from 1863 to 1865.

B.C. ARCHIVES

**314     United States. Army. Pacific Division**

[Letters from headquarters and from the Secretary of War forwarded to Captain A. H. Nickerson, commanding Camp Steele, San Juan Island, containing all necessary information in regard to the character of the joint military occupation of the islands.    n.p., 1868]

7 l.    23 cm.    Letters are dated 18 September 1864, 3 October 1865, 15 July 1868, and 26 September 1868.

B.C. ARCHIVES

**315     United States. Department of State**

The Northwest boundary. Discussion of the water boundary question: geographical memoir of the islands in dispute, and history of the military occupation of San Juan Island. Accompanied by a map and cross-sections of channels.    Washington, Government Printing Office, 1868.

x, 270 p.    maps (1 fold.) fold. plan.    23 cm.

One of the most extensive collections of relevant papers on the subject. It includes the report of the American commissioner for the Northwest Boundary Commission, Archibald Campbell.

Also appeared under title: *Message of the President of the United States, communicating . . . information in relation to the occupation of the Island of San Juan, in Puget Sound* ([United States] 40th Cong., 2d sess. Senate. Ex. doc. no. 29).

B.C. ARCHIVES

**316     Victoria. St. Andrew's Church**

Social re-union of members and friends of St. Andrew's Church in connection with the Church of Scotland, St. Nicholas Hall, Victoria, V.I., January 8th, 1868.    [Victoria] Printed at the British Colonist Office [1868]

[11] p.    25 cm.

B.C. ARCHIVES

**317     Victoria. St. John's Church**

Lent, 1868.    [Victoria, 1868]

[4] p. (folder)    19 cm.

B.C. ARCHIVES

**318     Waddington, Alfred [Penderill]**
         1801?-1872

Overland route through British North America; or, The shortest and speediest road to the East.    London, Longmans, Green, Reader, and Dyer, 1868.

48 p. fold. col. map. 20 cm.

The proposed railway route in British Columbia was via Yellow Head Pass and the upper Fraser to Bute Inlet.

B.C. ARCHIVES

## 319 Washington (Territory) Legislative Assembly

San Juan Island. Memorial of the legislature of Washington Territory, relative to the condition of citizens of the United States residing on San Juan Island. February 25, 1868—referred to the Committee on the Judiciary and ordered to be printed. [Washington, 1868]

2 p. 23 cm. ([United States] 40th Cong., 2d sess. House. Misc. doc. no. 79) Caption title.

U.B.C. SPECIAL COLLECTIONS

## 320 Whymper, Frederick
B. 1838

Travel and adventure in the territory of Alaska, formerly Russian America—now ceded to the United States—and in various other parts of the North Pacific. London, John Murray, 1868.

xix 331 p. illus., plates, fold. map. 23 cm. Binder's title: Travels in Alaska and the Yukon.

The first five chapters contain the author's reminiscences of his B.C. travels in the 1860's. They include an account of his trip to the interior of Vancouver Island in 1864 with Robert Brown's exploring expedition, and details of the Bute Inlet massacres.

Also: New York, Harper & Brothers, 1869. Second edition: New York, Murray, 1869. Also: New York, Harper & Brothers, 1871. French edition (Paris, Hachette, 1871) has title: *Voyages et aventures dans l'Alaska . . .* French abridgement by H. Vattemare (Paris, Hachette, 1880) has title: *Voyages et aventures dans la Colombia Anglaise, l'île Vancouver, le territoire d'Alaska et la Californie.*

B.C. ARCHIVES

## 321 Bates, H[enry] W[alter]
EDITOR 1825-1892

Illustrated travels; a record of discovery, geography, and adventure. London, Cassell, Petter, and Galpin [1869-75?]

6 v. illus. 32 cm.

Comprised of articles which first appeared in monthly parts. Volume 1 includes in four parts "The first journey of exploration across Vancouver Island," a popular account by Robert Brown of his 1864 expedition.

UNIVERSITY OF WASHINGTON LIBRARY

## 322 British Columbia. Lands and Works Department

Columbia River exploration, 1866. Reports and journals relating to the government exploration of the country lying between the Shuswap and Okanagan lakes and the Rocky Mountains. Victoria, Printed at the Government Printing Office [1869]

28 p. 32 cm. At head of title: British Columbia.

Includes the journals of Walter Moberly, James Turnbull, and Robert Howell. The expedition continued work begun in the previous year, the report for which was published in 1866 (entry 266). Both reports were reissued together in 1869 with a new title page and table of contents under title: *Columbia River exploration 1865-6* (Victoria, Printed at the Government Printing Office).

CANADIAN ARCHIVES

## 323 British Columbia. Lands and Works Department

Report and journal by the Hon. the Chief Commissioner of Lands and Works, of the proceedings in connection with the visit of His Excellency the late Governor Seymour to the North-west Coast in Her Majesty's ship Sparrowhawk. Victoria, Printed at the Government Printing Office, 1869.

8 p. 35 cm. At head of title: British Columbia. Report of Joseph W. Trutch.

Concerns "the settlement of the murderous quarrel carried on during the past twelve months between the Naas and Chimpsean Tribes."—p. [1]

B.C. ARCHIVES

## 324 British Columbian Investment & Loan Society

[Prospectus] Victoria, David W. Higgins, 1869.

8p. 20 cm.

B.C. ARCHIVES

## 325 Brown, Robert
1842-1895

On the geographical distribution and physical characteristics of the coal-fields of the North Pacific coast. Edinburgh, Printed by Neill and Company, 1869.

23 p. tables. 21 cm. Reprinted from: Edinburgh Geological Society. *Transactions.* 1868-69.

B.C. ARCHIVES

## 326 Canada. Governor-General
1868-1872 (LISGAR)

Message. San Juan Island. Claims of Canada for losses and damages sustained by Her Majesty's subjects in repelling Fenian invasion. Protection of the fisheries.   [Ottawa, Printed by Hunter, Rose & Co., 1869]

8 p.   25 cm.   Cover title.

Includes three joint reports from the Canadian delegates to London, George-Étienne Cartier and William McDougall.

## 327   Church Missionary Society

Metlahkatlah; ten years' work among the Tsimsheean Indians.   [London] Church Missionary House, 1869.

135 p.   fold. map.   18 cm.

Largely based on William Duncan's communications to the society.

A first edition probably appeared in 1868 (see entry 585). The fourth edition appeared in 1871 under title: *The British Columbia mission; or, Metlahkatlah;* half title: Metlahkatlah; or, Ten years' work among the Tsimsheean Indians of British Columbia. What is possibly a third edition is listed by Annie Harvie Foster in her typescript *British Columbia author's index* (p. 11) under title: *The Gospel in the far west Metlakatla; ten years work among the Tsimshean* (not found for examination).

## 328   Freemasons. British Columbia. Grand Lodge

Proceedings of the Provincial Grand Lodge of British Columbia, A.F. & A.M., R.S., at its Second Annual Communication held at the city of Victoria, May 1, A.L. 5869.   Victoria, J. E. M'Millan, 1869.

30 p.   21 cm.   At head of title: From the office of the Provincial Grand Secretary. Glued erratum changing the word "first" to "second" on t. p.

## 329   General testimonials . . .

General testimonials in favour of Gilbert Malcolm Sproat, Esq., respectfully submitted for the consideration of the Right Honourable, the Secretary of State for the Colonies.   London, 1869.

15 p. (incl. cover)   25 cm.   Cover title. At head of title: First series.

Sproat's name was put forward "by certain gentlemen" for the post of governor of British Columbia.

## 330   Great Britain. Colonial Office

British Columbia, &c. Return . . . Papers on the union of British Columbia with the Dominion of Canada. Ordered by the House of Commons to be printed, 3 August 1869. [London, 1869]

31 p.   34 cm.   ([Great Britain. Parliament, 1869. House of Commons papers] 390)

## 331   Great Britain. Foreign Office

British Columbia. Draft of a commission passed under the great seal of the United Kingdom of Great Britain and Ireland, appointing Anthony Musgrave, Esquire, to be governor and commander-in-chief of the colony of British Columbia and its dependencies.   [London, Printed by T. Harrison, 1869]

5, [1] p.   34 cm.   Title from p. [6]

## 332   Great Britain. Foreign Office

British Columbia. Draft of instructions passed under the royal sign-manual and signet to Anthony Musgrave, Esquire, as governor and commander-in-chief of the colony of British Columbia and its dependencies.   [London, Printed by T. Harrison, 1869]

10, [2] p.   34 cm.   Title from p. [12]

## 333   Great Britain. Foreign Office

Correspondence respecting the negotiations with the United States' government on the questions of the "Alabama" and British claims, naturalization, and San Juan water boundary. Presented to both Houses of Parliament by command of Her Majesty, 1869.   London, Printed by Harrison and Sons [1869]

v, 57 p.   34 cm.   ([Great Britain. Parliament. Command papers 4144]) At head of title: North America, no. 1 (1869)

## 334   Great Britain. Foreign Office

Despatch from Lord John Russell to Lord Lyons, dated November 22, 1860, respecting the San Juan water boundary. Presented to the House of Lords by command of Her Majesty, in pursuance of their address dated June 4, 1869. London, Printed by Harrison and Sons [1869]

[2] l.   34 cm.   ([Great Britain. Parliament. Command papers, 4144-1]) At head of title: North America, no. 2 (1869)

**335 Kennicott, [Robert]**
1835-1866

Slave Indians, Tenne [vocabulary. Washington, D.C., Smithsonian Institution, 1869?]

7 1. 31 cm. Caption title. Not seen.

**336 Law Society of British Columbia**

Rules. [Victoria] British Colonist Print [1869?]

18 p. 17 cm.

**337 Milton, [William Wentworth Fitzwilliam]**
VISCOUNT 1839-1877

A history of the San Juan water boundary question, as affecting the division of territory between Great Britain and the United States. Collected and compiled from official papers and documents printed under the authority of the governments respectively of Great Britain and Ireland and of the United States of America, and from other sources. London, Cassell, Petter, and Galpin, 1869.

446 p. 2 fold. maps. 23 cm.

**338 Seward, William H[enry]**
1801-1872

Alaska; speech . . . at Sitka, August 12, 1869. Washington, Philp & Solomons, 1869.

31 p. 23 cm. Cover title: Our North Pacific state; speeches of William H. Seward in Alaska, Vancouver's, and Oregon.

Contains Seward's speech at Victoria (p. 17-20). Also see note for entry below.

**339 Seward, [William Henry]**
1801-1872

Speech of Mr. Seward at Sitka, August 12th, 1869. [Victoria, Printed by David W. Higgins, 1869?]

8 p. 32 cm.

Text is the same as in pages 1-16 of above entry.

**340 Shareholder**
PSEUDONYM

The British Columbian Investment and Loan Society, incorporated under an ordinance of British Columbia; capital unlimited, consisting of permanent and accumulated stock, in shares of $50 each. Victoria, James E. McMillan, 1869.

15 p. 15 cm.

**341 Smith, J. Gregory**

Letter of J. Gregory Smith, president of the Northern Pacific Railroad, addressed to Hon. George F. Edmunds, enclosing two communications in relation to the treaty with Great Britain concerning the Island of San Juan. March 22, 1869—ordered to lie on the table and be printed. [Washington, 1869]

6 p. 23 cm. ([United States] 41st Cong. 1st sess. Senate. Misc. doc. no. 14) Caption title. The communications of George Gibbs and G. Clinton Gardner.

**342 United States. Coast and Geodetic Survey**

Pacific coast; coast pilot of Alaska, (first part) from southern boundary to Cook's Inlet, by George Davidson. Washington, Government Printing Office, 1869.

251 p. plates (part fold.) 27 cm.

Briefly descriptive of the inside passages to Alaska and of the settlement at Fort Simpson.

Second edition: 1883. Third edition: 1891.

**343 United States. Coast and Geodetic Survey**

Pacific coast; coast pilot of California, Oregon and Washington Territory, by George Davidson. Washington, Government Printing Office, 1869.

262 p. plates. 27 cm.

Numerous editions.

**344 United States. Department of State**

Northwest Boundary Commission. Message from the President of the United States concerning the Northwest Boundary Commission. February 13,1869—laid on the table and ordered to be printed. [Washington, 1869]

102 p. tables. 23 cm. ([United States] 40th Cong., 3d sess. House. Ex. doc. no. 86)

Contains reports from C. M. Walker and Archibald Campbell, United States commissioner, concerning expenditure.

## 345     United States. War Department

Letter of the Secretary of War, communicating, in compliance with a resolution of the Senate of the 10th instant, a report of the Chief of Engineers upon the military importance of San Juan Island. March 22, 1869—referred to the Committee on Foreign Relations, April 6, 1869—ordered to be printed. [Washington, 1869]

3 p. 23 cm. ([United States] 41st Cong. 1st sess. Senate. Ex. doc. no. 8) Caption title.

U.B.C. SPECIAL COLLECTIONS

## 346     Victoria. Angela College

Angela College, Victoria, Vancouver Island, for the education of young ladies. [Victoria] British Colonist Print [1869]

[3] p. (folder) 21 cm. Cover title. A prospectus for an Anglican school founded in 1860.

B.C. ARCHIVES

## 347     Waddington, Alfred [Penderill]
### 1801?-1872

Sketch of the proposed line of overland railroad through British North America. London, Longmans, Green, Reader, and Dyer, 1869.

24 p. tables. 20 cm.

A description of Waddington's proposed railway route, which, in British Columbia, was via the Yellow Head Pass and upper Fraser to Bute Inlet. Waddington's project aroused interest in London and New York, and in 1871 he went to Ottawa to seek a railway charter from the Canadian government. He died, however, before anything came of the scheme.

Second edition, with corrections: Ottawa, Printed by I. B. Taylor, 1871. 29 p.

B.C. ARCHIVES

## 348     Washington (Territory) Governor
### 1867-1869 (MOORE)

Memorial of Marshall F. Moore, Governor of Washington Territory, and other citizens of said Territory, remonstrating against any recognition of the claims of Great Britain to the Haro Archipelago and to San Juan Island. January 19, 1869—referred to the Committee on Foreign Relations and ordered to be printed. [Washington, 1869]

1 l. 23 cm. ([United States] 40th Cong., 3d sess. Senate. Misc. doc. no. 27)

U.B.C. SPECIAL COLLECTIONS

## 349     Alston, E[dward] Graham
### 1832-1873

A hand-book to British Columbia and Vancouver Island. [London] F. Algar, 1870.

18 p. fold. map. 20 cm. (On cover: Colonial hand-books) At head of title: Edition for 1870; issued February 1870.

There were earlier editions of this work. One appears to have been published in 1862, or earlier (see: London International Exhibition, 1862. *Catalogue of the Vancouver contribution . . .* , last p. 8).

B.C. ARCHIVES

## 350     [Bompas, William Carpenter]
### BISHOP 1834-1906

Beaver Indian primer. [London, 187-]

36 p. 16 cm. Not seen.

NEWBERRY LIBRARY CATALOGUE

## 351     British Columbia. Immigration Board

Assisted immigration. Victoria, 1870.

sheet. 35 x 22 cm. Signed in print: B. W. Pearse, deputy chairman.

States terms of assistance for those wishing to emigrate to British Columbia.

B.C. ARCHIVES

## 352     British Columbia. Laws, statutes, etc.

An act respecting the Methodist Church of Canada. [Victoria] Standard Print [1870]

14 p. 32 cm. Caption title.

B.C. ARCHIVES

## 353     British Columbia. Legislative Council

Debate on the subject of confederation with Canada. [Reported for the government by W. S. Sebright Green. Victoria, Government Printing Office, 1870]

27, 22, 23a p. 33 cm. Caption title. The *Government gazette extraordinary* for March and May, 1870. The third part appears with running title only: The Government gazette extraordinary.

Reprinted in 1870 by Richard Wolfenden (160 p.), and in 1912 by William H. Cullen (165 p.).

B.C. ARCHIVES

## 354     Brown, R[obert] C[hristopher] Lundin
### D. 1876

British Columbia; the Indians and settlers at Lillooet; appeal for missionaries. London, Printed by R. Clay, Sons, and Taylor, 1870.

16 p. 1 illus. 21 cm. Not seen.

BANCROFT LIBRARY CATALOGUE

**355    Corbett, G[riffith] O[wen]**

"The Red River Rebellion": the cause of it; in
a series of letters to the British government on the
importance of opening the overland route
through Rupert's America, from Canada to
British Columbia, for the introduction of means
for the administration of justice therein; the
promotion of emigration; and earnest appeals to
stay bloodshed in the Red River settlement, by
extending righteous rule to that country.    London,
Printed for the author by Cassell, Petter, & Galpin,
1870.

36 p.    21 cm.

B.C. ARCHIVES

**356    Cridge, Edward**
BISHOP    1817-1913

"Spiritualism"; or, Modern necromancy; a sermon
with preface and notes.    Victoria, Printed by
Higgins, 1870.

12p.    Cover title.    Not seen.

B.C. ARCHIVES

**357    Evans, Elwood**
1828-1898

The re-annexation of British Columbia to the
United States, right, proper and desirable; an
address delivered . . . before the Tacoma Library
Association. Olympia, W. T., January 18th, 1870.
Published by request.    [n.p., n.d.]

24 p.    22 cm.

B.C. ARCHIVES

**358    Fac simile . . .**

Fac simile of the Chinook jargon as used by the
Hudson Bay Company and all the Indian tribes
and early settlers of the Pacific Northwest.
Comp. by an old employee formerly of the
Hudson Bay Company.    [n.p., n.d.]

6 p.    13 cm.    Cover title.    Not seen.

LIBRARY OF CONGRESS

**359    Great Britain. Laws, statutes, etc.**

British Columbia . . . A bill intituled: An act to
make further provision for the government of
British Columbia. Brought from the Lords,
25 July 1870. Ordered by the House of Commons
to be printed, 3 August 1870.    [London, 1870]

2 p.    34 cm.    ([Great Britain. Parliament, 1870.
House of Commons] Bill 257)

SHORTT COLLECTION

**360    Great Britain. Privy Council**

Instructions to Mr. Blanchard [sic] governor of
Vancouver Island.    [Victoria, Printed by
Richard Wolfenden, n.d.]

6 p.    28 cm.    Caption title.

Although the instructions were issued in 1849, they
were printed after the government moved to Victoria
in May 1868 — perhaps at the time of agitation for
responsible government in 1870.

B.C. ARCHIVES

**361    Howard, Jacob M.**

San Juan Island; speech of Hon. Jacob M. Howard
of Michigan, delivered in executive session of
the Senate, April 16, 1869 (the injunction
of secrecy having been removed)    Washington,
F. & J. Rives & Geo. A. Bailey, 1870.

13 p.    23 cm.

U.B.C. SPECIAL COLLECTIONS

**362    Metlahkatlah . . .**

Metlahkatlah; the story of a mission in N.W.
America.    London, Society for Promoting
Christian Knowledge [1870]

Not seen.

BRITISH MUSEUM CATALOGUE

**363    Patterson, W[illia]m D.**
COMPILER

Map of the Cariboo and Omineca gold fields,
and the routes thereto. Compiled from reliable
authorities by Wm. D. Patterson, C. E.
Lithographed by F. W. Green, C. E.    Victoria,
Printed at the Standard Office, 1870.

fold. map (between covers. 15 x 10 cm.)    53 x 40
cm.    and sheet 25 x 26 cm.    Sheet has title: Distance
tables and miscellaneous information.

Reprinted in 1871.

B.C. ARCHIVES

**364    Travel and adventure . . .**

Travel and adventure in many lands; an
illustrated reading-book by many writers, suitable
for the upper classes of national schools and
also for use in night schools.    London, Society
for Promoting Christian Knowledge [1870]

124 p.    illus.    19 cm.

Contains five narratives relating to events in British
Columbia during the 1860's.

B.C. ARCHIVES

**365    United States. Department of State**

Correspondence concerning questions pending between Great Britain and the United States. Transmitted to the Senate in obedience to a resolution.    Washington, Government Printing Office, 1870.

23 p.    25 cm.    At head of title: Department of State.

Relates in part to the San Juan Island dispute.

U.B.C. SPECIAL COLLECTIONS

**366    United States. Treaties, etc.**

Postal convention between the United States of America and the provinces of Vancouver's Island and British Columbia. Signed at Washington on the 9th of June 1870, and at Victoria, the 25th of July 1870; approved by the President of the United States on the 5th of October 1870.    [Washington, 1870]

6 p.    26 cm.    Not seen.

LIBRARY OF CONGRESS

**367    Addresses and replies . . .**

Addresses and replies [on the occasion of Joseph W. Trutch's appointment as Lieutenant-Governor of British Columbia.    Victoria, Government Printing Office, 1871]

9 p.    33 cm.    Caption title. Not found in Holmes.

B.C. ARCHIVES

**368    B., J.**

The cruise round the world of the Flying Squadron, 1869-1870, under the command of Rear-Admiral G. T. Phipps Hornby.    [London] J. D. Potter, 1871.

290 p.    plates, port., fold. map.    23 cm.    In pref.: For the benefit of those who took part in the . . . expedition . . . these few facts, with the assistance of Henry Cavendish, have been compiled by . . . J. B.

Has a few pages on the squadron's Esquimalt visit.

B.C. ARCHIVES

**369    British Columbia**

British Columbia.    [n.p., 1871?]

16 p.    illus.    18 cm.    Caption title.

A pamphlet relating to the early missionary work of William Duncan and John Booth Good.

CANADIAN ARCHIVES

**370    British Columbia. Citizens**

Memorial in connection with the Omineca road petition.    [Victoria? 1871]

[3] p.    32 cm.    Caption title. Addressed to His Excellency Governor Musgrave and the Legislative Council of British Columbia. Signed: R. W. W. Carrall, member for Cariboo, C. F. Cornwall, member for Yale, R. J. Skinner, member for Kootenay [and others] Reader-printer copy examined. Original in Bancroft Library.

The petition referred to is printed in the Victoria *Colonist*, 12 January 1871, page 3.

UNIVERSITY OF VICTORIA LIBRARY

**371    British Columbia. Laws, statutes, etc.**

Appendix to the revised statutes of British Columbia, 1871; containing certain repealed colonial laws useful for reference, Imperial statutes affecting British Columbia, proclamations, &c.    Victoria, Printed by R. Wolfenden [1871]

234 p.    28 cm.    In Holmes.

U.B.C. SPECIAL COLLECTIONS

**372    British Columbia. Laws, statutes, etc.**

The laws of British Columbia, consisting of the acts, ordinances, & proclamations of the formerly separate colonies of Vancouver Island and British Columbia, and of the united colony of British Columbia, with table of acts, alphabetical index, and appendix. Compiled and published by the commissioners appointed under "The Revised Statutes Act, 1871."    Victoria, Printed at the Government Printing Office, 1871.

xxix, 638 p.    28 cm.    Commissioners: Henry Pering Pellew Crease, George Phillipps, and Edward Graham Alston. In Holmes.

New edition under title: *The consolidated statutes of British Columbia, consisting of the acts, ordinances & proclamations . . .* (Victoria, 1877). Continued by: *The statutes of British Columbia up to and including the year 1888* (Victoria, 1888?), and by: *The revised statutes of British Columbia . . .*

B.C. PROVINCIAL LIBRARY

**373    British Columbia. Legislative Council**

Series of resolutions respecting the admission of British Columbia into the union with Canada, to be proposed by Sir George Et. Cartier.    [n.p., 1871?]

6 p.    33 cm.    Caption title.

CANADIAN ARCHIVES

**374 British Columbia . . .**

British Columbia and the Canadian Pacific Railway. Complimentary dinner to the Hon. Mr. Trutch, Surveyor-General of British Columbia, given at the Russell House, Ottawa, on Monday, 10th April 1871. Reported for the Montreal Gazette. Montreal, The Gazette Printing House, 1871.

12 p. 26 cm.

Includes an address by Joseph William Trutch.

B.C. ARCHIVES

**375 Canada. Governor-General**
1868-1872 (LISGAR)

Message (Lisgar) The Governor General transmits, for the information of the House of Commons, the accompanying papers relative to the proposed union of British Columbia with the Dominion of Canada. Printed by order of Parliament. Ottawa, Printed by I. B. Taylor, 1871.

29 p. 26 cm.

B.C. ARCHIVES

**376 Canada. Parliament. Senate**

Debate in the Senate on the resolutions respecting British Columbia. Reported by J. G. Bourinot. Ottawa, Printed by the Times Printing & Publishing Co., 1871.

[140]-276 columns. 25 cm. Cover title.

Debates of 3-5 April 1871 on the resolutions providing for admission of British Columbia into confederation.

B.C. ARCHIVES

**377 Canadian Pacific Railway Company**

Exploratory survey of 1871; general instructions to engineers in charge of parties, transit-men and levelers. [Ottawa, 1871]

10 p. 20 cm. Signed in print: Sandford Fleming, engineer-in-chief.

Surveying parties were in British Columbia during 1871.

B.C. ARCHIVES

**378 Church Missionary Society**

British Columbia mission [letters from William Duncan, and an appeal for funds. London, 1871]

8 p. 20 cm. (Papers for deputations, no. 1) Caption title. At head of title: For private circulation only.

UNITED CHURCH ARCHIVES, TORONTO

**379 Claudet, F[rancis] G[eorge]**
1837-1906

"Gold," its properties, modes of extraction, value, &c., &c., by F. G. Claudet, superintendent of the government Assay Office, British Columbia. New Westminster, Printed at the office of the "Mainland Guardian," 1871.

32 p. 16 cm.

Reprinted in 1958 at the private press of Robert Reid and Takao Tanabe, Vancouver.

B.C. ARCHIVES

**380 Demers, Modeste**
BISHOP 1809-1871

Chinook dictionary, catechism, prayers and hymns. Composed in 1838 & 1839 by Rt. Rev. Modeste Demers. Rev., cor. and completed in 1867 by Most Rev. F. N. Blanchet, with modifications and additions by Rev. L. N. St. Onge. Montreal, 1871.

68 p. illus. 15 cm. At head of title: J. M. J. On cover: The Missionary's companion on the Pacific coast. Not seen.

LIBRARY OF CONGRESS

**381 A Dictionary of the Chinook jargon . . .**

A dictionary of the Chinook jargon; or, Indian trade language of the North Pacific coast. Victoria, Published by T. N. Hibben & Co. [1871?]

29 p. 21 cm. Cover title.

For the most part a reprint, with omissions, of George Gibbs' *Dictionary of Chinook jargon.*

There were at least twelve printings of this work between 1875 and 1906. A new edition appeared in 1887. A revised edition appeared in 1931 with title: *Chinook jargon, as spoken by the Indians of the Pacific coast; for the use of missionaries, traders, tourists and others who have business intercourse with the Indians; Chinook-English; English-Chinook.* This edition was reprinted in 1952.

B.C. ARCHIVES

**382 Haynes, William**
1835-1920

My log; a journal of the proceedings of the Flying Squadron. Devonport [Eng.] Clarke and Son, 1871.

xii, 142 p. illus., tables. 17 cm.

In verse. Four pages relate to the squadron's Esquimalt visit. The author was a bandsman on H.M.S. "Phoebe."

B.C. ARCHIVES

**383 Hudson's Bay Company**

Deed poll, by the governor and company of Hudson's Bay, for conducting their trade in North America, and for defining the rights and prescribing the duties of their officers. London, Printed by Sir Joseph Causton & Sons, 1871.

11 p. 26 cm. Cover title.

Reprinted with two amendments in 1887.

B.C. ARCHIVES

**384 Shotbolt, Tho[mas]**
1842-1922

An account of the establishment and subsequent progress of Freemasonry in the colony of British Columbia from its origin in 1859 to 1871. Victoria, Printed at the British Colonist Office, 1871.

18 p. 21 cm. At head of text: A statement of the position of the Masonic fraternity in the colony of Vancouver Island and British Columbia, compiled for the information of the craft, in consequence of a proposition by a certain brethren to form an independent Grand Lodge for the colony. On p. 18: Prepared by direction and under the inspection of the District Grand Master, and ordered to be issued from the District Grand Secretary's office, Victoria, British Columbia, 24th April 1871.

B.C. ARCHIVES

**385 Tolmie, W[illiam] F[raser]**
1812-1886

Testimonials; Dr. W. F. Tolmie. [Victoria] Victoria Daily Standard Print, 1871.

11 p. 20 cm.

Letters supporting William Tolmie's application for the position of superintendent of Indian Affairs.

B.C. ARCHIVES

**386 Vancouver Island. Citizens**

Sir, the following is a copy of a petition, signed by inhabitants of Vancouver Island, and forwarded to the government of Canada for the purpose of showing them the importance of making the western terminus of the Canadian Pacific railroad on Vancouver Island. To His Excellency Anthony Musgrave, Governor of British Columbia, &c., &c., &c. [Victoria, 1871?]

sheet. 35 x 22 cm.

B.C. ARCHIVES

**387 Achintre, A[uguste]**
1834-1886

From the Atlantic to the Pacific; a journey to Vancouver Island and British Columbia. [Montreal, G. E. Desbarats, 1872]

14 p. plates. 29 cm. Name of author on p. [7] Not seen.

Prospectus.

Also printed in French with dedication signed: A. Achintre.

LIBRARY OF CONGRESS

**388 Anderson, Alexander Caulfield**
1814-1884

The Dominion at the West; a brief description of the province of British Columbia, its climate and resources. The government prize essay, 1872. Victoria, Printed by Richard Wolfenden, 1872.

iv, 112, xlii p. 21 cm. Not found in Holmes.

B.C. ARCHIVES

**389 Bulkley, Tho[ma]s A.**

Victoria water supply; report . . . addressed to the Hon. the Chief Commissioner of Lands and Works, British Columbia, dated October 28th, 1872. Victoria, Printed at the "Victoria Daily Standard" Office, 1872.

22 p. 2 fold. maps, 2 fold. plans. 29 cm.

B.C. ARCHIVES

**390 Canada. Laws, statutes, etc.**

An act respecting the Canadian Pacific Railway (assented to 14th June 1872) [Ottawa, Printed by Brown Chamberlin, n.d.]

7 p. 25 cm. Caption title. At head of title: Anno tricesimo-quinto; Victoriæ Reginæ; cap. lxxi.

B.C. ARCHIVES

**391 Fleming, [Sir] Sandford**
1827-1915

Progress report on the Canadian Pacific Railway exploratory survey. Addressed to the Hon. H. L. Langevin, C.B., Minister of Public Works. Ottawa, 1872.

80 p. fold. map, fold. profile. 25 cm.

B.C. ARCHIVES

**392 Freemasons. British Columbia. Grand Lodge**

Proceedings of the Most Worshipful Grand Lodge of Ancient, Free and Accepted Masons of British Columbia held at Victoria, B.C. . . . 1872+ Victoria, Vancouver.

v. illus. 23 cm. annual. Title varies slightly. Various printers. No index.

Includes lodge histories and biographical articles which provide valuable additions to the historic records of

B.C. communities. Among the most important contributions are the reports of the Grand Historian (from 1916 to date). The historians are William Burns (for 1916-27), Robie L. Reid (for 1931-44), and W. G. Gamble, who was appointed in 1947.

B.C. ARCHIVES

## 393    Great Britain

Northwest American water boundary. Second and definite [definitive?] statement on behalf of the government of Her Britannic Majesty, submitted to His Majesty the Emperor of Germany under the Treaty of Washington of May 8, 1871. [Berlin? 1872?]

21, xxxviii p.    33 cm.    Not seen.

For the same text, see entries 406 and 434.

LIBRARY OF CONGRESS

## 394    Great Britain. Colonial Land and Emigration Commissioners

Colonization circular . . . no. 31, 1872.    [London, Printed by George E. Eyre and William Spottiswoode, 1872]

192 p.    tables.    21 cm.    At head of title: 1872. Index: p. 182-192.

Information on British Columbia and Vancouver Island is scattered.

B.C. ARCHIVES

## 395    Great Britain. Treaties, etc.

Treaty of Washington. Treaty between Her Majesty and the United States of America, signed at Washington, May 8, 1871.    [Ottawa, Dawson, 1872]

17 p.    24 cm.    Caption title. Colophon: Reprinted from the statute book of 35th Victoria (1872) by Samuel Edward Dawson, law printer to the Queen's Most Excellent Majesty.

CANADIAN ARCHIVES

## 396    Halcombe, J[ohn] J[oseph]
### D. 1909?

Stranger than fiction. Published under the direction of the Tract Committee.    London, Society for Promoting Christian Knowledge [1872]

256 p.    plates, ports.    18 cm.    Not seen.    Third edition in B.C. Archives examined.

An account of Metlahkatla and the work of William Duncan.

Third edition: 1873.    Fourth edition: 1874.    Also: 1877.    Also: 1878.    Also: 1880.

UNIVERSITY OF WASHINGTON LIBRARY

## 397    Johnson, R[ichard] Byron

Very far West indeed; a few rough experiences on the north-west Pacific coast.    London, Sampson Low, Marston, Low & Searle, 1872.

vi, 280 p.    19 cm.

Mainly concerned with the author's experiences in British Columbia, including those at the gold mines in the early 1860's. In his *British Columbia: a bibliographical sketch*, R. L. Reid writes that the work "may be classed, in some details, as the product of the imagination."—p. 34.

Second and third editions: 1872.    Fourth edition: 1872.    Fifth edition: 1873.    Appeared in Dutch with title: *Avonturen in Britisch-Columbia en op het Vancouver-Eiland* (Arnhem, Voltelen, 1873?). There were also two French editions: one was published in 1874.

B.C. ARCHIVES

## 398    Langevin, Sir H[ector] L[ouis]
### 1826-1906

British Columbia: report of the Hon. H. L. Langevin, Minister of Public Works. Printed by order of Parliament.    Ottawa, Printed by I. B. Taylor, 1872.

vi, 246 p.    tables.    25 cm.    Dictionary of Chinook jargon: p. 161-182.

Of Sir Hector Langevin's visit to British Columbia, Sir Sandford Fleming wrote: "It is chiefly remarkable as the first journey undertaken by a Canadian minister to the newly acquired western province of the Dominion. In the summer of 1871 the Minister of Public Works, visited the Pacific coast on behalf of the Government, with the view of acquiring some information concerning the new province, especially in relation to the Pacific Railway and its western terminus. His duty was to enquire into the requirements of the western province, and personally to ascertain what public works were imperative . . ." — *Presidential address*, p. 127.

The fifty-one appendices (p. 56-246) are chiefly composed of correspondence, official memoranda, tables, and extracts from publications.

B.C. ARCHIVES

## 399    McClellan, R[olander] Guy

The golden state; a history of the region west of the Rocky Mountains, embracing California, Oregon, Nevada, Utah, Arizona, Idaho, Washington Territory, British Columbia, and Alaska, from the earliest period to the present time . . .    Philadelphia, William Flint; Halifax, Nova Scotia [c1872]

685 p.    plates, ports., maps.    23 cm.

Also printed in 1872, 1874, 1875, and 1876.

B.C. ARCHIVES

**400   McDonald, Archibald**
1790-1853

Peace River; a canoe voyage from Hudson's Bay
to Pacific, by the late Sir George Simpson
(governor, Hon. Hudson's Bay Company) in 1828.
Journal of the late Chief Factor, Archibald
McDonald (Hon. Hudson's Bay Company) who
accompanied him. Edited, with notes, by
Malcolm McLeod.   Ottawa, J. Durie & Son, 1872.

xix, 119 p.   fold. map.   22 cm.   Errata slip.

"The editor's object in publishing the journal was
to draw attention to the potentialities of the Peace
River country, and the suitability of the Peace River
Pass for the proposed Canadian Pacific Railway."
—Peel, p. 21.

B.C. ARCHIVES


**401   Poole, Francis**
D. 1874

Queen Charlotte Islands; a narrative of discovery
and adventure in the North Pacific. Edited by
John W. Lyndon [pseud.]   London, Hurst and
Blackett, 1872.

xiv, 347 p.   plates, 2 maps.   22 cm.
John W. Lyndon was the pseudonym of John Wyse.

The author, an engineer, was employed in 1862 by
the Queen Charlotte Mining Company to mine copper
at Skincuttle Inlet. He lived there for eighteen
months with his white labourers, who, according to
Poole, were rebelliously inclined. The book, based on
Poole's diaries, is an account of the mining adventure
and of his relations with the Haida Indians during
this period.

B.C. ARCHIVES


**402   Tassé, Joseph**
1848-1895

Le Chemin de Fer Canadien du Pacifique.
Montréal, Eusèbe Senécal, 1872.

62 p.   23 cm.   Contents: Le chemin du Pacifique,
aperçu historique de l'entreprise. — Practicabilité de
la route. — Coûte de la ligne et son exploitation. —
Le chemin du Pacifique et le commerce asiatique. —
Les Territoires du Nord-ouest et la Colombie
Britannique.

CANADIAN ARCHIVES


**403   The Traveler's guide . . .**

The traveler's guide and Oregon railroad gazeeter
[sic] . . . no. 3.   Portland, Oregon, L. Samuel
[1872]

1 v.   17 cm.   Published monthly by L. Samuel,
general advertising agent.   Not seen.

BANCROFT LIBRARY CATALOGUE


**404   United States**

Memorial on the Canal de Haro as the boundary
line of the United States of America, presented in
the name of the American government to His
Majesty, William I, German emperor and king of
Prussia, as arbitrator, by the American
plenipotentiary, George Bancroft.   [Berlin,
Printed by R. v. Decker, 1872?]

32, 56 p.   8 maps (1 fold.)   29 cm.   Of the maps,
seven are photographs of maps of the Vancouver
Island region made before 1846.

For the same text, see entries 406 and 443.

Another edition: 27, 22 p. At head of title:
Confidential.   Also appeared in German with title:
*Denkschrift uber den Canal von Haro . . .*

B.C. ARCHIVES


**405   United States**

Reply of the United States to the case of the
government of Her Britannic Majesty, presented
to His Majesty the Emperor of Germany, as
arbitrator, under the Treaty of Washington,
June 12, 1872.   [Berlin, Printed by R. v. Decker,
1872]

44, [57]-120 p.   5 fold. maps, diagr.   29 cm.

For the same text, see entries 406 and 443.

Also appeared in German with title: *Gegenantwort
der Vereinigten . . .*

B.C. ARCHIVES


**406   United States. Department of State**

Papers relating to the Treaty of Washington.
Washington, Government Printing Office,
1872-74.

6 v.   fold. maps.   23 cm.   Volume 5: Berlin
arbitration; containing the memorial of the United
States on the Canal de Haro as its boundary-line; case
of the government of Her Britannic Majesty; reply
of the United States thereto; second and definitive
statement of the government of Her Britannic
Majesty; and correspondence.

VANCOUVER PUBLIC LIBRARY


**407   Victoria. Chamber of Commerce**

Constitution and by-laws of the Chamber of
Commerce of Victoria, Vancouver Island. Second
edition.   Victoria, Printed at the "Victoria Daily
Standard Office," 1872.

16 p.   17 cm.

B.C. ARCHIVES

**408 White, William**
COMPILER 1830-1912

Post office gazetteer of the Dominion of Canada.
Compiled from official records (by permission
of the Postmaster General) Montreal, Printed by
John Lovell, 1872.

174 p. 25 cm.

**409 Agricultural and Horticultural
Society of British Columbia**

First report of the Exhibition Committee for
1872, and prize list for the second provincial
exhibition to be held in the city of Victoria, V.I.,
on Thursday, the 25th of September 1873.
Victoria, Printed at the Victoria Standard
Office, 1873.

15 p. 21 cm. Not seen.

**410 Blake, Edward**
1833-1912

Three speeches . . . on the Pacific Scandal.
[n.p., 1873]

66 p. 22 cm. Caption title.

**411 British Columbia. Agent General
in London**

British Columbia; information for emigrants.
Issued by the Agent-General for the province
[Gilbert Malcolm Sproat. London, Printed by
William Clowes and Sons, 1873]

96 p. illus., fold. map, tables. 22 cm.

Also: London, 1875. 100 p.

**412 British Columbia. Laws,
statutes, etc.**

The land laws of British Columbia, together with
land office forms and regulations, 1873.
Victoria, Printed by Richard Wolfenden, 1873.

41 p. 18 cm. Not found in Holmes.

**413 British Columbia Protestant
Orphan's Home**

Report of the [1st]— annual meeting. 1873+
Victoria.

v. illus. 20, 23 cm. annual (irregular) Various
printers. An annual report is now published about

every tenth year only. A list of officers of the home,
1880-1957, in the report for 1957.

Provides proceedings, lists of subscribers, donations,
reports, by-laws, etc.

**414 Brown, R[obert] C[hristopher]
Lundin**
D. 1876

Klatsassan, and other reminiscences of missionary
life in British Columbia. London, Society for
Promoting Christian Knowledge, 1873.

viii, 199 p. plates, port., fold. map. 18 cm.

Mainly the story of a Chilcotin Indian, Klatsassan,
and his followers, who murdered several white
men. The author tried to convert the condemned
Indians to Christianity before their execution.

**415 Butler, [Sir] W[illiam] F[rancis]**
1838-1910

The wild north land; being the story of a winter
journey with dogs across northern North
America. London, Sampson Low, Marston,
Low & Searle, 1873.

x, 358 p. plates, port., fold. map. 23 cm.

In the spring of 1873 Butler left Fort Carleton and
journeyed north to Lake Athabasca. He ascended
the Peace River, followed the Finlay to Omineca, and
ascended a western tributary to Germansen. Travelling overland, he then turned south to Fort St. James
and Quesnel. From Quesnel he relied on established
transportation to take him to New Westminster.
About Butler, one bibliographer made the comment:
"One wishes he had written more about people and
less about dogs."

There have been at least eleven editions of this work,
four appearing in 1874.

**416 Canada. Governor-General**
1872-1878 (DUFFERIN)

Charter for the construction of the Pacific railway,
with papers and correspondence. Printed by order
of Parliament. Ottawa, Printed by I. B. Taylor,
1873.

40 p. 24 cm.

**417 Canada. Governor-General**
1872-1878 (DUFFERIN)

Message. Papers relative to the issue of a
commission to inquire into certain charges made
against members of Her Majesty's Privy Council
for Canada, respecting the granting of a charter and

contract to the Canadian Pacific Railway Company. Ottawa, Printed by I. B. Taylor, 1873.

10 p.   24 cm.   Not seen. Missing from Shortt collection.

PEEL

## 418   Canada. Governor-General
### 1872-1878   (DUFFERIN)

Message. Papers relative to the prorogation of Parliament on the 13th day of August 1873. Ottawa, Printed by I. B. Taylor, 1873.

99 p.   24 cm.

Relates to the Pacific Scandal.

B.C. ARCHIVES

## 419   Canada. Laws, statutes, etc.

[Letters patent incorporating the Canadian Pacific Railway Company.   n.p., 1873]

10 1.   34 cm.

B.C. ARCHIVES

## 420   Canada. Royal Commission to Inquire into and Report upon the Several Matters relating to the Canadian Pacific Railway

Report of the royal commissioners appointed by commission, addressed to them, under the great seal of Canada, bearing date the fourteenth day of August, A.D. 1873.   Ottawa, 1873.

xii, 220 p.   24 cm.   (Canada. House of Commons. Journal, 1873, Appendix 1)   Commissioners: Antoine Polette, James Gowan. Chairman: Charles Dewey Day.

Report and evidence on the charges made by Lucius Huntington of collusion between Canadian promoters and United States' capitalists with regard to the construction of the railway (the Pacific Scandal).

B.C. ARCHIVES

## 421   Canada. Department of the Secretary of State for the Provinces

Report of the Superintendent of Indian Affairs for British Columbia for 1872 & 1873. Printed by order of Parliament.   Ottawa, Printed by I. B. Taylor, 1873.

40 p.   25 cm.   Report of I. W. Powell.

B.C. ARCHIVES

## 422   Canadian Pacific Railway Company

The Canadian Pacific Railway.   Montreal, "Gazette" Printing House, 1873.

vi, 113 p.   fold. map.   23 cm.

Contains the royal letters patent constituting the charter of incorporation and embodying the agreement with the government, together with relevant federal legislation.

B.C. ARCHIVES

## 423   Comments on the proceedings . . .

Comments on the proceedings and evidence on the charges preferred by Mr. Huntington, M.P., against the government of Canada.   Montreal, "Gazette" Printing House, 1873.

16 p.   22 cm.

A pamphlet relating to the royal commission on the Pacific Scandal, and written in support of the Macdonald government.

B.C. ARCHIVES

## 424   Croasdaile, Henry E.

Scenes on Pacific shores, with a trip across South America, by Henry E. Croasdaile, retired lieutenant, R.N.   London, The Town and Country Publishing Company, 1873.

iv, 173 p.   front.   22 cm.

In two chapters the author gives an account of hunting, fishing and travel on Vancouver Island, and of a tour of duty in Esquimalt.

B.C. ARCHIVES

## 425   Cushing, Caleb
### 1800-1879

The treaty of Washington; its negotiation, execution, and the discussions relating thereto. New York, Harper & Brothers, 1873.

280 p.   21 cm.

Articles XXXIV to XLII of the treaty provided for arbitration to determine which channel would form the boundary line between Vancouver Island and the United States. Chapter 4 gives a history of the northwest boundary dispute and a review of the positions of the British and American governments (p. 220-225). The author was a leading advocate of the American claim.

B.C. ARCHIVES

## 426   Dallas, A[lexander] G[rant]
### 1816-1882

San Juan, Alaska, and the north-west boundary, by A. G. Dallas, late governor of Rupert's Land.   London, Henry S. King and Co., 1873.

11 p.   21 cm.

B.C. ARCHIVES

**427    Dictionary . . .**

Dictionary of the Chinook jargon or Indian trade language now in general use on the North-west Coast; adapted for general business. Olympia, W. T., T. G. Lowe & Co., 1873.

32 p.    22 cm.    Cover title.    Not seen.

BANCROFT LIBRARY CATALOGUE

**428    Eardley-Wilmot, S[ydney Marow]**
EDITOR    1847-1929

Our journal in the Pacific, by the officers of H.M.S. Zealous. Arranged and edited by Lieutenant S. Eardley-Wilmot.    London, Longmans, Green, 1873.

xiii, 333, xx p.    illus., plates, fold. map.    23 cm.

Two chapters describe the officers' activities while in British Columbia.

B.C. ARCHIVES

**429    Freemasons. Victoria. British Columbia Lodge No. 5**

By-laws of the British Columbia Lodge No. 5, Register Grand Lodge of British Columbia. Victoria, D. W. Higgins, 1873.

27 p.    13 cm.

B.C. ARCHIVES

**430    Freemasons. Victoria. Victoria Lodge No. 1**

By-laws of Victoria Lodge No. 1 (late 783, E.R.) F. and A.M., held under the jurisdiction of the Grand Lodge of British Columbia; instituted August 20th, 1860.    Victoria, Victoria Daily Standard Print, 1873.

30 p.    16 cm.

Also: Victoria, Colonist, 1895. 29 p.

B.C. ARCHIVES

**431    Grant, G[eorge] Monro**
1835-1902

Ocean to ocean; Sandford Fleming's expedition through Canada in 1872; being a diary kept during a journey from the Atlantic to the Pacific with the expedition of the engineer-in-chief of the Canadian Pacific and Intercolonial railways, by the Rev. George M. Grant, secretary to the expedition. With sixty illustrations.    Toronto, James Campbell & Son, 1873.

xiv, 371 p.    illus., plates, maps.    21 cm.

The expedition crossed the Rocky Mountains by the Yellow Head Pass, journeyed along the North Thompson River to Kamloops, and from there to Yale and the Pacific.

Several editions were published during the 1870's. Revised edition with introduction by William L. Grant and with bibliography: Toronto, The Radisson Society of Canada, 1925.

B.C. ARCHIVES

**432    Great Britain**

North-west American water boundary. Case of the government of Her Britannic Majesty, submitted to the arbitration and award of His Majesty the Emperor of Germany, in accordance with Article XXXIV of the treaty between Great Britain and the United States of America, signed at Washington, May 8, 1871. (For maps and charts referred to in this case, see North America no. 7) Presented to both House of Parliament by command of Her Majesty, 1873.    London, Printed by Harrison and Sons [1873]

iv, 41 p.    34 cm.    ([Great Britain. Parliament. Command papers] C. 690) At head of title: North America, no. 3 (1873) A.

For the same text, see entry 406.

B.C. ARCHIVES

**433    Great Britain**

North-west American water boundary. Maps annexed to the case of the government of Her Britannic Majesty . . . Presented to both Houses of Parliament by command of Her Majesty, 1873. London, Printed by Harrison and Sons [1873]

5 fold. maps.    34 cm.    ([Great Britain. Parliament. Command papers] C. 694) At head of title: North America, no. 7 (1873) E.

B.C. ARCHIVES

**434    Great Britain**

North-west American water boundary. Second and definitive statement on behalf of the government of Her Britannic Majesty, submitted to His Majesty the Emperor of Germany under the Treaty of Washington of May 8, 1871. Presented to both Houses of Parliament by command of Her Majesty, 1873.    London, Printed by Harrison and Sons [1873]

17, xxxiv p.    34 cm.    ([Great Britain. Parliament. Command papers] C. 692) At head of title: North American, no. 5 (1873) C.

For the same text, see entries 393 and 406.

B.C. ARCHIVES

**435    Great Britain**

North-western water boundary. Correspondence respecting the award of the Emperor of Germany on the matter of the boundary line between Great Britain and the United States, under the treaties of Washington of June 15, 1846, and May 6, 1871. Presented to both Houses of Parliament by command of Her Majesty, 1873. London, Printed by Harrison and Sons [1873]

12 p. 34 cm. ([Great Britain. Parliament. Command papers] C. 696) At head of title: North American, no. 9 (1873) G.

B.C. ARCHIVES

## 436 Great Britain. Treaties, etc.

Protocol signed at Washington on the 10th of March 1873, defining the boundary line through the Canal de Haro, in accordance with the award of the Emperor of Germany of October 21, 1872. Presented to both Houses of Parliament by command of Her Majesty, 1873. London, Printed by Harrison and Sons [1873]

3 p. 34 cm. ([Great Britain. Parliament. Command papers] C. 735) At head of title: North America, no. 10 (1873)

B.C. ARCHIVES

## 437 Lane, Charles C.

The mining laws of British Columbia contrasted with those of other countries. Victoria, Printed at the British Colonist Office, 1873.

13 p. 23 cm.

An appeal in the form of a letter for a change in British Columbia's Ordinance to Amend and Consolidate the Gold Mining Laws, 1865 (short title: Gold Mining Ordinance, 1865).

CANADIAN ARCHIVES

## 438 Lowe, Stahlschmidt...

Lowe, Stahlschmidt & Co.'s price current. Victoria, 1873.

[4] p. (folder) 28 cm. Caption title. Copy examined: no. 5, 7 January 1873.

B.C. ARCHIVES

## 439 Mills, David
### 1831-1903

The Pacific railway scandal; an address... delivered at Aylmer on the 14th October 1873. St. Thomas, Home Journal Presses Print, 1873.

11 p. 24 cm.

LIBRARY OF PARLIAMENT

## 440 Stannard, M.

Memoirs of a professional lady nurse. London, Simpkin, Marshall & Co., 1873.

viii, 239 p. illus. 19 cm.

In three chapters the author narrates her activities in British Columbia and comments upon Indian customs.

UNIVERSITY OF WASHINGTON LIBRARY

## 441 The Story of the Pacific Scandal...

The story of the Pacific Scandal; being a synopsis of the facts of the whole case. [n.p., n.d.]

sheet. 78 x 65 cm.

An attack on the Macdonald government.

B.C. ARCHIVES

## 442 United States

North-west American water boundary. Maps annexed to the memorial and reply of the United States' government... Presented to both Houses of Parliament by command of Her Majesty, 1873. London, Printed by Harrison and Sons [1873]

14 fold. maps. 34 cm. ([Great Britain. Parliament. Command papers] C. 695) At head of title: North America, no. 8 (1873) F.

B.C. ARCHIVES

## 443 United States

North-west American water boundary. Memorial on the Canal de Haro as the boundary line of the United States of America, presented in the name of the American government to His Majesty William I, German emperor and king of Prussia, as arbitrator, by the American plenipotentiary, George Bancroft. For map and charts referred to in this memoral, see North America, no. 8 [C. 695] Presented to both Houses of Parliament by command of Her Majesty, 1873. London, Printed by Harrison and Sons [1873]

36 p. 34 cm. ([Great Britain. Parliament. Command papers] C. 691) At head of title: North America, no. 4 (1873) B.

For the same text, see entries 404 and 406.

B.C. ARCHIVES

## 444 United States

North-west American water boundary. Reply of the United States to the case of the government of Her Britannic Majesty presented to His Majesty the Emperor of Germany as arbitrator, under the provisions of the Treaty of Washington, June 12, 1872. Presented to both Houses of Parliament by command of Her Majesty, 1873. London, Printed by Harrison and Sons [1873]

45 p. tables. 34 cm. ([Great Britain. Parliament. Command papers] C. 693) At head of title: North America, no. 6 (1873) D. Includes: Appendix to the reply.

For the same text, see entry 406.

B.C. ARCHIVES

**445    United States. Hydrographic Office**

Instructions pour naviguer sur les côtes de l'île Reine-Charlotte et d'Alaska, dans les îles Aléoutiennes, la mer de Behring et le détroit de Behring. Traduites de l'américain par M. le vicomte de La Tour du Pin. Publié sous le ministère du vice-amiral Pothuau, Ministre de la marine et des colonies.    Paris, Imprimerie nationale, 1873.

xi, 362 p.    26 cm.    (Dépôt des cartes et plans de la marine, no. 509)

CANADIAN ARCHIVES

**446    Victoria Fire Department (Victoria)**

Constitution, by-laws, and rules of order. Victoria, Printed at the Victoria Standard Office, 1873.

30 p.    16 cm.

B.C. ARCHIVES

**447    White, Thomas**
1830-1888

Our great West; a lecture delivered under the auspices of the Young Men's Christian Association of Christ Church Cathedral, on the evening of the 27th February 1873. Montreal, 1873.

32 p.    21 cm.    Not seen.

" . . . an extremely scarce work on British Columbia and the Northwest Territories. Much on the activities of the Hudson's Bay Company, the Rocky Mountain country, the exploration, routes, resources, gold rushes, etc."—Eberstadt, cat. 136, item 554.

LIBRARY OF CONGRESS

**448    Wood, E[dmund] B[urke]**
1820-1882

Speech in the House of Commons on the Pacific Scandal.    [Ottawa, 1873?]

32 p.    25 cm.    Caption title.

TORONTO PUBLIC LIBRARY

**449    Boddam-Whetham, J[ohn] W[hetham]**
B. 1843

Western wanderings; a record of travel in the evening land.    London, Richard Bentley and Son, 1874.

xii, 364 p.    plates.    23 cm.

Four chapters relate to Vancouver Island and mainland British Columbia.

B.C. ARCHIVES

**450    British Columbia. Quarantine Claims Commission**

The quarantine claims: "Prince Alfred," June 1872; judgment, December 24th, 1873.    Victoria, Printed at the "Victoria Standard" Office [n.d.]

11 p.    23 cm.    Cover title. Judgment delivered by Mr. Justice John H. Gray. Not found in Holmes.

Claims against the Dominion government arose over expenses incurred while quarantining passengers from a ship which had had a case of smallpox on board.

B.C. ARCHIVES

**451    British Columbia. Supreme Court**

Judgment: Bishop of Columbia versus Rev. Mr. Cridge. Judgment rendered on Saturday, October 24th, 1874, at 11:20 o'clock, A.M. [Victoria? 1874?]

viii, p.    23 cm.    Caption title. The judgment of Matthew Baillie Begbie.

Judgment in the case of an application on a bill filed by Bishop Hills against Rev. Edward Cridge to restrain him from officiating in Christ Church, Victoria, and from acting elsewhere in the diocese as a clergyman of the Church of England.

B.C. ARCHIVES

**452    British Columbia Pioneer Society**

Constitution, by-laws and rules of order of the British Columbia Pioneer Society, organized April 28, 1871.    Victoria, Board of Directors, 1874.

19 p.    14 cm.    Printers: Rose & Pottinger, Victoria.

Also: Victoria, M'Millan & Son, 1879. 22 p.    Also: Victoria, Munroe Miller, printer, 1893. 31 p.    Also: Victoria, Colonist Steam Presses, 1884. 24 p.

B.C. ARCHIVES

**453    British Columbia Rifle Association (Victoria)**

Programme of the annual meeting.    1874+ Victoria.

v.    17 cm.    Indexed on inside back cover after 1930. Title varies: 1894-1928? as *Prize list*.

Contains prize lists, descriptions of matches, contest regulations, and membership lists.

B.C. ARCHIVES

**454    British Columbia Terms of Union Preservation League**

[Preamble and by-laws.    n.p., 1874.]

4 p. (folder)    18 cm.

B.C. ARCHIVES

**455 Canada. Laws, statutes, etc.**

An act to extend certain laws relating to matters connected with Indians in the provinces of Manitoba and British Columbia, with proclamation suspending section eighth [*sic*] of said act.    Victoria, David W. Higgins, 1874.

14 p.    25 cm.    Cover title.

B.C. ARCHIVES

**456 Canada. Department of the Secretary of State**

Copies of all instructions on the practicability of a mixed land and water trans-continental communication with British Columbia, and for reports thereon.    Ottawa, Printed by I. B. Taylor, 1874.

6 p.    24 cm.    (Canada. Sessional papers, 1874, no. 51)    Not seen. Missing from Shortt Collection.

PEEL

**457 Cridge, E[dward]**
BISHOP   1817-1913

Diocesan synod; address of the Dean of Christ Church to the congregation.    [Victoria? 1874?]

[6] p.    22 cm.    Caption title.

The author's view of the aims of the synod, and his defense against a letter of censure from Bishop Hills.

B.C. ARCHIVES

**458 Fleming, [Sir] Sandford**
1827-1915

Memorandum of the Canadian Pacific Railway. [1 January 1874]    Ottawa, Printed by I. B. Taylor, 1874.

59 p.    21 cm.    At head of title: Confidential. Appendix A: Observations and practical suggestions on the subject of a railway through British North America, submitted ... in the year 1863 [p. 19-49] Appendix B: Canadian Pacific Railway; memorandum ... February 1873 [p. 53-59]

The author was requested to inform the government respecting the best means to be followed in the railroad's construction.

B.C. ARCHIVES

**459 Fleming, [Sir] Sandford**
1827-1915

Report of progress on the exploration and surveys up to January 1874.    Ottawa, Printed by MacLean, Roger & Co., 1874.

xi, 286 (i.e. 294) p.    fold. plates (incl. maps)    25 cm.    At head of title: Canadian Pacific Railway; Sandford Fleming, engineer-in-chief. Plates nos. 8, 10, 11, 13-16 in separate case. Appendices (contents in part): B. Peace River expedition, by C. Horetzky.

— E. Progress report on the surveys for 1872 in British Columbia, by Marcus Smith. — G. Detail report of operations in the Rocky Mountains ... during the year 1872, by Walter Moberly. — H. Detail report on the passes through the Cascade and year 1873, by Marcus Smith. — K. Special report on the passes through the Cascade and Rocky mountain chains, by Marcus Smith. — L. Extracts from report by Lieutenant H. Spencer Palmer, Royal Engineers, on the North Bentinck Arm and the route thence through the Cascade chain of mountains to the interior of British Columbia.

B.C. ARCHIVES

**460 Goudie, D. R.**

Goudie's perpetual sleigh road supersedes the railway, and is capable of carrying passengers at a rate of eighty to one hundred miles an hour; from the Atlantic to the Pacific Ocean in 40 to 45 hours, from Montreal to Fort Garry in 15 to 16 hours, from Toronto to Halifax, N.S., in 16 hours, or from London to St. John, N.B., in 20 hours. Patented, or patents applied for, in Canada, U.S., England, France, &c., &c. All rights, mechanical and literary are reserved.    Toronto, Printed at the office of the "Monetary Times," 1874.

90 p.    fold. diagr.    21 cm.    At head of title: Read, study, comprehend, then criticise.

LIBRARY OF PARLIAMENT

**461 Great Britain. Colonial Office**

Correspondence relative to the Canadian Pacific Railway. Presented to both Houses of Parliament by command of Her Majesty, March 1874. London, William Clowes & Sons, 1874.

266 p.    33 cm.    ([Great Britain. Parliament. Command papers] C. 911)

Relates to the Pacific Scandal.

SHORTT COLLECTION

**462 Halcombe, J[ohn] J[oseph]**
EDITOR   D. 1909?

The emigrant and the heathen; or, Sketches of the missionary life.    London, Society for Promoting Christian Knowledge [1874]

1v, 330 p.    plates.    19 cm.    Mission work in British Columbia; chiefly from the journals of the Rev. R. J. Dundas: p. 185-229.

B.C. ARCHIVES

**463 Hills, George**
BISHOP OF COLUMBIA   1816-1895

Synods: their constitution and objects; a sermon preached in Christ Church and St. John's, Victoria, January 1874.    [Victoria] Printed at the Victoria Standard Office, 1874.

vii p.    21 cm.    Cover title.

B.C. ARCHIVES

**464    The History of the Lake Superior ring . . .**

The history of the Lake Superior ring; an account of the rise and progress of the Yankee combination, headed by Hon. Alexander Mackenzie, premier of Canada, and the Browns, for the purpose of selling their interest and political power to enrich Jay Cook & Co. and other American speculators, changing the route of the Canada Pacific Railway, with a view of breaking up our great Dominion, and severing our connection with the British Empire; thorough exposé of Mackenzie's and Brown's treachery to their country. This pamphlet is stereotyped so that generations to come may look back with contempt upon a government that has united with the Republicans of the United States to destroy our prosperous country.    Toronto, Printed at [the Leader office] James Beaty, 1874.

14 p.    23 cm.

CANADIAN ARCHIVES

**465    Hodgins, Thomas**
1828-1910

Letters on English parliamentary precedents, as affecting the Canadian Pacific Scandal, by "Parliamentum" [pseud.]    Toronto, 1874.

32 p.    17 cm.    On p.[3]: These letters were originally published in the Globe newspaper during the discussions on the "Pacific Railway Scandal" last summer. At the request of some political friends, I have re-published them in pamphlet form, for use during the present election campaign [signed: Thomas Hodgins]

CANADIAN ARCHIVES

**466    Horetzky, Charles**
1839-1900

Canada on the Pacific: being an account of a journey from Edmonton to the Pacific by the Peace River Valley; and of a winter voyage along the western coast of the Dominion; with remarks on the physical features of the Pacific railway route and notices of the Indian tribes of British Columbia.    Montreal, Dawson Brothers, 1874.

x, 244 p.    fold. plan, fold. map.    19 cm.

"The writer organized and conducted the overland expedition of Mr. Sandford Fleming, from Fort Garry to Edmonton, during the summer of 1872; and it was at the instance of that gentleman, who desired to exhaust the whole field of enquiry, before deciding upon a route for the Canada Pacific road, that the journey . . . was undertaken." — pref.

B.C. ARCHIVES

**467    McLeod, M[alcolm]**
1821-1899

Pacific railway routes, Canada, by M. McLeod, "Britannicus" [pseud.] A series of letters published in the Montreal "Gazette." [n.p., 1874?]

21 p.    23 cm.    At head of text: Pacific railway routes, Canada; letters addressed to the editor of the Montreal Gazette, and published in that paper in the course of June and July 1874.

CANADIAN ARCHIVES

**468    Odd Fellows, Independent Order of. British Columbia. Grand Lodge**

Proceedings of the 1st— annual session.    1874+ Victoria, Vancouver.

v.    28 cm.    Various printers.

B.C. ARCHIVES

**469    Scammon, Charles Melville**
1825-1911

The marine mammals of the north-western coast of North America, described and illustrated; together with an account of the American whale-fishery.    San Francisco, John H. Carmany and Company, 1874.

319, v p.    illus., plates (part double) tables.    30 cm.

B.C. ARCHIVES

**470    Swan, James G[ilchrist]**
1818-1900

The Haidah Indians of Queen Charlotte's Islands, British Columbia; with a brief description of their carvings, tattoo designs, etc.    [Washington, Smithsonian Institution, 1874]

iii, 18 p.    7 plates (part col.)    33 cm. (Smithsonian contributions to knowledge [v. 21, art. 4]    Smithsonian Institution publication 267.

B.C. ARCHIVES

**471    Wilson, W[illia]m**

The Dominion of Canada and the Canadian Pacific Railway.    Victoria, Rose & Pottinger, 1874.

42 p.    23 cm.

An appeal for the railway's construction on the grounds of patriotism.

B.C. ARCHIVES

**472    Bancroft, Hubert Howe**
1832-1918

The native races of the Pacific states of North America.    New York, D. Appleton and Company, 1875-76.

5 v. illus., fold. maps, fold. table. 24 cm. Some copies of v. 1 are dated 1874. Authorities quoted: v. 1, p. [xvii]-xlix. According to W. A. Morris, this work was largely written by H. L. Oak, T. A. Harcourt, Albert Goldschmidt, W. M. Fisher and William Nemos (see *Oregon historical quarterly*, v. 4, p. 301-310)

"[Bancroft's] work is a most laborious encyclopaedia of all that is known up to to-day of the native races of the Pacific States, and it embraces all the inhabitants of the region to the west of the Mississippi from the Arctic Sea to the Isthmus of Panama. His aim . . . is not so much to write history as to provide materials out of which it may be eventually written by others."—*Edinburgh review*, v. 144, 1876, p. 283*f*.

Also: New York, A. L. Bancroft & Co., 1874-75.
Also: San Francisco, A. L. Bancroft & Co., 1883.
Also: San Francisco, History Co., 1886. Also published in Bancroft's *Works* as v. 1-5.

B.C. ARCHIVES

## 473    Canada. Governor-General
### 1872-1878    (DUFFERIN)

Message relative to the terms of union with the province of British Columbia. Printed by order of Parliament. Ottawa, Printed by Maclean, Roger & Co., 1875.

66 p. 25 cm. (Canada. Sessional papers, no. 19, 1875) Cover title.

Relates to the non-fulfilment of the terms of union.

B.C. ARCHIVES

## 474    Canadian Pacific Railway Company

Instructions from the Engineer in Chief to the staff. No. 1: Explorations and surveys. No. 2: The Purveyor's Branch. No. 3: Location and construction. No. 4: Organization of the engineering staff. No. 5: Location of stations. No. 6: Earthwork tables. [Ottawa, 1875]

36 p. illus., fold. profile, tables. 22 cm. The tables are unpaged, and each has t.p. with title: . . . Tables for facilitating the calculation of earthwork.

CANADIAN ARCHIVES

## 475    Cridge, Edward
### BISHOP 1817-1913 DEFENDANT

Trial of the Very Reverend Edward Cridge, Rector and Dean of Christ Church Cathedral, Victoria; documents, evidence, correspondence, and judgments, as used and given in the Bishop's Court, and in the Supreme Court of the province, before the Hon. Chief Justice Begbie. [Victoria] Printed at the Victoria Standard Office, 1875.

61, viii, [1] p. 21 cm. Cover title.

Another edition appeared with title: *Trial of the Very Reverend Edward Cridge, Rector and Dean of Christ Church Cathedral, Victoria; documents, evidence, correspondence, and judgments, as used and given in the Bishop's Court, and in the Supreme Court of the province, before the Hon. Chief Justice Begbie, an appilcation [sic] for injunction on 24th Oct. 1874, and final judgment of Mr. Justice Gray on 18 May 1875.* [Victoria] Printed at the Victoria Standard Office, 1875. 61, viii, 9 p.

B.C. ARCHIVES

## 476    Crouter, J[ohn] W[esley]

My policy for the construction of the Canada Pacific Railway as a government work, with irrefutable arguments in favor of this policy. [n.p., n.d.]

8 p. 24 cm. Caption title.

"I stand prepared to form a party which will hurl from political power every man, party and clique of men who shall refuse to build this railway as a government work."—p. 8.

BIBLIOTHÈQUE SAINT-SULPICE

## 477    Cubery, W[illia]m M.
### COMPILER

Cubery's visitors guide to Victoria. Compiled by Wm. M. Cubery of Cubery's Purchasing Agency [of San Francisco. Victoria, Published at the Colonist Office, 1875]

8 p. 26 cm. Caption title.

A business directory arranged by street location.

B.C. ARCHIVES

## 478    Dewdney, E[dgar]
### 1835-1916

Speech on the subject of the Canadian Pacific Railway, delivered by E. Dewdney, Esq., M.P., to his constituents at Cache Creek. New Westminster, "Mainland Guardian" Print, 1875.

28 p. 20 cm.

B.C. ARCHIVES

## 479    Friesach, Carl
### 1821-1891

Ein Ausflug nach Britisch-Columbien im Jahre 1858. Graz, Druckerei Leykam-Josefsthal, 1875.

53 p. 22 cm. Reprinted from the communications of the Philosophical Society. Graz, 1875.

"Much of Dr. Friesach's narrative is devoted to a description of matters he saw in Washington and Oregon, and to the general history and geography of the Pacific Northwest." — *British Columbia historical quarterly*, v. 5, p. 222.

TORONTO PUBLIC LIBRARY

**480   Great Britain. Parliament**

Correspondence respecting the Canadian Pacific Railway Act so far as regards British Columbia. Presented to both Houses of Parliament by command of Her Majesty, April 1875.   London Printed by Harrison and Sons [1875]

iv, 99 p.   32 cm.   ([Great Britain. Parliament. Command papers] C. 1217)

An important document with regard to the points at issue between the governments of Canada and British Columbia. Includes correspondence relating to Lord Carnarvon's arbitration, to J. D. Edgar's B.C. mission, and to the activities of George A. Walkem.

CANADIAN ARCHIVES

**481   [Johnson, M. E.]**
SUPPOSED AUTHOR

Dayspring in the far West; sketches of mission-work in north-west America, by M. E. J. London, Seeley, Jackson, and Halliday, 1875.

xi, 215 p.   plates, ports., fold. map.   20 cm. Chronological table of events connected with the Church Missionary Society's missions in north-west America: p. [203]-215. List of books made use of: p. [viii] Presentation inscription on fly-leaf of a copy in the Newberry Library is signed in manuscript: M. E. Johnson. The author was a woman.

Has four chapters on Metlahkatla.

B.C. ARCHIVES

**482   [McLeod, Malcolm]**
1821-1899

The Pacific railway; Britannicus' [pseud.] letters from the Ottawa Citizen.   Ottawa, Printed by the "Citizen" Printing and Publishing Company, 1875.

42 p.   22 cm.   Cover title.

B.C. ARCHIVES

**483   McLeod, M[alcolm]**
1821-1899

Pacific railway, Canada; selection from series of letters by "Britannicus" [pseud.] (from 1869 to 1875) on the subject, with additional remarks. [Ottawa, Printed by A. S. Woodburn, 1875]

36 p.   25 cm.   Cover title: Pacific railway, Canada; Britannicus letters, &c., thereon.

B.C. ARCHIVES

**484   Mason, Geo[rge]**
1829-1893

Ode on the loss of the steamship "Pacific," Nov. 4th, 1875.   Nanaimo, Printed by Geo. Norris, 1875.

4 p.   14 cm.   Cover title.

B.C. ARCHIVES

**485   Mason, Geo[rge]**
1829-1893

Prize poem. Lo! the poor Indian! Read before the Mechanics' Literary Institute, Victoria, Thursday, October 28, 1875.   Victoria, Alex. Rose, 1875.

8 p.   15 cm.

The effects of the white man's arrival on the Indian is set forth "to point a moral."

B.C. ARCHIVES

**486   Pinart, Alph[onse Louis]**
1852-1911

La chasse aux animaux marins et les pêcheries chez les indigènes de la côte nord-ouest d'Amérique.   Boulogne-sur-mer, Imp. de Charles Aigre, 1875.

15 p.   21 cm.

B.C. ARCHIVES

**487   Texada Iron Mines**

Texada iron mines, British Columbia. Agent for sale of Texada iron mines, Hon. A. DeCosmos, M.P., Victoria, B.C.   Montreal, Printed by Lovell Printing and Publishing Co., 1875.

34 p.   diagr., tables.   22 cm.

B.C. ARCHIVES

**488   Woods, C[harles] T[homas]**
1825-1895

A letter originally addressed to a member of the congregation of Holy Trinity Church, but now commended to the earnest consideration of all, by the Venerable C. T. Woods, M.A., rector of Holy Trinity, and Archdeacon of Columbia.   New Westminster, "Mainland Guardian" Print, 1875.

12 p.   21 cm.   Cover title.

The author evidently had been accused of leaning towards the practices of the Roman Catholic church. This letter is in defense of his teaching.

B.C. ARCHIVES

**489   Anderson, Alexander Caulfield**
1814-1884

Notes on north-western America.   Montreal, Mitchell & Wilson, 1876.

22 p.   22 cm.   Cover title.

"Descriptive matter intended to accompany a 'Skeleton Map of North-West America,' prepared by Mr. Anderson to send to the Philadelphia International Exhibition of 1876."—p. [1]

B.C. ARCHIVES

**490    Canada. Parliament. Senate**

Debate in the Senate on the Canadian Pacific Railway. The government policy criticised. [Ottawa, 1876]

70 p.    24 cm.    Caption title.

Pertains to British Columbia and the railway question.

B.C. ARCHIVES

**491    Canadian Pacific Railway Company**

Description of the country between Lake Superior and the Pacific Ocean on the line of the Canadian Pacific Railway. Compiled from the best authorities, and published by order of the Canadian government.    Ottawa, 1876.

xxxix, 143 p.    25 cm.    Chapter 5: The British Columbia section. Appendix to Chapter 5: Reports by Marcus Smith, Esq., of surveys in British Columbia during the years 1874-5.

Further information for intending contractors to supplement the technical reports of the engineer.

B.C. ARCHIVES

**492    Carnarvon Club (Victoria)**

Constitution.    [Victoria? 1876?]

3 p.    21 cm.    Cover title. At head of title: God save the Queen; Carnarvon terms or separation.

The club was organized in September 1876.

B.C. ARCHIVES

**493    Church of England. Synods. British Columbia**

Report of the . . . session of the . . . synod of the Diocese of British Columbia, held in the city of Victoria . . . with the address of the Bishop. Synod 1, session 1—Synod 5, session 3; 1875-92.    Victoria, 1876-92.

v.    Various printers. Microfilm copy examined.

The annual sessions include the proceedings.

B.C. ARCHIVES

**494    [Dewdney, Edgar]**
1835-1916

The railway in British Columbia.    [New Westminster, Printed at the 'Herald' Office, 1876]

6 p.    26 cm.    Cover title. At head of text: Letter from E. Dewdney, Esq., M.P., to the Hon. A. Mackenzie, premier of Canada; read at a public meeting, held in New Westminster, on the 10th of May, 1876, a report of which is annexed.

B.C. ARCHIVES

**495    [Dufferin and Ava, Frederick Temple Hamilton-Temple-Blackwood]**
1ST MARQUIS OF    1826-1902

Address of His Excellency the Governor-General of Canada on the subject of relations between the Dominion government and British Columbia, in respect to the Canadian Pacific Railway, delivered at Government House, Victoria, Sept. 20th, 1876, to a deputation of the Reception Committee. Victoria, Printed by Richard Wolfenden, 1876.

32 p.    19 cm.    In Holmes.

Also printed with an introduction under caption title: *Lord Dufferin's speech at Victoria* (Victoria, Printed by William H. Cullen, 1912). In 13 pages. Not in Holmes.

B.C. ARCHIVES

**496    Great Britain. Colonial Office**

Correspondence respecting the non-admission of fish and fish oils, the produce of British Columbia, into the United States, free of duty, under the Treaty of Washington, May 8, 1871. Presented to both Houses of Parliament by command of Her Majesty, 1876.    London, Printed by Harrison and Sons [1876]

12 p.    34 cm.    ([Great Britain. Parliament. Command papers] C. 1548) At head of title: North America no. 5 (1876)

B.C. ARCHIVES

**497    Kennedy, Sir W[illiam] R[obert]**
1838-1916

Sporting adventures in the Pacific, whilst in command of the "Reindeer."    London, Sampson Low, Marston, Searle, & Rivington, 1876.

303 p.    illus., plates.    22 cm.

One chapter on the author's activities on Vancouver Island in 1873.

B.C. ARCHIVES

**498    [McLeod, Malcolm]**
1821-1899

Pacific railway; extra tax for it, not necessary. British Columbia.    Ottawa, Printed by the Citizen Printing and Publishing Company, 1876.

15 p.    21 cm.    Cover title. Caption title: Britannicus' letters published in the Ottawa Citizen.

B.C. ARCHIVES

**499    Petitot, [Émile Fortuné Stanislas Joseph]**
1838-1917

Monographie des Déné-Dindjié.    Paris, Ernest Leroux, 1876.

109 p.   24 cm.   First appeared in five issues of a periodical not yet identified.

The work is divided into two parts: the first describes the Indians; the second relates to their origin. Petitot believed there was a possibility of the Indians being identified with the lost Ten Tribes of Israel.

B.C. ARCHIVES

### 500   Aube, Th[éophile]
#### 1826-1890

Notes sur le Centre-Amérique (Costa-Rica, Nicaragua et San-Salvador) Vancouver et la Colombie Anglaise.   Paris, Berger-Levrault, 1877.

59 p.   24 cm.   Cover title. Notes sur Vancouver et la Colombie Anglaise: p. [25]-59. Reprinted from *Revue maritime et coloniale*, December 1876, p. 613-636, and January 1877, p. 54-88.

A description of the province with particular reference to the importance of the Canadian Pacific Railway.

B.C. ARCHIVES

### 501   Canada. Department of Customs

Correspondence between the government and Mr. T. C. Dupont, or any other parties, with reference to his inspection of the customs stations between Victoria and Kootenay in 1876 . . .   Ottawa, Maclean, Roger, 1877.

40 p.   25 cm.   Not seen.

NOVA SCOTIA PUBLIC ARCHIVES

### 502   Canada. Executive papers

Correspondence relating to the Canadian Pacific Railway.   [Ottawa, 1877?]

16 p.   25 cm.   Cover title.

Documents from March to December 1876 which relate to British Columbia's attitude regarding the completion of the railway. The publication includes four letters from the Earl of Carnarvon to the Earl of Dufferin.

B.C. ARCHIVES

### 503   Dawson, George M[ercer]
#### 1849-1901

Mesozoic volcanic rocks of British Columbia and Chile. Relation of volcanic and metamorphic rocks.   [London, Truber & Co., 1877]

4 p.   22 cm.   Caption title. Cover title: Rocks of British Columbia & Chile. Reprinted from the *Geological magazine*, July 1877, p. 314-317.

B.C. ARCHIVES

### 504   Enterprise Gold and Silver Mining Company (Limited)

Prospectus, memorandum and articles of association of the Enterprise Gold and Silver Mining Company (Limited)   Victoria, Colonist Steam Presses, 1877.

17 p.   22 cm.

B.C. ARCHIVES

### 505   Fleming, [Sir] Sandford
#### 1827-1915

Report on surveys and preliminary operations on the Canadian Pacific Railway up to January 1877. Ottawa, Printed by MacLean, Roger & Co., 1877.

xvi, 431 p.   fold. maps.   26 cm.   Addressed to Alexander Mackenzie, Minister of Public Works.

In part, retrospective of work accomplished in British Columbia from 1871.

B.C. ARCHIVES

### 506   Foresters, Ancient Order of. New Westminster. Court Lord Dufferin No. 6304

By-laws, rules and regulations of Court Lord Dufferin No. 6304 of the Ancient Order of Foresters, held at the Foresters' Hall, New Westminster, British Columbia, in the Dominion of Canada.   New Westminster, Printed at the Office of the Mainland Guardian, 1877.

21 p.   22 cm.   Original examined. Xerox copy in the library, University of Victoria.

UNIVERSITY OF VICTORIA LIBRARY

### 507   Guide to the province . . .

Guide to the province of British Columbia for 1877-8. Compiled from the latest and most authentic sources of information.   Victoria, T. N. Hibben & Co., publisher, 1877.

xii, 408 p. (advertisements, p. 375-408)   23 cm. Chinook jargon dictionary: p. 222-250.

B.C. ARCHIVES

### 508   Journal . . .

Journal of the journey of His Excellency the Governor-General of Canada from Government House, Ottawa, to British Columbia and back. London, Webster & Larkin, 1877.

87 p. (interleaved with blank pages)   19 cm. Written by one of the party accompanying the Governor-General and the Countess of Dufferin.

B.C. ARCHIVES

**509  Knevett, J. S.**

British Columbia and Vancouver Island.
London, "Labour News" Publishing Offices, 1877.

12 p.  18 cm.  (At head of title: Pioneer paper, no. 16)

B.C. ARCHIVES

**510  Mason, George**
1829-1893

In memory of Sir James Douglas, K.C.B.
[n.p., 1877?]

[3] p.  25 x 15 cm.  Cover title.

Also appeared as a sheet (18 x 25 cm.) with title: *In memory of Sir John* [sic] *Douglas, K.C.B., died August 4th, 1877.*

B.C. ARCHIVES

**511  Nelson, Joseph**

Hudson's Bay Company and Sir Edward Watkin; statement in support of an application for the appointment of a select committee of the House of Commons to inquire into and report upon all the circumstances respecting the reconstruction of the Hudson's Bay Company by Mr. Edward Watkin in 1863 by which the capital of the company was thereby increased from £500,000 to £2,000,000 sterling without adding in any material degree to the resources of the company.
[London] E. D. Maddick and Co., 1877.

13 p.  33 cm.

Restrospective documents which, in part, reflect Edward Watkin's interest in the problem of communications with British Columbia.

LIBRARY OF PARLIAMENT

**512  Opinions . . .**

Opinions of the English press on the British Columbian railway question.  Victoria, Victoria "Standard" Print, 1877.

12 p.  20 cm.  Cover title.

B.C. ARCHIVES

**513  St. John, [Frederick Edward] Molyneux**
1838-1904

The sea of mountains; an account of Lord Dufferin's tour through British Columbia in 1876.  London, Hurst and Blackett, 1877.

2 v.  port.  20 cm.

B.C. ARCHIVES

**514  Tolmie, W[illia]m Fraser**
1812-1886

Candian Pacific Railway routes; the Bute Inlet and Esquimalt Route No. 6 and the Fraser Valley and Burrard Inlet Route No. 2, compared as to the advantages afforded by each to the Dominion and to the Empire.  Victoria, Colonist Steam Presses, 1877.

16 p.  25 cm.  Cover title.

B.C. ARCHIVES

**515  [Tolmie, William Fraser]**
1812-1886

Reply to letter of "Old Settler," published in the "Times" newspaper, on the selection of a terminus. on the Pacific coast for the proposed Canadian Pacific Railway, by A British North American [pseud.]  London, Benjamin Sulman [1877?]

34 p.  22 cm.  Letter of "Old Settler": p. [19]-22.

"A British North American" is identified by the Victoria *Colonist* (27 November 1877, p. 3) as being Tolmie. The B.C. Provincial Archives also attributes it to Tolmie from the evidence of his manuscript notes. Gilbert Malcolm Sproat was accused by the Victoria *Standard* (20 and 21 February 1877, p. 3, 3) of being the "Old Settler": he emphatically denied this epithet in the Victoria *Colonist*, calling the accusation "the deliberate concoctions of a scoundrel" (27 February 1877, p. 2).

B.C. ARCHIVES

**516  Victoria. Ordinances, etc.**

By-laws of the corporation of the city of Victoria, province of British Columbia.  Victoria, Daily Standard Printing House, 1877.

1 v. (various paging)  27 cm.  Title page and index printed for collection. Includes by-laws to no. 152 of 1888.

There are two other collections, variously bound, in the B.C. Provincial Archives. For a consolidation of by-laws see entry 1486.

B.C. ARCHIVES

**517  Victoria. Royal Hospital**

Rules for the government of the Royal Hospital, Victoria, B.C., established in 1859, supported by voluntary contributions and assisted by government grant.  Victoria, Printed at the Office of the Daily British Colonist, 1877.

8 p.  23 cm.

B.C. ARCHIVES

**518  Woods, C[harles] T[homas]**
1825-1895

Reasons for not joining "synod"; a letter to the Right Reverend the Lord Bishop of Columbia, by the Venerable C. T. Woods, M.A., Archdeacon of Columbia. New Westminster, "Mainland Guardian" Print, 1877.

8 p. 21 cm.

B.C. ARCHIVES

## 519 Baptist Missionary and Educational Society of Oregon, Washington, Idaho, and British Columbia

Minutes . . . being an account of the re-organization of the Baptist Convention of Oregon and Washington, and of the Oregon Baptist State S.S. Convention; synopsis of minutes of First Annual Meeting; and minutes of Second Annual Meeting of the Baptist Missionary and Educational Society of Oregon, Washington, Idaho, and B.C. Salem, Oregon, A. L. Stinson, 1878.

36 p. 22 cm.

B.C. ARCHIVES

## 520 British Columbia Milling and Mining Company, Limited

Prospectus, proposed act of incorporation, report of manager, memorandum, and articles of association of the British Columbia Milling and Mining Company, Limited; registered office, Victoria, British Columbia; incorporated January 1878. Victoria, Colonist Steam Presses, 1878.

30 p. illus. 21 cm.

B.C. ARCHIVES

## 521 British Columbia Mining Stock Board

Constitution and by-laws of the British Columbia Mining Stock Board. Victoria, Colonist Steam Presses, 1878.

24 p. 21 cm. Organized December 1877. Not seen.

BANCROFT LIBRARY CATALOGUE

## 522 Canada. Department of the Secretary of State

Return to an address of the House of Commons, dated 18th February 1878, for a copy of any reports in possession of the government, made in 1877 by Admiral de Horsey, respecting the port or ports most suitable for a terminus of the Canadian Pacific Railway in British Columbia, with a copy of any correspondence respecting the same with the Imperial Government. Printed by order of Parliament. Ottawa, Maclean, Roger & Co., 1878.

9, [1] p. 26 cm. Title from p. [10] At head of title: 5th session, 3rd Parliament, 41 Victoria, 1878.

U.B.C. SPECIAL COLLECTIONS

## 523 Canadian Pacific Railway Company

Reports and documents in reference to the location of the line, and a western terminal harbour, 1878. Ottawa, Printed by MacLean, Roger & Co., 1878.

104 p. fold. maps, tables. 26 cm. (Canada. Sessional papers, 1878, no. 20) At head of title: Canadian Pacific Railway; Sandford Fleming, C.M.G., engineer-in-chief.

Relates primarily to British Columbia.

B.C. ARCHIVES

## 524 Cariboo Quartz Mining Company, Limited

Memorandum and articles of association of the Cariboo Quartz Mining Comp'y (Limited) Victoria, Colonist Steam Presses, 1878.

13 p. illus., tables. 20 cm. Not seen.

BANCROFT LIBRARY CATALOGUE

## 525 Church of England. Liturgy and ritual. Thompson

The morning and evening prayer, and the litany, with prayers and thanksgivings. Translated into the Neklakapamuk tongue, for the use of the Indians of the St. Paul's mission, Lytton, British Columbia. Victoria, Printed by the St. Paul's Mission Press, 1878.

48 p. 21 cm. Presentation copy in the Bancroft Library is signed in writing on cover: From J[ohn] B[ooth] Good, the translator. Not seen.

BANCROFT LIBRARY CATALOGUE

## 526 Church of England. Liturgy and ritual. Thompson

The office for the Holy Communion. Translated into the Neklakapamuk tongue, for the use of the Indians of the St. Paul's Mission, Lytton, British Columbia. Victoria, B.C., Printed by the St. Paul's Mission Press, 1878.

46+ p. 22 cm. Only t. p., and p. 35-46 preserved. Translated by John Booth Good.

U.B.C. SPECIAL COLLECTIONS

## 527 Copper Gold and Silver Mining Company, Limited

Memorandum and articles of association . . . Incorporated March 1878. Victoria, Colonist Steam Presses, 1878.

14 p. illus., table. 21 cm. Not seen.

BANCROFT LIBRARY CATALOGUE

**528    Dawson, George Mercer**
1849-1901

On the superficial geology of British Columbia. [London, 1878]

[89]-123 p. illus., fold. map, diagrs. 22 cm. Caption title. Reprinted from: Geological Society of London. *Quarterly journal.* v. 34, 1878.

Concerns glaciation, glacial deposits, and striation.

B.C. ARCHIVES

**529    Dawson, George M[ercer]**
1849-1901

Travelling notes on the surface geology of the Pacific slope.    [Montreal] 1878.

11 p. diagrs. 22 cm. Caption title. Reprinted from the *Canadian naturalist,* new ser., v. 8, 1878, p. 389-399.

On the superficial deposits and general aspect of the country between northern California and British Columbia.

B.C. ARCHIVES

**530    De Cosmos, [Amor]**
1825-1897

Speech . . . on Mr. Hunter's survey of the Pine River Pass. Hansard report (corrected) [Wednesday, 13 March 1878.    Ottawa, MacLean, Roger & Co., 1878]

8 p. 25 cm. Caption title.

B.C. ARCHIVES

**531    De Cosmos, [Amor]**
1825-1897

Speech . . . on selecting the best harbor in British Columbia for a terminus of the Pacific railway. Hansard report (corrected) [Thursday, 28 February 1878.    Ottawa, MacLean, Roger & Co., 1878]

7 p. (incl. cover) 25 cm. Cover title.

B.C. ARCHIVES

**532    De Cosmos, [Amor]**
1825-1897

Speech . . . on the Pacific railway. Hansard report. [Wednesday, 8 May 1878.    Ottawa, MacLean, Roger & Co., 1878]

4 p. 25 cm. Caption title.

B.C. ARCHIVES

**533    De Cosmos, [Amor]**
1825-1897

Speech . . . on the Pacific railway route in British Columbia. Hansard report (corrected) [Monday,

25 February 1878.    Ottawa, MacLean, Roger & Co., 1878]

4 p. 25 cm. Caption title.

B.C. ARCHIVES

**534    De Cosmos, [Amor]**
1825-1897

Speeches . . . on De Horsey's report; trade of British Columbia; and money paid to British Columbia. Hansard report (corrected) [Monday, 18 February 1878; Tuesday, 19 February 1878. Ottawa, MacLean, Roger & Co., 1878]

12 p. 25 cm. Caption title.

The first speech concerns the question of a western railway terminus.

B.C. ARCHIVES

**535    De Cosmos, [Amor]**
1825-1897

Speeches . . . on the Esquimalt graving dock and the Canadian Pacific Railway, and the Alaska boundary line. Hansard report (corrected) [Thursday, 21 February 1878.    Ottawa, MacLean, Roger & Co., 1878]

10 p. 25 cm. Caption title.

B.C. ARCHIVES

**536    Eells, M[yron]**
1843-1907

Hymns in the Chinook jargon language. Compiled by Rev. M. Eels [*sic*]    Portland, Geo. H. Himes, 1878.

30 p. 15 cm. Contains English translation.

Second edition, revised and enlarged: Portland, David Steel, 1889. 40 p.

OREGON HISTORICAL SOCIETY

**537    Fernon, Thomas S[argent]**

No dynasty in North America; the West between salt waters; Hudson Bay a free basin like the Gulf of Mexico . . . Manitoba like Louisiana, a maritime state; North America for citizens, not subjects; the West and its ways out to the coast and in from the ocean; miscellany.    Philadelphia, Press of Henry B. Ashmead, 1878.

88 p. 25 cm.

Mentions British Columbia's natural affinity with the Pacific states.

CANADIAN ARCHIVES

**538  Freemasons. New Westminster. Union Lodge No. 9**

By-laws of Union Lodge No. 9, A.F. & A.M., New Westminster, B.C., approved by the Grand Lodge of B.C. Together with a Masonic burial service, arranged for this lodge.  New Westminster, Printed at the "Herald" Office, 1878.

33 p.   13 cm.

Also sheet inserted with title: *Proposed amendments to the by-laws.* 13 x 10 cm.

U.B.C. SPECIAL COLLECTIONS

**539  Jellett, J[onathan] H[enry]**

Pacific coast collection laws; a summary of the laws of California, Nevada, Oregon, Washington, Idaho, Montana, Utah, Wyoming, Arizona, British Columbia, Colorado, New Mexico, and Texas; including insolvency laws; also the jurisdiction of U.S. courts, with the names of reliable attorneys in the principal cities and towns throughout the Pacific coast, and a notary public for San Francisco. [Revised edition]   San Francisco, 1878.

342 p.   23 cm.   Part 12: British Columbia, prepared expressly for this work by M. W. T. Drake, Victoria [p. 319-326]

B.C. ARCHIVES

**540  Leggo, William**
1822-1888

The history of the administration of the Right Honorable Frederick Temple, Earl of Dufferin, late Governor General of Canada.   Montreal, Lovell Printing and Publishing Company, 1878.

901 p.   ports., facsim.   23 cm.

Has information on the railway question and on Lord Dufferin's visit to British Columbia in 1876.

U.B.C. SPECIAL COLLECTIONS

**541  Metlahkatlah . . .**

Metlahkatlah, die christliche Indianer-Kolonie in Britisch-Kolumbien.   Basel, 1878.

38 p.   Not seen.

BRITISH MUSEUM CATALOGUE

**542  Nuttall, R[eginald]**

British Columbia; its present condition and future policy.   Victoria, M'Millan & Son, 1878.

13 p.   21 cm.

The author advocated withdrawal from confederation with indemnity if the intentions of Canada were not confirmed by practical proofs of railway construction.

B.C. ARCHIVES

**543  Odd Fellows, Independent Order of. Victoria. Victoria Lodge No. 1**

Constitution and by-laws of Victoria Lodge No. 1, I.O.O.F., Victoria, British Columbia. Victoria, Standard Printing House, 1878.

72 p.   15 cm.

Also: Victoria, Wm. A. Calhoun, 1886. 59 p.

B.C. ARCHIVES

**544  [Sproat, Gilbert Malcolm]**
1834-1913

Memorandum on Indian reserves in the district of Yale.   Victoria, Colonist Steam Presses, 1878.

15 p.   22 cm.   Cover title.

An extract from a report on the subject of Indian reserves, submitted to the provincial government in 1877 by Malcolm Sproat and other Indian reserve commissioners.

B.C. ARCHIVES

**545  Stewart, George**
1848-1906

Canada under the administration of the Earl of Dufferin.   London, Sampson Low, Marston, Searle & Rivington, 1878.

696 p.   port.   23 cm.

Has a chapter on the highlights of the railway question, James Edgar's mission to British Columbia, the Carnarvon terms, etc.

Second edition: Toronto, Rose-Belford Publishing Company, 1879.

U.B.C. SPECIAL COLLECTIONS

**546  Victoria Daily Standard**

Standard extra . . . removal of steel rails stopped; Saturday morning, Nov. 2nd, 1878.   [Victoria, 1878]

sheet.   40 x 29 cm.

B.C. ARCHIVES

**547  Workingmen's Protective Association (Victoria)**

Constitution, by-laws and rules of order. Victoria, M'Millan & Son, 1878.

8, [1] p.?   13 cm.   Photostat copy seen. Original in the Vancouver City Archives.

The object of the association was the suppression of Chinese immigration. Its members were pledged not to employ Chinese workers or to patronize Chinese establishments.

B.C. ARCHIVES

**548   Bradstreet's reports . . .**

Bradstreet's reports of California, Colorado, Nebraska, Nevada, Oregon, the Territories, and British Columbia.   New York, The Bradstreet Company, 1879.

1 v. (various paging)   17 cm.   Copy examined: January 1879.

The section on British Columbia gives districts, routes, and the names of businesses and ratings as to their reliability.

B.C. ARCHIVES

**549   British Columbia. Board of Trade**

Acts of incorporation and by-laws of the British Columbia Board of Trade, Victoria, Vancouver Island, 1878, adopted at the quarterly general meeting, 2nd October 1879, and adjourned meeting 8th October 1879.   Victoria, British Colonist Steam Presses, 1879.

44 p.   21 cm.

B.C. ARCHIVES

**550   Canada. Parliament. Senate.
      Select Committee on Canadian
      Pacific Railway and Telegraph**

Minutes of evidence taken before the Select Committee of the Senate appointed to inquire into all matters relating to the Canadian Pacific Railway and telegraph west of Lake Superior. Printed by order of the Senate.   Ottawa, Printed by MacLean, Roger & Co., 1879.

133 p.   24 cm.   ([Parliament, 1878-79. Senate. Journals] Appendix no. 1)   Not seen.

LIBRARY OF CONGRESS

**551   Canada. Department of the
      Secretary of State**

Return (43 k) to an address of the of [sic] House of Commons dated 26th February 1879, for copy of any order in council passed in June 1876, locating the line of the Canada Pacific Railway between Thunder Bay and a point at or near Fort George in British Columbia, with all correspondence between the Dominion and [British] Columbia governments respecting the same, &c., &c. Printed by order of Parliament. Ottawa, Printed by MacLean, Roger & Co., 1879.

10 p.   tables.   25 cm.   Cover title.

B.C. ARCHIVES

**552   Church of England. Liturgy
      and ritual. Thompson**

The office for public baptism and the order of confirmation with select hymns and prayers.

Translated into the Neklakapamuk, or Thompson tongue, for the use of the Indians of the St. Paul's Mission, Lytton, British Columbia, by aid of the venerable Society for Promoting Christian Knowledge.   Victoria, Printed by the S. [sic] Paul's Mission Press (S.P.C.K.) Collegiate School, 1879.

32 p.   23 cm.   Translated by John Booth Good.

U.B.C. SPECIAL COLLECTIONS

**553   Cooke, Robert**
      1820?-1882

Sketches of the life of Mgr. de Mazenod, Bishop of Marseilles, and founder of the Oblates of Mary Immaculate, and the missionary labours and travels of members of that Society . . . London, Burns & Oates, 1879-82.

2 v.   port.   21 cm.   On t. p. of v. 1: . . . in Canada, Labrador, the Red River regions, Saskatchewan, on the borders of the Great Slave and the Great Bear lakes, in the Mackenzie regions, to the confines of the Arctic Ocean, and in British Columbia.

NATIONAL LIBRARY

**554   Dawson, George M[ercer]**
      1849-1901

Notes on the glaciation of British Columbia. [Montreal, 1879]

8 p.   22 cm.   Caption title. Reprinted from the *Canadian naturalist,* new ser., v. 9, p. 32-39.

B.C. ARCHIVES

**555   Dewdney, E[dgar]**
      1835-1916

Pacific railway route, British Columbia. [n.p., 1879?]

8 p.   22 cm.   Cover title. Addressed to: The Hon. Senators and Members of the House of Commons.

On the advantages of the Fraser River route with Burrard Inlet as the railway terminus.

B.C. ARCHIVES

**556   Fleming, [Sir] Sandford**
      1827-1915

Report in reference to the Canadian Pacific Railway. 1879.   Ottawa, Printed by MacLean, Roger & Co., 1879.

ii, 142 p.   fold. map.   26 cm.   Addressed to the Minister of Public Works.

B.C. ARCHIVES

**557    Great Britain. Hydrographic Office**

Extracts from the "Vancouver Island pilot," compiled from surveys made by Captain George Henry Richards, R.N., in H.M.'s ships "Plumper" and "Hecate," between the years of 1858 and 1864, and published by order of the Lords Commissioners of the Admiralty—(pp. 68-70, and 108-117)   [n.p., n.d.]

4 p.   24 cm.   Caption title.

The copy of the excerpt examined in the B.C. Archives was bound with *Island railway papers,* compiled by Amor De Cosmos.

It was undoubtedly printed to strengthen the arguments for the construction of the Vancouver Island section of the Canadian Pacific Railway.

B.C. ARCHIVES

**558    Hall, E[dward] Hepple**

Lands of plenty; British North America for health, sport, and profit. A book for all travellers and settlers.   London, W. H. Allen & Co.; Toronto, James Campbell & Son, 1879.

xii, 192 p.   2 fold. maps (1 in pocket)   20 cm. Chapter 6: British Columbia and Vancouver's Island [p. 107-134]

B.C. ARCHIVES

**559    Hewson, M. Butt**

Notes on the Canadian Pacific Railway.   Toronto, Patrick Boyle, 1879.

39 p.   22 cm.

Criticizes the railway route and advocates a more northerly one via the Peace River Pass.

CANADIAN ARCHIVES

**560    Victoria. Collegiate School**

[Prospectus]   Victoria, 1879.

[2] p. (folder)   26 cm.   The Rev. H. Herbert Mogg, principal. Dated: May 1st, 1879.

B.C. ARCHIVES

**561    Blake, Edward**
1833-1912

Pacific railway; speech delivered in the House of Commons . . . on Thursday and Friday, 15th and 16th April 1880. From the official report of debates.   [Ottawa, 1880]

44 p.   23 cm.   Caption title.

A speech on a motion to postpone railway construction in British Columbia.

LIBRARY OF PARLIAMENT

**562    Butler, [Sir] W[illiam] F[rancis]**
1838-1910

Far out; rovings retold.   London, Wm. Isbister, Limited, 1880.

xxiv, 386 p.   21 cm.

Has several chapters on the author's trip across the Rockies to the Pacific which contain a description of the Cariboo country and Quesnel in the early 1870's.

Also: 1880. xx, 329 p.   Also: 1881. xx, 329 p.

B.C. ARCHIVES

**563    Canada. Department of Railways and Canals**

Articles of agreement entered into in connection with the Canadian Pacific Railway. Printed by order of Parliament.   Ottawa, Printed by Maclean, Roger & Co., 1880.

98 p.   25 cm.

Also includes construction specifications. Several agreements relate to construction in British Columbia.

B.C. ARCHIVES

**564    Canada. Department of Railways and Canals**

Report and documents in reference to the Canadian Pacific Railway. Sandford Fleming, C.M.G., engineer-in-chief.   Ottawa, Printed by MacLean, Roger & Co., 1880.

xii, 30, 30a-30i, 31-373 p.   fold. maps, fold. diagrs. 26 cm.   Report presented by Sir Charles Tupper, Minister of Railways and Canals.

The general report includes coverage of explorations in northern British Columbia and Peace River district. Several of the appendices relate to exploration in the province, and two by George M. Dawson, to agriculture.

B.C. ARCHIVES

**565    Canada. Department of the Secretary of State**

Tenders for works on the Canadian Pacific Railway since January 1879. Printed by order of Parliament.   Ottawa, Printed by Maclean, Roger & Co., 1880.

203 p.   tables (part fold.)   25 cm.

B.C. ARCHIVES

**566    The Canadian Pacific Railway . . .**

The Canadian Pacific Railway.   [n.p., 1880?]

64 p.   25 cm.   On p. [2]: The following papers, with slight modifications, and the exception of article

no. xi, have lately appeared in the Morning Chronicle of Quebec.

Supports M. Butt Hewson's objections to the railway route.

B.C. ARCHIVES

567     Church of England. Book of
        Common Prayer. Selections.
        Thompson

Offices for the solemnization of matrimony, the visitation of the sick, and the burial of the dead. Translated into the Nitlakapamuk or Thompson Indian tongue, by J. B. Good, S.P.G., missionary, Yale-Lytton, by aid of a grant from the ven. Society for Promoting Christian Knowledge.    Victoria, Printed by the St. Paul's Mission Press, 1880.

15 p.    21 c.m.

B.C. ARCHIVES

568     Church of England. Liturgy
        and ritual. Beaver

Manual of devotion in the Beaver Indian dialect. Compiled from the manuals of the Venerable Archdeacon Kirby by the Bishop of Athabasca [William Carpenter Bompas] for the use of the Indians in the Athabasca Diocese.    London, Society for Promoting Christian Knowledge [1880?]

48 p.    illus.    15 cm.    Text in syllabic characters.

TORONTO PUBLIC LIBRARY

569     Dawson, George M[ercer]
        1849-1901

Note on the distribution of some of the more important trees of British Columbia. Printed in advance of the Report of progress of the Geological Survey of Canada for 1879-80. [Montreal, 1880]

11 p.    fold. map.    22 cm.    Caption title. Reprinted from the *Canadian naturalist,* new ser., v. 9, p. [321]-331.

B.C. ARCHIVES

570     De Cosmos, Amor
        1825-1897

Esquimalt and Nanaimo Railway; remarks made in the House of Commons . . . on Wednesday, 5th May 1880. From the official report of the debates.    [Ottawa, 1880]

4 p.    (folder)    25 cm.    Caption title.

Another copy has caption title: *Esquimalt-Nanaimo section of Canadian Pacific Railway; speech delivered in the House of Commons . . . on Wednesday, 5th May 1880.* Page 1 of this printing is the verso of page 27 of De Cosmos' *Canadian Pacific Railway; speeches . . .* (see note of entry 572).

B.C. ARCHIVES

571     De Cosmos, A[mor]
        COMPILER    1825-1897

Extracts from debates in Dominion Parliament and British Columbia Legislative Council in 1871 on the railway land clause of the terms of union of British Columbia with Canada.    Ottawa Printed by Maclean, Roger & Co., 1880.

vii, 24 p.    tables.    25 cm.

B.C. ARCHIVES

572     De Cosmos, [Amor]
        1825-1897

Pacific railway, speech delivered in the House of Commons . . . on Friday and Monday, 16th and 19th April, 1880. From the official report of the debates.    [Ottawa, 1880]

27 p.    tables.    25 cm.    Caption title.    Errata slip.

Another copy has caption title: *Canadian Pacific Railway; speeches delivered in the House of Commons . . . on Friday and Monday, 16th and 19th April 1880.*

B.C. ARCHIVES

573     Fleming, [Sir] Sandford
        1827-1915

(Circular) Canadian Pacific Railway; Ottawa, 1st July, 1880; to the members of the engineering staff and other officers.    [Ottawa, 1880]

7 p.    23 cm.    Caption title.

Tells of the author's dismissal as engineer-in-chief of the C.P.R. and of his decision to leave the government service.

CANADIAN ARCHIVES

574     Fleming, [Sir] Sandford
        1827-1915

Memorandum addressed to the Honourable the Minister of Railways and Canals by the Engineer-in-Chief of the Canadian Pacific Railway. Ottawa, Printed by MacLean, Roger & Co., 1880.

17 p.    illus.    25 cm.

An answer to charges made by a member of Parliament.

CANADIAN ARCHIVES

575     Good, J[ohn] B[ooth]
        1833-1916

A vocabulary and outlines of grammar of the Nitlakapamuk, or Thompson tongue (the Indian language spoken between Yale, Lillooet, Cache Creek and Nicola Lake) together with a phonetic Chinook [jargon] dictionary, adapted for use in the province of British Columbia, by J. B. Good, S.P.G., missionary, Yale-Lytton. By aid of a grant from the Right Hon. Superintendent of Indian Affairs, Ottawa. Victoria, Printed by the St. Paul's Mission Press (S.P.C.K.) Collegiate School, 1880.

46 p.   21 cm.

## 576    Gordon, Daniel M[iner]
### 1845-1925

Mountain and prairie; a journey from Victoria to Winnipeg via Peace River Pass. Montreal, Dawson Brothers, 1880.

x, 310 p.   plates, 4 fold. maps.   19 cm.

The final selection of a Pacific terminus for the C.P.R. was reserved until a northern route was examined. The author accompanied the expedition appointed to make the examination, travelling by boat from Port Simpson up the Skeena as far as the Forks from where he went on foot to Lake Babine. From Lake Babine he travelled to Fort Macleod where the party divided: some proceeded across the Rockies via Pine River Pass, while the others, including the author, descended the Peace River to Dunvegan.

Also: London, Sampson Low, Marston, Searle, & Rivington, 1880.

## 577    Hewson, M. Butt

The Canadian Pacific Railway. Toronto, Patrick Boyle, 1880.

vii, 56 p.   fold. map.   22 cm.

The author objected to the proposed railway route, desiring a more northerly one where construction would pause at Pine River Pass. See entry 566.

## 578    Horetzky, C[harles]
### 1839-1900

Some startling facts relating to the Canadian Pacific Railway and the north-west lands; also, a brief discussion regarding the route, the western terminus, and the lands available for settlement. Ottawa, Printed at the office of the "Free Press," 1880.

76 p.   21 cm.

The author, who was connected with C.P.R. surveys from 1872-1880, advocated a northern route to the Pacific via Pine River Pass.

## 579    Jackson, Sheldon
### 1834-1909

Alaska, and missions on the North Pacific coast, New York, Dodd, Mead & Company [c1880]

327 p.   illus., ports., fold. map.   20 cm.

Has two chapters on the B.C. missions established by the Methodist Church and the Church Missionary Society of England.

Also: New York, Dodd, Mead & Company, 1884?

## 580    Jenns, E[ustace] A[lvanley]
### 1860-1930

Evening to morning and other poems. Victoria, Published by T. N. Hibben & Co., 1880.

[33] p.   18 cm.   Cover title: Poems.

## 581    McLean, Allan [and others]
### ACCUSED

In the Supreme Court of British Columbia; the Queen vs. Allan McLean, Archibald McLean, Charles McLean, and Alexander Hare, indicted, found guilty, and sentenced to death for the murder of John Ussher. Judgment of the court, delivered on the 26th June 1880, on showing cause against a rule nisi for a habeas corpus on behalf of the prisoners for their discharge. Edited from notes of the judges by the Hon. Henry P. Pellew Crease, one of the judges of the said court. Victoria, McMillan & Son, 1880.

126 p.   21 cm.

## 582    McLeod, Malcolm
### 1821-1899

The problem of Canada. Ottawa, Citizen Printing and Publishing Company, 1880.

72 p.   22 cm.   Errata slip.

Stresses the importance of the Canadian Pacific Railway.

## 583    The Pacific railway . . .

The Pacific railway; speeches delivered by Hon. Sir Charles Tupper . . . H. L. Langevin . . . J. B. Plumb . . . Thomas White . . . during the debate in the House of Commons, session 1880. Montreal, Printed by the Gazette Printing Company, 1880.

100 p.   22 cm.   Cover title.

On C.P.R. policy.

## 584    Rattray, W[illiam] J[ordan]
### 1835-1883

The Scot in British North America. Toronto, Maclear and Company [1880-84]

4 v. fronts. (ports.) 24 cm. Personal name index in v. 4.

Volume 4 is on the "North-west," and includes chapters with biographical information on people connected with the C.P.R. and British Columbia.

B.C. ARCHIVES

## 585    [Stock, Eugene]
### 1836-1928

Metlakahtla and the North Pacific mission of the Church Missionary Society.    London, Church Missionary House, 1880.

130 p.    fold. map.    22 cm.    On verso of t. p.: The third, fourth, and fifth chapters . . . are substantially a reprint of parts of a pamphlet entitled, "Metlakahtla, or, Ten years' work among the Tsimshean Indians," published by the Church Missionary Society in 1868. Attributed to Eugene Stock by William Ridley in his *Snapshots from the North Pacific,* p. 2. Note on verso of t. p. signed in print: E. S.

Chiefly about the establishment and growth of Metlahkatla. The book also mentions the missions of Kincolith on the Nass River, Masset on Graham Island, and Fort Rupert, northern Vancouver Island.

Second edition: 1881.    130 p.

TORONTO PUBLIC LIBRARY

## 586    Victoria and Esquimalt Telephone Company, Limited

List of subscribers, May 1880.    [Victoria, 1880]

sheet.    18 x 11 cm.    Mounted on board.

The company was formed in May of 1880: this list of subscribers was its first.

B.C. ARCHIVES

## 587    British Columbia. Legislative Assembly

Petition of Legislative Assembly of British Columbia to the Queen; respecting Canadian Pacific Railway, March 25, 1881.    [Victoria, 1881]

sheet (2 p.)    24 x 16 cm.    Caption title. Signed in print: Fredck. Williams, speaker of Legislative Assembly. Bound in B.C. Archives with De Cosmos' *Island railway papers.*    Not found in Holmes.

B.C. ARCHIVES

## 588    Canada. Department of Railways and Canals

Canadian Pacific Railway from Emory's Bar at the west end of Contract 60 to Port Moody (Burrard Inlet) British Columbia; specification for the construction of the work.    [Ottawa, 1881?]

18 p.    25 cm.    Caption title. Dated on p. 16: 1 December 1881. Signed in print: Collingwood Schreiber, chief engineer.

SHORTT COLLECTION

## 589    Canada. Department of the Secretary of State

Return to an address of the House of Commons, dated 16th December 1880, for copies of any correspondence with the government of British Columbia, or with any persons in that province respecting the Island railway.    [Ottawa, 1881]

25 p.    table.    24 cm.    Caption title. The copy in the Library of Parliament has in manuscript above caption title: Published by A. deCosmos, March 29, 1881. List of disasters to vessels that have occurred . . from Race Rocks to Nanaimo since the year 1858: p. 9-11.

Includes communications dated from 1873.

B.C. ARCHIVES

## 590    Canada. Department of the Secretary of State

Returns and addresses to the House of Commons relative to the surveys and appropriations of lands for the construction of the Canadian Pacific Railway in the province of Manitoba, North-west Territory, and British Columbia. Printed by order of Parliament.    Ottawa, Printed by MacLean, Roger & Co., 1881.

51 p.    tables.    25 cm.

B.C. ARCHIVES

## 591    Canadian Pacific Railway Company

By-laws.    Ottawa, Maclean, Roger & Co., 1881.

13 p.    22 cm.    Cover title.

B.C. ARCHIVES

## 592    Dawson, Aeneas McDonell
### 1810-1894

The North-west Territories and British Columbia. Ottawa, Printed by C. W. Mitchell, 1881.

iv, 232 p. (advertisements, p. 219-232)    20 cm.

Describes resources, climate, geographical features, the native population, etc.

B.C. ARCHIVES

## 593    Dawson, G[eorge] M[ercer]
### 1849-1901

The superficial geology of British Columbia and adjacent regions.    [London?] 1881.

272-285 p. 23 cm. Caption title: Additional observations on the superficial geology . . . Reprinted from the *Quarterly journal of the Geological Society,* May 1881.

### 594 De Cosmos, [Amor]
1825-1897

Index prepared by Mr. De Cosmos to papers published in 1880 by order of the Legislative Assembly of British Columbia in connection with the construction of the Canadian Pacific Railway between the Dominion, Imperial, and provincial governments. [Ottawa, 1881]

ix p. 25 cm. Running head: Index to railway papers. On p. ix: Printed at Ottawa, May 1881, for Mr. De Cosmos.

### 595 [De Cosmos, Amor]
COMPILER 1825-1897

[Island railway papers, 1872-1881. Ottawa, n.d.]

viii, 148 p. 24 cm. No t. p. Index: p. [i] Index of subjects: p. [iii]-viii. Copy examined has printed marginal notes glued in.

Extracts, mainly from the Parliamentary debates and newspapers, on the subject of the Esquimalt and Nanaimo Railway, the Vancouver Island section of the Canadian Pacific Railway.

### 596 [De Cosmos, Amor]
1825-1897

Memorandum on "A report of a committee of the Honorable the Privy Council for Canada, approved by His Excellency the Governor-General on the 19th May 1881; and generally in support of the recent petition of the Legislative Assembly of British Columbia to Her Majesty the Queen." [n.p., 1881]

44, [4] p. 25 cm. Caption title. Copy in the University of British Columbia's Special Collections has manuscript note signed: A. De Cosmos. De Cosmos refers to the memorandum in: British Columbia. Sessional papers, 1882, p. 341.

Concerns a petition calling for an immediate start on railway construction between Nanaimo and Victoria, and between Port Moody and Yale, the regulations of the province's own customs and excise tariffs, and payment from the Dominion government to compensate for the delay in railway construction.

### 597 D'Herbomez, L[ouis] J[oseph]
COMPILER 1822-1890

Secular schools versus denominational schools. Saint Mary's Mission, Printed with the press of Saint Mary's Mission, B.C., partly by the pupils of the Indian school of that mission, 1881.

28 p. 20 cm. On t. p.: Evangelizare pauperibus misit me; pauperes evangelizantur. O.M.I.

### 598 Handbook to Canada . . .

Handbook to Canada; a guide for travellers and settlers in the provinces of Ontario, North-west Territory, Manitoba, Quebec, Nova Scotia, New Brunswick, British Columbia, Prince Edward Island, &c., &c. With new map showing the railway system, &c. London, S. W. Silver and Co., 1881.

viii, 288 p. fold. map, tables. 19 cm. Cover title: S. W. Silver & Co.'s Canada.

Second edition: 1884. viii, 292 p.

### 599 Langelier, [Sir] F[rançois] Charles Stanislas]
1838-1915

Le Pacifique: historique de la question.—Plan de M. Mackenzie en 1874.—Syndicat de St. Paul.—Syndicat canadien.—Plan de l'opposition. Conférence donnée au Club de Réforme, à Québec, le 4 février 1881. Québec, Imprimerie de "L'Électeur, ["] 1881.

41 p. 21 cm. Cover title.

### 600 McLelan, Archibald Woodbury
1824-1890

Speech . . . on the second reading of a bill to incorporate the Pacific Railway Company, in the Senate, Ottawa, Wednesday & Thursday, Feb. 9 & 10, 1881. Reported by A. & Geo. C. Holland. [n.p.] 1881.

28 p. diagr. 23 cm.

### 601 The Proposed contract . . .

The proposed contract for building and operating the Canadian Pacific Railway. Lachine, 1881.

[3] p. 35 cm. Caption title. At head of title: Memorandum.

A criticism of the contract by Conservatives.

### 602 Tupper, Sir Charles
BARONET 1821-1915

The Pacific railway; speech delivered . . . during the debate in the House of Commons, session

1880-1. Ottawa, Printed by Maclean, Roger & Co., 1881.

82 p. 21 cm. Cover title.

On railway construction policy.

CANADIAN ARCHIVES

## 603 Victoria. Board of Trade

Report. 1881-1919. Victoria, Colonist Printing and Publishing Co.

v. illus. 22 cm. annual. Printer varies. Index in each annual issue. Vol. 1-22 as *Annual report* of the British Columbia Board of Trade. Continued as *Report* of the Victoria Chamber of Commerce. Binder's title: British Columbia Board of Trade. Annual reports.

Includes survey of business, fisheries, industries, and agriculture; surveys labour, immigration, trade outlook, and gives tables, statistics, and financial statements in appendices.

B.C. ARCHIVES

## 604 Victoria Amateur Orchestral Society

Constitution and by-laws of the Victoria Amateur Orchestra Society, organized April 8th, 1878. Victoria, M'Millan & Son, 1881.

10 p. 13 cm.

B.C. ARCHIVES

## 605 Victoria and Esquimalt Telephone Company, Limited

Telephone exchange; rules, regulations, stations, etc., for the guidance of subscribers. Victoria, [1881]

28 p. (incl. advertisements) 21 cm.

B.C. ARCHIVES

## 606 Weiler, John (firm)

Catalogue of John Weiler, Fell's Block, Fort Street, corner of Broad, Victoria, B.C.; importer, dealer in and jobber of crockery, glassware, plated ware, wall-paper, furniture, and house furnishing goods of every description. Victoria, McMillan & Son, 1881.

19 p. 21 cm. Cover title.

A list of stock exclusive of price.

B.C. ARCHIVES

## 607 The Bank of British North America
### DEFENDANT

In the Supreme Court of Canada, on appeal from the Supreme Court of British Columbia;

between the Bank of British North America (defendants) appellants, and Samuel Walker (plaintiff) respondent. Case. Edwin Johnson, Victoria, B.C., appellants' solicitor; Pinhey & Christie, Ottawa agents. Victoria, J. E. McMillan, 1882.

54 l. 28 cm.

B.C. ARCHIVES

## 608 Bastian, [Adolf]
### 1826-1905

Die Haida's. [n.p., 1882]

[278]-298 p. 26 cm. Caption title. At head of title: Hr. Bastian spricht, unter Vorlage zahlreicher Gegenstände, über [die Haida's] Reprinted from the *Verhandlungen der Berliner Gesellschaft für Anthropologie, Ethnologie und Urgeschichte,* April 1882.

B.C. ARCHIVES

## 609 Bible. New Testament. Matthew. Kwakiutl

The Gospel according to St. Matthew. Translated into the Qā-gūtl (or Quoquols language) by the Rev. A. J. Hall, C. M. S. missionary at Fort Rupert, Vancouver's Island. London, Printed for the British and Foreign Bible Society, 1882.

121 p. 17 cm.

B.C. ARCHIVES

## 610 British Columbia. Supreme Court

In the Supreme Court of British Columbia; Sewell and others, plaintiffs, *vs.* the B.C. Towing and Transportation Co., Limited, and the Moodyville Saw Mill Co., Limited, defendants; commonly called the Thrasher Case. Judgments of Sir M. B. Begbie, C.J., and of Crease and Gray, Justices (McCreight, J., abs.) relative to the unconstitutionality of certain acts of the provincial Legislature affecting the Supreme Court. 10th February, 1882. Victoria, The Colonist Steam Presses [1882]

82 p. 21 cm. Cover title.

B.C. ARCHIVES

## 611 Canada. Canadian Pacific Railway Royal Commission

Report . . . Ottawa, Printed by S. Stephenson, Chatham, Ont., 1882.

3 v. 25 cm. Commissioners: George M. Clark, Samuel Keefer, Edward Miall.

The commission was appointed "to make enquiry into and concerning all facts connected with, and the conduct and prosecution of, the Canadian Pacific

Railway from its inception . . ." — p. 29. The report
has information on surveys, location of the route, and
on contracts. The introduction of 25 pages by N.
Flood Davin gives a valuable review of events
connected with overland communication to the
Pacific.

CANADIAN ARCHIVES


## 612    Canada. Laws, statutes, etc.

The Canadian Pacific Railway; contract between
the government of the Dominion of Canada
and the Canadian Pacific Railway Company;
also the Consolidated Railway Act (1879)
and the act of 1881 amending it.    Ottawa,
Printed by MacLean, Roger & Co., 1882.

xix, 155 p.    25 cm.

SHORTT COLLECTION


## 613    Canada. Department of the Secretary of State

Returns relative to the letting of the railway
work between Emory's Bar and Port Moody, B.C.
Printed by order of Parliament.    Ottawa,
Printed by MacLean, Roger & Co., 1882.

60 p.    tables.    25 cm.

Relates to the status of a deposit cheque submitted
with the lowest tender.

B.C. ARCHIVES


## 614    Chittenden, Newton H.

Settlers, prospectors, and tourists guide; or,
Travels through British Columbia. Circular 10
of "The worlds guide for home, health and
pleasure seekers," containing new and valuable
information concerning this comparatively
unknown region, its physical features, climate,
resources and inhabitants.    Victoria, 1882.

84 p.    23 cm.    Cover title.

Another edition, issued the same year, has title:
*Travels in British Columbia and Alaska.*

B.C. ARCHIVES


## 615    The Church and the Indians . . .

The church and the Indians; the trouble at
Metlakahtla.    [Victoria, 1882]

8 p.    23 cm.    Caption title.    Reprinted from
the Victoria *Colonist*, 26 July 1882.

A report of accounts by Bishop Cridge and Senator
Macdonald of their visit to William Duncan's mission.

B.C. ARCHIVES


## 616    Fleming, [Sir] Sandford
### 1827-1915

Letter to the Secretary of State, Canada, in
reference to the report of the Canadian Pacific
Railway royal commission. Printed by order
of Parliament.    Ottawa, Printed by MacLean,
Roger & Co., 1882.

50 p.    tables.    25 cm.

Written in defense of the commission's charges
against the author.

B.C. ARCHIVES


## 617    History . . .

History of a contract.    [n. p., 1882?]

14 p.    22 cm.    Cover title.

Concerns the status of a deposit cheque
submitted by Messrs. McDonald and Charlebois
with a tender for the construction of the C.P.R. from
Emory's Bar (Emory Creek) to Port Moody.

Also published in French under title: *Histoire
d'un contrat.*

LIBRARY OF PARLIAMENT


## 618    Hittell, John S[hertzer]
### 1825-1901

The commerce and industries of the Pacific coast
of North America; comprising the rise, progress,
products, present condition, and prospects of
useful arts on the western side of our continent,
and some account of its resources; with elaborate
treatment of manufactures; briefer consideration
of commerce, transportation, agriculture, and
mining; and mention of leading establishments
and prominent men in various departments of
business.    San Francisco, A. L. Bancroft & Co.,
1882.

819 p.    illus., plates, 2 double maps.    30 cm.

The information is arranged under various
commercial activities. The author's main source for
information on British Columbia was *Guide to
the province of British Columbia for 1877-8*
(entry 507).

Second edition: 1882.

B.C. ARCHIVES


## 619    [McAdam, J. T.]

Canada: the country, its people, religions, politics,
rulers, and its apparent future; being a compendium
of travel from Atlantic to the Pacific, the Great
Lakes, Manitoba, the North-west, and British
Columbia, with a description of their resources,
trade, statistics, etc., viewed in its business, social
and political aspects; the various cities and resorts,
salmon rivers, etc. . . . . By Captain "Mac."
[pseud.]    Montreal, 1882.

353 p.   illus., plates.   23 cm.   At head of title: Enlarged edition.

B.C. ARCHIVES

620     [Ridley, William]
       BISHOP OF CALEDONIA   1836-1911

Senator Macdonald's misleading account of his visit to Metlakatla exposed by the Bishop of Caledonia.   [n.p.] 1882.

12 p.   19 cm.

In effect a listing of the wrongs committed by the missionary William Duncan in the eyes of the Church Missionary Society.

B.C. ARCHIVES

621     Tupper, Sir Charles
       BARONET   1821-1915

Official report of the speech delivered ... on the Canadian Pacific Railway. House of Commons, session 1882. [Tuesday, 18 April 1882] Ottawa, Printed by MacLean, Roger & Co., 1882.

56 p.   table.   22 cm.   Cover title.

On the railway's construction and route.

A revised and abridged edition: Ottawa, 1882. 27 p.

B.C. ARCHIVES

622     Victoria. College School

Appeal in behalf of the building fund of the College School, Victoria.   [Victoria, 1882]

sheet.   35 x 22 cm.

B.C. ARCHIVES

623     Victoria. Royal Jubilee Hospital

Report.   1882+   Victoria.

v.   illus.   22-28 cm.   annual.   1922-33 not published. Title varies slightly. Name varies: Provincial Royal Jubilee Hospital, 1890-1937.

B.C. PROVINCIAL LIBRARY

624     The Williams' official British Columbia directory

The Williams' official British Columbia directory, 1882/83-1899, containing general information and directories of the various cities and settlements in the province, with a classified business directory. Compiled and published by R. T. Williams.   Victoria, Williams' B.C. Directory Co., 1882-99.

9 v.   24 cm.   Printer varies. Issued for the year 1882/83, 1884/85, 1889, 1891, 1892, 1894, 1895, 1897-98, and 1899. Title varies: 1882/83

and 1884/85 as *The British Columbia directory*; 1889 as *Williams' British Columbia directory*. Binder's title, 1889-94: *Williams' British Columbia directory and street index*. Incorporated into *Henderson's British Columbia gazetteer and directory*, 1900. Subtitles vary.

Provides lists of government officials, teachers, officers of armed forces, societies, consuls, members of the Legislative Assembly, and judges, as well as providing a wide range of information about various B.C. localities.

B.C. ARCHIVES

625     Anderson, Alexander Caulfield
       1814-1884

A brief account of the province of British Columbia; its climate and resources. An appendix to the British Columbia directory, 1882-83. Victoria, Published by R. T. Williams, 1883.

33 p.   fold. map.   23 cm.   Some copies contain plates.

B.C. ARCHIVES

626     Aspdin, James

Emigration: who should emigrate; how to emigrate; where to emigrate.   Sheffield, James S. Garrard, 1883.

50 p.   21 cm.

A small section on British Columbia.

B.C. ARCHIVES

627     Berlin. K. Museen. Museum für Völkerkunde. Ethnologische Abteilung

Amerika's Nordwest-Küste: neueste Ergebnisse ethnologischer Reisen, aus den Sammlungen der Königlichen Museen zu Berlin, herausgegben von der Direction der ethnologischen Abtheilung. Berlin, Verlag von A. Asher & Co., 1883.

13 p.   13 plates (5 col.)   51 x 38 cm.   In portfolio. Each plate preceded by leaf with explanatory letterpress. Explanatory text by Eduard Krause and Albert Gruenwedel. Preface by Adolf Bastian.

The plates show masks, totem poles, wooden figures, and other objects — many from Fort Rupert — collected by Johan Adrian Jacobsen (see entries 627 and 1728 for his publications).

English translation under title: *The north-west coast of America; being the results of recent ethnological researches* ... (London, Asher & Co., 1883; and: New York, Dodd, Mead & Company, 1882?).

B.C. ARCHIVES

## 628 Bridges, F.D.

Journal of a lady's travels round the world. With illustrations from sketches by the author. London, John Murray, 1883.

xi, 413 p. illus., plates, map. 22 cm.

Recollections of a trip by steamer and coach from Victoria to Boston Bar in July 1880 comprise two chapters. There is some information on the Thompson Indians.

B.C. PROVINCIAL LIBRARY

## 629 Canada. Department of Agriculture

Province of British Columbia; information for intending settlers. Ottawa, 1883.

32 p. fold. map. 21 cm. Cover title. At head of title: Dominion of Canada.

Also: 1884. 32 p. map. Also: 1886. 32 p. map. Also: 1886. 32 p. 2 maps (1 col. fold.) Also: 1887. 32 p. map. An edition was published in French in 1886, and one in German in 1883.

B.C. ARCHIVES

## 630 Canada. Parliament. House of Commons. Immigration and Colonization Committee

Evidence of Dr. Dawson . . . Ottawa, Printed by MacLean, Roger & Co., 1883.

21 p. 25 cm. At head of title: Dominion of Canada, province of British Columbia.

Relates to the geography, climate, and resources of the province.

B.C. ARCHIVES

## 631 Canada. Department of the Secretary of State

Sessional papers relating to the Canadian Pacific Railway, 1882-83. Printed by order of Parliament. Ottawa, Printed by MacLean, Roger & Co., 1883.

213 p. 25 cm.

SHORTT COLLECTION

## 632 Church of England in Canada. Dioceses. New Westminster

Journal of the first meeting of the diocesan synod held at New Westminster, October 3rd, in the year of Our Lord, 1882. New Westminster, Printed at the Office of the British Columbian, 1883.

26 p. 22 cm.

B.C. ARCHIVES

## 633 Collins, J[oseph] E[dmund]
### 1855-1892

Life and times of the Right Honourable Sir John A. Macdonald, premier of the Dominion of Canada. Toronto, Rose Publishing Company, 1883.

642 p. port. 23 cm.

Has information on the Canadian Pacific Railway, "Pacific Canada," and the province's entrance into confederation.

A revised edition with additions by G. Mercer Adam was published in 1891 under title: *Canada's patriot statesman* (Toronto, Rose; and also: London, McDermid & Logan).

CANADIAN ARCHIVES

## 634 New Westminster. Board of Trade

Acts of incorporation and by-laws, 1883. New Westminster, British Columbian Newspaper and Job Printing Office, 1883.

44 p. 21 cm.

Provides a membership list and rules and regulations applying to the port.

Also: New Westminster, Commercial Printing Company, 1897. 27 p.

B.C. PROVINCIAL LIBRARY

## 635 Resources of British Columbia

Resources of British Columbia. v. 1-3, no. 3; March 1883—July 1885. Victoria, Munroe Miller.

v. illus., maps (part fold.) 30 cm. monthly. Not indexed.

Contemporary accounts of manufacturing, wages, fisheries, shipping (with steamer schedules), sheep raising, mining, etc.

B.C. ARCHIVES

## 636 Victoria (city)

Report for the year. 1882+ Victoria, 1883+

v. 22, 26 cm. annual. Cover title, 1960+ Title varies: 1883 as *Annual message by Noah Shakespeare, mayor of the city of Victoria, British Columbia;* 1884-86 as *Annual report of . . . mayor . . .* ; 1887+ as *Annual report.* At head of t. p. or cover title, 1887+: The Corporation of the City of Victoria.

Reports for 1883-6 concern public property, street work, public services, liquor laws, and finances; those from 1887 include cash statements and reports of department heads.

B.C. ARCHIVES

**637    Victoria. College School**

The calendar . . . for the year of Our Lord, 1883. [Victoria, Printed by J. E. McMillan] 1883.

10 p.    17 cm.

B.C. ARCHIVES

**638    Vis, Gerrit Willem**

Translation of a letter . . . to Messrs. Adolph Boissevain and Co. and H. Öyens and Sons, Amsterdam.    [n.p., 1883?]

20 p.    fold. map, tables.    21 cm.

A report on personal investigations as to the condition and future prospects of the C.P.R.

B.C. ARCHIVES

**639    [Argyll, John George Edward Henry Douglas Sutherland Campbell]**
9TH DUKE OF    1845-1914

Canadian pictures, drawn with pen and pencil, by the Marquis of Lorne, K.T. With numerous illustrations from objects and photographs in the possession of, and sketches by, the Marquis of Lorne, Sydney Hall, etc. Engraved by Edward Whymper.    London, The Religious Tract Society [1884]

viii, 224 p.    illus., plates, maps (1 fold.)    29 cm. Chapter 10: British Columbia [p. 195-214]

The text gives a commentary on Indians and Chinese in British Columbia, ports, industry, and history.

B.C. ARCHIVES

**640    Baillie-Grohman, W[illia]m A[dolph]**
1851-1921

[Letter to the Chief Commissioner of Lands and Works, Victoria, B.C.    Victoria, 1884]

3 p. (folder)    27 cm.

A proposal from the Kootenay Lake Syndicate respecting partially free grants of lands which the syndicate hoped to acquire from the government.

B.C. ARCHIVES

**641    Barneby, W[illiam] Henry**
1843-1914

Life and labour in the far, far West; being notes of a tour in the western states, British Columbia, Manitoba, and the North-west Territory. London, Cassell & Company, 1884.

xvi, 432 p.    fold. map (in pocket)    22 cm. Appendix C: The Kootenay Lake district, by Mr. W. A. Baillie-Grohman.

Second edition: London, Cassell and Company, 1884.

B.C. ARCHIVES

**642    Barneby, W[illiam] Henry**
1843-1914

Notes from a journal in North America in 1883. Hereford, Printed at the office of the "Hereford Times" [1884]

91 p.    21 cm.    Reprinted from the Hereford *Times*. A portion of the material was afterwards incorporated in his *Life and labour in the far, far West* (London, 1884)    Not seen.

LIBRARY OF CONGRESS

**643    Barrows, William**
1815-1891

Oregon; the struggle for possession.    Boston, Houghton, Mifflin and Company, 1884.

viii, 363 p.    double map.    19 cm.    (American commonwealths [v. 2])    Authorities: p. [iii]-vi.

Has a chapter on the San Juan Island dispute.

Numerous editions.    Tenth edition: 1898.

B.C. ARCHIVES

**644    Berlin. Straatliche Museen**

Amerika's Nordwest-Küste . . . Neue Folge. [11 plates with explanatory text by Eduard Krause. With preface by Adolf Bastian]    Berlin, 1884.

Not seen.

BRITISH MUSEUM CATALOGUE

**645    Bull, William K[ing]**
1811-1899

A lecture on the subject of "current events," delivered at the Mechanics' Literary Institute of Victoria, British Columbia, December 11th, 1883.    Victoria, R. H. McMillan, 1884.

19 p.    19 cm.

B.C. ARCHIVES

**646    Busk, Charles Westly**
1852-1934

Notes of a journey from Toronto to British Columbia via the Northern Pacific Railway (June to July 1884); being letters to his sister and mother from Charles Westly Busk.    London, Printed by Taylor and Francis, 1884.

48 p.    illus.    22 cm.    For private circulation.

Although the two letters are written from Victoria, only four pages describe Victoria and the lower mainland. To the author, Victoria "looks like one of those mushroom cities in America would look like if from any cause the railway were to stop running for six months." — p. 46.

### 647    Canada. Department of Justice

Report of the Minister of Justice with reference to the arrangement made for the settlement of matters in difference between the government of Canada and the government of British Columbia. Vancouver Island railway, Esquimalt graving dock, railway lands, judicial districts. Printed by order of Parliament.    Ottawa, Printed by Maclean, Roger & Co., 1884.

21 p.    fold. map.    25 cm.    (Canada. Parliament. Sessional papers, 1884, no. 15)    Alexander Campbell, Minister of Justice.

### 648    Canada. Department of the Secretary of State

Sessional papers relating to the Canadian Pacific Railway, 1883-84. Printed by order of Parliament. Ottawa, Printed by MacLean, Roger & Co., 1884.

93 p.    tables.    25 cm.

### 649    Canadian Pacific Railway Company

[Reports relating to the work remaining to be done by the company, and to the character of the country on the western section of the line.    Montreal, 1884]

16 p.    22 cm.    No cover or t. p. on copy examined. Title from p. [1] Reports signed in print: W. C. Van Horne, vice-president; S. B. Reed, C. E.

Relates entirely to British Columbia.

### 650    Chittenden, Newton H.

Health seekers', tourists' and sportsmen's guide to the sea-side, lake-side, foothill, mountain, and mineral spring health and pleasure resorts of the Pacific coast. Second edition.    San Francisco, C. A. Murdock & Co., 1884.

311 p.    illus., plates (part fold.) ports., maps. 24 cm.

Has a section on British Columbia (p. 295-311).

### 651    Churchman's gazette . . .

The churchman's gazette and New Westminster diocesan chronicle.    March 1884—February 1892.    New Westminster, The Anglican Diocese.

v.    monthly.    Microfilm examined. No index.

### 652    Davies (J. P.) & Co. (Victoria)
AUCTIONEERS

Valuable property in the city of Victoria and districts of Victoria, Sooke, and New Westminster. In the Supreme Court of British Columbia, pursuant to an order made in an action Naylor v. Jackson and others, with the approbation of the Judge, I will sell at salesroom Wharf Street, on Saturday, August 2d, 1884, at noon, the freehold and other property belonging to the estate of the late Henry Rhodes Esq. Particulars and conditions of sale contained herein. Joshua Davies, auctioneer.    [Victoria] The Colonist Print [1884]

14 p. (incl. cover)    plans.    26 cm.    Cover title.

### 653    Fleming, [Sir] Sandford
1827-1915

England and Canada; a summer tour between old and new Westminster. With historical notes. Montreal, Dawson Brothers, 1884.

xi, 449 p.    fold. map.    20 cm.

About one-third of the book relates to British Columbia.

Also: London, Low, Marston, Searle & Rivington, 1884.

### 654    George, Henry
1839-1897

Scotland and Scotsmen.    Victoria, Anti-Poverty Club [1884?]

27 p.    port.    18 cm.    Cover title. Book notices: p. 25-27.    Not seen.

### 655    [Gill, John Kaye]
COMPILER    1851-1929

Dictionary of the Chinook jargon with examples of its use in conversation. Compiled from all existing vocabularies, and greatly improved by the addition of necessary words never before published. Tenth edition.    Portland, Ore., J. K. Gill & Co., 1884.

60 p.    17 cm.

The eighth edition was published in 1881 in continuation of the dictionaries issued by the firm of S. J. M'Cormick (see entry 32). A ninth edition, published in 1882, is listed in Pilling's *Chinookan languages* and in Smith under title: *Gill's dictionary of the Chinook jargon . . .*    The eighteenth edition was published in 1960.

**656  Good Templars, Independent Order of. Washington Territory and British Columbia. Grand Lodge**

Journal of proceedings of the Grand Lodge of Washington and British Columbia, I.O.G.T.; fifteenth annual session, held in Seattle, August 12th, 13th and 14th, 1884. Dillis B. Ward, grand secretary.   Seattle, Globe Printing Company, 1884.

[3], 616-641 p.   22 cm.

B.C. ARCHIVES

**657  Harrison, Charles**

The Hydah mission, Queen Charlotte Islands; an account of the mission and people, with a descriptive letter from the Rev. Charles Harrison.   London, Church Missionary Society [1884?]

23 p.  illus.  19 cm.

B.C. ARCHIVES

**658  Holbrook, Henry**
B. 1820

British Columbia gold mines; a paper read before the Liverpool Geological Association. The richness of the mines, the hydraulic gold washing and general resources of the province fully laid down, so as to bring such (for inquiry) to the notice of capitalists in Great Britain, and showing British Columbia to be the garden and golden province of Canada.   Liverpool, Printed by B. Haram [1884]

24 p.  tables.  22 cm.

B.C. ARCHIVES

**659  Illustrated British Columbia**

Illustrated British Columbia.   Victoria, J. B. Ferguson & Co. [1884]

273-304 p.  8 plates.  30 cm.  Cover title. Reprinted from the *West Shore*, v. 10, September 1884.

Describes the province by region with reference to industries and resources.

B.C. ARCHIVES

**660  Ives, William B[ullock]**
1841-1899

Speech on the Canadian Pacific Railway delivered in the House of Commons, Ottawa, on February 8, 1884.   [Montreal, Gazette Printing Co., 1884]

44 p.  22 cm.

B.C. ARCHIVES

**661  Jacobsen, [Johan Adrian]**
B. 1853

Captain Jacobsen's Reise an der Nordwestküste Amerikas, 1881-1883, zum Zwecke ethnologischer Sammlungen und Erkundigungen, nebst Beschreibung persönlicher Erlebnisse, für den deutschen Leserkreis bearbeitet, von A. Woldt. Leipzig, Max Spohr, 1884.

viii, 431 p.  illus., 3 maps (1 fold.)  22 cm.

The object of Jacobsen's travels was to collect native implements and art work for the Royal Berlin Ethnological Museum. The book, the first seven chapters of which describe mainland British Columbia, Vancouver Island, and Indians, was written from his diaries.

Danish-Norwegian translation: Kristiania, Forlagt af Alb. Cammermeyer, 1887. xxxviii, 329 p. Title: *Kaptein Jacobsen's reiser til Nordamerikas nordvestkyst, 1881-83.*

B.C. ARCHIVES

**662  James, J[ohn] C[ollinson]**
1846-1883

The Western Division of the Canadian Pacific Railway, by the late J. C. James and Alan Macdougall.   London, Published by the Institution, 1884.

26 p.  21 cm.  Cover title: James and Macdougall on the Canadian Pacific Railway. On t. p.: Excerpt minutes of Proceedings of the Institution of Civil Engineers, v. 76, session, 1883-4, pt. 2.

CANADIAN ARCHIVES

**663  Leighton, Caroline C.**

Life at Puget Sound, with sketches of travel in Washington Territory, British Columbia, Oregon, and California, 1865-1881.   Boston, Lee and Shepard, 1884.

ix, 258 p.  18 cm.

Several pages describe Victoria in 1868.

B.C. ARCHIVES

**664  Mohr, N.**

Ein Streifzug durch den Nordwesten Amerikas; festfahrt zur Northern Pacific-Bahn im Herbste 1883.   Berlin, Robert Oppenheim, 1884.

vi, 394 p.  20 cm.

Several pages about Vancouver Island.

B.C. ARCHIVES

**665  Morris, Alexander**
1826-1889

Nova Britannia; or, Our new Canadian Dominion foreshadowed; being a series of lectures, speeches and addresses. Edited, with notes and an introduction by a member of the Canadian press.    Toronto, Hunter, Rose & Co., 1884.

xii, 187 p.    19 cm.

Includes "The Hudson's Bay and Pacific territories," which was separately published in 1859 (entry 94).

B.C. ARCHIVES

### 666    Peebles, D. Bruce

From Edinburgh to Vancouver's Island; some notes of a trip on the occasion of the driving of the last spike in the Northern Pacific Railway. Read before the Royal Scottish Society of Arts, Edinburgh.    Edinburgh, Printed by Neill and Company, 1884.

[75]-114 p.    Cover title. On cover: Reprinted from the Transactions of the society, session 1883-84.

Two pages relate to a Victoria visit.

TORONTO PUBLIC LIBRARY

### 667    Phillipps-Wolley, [Sir] Clive [Oldnall Long]
1854-1918

Trottings of a tenderfoot; or, A visit to the Columbian fiords.    London, Richard Bentley and Son, 1884.

v, 252 p.    20 cm.

A record of two months' travel and hunting on Vancouver Island and amongst the coastal mountains.

Another edition was published in 1884 under title: *The trottings of a tenderfoot; a visit to the Columbian fiords and Spitzbergen* (London, Richard Bentley and Son). In v, 350 pages. It has a section entitled "The Spitzbergen swindle" (p. 253-350).

B.C. ARCHIVES

### 668    Pierrepont, Edward [Willoughby]
1860-1885

Fifth Avenue to Alaska. With maps by Leonard Forbes Beckwith.    New York, G. P. Putnam's Sons, 1884.

vi, 329 p.    4 fold. maps.    21 cm.

Has a chapter on the author's impressions of Vancouver Island.

B.C. ARCHIVES

### 669    Rand & Lipsett (firm)

Messrs. Rand & Lipsett, real estate brokers and financial agents, beg to inform you . . . Victoria, 1884.

sheet (2 p.)    26 x 21 cm.    Caption title.    At head of title: C. D. Rand, notary public; R. Lipsett; Victoria, B.C., Sept. 25th, 1884.

U.B.C. SPECIAL COLLECTIONS

### 670    Stevens, Robert J[ulius]
1824-1889

Social letter to unanswered correspondents in America, by Robert J. Stevens, consul of the United States for Victoria, B.C., and its dependencies.    Victoria, Published by Faust of Guttemburg, 1884.

45 p.    fold. map.    20 cm.    On cover: Xmas, 1884.    Not seen.

BANCROFT LIBRARY CATALOGUE

### 671    Tolmie, W[illiam] Fraser
1812-1886

Comparative vocabularies of the Indian tribes of British Columbia. With a map illustrating distribution, by W. Fraser Tolmie and George M. Dawson. Published by authority of Parliament.    Montreal, Dawson Brothers, 1884.

131 p.    fold. map.    24 cm.    At head of title: Geological and Natural History Survey of Canada.

The book contains a short series of the principal words of all Indian languages and dialects in the province.

B.C. ARCHIVES

### 672    A Tour . . .

A tour through Canada, from Nova Scotia to Vancouver Island. Reprinted by permission from the columns of the Canadian gazette, London, England.    [London, Printed by Cassell & Company] 1884.

viii, 72 p.    illus.    22 cm.

Contains only a brief description of British Columbia at a time when the C.P.R. had yet to be completed.

B.C. ARCHIVES

### 673    Union Club of British Columbia

Constitution, by-laws and list of members of the Union Club of British Columbia, established 1879.    [n.p., 1884]

31 p.    14 cm.

Also: 1887. 35 p.    Also: 1892. 39 p.    Also: 1907. 40 p.    Also: 1911. 43 p.    Also: 1919. 59 p.    Also: 1926. 58 p.    Also: 1924. 58 p.    Also: 1929. 60 p.

B.C. ARCHIVES

### 674    Victoria Theatre Company

Memorandum and articles of association. Victoria, Colonist, 1884.

17 p.    Not found for examination.

B.C. ARCHIVES

**675  Wardman, George**
B. 1838

A trip to Alaska; a narrative of what was seen and heard during a summer cruise in Alaskan waters.   San Francisco, Samuel Carson & Co., 1884.

237 p.   19 cm.

Includes a description of B.C. coastal waters (1879).

Also: Boston, Lee and Shepard, 1884.   Also: 1885.

B.C. ARCHIVES

**676  Bible. New Testament. Matthew. Tsimshian**

Am da malshk ga na damsh St. Matthew; ligi, The Gospel according to St. Matthew. Translated into Zimshian [by William Ridley]   London, Society for Promoting Christian Knowledge, [1885]

59 p.   17 cm.

B.C. ARCHIVES

**677  British Association for the Advancement of Science**

Report of the north-western tribes of Canada. 1st, 4th-12th.   London, Offices of the Association [1885-98]

10 v.   illus., plates, maps, diagrs., tables (part fold.) 22-23 cm.   Title varies slightly. No 2d report was published in any form. The 3d report does not appear to have been issued separately and can be found in the association's report for 1887, p. 173-200. Partial listing of contents for this series on p. 1-2 of the 10th report. Index to the 4th to 12th reports in the 12th report. Reprinted from: *Report of the . . . meeting of the British Association for the Advancement of Science.*

Papers on the physical characteristics, language, industry, and social conditions of Indian tribes in British Columbia by Franz Boas, A. F. Chamberlain, Livingston Farrand, Horatio Hale, and E. F. Wilson.

B.C. ARCHIVES

**678  British Columbia. Asylum for the Insane (New Westminster)**

By-laws, rules and regulations of the Provincial Lunatic Asylum, New Westminster, B.C. [by] R. I. Bentley, Medical Superintendent.   New Westminster, British Columbian Steam Print, 1885.

12 p.   22 cm.

B.C. ARCHIVES

**679  British Columbia. Executive Council**

Copy of a report of a committee of the Honourable the Executive Council of British Columbia, on the question of the boundary between Alaska and Canada.   [Victoria, 1885]

12 p.   27 cm.   [British Columbia. Sessional papers, 1885]   Cover title.   Not found in Holmes.

B.C. ARCHIVES

**680  British Columbia . . .**

British Columbia, Kootenay district, townsite of Farwell.   Victoria, Farwell & Co., 1885.

12 p.   fold. map.   22 cm.   Cover title: The future chief city of the interior of British Columbia, Farwell, at second crossing of Columbia River, the meeting point of Canadian and American commercial highways. On t. p.: Victoria, Colonist Steam Presses.

TORONTO PUBLIC LIBRARY

**681  Canada. Department of the Interior**

Regulations for the disposal of Dominion lands within the railway belt in the province of British Columbia, 1885.   [Ottawa, 1885]

31 p.   25 cm.

B.C. ARCHIVES

**682  Canada. Royal Commission on Chinese Immigration**

Report of the Royal Commission on Chinese Immigration; report and evidence.   Ottawa, Printed by order of the Commission, 1885.

cxxxiv, cii, 487 p.   25 cm.   (Canada. Sessional papers, 1884-85, no. 54a)   Commissioners: J. A. Chapleau and J. H. Gray. Commissioner John Hamilton Gray's report: Respecting Chinese immigration in British Columbia [p. i-cii]

B.C. ARCHIVES

**683  Canadian Pacific Railway Company**

By the West to the East; memorandum on some Imperial aspects of the completion of the Canadian Pacific Railway. November 1885. [n. p., 1885]

11 p. (incl. cover)   22 cm.   Cover title.

Another edition is dated April 1885: London, Blacklock, 1885. 8 p.

B.C. ARCHIVES

**684  Chapleau, [Sir Joseph Adolphe]**
1840-1898

Discours . . . sur les résolutions du Chemin de Fer Canadien du Pacifique. Chambre des Commumes [sic] 16 juin 1885.   Ottawa, MacLean, Roger, 1885.

68 p. tables. 22 cm. Cover title.

Also printed in English. 64 p.

B.C. ARCHIVES

### 685　Chittenden, Newton H.

Settlers, miners and tourists guide; from ocean to ocean by the C.P.R., the great trans-continental short line through a region of unsurpassed attractions for settler, miner and tourist. Circular 14 of the "World's guide for home, health and pleasure seekers." [Ottawa, James Hope & Co., 1885]

112 p. (incl. advertisements) illus. 23 cm. British Columbia: p. 62-112. At head of text on p. 62: From Chittenden's Travels in British Columbia and Alaska, 1882-83.

CANADIAN ARCHIVES

### 686　Foresters, Ancient Order of. Nanaimo. Home No. 5886

Constitution and by-laws of Court Nanaimo Foresters' Home No. 5886 of the Ancient Order of Foresters; instituted June 24th, 1875 ... [Nanaimo] Nanaimo Free Press Steam Print, 1885.

43 p. 15 cm.

B.C. ARCHIVES

### 687　Hay, James

Notes of a trip from Chicago to Victoria, Vancouver's Island, and return, 1884. Printed for private circulation. Chicago, Rand, McNally & Co., 1885.

77 p. illus. 22 cm. Not seen.

LIBRARY OF CONGRESS

### 688　Krause, Aurel
1848-1908

Die Tlinkit-Indianer; Ergebnisse einer Reise nach der Nordwestküste von Amerika und der Beringstrasse, ausgeführt im Auftrage der Bremer Geographischen Gesellschaft in den Jahren 1880-1881, durch die Doctoren Arthur und Aurel Krause, geschildert von Dr. Aurel Krause. Jena, Hermann Costenoble, 1885.

xvi, 420 p. illus., 4 plates, fold. map, tables. 24 cm. Verzeichnis der benutzen Litteratur: p. [392]-404.

English edition appeared under title: *The Tlingit Indians* (Seattle, Published for the American Ethnological Society by the University of Washington Press, 1956).

B.C. ARCHIVES

### 689　Moberly, Walter
1832-1915

The rocks and rivers of British Columbia. London, Printed by H. Blacklock & Co., 1885.

104 p. illus., 2 fold. maps. 22 cm. Some copies, with no maps and 1 illus., have 102 pages.

Recounts the experiences and travels of the author who conducted explorations and surveys in the province from 1857 to 1872.

B.C. ARCHIVES

### 690　Panton, J[ames] Hoyes
1847-1898

Rambles in the North-west, across the prairies, and in the passes of the Rocky Mountains. Guelph, Ont., Mercury Steam Printing House, 1885.

20 p. 23 cm. Cover title. Caption title: Rambles across the prairie, up the Bow River, over the summit of the Rockies, and down the Kicking Horse Pass into British Columbia.

B.C. ARCHIVES

### 691　Royal Agricultural and Industrial Society of British Columbia (New Westminster)

Programme, rules and regulations of the provincial exhibition. 1885?-1929? New Westminster, The Commercial Company, Ltd., Dingle & Galbraith.

v. illus. 22, 17 cm. annual. Copies examined for 1894, 1901. Printer varies. Society reformed 17 April 1956, after being inactive from 1929.

Contains the society's constitution, rules and regulations for exhibitions, prizes and judging; includes livestock, vegetable, and machinery prize lists, and description of New Westminster.

B.C. ARCHIVES

### 692　Scidmore, E[liza] Ruhamah
1856-1928

Alaska; its southern coast and Sitkan Archipelago. Boston, D. Lothrop and Company [c1885]

viii, 333, vi p. illus., plates, double map. 19 cm.

Includes short descriptions of Victoria, Nanaimo, Metlahkatla, and coastal waters.

B.C. ARCHIVES

### 693　Shall we emigrate?

Shall we emigrate? A tour through the states of America, to the Pacific coast of Canada, by a family man. Dublin, George Herbert, 1885.

32 p. 22 cm.

B.C. ARCHIVES

**694  Stevenson, E[ady]**

Religion and rum; or, The influence of religion on the use of alcoholic liquors as a beverage. A lecture . . . delivered in Philharmonic Hall, March 26th, 1884.   Victoria, Cohen & Salmon, 1885.

38 p.   17 cm.

B.C. ARCHIVES

**695  Tolmie, William Fraser**
1812-1886

Utilization of the Indians of British Columbia. Victoria, Munroe Miller, 1885.

9 p.   21 cm.

A plea for the teaching of Indians in secular subjects.

B.C. ARCHIVES

**696  United States. Army. Department of the Columbia**

Report of a military reconnaissance in Alaska, made in 1883 by Frederick Schwatka. Washington, Government Printing Office, 1885.

121 p.   illus., 20 fold. maps.   24 cm.   ([United States] 48th Cong., 2d sess. Senate. Ex. doc. no. 2)

Has comments on Indians living in British Columbia.

OREGON HISTORICAL SOCIETY

**697  Veritas, Philo.**
PSEUDONYM

The Canadian Pacific Railway; an appeal to public opinion against the railway being carried across the Selkirk Range, that route being objectionable from the danger of falls from glaciers and from avalanches; also, generally on other matters, by Philo. Veritas [pseud.]   Montreal, Wm. Drysdale & Co., 1885.

100 p.   fold. map, tables.   22 cm.

B.C. ARCHIVES

**698  [Argyll, John George Edward Henry Douglas Sutherland Campbell]**
9TH DUKE OF   1845-1914

Our railway to the Pacific, by the Marquis of Lorne. With illustrations by H.R.H. Princess Louise.   London, Isbister and Company, 1886.

32 p.   illus.   24 cm.   Reprinted from *Good words,* v. 27, 1886, p. 73-81, 160-168.

B.C. ARCHIVES

**699  Baillie-Grohman, W[illia]m A[dolph]**
1851-1921

The Kootenay valleys in Kootenay district, British Columbia.   London, Printed by Witherby & Co., 1886.

6 p.   fold. map.   28 cm.   Cover title. At head of text: Mr. W. A. Baillie-Grohman's descriptive report on the Kootenay valleys in British Columbia, and the 73,025 acres of agricultural and forest land secured to the Kootenay Syndicate (Limited) by a special, partially free grant from the government of British Columbia.

B.C. ARCHIVES

**700  Bible. New Testament. Mark. Beaver**

The Gospel according to St. Mark. Translated by the Rev. Alfred C. Garrioch into the language of the Beaver Indians of the Diocese of Athabasca.   London, Society for Promoting Christian Knowledge [1886]

47 p.   16 cm.   Text in syllabic characters.

Also printed in roman characters in 1886.

B.C. ARCHIVES

**701  Boas, Franz**
1858-1942

Die Anthropologische untersuchung der Bella-Coola.   [Berlin, 1886]

206-215 p.   table.   26 cm.   Caption title. Reprinted from the *Verhandlungen der Berliner Gesellschaft für Anthropologie, Ethnologie und Urgeschichte,* March 1886.

Brief notes on Bella Coola Indian traditions.

B.C. ARCHIVES

**702  Boas, Franz**
1858-1942

Sprache der Bella-Coola-Indianer.   [Berlin, 1886]

[202]-206 p.   plate, map.   26 cm.   Caption title. Reprinted from the *Verhandlungen der Berliner Gesellschaft für Anthropologie, Ethnologie und Urgeschichte,* March 1886.

B.C. ARCHIVES

**703  British Columbia St. George's Society**

Constitution, by-laws, and standing rules and orders.   Victoria, Wm. A. Calhoun, 1886.

16, [3] l.   15 cm.

B.C. ARCHIVES

**704    Bull, William K[ing]**
1811-1899    APPELLANT

In the Privy Council, in appeal from the
Supreme Court of British Columbia; between
William K. Bull, appellant, and Wing Chong,
alias Chu Lay, respondent.    [n.p., 1886]

2, 20 p.    27 cm.    Caption title.

Concerns the B.C. Chinese Regulation Act of 1884
which Justice Crease had ruled *ultra vires*.

B.C. ARCHIVES

**705    Cameron, D[onald] R[oderick]**
1834-1921

Report on the location of the British-Alaskan
boundary under the Anglo-Russian convention
of 1825. Colonial Office, September 1886.
[London, Eyre and Spottiswoode, 1886]

vi, 83 p.    17 maps (part fold.) in pocket, tables.    34
cm.    (At head of title: North America, no. 119)

CANADIAN ARCHIVES

**706    The Canadian Pacific Railway
Company**

Memorandum; the trans-Pacific connections
of the Canadian Pacific Railway. February 1886.
[n.p., 1886]

47 p.    tables.    23 cm.    Cover title. At head
of title: Private.

Concerns trade, mail and passenger service, routes
to the Orient and Australia, and aspects of defense.

B.C. ARCHIVES

**707    The Canadian Pacific Railway
Company**

The province of British Columbia, Canada:
its resources, commercial position and climate,
and description of the new field opened up
by the Canadian Pacific railways. With maps
and information for intending settlers.
[n.p., 1886?]

48 p.    illus., fold. maps.    Cover title: British
Columbia; farms, fisheries, forests, mines. One
of the maps is dated 1886.

NATIONAL LIBRARY

**708    Church Missionary Society**

Report of the deputation to Metlakatla
(General Touch and the Rev. W. R. Blackett)
[n.p., 1886]

44 p.    21 cm.    Caption title. At head of title:
Private; for the use of the committee.

A condemnation of William Duncan's activities in
secular affairs, of his views with respect to the

observance of certain church rituals, and of his
preaching methods.

B.C. ARCHIVES

**709    Craib, W[illia]m**

Island Mountain Mine, Cariboo district, B.C.;
reports of Wm. Craib and Geo. A. Koch on the
property.    Victoria, 1886.

9 p.    22 cm.    Cover title.

The mine was located about five miles from
Barkerville. Assays showed the presence of gold and
silver.

U.B.C. SPECIAL COLLECTIONS

**710    Dawson, George M[ercer]**
1849-1901

The Canadian Rocky Mountains [with special
reference to that part of the range between the
forty-ninth parallel and the head-waters of the
Red Deer River.    Montreal? 1886?]

16 p.    22 cm.    Cover title. Read before Section C,
British Association, Birmingham Meeting, 1886,
Reprinted from the *Canadian record of science*.

On geological formations and mountain passes.
It also includes a summary of contemporary
knowledge concerning the Rockies.

B.C. ARCHIVES

**711    Duck, Simeon**
1834-1905

Finances of the province of British Columbia;
budget speech delivered by the Hon. Simeon
Duck, Minister of Finance, in the provincial
legislature, on Monday, March 29th, 1886.
Victoria, Munroe Miller, 1886.

47 p.    20 cm.

B.C. ARCHIVES

**712    Esquimalt and Nanaimo Railway
Company**

Rules and regulations for the guidance of
employes [*sic*]    [n.p., 1886]

48 p.    16 cm.

B.C. ARCHIVES

**713    Findlay, Alexander G[eorge]**
1812-1875

A directory for the navigation of the North Pacific
Ocean. Third edition.    London, Printed for R. H.
Laurie, 1886.

xxxii, 1315 p.    plates, maps (part fold.) tables.
25 cm.

B.C. ARCHIVES

**714    Forrest, James**
EDITOR 1825-1917

Railway construction and working; comprising the following papers: I. The construction and operation of railways in countries where small returns are expected, by Robert Gordon. II. The laying-out, construction and equipment of railways in newly-developed countries, by James Robert Mosse. III. The Rocky-Mountain Division of the Canadian Pacific Railway, by Granville Carlyle Cuningham. With an abstract of the discussion upon the papers.   London, Published by the Institution, 1886.

65 p. illus., fold. plans. 21 cm.   Reprinted from: Institute of Civil Engineers. *Proceedings.* v. 85, sess. 1885-6, pt. 3.

CANADIAN ARCHIVES

**715    Gerrish, Theodore**
1846-1923

Life in the world's wonderland; a graphic description of the great Northwest, from the Mississippi River to the Land of the Midnight Sun . . .   [n.p., 1886?]

421 p. illus. 24 cm.

A book for tourists which includes a description of the inside passage to Alaska.

There were at least three further editions.

B.C. ARCHIVES

**716    Lansdowne, [Henry Charles Keith Petty-Fitzmaurice]**
5TH MARQUIS OF 1845-1927

Canadian North-west and British Columbia; two speeches by His Excellency the Marquis of Lansdowne.   Ottawa, Department of Agriculture, 1886.

32 p. fold. map. 22 cm.   Cover title.

B.C. ARCHIVES

**717    [Le Jeune, Jean-Marie Raphael]**
1855-1930

Practical Chinook [jargon] vocabulary, comprising all & the only usual words of that wonderful language arranged in a most advantageous order for the speedily learning of the same. After the plan of Right Rev. Bishop Durieu, O.M.I., the most experienced missionary & Chinook speaker in British Columbia. Kamloops, 1886.

16 p.   Cover title. Mimeographed.   Not seen. From Pilling's *Chinookan languages.* Paul Durieu desclaimed authorship (*ibid.,* p. 45).

Second edition has title: *Chinook [jargon] vocabulary; Chinook-English. From the original of Rt.*

*Rev. Bishop Durieu, O.M.I., with Chinook words in phonography, by J. M. R. Le Jeune* (Kamloops, 1892). In 16 pages.

PILLING'S CHINOOKAN BIBLIOGRAPHY

**718    Lowe, T.**

A mechanic's tour round the world; being notes and sketches about life in South Africa, Canada (including British Columbia) United States of America, Australia, etc.   London, Wyman & Sons, 1886.

viii, 149 p. 17 cm.

Written for the intended emigrant.

NATIONAL LIBRARY

**719    Martley, John**
1859-1896

In the Supreme Court of Canada, on appeal from the Supreme Court of British Columbia; between John Martley and Truman Celah Clark (defendants) appellants, and Robert Carson and Joseph Eholt (plaintiffs) respondents. Case. Messrs. Davie & Pooley, solicitors for appellant Martley; Charles Wilson, solicitor for appellant Clark; Messrs. McIntyre & Lewis, Ottawa agts. for appellants' solicitors; Messrs. Drake, Jackson & Helmcken, solicitors for respondents; Messrs. Stewart & Chrysler, Ottawa, agents.   Victoria, Daily Evening Post Job Print, 1886.

[59] 1.   30 cm.

B.C. ARCHIVES

**720    New Westminster Gas Company, Limited**

Articles of association; incorporated March 16th, 1886, registered under the "Companies' Act, 1878."   Victoria, Munroe Miller, 1886.

17 p.   23 cm.

B.C. ARCHIVES

**721    P., M.**

A winter trip on the Canadian Pacific Railway; Christmas and New Year in the snow, 1885-6. Written for private circulation . . .   [n.p., 1886?]

29 p.   19 cm.

An account of a month's rail journey from Golden, B.C., to Halifax, N.S. The author was not optimistic about the future of winter rail travel through the Rockies.

B.C. ARCHIVES

**722    Railway and navigation guide . . .**

Railway and navigation guide for Puget Sound and British Columbia; Seattle, Victoria; contains the latest time tables of all railway, steamship, and stage lines; together with distance tables, mail schedules, rates of fare, and general rallway [*sic*] and shipping information; distributed on ocean, sound, and river steamers, railways, and stages, to hotel, and leading business houses throughout the Northwest.   Seattle, W. T., Victoria, William C. Haywood & Co., 1886.

42 p. (incl. advertisements)   tables.   20 cm. Copy examined: v. 2, no. 12, December 1886. On t. p.: revised and published monthly.

B.C. ARCHIVES

### 723   St. John, [Frederick Edward] Molyneux
COMPILER   1838-1904

The province of British Columbia, Canada; its resources, commercial position and climate, and description of the new field opened up by the Canadian Pacific Railway, with information for intending settlers, based on the personal investigations of the writer, and upon the reports of scientific explorers and government surveyors. [n.p., 1886]

56 p.   plates, fold. map, tables.   22 cm.   Cover title: British Columbia; information for miners, agriculturists, tourists, sportsmen.

Also: 52 p. With 2 maps.   Also: 1899? 48 p.

B.C. ARCHIVES

### 724   Sharpe, J.

Model farming a science. In a nation's prosperity much depends upon her agricultural progress. This pamphlet is the first one published in British Columbia on "the model farm and soiling system," with a balance sheet, and a rotation plan of cropping the fields of the farm for three consecutive seasons.   [Victoria] R. T. Williams, 1886.

36 p.   tables.   22 cm.

B.C. PROVINCIAL LIBRARY

### 725   The Times (London)

A Canadian tour; a reprint of letters from the special correspondent of The Times.   London, Printed and published by George Edward Wright at The Times Office, 1886.

58 p.   double map.   29 cm.   Cover title.

The author travelled on the C.P.R. to the West Coast in September 1886. Over one-third of the publication relates to British Columbia.

NATIONAL LIBRARY

### 726   Trout, P[eter] L[aird]
D. 1925

Prospectors' manual; being a full and complete history and description of the newly discovered gold mines on Granite Creek, the canyon of the Tulameen River, and other new mineral discoveries in the Similkameen country, with full instructions as how to get there and what to do on arriving there; also, its many advantages as an agricultural, stock raising and lumbering country; designed for the use of emigrants, tourists, sportsmen and goldseekers.   [Victoria?] 1886.

64 p.   maps.   22 cm.

B.C. ARCHIVES

### 727   United States. Department of State

Message from the President of the United States, transmitting a report of the Secretary of State relative to the frontier line between Alaska and British Columbia.   [Washington, Government Printing Office, 1886]

20 p.   23 cm.   ([United States] 49th Cong., 1st sess. Senate. Ex. doc. no. 143)   Caption title.

Contains correspondence between the American and British governments.

B.C. ARCHIVES

### 728   Victoria. Corrig School

Catalogue of Corrig School, Victoria, B.C., an English and classical boarding school for boys, 1886.   [Victoria, 1886]

[16] p.   21 cm.   On cover: Corrig School, Victoria, B.C.; testimonials.

B.C. ARCHIVES

### 729   Victoria. Sewerage Committee

Report . . . with estimated cost and proposed sewerage districts; October 13th, 1886.   Victoria, Daily Post Print, 1886.

5 p.   21 cm.   Cover title. Signed in print: D. W. Higgins, W. A. Robertson, R. Lipsett.

B.C. ARCHIVES

### 730   Adair, William Butler
PLAINTIFF

In the Supreme Court of British Columbia; between William Butler Adair, plaintiff, respondent, and Andrew Welch and Robert Paterson Rithet, carrying on business as Welch, Rithet and Company, and John Adair, Junior, lately carrying on business as Adair and Company, on Fraser River, and Joseph Despard Pemberton (by original action) and between the said Andrew Welch and Robert Paterson Rithet, plaintiffs, appellants, and the said William Butler Adair, defendant, respondent (by counter claim). Case on appeal. Messrs. Drake, Jackson & Helmcken, solicitors for appellants; Messrs. Davie

& Pooley, solicitors for respondents; Theodore Davie, Esq., solicitor for defendant, Adair & Company.   Victoria, Munro Miller [1887]

37 1.   30 cm.

B.C. ARCHIVES

## 731      Bancroft, Hubert Howe
### 1832-1918

History of British Columbia, 1792-1887. San Francisco, The History Company, 1887.

xxxi, 792 p.   maps (1 fold.)   23 cm.   (The works of Hubert Howe Bancroft, v. 32) Authorities quoted: p. xxiii-xxxi. Bibliography: p. 763-774. Chapter headings: Summary of early voyages. — General view of the Northwest Coast. — Occupation of the Domain, 1841. — Camosun and Esquimalt, 1842. — Founding of Fort Camosun, 1843. — Affairs at Camosun, 1844. — Camosun, Albert, Victoria, 1845. — The Shushwap conspiracy, 1846. — Anderson's explorations, 1846-1847. — Yale and Hope established, 1848-1849. — Establishing Forts Rupert and Nanaimo, 1849-1852. — Crown grant of Vancouver Island to the Hudson's Bay Company, 1849. — The colony of Vancouver Island under the Hudson's Bay Company regime, 1849-1859. — Two original characters. — Settlement of Vancouver Island, 1849-1857. — Government established, 1840-1852. — James Douglas. — The Island under Douglas, 1851-1859. — The judiciary, 1853-1859. — The great gold establishment, 1858. — Death of the monopoly — the colony of British Columbia established, 1857-1858. — Government of the mainland, 1858-1863. — Administration of justice, 1856-1880. — Fraser River mining and settlement, 1858-1868. — Gold in the Cariboo country. — Mining in the Cariboo, 1863-1882. — Upper Columbia mines, 1864-1882. — Gold discoveries in the far north, 1861-1882. — Coal. — Union and confederation, 1863-1871. — The San Juan Island difficulty, 1854-1872. — The Canadian Pacific Railway, 1871-1874. — The Canadian Pacific Railway, 1874-1885. — Politics and government, 1870-1886. — Settlement, missions, and education, 1861-1886. — Industries, commerce, and finance, 1880-1886.

Hubert Bancroft is credited with writing about half this volume. He was helped by Alfred Bates, William Nemos, and Amos Bowman, who were responsible for the remainder (see *Oregon historical quarterly*, v. 4, p. 287-364).

Reprinted separately in 1890. Also published as the second volume of Bancroft's *History of the Pacific states of North America*.

B.C. ARCHIVES

## 732      Bates, E[mily] Katharine

A year in the great republic, by E. Catherine Bates.   London, Ward & Downey, 1887.

2 v.   20 cm.

Volume 2 has several pages describing the author's Victoria visit.

UNIVERSITY OF WASHINGTON LIBRARY

## 733      [Beadle, Charles]

A trip to the United States in 1887.   [London] Printed for private circulation by [J. S. Virtue and Co., 1887]

210 p.   20 cm.

In a few pages the author touches on his travels through British Columbia.

B.C. ARCHIVES

## 734      Beaugrand, Honoré
### 1849-1906

Across the continent via the Canadian Pacific Railway; a lecture delivered . . . under the auspices of the Montreal District Board of Trade, 23rd March 1887.   [Montreal? 1887]

9 p.   21 cm.

Impressions of a winter railway traveller. A good proportion of the pamphlet describes British Columbia.

CANADIAN ARCHIVES

## 735      Beaugrand, Honoré
### 1849-1906

De Montréal à Victoria par le transcontinental canadien; conférence faite par M. Honoré Beaugrand, ancien maire de Montréal devant la Chambre de Commerce du district de Montréal. Montréal, 1887.

52 p.   plates.   21 cm.

About half of the publication relates to British Columbia.

Also appears in Beaugrand's *Mélanges* (entry 773).

B.C. ARCHIVES

## 736      Bible. New Testament. Luke. Tsimshian

Am da malshk ga na damsh St. Luke; ligi, The Gospel according to St. Luke. Translated into Zimshian [by William Ridley]   London, Society for Promoting Christian Knowledge [1887]

63 p.   18 cm.

B.C. ARCHIVES

## 737      Bible. New Testament. Mark. Tsimshian

Am da malshk ga na damsh St. Mark; ligi, The Gospel according to St. Mark. Translated into Zimshian [by William Ridley]   London, Society for Promoting Christian Knowledge [1887]

40 p.   Not seen.

BRITISH MUSEUM CATALOGUE

**738 Blavatsky, H[elena] P[etrovna (Hahn)]**
1831-1891

To the Archbishop of Canterbury—an open letter (reprinted from "Lucifer" magazine, 1887) Victoria, The "H.P.B." Library [n.d.]

14 p. 23 cm. (The Blavatsky pamphlets, no. 1) Cover title.

On the position of theosophy in regard to Christianity.

B.C. ARCHIVES

**739 The British Columbia directory . . .**

The British Columbia directory, containing a general directory of business men and householders in the principal cities and every important district, with provincial and dominion officials and general information about the province, 1887. Victoria, E. Mallandaine and R. T. Williams, 1887.

x, 308 p. 23 cm. Binder's title: Mallandaine's British Columbia directory, 1887.

B.C. ARCHIVES

**740 British Columbia Mainland Pioneer and Benevolent Society**

Constitution, by-laws, and rules of order of the British Columbia Mainland Pioneer and Benevolent Society, organized April 1887. Published by order of the Board of Directors, Kamloops, B.C., 1887. Kamloops, Inland Sentinel Print, 1887.

23 p. (p. 12-16 blank) 14 cm.

B.C. ARCHIVES

**741 Canada**

Correspondence relative to the seizure of British American vessels in Behrings Sea by the United States authorities in 1886. Ottawa, Printed by Maclean, Roger & Co., 1887.

47 p. fold. map. 25 cm. (Canada. Sessional papers, 1887, no. 48) Cover title.

B.C. ARCHIVES

**742 Canada. Department of Public Works**

Rules and regulations for the management and working of the graving dock at Esquimalt, B.C. Victoria, The Colonist Steam Print, 1887.

15 p. 14 cm.

Also: Ottawa, Government Printing Bureau, 1899. 8 p.

B.C. ARCHIVES

**743 Canadian Pacific Railway Company**

The Canadian Pacific, the new highway to the East, across the mountains, prairies & rivers of Canada. [Montreal, 1887]

45 p. illus., map (on inside back cover) Cover title.

Also: 1180. 50 p. Numerous editions. Later editions published under titles: *The Canadian Pacific, the new highway to the Orient . . . ;* and, *The new highway to the Orient.*

B.C. ARCHIVES

**744 Corrig school record**

Corrig school record. 1887-189–. Victoria, Record Pub. Co.

v. 31 cm. quarterly. Possible terminal date: 5 May 1890. Private school publication.

B.C. ARCHIVES

**745 Dawson, George M[ercer]**
1849-1901

Note on the occurrence of jade in British Columbia and its employment by the natives. With quotations & extracts from a paper by Prof. A. B. Meyer, on nephrite & analogous minerals from Alaska. [n.p., 1887]

15 p. diagr. 21 cm. Cover title. Reprinted from the *Canadian record of science*, v. 2, 1887.

B.C. ARCHIVES

**746 Dawson, George M[ercer]**
1849-1901

Notes on the Indian tribes of the Yukon district and adjacent northern portion of British Columbia. [n.p., 1887]

23 p. 24 cm. Caption title. Short vocabularies of the Tahl-tan, Ti-tsho-ti-na, and Ta-gish obtained in 1887: p. [18]-23.

Reprint of Appendix 2 of *Report on an exploration in the Yukon District, N.W.T., and adjacent northern portion of British Columbia* in: Canada. Geological Survey. *Annual report. 1887-8.* new ser., v. 3, pt. 1, rept. B, p. [191B]-213B.

B.C. ARCHIVES

**747 Findlay, George James [and others]**
PLAINTIFFS

In the Supreme Court of British Columbia, on appeal to the divisional court; between George James Findlay, John Henry Durham, and John Henry Brodie, plaintiffs, and Peter Birrell and Joseph A. Boscowitz, Defendantt [*sic*] Case on appeal. Drake, Jackson & Helmcken, solicitors for plaintiffs; J. Roland Hett, solicitor for defendant Boscowitz.    Victoria, Munroe Miller, 1887.

18 1.    28 cm.

B.C. ARCHIVES

748      Garner, Charles
         1885-1905

The Queen's highway; from ocean to ocean, by Stuart Cumberland [pseud.]    London, Sampson Low, Marston, Searle, & Rivington, 1887.

431 p.    illus., plates, fold. map.    22 cm.

A journalist's description of the C.P.R. line from west to east. Nearly one-half of the book relates to British Columbia.

New and cheaper edition: 1888.

B.C. ARCHIVES

749      Great Britain. Foreign Office

Correspondence respecting the boundary between the British possessions in North America and the territory of Alaska . . .    [London, 1887-1903]

14 pts. in 3 v.    fold. maps.    33 cm.    Parts 2-14 have title: Further correspondence . . .    At head of title: Printed for the use of the Foreign Office [date] confidential [number related to Foreign Office confidential document, and part number]    Binder's title on cover: Alaska boundary . . . Foreign Office confidential series relating to the Alaska boundary; part[s] . . .

Series has index in Vancouver Public library with title: *Alaska boundary; Foreign Office confidential series. Index to vols. I, II, and III.* At head of title: Confidential. In 79 pages.

VANCOUVER PUBLIC LIBRARY

750      Hayden, Isaac J.
         PLAINTIFF

In the Supreme Court of British Columbia, on appeal to the full court; between Isaac J. Hayden, plaintiff and appellant, and the Canadian Pacific Railway Company, Sir Donald A. Smith, and Richard B. Angus, defendants and respondents. Case on appeal. J. P. Walls, solicitor for plaintiff; Drake, Jackson & Helmcken, solicitors for defendants.    Victoria, Jas. A. Cohen, printer, 1887.

23 1.    28 cm.

B.C. ARCHIVES

751      Higgins, David Williams
         1834-1917   DEFENDANT

In the Supreme Court of Canada, on appeal from the Supreme Court of British Columbia; between David Williams Higgins (defendant) appellant, and the Honourable George Anthony Walkem (plaintiff) respondent. Case on appeal from the order discharging the order nisi for a new trial. Theodore Davie, solicitor for the appellant; H. Dallas Helmcken, solicitor for the respondent. Victoria, "The Colonist" Steam Printing House, 1887.

71 1.    28 cm.

B.C. ARCHIVES

752      Hudson's Bay Company

Rules and regulations subject to the provisions of the deed poll.    Winnipeg, Printed by The Call Printing Company, 1887.

18 1.    26 cm.    Cover title.

B.C. ARCHIVES

753      Ingersoll, Ernest
         1852-1946

An excursion to Alaska by the Canadian Pacific Railway.    Montreal, Issued by the Passenger Department, Canadian Pacific Railway, 1887.

62 p.    illus., fold. maps.    16 cm.    (Canadian Pacific primers, no. 1)

Also: 1888.

B.C. ARCHIVES

754      Metlakahtla . . .

Metlakahtla and the Church Missionary Society [being a defence of the position taken by the native Christians and their teachers, and an answer to the charges brought against them] Victoria, Munroe Miller, 1887.

44 p.    22 cm.    Cover title. Contents: A reply to the article on Metlakahtla in the Church Missionary Intelligencer of September 1885, by Robert Tomlinson [p. 2-12] — Copies of correspondence between the deputies and the native Christians and Mr. Tomlinson [p. 12-42]    Introductory paragraph is signed by William Duncan and Robert Tomlinson.

B.C. ARCHIVES

755      Perry, Charles E[benezer]
         COMPILER   1835-1917

Railways of Canada; their cost, amounts of aid given in cash and land, &c. Compiled from the latest authorities.    Victoria, The Colonist Steam Presses, 1887.

18 p.    tables (1 fold.)    21 cm.

Written to stimulate interest in B.C. railway investment.

B.C. ARCHIVES

**756  Picken, M.**
COMPILER

City of Vancouver, terminus of the Canadian
Pacific Railway; British Columbia hand book.
Vancouver, Daily News Office, 1887.

88 p. (p. 65-88 advertisements)  fold. map.  23 cm.

B.C. ARCHIVES

**757  Roberts, Morley**
1857-1942

The western Avernus; or, Toil and travel in further
North America.  London, Smith, Elder & Co.,
1887.

307 p.  fold. map.  21 cm.

Mainly concerned with the author's experiences as a
member of a railway gang in the Rockies and during
his walk through the Selkirks and the Fraser Canyon to
the Coast.

New Edition: Westminster, Archibald Constable and
Co., 1896. xi, 277 p.  Also: London, Brown,
Langham & Company, 1904.  viii, 277 p.  Also:
London, Dent, 1924. viii, 238 p. (Everyman's library.
Travel)

B.C. ARCHIVES

**758  Seton-Karr, H[eywood]
W[alter]**
B. 1859

Shores and alps of Alaska.  London, Sampson
Low, Marston, Searle, & Rivington, 1887.

xiv, 248 p.  illus., plates, ports., maps (1 fold.)  23
cm.

Briefly mentions the author's rail journey through
British Columbia and his boat trip along the B.C.
coast.

Also: London, Sampson Low; Chicago, A. C.
McClurg & Co., 1887.

B.C. ARCHIVES

**759  Sheldon, John Prince**
1841-1913

From Britain to British Columbia.  [Ottawa]
Published by the Government of Canada, 1887.

76 p.  illus., fold. map.  22 cm.  Cover title.
Printed in London by McCorquodale & Co. At head of
text: From Britain to British Columbia; or, Canada as
a domain for British farmers, sportsmen, and tourists.

B.C. ARCHIVES

**760  Sketch . . .**

Sketch of the Alaskan missions, with an account
of the death of the late Most Rev. Charles J.
Seghers, Archbishop-Bishop of Vancouver
Island, B.C.  [n.p., 1887]

11 p.  22 cm.  Cover title.

B.C. ARCHIVES

**761  Spragge, [Ellen Elizabeth
(Cameron)]**
1854-1932

From Ontario to the Pacific by the C.P.R.
[by] Mrs. Arthur Spragge.  Toronto, C. Blackett
Robinson, 1887.

186 p.  fold. map.  15 cm.

Two-thirds of the book is devoted to a description of
British Columbia.

B.C. ARCHIVES

**762  Tanner, Henry**

British Columbia; its agricultural and commercial
capabilities and the advantages it offers for
emigration purposes.  Montreal Dawson Brothers,
1887.

45 p.  illus., fold. map.  22 cm.

Also: London, Kenning, 1887. 45 p. At head
of title: A sequel to "The Canadian North-west."
Also: Montreal, 1890.

B.C. ARCHIVES

**763  United States. Department of
State**

Papers relating to Behring Sea fisheries.
Washington, Government Printing Office, 1887.

128 p.  23 cm.

B.C. ARCHIVES

**764  Vancouver, B.C. . . .**

Vancouver, B.C., the Pacific coast terminus of the
C.P.R., the largest single line of railway in the
world and the only truly transcontinental railway
in America.  Vancouver, Ross & Ceperley, real
estate, financial and insurance agents [1887?]

32 p. (folder)  illus., map.  25 x 11 cm.  Map of
Vancouver on verso of pages is dated 24 February
1887. Map has title: City of Vancouver; Canadian
Pacific town site. Three smaller maps are inset. In the
Arkin Collection.

MCGILL UNIVERSITY LIBRARY

**765  Victoria's jubilee**

Victoria's jubilee, 1837-1887.  Victoria, Jas. A.
Cohen [1887]

38 p. (incl. advertisements)  24 cm.  Cover title.

Published for free distribution on the occasion
of Queen Victoria's jubilee.

B.C. ARCHIVES

**766  Walkem, George Anthony**
1834-1908  PLAINTIFF

In the Supreme Court of British Columbia, on appeal to the full court; between the Honorable George Anthony Walkem, plaintiff, and David William Higgins, defendant. Case on appeal. H. Dallas Helmcken, solicitor for plaintiff; Theodore Davie, solicitor for defendant.  Victoria, "The Colonist" Steam Printing House, 1887.

55 1.  28 cm.  Cover title.

B.C. ARCHIVES


**767  Watkin, Sir E[dward] W[illiam]**
1819-1901

Canada and the States; recollections, 1851 to 1886.  London, Ward, Lock and Co. [1887]

xvi, 524 p.  port., fold. maps.  22 cm.

Includes information on Hudson's Bay Company lands and on the beginnings of the C.P.R.

B.C. ARCHIVES


**768  Wellcome, [Sir] Henry S[olomon]**
1853?-1936

The story of Metlakahtla.  London, New York, Saxon & Co., 1887.

xx, 483 p.  plates, ports.  20 cm.

Gives William Duncan's side of his dispute with the Church Missionary Society.

Second edition: 1887.  Third edition: 1887. Fourth edition: n.d.

B.C. ARCHIVES


**769  Adams, Emma H[ildreth (Drake)]**
1827-1900?

To and fro, up and down, in southern California, Oregon, and Washington Territory, with sketches in Arizona, New Mexico, and British Columbia. San Francisco, Hunt & Eaton [c1888]

608 p.  illus.  21 cm.

Four chapters relate to British Columbia.

Chapters 1-31 (p. 11-278) were previously published under title: *To and fro in southern California, with sketches in Arizona and New Mexico* (Cincinnati, 1887).

Another edition: Cincinnati, Cranston & Stowe, c1888.

B.C. ARCHIVES


**770  Aubertin, J[ohn] J[ames]**

A fight with distances; the States, the Hawaiian Islands, Canada, British Columbia, Cuba, the Bahamas.  London, Kegan Paul, Trench & Co., 1888.

viii, 352 p.  plates, maps.  20 cm.  Chapter 6: British Columbia — The Canadian Pacific Railway [p. 106-121]

Contains an account of a railway trip through British Columbia in July 1887.

B.C. ARCHIVES


**771  Backus, John P.**
PLAINTIFF

In the Supreme Court of British Columbia, on appeal to the full court; between John P. Backus, plaintiff, and the Canadian Pacific Railway Company, defendants. Case on appeal. Theodore Davie, agent for W. Norman Bole, solicitor for plaintiff; Robert Edwin Jackson, solicitor for defendants.  Victoria, "The Colonist" Steam Printing House, 1888.

9 1.  28 cm.

B.C. ARCHIVES


**772  [Baillie-Grohman, William Adolph]**
1851-1921

The Kootenay valleys and the Kootenay district in British Columbia. With maps.  London, Kootenay Valleys Company (Limited) [1888]

31 p.  22 cm.  Maps lacking in copy examined.

Written to support the author's reclamation and settlement scheme.

B.C. ARCHIVES


**773  Beaugrand, H[onoré]**
1849-1906

Mélanges: trois conférences. I—De Montréal à Victoria. II—Le journal, son origine et son histoire. III—Anita: souvenirs d'un contre-guérillas.  Montréal, 1888.

149 p.  plates.  22 cm.  Part 1 has t. p.: De Montréal à Victoria par le transcontinental canadien; conférence faite devant la Chambre de Commerce du district de Montréal, le 23 mars 1887 (see entry 735)

LIBRARY OF PARLIAMENT


**774  British Columbia. Board of Trade**

Minute of Council . . . re China-Japan mail steamship service.  [n.p., 1888]

[4] p. (folder)  36 cm.  Cover title.

Concerns a petition to make Victoria a port of call on the route between Vancouver and the Orient.

B.C. ARCHIVES

775    Bryce, George
1844-1931

Holiday rambles between Winnipeg and Victoria.
I: Prairie and Mountain. II: Lo! the poor Indian.
Winnipeg, 1888.

87 p.   22 cm.

The portion of the book pertaining to Indians
does not relate to those of British Columbia.

B.C. ARCHIVES

776    Caine, W[illiam] S[proston]
1842-1903

A trip round the world in 1887-8. Illustrated by
John Pedder, H. Sheppard Dale, Geo. Bickham,
and the author.   London, New York,
George Routledge, 1888.

xxiv, 398 p.   illus., plates.   22 cm.   Letters which
originally appeared in the *Barrow news,* dating from
August 1887 to March 1888.

Two chapters relate to British Columbia.

Second and third editions: 1888.   Also: 1892.

CANADIAN ARCHIVES

777    Canada

Correspondence relative to the seizure of British
American vessels in Behrings Sea by the
United States authorities in 1886-87.   Ottawa,
Printed by Brown Chamberlin, 1888.

114 p.   25 cm.   (Canada. Sessional papers,
1888, no. 65, 65a, 65b, 65c)   Cover title.

B.C. ARCHIVES

778    [Carmichael, James]
1835-1908

A holiday trip: Montreal to Victoria and return,
via the Canadian Pacific Railway, midsummer,
1888.   [Montreal, Printed by the Gazette Printing
Company, 1888]

32 p.   illus.   27 cm.   Cover title.   On p. 1:
For private circulation.

B.C. ARCHIVES

779    Catholic Church. Liturgy
and ritual. Okanagon

I smemeies, i nkaumen i snkuenzin l okenakan
nkolkoeltens. Preces in linguam Indorum
Okenakan versae, a P. de Rouge, S. J.   [Paris, G.
Picquoin, n.d.]

44 p.   20 cm.   At head of title: A.M.D.G.

A manual of prayers, etc., in Latin and Okanagon.
The contents are outlined in Sister Maria Ilma
Raufer's *Black robes and Indians of the last frontier*
(Milwaukee, The Bruce Publishing Company, 1966),
p. 218.

B.C. ARCHIVES

780    Chicago and North-Western
Railway Company

The Pacific Northwest; some facts regarding
Oregon, Washington Territory and British
Columbia.   [n.p., 188–]

16 p.   maps (on back cover)   20 cm.   Caption
title. Front cover lacking on copy examined.

LIBRARY OF PARLIAMENT

781    Dawson, Geo[rge Mercer]
1849-1901

Glaciation of British Columbia and adjacent
regions.   [London, Trübner & Co., 1888]

[347]-350 p.   22 cm.   Cover title. Caption title:
Recent observations on the glaciation of British
Columbia . . .   Reprinted from the *Geological
magazine,* v. 5, 1888.

B.C. ARCHIVES

782    Dawson, George M[ercer]
1849-1901

Notes and observations on the Kwakiool people
of Vancouver Island.   Montreal,
Dawson Brothers, 1888.

36 p.   plate, table.   31 cm.   Cover title.
Contains: Vocabulary of about seven hundred
words of the Kwakiool language [p. 27-36] From:
The Royal Society of Canada. *Proceedings and
transactions.* ser. 1, v. 5, sec. 2, 1887.

B.C. ARCHIVES

783    Description of country . . .

Description of country tributary to the proposed
Shuswap and Okanagan Railway, Yale district,
British Columbia.   [n.p., 1888]

23 p.   fold. map.   21 cm.   On p. [3]: The
following description . . . is taken from the *Victoria
Daily Times* of December the 31st, 1887. Report of
government engineer [A. S.] Farwell: p. [17]-23.
Statement of Mr. [M.] Lumby, a pioneer farmer:
p. [10]-16.

LIBRARY OF PARLIAMENT

784    Freemasons. Vancouver. Mount
Hermon Lodge No. 7

By-laws of Mount Hermon Lodge, A.F. & A.M.,
No. 7, Grand Register, British Columbia.
Vancouver, R. Mathison, Jr., the printer, 1888.

14 p.   15 cm.

B.C. ARCHIVES

785    Great Britain. Hydrographic
Office

The British Columbia pilot; including the coast
of British Columbia, from Juan de Fuca Strait

to Portland Canal, together with Vancouver and Queen Charlotte Islands. Compiled from Admiralty surveys [and prepared by F. W. Jarrard and W. H. Sharp] London, Printed by J. D. Potter, 1888.

xiii, 586 p. fold. map., tables. 24 cm.

Second edition (3 pts.): 1898, 1899, 1903. Third edition: 1905; and supplement: 1908. Several subsequent editions. With the fourth edition the work appeared in two volumes.

B.C. ARCHIVES

786    [Ham, George Henry]
       1847-1926

The new West, extending from the Great Lakes across plain and mountain to the golden shores of the Pacific; wealth and growth; manufacturing and commercial interests; historical; statistical; biographical. Winnipeg, Canadian Historical Publishing Co., 1888.

205 p. plates (part fold.) ports., fold. maps. 27 cm.

A business directory for the larger towns on the C.P.R. line.

B.C. ARCHIVES

787    Henderson's Vancouver City
       directory . . .

Henderson's Vancouver City directory for 1888-1923; comprising a complete street and avenue directory of the city and adjoining districts, an alphabetically arranged list of business firms and companies, professional men and private citizens, and a complete classified business directory and buyer's guide. Vancouver, Henderson Directory Co.

30 v. 23 cm. annual. Title varies: 1909-10 as *Henderson's city of Vancouver and North Vancouver directory;* 1911-23 as *Henderson's greater Vancouver directory.* Subtitle varies. Superseded by *Wrigley-Henderson's British Columbia directory* (binder's title: Wrigley-Henderson's Vancouver City, Victoria City, and British Columbia directory) 1924-25; by *Wrigley's British Columbia directory,* 1926-32; and by *Wrigley's greater Vancouver and New Westminster directory,* 1932-48. Current directories published by B.C. Directories, Ltd.

B.C. ARCHIVES

788    Hulot, Étienne [Gabriel Joseph]
       BARON 1857-1918

De l'Atlantique au Pacifique à travers le Canada et le nord des États-Unis. Paris, E. Plon, Nourrit, 1888.

339 p. 2 maps. 19 cm.

One chapter relates to a Victoria visit. The author travelled by the Northern Pacific Railway.

Second edition: 1888.

NATIONAL LIBRARY

789    Keefer, Thomas C[oltrin]
       1821-1915

The Canadian Pacific Railway; address at the annual convention at Milwaukee, Wisconsin, June 28, 1888. [n.p., 1888]

[55]-88 p. illus., plates, 3 fold. maps, diagrs., tables. 24 cm. Reprinted from: American Society of Civil Engineers. *Transactions.* v. 19, August 1888.

A technical paper on the railroad's construction.

B.C. ARCHIVES

790    Kurtz, J[ohn]
       1832?-1891

Catalogue of British Columbia minerals as exhibited in specimen case at Kurtz & Co.'s cigar store, corner Government and Trounce streets, Victoria, B.C. [Second edition. Victoria, The Colonist, 1888]

22 p. 15 cm. Cover title.

B.C. ARCHIVES

791    Lees, J[ames] A[rthur]
       B. 1852

B.C., 1887; a ramble in British Columbia, by J. A. Lees and W. J. Clutterbuck. With map and 75 illustrations from sketches and photographs by the authors. London, Longmans, Green, and Co., 1888.

viii, 387 p. illus., plates, fold. map. 20 cm.

Primarily relates to the authors' travels in the East Kootenay region.

There were two issues in 1888. New edition: 1889. Also: 1892. A Norwegian translation was published under title: *Tre i Kanada, af forfatterne til "Tre i Norge"* (Kristiania, Alb. Cammermeyer, 1890).

B.C. ARCHIVES

792    Literary news . . .

Literary news: an eclectic review of current literature. Victoria, Published by the B.C. Stationery Co., 1888

65-96 p. illus. 26 cm. Cover title. Copy examined: v. 9, no. 3, March 1888. Appears to be a B.C. edition of a periodical printed in St. Paul, Minn.

Includes short literary selections, book reviews.

B.C. ARCHIVES

793    Mohun, E[dward]
       1838-1927

The sewage system of Vancouver, B.C. [Montreal, 1888]

27 p. 24 cm. Caption title: Mohun on Vancouver Sewage. From: Canadian Society of Civil Engineers. *Transactions.* 1888. v. 2, p. [243]-267.

B.C. ARCHIVES

794      Murray, W[illiam] H[enry]
H[arrison]
1840-1904

Daylight land; the experiences, incidents, and
adventures, humorous and otherwise, which
befel Judge John Doe, tourist, of San Francisco;
Mr. Cephas Pepperell, capitalist, of Boston;
Colonel Goffe, the man from New Hampshire, and
divers others, in their parlor-car excursion over
prairie and mountain, all of which I saw, and one
of whom I was. Illustrated . . . under the
supervision of J. B. Millet.     Boston, Cupples and
Hurd, 1888.

338 p.    illus., plates.    23 cm.

About one-third of the book relates to British
Columbia.

Also: London, Chatto & Windus, 1888.

B.C. ARCHIVES

795      Oppenheimer, D[avid]
1834-1897

Vancouver, its progress and industries; a record
unparalleled in the history of Canada; some facts
concerning the country surrounding and tributary
to Vancouver City and the province of British
Columbia generally.     Vancouver, Printed at the
office of the News-Advertiser, 1888.

16 p.    tables.    22 cm.    Cover title. At head of title:
Province of British Columbia.

Mainly comprised of three speeches.

B.C. ARCHIVES

796      Phillipps-Wolley, Sir Clive
[Oldnall Long]
1854-1918

A sportsman's Eden.     London, Richard Bentley
and Son, 1888.

xv, 261 p.    tables.    23 cm.

Letters describing a hunting trip in B.C.

B.C. ARCHIVES

797      [Prosch, Thomas Wickham]
1850-1915
The complete Chinook jargon or Indian trade
language of Oregon, Washington, British
Columbia, Alaska, Idaho, and other parts of the
North Pacific coast. The best yet issued.     Seattle,
G. Davies & Co., 1888.

40 p.    15 cm.    On cover: Dictionary of the Chinook
. . . Attributed in Smith to Griffith Davies.

UNIVERSITY OF WASHINGTON LIBRARY

798      Shaw, Campbell

A romance of the Rockies.     Toronto, William
Bryce [1888]

102 p.    18 cm.

In 1879 two young men, one of whom leads a small
C.P.R. survey party, meet on the British Columbia-
Alberta border.

B.C. ARCHIVES

799      [Strathcona and Mount Royal,
Donald Alexander Smith]
1ST BARON    1820-1914    PLAINTIFF

In the Supreme Court of British Columbia, on
appeal to the full court; between Donald A.
Smith and Richard B. Angus, plaintiffs and
respondents, and Samuel Greer, defendant
and appellant. Case on appeal. J. Roland Hett,
solicitor for appellant; Drake, Jackson &
Helmcken, solicitors for respondents.     Victoria,
James A. Cohen, 1888.

14 1.    28 cm.

The defendant claimed buildings on land held
in trust by the plaintiffs for the C.P.R.

B.C. ARCHIVES

800      Turner-Turner, J.

Three years' hunting and trapping in America
and the great North-west. Illustrated by
Constance Hoare.     London, Maclure & Co., 1888.

viii, 182 p.    illus., port.    28 cm.

Mostly on the author's B.C. travels, which extended
along the coast, up the Skeena River to Babine Lake,
and south through central British Columbia. Among
other places, he visited Metlahkatla, Fort George,
Alexandria, Kamloops, Vancouver, and Victoria.

B.C. ARCHIVES

801      Vancouver. Board of Trade

Act of incorporation and by-laws of the
Vancouver Board of Trade, Vancouver, B.C.,
1887; adopted and confirmed at the meetings
of 23rd and 25th November 1887.     Vancouver,
Herald Printing and Publishing Co., 1888.

42 p.    22 cm.

Also: *By-laws and act of incorporation . . .*
(Vancouver, Evans & Hastings, 1899).    31 p.

B.C. ARCHIVES

802      Vancouver city directory . . .

Vancouver city directory—1888. Compiled for
R. T. Williams by Thomas Draper, containing a

complete business and general directory of the city of Vancouver, B.C.   Victoria, Vancouver, R. T. Williams, 1888.

xx, 48 p.   23 cm.

B.C. ARCHIVES

803   Victoria Society for the Prevention of Cruelty to Animals

Constitution and by-laws . . . adopted Sept. 24th, 1888.   Victoria, H. G. Waterson, printer, 1888.

11 p.   15 cm.

B.C. ARCHIVES

804   Ballou, Maturin M[urray]
1820-1895

The new Eldorado; a summer journey to Alaska. Boston, Houghton, Mifflin and Company, 1889.

xi, 352 p.   21 cm.

Includes a brief description of the author's travels in British Columbia.

This work ran to numerous editions in the first ten years.

B.C. ARCHIVES

805   Barneby, W[illiam] Henry
1843-1914

The new far West and the old far West; being notes of a tour in North America, Japan, China, Ceylon, etc.   London, E. Stanford, 1889.

x, 316 p.   plates, fold. maps.   23 cm.

Several chapters relate to Victoria, Vancouver, and the author's travels in B.C. by the C.P.R.

B.C. ARCHIVES

806   Bates, E[mily] Katharine

Kaleidoscope; shifting scenes from East to West. London, Ward and Downey, 1889.

xii, 275 p.   23 cm.   Chapter 8: Over the Rockies by the Canadian Pacific Railway.

B.C. ARCHIVES

807   Bible. New Testament. John. Tsimshian

Am da malshk ga na damsh St. John; ligi, The Gospel according to St. John. Translated into Zimshian [by William Ridley]   London, Society for Promoting Christian Knowledge, 1889.

47 p.   18 cm.

B.C. ARCHIVES

808   Biggar, E[merson] B[ristol]
EDITOR   1853-1921

Canada; a memorial volume. General reference book of Canada, describing the Dominion at large, and its various provinces and territories; with statistics relating to its commerce and the development of its resources.   Montreal, E. B. Biggar, publisher, 1889.

[953] p.   illus., plates, maps (part. fold.) facsim. 22 cm.   In 11 separately paged sections. Section 9: British Columbia [p. 1-20]

Also published with subtitle: *General reference book of Canada* . . . (London, Stanford, 1889). [958] p.

NATIONAL LIBRARY

809   Boas, Franz
1858-1942

Notes on the Snanaimuq.   [n.p., 1889]

[321]-328 p.   Caption title. Reprinted from the *American anthropologist*, v. 2, October 1889.

B.C. ARCHIVES

810   Boas, Franz
1858-1942

Über seine Reisen in Britisch-Columbien. [Berlin, 1889]

12 p.   23 cm.   Reprinted from the *Verhandlungen der Berliner Gesellschaft für Anthropologie, Ethnologie und Urgeschichte*, Heft 6, 1889.

B.C. ARCHIVES

811   Briggs, Horace

Letters from Alaska and the Pacific coast. Buffalo [Press of E. H. Hutchinson] 1889.

87 p.   21 cm.

The author briefly describes Victoria and William Duncan's conflict with the Church Missionary Society.

B.C. ARCHIVES

812   British Columbia Fruit Growers' Association

Constitution and by-laws of the Fruit-Growers' Association of the province of British Columbia, adopted at a general meeting of the society held in Vancouver on the 1st day of February 1889. Vancouver, World Printing and Publishing Co., 1889.

10 p.   17 cm.

B.C. PROVINCIAL LIBRARY

**813**   British Columbia...

British Columbia; its resources and capabilities. Reprinted from "Canada: a memorial volume." Montreal, 1889.

20 p.   illus., table.   22 cm.   Cover title.

B.C. ARCHIVES

**814**   Canada. Department of the Interior

Regulations for the disposal of Dominion lands within the railway belt in the province of British Columbia, approved by order in council dated 17th September 1887, and amended by order in council dated 18th March 1889, under the authority of sub-section 4 of section 1, chapter 56 of the Revised statutes of Canada.   [Ottawa, 1889?]

30 p.   25 cm.

B.C. ARCHIVES

**815**   [Church, Herbert E.]
B. 1868

Making a start in Canada; letters from two young emigrants [by Herbert E. Church and Richard Church] With an introduction by Alfred J. Church.   London, Seeley & Co., 1889.

xx, 224 p.   19 cm.   Part 2: Exploring British Columbia [p. 89-135]

Part 2 depicts adventures on Vancouver and Texada Islands.

B.C. ARCHIVES

**816**   Church of England. Liturgy and ritual. Slave

Lessons and prayers in the Tenni or Slavi language of the Indians of Mackenzie River in the North-west Territory of Canada.   [London] Society for Promoting Christian Knowledge [1889]

81 p.   17 cm.

The Slave language is spoken by the Athapaskan Indians living in the extreme northeast of the province.

B.C. ARCHIVES

**817**   Cranbrook and Fort Steele Estates and Townsite Company, Limited

Prospectus of the ... Company (limited liability) Kootenay, B.C. [incorporated under the Companies Act (British Columbia) 1878.   n.p., n.d.]

4 l.   36 x 22 cm. fold. to 22 x 9 cm.

B.C. ARCHIVES

**818**   Dawson, George M[ercer]
1849-1901

Glaciation of British Columbia.   London, Trübner [1889]

[350]-352 p.   22 cm.   Cover title. Caption title: Glaciation of high points in the southern interior of British Columbia. Reprinted from the *Geological magazine,* decade 3, v. 6, no. 302.

LIBRARY OF PARLIAMENT

**819**   Dawson, George M[ercer]
1849-1901

On the earlier Cretaceous rocks of the northwestern portion of the Dominion of Canada.   [n.p., 1889]

[119]-126 p.   map, table.   24 cm.   Reprinted from the *American journal of science,* v. 38, 1889.

LIBRARY OF PARLIAMENT

**820**   Dickinson, Robert
PLAINTIFF

In the Supreme Court of British Columbia, re Ellard trusts. Case on appeal. Theodore Davie, Q.C., solicitor for applicants.   [Victoria, 1889?]

18 l.   26 cm.   Cover title. At head of text: ... on appeal to the divisional court, in the matter of the trusts of the will of James Ellard, late of the city of New Westminster, deceased, and in the matter of the Trustee Act, 1850; and between Robert Dickinson and George Turner, plaintiffs, and Mary Ellard, James Ellard [and others] defendants.

U.B.C. SPECIAL COLLECTIONS

**821**   Edwards, Sir Henry

A two months' tour in Canada and the United States in the autumn of 1889.   London, Chapman and Hall, 1889.

62 p.   20 cm.

Contains brief observations of a railroad traveller in British Columbia (p. 26-34).

B.C. ARCHIVES

**822**   Greer, Samuel

The celebrated Greer case; the subject and the crown; the government of British Columbia and the C.P. Railway Co. versus Samuel Greer; the rights of the subject in jeopardy by an unprincipled government and an ironclad monopoly.   [n.p., 1889?]

12 p.   23 cm.

Relates to a claim to 160 acres of land at English Bay which had been conveyed to Greer by deed from Indians.

B.C. ARCHIVES

**823 The Guardian Assurance Company of London**
DEFENDANTS

In the Supreme Court of British Columbia, on appeal to the full court; between the Guardian Assurance Company of London (defendants) appellants, and Stephen Jones (plaintiff) respondent. Case on appeal. Geo. Jay, Jr., solicitor for appellants; Fred. G. Walker, solicitor for respondent. Victoria, "The Colonist" Steam Printing House, 1889.

40 1. 28 cm.

B.C. ARCHIVES

**824 Hall, Alfred J[ames]**
D. 1918

A grammar of the Kwagiutl language. Montreal, Dawson Brothers, 1889.

59-105 p. 30 cm. From: Royal Society of Canada. *Proceedings and transactions*. ser. 1, v. 6, sec. 2, 1888.

B.C. ARCHIVES

**825 Harrison, Carter H[enry]**
1825-1893

A race with the sun; or, A sixteen months' tour from Chicago around the world ... New York, G. P. Putnam's Sons, 1889.

xiii, 569 p. plates. 26 cm.

Five chapters contain letters recording the impressions of a railroad tourist in British Columbia (p. 1-28).

B.C. ARCHIVES

**826 Henderson's British Columbia gazetteer ...**

Henderson's British Columbia gazetteer and directory for 1889-1910, including condensed business directories of the cities of Vancouver and Victoria and a complete classified business directory. Vancouver, Victoria, Henderson Publishing Company.

13 v. 23 cm. annual (irregular) *Henderson's Victoria City and Vancouver Island gazetteer and directory, 1910-1911,* numbered as v. 14, but gives narrower coverage. Incorporated *William's official British Columbia directory* in 1900. Superseded by *Wrigley's British Columbia directory, 1918-23;* by *Wrigley-Henderson's British Columbia directory, 1924-25;* and by *Wrigley's British Columbia directory, 1926-32,* which was incorporated into the *Sun British Columbia directory, 1934-48.* Current directories (1950+) published by B.C. Directories Ltd.

B.C. ARCHIVES

**827 Hudson's Bay Company**

Circular letter. [Winnipeg, 1889]

[4] p. 27 cm. Caption title. Signed in print: J. Wrigley, commissioner. Issued 20 June 1889.

An explanation of *Rules and regulations* (entry 752).

B.C. ARCHIVES

**828 Huleatt, Hugh**

British Columbia, Alaska, and the London Artizan colony at Moosomin, Assiniboia; seven letters. Chilworth, London, Printed by Unwin Brothers, 1889.

40 p. 13 cm.

An account of the author's visit in 1888 to fourteen families which he had helped to settle in Assiniboia four years previously through the London Artizan Colonist Society, and of his impressions of settlement opportunities, including those offered in British Columbia.

CANADIAN ARCHIVES

**829 Knights of Pythias. Comox. Comox Lodge No. 5**

Constitution and by-laws of Comox Lodge No. 5, K. of P., Comox, B.C.; instituted at Comox, British Columbia, August 25, 1888. Victoria, H. G. Waterson [1889?]

28, 23 p. 14 cm. Cover title. Has two title pages. On first p.[1]: Constitution for the government of lodges, Knights of Pythias, subordinate to and working under the Grand Lodge of Washington, adopted at Grand Lodge Session, May 22, 1885; amended May 16, 1888; promulgated August 1, 1888. Seattle, The Wm. H. Hughes Printing Company, 1888. Second t. p. same as cover. Original examined. Xerox copy in the library, University of Victoria.

UNIVERSITY OF VICTORIA LIBRARY

**830 Law Society of British Columbia**

Legal Professions Act of British Columbia, and rules. Victoria, Munroe Miller, 1889.

29 p. 23 cm. Members of the Bar and list of solicitors of British Columbia, 1889: p. 16. Rules of the Law Society ... : p. [17]-22.

Also see entries 990 and 1297.

B.C. ARCHIVES

**831 Lukens, Matilda Barns**

The inland passage; a journal of a trip to Alaska. [n.p.] 1889.

84 p. 15 cm.

Several pages relate to a description of Victoria and the B.C. coast.

B.C. ARCHIVES

**832**   [MacInnes, Donald]
SUPPOSED AUTHOR   1824-1900

Notes of our trip across British Columbia from Golden, on the Canadian Pacific Railway, to Kootenai, in Idaho, on the Northern Pacific Railway, and of our visit to the American national park, "The Yellowstone," in Wyoming, thence home via St. Paul and the new Soo line. Hamilton, Spectator Printing Company, 1889.

34 p.   illus., fold. map.   22 cm.   Cover title: A trip across British Columbia. The Public Archives of Canada attributes this work to Senator MacInnes from the evidence of a manuscript note on the title page of its copy.

B.C. ARCHIVES

**833**   McLeod, Malcolm
1821-1899

Memorial to the government and Parliament of Canada . . . for indemnity for service in initiating the Canadian Pacific Railway, &c., &c. Ottawa, Printed by A. S. Woodburn, 1889.

24 p.   22 cm.

B.C. ARCHIVES

**834**   Map and Information . . .

Map and information concerning the city and district of New Westminster and province of British Columbia.   New Westminster, Columbian Print, 1889.

col. map.   29 x 83 cm.   fold. to 19 x 11 cm.

Information on verso of map sheet.

B.C. ARCHIVES

**835**   Methodist Missionary Society

Letter from the Methodist Missionary Society to the Superintendent-General of Indian Affairs respecting British Columbia troubles. With affidavits, declarations, etc.   [Toronto, 1889]

viii, 77 p.   25 cm.

Written in criticism of the Indian Agents' attitude to the Methodist missions and of the government position with respect to Indian lands.

B.C. ARCHIVES

**836**   [Morris, W. J.]

The Winnipeg and North Pacific Railway, the great highway of the new North-west; the route and its advantages; the country and its resources. Toronto, Spectator Printing Co. [1889?]

12 p.   fold. map, fold. diagr.   25 cm.   Cover title.

A prospectus calling for a railway line from Winnipeg to the mouth of the Skeena River.

B.C. ARCHIVES

**837**   Oppenheimer, D[avid]
1834-1897

The mineral resources of British Columbia; practical hints for capitalists and intending settlers. With appendix containing the mineral laws of the province and the Dominion of Canada. Vancouver, News-Advertiser, 1889.

50 p.   22 cm.

B.C. ARCHIVES

**838**   Oppenheimer, D[avid]
COMPILER   1834-1897

Vancouver City, its progress and industries, with practical hints for capitalists and intending settlers. Vancouver, News-Advertiser, 1889.

64 p. (incl. advertisements)   tables.   22 cm. At head of title: Province of British Columbia.

CANADIAN ARCHIVES

**839**   A Rousing meeting . . .

A rousing meeting; the Victoria Theatre crowded to the doors; Hon. Mr. Davie explains his views to the electors in a clear, convincing speech that carries conviction to his auditors; the Attorney-General warmly received.   [Victoria, 1889]

8 p.   23 cm.   Caption title. Cover wanting. First appeared in the Victoria *Colonist,* 13 August 1889.

A report of an election meeting on the subject of the Canadian Western Railway.

B.C. ARCHIVES

**840**   Seton-Karr, H[eywood] W[alter]
B. 1859

Ten years' wild sports in foreign lands; or, Travels in the eighties.   London, Chapman and Hall Limited, 1889.

333 p.   22 cm.   Chapter 14: In British Columbia amongst the wild white goats of the Cascades [p. 269-309]

Chapter 14 contains an account of hunting, fishing, and canoeing.

B.C. ARCHIVES

**841**   Shannon, W[illia]m
1841-1928

British Columbia and its resources. Compiled by and printed for Messrs. [William] Shannon & [Charles] MacLachlan [real estate and financial agents] Vancouver, B.C.   London, Geo. Barber, 1889.

30 p.   fold. map.   19 cm.

B.C. ARCHIVES

**842** Shields, G[eorge] O[liver]
1846-1925

Cruising in the Cascades; a narrative of travel,
exploration, amateur photography, hunting, and
fishing, with special chapters on hunting the grizzly
bear, the buffalo, elk, antelope ...   Chicago,
Rand, McNally & Company, 1889.

339 p.   illus., port.   23 cm.

A quarter of the book is devoted to the author's
description of hunting in the Harrison Lake area. It
also describes Lillooet Indians.

Also: London, Sampson Low, Marston, Searle
& Rivington, 1889.

B.C. ARCHIVES

**843** Single tax advocate

Single tax advocate.   v. 1-?; 1889-?   New
Westminster, J. Turnbull.

v.   monthly.   v. 1, no. 10, on microfilm, examined.
First issue: April 1889.

Has local news, notes on single tax clubs, and
criticisms of socialism. The motto was: Free trade,
free land, free men.

B.C. ARCHIVES

**844** Smith, H[enry] B[adeley]

Vancouver water works.   Montreal, Printed for
the Society by John Lovell & Son, 1889.

80 p.   2 fold. plans, 3 fold. diagrs.   24 cm.
At head of title: Canadian Society of Civil Engineers.
From the Society's *Transactions,* v. 3, session 1889,
v. 4, session 1890.

U.B.C. SPECIAL COLLECTIONS

**845** Tate, C[harles] M[ontgomery]
1852-1933

Chinook as spoken by the Indians of Washington
Territory, British Columbia and Alaska; for the
use of traders, tourists and others who have
business intercourse with the Indians.
Chinook-English; English-Chinook.   Victoria,
M. W. Waitt & Co. [c1889]

47 p.   17 cm.   Caption title: Revised dictionary of
the Chinook jargon.

Also: Victoria, Printed by Thos. R. Cusack, 1914.
48 p.   Also: Victoria, Diggon's Limited, 1931. 30 p.

B.C. ARCHIVES

**846** United States. President
1885-1889   (CLEVELAND)

Message from the President of the United States
transmitting, in response to Senate resolution of
January 2, 1889, a report upon the seal fisheries
in Bering Sea.   [Washington, Government
Printing Office, 1889]

281 p.   fold. map.   23 cm.   ([United States]
50th Cong., 2d sess. Senate. Ex. doc. no. 106)

Correspondence relating to the right of fishing, taking
seals, and navigation in the waters of the Bering Sea,
which includes Canadian communications regarding
the seizure of sealing vessels.

DEPARTMENT OF FISHERIES LIBRARY, OTTAWA

**847** United States. Department of State

Message from the President of the United States,
transmitting report on the boundary line between
Alaska and British Columbia.   Washington,
Government Printing Office, 1889.

40 p.   9 fold. maps.   23 cm.   ([United States]
50th Cong., 2d sess. Senate. Ex. doc. no. 146)
Cover title.

Includes the accounts of conferences between
William Healey Dall of the U.S. Geological Survey
and George M. Dawson.

B.C. ARCHIVES

**848** Vancouver. Board of Trade

Report.   1st+ 1889+   Vancouver.

v.   illus., plates, maps.   23 cm.   annual.   Various
printers. Probably not published separately 1893-96;
not published separately 1918-47. Also appeared in
the Vancouver daily newspapers before 1900.

Contains lists of members, summaries of bank
clearings, mineral production, business failures,
descriptions of the northern interior and agriculture,
shipping reports, summaries of city land values, and
lists of churches and hospitals.

B.C. PROVINCIAL LIBRARY

**849** Vancouver Art Association

Constitution, rules, and list of members of
the Vancouver Art Association, established,
January 18, 1889.   Vancouver [1889?]

7 p.   22 cm.

B.C. ARCHIVES

**850** Vancouver Cricket Club

Constitution and rules.   Vancouver, 1889.

7 p.   13 cm.   Not found for examination.

B.C. ARCHIVES

**851** Wilson, W[illia]m

A mining case of importance, Wilson v. Whitten;
judgments thereon criticized by the plaintiff.
Victoria, "The Colonist" Steam Printing House,
1889.

32 p.   22 cm.   Cover title.

B.C. ARCHIVES

852     Withrow, W[illiam] H[enry]
1839-1908

Our own country, Canada, scenic and descriptive; being an account of the extent, resources, physical aspect, industries, cities and chief towns of the provinces of Nova Scotia, Prince Edward Island, Newfoundland, New Brunswick, Quebec, Ontario, Manitoba, the North-west Territory, and British Columbia; with sketches of travel and adventure.   Toronto, William Briggs, 1889.

606 p.   illus., plates, ports., diagr., plan.   24 cm.

B.C. ARCHIVES

853     Woodman, Abby (Johnson)
B. 1828

Picturesque Alaska; a journal of a tour among the mountains, seas and islands of the Northwest, from San Francisco to Sitka.   Boston, New York, Houghton, Mifflin and Company, 1889.

212 p.   plates, double map.   19 cm.

A section on Victoria and B.C. coastal waters.

U.B.C. SPECIAL COLLECTIONS

854     Blaikie, W[illiam] G[arden]
1820-1899

Summer suns in the far West; a holiday trip to the Pacific slope.   London, Thomas Nelson and Sons, 1890.

160 p.   plate (fold.)   19 cm.

One chapter relates to British Columbia.

B.C. ARCHIVES

855     Boas, Franz
1858-1942

The use of masks and the head-ornaments on the north-west coast of America.   [n.p., 1890]

9 p.   2 plates (1 col.)   33 cm.   Reprinted from *Internationales Archiv für Ethnographie,* v. 3, 1890, p. 7-15.

B.C. ARCHIVES

856     The British colonist . . .

The British colonist in North America; a guide for intending emigrants.   London, Swan Sonnenschein & Co., 1890.

320 p.   2 fold. maps.   19 cm.

The first chapter describes conditions in British Columbia.

B.C. ARCHIVES

857     British Columbia . . .

British Columbia and Alaska Indian bazaar. Victoria, Victoria Loan and Security Co., Ltd. [n.d.]

[8] p. (incl. cover)   illus. (on cover)   14 cm. Cover title.

Tourist brochure. The Indian display was assembled by F. Landsberg.

B.C. ARCHIVES

858     British Columbia Fruit Growers' Association

List of premiums offered by the Fruit Growers' Association of the province of British Columbia; open to the whole province; exhibition to be held in the city of New Westminster, on the 6th and 7th August 1890 . . .   Vancouver, News-Advertiser, 1890.

9 p.   22 cm.

B.C. PROVINCIAL LIBRARY

859     British Columbia Fruit Growers' Association

Report.   1st—40th; 1890-1945.   Vancouver, News-Advertiser; Victoria, Queen's printer.

40 v.   illus., plates.   21-26 cm.   annual (irregular) Title varies: 2d — 6th, Report of the Horticultural Society and Fruit Growers' Association; 7th to ?, Report of the British Columbia Fruit Growers' and Horticultural Society. The 7th report covers period May 1895 — August 1897. If not found separately, reports may be located in the British Columbia *Sessional papers.*

B.C. PROVINCIAL LIBRARY

860     Butterworth, Hezekiah
1839-1905

Zigzag journeys in the great Northwest; or, A trip to the American Switzerland.   Boston, Dana Estes and Company [c1890]

319 p.   illus., plate, ports.   22 cm.

Designed for the young reader. About one-third of the book is concerned with British Columbia.

B.C. ARCHIVES

861     Canada. Department of the Interior

Regulations for the survey, administration, disposal and management of the Dominion lands within the forty-mile railway belt in the province of British Columbia, 1890.   Ottawa, 1890.

21 p.   25 cm.   Not seen.

QUEEN'S UNIVERSITY LIBRARY

**862　Catholic Church. Catechisms. Athapaska**

[Lœkateshisyaz keiskœz.　Stuart's Lake Mission, 1890]

18 p.　Not seen.　From Pilling's *Athapascan languages*, p. 66. Translation of title: The little catechism. The work of Adrian Gabriel Morice.

PILLING'S ATHAPASCAN BIBLIOGRAPHY

**863　Catholic Church. Liturgy and ritual. Athapasca**

Preces post privatam missam recitandæ [Stuart's Lake Mission, 1890]

sheet.　Not seen.　From Pilling's *Athapascan languages*, p. 66. The work of Adrian Gabriel Morice.

Described by Pilling as "A prayer in the Déné language, syllabic characters, followed by a prayer in Latin, roman characters."

PILLING'S ATHAPASCAN BIBLIOGRAPHY

**864　Catholic Church. Liturgy and ritual. Latin**

Latin manual.　[Kamloops, 189-]

16 p.　19 cm.　Caption title. Mimeographed. Latin transcribed into Duployan shorthand. The work of Jean-Marie Raphael Le Jeune.

B.C. ARCHIVES

**865　Church of England. Book of Common Prayer. Selections. Niska**

A Nish'ga version of portions of the Book of Common Prayer. Translated by J. B. McCullagh. London, Society for Promoting Christian Knowledge [1890]

79, 14 p.　17 cm.　Text in the Niska dialect of the Tsimshian language. Includes hymns.

B.C. ARCHIVES

**866　Church of England. Book of Common Prayer. Selections. Tsimshian**

A Zimshian version of portions of the Book of Common Prayer.　London, Society for Promoting Christian Knowledge [n.d.]

35 p.　17 cm.　The translator was probably William Ridley.

B.C. ARCHIVES

**867　Church of England. Liturgy and ritual**

Office to be used in laying the corner-stone of a church.　[Victoria?] 1890.

8 p. (incl. cover)　17 cm.　Cover title.

B.C. ARCHIVES

**868　Collis, Septima Maria (Levy)**
1842-1917

A woman's trip to Alaska; being an account of a voyage through the inland seas of the Sitkan archipelago in 1890. Illustrated by American Bank Note Co., New York.　New York, Cassell Publishing Company [c1890]

[14], 194 p.　illus., fold. plate, ports., map.　22 cm.

Mentions Vancouver, Victoria, and B.C. Indians.

CANADIAN ARCHIVES

**869　Cridge, E[dward]**
BISHOP　1817-1913

To the congregation of the Church of Our Lord, Victoria, B.C.　[Victoria, 1890]

[2] 1. (folder)　28 cm.　Caption title.

A letter telling of the appointment of an assistant clergyman.

B.C. ARCHIVES

**870　Dawson, George M[ercer]**
1849-1901

Notes on the Cretaceous of the British Columbian region; the Nanaimo group.　[n.p., 1890]

[179]-183 p.　21 cm.　Reprinted from the *American journal of science*, v. 39, 1890.

LIBRARY OF PARLIAMENT

**871　Dawson, George M[ercer]**
1849-1901

On the glaciation of the northern part of the Cordillera, with an attempt to correlate the events of the glacial period in the Cordillera and Great Plains.　[n.p., 1890]

[153]-162. p.　21 cm.　Cover title. On p. [153]: This article may be considered as a partial abstract of a paper read by the author before the Royal Society of Canada, May 29th, 1890.　Reprinted from the *American geologist*, September 1890.

LIBRARY OF PARLIAMENT

**872　Dawson, George M[ercer]**
1849-1901

On the later physiographical geology of the Rocky Mountain region in Canada, with special reference to changes in elevation and the history of the glacial period. [Montreal, 1890]

3-74 p. 30 cm. Cover title. From: Royal Society of Canada. *Proceedings and transactions.* ser. 1, v. 8, sec. 4, 1890.

B.C. ARCHIVES

873     Finck, Henry T[heophilus]
1854-1926

The Pacific coast scenic tour; from southern California to Alaska, the Canadian Pacific Railway, Yellowstone Park and the Grand Canyon. New York, Charles Scribner's Sons, 1890.

xiv, 309 p. plates, map. 21 cm.

One chapter includes a description of the author's railway journey through British Columbia.

Also: New York, Scribner's, 1891. Also: London, Low, Marston, Searle & Rivington, 1891. Also: New York, Scribner's, 1907.

B.C. ARCHIVES

874     Fleming, Sir Sandford
1827-1915

Presidential address before the Royal Society of Canada, with papers from the Transactions. Vol. 7, section II: Expeditions to the Pacific. Vol. 7, section III: A problem in political science. Montreal, Dawson Brothers, 1890.

1-11, 90-141, 33-40 p. fold. map. 31 cm. Cover title. Contents: Address to the President. — Expeditions to the Pacific ... — A problem in political science.

The section entitled "Expeditions to the Pacific ..." gives a valuable review of journeys to the Pacific through what is now Canadian territory. It includes coverage of railway surveys and of expeditions made in connection with the Canadian Geological Survey.

U.B.C. SPECIAL COLLECTIONS

875     Gosnell, R. E[dward]
1860-1931

British Columbia; a digest of reliable information regarding its natural resources and industrial possibilities. Vancouver, News-Advertiser, Printing and Publishing Company, 1890.

47 p. 20 cm. Cover title.

B.C. ARCHIVES

876     Great Britain. Foreign Office

Correspondence respecting the Behring Sea seal fisheries, 1886-90. Presented to both Houses of Parliament by command of Her Majesty, August 1890. London, Printed by Harrison and Sons [1890]

xiii, 532 p. 34 cm. ([Great Britain. Parliament. Command papers] C. 6131) At head of title: United States, no. 2 (1890)

B.C. ARCHIVES

877     Great Britain. Foreign Office

Correspondence respecting the seizure of the British schooner "Araunah," off Copper Island, by the Russian authorities. Presented to the House of Commons by command of Her Majesty, in pursuance of their address dated May 13, 1890. London, Printed by Harrison and Sons [1890]

25 p. diagr. 34 cm. ([Great Britain. Parliament. Command papers] C. 6041) At head of title: Russia, no. 1 (1890)

Relates to the Bering Sea controversy. The "Araunah" was a Victoria-based sealing schooner.

B.C. ARCHIVES

878     Green, William Spotswood
1847-1919

Among the Selkirk glaciers; being the account of a rough survey in the Rocky Mountain regions of British Columbia. London, New York, Macmillan, 1890.

xv, 251 p. plates, fold. map. 20 cm.

B.C. ARCHIVES

879     Hale, Horatio [Emmons]
1817-1896

An international idiom; a manual of the Oregon trade language, or "Chinook jargon." London, Whittaker & Co., 1890.

63 p. 19 cm. Errata slip.

B.C. ARCHIVES

880     Henderson's Victoria directory

Henderson's Victoria directory 1890-1921. Victoria, Henderson Directory Co.

22 v. 24 cm. annual (irregular) Title varies: 1905/1906, 1908, as *Henderson's city of Victoria and suburban directory;* 1912-15 as *Henderson's greater Victoria directory and Vancouver Island gazetteer;* 1917-21 as *Henderson's greater Victoria city directory.* Superseded by *Wrigley-Henderson Victoria street and avenue directory,* 1924-32, and by *Wrigley's greater Victoria directory,* 1933/34-1949, published by Sun Directories Ltd. Current directories (1950+) published by B.C. Directories Ltd. Subtitles vary.

B.C. ARCHIVES

**881    Hymns in the Tenni . . .**

Hymns in the Tenni or Slavi language of the Indians of Mackenzie River, in the North-west Territory of Canada.   London, Society for Promoting Christian Knowledge [189-?]

118 p.   Not seen.

Possibly by Rev. W. D. Reeve or Bishop Bompas. See Pilling's *Athapascan languages*, p. 42.

**882    James Bay Athletic Association, Limited**

Constitution, by-laws, and rules of the James Bay Athletic Association, l'd, Victoria, B.C., incorporated January 21, 1890; adopted March 4th, 1890.   [Victoria] Munroe Miller [1890?]

13, ii p.   13 cm.

Also: Victoria, Munroe Miller, 1892. 22 p.   Also: Victoria, The Colonist Printing & Publishing Co., 1903. 46 p.

**883    Jennings, D[ennis]**

Manners and customs of the Indians of Simpson district, B.C.   [Toronto, Woman's Missionary Society of the Methodist Church, n.d.]

15 p.   13 cm.   (Our work)   Caption title.

**884    Kerr, J[ohn] B[laine]**

Biographical dictionary of well-known British Columbians; with a historical sketch. Vancouver, Kerr & Begg, 1890.

xxx, 326 p.   42 ports.   23 cm.

**885    MacManus, Robert H.**
1840-1897

The tourists' pictorial guide and hand book to British Columbia, and the shores of the northern Pacific waters.   Victoria, "The Tourists' Pictorial Guide" Publishing Co., 1890.

48 p.   18 cm.   Stamped on cover of copy examined: Un-revised copy; Part I & II.

**886    Medical directory**

Medical directory.   1890+   New Westminster, Victoria, Vancouver, College of Physicians and Surgeons.

v.   22, 25 cm.   annual (irregular)   Cover title. Various printers. Title varies: 1890-1922 as *British Columbia medical register*; 1923-51 as *Medical register of British Columbia*. Minutes of council and executive meetings and auditor's reports included in 1909/10, 1916/17, 1923-33, 1936/37, 1940-43, 1946. On cover 1891-96, 1916/17: Medical Council, British Columbia.

**887    Miners' Association of British Columbia. Revelstoke Camp**

Constitution and by-laws.   [Revelstoke, 1890]

6 p.   14 cm.   Cover title.

**888    Morice, A[drian] G[abriel]**
1859-1938

A new improved and easy alphabet or syllabary, suggested to the "Cherokee nation" by a friend and earnest sympathizer.   [Stuart's Lake Mission, 1890]

sheet.   24 x 16 cm.   (Stuart's Lake Mission print, no. 9)   Not seen. From Pilling's *Athapascan languages*, p. 66.

**889    Morice, Adrian Gabriel**
1859-1938

The new methodical, easy and complete Déné syllabary.   Stuart's Lake Mission, 1890.

3 p.   Not seen. From Morice's *Dans le champ des lettres canadiennes*, p. 107, where it is described as: La toute première apparition des caractères syllabique du P. Morice.

Reprinted in Pilling's *Athapascan languages*, p. 67-69.

**890    Morice, Adrian Gabriel**
1859-1938

[Pe tœstlœs oetsôtœléh.   Stuart's Lake Mission, 1890]

32 p.   Text in Déné syllabic characters.   Not seen. From Pilling's *Athapascan languages*, p. 66. In Morice's *Dans le champ des lettres canadiennes*, p. 107, the title is given as: *Pê test' les et' sôtel-éh*.

Pilling described this book as "a sort of primer containing spelling and elementary reading lessons." According to the Preface of the second edition, which was published under title *Carrier reading-book* (entry 1124), this was the first book printed in the Déné syllabary (as distinct from the first appearance of the syllabary in explanatory form, which is listed as entry 888).

891 New Westminster and Burrard Inlet Telephone Company, Limited

General instructions, tariff of charges, terms of conditions of lease of instruments; exchange lists. [New Westminster] Mathison, the printer, April 1890.

29 p.   17 cm.   Cover title.

B.C. ARCHIVES

892 North Pacific almanac . . .

North Pacific almanac and statistical handbook for 1890, containing valuable information about Oregon, Washington, Idaho, Alaska, and British Columbia. First edition.   Portland, Oregon, North Pacific Publishing Co., 1890.

224 p.   tables.   22 cm.   At head of title: Annual. British Columbia: p. 188-198.

OREGON HISTORICAL SOCIETY

893 Phillipps-Wolley, [Sir] C[live Oldnall Long]
1854-1918

Snap, a legend of the Lone Mountain. With thirteen illustrations by H. G. Willink.   London, Longmans, Green, and Co., 1890.

x, 310 p.   illus., plates.   19 cm.

Juvenile fiction. The daily life of two English boys who come to a ranch in the Thompson River area at the end of the Nineteenth Century.

New impression: New York, Longmans, Green, and Co., 1899.

B.C. ARCHIVES

894 Pierce, J. H.

Thirteen years of travel and exploration in Alaska. Edited by Prof. and Mrs. J. H. Carruth. Lawrence, Kansas, Journal Publishing Company, 1890.

224 p.   illus.   19 cm.

In two chapters, the author briefly describes his activities at the Cassiar gold mines and a sled trip up the Stikine River.

B.C. ARCHIVES

895 Procter, W. C.
EDITOR

Round the globe, through greater Britain. London, Wm. Isbister [189-]

384 p.   illus.   19 cm.   Our railway to the Pacific, by the Marquis of Lorne [p. 65-116]

Has a brief description of the C.P.R.'s route in British Columbia.

NATIONAL LIBRARY

896 Roberts, Morley
1857-1942

The prey of the strongest.   London, Hurst and Blackett [n.d.]

335 p.   21 cm.

"I offer you this, which . . . takes for its subjects a Sawmill and the life we lived who worked in one on the lower Fraser . . ." — pref.

Also: 1906. viii, 325 p.

B.C. ARCHIVES

897 Sessions, Francis C[harles]
1820-1892

From Yellowstone Park to Alaska. Illustrated by C. H. Warren.   New York, Welch, Fracker Company, 1890.

186, ix p.   plates.   20 cm.

Contains some information on the missionary work of William Duncan.

B.C. ARCHIVES

898 Shields, G[eorge] O[liver]
EDITOR   1846-1925

The big game of North America; its habits, habitat, haunts, and characteristics; how, when, and where to hunt it, by Judge John Dean Caton [and others]   London, Sampson Low, Marston, Searle, & Rivington, 1890.

581 p.   illus., plates.   24 cm.

In part descriptive of big game found in British Columbia, including the grizzly bear, Rocky Mountain goat, Rocky Mountain sheep, and the black bear.

Also: Chicago, New York, Rand McNally, 1890.

B.C. ARCHIVES

899 [Somerset, Susan Margaret (McKinnon)] Saint Maur
DUCHESS OF

Impression of a tenderfoot during a journey in search of sport in the far West, by Mrs. Algernon St. Maur.   London, John Murray, 1890.

xv, 279 p.   illus., plates, fold. map.   22 cm.

Over half the book is devoted to describing the author's travels in British Columbia.

B.C. ARCHIVES

900 United States. Department of State

Seal fisheries of Behring Sea. Message from the President of the United States transmitting a letter from the Secretary of State, with accompanying papers, touching the subjects in dispute between the government of the United

States and the government of Great Britain in the Behring Sea, including all communications since March 4, 1889. Washington, Government Printing Office, 1890.

96 p. fold. map. 23 cm. ([United States] 51st Cong., 1st sess. House. Ex. doc. no. 450)

B.C. ARCHIVES

## 901 Verne, Jules
1828-1905

Caesar Cascabel. Translated from the French by A. Estoclet. Illustrated by George Roux. New York, Cassell Publishing Company [1890]

iv, 373 p. 80 plates. 22 cm.

Fiction. The first eight chapters describe the 1867 caravan journey of an itinerant showman and his family from California through the interior of British Columbia to Alaska. Hatred for anything British is evident in the travellers' desire to hurry through the British possession to reach Russian territory.

B.C. ARCHIVES

## 902 Victoria. Public Library

Catalogue of books in the Free Public Library of Victoria City. Victoria, H. G. Waterson, 1890.

168 p. 17 cm.

Also: Victoria, Province Publishing Co., 1897. 213 p.

B.C. PROVINCIAL LIBRARY

## 903 Victoria and Esquimalt Telephone Company, Limited

List of subscribers, issued 1st July 1890. [Victoria, 1890]

sheet. 20 x 14 cm. Mounted on board.

B.C. ARCHIVES

## 904 Victoria tramway . . .

Victoria tramway, railway and steamboat guide. Victoria, Jas. A. Cohen, 1890.

12 p. (incl. advertisements) 17 cm. Cover title. On cover: Revised monthly.

B.C. ARCHIVES

## 905 Wade, Mark S[weeten]
1858-1929

Notes on medical legislation in British Columbia. [Victoria, 1890]

14 p. 24 cm. Cover title.

A plea for new and revised medical legislation.

B.C. ARCHIVES

## 906 Webb, William Seward
1851-1926

California and Alaska, and over the Canadian Pacific Railway. New York, G. P. Putnam's Sons, 1890.

190 p. illus., 92 plates. 23 cm.

Contains two chapters on the railway route in B.C.

Popular edition: 1891. xiv, 268 p. illus., 11 plates.

B.C. ARCHIVES

## 907 Western world

Western world. v. 1-5, no. 58? March 1890-[1894?] Winnipeg, Vancouver, Acton Burrows.

5 v. illus. 34 cm. monthly.

Includes notes and descriptions of B.C. towns, industries and scenes in the 1890's.

B.C. ARCHIVES

## 908 Williams' Vancouver & New Westminster . . . directory

Williams' Vancouver & New Westminster cities directory, 1890; containing general provincial information. Compiled for R. T. Williams, publisher, by Thomas Draper. Vancouver, Trythall, City Printing Works, 1890.

310 p. 22 cm.

B.C. ARCHIVES

## 909 Williams' Victoria . . .

Williams' Victoria and Nanaimo cities directory, 1890; containing general provincial information, with a classified business directory. Compiled for R. T. Williams, publisher, by Thomas Draper. Victoria, "The Colonist" Steam Printing House, 1890.

328 p. 23 cm.

Has some information on agricultural associations, building societies, boards of trade, dominion and provincial cabinets, registered companies, land laws, foreign consuls, mayors, government agents, courts, clubs, and libraries.

B.C. ARCHIVES

## 910 Adams, Frank D[awson]
1859-1942

On some granites from British Columbia and the adjacent parts of Alaska and the Yukon district. [n.p., 1891]

[343]-358 p. 2 diagrs. 22 cm. Cover title. Reprinted from the *Canadian record of science*, September 1891.

NATIONAL LIBRARY

911    The Association of Provincial Land Surveyors of British Columbia

Constitution and by-laws; list of members. [n.p., 1891]

17 p.    16 cm.

B.C. ARCHIVES

912    Bible. New Testament. Matthew. Haida

Saint Matthew gie giatlan las. St. Matthew, Haida. [Translated by the Rev. Charles Harrison] London, British and Foreign Bible Society, 1891.

143 p.    16 cm.

B.C. ARCHIVES

913    Boas, Franz
1858-1942

Physical characteristics of the Indians of the North Pacific coast.    [Washington, 1891]

[24]-32 p.    25 cm.    Caption title. Reprinted from the *American anthropologist*, v. 4, 1891.

B.C. ARCHIVES

914    British Columbia Agricultural Association (Victoria)

British Columbia Agricultural Association; review of its history; what it has accomplished; the new grounds and Crystal Palace.    Victoria, 1891.

sheet (2 p.)    illus. (on p. 2)    48 x 59 cm.

B.C. ARCHIVES

915    British Columbia . . .

British Columbia as a field for emigration and investment.    Victoria, Printed by Richard Wolfenden, 1891.

60 p.    tables.    21 cm.    Not found in Holmes.

B.C. ARCHIVES

916    British Columbia commercial journal

British Columbia commercial journal.    v. 1-4; 17 March 1891—12 March 1895.    Victoria.

4 v.    weekly.    No more published? No index. On microfilm.

Includes statistics for agriculture, fisheries, mining, and imports and exports; comments on trade, notices of appointments, legislation, shipping, etc.

B.C. ARCHIVES

917    Burall, W. T.

A trip to the far west of British Columbia; a 13,000 miles tour [through the mountains, over the prairies, and across the rivers of Canada] Wisbech, William Earl [1891]

26 p.    illus.    22 cm.    Includes: A five weeks' stay at Vancouver [p. 15-19]

B.C. ARCHIVES

918    Canada

Correspondence relative to the seizure of British American vessels in Behrings Sea by the United States authorities in 1886-91.    Ottawa, Brown Chamberlain, 1891.

xxxv, 498 p.    26 cm.    Not seen.

NATIONAL LIBRARY

919    Canada. Department of Agriculture

The visit of the tenant-farmer delegates to Canada in 1890. The reports of Mr. George Brown [and others] on the agricultural resources of Canada: Prince Edward Island, Nova Scotia, New Brunswick, Quebec, Ontario, Manitoba, the North-west Territories, and British Columbia. Published by authority of the government of Canada (Department of Agriculture)    [London, McCorquodale, 1891]

262 p.    illus., plate, fold. map.    22 cm.    On cover: Canada in 1890; the reports of the tenant farmers' delegates.

Contains the reports of eleven men connected with agriculture in the United Kingdom. The reports describe the agricultural resources in Canada and the advantages the country offers for the settlement of farmers, farm labourers, and others of the working class. Each report deals with the various provinces visited by the particular delegate.

The Preface states that the reports were also issued in four parts for general circulation. Parts 1 and 2 were intended for distribution in England; Part 3 in Scotland, and Part 4 in Ireland. Part 1 contains the reports of William Edwards, G. Hutchinson, William Scotson, and J. T. Wood; Part 2, those of Arthur Daniel, Francis Fane, Robert Pitt, and H. Simmons; Part 3, those of George Brown, and John Speir; and Part 4, those of Major Stevenson, and George Brown. A small number of Major Stevenson's reports were printed in a separate pamphlet numbered "IV A."

The Canadian edition was published under title: *Tenant-farmer delegates' visit to Canada in 1890 . . .* (Ottawa, Printed by S. E. Dawson, 1892). In 230 pages.

CANADIAN ARCHIVES

**920**  Canada. Parliament. House of Commons. Select Standing Committee on Privileges and Elections

Reports . . . relative to certain statements and charges made in connection with the tenders and contracts respecting the Quebec harbour works and the Esquimalt graving dock (referred on the 11th May 1891) also relative to the resignation of Honourable Thomas McGreevy (referred on the 19th August 1891) With minutes of proceedings and evidence attached.   Ottawa, Brown Chamberlin, 1891.

cxv (i.e. 226), vi, 1359 p.   plans.   25 cm.   Pages ivA-ivNN, lxxxiiA-lxxxiiSS inserted.

NATIONAL LIBRARY

**921**  The Canadian guide-book

The Canadian guide-book . . . A guide to eastern Canada and Newfoundland . . . by Charles G. D. Roberts . . . and western Canada to Vancouver's Island . . .   New York, D. Appleton & Company, 1891-1919.

v.   illus., plates, maps (part fold.) fold. plans.   18 cm.   Binder's title: Appleton's Canadian guide books. Title varies: 1891, *The Canadian guide-book; the tourist's and sportsman's guide to eastern Canada and Newfoundland . . .*; 1892-94, *The Canadian guide-book; pt. 1, Eastern Canada . . .* by Charles G. D. Roberts; pt. 2, *Western Canada . . .* by Ernest Ingersoll . . .   Only 1892 edition, pt. 2, examined.

The 1892 edition, Part 2, has about one hundred pages on British Columbia.

U.B.C. SPECIAL COLLECTIONS

**922**  Catholic Church. Catechisms. Carrier

Le petit catéchisme à l'usage des sauvages Porteurs; texte & traduction avec notes suivi des prières du matin et du soir.   Mission du Lac Stuart, 1891.

144 p.   16 cm.   (Typographie de la Mission du Lac Stuart, no. 10)   Text in Carrier and French, usually on facing pages. The work of Adrian Gabriel Morice.

B.C. ARCHIVES

**923**  Catholic Church. Liturgy and ritual

Chinook hymns.   Kamloops, 1891.

[32] p.   11 cm.   Cover title. Mimeographed. Chinook jargon in Duployan shorthand. Translated and transcribed by Jean-Marie Raphael Le Jeune. Not seen.

Fourth edition: 1893. 16 p.   Sixth edition: 1895. 16 p.

LIBRARY OF CONGRESS

**924**  Catholic Church. Liturgy and ritual. Stalo

Prayers in Stalo, by Rt. Rev. Bishop Durieu. [Kamloops, 1891]

16 p.   19 cm.   Caption title.   Not seen.

"Transcribed into Stalo by Father Le Jeune . . . who reproduced it by aid of the mimeograph." — Pilling's *Salishan languages*, p. 16.

LIBRARY OF CONGRESS

**925**  Church of England. Book of Common Prayer. Selections. Kwakiutl

A Kwagūl version of portions of the Book of Common Prayer. [Translated by Alfred James Hall] London, Society for Promoting Christian Knowledge [1891]

62 p.   17 cm.

B.C. ARCHIVES

**926**  [Coombs, Samuel F.]

Dictionary of the Chinook jargon as spoken on Puget Sound and the Northwest, with original Indian names for prominent places and localities with their meanings; historical sketch, etc. Seattle, Wash., Loman & Hanford Stationery & Printing Co. [1891]

38 p.   15 cm.   Cover title: Chinook dictionary and original Indian names of western Washington. James Pilling in *Chinookan languages* attributes this work to S. F. Coones.

B.C. ARCHIVES

**927**  Dawson, George M[ercer]
1849-1901

Note on the geological structure of the Selkirk Range.   Rochester, Published by the Society, 1891.

165-176 p.   diagr., table.   26 cm.   Reprinted from: Geological Society of America. *Bulletin.* v. 2, 1891.

LIBRARY OF PARLIAMENT

**928**  Dawson, G[eorge Mercer]
1849-1901

Notes on the Shuswap people of British Columbia. [Montreal, 1891]

3-44 p.   illus., map.   30 cm.   Cover title.   List of two hundred and twenty place names in the Shuswap country, British Columbia: p. 40-44. From: Royal Society of Canada. *Proceedings and transactions.* ser. 1, v. 9, sec. 2, 1891.

U.B.C. SPECIAL COLLECTIONS

**929    Dufferin and Ava, [Hariot Georgina (Hamilton) Hamilton-Temple-Blackwood]**
MARCHIONESS OF   D. 1936

My Canadian journal, 1872-8; extracts from my letters home, written while Lord Dufferin was Governor-General. With illustrations from sketches by Lord Dufferin, portraits and map. London, John Murray, 1891.

18, 422 p.   illus., plates, 2 ports., fold. map.   23 cm.

Includes an account of the 1876 visit to the Pacific coast.

Also: New York, D. Appleton and Company, 1891. xvi, 451 p.

B.C. ARCHIVES


**930    Finlayson, Roderick**
1818-1892

Biography.   [Victoria? 1891]

27 p.   22 cm.

A summary of the author's years with the Hudson's Bay Company. In 1843 he accompanied James Douglas to found Fort Victoria and remained at the Fort as second-in-command to Charles Ross. When Ross died in 1844, Finlayson became the senior officer until the return of Douglas in 1849. Finlayson remained with the Hudson's Bay Company until his retirement in 1872. He was active in public affairs during his service with the company and afterwards.

Reprinted in the *Washington historian*, v. 2, 1900, p. 29-33, 70-84.

B.C. ARCHIVES


**931    First British Columbia Society of Spiritualists**

By-laws of the First British Columbia Society of Spiritualists of Victoria, B.C.   Victoria, Jas. A. Cohen, printer, 1891.

9 p.   16 cm.   Original examined. Xerox copy in the library, University of Victoria.

UNIVERSITY OF VICTORIA LIBRARY


**932    Forester, Harry**

Ocean jottings from England to British Columbia; being the record of a voyage from Liverpool to Vancouver's Island via the Straits of Magellan [in] the steamship "West Indian," and embracing scenes and incidents of the Chilean Revolution (1891)   Vancouver, Printed by the Telegram Printing and Publishing Co., 1891.

111 p.   22 cm.

B.C. ARCHIVES


**933    Foursin, Pierre**

La colonisation française au Canada; Manitoba, Territoires du Nord-ouest, Colombie Anglaise. Imprimé par ordre du Parlement.   Ottawa, Imprimé par Brown Chamberlain, 1891.

45 p.   illus.   27 cm.

The author, a Frenchman, joined the delegation of farmers which toured Canada in 1890 by the invitation of Sir Charles Tupper.

SHORTT COLLECTION


**934    [Gosnell, R. Edward]**
1860-1931

Land of the Okanagan, British Columbia. [Vancouver, Okanagan Land and Development Co., 1891]

48 p.   illus.   22 cm.   Cover title. Colophon: Vancouver, Daily Telegram Print. Author's name is from a manuscript note on a copy examined in the Public Archives of Canada.

B.C. ARCHIVES


**935    Great Britain. Foreign Office**

Further correspondence respecting the Behring Sea seal fisheries. (In continuation of "United States no. 1 (1891)" C. 6253) Presented to both Houses of Parliament by command of Her Majesty, June 1891.   London, Printed by Harrison and Sons [1891]

61 p.   34 cm.   ([Great Britain. Parliament. Command papers] C. 6368) At head of title: United States, no. 2 (1891)

B.C. ARCHIVES


**936    Great Britain. Foreign Office**

Further correspondence respecting the Behring Sea seal fisheries. Presented to both Houses of Parliament by command of Her Majesty, March 1891.   London, Printed by Harrison and Sons [1891]

92 p.   34 cm.   ([Great Britain. Parliament. Command papers] C. 6253) At head of title: United States, no. 1 (1891)

B.C. ARCHIVES


**937    Headland, Emily**

Brief sketches of C.M.S. missions, designed to provide material for missionary addresses. With a preface by Eugene Stock. Part III.   London, James Nisbet & Co., 1891.

201 p.   fold. map.   18 cm.   Errata slip.

One chapter on the Church Missionary Society's North Pacific missions.

B.C. ARCHIVES

**938 Kamloops Wawa**

Kamloops Wawa. no. 1-507; 2 May 1891—
April 1923. Kamloops, St. Louis Mission.

9 v. in 6. 18, 21 cm. irregular: monthly, 1891;
weekly, 1892-93; monthly, 1894-1900; quarterly,
1901-1904. Publication stopped in 1904, but special
issues appeared from time to time. Largely
mimeographed. Text mainly in Duployan shorthand,
a transcription of Chinook jargon and various Indian
languages. Later issues have some French and English
text.

A periodical, the work of Jean-Marie Raphael
Le Jeune, giving religious readings, news, etc.
In September 1894 the paper was printed by
photoengraving at 2,000 copies per month. Until 1898
it enjoyed increasing popularity, reaching a monthly
circulation of 3,000 copies.

B.C. ARCHIVES

**939 [Le Jeune, Jean-Marie Raphael]**
1855-1930

Elements of shorthand. Part I. Kamloops, 1891.

[32] p. (plus cover) 11 cm. Cover title.
Mimeographed. Duployan shorthand with phonetic
equivalents in italics. Bound in the University of
Washington Library in *Kamloops miscellany*, v. 1.

For second edition see entry 1119.

UNIVERSITY OF WASHINGTON LIBRARY

**940 [Le Jeune, Jean-Marie Raphael]**
1855-1930

[Shorthand primer for the . . . language.
Kamloops, n.d.]

[4] p. 19 cm. Mimeographed. Bound in the
University of Washington Library in *Kamloops
miscellany*, v. 2, as part of "Shushwap manual." It is,
however, probably a primer for the Thompson
language. Such a publication was noted by Marcel
Bernad in his *Bibliographie des missionnaires oblats
de Marie Immaculée* (Liege, 1922) p. 60.

UNIVERSITY OF WASHINGTON LIBRARY

**941 Lewis & Dryden's . . .**

Lewis & Dryden's official railway guide for the
North Pacific coast; containing railway time
schedules, connections, distance and fares, ocean
and inland navigation and stage routes; also a
complete ABC guide for Oregon, Washington,
Idaho, Montana, and British Columbia. Portland,
Ore., Lewis & Dryden Printing Co., 1891.

198 p. (incl. advertisements) illus., maps, tables.
23 cm. Copy examined: v. 12, no. 4, April 1891.
On t. p.: published monthly.

B.C. ARCHIVES

**942 Natural History Society of British Columbia**

Papers and communications read before the
Natural History Society of British Columbia.
Victoria, Jas. A. Cohen, 1891.

49 p. illus. 21 cm. Copy examined in B.C.
Archives: v. 1, no. 1. No more published.

Includes papers on birds, fishes, ethnology, and
entomology.

B.C. ARCHIVES

**943 New Westminster. Chamber of Commerce**

Report. 8th+ 1891+ New Westminster.

v. illus. 23 cm. annual. Various printers.
Eighth annual report was the first to be published.
Sixteenth report covers the years 1897-98. Name
varies: 1883-1959 as Board of Trade.

Includes secretary's reports, memoranda to federal
and provincial governments, and statistics.

B.C. ARCHIVES

**944 Palmer, W[illia]m Harry**

Pages from a seaman's log; being the first eighteen
months of the cruise of H.M.S. Warspite in the
Pacific. Victoria, Munroe Miller, 1891.

64 p. fold. plate. 17 cm.

A few pages describe a seaman's life while in
Esquimalt and Victoria.

B.C. ARCHIVES

**945 Pharmaceutical Association of the Province of British Columbia**

British Columbia Pharmacy Act, and by-laws of
the British Columbia Pharmaceutical Association.
Victoria, Jas. A. Cohen, printer, 1891.

22 p. 15 cm.

B.C. ARCHIVES

**946 Roper, Edward**

By track and trail; a journey through Canada.
With numerous original sketches by the author.
London, W. H. Allen & Co., 1891.

xiv, 455 p. illus., plates, fold. map. 24 cm.

About one-half of the book describes British
Columbia.

B.C. ARCHIVES

**947 Rux**
PSEUDONYM

Roughing it after gold by Rux [pseud.] London,
Sampson Low, Marston, Searle & Rivington, 1891.

viii, 152 p.   19 cm.

On pages 107-152 the author describes various adventures in British Columbia, including a trip to the Cassiar district in the mid-1870's.

VANCOUVER PUBLIC LIBRARY

948    Seton-Karr, H[eywood] W[alter]
       B. 1859

Bear-hunting in the White Mountains; or, Alaska and British Columbia revisited.    London, Chapman and Hall Limited, 1891.

vi, 156 p.    illus., plates, fold. map.    21 cm.
Plates appear without captions in some copies.

In about one-third of the book, Seton-Karr describes his travels along the coast of Vancouver Island to the Chilcat country and his fishing and hunting expeditions in areas in the Interior which had been made accessible by the Canadian Pacific Railway.

VANCOUVER PUBLIC LIBRARY

949    Sons of England Benevolent
       Society. Pride of the Island
       Lodge No. 131

By-laws of Pride of the Island Lodge No. 131, Sons of England Benevolent Society; instituted January 15th, 1891; established A.D. 1874; under the supreme jurisdiction of the Grand Lodge of Canada. Meetings held in St. George's Hall . . . Victoria, James A. Cohen, printer, 1891.

8 p.    15 cm.    At head of title: Red rose degree.
Original examined. Xerox copy in the library, University of Victoria.

UNIVERSITY OF VICTORIA LIBRARY

950    [Toestlœs-Nahwoelnœk . . .]

[Toestlœs-Nahwoelnœk; or, Carrier review] 1891-1894.    Stuart's Lake, B.C., Adrian Gabriel Morice.

[9]-200 p.    illus.    23 cm.    24 issues.    No. 1 begins with p. 9. Title as given in Pilling's *Athapascan languages*, p. 72. In the bibliography of Morice's *Dans le camp des lettres canadiennes* (Winnipeg, 1936) p. 107, the title is given as "*Test'les nahwelnek*," with the French translation of "le papier que raconte."

An eight-page periodical, printed entirely in the Déné syllabic characters invented by Father Morice. The contents are varied, ranging from news events to hymns and bible questions.

B.C. ARCHIVES

951    Turner, George H.

Before the council; or, Social life in Victoria. [Victoria?] 1891.

72 p.    2 plates.    17 cm.

A religious tract decrying social evils. The title refers to a hearing before the Victoria City Council of a delegation from the Temperance and Moral Reform Association which protested prostitution in Victoria.

B.C. ARCHIVES

952    United States. Hydrographic
       Office

The coast of British Columbia, including the Juan de Fuca Strait, Puget Sound, Vancouver and Queen Charlotte Islands. Compiled by R. C. Ray . . . under the direction of Richardson Clover, hydrographer.    Washington, Government Printing Office, 1891.

vi, 484 p.    fold. chart.    23 cm. ([Publications] no. 96)    Not seen.

Supplement: *The coast of British Columbia* (Washington, 1901). In 84 leaves.

BANCROFT LIBRARY CATALOGUE

953    United States. Department of State

Seal fisheries of the Behring Sea. Message from the President of the United States, transmitting a letter from the Secretary of State submitting the official correspondence between the government of the United States and the government of Great Britain touching the seal fisheries of the Behring Sea since the nineteenth of July last [1890] Washington, Government Printing Office, 1891.

53 p.    2 fold. maps.    23 cm.    ([United States] 51st Cong., 2d sess. House. Ex. doc. 144)    Not seen.

LIBRARY OF CONGRESS

954    Vancouver Daily World

The financial, professional, manufacturing, commercial, railroad and shipping interests of Vancouver, B.C.    Vancouver [1891]

24 p.    illus., 7 plates, ports., tables.    29 cm.    Cover title. At head of title: The Vancouver Daily World. Caption title: Vancouver City; its wonderful history and future prospects . . .    Includes: Vancouver's progress; brief outline of its wonderful history [p. 1-3]

B.C. ARCHIVES

955    Vancouver Waterworks Company

Memorandum.    [Vancouver, 1891?]

48 p.    24 cm.    Caption title.

Relates to the purchase of the company by the city of Vancouver; includes the company's history.

B.C. ARCHIVES

956    Victoria (city)

Victoria illustrated; published under the auspices of the corporation of the city of Victoria, containing a general description of the province of British Columbia, and a review of the resources, terminal advantages, general industries, and climate of Victoria, the "Queen city" and its tributary country. Victoria, Ellis & Co., "The Colonist," 1891.

96 p. illus., ports. 30 cm. Cover title: Victoria, the Queen city.

B.C. ARCHIVES

957     Victoria. Provincial Royal Jubilee Hospital

Bye-laws; Victoria, British Columbia, February 1891; finally considered and approved by the Board of Directors at their regular monthly meeting, held at the hospital on the 2nd day of March 1891; H. M. Yates, secretary; Thomas R. Smith, president. Victoria, "The Colonist" Steam Printing House, 1891.

16 p. 22 cm.

B.C. ARCHIVES

958     Victoria Gun Club and Game Protective Association

Constitution and by-laws. Victoria, Waterson, 1891.

32 p. Not found for examination.

B.C. ARCHIVES

959     Victoria home journal

Victoria home journal, devoted to social, political, literary, musical and dramatic gossip. v. 1-4; 1891-95. [n.p.]

4 v. 29 cm. weekly. Title varies: no. 17-24 as *Pacific harbour light.*

B.C. ARCHIVES

960     Wagstaff, J[ohn]
            D. 1925?

English lands & English homes in the far West; being the story of a holiday tour in Canada. With an introduction by Joseph Wright. Macclesfield, Printed and published by Claye, Brown, and Claye, "Courier" Office, 1891.

76 p. 21 cm. Chapter 5: Through the mountains. Chapter 6: Victoria, B.C.

The National Library bibliography notes that an earlier edition was published in Canada.

CANADIAN ARCHIVES

961     Walker, W[alter] J[ames]
            B. 1852

Some thoughts and suggestions on municipal reform in British Columbia. New Westminster, Lewis & Greig, 1891.

16 p. 23 cm.

B.C. PROVINCIAL LIBRARY

962     Women's Christian Temperance Union of British Columbia

Yearbook and proceedings of the 3d— annual convention. 1891+ New Westminster, Plowright Printing Co., Ltd., and the Columbian Co., Ltd.

v. 21 cm.

Contains directories of officers, financial statements, resolutions, and the constitution, by-laws and regulations.

B.C. ARCHIVES

963     [Wrigley, Howard]
            SUPPOSED AUTHOR

Log of a voyage to British Columbia in the "West Indian," 1890-91. Liverpool, Printed by W. P. Platt, 1891.

vi, 52 p. illus. 19 cm. Attributed to Howard Wrigley by the University of British Columbia Library.

A passenger's journal, a third of which describes his activities while on Vancouver Island

U.B.C. SPECIAL COLLECTIONS

964     Beanlands, [Arthur John]
            1857-1917

British Columbia; a problem of colonial development. [London, Royal Colonial Institute, 1892]

12 1. 22 cm. Caption title. At head of text: To be read at a meeting of the Royal Colonial Institute ... Lieut.-General R. W. Lowry, C.B., in the chair.

Also printed in: Royal Colonial Institute. *Journal.* v. 23, pt. 4, 1892, p. 217-229.

B.C. ARCHIVES

965     Boas, Franz
            1858-1942

Vocabularies of the Tlingit, Haida and Tsimshian languages. [Philadelphia, 1892]

173-208 p. 23 cm. Caption title. Reprinted from: American Philosophical Society. *Proceedings.* v. 29. Not seen.

LIBRARY OF CONGRESS

966     British Columbia Mercantile Agency

The British Columbia Mercantile Agency, 58 Cordova Street, Vancouver, B.C. Telephone 159. George Giles, general manager; Geo. B. Cross, local manager; Wm. Brown, mgr., Collecting Dept. Victoria, The Colonist Presses, 1892.

68 p. (interpaged with blank leaves) 20 cm.

A directory of credit ratings of lower mainland residents.

B.C. ARCHIVES

**967    Canadian Pacific Railway Company**

British Columbia, the Pacific province of the Dominion of Canada; its position, resources and climate; a new field for farming, ranching and mining along the line of the Canadian Pacific Railway; full information for intending settlers. [Montreal] 1892.

32 p.   illus., fold. map.   22 cm.

Also: 1893. 31 p.   Also: 1894. 32 p.   Also: 1895. 32 p.   Titles of later editions vary slightly.

NATIONAL LIBRARY

**968    [Canestrelli, Philippo]**
1839-1918

Yakasinkinmiki [Kootenai catechism of Christian doctrine.   Desmet, Idaho, Desmet Mission Print, 1892]

16 p.   21 cm.   Title from heading which begins text on p. [1] Often erroneously attributed to Father J. Bandini (see Wilfred Schoenberg's *Jesuit mission presses in the Pacific Northwest* (Portland, Ore., Champoeg Press, 1957) p. 67)

VANCOUVER PUBLIC LIBRARY

**969    Catholic Church. Catechisms. Thompson**

First catechism in Thompson language. [Kamloops, 1892]

32 p.   18 cm.   Caption title.   Mimeographed. Text in Duployan shorthand. Translated by Jean-Marie Raphael Le Jeune.

B.C. ARCHIVES

**970    Catholic Church. Liturgy and ritual. Shuswap**

Prayers in Shushwap.   [Kamloops, 1892-189-]

80 p.   18 cm.   Caption title. Mimeographed. Text in Duployan shorthand with English and Latin headings in italics. The work of Jean-Marie Raphael Le Jeune. Contents: Morning prayers [p. 1-16] — Night prayers [p. 17-32] — Prayers before communion [p. 33-39] — After communion [p. 40-45] — Hymn [p. 46-47] — Helas quelle douleur [p. 48] — Stations of the cross [p. 49-64] — Preparation for confession [p. 65-80]

In *Salishan languages* Pilling lists the contents in 48 pages. The "Night prayers" first appeared separately in 16 pages and was later incorporated as pages 17-32 (see entry below).

B.C. ARCHIVES

**971    Catholic Church. Liturgy and ritual. Shuswap**

Prayers in Shushwap. [Part] I: Night prayers. [Kamloops, 1892?]

16 p.   18 cm.   Caption title. Mimeographed. Text in Duployan shorthand with Latin and English headings in italics. The work of Jean-Marie Raphael Le Jeune. Bound in the University of Washington Library in *Kamloops miscellany,* v. 2.

Also see entry 970.

UNIVERSITY OF WASHINGTON LIBRARY

**972    Catholic Church. Liturgy and ritual. Thompson**

Prayers for communion in Ntlakapmah or Thompson.   [Kamloops, n.d.]

33-[48] p.   19 cm.   Caption title. Mimeographed. Text in Duployan shorthand with headings in English italics. The work of Jean-Marie Raphael Le Jeune. Bound in the University of Washington Library in *Kamloops miscellany,* v. 2.

Presumably printed to follow *Prayers in Thompson, or Ntlakapmah* (entry below).

UNIVERSITY OF WASHINGTON LIBRARY

**973    Catholic Church. Liturgy and ritual. Thompson**

Prayers in Thompson, or Ntlakapmah. [Kamloops, 1892]

32 p.   18 cm.   Caption title. Mimeographed. Text in Duployan shorthand with English headings in italics. The work of Jean-Marie Raphael Le Jeune. Contents: Morning prayers [p. 1-16] — Night prayers in Ntlakapmah or Thompson language [p. 17-32]

*Prayers for communion in Ntlakapmah or Thompson* was presumably designed to follow this publication (entry 972).

Third edition: 1894. 18 p.

B.C. ARCHIVES

**974    Church of England. Book of Common Prayer. Selections. Tsimshian**

Shãõnshkgum shagait gigiengwaklthit, dīlth wila ontk ga Sacramentsit, dīlth gik nagazãout hoiya dit dilth wilalau churchit, nīwalda hoi Churchum Englandit. (Portions of the Book of Common Prayer in the Zimshian language)   London, Society for Promoting Christian Knowledge, 1892.

218 p.   19 cm.

B.C. ARCHIVES

**975    Church of England in Canada. Dioceses. British Columbia**

Report of the third session of the Fifth Synod of the Diocese of British Columbia, held in the city of Victoria, June 14 and 15, 1892; with

the address of the Bishop.   Victoria, Ellis &
Co., printers, Colonist Office, 1892.

50 p.   21 cm.

976      Commercial

The Kootenay country of British Columbia.
A volume devoted to its resources and possibilities.
Winnipeg, James E. Steen, publisher, 1892.

[28] p. (incl. plates)   illus., 2 plates.   30 cm.
Cover title. A supplement to the *Commercial*
journal. Dated on cover: July 15th, 1892.

977      Dewar, J[ames] Cumming

Voyage of the Nyanza, R.N.Y.C.; being the
record of a three years' cruise in a schooner yacht
in the Atlantic and Pacific, and her subsequent
shipwreck.   Edinburgh, William Blackwood and
Sons, 1892.

xviii, 466 p.   illus., plates, map.   23 cm.

Pages 309-314 relate to Vancouver Island.

978      Everett, T. Thomson
         EDITOR

Victoria illustrated; a brief history of Victoria
from 1842.   Toronto, Victoria Publishing
Company, 1892.

32 p.   illus.   29 cm.

979      Great Britain. Bering Sea
         Commissioners

Report of the Behring Sea Commission, 1892.
[London, 1892]

235 p.   fold. maps, fold. diagr.   33 cm.   At head
of title: Printed for the use of the Foreign Office;
June 1892; confidential. Commissioners: George
Baden-Powell and George Mercer Dawson.

On seal life and methods of pelagic sealing.

For a supplementary report, see entry 1046.

980      Great Britain. Foreign Office

[Behring Sea arbitration. British case. First
to sixth] draft for case. Tribunal of arbitration
under treaty convention between Great Britain
and the United States of America relating to
Behring Sea.   [London, 1892-93?]

6 v.   33 cm.   Caption title. A manuscript
letter bound in with the second draft is addressed
to Charles Tupper. It advised him of the imperfect
printing of the draft. It is dated 27 July 1892.

981      Great Britain. Foreign Office

Copy of a despatch from Her Majesty's minister at
Washington inclosing a treaty between Her
Majesty and the United States of America for
arbitration concerning the seal fisheries in
Behring's Sea. Presented to both Houses of
Parliament by command of Her Majesty, March
1892.   London, Printed by Harrison and Sons
[1892]

5 p.   34 cm.   ([Great Britain. Parliament. Command
papers] C. 6634) At head of title: United States, no. 2
(1892)

982      Great Britain. Foreign Office

Further correspondence respecting the Behring Sea
seal fisheries. (In continuation of "United States
no. 2 (1891)" C. 6368, and including the papers
contained in "United States nos. 1 and 2 (1892)"
C. 6633 and 6634) Presented to both Houses of
Parliament by command of Her Majesty, April
1892.   London, Printed by Harrison and Sons
[1892]

x, 191 p.   map.   34 cm.   ([Great Britain.
Parliament. Command papers] C. 6635) At head
of title: United States, no. 3 (1892)

983      Great Britain. Foreign Office

Telegraphic correspondence respecting seal
fishing in Behring's Sea during the season of
1892. Presented to both Houses of Parliament
by command of Her Majesty, March 1892.
London, Printed by Harrison and Sons [1892]

11 p.   34 cm.   ([Great Britain. Parliament.
Command papers] C. 6633) At head of title:
United States, no. 1 (1892)

984      Hart, A[lbert] B[ushnell]
         EDITOR   1854-1943

Extracts from official papers relating to the Bering
Sea controversy, 1790-1892.   New York, A.
Lovell & Co., 1892.

26 p.   18 cm.   (American history leaflets . . .
edited by A. B. Hart and E. Channing . . . no. 6,
November 1892)   Caption title.   Not seen.

985      Holbrook, Mary H.

Jottings by the way.   [Portland, Oregon, The
author, 1892]

21 p.   14 x 19 cm.   Cover title.

An account of an excursion along the British
Columbia coast in 1891.

**986** International Coast Seamen and Sealers' Union of British Columbia

Constitution and by-laws of the International Coast Seamen and Sealers' Union of British Columbia, organized October 7, 1892.    Victoria, H. G. Waterson, printer, 1892.

48 p.    13 cm.

B.C. ARCHIVES

**987** Kamloops phonographer

Kamloops phonographer.    June 1892— January 1893.    Kamloops, St. Louis Mission, Jean-Marie Raphael Le Jeune.

1 v.    18 cm.    Mimeographed. Introductory number: June 1892. No. 1: July 1892.

Designed to show the method of teaching Duployan shorthand to the Indians. For more information see Pilling's *Chinookan languages,* p. 49.

B.C. ARCHIVES

**988** Knights of Pythias. Victoria. Far West Lodge No. 1

By-laws of Far West Lodge No. 1, Knights of Pythias.    Victoria, Munroe Miller, 1892.

16 p.    16 cm.    Original examined. Xerox copy in the library, University of Victoria.

Also: 1908. 18 p.

UNIVERSITY OF VICTORIA LIBRARY

**989** Langley Agricultural Association

Prize list.    1892-1951?    Langley.

v.    22 cm.    annual.    Various printers. Title varies slightly.

B.C. ARCHIVES

**990** Law Society of British Columbia

Law Society of British Columbia; acts relating thereto; rules of the society; list of benchers, and practicing members thereof, 1892.    Victoria, Munroe Miller, 1892.

iv, 36 p.    22 cm.    Cover title: Acts and rules, 1892, Law Society of B.C.

Also see entries 830 and 1297.

B.C. ARCHIVES

**991** Law Society of British Columbia. Library

Catalogue of the library of the Law Society of British Columbia. With an index of subjects and table of abbreviations. Compiled by Gordon Hunter.    Victoria, Printed for the Society by Munroe Miller, 1892.

124 p.    22 cm.

CANADIAN ARCHIVES

**992** Le Jeune, J[ean]-M[arie] R[aphael]
1855-1930

Chinook primer, by which the natives of British Columbia, and any other persons speaking the Chinook [jargon] are taught to read and write Chinook in shorthand in the space of a few hours. Kamloops, St. Louis Mission, 1892.

[2], 8, [2] p. (incl. cover)    18 cm.    Cover title. Mimeographed. In Chinook jargon with headings in italics. Bound in the University of Washington Library in *Kamloops miscellany,* v. 1.

UNIVERSITY OF WASHINGTON LIBRARY

**993** [Le Jeune, Jean-Marie Raphael]
1855-1930

[Joseph sold by his brethren; an act played by the Shuswap Indians in 1892.    Kamloops, 1892]

20 p.    18 cm.    Mimeographed. Title written on cover in manuscript. Text is entirely in Duployan shorthand, a transcription of the Shuswap language. Bound in the University of Washington Library in *Kamloops miscellany,* v. 1.

UNIVERSITY OF WASHINGTON LIBRARY

**994** McLeod, Malcolm
1821-1899

Oregon indemnity; claim of chief factors and chief traders of the Hudson's Bay Company thereto, as partners under the treaty of 1846.    [Ottawa] 1892.

57 p.    22 cm.

B.C. ARCHIVES

**995** Morice, A[drian] G[abriel]
1859-1938

Carrier sociology and mythology [with map. n.p., 1892]

109-126 p.    col. map.    30 cm.    Cover title. Caption title: Are the Carrier sociology and mythology indigenous or exotic? From: The Royal Society of Canada. *Proceedings and transactions.* ser. 1, v. 10, sec. 2, 1892.

B.C. ARCHIVES

**996** New Westminster. Board of Trade

British Columbia; some statistics about business chances in the city and district of New Westminster, B.C.    New Westminster, The Commonwealth Company, 1892.

10 p.    21 cm.    Cover title.

B.C. ARCHIVES

**997     Parrish, H. E.**

Report on Yakoun coalfields, Graham Island, Queen Charlotte district.     [n.p., 1892?]

7, [1] p.     26 cm.     Caption title.

B.C. ARCHIVES


**998     Pike, Warburton [Mayer]**
1861-1915

The Barren Ground of northern Canada. London, New York, Macmillan and Co., 1892.

ix, 300 p.     2 fold. maps.     23 cm.     Errata slip.

Returning from the Barren Lands, Pike decided to travel on the Peace, Parsnip, and Pack rivers to McLeod Lake, and then to run down the Fraser River to Quesnel. In part of the book, Pike graphically describes his party's condition in winter time when they missed the Pack River, became lost, and were close to dying of starvation.

Also: New York, E. P. Dutton, 1917.

B.C. ARCHIVES


**999     Pilling, James Constantine**
1846-1895

Bibliography of the Athapascan languages. Washington, Government Printing Office, 1892.

xii, 125 p.     facsims.     25 cm.     ([United States] Bureau of American Ethnology. [Bulletin, no. 14])

Lists all types of sources, including manuscripts, which contain vocabularies.

B.C. ARCHIVES


**1000     Ralph, Julian**
1853-1903

On Canada's frontier; sketches of history, sport, and adventure, and of the Indians, missionaries, fur traders, and new settlers of western Canada.     New York, Harper & Brothers, 1892.

x, 325 p.     illus., plates.     23 cm.

Two chapters describe life in British Columbia.

B.C. ARCHIVES


**1001     Raymond & Whitcomb Company**

Raymond's vacation excursions: California, the Pacific Northwest, and Alaska; three spring tours, leaving Boston April 25, 1892; also tour via Canadian Pacific Railway, leaving Boston May 23, 1892.     Boston [1892?]

208 p.     11 x 14 cm.

One of the tours includes a trip to British Columbia. Brief historical notes describe the development of Victoria and Vancouver Island.

B.C. ARCHIVES


**1002     Roberts, Morley**
1857-1942

The mate of the Vancouver.     London, Lawrence & Bullen, 1892.

268 p.     20 cm.

Fiction. In the 1880's the hero leaves his ship at Victoria and travels to the interior of British Columbia to make his fortune.

Also: New York, Street & Smith, 1900. 263 p.

B.C. ARCHIVES


**1003     St. Onge, Louis Napoléon**
B. 1842

History of the Old Testament. Age 1: from Adam to Abraham, containing 2083 years.     [Kamloops, 1892]

24 p.     Caption title. Mimeographed? Text in Chinook jargon, Duployan stenographic characters.     Not seen. From Pilling's *Chinookan languages*.

Forms a supplement to the Kamloops *Wawa*, v. 2, nos. 1-6 (nos. 33-38 of the series), 3 July to 7 August 1892.

PILLING'S CHINOOKAN BIBLIOGRAPHY


**1004     Sir William Wallace Benefit Society**

Constitution and by-laws.     Victoria, H. G. Waterson, printer, 1892.

15 p.     14 cm.

The membership was limited to Scotsmen or their sons and grandsons.

B.C. ARCHIVES


**1005     Slough Creek Mining Company**

Prospectus of the Slough Creek Mining Company, incorporated January 1892. [Third edition] Tacoma [189-]

[18] p.     plate, fold. map.     22 cm.     Cover title.

B.C. ARCHIVES


**1006     South Fork Hydraulic and Mining Company, Limited**

Articles of association . . . registered office, Quesnelle Forks; incorporated June 23rd, 1892. Victoria, "The Colonist" Print, 1892.

8 p.     16 cm.

B.C. ARCHIVES

**1007    Stanton, Stephen Berrien**
B. 1864

The Behring Sea controversy.    New York, Albert B. King, 1892.

102 p.    21 cm.    List of authorities: p. [101]-102.

B.C. ARCHIVES


**1008    United States. President**
1889-1893    (HARRISON)

Message from the President of the United States, transmitting a convention signed at Washington, February 29, 1892, between the governments of the United States and Her Britannic Majesty submitting to arbitration the questions which have arisen between those governments concerning the jurisdictional rights of the United States in the waters of the Bering Sea, etc.    [Washington, 1892]

102 p.    fold. map.    23 cm.    ([United States] 52d Cong., 1st sess. Senate. Ex. doc. no. 55)
Caption title.

B.C. ARCHIVES


**1009    United Workmen, Ancient Order of. British Columbia. Grand Lodge**

Constitution of the Grand Lodge of British Columbia of the A.O.U.W., together with constitution for subordinate lodges, beneficiary rules and laws of the Grand Lodge.    Victoria, Jas. A. Cohen, printer, 1892.

88 p.    15 cm.

Also: Victoria, G. S. R. Co., n.d. 96 p.    Also: Victoria, Cusack Press, 1902. 104 p.    Also: Victoria, Cusack Press, 1907. 116 p.    Also: Victoria, Victoria Printing & Publishing Company, 1911? 136 p.    Also: Victoria, Thos. R. Cusack Presses, 1918? 148 p. Also: Victoria, Victoria Printing & Publishing Company, 1923? 150 p.    Also: Victoria, Victoria Printing & Publishing Co., 1938? 150 p.    Title for the last two editions: *Constitution and beneficiary by-laws* . . .

B.C. ARCHIVES


**1010    United Workmen, Ancient Order of. British Columbia. Grand Lodge**

Proceedings of the . . . Grand Lodge, A.O.U.W., of the Province of British Columbia.    1892+
Victoria, Munroe Miller, etc.

v.    tables.    21 cm.    annual.    Printer varies.

B.C. ARCHIVES


**1011    Victoria. British Columbia Protestant Orphans' Home**

Constitution and by-laws.    [Victoria, 1892]

sheet.    41 x 47 cm.    Copy examined is printer's proof.

Another copy on two leaves.    Also: Victoria, 1907?

B.C. ARCHIVES


**1012    Victoria Lawn Tennis Club**

Victoria Lawn Tennis Club [rules.    Victoria? n.d.]

6 p.    16 cm.    Lists 13 rules.

The club was founded prior to February 1892 when a reference first appears to it in the Victoria *Colonist*.

Another edition of seven pages lists 14 rules.

UNIVERSITY OF VICTORIA LIBRARY


**1013    Westminster Club**

Constitution, by-laws, and list of members of Westminster Club, established 1889.    New Westminster, Lewis & Greig, 1892.

25 p.    14 cm.

B.C. ARCHIVES


**1014    Aberdeen and Temair, Ishbel Marie (Marjoribanks) Gordon**
MARCHIONESS OF    1857-1939

Through Canada with a Kodak.    Edinburgh, W. H. White & Co., 1893.

viii, 249 p.    illus., ports.    19 cm.    A collection of papers first published in the magazine *Onward and upward*, 1891-2. Chapter 10: The Rocky Mountains. Chapter 11: A visit to British Columbia. Chapter 12: Guisachan farm.

Recollections of holiday trips. Chapter 12 describes life on an Okanagan farm.

CANADIAN ARCHIVES


**1015    Adams, Daniel Fowler**
D. 1905    PLAINTIFF

In the Supreme Court of British Columbia, on appeal to the full court; between Daniel Fowler Adams, plaintiff, and Simeon Duck, defendant (by original action) and between the said Simeon Duck, plaintiff, and the said Daniel Fowler Adams, defendant (by counter claim) Case on appeal. H. B. W. Aikman, solicitor for appellant (plaintiff) S. Perry Mills, solicitor for respondent (defendant) Victoria, James A. Cohen's Electric Print, 1893.

126 l.    27 cm.

B.C. ARCHIVES

**1016**   [Beanlands, Arthur John]
1857-1917

British Columbia, its present resources and future possibilities; a brief attempt to demonstrate the value of the province. Published by direction of the provincial government.   Victoria, "The Colonist" Printing and Publishing Co., 1893.

109 p.   illus., fold. map, tables.   23 cm.

B.C. ARCHIVES

**1017**   Bering Sea Commission

Behring Sea arbitration. Report of the Behring Sea Commission, and report of British commissioners of June 21, 1892. With five maps and diagrams and appendices. Presented to both Houses of Parliament by command of Her Majesty, March 1893.   London, Printed by Harrison and Sons [1893]

vii, 241 p.   fold. maps, diagrs. (part fold.) tables. 34 cm.   ([Great Britain. Parliament. Command papers] C. 6919) At head of title: United States, no. 2 (1893)   British commissioners: George Baden-Powell and George M. Dawson. Copy in Canadian Archives has index (p. xxix-xliii) inserted between p. iv-v.

Another copy has t. p. lacking imprint and only brief statement "With Appendices."

B.C. ARCHIVES

**1018**   Bering Sea Tribunal of Arbitration

Behring Sea arbitration. Award of the tribunal of arbitration, constituted under Article I of the treaty concluded at Washington on the 29th February 1892, between Her Britannic Majesty and the United States of America. Presented to both Houses of Parliament by command of Her Majesty, August 1893.   London, Printed by Harrison and Sons [1893]

15 p.   34 cm.   ([Great Britain. Parliament. Command papers] C. 7107) At head of title: United States, no. 10 (1893)

B.C. ARCHIVES

**1019**   Bering Sea Tribunal of Arbitration

Réception officielle à Paris du Tribunal d'arbitrage pour les pêcheries de la mer de Behring. (23 mars 1893)   Paris, Imprimerie Nationale, 1893.

15 p.   28 cm.

SHORTT COLLECTION

**1020**   Bering Sea Tribunal of Arbitration

Report of the proceedings of the tribunal of arbitration, convened at Paris, 1893.   [Paris]

Chamerot & Renouard [1893?]

8 pts. in 6 v.   33 cm.   At head of title: Hôtel du Ministère des affaires étrangères, Paris. Continuous paging. Vols. 2-6 have title pages in French and English.

VANCOUVER PUBLIC LIBRARY

**1021**   Bible. Old Testament. Selections. Haida

Old testament stories in the Haida language, by Rev. C. Harrison.   London, Society for Promoting Christian Knowledge, 1893.

92 p.   17 cm.

B.C. ARCHIVES

**1022**   [Blowitz, Henri Georges Stephane Adolphe Opper de]
1825-1903

The Behring Sea arbitration; letters to The Times by its special correspondent, together with the award. Reprinted by permission of the proprietors.   London, William Clowes & Sons; Victoria, T. N. Hibben & Co., 1893.

87 p.   19 cm.

Also: London, The Times, 1893.

B.C. ARCHIVES

**1023**   Boas, Franz
1858-1942

Vocabulary of the Kwakiutl language. [Philadelphia, 1893]

34-82 p.   23 cm.   Caption title.   Reprinted from: American Philosophical Society. *Proceedings*. v. 31. Not seen.

LIBRARY OF CONGRESS

**1024**   Buel, J[ames] W[illiam]
1849-1920

America's wonderlands; a pictorial and descriptive history of our country's scenic marvels as delineated by pen and camera. More than 500 magnificent photographic views.   Vancouver, J. W. MacGregor Pubg. Co. [1893]

503 p.   illus., plates.   24 x 32 cm.

No reference to British Columbia scenery.

B.C. ARCHIVES

**1025**   Canada. British Columbia Fishery Commission

Report 1892.   Ottawa, Printed by S. E. Dawson, 1893.

xx, 433 p.   25 cm.   (Canada. Sessional papers,

no. 10c, 1893)    At head of title: British Columbia Fishery Commission. Chairman: Samuel Wilmot.

The commission was appointed to make recommendations for the regulation and supervision of fisheries. The report includes a résumé of the growth of salmon fisheries from 1876 to 1891.

DEPARTMENT OF FISHERIES LIBRARY, OTTAWA

### 1026    Canada. Department of the Interior

Regulations for the survey, administration, disposal and management of the Dominion lands within the forty-mile railway belt in the province of British Columbia, 1893.    [Ottawa. 1893]

23 p.    25 cm.    Not seen.

LIBRARY OF CONGRESS

### 1027    Carter, James C[oolidge]
#### 1827-1905

Fur-seal arbitration. Oral argument of James C. Carter . . . on behalf of the United States before the tribunal of arbitration convened at Paris under the provisions of the treaty between the United States of America and Great Britain, concluded February 29, 1892.    Paris, Chamerot & Renouard, printers, 1893.

379 p.    26 cm.    Not seen.

LIBRARY OF CONGRESS

### 1028    Catholic Church. Catechisms. Shuswap

First catechism in Shushwap.    [Kamloops, 1893]

32 p.    18 cm.    Caption title.    Mimeographed. Text in Duployan shorthand with English headings in italics. The work of Jean-Marie Raphael Le Jeune.

B.C. ARCHIVES

### 1029    Catholic Church. Liturgy and ritual

Benediction of a church.    [Kamloops, n.d.]

16 p.    18 cm.    Caption title.    Mimeographed. Text in Duployan shorthand. The work of Jean-Marie Raphael Le Jeune. Includes music.

B.C. ARCHIVES

### 1030    Catholic Church. Liturgy and ritual. Okanagon

Prayers in Okanagon language.    [Kamloops, 1893]

80 p.    18 cm.    Caption title. Mimeographed. Text in Duployan shorthand; Latin and English headings in italics. The work of Jean-Marie Raphael Le Jeune.

B.C. ARCHIVES

### 1031    Church of England in Canada. Dioceses. British Columbia

Report of the special session of the synod of the Diocese of British Columbia held in the city of Victoria, November 22nd and 23rd, 1892, for the election of a bishop . . . also, report of the first session of the Sixth Synod of the Diocese of British Columbia, held in the city of Victoria, June 29th and 30th, 1893, with the address of the Bishop. [Victoria] The Colonist Print [1893?]

73 p.    20 cm.    Cover title. Includes two title pages. On p. [1]: Journal of a special meeting of the synod of the Diocese of British Columbia held for the election of a bishop to fill the vacancy in the see caused by the resignation of the Right Reverend George Hills, D.D., first Bishop, on the 22nd and 23rd days of November 1892. Victoria, The "Colonist" Presses, 1893.    On p. [27]: Report of the first session of the Sixth Synod of the Diocese of British Columbia, held in the city of Victoria, June 29th and 30th, 1893, with the address of the Bishop. Victoria, The "Colonist" Presses, 1893.

CANADIAN ARCHIVES

### 1032    Cogswell, O[liver] H.
#### 1857-1940

History of British Columbia, adapted for the use of schools.    Victoria, The "Colonist" Presses, 1893.

101 p.    18 cm.

Second edition: 1894.

B.C. ARCHIVES

### 1033    Commercial

Special supplement . . . relating to Vancouver Island, the adjacent coast and northern interior of British Columbia.    [Winnipeg] 1893.

[42] p.    illus.    30 cm.    Cover title. Issue dated 24 June 1893.

B.C. ARCHIVES

### 1034    Currie, Geo[rge] G[raham]
#### 1867-1926

How I once felt; songs of love and travel. Montreal, John Lovell & Son, printers, 1893.

142 p.    illus.    20 cm.    Includes: The "Beaver." — Vancouver.

Poetry.

B.C. ARCHIVES

### 1035    Davie, Theodore
#### 1852-1898

Facts and figures; a mass meeting addressed by the Premier at New Westminster; equal justice by the administration to all sections of the province alike clearly proved; parliament buildings and redistribution policy of the government triumphantly vindicated.   [n.p., 1893?]

8 p.   24 cm.   Caption title.

B.C. ARCHIVES

### 1036   Downie, William
1819-1893

Hunting for gold; reminisences [*sic*] of personal experience and research in the early days of the Pacific coast, from Alaska to Panama. [Edited by C. M. Waage]   San Francisco, California Publishing Co., 1893.

407 p.   illus., port.   23 cm.   Some of my early friends: p. 379-397.

William Downie's capabilities as an explorer were officially recognized by Governor Douglas who sent him on various expeditions. Under Douglas' instructions, Downie and J. W. McKay located the Harrison-Lillooet route to the Fraser River gold mines. In 1861 Downie began to mine in the Cariboo; in 1878, or shortly after, he was at the Cassiar mines, and in 1886 he reported to the government on the gold discoveries of the Similkameen country. Downie's B.C. experiences are covered in about one hundred pages of the book.

B.C. ARCHIVES

### 1037   Edwords, Clarence E[dgar]
B. 1856

Camp-fires of a naturalist; the story of fourteen expeditions after North American mammals. From the field notes of Lewis Lindsay Dyche, professor of zoology and curator of birds and mammals in the Kansas State University.   New York, D. Appleton and Company, 1893.

ix, 304 p.   plates.   20 cm.

Has several chapters on hunting and specimen collecting in the international boundary area of the Similkameen district.

B.C. ARCHIVES

### 1038   Foresters, Ancient Order of. Victoria. Court Hon. Robert Dunsmuir No. 7854

Constitution and by-laws of Court Hon. Robert Dunsmuir No. 7854 of the Ancient Order of Foresters; instituted Sept. 26th, 1891. Regular meetings 2 & 4 Wednesday, at 7:30 P.M., Foresters' Hall, Wellington, 1892.   Victoria, Munro[e] Miller, 1893.

41 p.   14 cm.   Original examined. Xerox copy in the library, University of Victoria.

UNIVERSITY OF VICTORIA LIBRARY

### 1039   Freemasons. British Columbia. Grand Lodge

22nd Annual Communication of the M.W. Grand Lodge of British Columbia, A. F. & A. M.; laying corner stone of the British Columbia Protestant Orphans' Home, Hillside Avenue, Victoria, B.C., on Saturday, June 24th, 1893, at 3 P.M.   Victoria, The Colonist Printing and Publishing Co., 1893.

11 p.   22 cm.   Cover title.

B.C. ARCHIVES

### 1040   Great Britain

Behring Sea arbitration. Argument of Her Majesty's government. Presented to both Houses of Parliament by command of Her Majesty, March 1893.   London, Printed by Harrison and Sons [1893]

iii, 162 p.   34 cm.   ([Great Britain. Parliament. Command papers] C. 6921) At head of title: United States, no. 4 (1893)

B.C. ARCHIVES

### 1041   Great Britain

Behring Sea arbitration. Case presented on the part of the government of Her Britannic Majesty to the tribunal of arbitration constituted under Article I of the treaty concluded at Washington on the 29th February 1892, between Her Britannic Majesty and the United States of America. Presented to both Houses of Parliament by command of Her Majesty, March 1893.   London, Printed by Harrison and Sons [1893]

161 p.   34 cm.   ([Great Britain. Parliament. Command papers] C. 6918) At head of title: United States, no. 1 (1893)

B.C. ARCHIVES

### 1042   Great Britain

Behring Sea arbitration. Counter-case presented on the part of the government of Her Britannic Majesty to the tribunal of arbitration constituted under Article I of the treaty concluded at Washington on the 29th February 1892, between Her Britannic Majesty and the United States of America. Presented to both Houses of Parliament by command of Her Majesty, March 1893. London, Printed by Harrison and Sons [1893]

iii, 315 p.   34 cm.   ([Great Britain. Parliament. Command papers] C. 6920) At head of title: United States, no. 3 (1893)

B.C. ARCHIVES

### 1043   Great Britain

Case presented on the part of the government of Her Britannic Majesty to the tribunal of arbitration constituted under Article I of the treaty concluded at Washington on the 29th February 1892, between Her Britannic Majesty and the United States of America [and appendices.   London? 189-]

5 v.   2 fold. maps.   33 cm.   At head of title of v. 2-3: Behring Sea arbitration.   Not seen.

Also published in French.

### 1044     Great Britain

Counter-case presented on the part of the government of Her Britannic Majesty to the tribunal of arbitration constituted under Article I of the treaty concluded at Washington on the 29th February 1892, between Her Britannic Majesty and the United States of America [and appendices. London? 189-]

3 v.   tables (part fold.)   33 cm.   At head of title of appendices: Behring Sea arbitration.   Not seen.

The counter-case, without appendices, was also published in French.

### 1045     Great Britain

Reports, treaties, &c.   [London, 1893?]

227 p.   33 cm.

Probably issued for the use of the Foreign Office. It relates to the Alaska boundary question and contains reports of D. R. Cameron (1886), Otto J. Klotz on his trip to Alaska (1889), George M. Dawson (1887 and 1889), and W. F. King, astronomer for the Canadian government (1891). There is considerable correspondence from Hudson's Bay House relating to the location of the early fur-trading posts and to the rights and privileges of the Hudson's Bay Company.

### 1046     Great Britain. Bering Sea Commissioners

Behring Sea arbitration. Supplementary report of the British Behring Sea commissioners, January 31, 1893.   [London? 1893]

68 p.   33 cm.   British commissioners: George Baden-Powell, George M. Dawson.

### 1047     Great Britain. Foreign Office

Behring Sea arbitration. Appendix to counter-case of Her Majesty's government.   [London, 1893?]

2 v.   33 cm.

### 1048     Great Britain. Foreign Office

Behring Sea arbitration. Appendix to the case of Her Majesty's government.   [London, 1893?]

4 v.   fold. maps.   33 cm.   Descriptive contents: v. 1. Miscellaneous correspondence. — v. 2. Great Britain and United States correspondence with Russia. — v. 3. Papers presented to the British Parliament: United States no. 2 (1890); United States nos. 1-3 (1891-92); Treaty series no. 8 (1892) — v. 4. Maps.

### 1049     Great Britain. Foreign Office

Behring Sea [arbitration] British counter-case. Drafts.   [London, 1893?]

1 v. (leaves, variously numbered)   34 cm.   Title from separately printed t. p. The drafts were for the use of Charles Tupper.

### 1050     Great Britain. Foreign Office

Behring Sea arbitration. Indexes to the British case, counter-case, and argument, and to the report of the Behring Sea Commission, and report of the Behring Sea commissioners.   [London, 1893?]

xliii p.   33 cm.

### 1051     Great Britain. Foreign Office

Behring Sea arbitration. Map of the northern portion of the North Pacific Ocean, annexed as part of the appendix to the case of Her Majesty's government. Presented to both Houses of Parliament by command of Her Majesty, March 1893.   London, Printed by Harrison and Sons [1893]

fold. map.   34 cm.   ([Great Britain. Parliament. Command papers] C. 6922) At head of title: United States, no. 5 (1893)

### 1052     Great Britain. Foreign Office

Behring Sea [arbitration] Memoranda on questions 1 to 5.   [London, 1893?]

1 v. (leaves, variously numbered)   34 cm.   Title from head of text of a list of contents on first printed page.

### 1053     Great Britain. Foreign Office

Behring Sea [arbitration] Memoranda, proposed regulations.   [London, 1893?]

1 v. (leaves, variously numbered)   34 cm.   Title from head of text of a list of contents on first printed page.

## 1054     Great Britain. Foreign Office

Behring Sea arbitration. Papers relating to the proceedings of the tribunal of arbitration, constituted under Article I of the treaty concluded at Washington on the 29th of February 1892, between Her Britannic Majesty and the United States of America. Presented to both Houses of Parliament by command of Her Majesty, September 1893.   London, Printed by Harrison and Sons [1893]

iv, 105 p.   34 cm.   ([Great Britain. Parliament. Command papers] C. 7161) At head of title: United States, no. 11 (1893)

B.C. ARCHIVES

## 1055     Great Britain. Foreign Office

Correspondence respecting an agreement for the protection of Russian sealing interests in the North Pacific Ocean during the year 1893. Presented to both Houses of Parliament by command of Her Majesty, June 1893.   London, Printed by Harrison and Sons [1893]

29 p.   34 cm.   ([Great Britain. Parliament. Command papers] C. 6952) At head of title: Russia, no. 1 (1893)

B.C. ARCHIVES

## 1056     Great Britain. Foreign Office

Correspondence respecting the seizures of British sealing vessels by Russian cruisers in the North Pacific Ocean. Presented to both Houses of Parliament by command of Her Majesty, June 1893. London, Printed by Harrison and Sons [1893]

iv, 116 p.   34 cm.   ([Great Britain. Parliament. Command papers] C. 7028) At head of title: Russia, no. 2 (1893)

The Russsians seized British vessels registered in the port of Victoria, claiming their crews were fishing in Russian Pacific waters without the required permission or licenses.

B.C. ARCHIVES

## 1057     Great Britain. Foreign Office

Despatch from Sir R. Morier, inclosing the reply of the Russian government in regard to the seizures of British sealing vessels by Russian cruisers in the North Pacific Ocean. Presented to both Houses of Parliament by command of Her Majesty, June 1893.   London, Printed by Harrison and Sons [1893]

15 p.   34 cm.   ([Great Britain. Parliament. Command papers] C. 7029) At head of title: Russia, no. 3 (1893)

B.C. ARCHIVES

## 1058     Great Britain. Treaties, etc.

Convention between Great Britain and the United States of America respecting the boundary between the two countries (Alaska and Passamaquoddy Bay) Signed at Washington, July 22, 1892; ratifications exchanged at Washington, August 23, 1892. Presented to both Houses of Parliament by command of Her Majesty, February 1893.   London, Printed by Harrison and Sons [1893]

2 p.   25 cm.   ([Great Britain. Parliament. Command papers] C. 6845) Treaty series no. 16, 1892.

For the supplementary convention, see entry 1115.

B.C. ARCHIVES

## 1059     Hagaga

Hagaga.   1893-1910?   Aiyansh Mission, Nass River, B.C., Printed and published by James Benjamin McCullagh.

v.   19-38 cm.   monthly (irregular)   Earliest copy examined (no. 2, 1 September 1893) has text in English. In other early copies text is in Niska dialect and English.

"In 1909 the *Hagaga* was revised under a new name and form, entitled '*Hagaga,* the Aiyansh Parish Magazine and Indian's Own Paper.' It was printed in English, the printers being four of the old Mission boys. The magazine consisted of eight pages of three columns each." — J. W. W. Moeran, *McCullagh of Aiyansh,* p. 48.

B.C. ARCHIVES

## 1060     Handbook to British Columbia . . .

Handbook to British Columbia; a general guide containing railway, steamer and stage time tables, distances, fares and other general information about the province . . .   v. 1-?; 1893-?   Victoria, Vancouver.

v.   20 cm.   monthly (irregular)   Edited by Alexander Begg. Title varies: April, May and June 1893, as *Begg & Lynch's handbook and general guide to British Columbia,* with running title: Handbook of British Columbia; July 1893, as *Begg's monthly and general guide to British Columbia* (Victoria, The B.C. Guide Publishing Company); August-September 1894 as *Handbook to British Columbia* (Victoria, Vancouver, Begg & Hoare)

B.C. ARCHIVES

## 1061     Harlan, [John Marshall]
### 1833-1911

Bering Sea Tribunal of Arbitration. Opinions of Mr. Justice Harlan at the conference in Paris of the Bering Sea Tribunal of Arbitration, constituted by the treaty of February 29, 1892, between Her Britannic Majesty and the United States of America . . .   Washington, Government Printing Office, 1893.

228 p.   26 cm.

B.C. ARCHIVES

**1062**  Hodgins, J[ohn] George
1821-1912

Hand book of the Church of England missions in the eleven dioceses of Selkirk, Mackenzie River, Moosonee, Caledonia, Athabasca, Columbia, New Westminster, Saskatchewan, Calgary, Qu'Appelle, and Rupert's Land; with illustrative extracts from the report of the Indian Department at Ottawa, and from the reports of the four great Church of England missionary societies, etc., in England for the year 1893.  Toronto, Printed for the Woman's Auxiliary of the Diocese of Toronto by Rowsell & Hutchison, 1893.

62 p.  22 cm.  Geographical references to missions in the dioceses: p. 62.

Presents extracts from various reports on the extent of activities in missions and schools, and lists clergy and lay workers.

LIBRARY OF PARLIAMENT

**1063**  Knights of Pythias. British Columbia. Grand Lodge

Constitution for the government of lodges, Knights of Pythias, subordinate to and working under the Grand Lodge of British Columbia; adopted at Grand Lodge Session, May 19th, 20th and 21st, 1891.  Vancouver, Daily Telegram Print [1893]

51 p.  15 cm.  Original seen. Xerox copy in the library, University of Victoria.

UNIVERSITY OF VICTORIA LIBRARY

**1064**  Knights of Pythias. Victoria. Sunset Lodge No. 10

By-laws of Sunset Lodge No. 10; instituted March 5, 1892; Knights of Pythias; Victoria, B.C.  Victoria, James A. Cohen, printer, 1893.

20 p.  15 cm.  Original examined. Xerox copy in the library, University of Victoria.

UNIVERSITY OF VICTORIA LIBRARY

**1065**  Le Jacq, J[ean] M. J.
D. 1899

Our Lady of Lourdes, by Rev. Father J. M. J. le Jacq, O.M.I. . . .  Kamloops, St. Louis Mission, 1893.

64 p.  19 cm.  At head of title: Chinook library. In Duployan shorthand.

B.C. ARCHIVES

**1066**  Le Jeune, J[ean]-M[arie] R[aphael]
1855-1930

Chinook first reading book, including Chinook hymns, syllabary and vocabulary.  Kamloops, 1893.

16 p.  19 cm.  Caption title. Mimeographed. Chinook jargon transcribed into Duployan shorthand with headings in italics. Bound in the University of Washington Library in *Kamloops miscellany*, v. 2.

UNIVERSITY OF WASHINGTON LIBRARY

**1067**  [McCullagh, James Benjamin]
1854-1921

[Miscellaneous hymns.  Aiyansh Mission, B.C., n.d.]

4 sheets.  20 x 11-12 cm.  Hymns numbered. Printed in the Niska dialect of the Tsimshian language on lined copy paper. B.C. Provincial Archives has: 1: How sweet the name. 4: Rock of ages. 5: My God accept my heart this day. 8: Jesus lover of my soul.

B.C. ARCHIVES

**1068**  McNamara, James
PLAINTIFF

In the Supreme Court of British Columbia, on appeal to the full court; between James McNamara (plaintiff) respondent, and the corporation of the city of New Westminster (defendants) appellants. Case on appeal. Messrs. Corbould, McColl, Wilson & Campbell, solicitors for appellants; E. A. Jenns, solicitor for respondent.  New Westminster, Printed by Fred. Jackson, Royal City Printing Works, 1893.

83 l.  28 cm.  Cover title.

B.C. ARCHIVES

**1069**  Mainland Steamshipmen's Protective and Benevolent Association of British Columbia

Constitution and by-laws and rules of order of the Mainland Steamshipmen's Protective and Benevolent Association of British Columbia; organized November 13th, 1892; Vancouver, B.C. Vancouver, Evans & Hastings, printers, 1893.

27 p.  1 illus.  15 cm.  Original examined. Xerox copy in the library, University of Victoria.

UNIVERSITY OF VICTORIA LIBRARY

**1070**  Morgan, [John Tyler]
1824-1907

Bering Sea Tribunal of Arbitration. Opinions of Senator Morgan at the conference in Paris of the Bering Sea Tribunal of Arbitration, constituted by the treaty of February 29, 1892, between Her Britannic Majesty and the United States of America. Washington, Government Printing Office, 1893.

129 p.  26 cm.

U.B.C. SPECIAL COLLECTIONS

**1071** Natural History Society of British Columbia

Bulletin.  no. [1]-[3]; 1893-1910.  Victoria.

3 v.  plates.  23, 25 cm.  irregular.

B.C. ARCHIVES

**1072** Nelson, Joseph

Proposed Hudson's Bay and Pacific railway and new steamship route.  [London, Economic Printing & Publishing Co.] 1893.

84 p.  fold. map.  24 cm.  At head of title: Direct route through the North-west Territories of Canada to the Pacific Ocean.

A proposal for a railway line from Port Churchill to Calgary, a junction of the C.P.R., and for steamer service between Churchill and the United Kingdom.

Also: London, H. Little, 1894. 78 p.

B.C. ARCHIVES

**1073** Odd Fellows, Canadian Order of. Victoria. Loyal Fernwood Lodge No. 178

By-laws and order of business of the Loyal Fernwood Lodge of the Canadian Order of Odd-Fellows, Manchester Unity.  Victoria, H. G. Waterson, printer, 1893.

20 p. (incl. cover)  13 cm.  Cover title.  Original examined. Xerox copy held by the library, University of Victoria.

UNIVERSITY OF VICTORIA LIBRARY

**1074** Odd Fellows, Independent Order of. Nanaimo. Centennial Lodge No. 20

Constitution, by-laws, rules of order, etc., of Centennial Lodge No. 20, I.O.O.F., under the jurisdiction of the Grand Lodge of British Columbia; instituted at Nanaimo, B.C., June 28th, 1892.  Nanaimo, Printed at the Free Press Office, 1893.

56 p.  16 cm.  List of members: p. [49]-51. Original examined. Xerox copy in the library, University of Victoria.

UNIVERSITY OF VICTORIA LIBRARY

**1075** Odd Fellows, Independent Order of. Victoria. Columbia Lodge No. 2

Constitution, by-laws and rules of order of Columbia Lodge No. 2 of the Independent Order of Odd Fellows, under the jurisdiction of the Grand Lodge of British Columbia, located at Victoria, B.C. Victoria, Printed at 28 Broad Street, 1893.

76 p.  facsim.  15 cm.

B.C. ARCHIVES

**1076** Odd Fellows, Independent Order of. Victoria. Loyal "Occidental" Lodge No. 7177

By-laws.  Victoria, H. G. Waterson, printer, 1893.

27 p.  12 cm.  After t. p. printing on verso of pages only.

B.C. ARCHIVES

**1077** Official programme . . .

Official programme of the citizens' celebration to be held in conjunction with the annual exhibition of the Royal Agricultural and Industrial Society of British Columbia at New Westminster, Sept. 26th to 29th, 1893.  [New] Westminster, Printed by Fred. Jackson [1893]

32 p. (incl. advertisements)  15 cm.  Cover title. Contents: Jackson's official programme [p. 3-15] — Philip, Gibson & Company [property list: p. 16-32]

B.C. ARCHIVES

**1078** Okanagan Falls . . .

Okanagan Falls, British Columbia; mining, grazing, fruit-raising, manufacturing.  [Vancouver, News-Advertiser, 1893]

7 p.  illus.  22 cm.  Cover title.

B.C. ARCHIVES

**1079** Okanagan mining review

Okanagan mining review.  v. 1, no. 1–11; August 1893—November 1893.  Okanagan Falls, B.C.

v.  weekly.  Microfilm copy examined.

B.C. ARCHIVES

**1080** Palmer, H[enry] T[homas]

A marvellous experience, containing light and food for Christians, sceptics, and worldlings. Vancouver, Trythall City Printing Works [1893?]

218 p.  20 cm.

B.C. ARCHIVES

**1081** Pilling, James Constantine
1846-1895

Bibliography of the Chinookan languages (including Chinook jargon)  Washington, Government Printing Office, 1893.

xiii, 81 p.  facsims.  25 cm.  ([United States] Bureau of American Ethnology. [Bulletin, no. 15])

Lists all types of sources, including manuscripts, which contain vocabularies. It offers valuable background to the compilation of Chinookan jargon dictionaries as well as providing biographical information on the compilers.

B.C. ARCHIVES

**1082    Pilling, James Constantine**
1846-1895

Bibliography of the Salishan languages.
Washington, Government Printing Office, 1893.

xi, 86 p.    25 cm.    ([United States] Bureau of
American Ethnology. [Bulletin, no. 16])

Lists all types of sources, including manuscripts,
which contain vocabularies.

B.C. ARCHIVES

**1083    Routhier, [Sir] A[dolphe]
        B[asile]**
1839-1920

De Québec à Victoria.    Québec, L.-J. Demers &
Frère, 1893.

392 p.    22 cm.

Four chapters relate to British Columbia.

B.C. ARCHIVES

**1084    Scidmore, Eliza Ruhamah**
1856-1928

Appleton's guide-book to Alaska and the
Northwest Coast, including the shores of
Washington, British Columbia, southeastern
Alaska, the Aleutian and the Seal Islands, the
Bering and Arctic coasts.    New York, D.
Appleton and Company, 1893.

v, 156 p.    plates, maps (part fold.)    18 cm.

Also: 1896.    Also: 1897.    New edition, with a
chapter on the Klondike: 1898.    Also: 1899.
English edition published under title: *The guide-book
to Alaska and the Northwest Coast* . . . (London,
Heinemann, 1893).

B.C. ARCHIVES

**1085    Strong, James C[lark]**
B. 1826

Wah-kee-nah and her people; the curious customs,
traditions, and legends of the North American
Indians.    New York, G. P. Putnam's Sons, 1893.

xiii, 275 p.    port.    20 cm.

Mentions Indian tribes of the B.C. coast.

B.C. ARCHIVES

**1086    United States**

Behring Sea arbitration. Argument of the United
States before the tribunal of arbitration convened at
Paris under the provisions of the treaty between the
United States of America and Great Britain,
concluded February 29, 1892. Presented to both
Houses of Parliament by command of Her Majesty,
March 1893.    London, Printed by Harrison and
Sons [1893]

iv, 327 p.    25 cm.    ([Great Britain. Parliament.
Command papers] C. 6951)    At head of title: United
States, no. 8 (1893)

B.C. ARCHIVES

**1087    United States**

Behring Sea arbitration. The case of the United
States before the tribunal of arbitration convened at
Paris under the provisions of the treaty between the
United States of America and Great Britain,
concluded February 29, 1892, including the reports
of the Bering Sea Commission. Presented to both
Houses of Parliament by command of Her Majesty,
March 1893.    London, Harrison and Sons [1893]

xvii, 433 p.    25 cm.    ([Great Britain. Parliament.
Command papers] C. 6949) At head of title:
United States, no. 6 (1893)

B.C. ARCHIVES

**1088    United States**

Behring Sea arbitration. The counter case of the
United States before the tribunal of arbitration
convened at Paris under the provisions of the treaty
between the United States of America and Great
Britain, concluded February 29, 1892. Presented to
both Houses of Parliament by command of Her
Majesty, March 1893.    London, Harrison and
Sons [1893]

ix, 152 p.    25 cm.    ([Great Britain. Parliament.
Command papers] C. 6950) At head of title:
United States, no. 7 (1893)

B.C. ARCHIVES

**1089    United States**

Fur-seal arbitration. Argument of the United
States before the tribunal of arbitration convened
at Paris under the provisions of the treaty between
the United States of America and Great Britain,
concluded February 29, 1892.    Washington,
Government Printing Office, 1893.

v, 327 p.    25 cm.    Not seen.

LIBRARY OF CONGRESS

**1090    United States**

Fur-seal arbitration. The counter case of the United
States before the tribunal of arbitration to convene
at Paris under the provisions of the treaty between
the United States of America and Great Britain,
concluded February 29, 1892, including appendix.
Washington, Government Printing Office, 1893.

xi, 470 p.    plates, facsims.    *and* 4 portfolios of
maps.    26 cm.

NATIONAL LIBRARY

1091 United States. Treasury Department. Special Agents Division

Behring Sea arbitration. Report on the condition of the fur-seal fisheries of the Pribylov Islands in 1890, by Henry W. Elliott, special agent appointed under an act of Congress of the United States, approved April 5, 1890. Produced on the 4th April 1893, by the agent of the United States to the Tribunal of Arbitration convened at Paris.　Paris, Chamerot & Renouard, 1893.

xv, 338 p.　24 cm.

NATIONAL LIBRARY

1092 Victoria. Congregation Emanu-El

Constitution and by-laws; organized 5622-1862; incorporated 5624-1864.　Victoria [Jas. A. Cohen, 1893]

22 p.　26 cm.　Cover title. Microfilm copy examined.

B.C. ARCHIVES

1093 Whiteaves, Joseph Frederick
1835-1909

Notes on some marine invertebrata from the coast of British Columbia.　[n.p., 1893?]

133-137 p.　plate.　22 cm.　Reprinted from the *Ottawa naturalist*, v. 7, no. 9, 1893.　Not seen.

QUEEN'S UNIVERSITY LIBRARY

1094 Wishart, Andrew

The Behring Sea question; the arbitration treaty and the award.　Edinburgh, William Green & Sons [1893]

54 p.　fold. map.　22 cm.　Includes as an appendix the treaty signed in Washington, 29 February 1892.

A summary of events from a legal point of view.

B.C. ARCHIVES

1095 Art, Historical and Scientific Association of Vancouver

Constitution, 1894.　[Vancouver] News-Advertiser Press [1894?]

8 p.　14 cm.　Cover title.

B.C. ARCHIVES

1096 Baker, James
1830-1906

International bimetallism; speech of Lt.-Colonel the Hon. James Baker, in the Legislative Assembly of British Columbia, January 24th, 1894. [n.p., n.d.]

18 p.　23 cm.　Cover title.

B.C. ARCHIVES

1097 Begg, Alexander
1825-1905

History of British Columbia from its earliest discovery to the present time.　Toronto, William Briggs, 1894.

568 p.　illus., ports., fold. map.　23 cm.

A popular account which contains numerous quotations from pioneer journals and letters.

Also: London, Sampson, c1894.

B.C. ARCHIVES

1098 Bella Coola Colony, British Columbia

Bella Coola Colony of British Columbia; constitution and by-laws.　[Bella Coola, 1894?]

sheet.　34 x 21 cm.

The association's purpose was to encourage Norwegian emigration to Bella Coola.

B.C. ARCHIVES

1099 Bering Sea Tribunal of Arbitration

Sentence, déclarations et protocoles des séances. Paris, Imprimerie Nationale, 1894.

240 p.　33 cm.　At head of title: Tribunal arbitral des pêcheries de Behring . . .　Text in English and French. Binder's title: Protocols and award. John W. Foster, agent for the United States; Charles H. Tupper, agent for Great Britain.

VANCOUVER PUBLIC LIBRARY

1100 Betts, Emery C.

Prospecting for minerals in British Columbia; or, Fourteen days in the hills; its pains, pleasures and results. (A true story descriptive of mining life) Minneapolis, Minn., Betts Publishing Company [1894]

84 p.　illus.　17 cm.　Not seen.

YALE WESTERN AMERICANA CATALOGUE

1101 Bible. New Testament. Luke. Kwakiutl

The Gospel according to Saint Luke. Translated into the Kwā Gūtl language, north of Vancouver Island [by Alfred James Hall]　London, British and Foreign Bible Society, 1894.

138 p.　Not seen.

BRITISH MUSEUM CATALOGUE

**1102    Boas, Franz**
1858-1942

Chinook texts.    Washington, Government
Printing Office, 1894.

278 p.   port.   25 cm.   ([United States]
Bureau of American Ethnology.
Bulletin no. 20)

The Chinook texts were translated into English
literally and in free form by means of the Chinook
jargon. Examination of them shows the similarity
between Chinook words and jargon words.

B.C. ARCHIVES

**1103    British Columbia. Provincial
         Archives**

Report.    1893/94-1921.    Victoria,
R. Wolfenden.

v.   26 cm.   annual (irregular)   Title varies: For
1893/94-1909 as *Report on the library of the
Legislative Assembly . . .*   For 1910-13 as *Report
of the Provincial Archives Department.* The reports
for 1893/94-1909 include the Archives under the
heading, "Northwest collection." The Provincial
Archives became separate from the Provincial
Library in 1908, and published reports separately in
1910 and 1913. The report for 1921 was entitled
*Report of the Provincial Library and Archives.*
Reports were printed for the years 1893/94, 1895,
1896, 1897, 1898, 1899-1900, 1900-1901, 1902-1903,
1907, 1909, 1910, 1913, with 1921 being a joint
report. Most reports are also in the Clerk's papers, and
those for 1910, 1913 and 1921 are also in the
*Sessional papers* of British Columbia.

See especially following reports which contain
material not published elsewhere: 1900-1901,
Appendix 4: "Titles of works relating to the history
and discovery of British Columbia and the
North-west portion of America"; 1910, Appendix A:
"Papers relating to Vancouver Island," "Papers
relating to the colony of British Columbia," and
"Papers relating to the province of British Columbia."
Appendix B contains important letters, transcripts and
miscellaneous papers. 1913, section 2: "Papers relating
to the colonization of Vancouver Island," with letters
by Lieut. Adam Dundas, Sir George Simpson, Charles
Enderby, James E. Fitzgerald, W. Colquhoun Grant,
Right Rev. Modeste Demers, James Douglas and
David Thompson. The same section has a "Report on
Vancouver Island."

B.C. ARCHIVES

**1104    British Columbia law notes**

British Columbia law notes.   v. 1, no. 1-2;
February—March 1894.    Victoria,
Munroe Miller.

1 v.   24 cm.   bi-monthly.   Only two published.
Index on back cover of no. 2.

Includes abstracts of court proceedings.

B.C. ARCHIVES

**1105    British Columbia . . .**

British Columbia; mineral and agricultural
wealth; the Canadian national park [Banff]
Illustrated. From "Winnipeg Saturday night."
[Winnipeg, 1894]

24, [2] p. (last two pages numbered 13,14)   illus.,
ports., map.   34 cm.   Cover title. Reprinted from
*Winnipeg Saturday night*, v. 2, no. 3, September-
October 1894.

B.C. ARCHIVES

**1106    Canada. Department of Marine
         and Fisheries**

Pilotage by-laws for the district of Yale and New
Westminster, established by the Pilotage Authority
under the Dominion Act, 36 Vic., cap. 54, intitled
"An Act Respecting Pilotage, 1873," with several
amendments and subsequent orders in council.
Approved Saturday, 28th day of April 1894.
Vancouver, Thomson Bros., printers, 1894.

14 p.   14 cm.   Cover title.

B.C. ARCHIVES

**1107    Canada. Royal Commission on
         the Liquor Traffic**

Minutes of evidence: Province of Manitoba,
North-west Territories, and British Columbia.
Ottawa, Printed by S. E. Dawson, 1894.

700 p.   24 cm.   (Canada. Sessional papers, 1894,
no. 21, v. 3 of the evidence)   Not seen.   Missing
from Shortt collection.

PEEL

**1108    Canestrelli, Philippo**
1839-1918

Linguae Ksanka (Kootenai); elementa
grammaticae. Auctore Philippo Canestrelli
e Societate Jesu.   Santa Clara, Calif., Typis N. H.
Downing, 1894.

144 p.   21 cm.

A grammar with Latin text. Until 1958 only seven
copies and one fragment were known to exist. In
that year the Director of the Oregon Province
Archives discovered unbound copies for which he
had been searching for some years. They were
bound and sold in 1959 by the Archives with a
facsimile of the original title page under title:
*A Kootenai grammar.*

UNIVERSITY OF WASHINGTON LIBRARY

**1109    Church of England. Liturgy
         and ritual. Haida**

A child's manual.   Massett, Queen Charlotte
Islands, 1894.

12 p.   17 cm.   Cover title. Mimeographed writing.
Text in Haida. Possibly the work of John Henry Keen.

B.C. ARCHIVES

**1110 Church of England. Liturgy and ritual. Salish.**

Sh' atjinkujĭn; parts of the communion service of the Church of England. Privately printed for the use of the Lower Fraser Indians in the All Hallows' Mission Chapel, Yale, B.C. Not published. [London, Darling & Son, Ltd.] 1894.

8 l. 19 cm. Cover title. Text is probably in the Stalo dialect of the Halkomelem language of the Coast Salish Indians.

B.C. ARCHIVES

**1111 The Cost of the Nakusp and Slocan Railway ...**

The cost of the Nakusp and Slocan Railway as sworn to by engineers, and compared with the cost of other railways. [n.p., 1894?]

sheet. 36 x 27 cm.

B.C. ARCHIVES

**1112 Dale, John**

Round the world by doctors' orders; being a narrative of a year's travel in Japan, Ceylon, Australia, China, New Zealand, Canada, the United States, etc., etc. London, Elliot Stock, 1894.

viii, 350 p. illus., plates. 24 cm.

Several pages relate to the author's travels in British Columbia.

B.C. ARCHIVES

**1113 Eells, Myron**
1843-1907

The Chinook jargon. [n.p., 1894?]

[300]-312 p. 24 cm. Caption title. Bibliography — dictionaries and vocabularies: p. 311-312. Reprinted from the *American anthropologist* for July 1894. Not seen.

LIBRARY OF CONGRESS

**1114 Government policy reviewed ...**

Government policy reviewed; being a series of articles on the political situation in this province, as reprinted from the "Colonist." Victoria, "The Colonist" Steam Presses, 1894.

20 p. 22 cm. Cover title. Six articles.

B.C. ARCHIVES

**1115 Great Britain. Treaties, etc.**

Convention between Great Britain and the United States supplementary to the convention respecting boundaries of July 22, 1892 (Alaska and Passamaquoddy Bay) Signed at Washington, February 3, 1894; ratifications exchanged at Washington, March 28, 1894. Presented to both Houses of Parliament by command of Her Majesty, April 1894. London, Printed by Harrison and Sons [1894]

2 p. 25 cm. ([Great Britain. Parliament. Command papers] C. 7311) Treaty series no. 10, 1894.

For the convention of 22 July 1892, see entry 1058.

B.C. ARCHIVES

**1116 Indian bazaar**

Indian bazaar. [Victoria, J. J. Hart & Co., 1894?]

44 p. 14 cm. Cover title. The home of the Haidas, by Rev. Charles Harrison: p. 11-33.

Haida legends and beliefs written to publicize the sale of Indian material by J. J. Hart & Co.

B.C. ARCHIVES

**1117 Ingall, E[lfric] D[rew]**
1858-1944

Silver mining in British Columbia. [Ottawa? 1894]

4 p. (folder) 22 cm. Caption title. Paper read before the General Mining Association of Quebec, 10 July 1894.

LIBRARY, GEOLOGICAL SURVEY OF CANADA

**1118 [Jones, Edward Gardiner]**
EDITOR

The Oregonian's handbook of the Pacific Northwest. [Portland, The Oregonian Publishing Co., c1894]

631 p. illus., ports. 21 cm. Not seen.

Pages 568-588 relate to British Columbia.

OREGON HISTORICAL SOCIETY

**1119 [Le Jeune, Jean-Marie Raphael]**
1855-1930

Elements of shorthand; or, A phonetic syllabary after the Duployan system of phonography. Second edition. Kamloops, 1894.

16 p. (plus cover) 16 cm. Mimeographed. Duployan shorthand with phonetic equivalents in italics. Bound in the University of Washington Library in *Kamloops miscellany*, v. 1.

The first edition is listed as entry 939.

UNIVERSITY OF WASHINGTON LIBRARY

**1120    McCain, Charles W.**
COMPILER    1867-1933

History of the SS. "Beaver"; being a graphic and vivid sketch of this noted pioneer steamer and her romantic cruise for over half a century on the placid island-dotted waters of the North Pacific. Vancouver [Evans & Hastings] 1894.

99 p.   plates, ports.   17 cm.   On t.p.: Also containing a description of the Hudson's Bay Company from its formation in 1670, down to the present time; biography of Captain McNeill; the narrative of a Fraser River prospector of 1859; historical momentoes of the Beaver's copper remains; the sad ending of the author's last trip in search of old-time naval relics; important developments in steam since its introduction in 1769, etc.

B.C. ARCHIVES

**1121    MacMaster, [Sir] Donald**
1846-1922

The seal arbitration, 1893.    Montreal, Wm. Foster Brown & Co., 1894.

65 p.   fold. map.   22 cm.   Cover title.

A legal synopsis with comments. The Appendix lists the members of the Tribunal of Arbitration.

CANADIAN ARCHIVES

**1122    [Martley, John]**
1859-1896

Songs of the Cascades. First part. By Erl Viking [pseud.]    London, Horace Cox, 1894.

x, 188 p.   18 cm.   Contents in part: An appeal case (Lillooet, August 1892) — H. P. C. [Henry Pennant Cornwall] — Mr. Doolan's lament [and its sequel] A wail from New Westminster. — At Lillooet, 8th August 1892. Part 3: Sketches and portraits [of well-known persons of the time — The Hon. P. O. Reilly, the Hon. C. T. Cornwall, the Hon. J. E. Pooley, the Ven. Archdeacon Woods, Sir Matthew Baillie Begbie. These were all identified in the author's own handwriting in a personal copy belonging to Kathleen O'Reilly]

Poetry.

B.C. ARCHIVES

**1123    Minnie (ship)**

In the Supreme Court of Canada, on appeal from the British Columbia Admiralty District of the Exchequer Court of Canada; between the ship "Minnie," her equipment and everything on board of her and the proceeds thereof (defendant) appellant, and Our Sovereign Lady, the Queen, (plaintiff) respondent. Action for condemnation. Case on appeal. Arthur Louis Belyea, Victoria, B.C., solicitor for appellant; McIntyre, Code & Orde, Ottawa, Ont., agents; Chas. E. Pooley, Victoria, B.C., solicitor for respondent; O'Connor

& Hogg, Ottawa, agents.    Victoria, The Colonist Printing and Publishing Company, 1894.

48 l.   28 cm.

The Victoria-based ship was condemned for contravention of the Seal Fishery (North Pacific) Act of 1893.

B.C. ARCHIVES

**1124    Morice, A[drian] G[abriel]**
1859-1938

Carrier reading-book. Second edition.    Stuart's Lake Mission, 1894.

192 p.   illus.   15 cm.   (Stuart's Lake Mission print, no. 13)    Except for the Preface and text headings, the work is in Déné syllabic characters. Déné syllabary: p. [11]-12.

The first edition appeared under title: *Pe tœstlœs œtsôtœléh* (entry 890).

B.C. ARCHIVES

**1125    Morice, Adrian Gabriel**
1859-1938

Notes, archaeological, industrial and sociological, on the western Dénés; with an ethnographical sketch of the same.    [Toronto, Copp, Clark, 1894]

222 p.   illus.   27 cm.   (Canadian Institute. *Transactions.* 1892-93. v. 4, pt. 1, no. 7)

B.C. ARCHIVES

**1126    Munroe, Kirk**
1850-1930

The fur-seal's tooth; a story of Alaskan adventure. New York, Harper & Brothers, 1894.

viii, 267 p.   illus., plates, map.   19 cm.

Fiction. Part of the book is concerned with British Columbia.

NATIONAL LIBRARY

**1127    Opposition slanders refuted . . .**

Opposition slanders refuted; the Pooley scandal; the Baker scandal; intestate estates; suitors' funds, minor slanders; who are the scandal-mongers?; speech of the premier on the budget; carrying the war to Egypt; comparison of travelling expenses under opposition regime and now; $3,500 for one trip to England and not an item of detail; $1,100 for one trip to Ottawa; what government used the intestate estates funds without authority?; robbing the dead; political anarchism.    [n.p., 1894]

7 p.   23 cm.   Caption title.

Report of remarks made by Theodore Davie, premier, and Robert Beaven in a debate on the budget.

B.C. ARCHIVES

**1128**   Phillipps-Wolley, [Sir] Clive
[Oldnall Long]
1854-1918

Big game shooting.   London, Longmans, Green
and Co., 1894.

2 v.   illus., plates.   20 cm.   (Half title: The
Badminton Library of sports and pastimes)

Chapter 18 of Volume 1, "Big game of North
America" (p. 346-427), relates in part to a
description of animals found in British Columbia.

Second edition: 1895.

**1129**   Phillipps-Wolley, Sir C[live
Oldnall Long]
1854-1918

Gold, gold, in Cariboo; a story of adventure in
British Columbia. With six illustrations by Godfrey
C. Hindley.   London, Blackie & Son
Limited, 1894.

288 p.   6 plates.   20 cm.

Fiction. In 1862 two young Englishmen set out from
Victoria to go to the upper reaches of the Fraser
River to search for gold in the Cariboo.

Also: London, Blackie & Son Limited, n.d. 288 p.

**1130**   Pilling, James Constantine
1846-1895

Bibliography of the Wakashan languages.
Washington, Government Printing Office, 1894.

x, 70 p.   facsims.   25 cm.   ([United States] Bureau
of American Ethnology. [Bulletin, no. 19])

In part, lists monographs, periodical articles, and
manuscripts containing words in the Kwakiutl,
Nootka, and Bella Coola Indian languages.

**1131**   The Province

The province.   v. 1-5; 3 March 1894—26 March
1898?   Victoria, The Province Publishing Co.

5 v.   31 cm.   Last issue examined: v. 5, no. 13,
26 March 1898. Edited by Arthur Hodgins Scaife
from 1894-97.

A paper-covered journal, the forerunner of the
Vancouver *Province* (see Index under "Scaife,
Arthur Hodgins").

**1132**   [Scaife, Arthur Hodgins]

Three letters of credit and other stories, by "Kim
Bilir" [pseud.]   Victoria, Province Publishing
Co., 1894.

123 p.   19 cm.   First published in the *Province*
(Victoria; journal) Contents: Three letters of credit.
— An old string re-strung. — The seventieth time
seven. — How's that? — How Greek met Greek.

**1133**   Schulenburg, A[lbrecht]
C[onon]
GRAF VON DER   1865-1902

Die Sprache der Zimshian-Indianer in Nordwest-
Amerika.   Braunschweig, Richard Sattler, 1894.

16, viii, 372 p.   30 cm.

Grammar and dictionary of the Tsimshian language.

**1134**   [Smith, Henry Erskine]
1842-1932

On and off the saddle; characteristic sights and
scenes from the great Northwest to the Antilles, by
Lispenard Rutgers [pseud.]   New York, G. P.
Putnam's Sons, 1894.

viii, 201 p.   plates.   17 cm.   A Rocky-Mountain
picture; winter scenes among the glaciers of the
Selkirks in British Columbia: p. 166-171.

**1135**   Tupper, Sir Charles Hibbert
1855-1927

Speech of Sir Charles Hibbert Tupper, Minister of
Marine and Fisheries, delivered in the Victoria
Theatre on the evening of Monday, 10th December,
1894.   [Victoria, Victoria Liberal-Conservative
Association, 1894?]

15 p.   22 cm.   Caption title.

**1136**   Vancouver Pioneer Society

Constitution, by-laws and rules of order of the
Vancouver Pioneer Society; organized Oct. 26,
1893. Published by order of the Board of Directors.
Vancouver, Thomson, 1894.

20 p.   11 cm.   Cover title.   Not seen.

**1137**   [Venning, Robert Norris]
B. 1854

Report of the British agent to the Russian seal
islands under the provisional agreement entered
into between Her Majesty's government and that of
Russia for the protection of the seal fisheries during
1893. With appendices.   Ottawa, Government
Printing Bureau, 1894.

111 p.   tables (1 fold.)   33 cm.

**1138    Victoria. Corrig College**

[Prospectus.    Victoria, 1894?]

4 p. (folder)    27 cm.    J. W. Church, headmaster.

B.C. ARCHIVES


**1139    Victoria City School District. Board of Trustees**

Report.    1894-1945.    Victoria.

v.    illus.    22, 24 cm.    annual.    Printer varies.
Superseded in 1945 by *Annual report of the Board of School Trustees of School District no. 61.*

B.C. ARCHIVES


**1140    Williams, John G.**
B. 1824

The adventures of a seventeen-year-old lad and the fortunes he might have won.    Boston, Printed for the author by the Collins Press, 1894.

308 p.    illus., port.    24 cm.    Not seen.

Includes accounts of gold mining in California and the Fraser River district.

B.C. ARCHIVES


**1141    Aberdeen Claims**

Prospectus of the Aberdeen Claims, Cariboo district, B.C., junction of Slough Creek and Willow River.    [Victoria, Chas. Ramos, printer] 1895.

[8] p.    fold. map.    10 x 23 cm.

B.C. ARCHIVES


**1142    Badminton Club of Victoria**

Articles of constitution, and by-laws of the Badminton Club of Victoria, B.C., established May 15, 1894.    Victoria, The Province Publishing Company [n.d.]

11 1.    15 cm.    Copy examined has folder insert (2 p.) with headings: Committee. List of members, March 8th, 1895.

B.C. ARCHIVES


**1143    Baker, James**
1830-1906

Report on the mining industries of Kootenay. Victoria, "The Colonist" Steam Presses, 1895.

8 p.    22 cm.

UNIVERSITY OF WASHINGTON LIBRARY


**1144    Bering Sea Tribunal of Arbitration**

Fur seal arbitration. Proceedings of the tribunal of arbitration, convened at Paris under the treaty between the United States of America and Great Britain, concluded at Washington, February 29, 1892, for the determination of questions between the two governments concerning the jurisdictional rights of the United States in the waters of the Bering Sea.    Washington, Government Printing Office, 1895.

16 v.    plates, fold. maps, diagrs., facsims., tables. 24 cm.    ([United States] 53d Cong., 2d sess. Senate. Ex. doc. 177, pts. 1-16)

B.C. ARCHIVES


**1145    Boas, Franz**
1858-1942

Indianische sagen von der Nord-Pacifischen Küste Amerikas.    Berlin, A. Asher & Co., 1895.

vi, 363 p.    map.    26 cm.    The material first appeared in the *Verhandlungen der Berliner Gesellschaft für Anthropologie, Ethnologie und Urgeschichte* in the years from 1891 to 1895.

B.C. ARCHIVES


**1146    Bovey, H[enry] T[aylor]**
1852-1912

The strength of Canadian douglas fir, red pine, white pine and spruce.    [n.p., 1895]

104 p.    illus., diagrs., tables.    34 cm.    Cover title.
Reprinted from: Canadian Society of Civil Engineers. *Transactions.* v. 9, 1895.

The results of experiments conducted at McGill University.

CANADIAN ARCHIVES


**1147    The British Columbia almanac . . .**

The British Columbia almanac, specially compiled for this province with other information, 1895-98.    Victoria, The Colonist Printing & Publishing Co., 1895-98.

4 v.    21 cm.    annual.    No more published?

The almanac includes game laws, laws relating to placer mining and claims, and abstracts of land regulations.

B.C. ARCHIVES


**1148    Canada. Department of Public Printing and Stationery**

Electoral atlas of the Dominion of Canada, as divided for the revision of the voters' lists made in the year 1894. Ottawa, Government Printing Bureau, 1895.

1 v. (unpaged)    203 maps.    27 x 36 cm.

## 1149    Chapman, John

Reflections from sunny memories of a tour through Canada, British Columbia, and the United States of America. Edited by Henry Tuckett.    Torquay [Eng.] Standard Printing, Publishing, and Newspaper Company, 1895.

43 p.    22 cm.    Reprinted from the *Devon County Standard* and other newspapers.    Not seen.

## 1150    Church of England. Liturgy and ritual. Tsimshian

Wila yelth; gigiangwaklthum hialthukq; alth tkanitqushlth sha alth tkash golth.    [Aiyansh Mission, B.C., n.d.]

21 p.    21 cm.    Caption title.    Translated by James Benjamin McCullagh and from his press.

Prayers and psalms in the Niska dialect of the Tsimshian language.

## 1151    Costello, J[oseph] A.

The Siwash; their life, legends, and tales. Puget Sound and Pacific Northwest.    Seattle, The Calvert Company, 1895.

vii, 169 p.    illus., plates, ports.    24 cm.

Also: 1896.

## 1152    Eummelen, H.

Sick room altar manual, with prayers, formulas, instructions in administering the sacraments, and a complete course of instructions to nurses in attending the sick. Dedicated to the Sacred Heart. Vancouver, 1895.

89 p.    illus., port.    15 cm.    On verso of t.p.: Imprimatur Paul Durieu, Bishop of New Westminster, B.C.; Vancouver, B.C., June 18th, 1895.

## 1153    Field, Henry Martyn
### 1822-1907

Our western archipelago.    New York, Charles Scribner's Sons, 1895.

ix, 250 p.    plates, map.    21 cm.

An account of a trip through Canada to Alaska.

## 1154    Freemasons. Victoria. Victoria-Columbia Lodge No. 1

By-laws of Victoria-Columbia Lodge No. 1, A.F. & A.M., B.C.R.    Victoria, The Colonist Steam Presses, 1895.

29 p.    14 cm.

## 1155    George, William

A sealer's journal; or, A cruise of the schooner "Umbrina."    Victoria, H. G. Waterson, printer, 1895.

136 p.    18 cm.

A record of daily life kept by the cabin boy of a Victoria-based sealer.

## 1156    Great Britain. Foreign Office

Correspondence respecting claims for compensation on account of British vessels seized in Behring Sea by United States' cruisers. Presented to both Houses of Parliament by command of Her Majesty, September 1895. London, Printed by Harrison and Sons [1895]

iv, 43 p.    34 cm.    ([Great Britain. Parliament. Command papers] C. 7836) At head of title: United States, no. 1 (1895)

## 1157    Great Britain. Foreign Office

Correspondence respecting the agreement with Russia relative to the seal fishery in the North Pacific. (In continuation of "Russia no. 3 (1893)" C. 7029) Presented to both Houses of Parliament by command of Her Majesty, June 1895.    London, Printed by Harrison and Sons [1895]

v, 52 p.    34 cm.    ([Great Britain. Parliament. Command papers] C. 7713) At head of title: Russia, no. 1 (1895)

## 1158    Harrison, C[harles]

Haida grammar. Edited by Alex. F. Chamberlain [with] prefatory note by [the] editor.    [n.p.] 1895.

123-226 p.    25 cm.    Cover title. From: Royal Society of Canada. *Proceedings and transactions.* ser. 2, v. 1, sec. 2, 1895.

**1159    Hill-Tout, Charles**
1858?-1944

Later prehistoric man in British Columbia.
[n.p.] 1895.

103-122 p.   25 cm.   Cover title. From: The Royal
Society of Canada. *Proceedings and transactions.*
ser. 2, v. 1, sec. 2, 1895-6. Contains: Remarks on a
skull from British Columbia, by Franz Boas [p. 122]

On middens and tumuli in the vicinity of the lower
Fraser River.

B.C. ARCHIVES

**1160    Howard, Leland Ossian**
1857-1950

Legislation against injurious insects; a compilation
of the laws and regulations of the United States and
British Columbia.   Washington, Government
Printing Office, 1895.

46 p.   23 cm.   (United States. Department of
Agriculture. Division of Entomology. Bulletin no. 33)
Not seen.

LIBRARY OF CONGRESS

**1161    Kamloops. Citizens' Committee**

General statistics and other information regarding
the suitability of Kamloops as a health resort.
Compiled by E. Furrer, T. W. Lambert [and others]
a committee appointed by the citizens of Kamloops.
Kamloops, Inland Sentinel Print [1895]

8 p.   21 cm.   Cover title.

Also: 1896. [12] p.

B.C. ARCHIVES

**1162    Kamloops Wawa directory**

Kamloops Wawa directory.   January 1895.
[Kamloops? 1895]

8 l. (i.e. 11 p.)   19 x 25 cm.   The 11 pages are on
5 leaves, printed on one side only (p. 1-2, 7-8, and 9
in duplicate) The work of Jean-Marie Raphael
Le Jeune. No more published? Not seen.

LIBRARY OF CONGRESS

**1163    Lefevre, Lily Alice [ (Cooke) ]**
D. 1938

The Lions' Gate and other verses.   Victoria,
Province Publishing Co., 1895.

95 p.   16 cm.

The first poem describes the mountain called "the
Lions" on the north shore of Vancouver; "Eagle Pass"
tells of the accidental finding and naming of
Eagle Pass.

B.C. ARCHIVES

**1164    Mining and industrial record**

Mining and industrial record.   v. 1-37, no. 10;
October 1895—October 1932.   Vancouver.

v. illus.   30 cm.   monthly.   Title varies: v. 1-15
(1895—August 1908) as *British Columbia mining
record;* v. 16-17 (August 1910—July 1912) as
*British Columbia mining and engineering record;*
v. 18-19, no. 2 (August 1912—October 1913) as
*Mining and engineering record;* v. 19, no. 3—v. 21,
no. 4 (October 1913—August 1916) as *Mining
engineering and electrical record;* v. 21, no. 5—v. 29,
no. 3 (September/October 1916—March 1926) as
*Mining and electrical record.* Several suspensions in
publication. Absorbed *Economic and financial record,*
March 1925 (v. 28, no. 1-2 repeated in numbering)
Not indexed.

B.C. ARCHIVES

**1165    Nanaimo Poultry Society
Limited**

Prize list and rules of the Second Annual
Exhibition to be held at Nanaimo, B.C., on
February 12, 13 & 14, 1895 . . .   Nanaimo, Free
Press Print [1895]

12 p.   21 cm.   Cover title.

B.C. ARCHIVES

**1166    Odd Fellows, Independent Order
of. Nanaimo. Cedar Lodge
No. 35**

Constitution, by-laws, rules of order and order
of business of Cedar Lodge No. 35, Independent
Order of Odd-Fellows, Cedar district, Nanaimo,
B.C.; instituted March 21st, 1895.   [Nanaimo]
Nanaimo Free Press Book and Job Printing
Office, 1895.

47, [1] p.   16 cm.   List of members: p. [48] Original
examined. Xerox copy in the library, University
of Victoria.

UNIVERSITY OF VICTORIA LIBRARY

**1167    Odd Fellows, Independent Order
of. Vancouver**

Lodge history of the Independent Order Odd
Fellows, Knights of Pythias, and A.O.U.W.,
Vancouver, B.C., with a short history of their
organization; biographical sketches of members.
Vancouver, Order Publishing Company, 1895.

39 p.   15 cm.   Contents: Vancouver Lodge No. 8,
I.O.O.F., by D. Menzies. — Western Star Lodge No.
10, I.O.O.F., by H. B. Gilmour. — Mt. Pleasant Lodge
No. 19, I.O.O.F., by Richard Mills. — Pacific Lodge
No. 26, I.O.O.F. — Granville Lodge No. 3, K. of P.,
by W. F. M'Neil. — Rathbone Lodge No. 7, K. of P.,
by S. R. Robb. — Mt. Pleasant Lodge No. 11, K. of P.,
by I. Mills. — Crusader Lodge No. 19, K. of P., by
J. E. Evans. — Perseverance Lodge No. 11,
A.O.U.W., by F. L. Budlong. — Granville Lodge
No. 2, A.O.U.W.

U.B.C. SPECIAL COLLECTIONS

**1168  Parkin, [Sir] George R[obert]**
1846-1922

The great Dominion; studies of Canada.    London, Macmillan and Co., 1895.

viii, 251 p.    fold. maps.    20 cm.

One chapter on British Columbia; another on the Canadian Pacific Railway.

B.C. ARCHIVES

**1169  [Pascoe, Charles Frederick]**
COMPILER  B. 1854

Classified digest of the records of the Society for the Propagation of the Gospel in Foreign Parts, 1701-1892 (with much supplementary information) [Edited by H. W. Tucker] Fifth edition.    London, Published at the Society's Office, 1895.

xvi, 984 p.    illus., ports.    23 cm.

Chapter 22 deals with British Columbia.

After passing through seven editions the book was revised and appeared as *Two hundred years of the S. P. G.; an historical account of the Society for the Propagation of the Gospel in Foreign Parts, 1701-1900* (London, 1901). In xli, 1429 pages. List of references: p. 1301-1389.

B.C. ARCHIVES

**1170  St. Barbe, Charles**
EDITOR  D. 1929

The Kootenay mines; a sketch of their progress and condition to-day [with letters from the Similkameen and Kettle River camps from the special correspondent of "The Miner"]    Nelson, The Miner Print. & Pub. Co., 1895.

26 p.    map.    23 cm.    Cover title.

B.C. ARCHIVES

**1171  [Scaife, Arthur Hodgins]**

As it was in the Fifties, by "Kim Bilir" [pseud.] Victoria, The Province Publishing Company, 1895.

287 p.    23 cm.    First appeared in serial form in the *Province* (Victoria; journal)

Fiction. Part of the story takes place in British Columbia during the Cariboo gold rush days.

B.C. ARCHIVES

**1172  [Scaife, Arthur Hodgins]**

Gemini and lesser lights, by "Kim Bilir" [pseud. Victoria, Province Publishing Company, 1895]

187 p.    22 cm.    First published in the *Province* (Victoria; journal)

A collection of short stories.

B.C. PROVINCIAL LIBRARY

**1173  The seal arbitration**

The seal arbitration.    [n.p., n.d.]

68 p.    23 cm.

A summary from an anti-American point of view.

U.B.C. SPECIAL COLLECTIONS

**1174  Sladen, Douglas [Brooke Wheelton]**
1856-1947

On the cars and off; being the journal of a pilgrimage along the Queen's highway to the East, from Halifax in Nova Scotia to Victoria in Vancouver's Island.    London, New York, Ward, Locke & Bowden Limited, 1895.

xviii, 447 p.    illus., plates, port., maps.    24 cm.

About one-quarter of the book relates to British Columbia.

Another edition, with additional matter on the Klondike by P. A. Hurd: London, New York, Ward, Locke & Bowden, 1898? In xviii, 512 pages.

B.C. ARCHIVES

**1175  Slater, John B.**

Natural resources of Stevens County, Washington, and the famous mining region of Trail Creek, B.C. Spokane, Spokane Printing Co., 1895.

62 p.    illus.    Not seen. Copy in the Spokane Public Library.

SMITH

**1176  Slivers**
PSEUDONYM

Fables of the Nechaco; a complete novel of one of the most remarkable and romantic districts on the American continent.    Vancouver, Produced by the Dominion Stock and Bond Corporation [n.d.]

46 p.    illus.    21 cm.    Not seen.

VANCOUVER PUBLIC LIBRARY

**1177  Somerset, H[enry Charles Somers Augustus]**

The land of the muskeg. With a preface by A. Hungerford Pollen. With one hundred and ten illustrations from sketches by A. H. Pollen and instantaneous photographs, and four maps. London, William Heinemann, 1895.

xxxi, 248 p.    illus., ports., maps (part. fold.) 24 cm.

Passing some of the camp sites of George Dawson, the author and his party made a harrowing journey from Dunvegan to the Pine, along the Pine and Misinchinka rivers to Fort McLeod. From Fort

McLeod they travelled to Quesnel via Fort St. James and the Stuart River.

Second edition: 1895.

## 1178 United States. Department of State

Message from the President of the United States, in response to Senate resolution of January 8, 1895, transmitting information relating to the enforcement of the regulations respecting fur seals, adopted by the governments of the United States and Great Britain in accordance with the decision of the tribunal of arbitration convened at Paris, with other information called for by said resolution. [Washington, Government Printing Office, 1895]

438 p. maps, tables. 23 cm. ([United States] 53d Cong., 3d sess. Senate. Ex. doc. no. 67) At head of title: Regulations of fur seals.

Includes reports on the activities of various Victoria-based sealing schooners; mentions the smuggling of liquor from Fort Simpson to Alaska (p. 279*f*).

## 1179 United States. Treasury Department

Appropriation for claims arising out of the Behring Sea controversy. Letter from the Secretary of the Treasury, transmitting a communication from the Secretary of State in regard to an appropriation for the payment by the United States of all claims that may be made by Great Britain arising out of the Bering Sea controversy. February 13, 1895, referred to the Committee on Appropriations and ordered to be printed. [Washington, 1895]

13 p. 23 cm. ([United States] 53d Cong., 3d sess. House. Ex. doc. no. 310) Caption title.

## 1180 United States. Treasury Department

Survey of boundary line between Alaska and British Columbia; letter from the Acting Secretary of the Treasury, transmitting a communication from the Secretary of State, submitting an estimate of appropriation for survey of the boundary line between Alaska and British Columbia. [Washington, 1895]

2 p. 23 cm. ([United States] 54th Cong., 1st sess. House. Doc. no. 40) Caption title.

## 1181 Victoria (city)

Municipal voters list of the city of Victoria, British Columbia, for the year 1895, for South Ward. [Victoria] Roarke & Co. [1895]

32 p. 24 cm. Cover title.

## 1182 Victoria Liberal-Conservative Association

The Victoria Liberal-Conservative Association, Victoria, B.C., organized September 28th, 1894; constitution and by-laws of the association, and by-laws governing nominating committees. Victoria, The Colonist Printing and Publishing Co., 1895.

12 p. 14 cm.

## 1183 Wilson, E[dward] F[rancis]
### COMPILER

Salt Spring Island, British Columbia. [Victoria] The Colonist Presses, 1895.

30 p. illus., plate, port., fold. map. 23 cm. Cover title.

Description with some historical information.

## 1184 Withrow, W[illiam] H[enry]
### EDITOR 1839-1908

The native races of North America. Toronto, Methodist Mission Rooms, 1895.

200 p. illus., ports., diagrs. 19 cm.

Includes chapters descriptive of Indian life and Methodist missions in British Columbia.

Also: Toronto, Briggs, 1895.

## 1185 Wright, Edgar Wilson
### EDITOR 1863-1930

Lewis & Dryden's marine history of the Pacific Northwest; an illustrated review of the growth and development of the maritime industry from the advent of the earliest navigators to the present time, with sketches and portraits of a number of well known marine men. Portland, Ore., Lewis & Dryden Printing Company, 1895.

xxiii, 494 p. illus., ports. 33 cm.

A valuable and detailed source of marine history.

Reprinted with corrections: New York, Antiquarian Press, 1961.

**1186**   **Yale Lillooet District Pioneer Society**

Constitution, by-laws, and rules of order of the Yale and Lillooet Pioneer Society, as revised December 23rd, 1895.   Ashcroft, Published by order of the Board of Directors, 1895.

13 p.   15 cm.   Colophon: Mining Journal, Ashcroft.

The society was organized in January 1889.

**1187**   **Alaskan-Canadian Boundary Commission**

Rapport conjoint des commissaires nommés en vertu de l'article 1 de la convention entre les États-Unis d'Amerique et le Royaume 'Uni de la Grande-Bretagne et d'Irlande, pour définir la ligne frontière entre les États-Unis et le Canada qui divise l'Alaska de la Colombie Britannique, ainsi que la minute du conseil qui s'y rapporte, approuvée le 25 février 1896. Imprimé par ordre du Parlement.   Ottawa, Imprimé par S. E. Dawson, 1896.

7, [1] p.   27 cm.   (Canada. Sessional papers, 1896, no. 74)   Title from p. [8] Report signed by William Ward Duffield, United States commissioner, and William Frederick King, British commissioner.

Also appeared separately in English.

**1188**   **Anacortes Packing Company, Limited**

[Memorandum and articles of association. Victoria, 1896]

[5] p.   33 cm.

**1189**   **Arion Club (Victoria)**

By-laws, adopted 20th February, 1893, revised 18th September, 1895.   Victoria, The Colonist Printing and Publishing Co., 1896.

10 p.   15 cm.

A men's choir club.

**1190**   **Baets, Maurice de**
1863-1931

Mgr. Seghers, l'apôtre de l'Alaska.   Paris, H. Oudin, 1896.

xcii, 237 p.   plates, ports., 2 fold. maps, facsims. 25 cm.

A biography of Charles John Seghers, Bishop and Archbishop of Vancouver Island, who was murdered in 1886.

The English translation by Sister Mary Mildred has title: *The apostle of Alaska; the life of the Most Reverend Charles John Seghers* (Paterson, New Jersey, St. Anthony Guild Press, 1943). On title page: "A translation of Maurice De Baets' 'Vie de Monseigneur Seghers'."

**1191**   **Baker, James**
1830-1906

Evolution of mind; speech of Lieut.-Colonel Hon. James Baker, at a meeting of the Mainland Teachers' Institute, held at Vancouver, January 6th, 1896.   [Vancouver? 1896]

13 p. (incl. cover)   26 cm.   Cover title.

**1192**   **Baker, Marcus**
1849-1903

The Alaskan boundary.   [New York, 1896]

16 p.   maps.   25 cm.   Cover title. Reprinted from *Bulletin of the American Geographical Society*, v. 28, 1896, p. 130-145.   Not seen.

**1193**   **Begg, Alexander**
1825-1905

Report relative to the Alaska boundary question. [Victoria, Printed by Richard Wolfenden, 1896]

17 p.   28 cm.   Caption title. Addressed to the Hon. J. H. Turner, Minister of Finance. Not found in Holmes.

**1194**   **Bering Sea Claims Commission**

[Record of oral testimony by witnesses at Victoria, B.C.   n.p., 1896?-97?]

1120 p.   32 cm.   Binder's title. On spine: Vol. 1.

**1195**   **Bering Sea Claims Commission**

[Records of the convention; arguments by counsel, British and American; detailed statements as drafted.   n.p., 1896?-97?]

4 v.   32 cm.   Binder's titles. George Edwin King, British commissioner; William L. Putnam, American commissioner.

The commission first met in Victoria, B.C., on 23 November 1896.

**1196** Bible. New Testament. Okanagon

Okanagan Gospel readings. [Kamloops, B.C., n.d.]

64 p. 19 cm. Caption title. Mimeographed. In Duployan shorthand; English headings. The work of Jean-Marie Raphael Le Jeune.

B.C. ARCHIVES

**1197** Boas, Franz
1858-1942

Die Entwicklung der Geheimbünde der Kwakiutl-Indianer. Berlin, Dietrich Reimer, 1896.

9 p. 28 cm. Reprinted from: *Festschrift für Adolf Bastian zu 70 Geburtstag* . . . (Berlin, 1896) p. 435-444.

B.C. ARCHIVES

**1198** Boddy, Alexander A[lfred]

By ocean, prairie and peak; some gleanings from an emigrant chaplain's log, on journeys to British Columbia, Manitoba, and eastern Canada. London, Society for Promoting Christian Knowledge, 1896.

204 p. illus., fold. map. 19 cm.

B.C. ARCHIVES

**1199** British Columbia. Board of Trade

Report of the committee appointed by the B. C. Board of Trade to enquire into the resources and trading prospects of the Yukon. [n.p., 1896]

8 p. fold. map. 16 cm. Caption title. Report signed in print: G. L. Milne, chairman.

CANADIAN ARCHIVES

**1200** British Columbia Curling Association (Nelson)

Manual and prize list of the 1st—28th annual bonspiel. Nelson, etc.

v. illus. 23 cm. Name varies: formerly Kootenay Curling Association. B.C. Provincial Archives has only the 28th (1923) manual.

B.C. ARCHIVES

**1201** British Columbia Fruit Exchange Society, Limited

Objects, rules and by-laws. [New Westminster? Baillie, Wilson & Hawson, printer, 1896?]

20 p. 15 cm. Caption title. Not seen.

LIBRARY OF CONGRESS

**1202** Canada. Department of the Interior

Letters from settlers in Canada; official and other information for intending settlers in Manitoba, North-west Territories, British Columbia, and the other provinces of Canada. Issued by the authority of the Minister of the Interior of Canada. London, Printed by McCorquodale & Co., 1896.

46 p. 22 cm. On p. [2]: This pamphlet has been prepared to supplement the other pamphlets issued under the auspices of the Imperial and Dominion governments, in regard to the advantages offered to settlers in the different provinces of Canada.

Mainly concerns Manitoba and the Northwest; pages 29-33 relate to British Columbia.

CANADIAN ARCHIVES

**1203** Canada. Department of Justice

Correspondence, reports of the Ministers of Justice, and orders in council upon the subject of Dominion and provincial legislation, 1867-1895. Compiled under the direction of the Honourable the Minister of Justice by W. E. Hudgins. Ottawa, 1896-1922.

2 v. 26 cm.

Includes correspondence and despatches regarding the fate of B.C. legislation.

B.C. ARCHIVES

**1204** Capital Lacrosse Club (Victoria)

Constitution and by-laws . . . adopted May 15th, 1896. Victoria, B. C. Victoria, "The Province" Publishing Co., 1896.

10 p. (incl. cover) 15 cm. Cover title.

B.C. ARCHIVES

**1205** Catholic Church. Liturgy and ritual

Polyglott [*sic*] manual. [Kamloops, 1896-97]

183, 30, 33, 31, 32, 63, 153 p. 15 cm. Binder's title. Photoengraved. In twelve parts with separate title pages. Some parts have irregular, continuous paging at foot of page. Except for the English manual, the text is in Duployan shorthand. The work of Jean-Marie Raphael Le Jeune. Contents: [pt. 1] English manual; or, Prayers and catechism in English typography (1896) 19 p. — [pt. 2] Prayers and catechism in English (phonography) (1896) [21]-40 p. — [pt. 3] Chinook manual; or, Prayers, hymns and catechism in Chinook (1896) [43]-100 p. — [pt. 4] Latin manual; or Hymns and chants in use by the Indians of British Columbia (1896) [103]-183 p. — [pt. 5] Stalo manual; or, Prayers, hymns and the catechism in the Stalo or Lower Fraser language (1897) 30 p. — [pt. 6] Thompson manual; or, Prayers, hymns and catechism in the Thompson or Ntla Kapmah language (1897) 33 p. (not incl. t. p.) — [pt. 7] Lillooet manual; or, Prayers, hymns and the catechism in the Lillooet or Stlatliemoh language (1897) 31 p. — [pt. 8] Okanagan manual; or, Prayers and hymns and catechism in the Okanagan language (1897) 32 p. — [pt. 9] Shushwap manual; Prayers, hymns and catechism in Shushwap (1896) [3]-63 p. — [pt. 10] Skwamish manual; or, Prayers, hymns and catechism in Skwamish (1896) 56 p. — [pt. 11] Sheshel manual; or, Prayers, hymns and catechism in the Sechel [sic] language (1896) [57]-109 p. — [pt. 12] Slayamen manual; or, Prayers, hymns and catechism in the Slayamen language (1896) [111]-153 p.

The twelve parts were issued separately. According to the Bancroft Library catalogue, the English, Chinook, Latin, and Thompson manuals were also issued together in one volume (pts. 1, 3, 4, and 6), as were the Okanagan, English, Chinook, and Latin manuals (pts. 8, 1, 3, and 4).

B.C. ARCHIVES

## 1206    Catholic Church. Liturgy and ritual. Latin

Messe royale.    [Kamloops, n.d.]

8 p.    18 cm.    Caption title. Mimeographed. Music for hymns and chants with Latin words in Duployan shorthand. The work of Jean-Marie Raphael Le Jeune.

B.C. ARCHIVES

## 1207    Catholic Church. Liturgy and ritual. Latin

Missa de requiem.    [Kamloops, n.d.]

16 p.    18 cm.    Caption title. Mimeographed. Music for hymns and chants with Latin words in Duployan shorthand. The work of Jean-Marie Raphael Le Jeune.

B.C. ARCHIVES

## 1208    Chilliwack Telephone Company, Ltd.

Rules governing subscribers [and list of subscribers. n.p., 1896?]

11 p.    14 cm.    Caption title.

B.C. ARCHIVES

## 1209    Church of England. Liturgy and ritual. Tsimshian

Appendix a shimalgiagum liami. Hymns in Zimshian for the use of the church at Metlakatla. Translated by William Ridley.    Metlakatla, B.C., Printed at the Bishop's Press [n.d.]

10 p.    17 cm.

B.C. ARCHIVES

## 1210    Circular letter . . .

Circular letter to the people of British Columbia. [Victoria, 1896]

[4] p. (folder)    26 cm.    Cover title. In manuscript on cover: Issued Oct. 6, 1896, Victoria.

A petition to the government to assist in the building of 'The Peoples' Railway' from "a point on the Gulf of Georgia to New Westminster, and from Vancouver to a junction at New Westminster and thence easterly through the fertile municipalities lying between the Fraser River and the international boundary line to pass through the Hope Mountains, thence by way of the valleys of the Tulameen and Similkameen River . . . to a point near the Columbia River . . . " — p. [2].

B.C. ARCHIVES

## 1211    Colmer, J[oseph] G[rose]
### 1856-1937

Across the Canadian prairies; a two months' holiday in the Dominion.    London, Published by the European Mail Ltd. [1896]

85 p.    port., map,    19 cm.

Of the twenty-six chapters, five are on British Columbia.

B.C. ARCHIVES

## 1212    Davie, [Theodore]
### 1852-1898

The Paris Belle Mine; text of Chief Justice Davie's judgment in this important mining case; his reasons for declaring the location of the claim illegal and void.    [n.p., 1896]

8 p.    22 cm.    Cover title.

The case was *Nelson & Fort Sheppard Railway Co. vs. Jerry et al.*

B.C. ARCHIVES

## 1213    Duncan, Eric
### 1858-1944

Rural rhymes and the sheep thief.    Toronto, William Briggs, 1896.

64 p.    8 cm.    Author's note: These "Rural Rhymes" are not the rose-tinted reveries of a rusticating rhapsodist, but the regular, rough reminiscences of a real rancher, written by himself.

B.C. ARCHIVES

## 1214    Egerton, [Mary Augusta Phipps (Hornby)]

Admiral of the Fleet, Sir Geoffrey Phipps Hornby, G.C.B.; a biography, by Mrs. Fred. Egerton. Edinburgh, William Blackwood and Sons, 1896.

xi, 404 p.    ports.    23 cm.

Hornby figured prominently in the San Juan controversy.

B.C. ARCHIVES

**1215    Esquimalt and Nanaimo Railway Company**

Vancouver Island as a home for settlers.    Victoria, Colonist Presses [1896]

24 p.    illus., map., fold. plans.    23 cm.    Cover title.

B.C. ARCHIVES


**1216    Great Britain. Treaties, etc.**

Convention between Great Britain and the United States for the submission to arbitration of British claims in connection with the Behring Sea seal fishery. Signed at Washington, February 8, 1896; ratifications exchanged at London, June 3, 1896. Presented to both Houses of Parliament by command of Her Majesty, June 1896.    London, Printed by Harrison and Sons [1896]

5 p.    26 cm.    ([Great Britain. Parliament. Command papers] C. 8101)    Treaty series no. 10, 1896.

B.C. ARCHIVES


**1217    Great Northern Railway Company**

The Kootenai country; Fort Steele, Libby Creek, Yakt, Rossland, Nelson, Kaslo, Slocan; Montana, Idaho, British Columbia, reached by Great Northern Railway from the East and West.    Chicago, Rand, McNally & Co. [1896]

10 p. (folder)    map (on verso of pages)    22 x 10 cm.    Cover title.

B.C. ARCHIVES


**1218    Haller, Granville O[wen]**
1820-1897

San Juan and secession; possible relation to the war of the rebellion. Did General Harney try to make trouble with English to aid the conspiracy? A careful review of his orders and circumstances attending the disputed possessions during the year 1859.    [n.p., R. L. M'Cormick, 1896]

15 p. (incl. cover)    23 cm.    Cover title. Reprinted from the Tacoma *Sunday Ledger*, 19 January 1896.

B.C. ARCHIVES


**1219    Harris, J[osiah]**

Lecture delivered at the Imperial Institute on the 17th February 1896 . . . on the new British route to the Pacific . . .    [London] Printed by Spottiswoode & Co., 1896.

23 p.    21 cm.    At head of text on p. 10: Evidence as to the commercial practicability of the navigation of the Straits and Hudson's Bay.

NATIONAL LIBRARY


**1220    Hebrew Ladies Association (Victoria)**

Constitution, by-laws and rules of order; organized November 1890.    Victoria, Times Job Department, 1896.

1 v. (unpaged)    26 cm.    Cover title.    Microfilm copy examined.

B.C. ARCHIVES


**1221    Hogan, James Francis**
1855-1924

The sister dominions; through Canada to Australia by the new Imperial highway.    London, Ward and Downey Limited, 1896.

234 p.    20 cm.    Chapter 8: Over the Rockies [p. 91-97]

Chapter 8 contains the observations of a railroad traveller.

B.C. ARCHIVES


**1222    Kitamaat Mission**

Kitamaat mission. Ahmakatle Hallelas'l wah gaedzowah; nakwa kuddielth.    [Kitamat? 189-]

[2] p. (folder)    23 cm.    Caption title.

Probably from Rev. George H. Raley's press. Appears to be statements with responses.

MCGILL UNIVERSITY. LANDE COLLECTION


**1223    [Le Jeune, Jean-Marie Raphael]**
1855-1930

The Wawa shorthand first reading book, by the editor of the Kamloops "Wawa."
Kamloops, 1896.

16 p. (incl. cover)    20 cm.    Cover title.

B.C. ARCHIVES


**1224    [Le Jeune, Jean-Marie Raphael]**
1855-1930

The Wawa shorthand instructor; or, The Duployan stenography adapted to English, by the editor of the Kamloops "Wawa." First edition.
Kamloops, 1896.

24 p.    19 cm.    Cover title.

B.C. ARCHIVES


**1225    Leghait, M. A.**

Compte rendu d'un voyage d'exploration dans la Colombie Britannique, le nord-ouest des États-Unis et la Californie, par M. A. Leghait, ministre de Belgique aux États-Unis d'Amérique. Extrait du Recueil consolaire belge.    Bruxelles, P. Weissenbruch, 1896.

57 p.   23 cm.

Includes a brief report on Vancouver and Victoria.

1226   Lévis-Mirepoix, Gaston Gustave
MARQUIS DE   B. 1844

Visite au Canada suivie d'une course aux montagnes Rocheuses et à l'océan Pacifique en 1895.   Chateaudun, Société Typographique, 1896.

ii, 194 p.   21 cm.   Chapter 6: Victoria; Vancouver; la forêt-vierge; les montagnes-Rocheuses; Banff [p. 133-144]

1227   McInnes, W[illiam] W[allace Burns]
1871-1954

An address to the electors of Vancouver District by the Liberal candidate; the issues of the coming campaign clearly defined, the requirements of this district set forth, an appeal to the independent electorate, a frank declaration of principles. [Nanaimo, R. Lukey, printer, 1896]

30 p.   port. (on cover)   22 cm.   Cover title.

1228   Maclean, John
1851-1928

Canadian savage folk: the native tribes of Canada. Toronto, William Briggs, 1896.

641 p.   illus., port.   23 cm.   Language and literature of western Canada: p. 496-540. Bibliographies: p. 456-485, 499-540.

1229   McNaughton, Margaret [(Peebles)]

Overland to the Cariboo; an eventful journey of Canadian pioneers to the gold-fields of British Columbia in 1862.   Toronto, William Briggs, 1896.

176 p.   illus., plates, ports., map.   20 cm. Chapter 8: Biographical sketches of some of the "Overlanders." Chapter 10: Extracts from Sawney's letters and Cariboo rhymes, by James Anderson.

Written by the wife of one of the participants, the book is a narrative depicting the hardships endured by some 150 adventurers and pioneers during their journey from Fort Garry to the gold fields.

1230   McPhillips, A[lbert] E[dward]
1861-1938

The Manitoba question; true side of the case; Mr. Bodwell's fallacies exposed; Mr. Joseph Martin and his methods.   Victoria, The Colonist Steam Presses, 1896.

15 p.   21 cm.   Cover title. Caption title: The Manitoba school case; a reply to Mr. E. V. Bodwell's argument against the school system in operation in Manitoba prior to 1890 . . .

A political attack.

1231   Maxwell, Geo[rge] R.

Inaugural address . . . in the Market Hall, Vancouver, B.C., May 5th, 1896.   [n.p., 1896]

4 p. (folder)   23 cm.   Caption title.

An election speech by a candidate in the federal riding of Burrard District.

1232   Merchant's agency red book

Merchant's agency red book; a gazetteer and trade directory of British Columbia.   Victoria, T. R. Cusack, printer, 1896.

1 v. (various paging; incl. advertisements)   21 cm. On t.p.: issued semi-annually. No more published? Text in red print.

1233   Merriam, J[ohn] C[ampbell]
1869-1945

Note on two Tertiary faunas from the rocks of the southern coast of Vancouver Island.   Berkeley, The University, 1896.

[101]-108 p.   27 cm.   (University of California. Bulletin of the Department of Geology, v. 2, no. 3) Cover title.   Not seen.

1234   Mockridge, Charles H[enry]
1844-1913

The bishops of the Church of England in Canada and Newfoundland; being an illustrated historical sketch of the Church of England in Canada, as traced through her episcopate.   Toronto, F. N. W. Brown [1896]

xi, 380 p.   illus., ports.   23 cm.

Contains brief biographical information on George Hills, William Perrin, Acton Sillitoe, and John Dart.

**1235    Mohun, Edward**
1838-1927

The sewerage system of Victoria, British Columbia. [n.p., 1896?]

16 p.    21 cm.

B.C. ARCHIVES

**1236    New Westminster (city)**

Financial statement and annual report.    1896+ New Westminster.

v.    25, 37 cm.    Title varies slightly.

B.C. PROVINCIAL LIBRARY

**1237    Phillips, Walter Shelley**
1867-1940

Totem tales; Indian stories Indian told, gathered in the Pacific Northwest. Fully illustrated by the author.    Chicago, Star Publishing Co., 1896.

326 p.    plates.    20 cm.

Published in 1902 under title: *Indian fairy tales* . . . Also: 1904. 326 p.

B.C. ARCHIVES

**1238    Pike, Warburton, [Mayer]**
1861-1915

Through the subarctic forest; a record of a canoe journey from Fort Wrangel to the Pelly Lakes and down the Yukon River to the Behring Sea. London, Edward Arnold, 1896.

xiv, 295 p.    plates, 2 fold. maps.    23 cm.

The author's account of two summers and a winter exploring and hunting. In British Columbia his travels took him up the Stikine River to Telegraph, then along the Telegraph Trail to Dease River. He descended the Dease through the Cassiar district to its junction with the Liard, at which point he set up a winter camp.

B.C. ARCHIVES

**1239    Squire, Watson C[arvosso]**
1838-1926

The Alaska boundary; speech of Hon. Watson C. Squire of Washington, in the Senate of the United States, January 3, 1896.    Washington, 1896.

14 p. (incl. cover)    23 cm.    Cover title.

B.C. ARCHIVES

**1240    Teit, James [Alexander]**
1864-1922

A rock painting of the Thompson River Indians, British Columbia.    New York, 1896.

227-230 p.    22 cm.    Cover title. Author's edition. Edited, from notes of the collector, by Franz Boas. Reprinted from: American Museum of Natural History. *Bulletin.* v. 8, 1896.

B.C. ARCHIVES

**1241    Trail. Board of Trade**

A land of gold! Trail Creek, B.C.; the best and cheapest route to the towns and mines of Trail Creek, B.C.    [Trail, "News" Print] 1896.

[16] p. (incl. cover)    13 cm.    Cover title.

B.C. ARCHIVES

**1242    The Trail Creek mines . . .**

The Trail Creek mines, British Columbia; their history and development, with a description of the mining laws of British Columbia. A supplement to J. A. Kirk's map of the Trail Creek Mining Camp. [Victoria] The Colonist Presses, 1896.

52 p. (incl. advertisements)    fold. map.    23 cm. Cover title.

B.C. ARCHIVES

**1243    United States. Revenue-Cutter Service**

Fur-seal, sea otter, and salmon fisheries. Acts of Congress, President's proclamations, regulations governing U.S. vessels, acts of Parliament, orders in council, pertaining to the fur-seal fisheries in Behring Sea and North Pacific Ocean; sea otter regulations, laws as to salmon fisheries in Alaska. Washington, Government Printing Office, 1896.

78 p.    23 cm.    [Treasury Department. Doc. no. 1850. Office of Division of Revenue Cutter Service] Not seen.

LIBRARY OF CONGRESS

**1244    United States. Treasury Department**

Alaska boundary survey. [A report from Mr. Cannon, Committee on Appropriations, recommending the passage of S.R. 39 allowing for $75,000 to defray the joint expense of locating boundary line.    Washington, 1896.]

[1] p.    23 cm.    ([United States] 54th Cong., 1st sess. House. Report no. 326)

B.C. ARCHIVES

**1245    United States. Treasury Department**

Reports of agents, officers, and persons acting under the authority of the Secretary of the Treasury in relation to the condition of seal life on the rookeries of the Pribilof Islands, and to pelagic sealing in Bering Sea, and the North Pacific Ocean in the years 1893-1895. In two parts. Washington, Government Printing Office, 1896.

2 v. illus., plates, fold. maps., fold. diagrs., tables. 24 cm. *and* atlas (fold. photographs only) 24 x 31 cm. ([United States] 54th Cong., 1st sess. Senate. Doc. 137, pts. 1 and 2) Reports of C. S. Hamlin, J. B. Crowley, Joseph Murray, and C. H. Townsend.

Includes details of the value of the seal catches made by Victoria-based schooners.

B.C. ARCHIVES

### 1246    The Vancouver city directory . . .

The Vancouver city directory, March 1896; containing provincial and local information with a classified business directory of the province. Vancouver, Published by Hodgson & Co. [1896]

xvi, 239 p.   23 cm.

B.C. ARCHIVES

### 1247    Venning, R[obert] N[orris]
#### B. 1854

The Behring Sea question, embracing the fur sealing industry of the North Pacific Ocean and the international agreement between Russia and Great Britain.   Ottawa, Government Printing Bureau, 1896.

50 p.   25 cm.   At head of title: From Report of the Department of Marine and Fisheries, 1895.

DEPARTMENT OF FISHERIES LIBRARY, OTTAWA

### 1248    Victoria. Collegiate School

Prospectus of the Collegiate School for Boys. [Victoria, 1896]

[3] p. (folder)   27 cm.   Cover title. Under the management of the Rev. C. Ensor Sharp and J. W. Laing. Dated: September 1st, 1896.

B.C. ARCHIVES

### 1249    Victoria. Collegiate School

[Testimonials for J. W. Laing.   Victoria, 1896]

[4] p. (folder)   21 cm.

B.C. ARCHIVES

### 1250    Wilcox, Walter Dwight
#### 1869-1949

Camping in the Canadian Rockies; an account of camp life in the wilder parts of the Canadian Rocky Mountains, together with a description of the region about Banff, Lake Louise and Glacier, and a sketch of the early explorations. With twenty-five full-page photogravures, and many text illustrations

from photographs by the author.   New York, G. P. Putnam's Sons, 1896.

xiii, 283 p.   illus., plates.   26 cm.

Along with the works of John Palliser and George Mercer Dawson, this book is one of the best early sources of information on the Alberta-British Columbia border region.

Second edition: London, G. P. Putnam's Sons, 1897. With map.

Also see entry 1480.

B.C. ARCHIVES

### 1251    Woodward, Henry

On some podophthalmatous Crustacea from the cretaceous formation of Vancouver and Queen Charlotte Islands.   [n.p., 1896]

[221]-228 p.   22 cm.   Caption title. At head of title: From the Quarterly journal of the Geological Society for May 1896, v. 52.

NATIONAL LIBRARY

### 1252    Alaska . . .

Alaska, the Eldorado of the midnight sun; marvels of the Yukon, the Klondike discovery, fortunes made in a day, how to go, what to take and what it costs, routes, rates and distances, attractions and dangers, land laws; practical counsel for prospectors, tourists and stay-at-homes.   New York, The Republic Press, 1897.

62 p. (incl. advertisements)   illus., tables.   24 cm. Cover title: Ho! for Alaska; how to go, what to take, what it costs, what you find.

In the section briefly describing the Stikine River route is the sentence: "Then Teslin Lake is reached, and it is plain sailing clear to Dawson City."

B.C. ARCHIVES

### 1253    Anaconda Commercial Club

A brief description of the Boundary Creek district, British Columbia. [Compiled by the Anaconda Commercial Club, Anaconda, B.C.   Anaconda, "Boundary Creek Times" Print, 1897]

17 p.   14 cm.

Enumerates mining claims in the area.

B.C. ARCHIVES

### 1254    B. C. and Dominion Exploration Company, Limited

The B.C. and Dominion Exploration Company, Limited; the following information as to British

Columbia is taken from public and other sources. [London, 1897?]

Sheet (2 p.)   35 x 22 cm.

The above was found together with the entry below.

## 1255   B. C. and Dominion Exploration Company, Limited

Prospectus.   London, Wertheimer, Lea & Co. [1897]

2, [2] p. (folder)   35 cm.   Title from p. [4] Caption title: B.C. and Dominion Exploration Company, Limited; incorporated under the Companies Acts, 1862 to 1893; capital, £50,000 ...   At head of caption title: Private.   Included as separate sheet: Form of application for shares ...   [1] p. 35 x 22 cm.

Found together with the entry above.

## 1256   Begg, Alexander
### 1825-1905

Sequel to an open letter to members of the Honorable Legislative Assembly of British Columbia; colonization and deep sea fisheries, etc. Victoria, 1897.

Sheet.   33 x 16 cm.

## 1257   Bible. New Testament. Acts. Kwakiutl

Yikā qāyīlelas wūtla sa apostles. The Acts of the Apostles translated [by Alfred James Hall] into the Kwagutl language, north of Vancouver Island. London, British and Foreign Bible Society, 1897.

139 p.   16 cm.

## 1258   Big game shooting ...

Big game shooting and fishing in British Columbia. [n.p., 1897?]

3 p. (folder)   27 cm.   Caption title. Possibly printed in London.

A publication advertising the services of "Messrs. Inskip and Tait," Spence's Bridge, as guides and outfitters. In *Williams' official British Columbia directory, 1897-8*, there is a Harry V. Inskip, hunter, listed. The "Tait" referred to is the anthropologist and hunter, James Alexander Teit.

## 1259   Boas, Franz
### 1858-1942

The decorative art of the Indians of the North Pacific coast. Author's edition.   New York, 1897.

123-176 p.   illus.   25 cm.   Cover title. Reprinted from: American Museum of Natural History. *Bulletin.* v. 9, art. 10. Not seen.

## 1260   Bonnaud, Dominique

D'océan à océan; impressions d'Amérique. Préface d'Armand Silvestre.   Paris, Paul Ollendorf, 1897.

586 p.   19 cm.

About fifty pages relate to British Columbia.

A note on the Library of Congress catalogue card reads: "First edition appeared 1895 in Bibliothèque de la Vie moderne."

## 1261   British Association for the Advancement of Science

Report on the ethnological survey of Canada. 1897-1902.   London, Offices of the Association, 1897-1902.

6 v.?   22 cm.   The reports of 1897 and 1901 may not have been separately published.

The report of 1898 includes Charles Hill-Tout's paper on Haida stories and beliefs; and those of 1899, 1900, and 1902, his notes on Salish Indians.

Also contained in the association's reports of meetings.

## 1262   British Columbia. Board of Trade

Victoria, British Columbia, Canada, the head quarters for miners' outfits.   [Victoria, Colonist Litho., 1897?]

[3] p. and cover (folder)   illus., map.   29 x 23 cm. fold. to 23 x 10 cm.   Cover title. On back cover when folded: Klondyke, Cassiar, Omineca, and Cariboo gold fields, shewing routes from Victoria, B. C.

A brochure promoting Victoria as the key to the gold fields.

## 1263   British Columbia Development Association, Limited (London)

Klondyke; the Yukon (Klondyke) mines, and how to reach them.   London, Crowther & Goodman [1897?]

32 p.   fold. map.   17 cm.

**1265    British Columbia ...**

British Columbia; Kamloops mining camp. Kamloops, Baillie & Bennett, 1897.

64 p. (incl. advertisements)    illus., ports., 2 fold. maps.    30 cm.

Includes biographical sketches.

B.C. ARCHIVES


**1266    British Columbia mining journal**

Overland to Klondike, through Cariboo, Omineca, Cassiar, and Lake Teslin; the poor man's route, 1898.    Peoria, J. W. Franks & Sons, printers [1897?]

34 p.    illus., map.    23 cm.    Cover title. Preface dated: 10th Dec. 1897.

B.C. ARCHIVES


**1267    British Columbia Society for the Prevention of Cruelty to Animals. Victoria Branch**

The Victoria Branch of the British Columbia Society for the Prevention of Cruelty to Animals, incorporated by an act of Parliament, February 1895.    Victoria, Cusack, printer, 1897.

26 p.    15 cm.

Includes its act of incorporation, constitution, and by-laws, as well as other information.

B.C. ARCHIVES


**1268    Campbell, John**
1840-1904

The origin of the Haidahs of the Queen Charlotte Islands.    [n.p.] 1897.

91-112 p.    25 cm.    Cover title. Includes: A comparison of the Haidah dialects with the Malay-Polynesian and Melanesian languages [p. 97-112] From: The Royal Society of Canada. *Proceedings and transactions.* ser. 2, v. 3, sec. 2, 1897-8.

B.C. ARCHIVES


**1269    Canada. Department of the Interior**

Information respecting the Yukon district, from the reports of Wm. Ogilvie, Dominion land surveyor, and from other sources.    Ottawa, Government Printing Bureau, 1897.

65 p.    plates, maps (1 double)    25 cm.    Mr. Ogilvie's exploration of 1887: p. 9-48.

Ogilvie's report was an often cited document during the Klondike gold rush days.

B.C. ARCHIVES


**1270    Canada. Royal Commission on Claims of Settlers on Lands within the Esquimalt and Nanaimo Railway Company Belt, British Columbia**

Report of Mr. T. G. Rothwell, commissioner [with copies of documents therein referred to.    Ottawa, Government Printing Bureau, 1897?]

40 p.    25 cm.    Commissioner: Thomas Gainsford Rothwell.

B.C. ARCHIVES


**1271    Canadian Pacific Railway Company**

British Columbia, Canada's most westerly province; its position, advantages, resources and climate; new fields for mining, farming and ranching along the lines of the Canadian Pacific Railway; information for prospectors, miners, and intending settlers. [Montreal] 1897.

36 p.    illus., maps (1 fold.)    23 cm. Also: 1898. 48 p.    Also: 1899. 63 p.    Also: 1900. 64 p.

NATIONAL LIBRARY


**1272    Canadian Pacific Railway Company**

Gold in Cariboo and Kootenay reached only by the Canadian Pacific Railway.    [n.p., 1897]

[28] p. (folder)    illus., maps.    23 cm.    Not seen.

YALE WESTERN AMERICANA CATALOGUE


**1273    Canadian Pacific Railway Company**

To the Klondike and gold fields of the Yukon. [Montreal, 1897?]

27 p.    illus., map (on inside cover)    23 x 11 cm. Cover title.

This appears to be the first of many editions. The fourth edition, the sixth edition (February 12, 1898), and tenth edition (May 4, 1898) have title: *Yukon gold fields; handbook of information.* On cover: Illustrated and with maps and charts of the routes.

B.C. ARCHIVES


**1274    Cowie, Isaac**
COMPILER 1848-1917

The grain, grass, and gold fields of south-western Canada; Edmonton, Alberta, Canada, described as a mixed farming and mining country, with a brief notice of Kootenay and Cariboo mining districts of British Columbia, as the near and natural markets for Edmonton produce. Also a description of the all Canadian routes from Edmonton to the Yukon gold fields. A handbook for agriculturists and gold miners, with information for railway and other capitalists, tourists, sportsmen, big game hunters, scientific explorers and others seeking fresh fields for their energies under the flag. Edmonton, 1897.

54 p.   illus.   22 cm.

CANADIAN ARCHIVES

## 1275   Crewe, E. O.

Gold fields of the Yukon, and how to get there. Chicago, O. C. Cole & Co. [c1897]

61 p.   illus., maps.   18 cm.

B.C. ARCHIVES

## 1276   Crow's Nest Pass Coal Company, Limited

Special rules to be observed by the owners, managers, overmen, master mechanics, firebosses & workmen of the collieries . . .   [n.p., n.d.]

12 p.   19 cm.   Cover title.

Rules imposed by the company to comply with the provincial Coal Mines Regulation Act, 1897.

B.C. ARCHIVES

## 1277   Diamond jubilee . . .

Diamond jubilee of Her Majesty Queen Victoria, Sunday, June 20th, 1897, Victoria, British Columbia; order of service arranged by Barlow Cumberland, Supreme Grand President of the Sons of England . . .   Victoria, 1897.

sheet (2 p.)   28 x 21 cm.

U.B.C. SPECIAL COLLECTIONS

## 1278   Directory of mines . . .

Directory of mines, a guide for the use of investors and others interested in the mines of British Columbia. Edited byAlexander Begg. 1897. Vancouver, Victoria, Mining Record Limited.

1 v.   map (part fold.)   20 cm.   quarterly.   After four numbers, no more published.

Contains a synopsis of the mining laws, and the placer claims of British Columbia, Northwest Territories, and the Yukon; includes map showing several non-existent routes to the Yukon, and gives stock quotations, list of post offices, etc.

B.C. ARCHIVES

## 1279   Directory of . . . Revelstoke

Directory of the city of Revelstoke, B.C., 1897-[1900?]   Revelstoke, Printed at the office of the Revelstoke Semi-Weekly Herald.

v.   fold. map.   22 cm.   No. t.p. in copy examined. Compiled by Richard Parmater Pettipiece.

In three sections: "The city of Revelstoke," "Business directory," and "Name directory."

B.C. ARCHIVES

## 1280   Donan, Patrick

The new bonanzaland; with a brief dissertation on booms.   Portland, Oregon, Oregon Railroad and Navigation Company, 1897.

68 p.   illus., fold. map.   18 cm.   On cover: Mining belts of the Pacific Northwest; Kootenai, British Columbia; Coeur d'Alene, Idaho; Baker County, eastern Oregon; southern Oregon; gold reached via the Oregon Railroad & Navigation Co.

B.C. ARCHIVES

## 1281   Dorsey, G[eorge] A[mos]
### 1868-1931

The geography of the Tsimshian Indians. [Chicago, 1897]

7 p.   double map.   25 cm.   Cover title. Reprinted from the *American antiquarian*, September and October 1897.

B.C. ARCHIVES

## 1282   Filley & Ogden
### COMPILER

Latest mining laws of British Columbia, United States and state of Washington. With complete legal forms, definitions of mining terms, etc. Comp. by Filley & Ogden, Olympia, Washington.   Olympia, Wash., O. C. White, state printer, 1897.

iv, 98 p.   26 cm.   At head of title: Practical information for the prospector, miner and investor. Not seen.

LIBRARY OF CONGRESS

## 1283   Gairdner, Geo[rge] W.

The Gairdner & Harrison prospectors' guide map and pamphlet to the Omineca, Cassier [sic] Liard, Klondyke and Yukon gold fields via the Edmonton route [by] Geo. W. Gairdner [and] A. G. Harrison.   Edmonton, Alta. [Bulletin Print, 1897]

16 p.   22 cm.   Cover title.

U.B.C. SPECIAL COLLECTIONS

## 1284   Gosnell, R. E[dward]
### 1860-1931

Compiled from the Year book of British Columbia and manual of provincial information, to which is added a chapter containing much special information respecting the Canadian Yukon and northern territory generally.   Victoria, 1897.

285 p. illus., fold. plate, ports., maps (1 fold.) tables. 25 cm. Cover title: The year book of British Columbia; compendium.

See entry 1484.

B.C. ARCHIVES

## 1285 Gosnell, R. E[dward]
1860-1931

Year book of British Columbia and manual of provincial information. 1897-1914. Victoria, King's printer.

5 v. illus., plates, maps (part fold.) 23 cm. Publications for the years 1897 (500 p.), 1897-1901 (406 p.), 1903 (394 p.), 1911 (coronation edition of 358 p.), and 1911-1914 (406 p.) Compendiums are separately listed as entries 1284 and 1484. Continued as *Manual of provincial information.* Table of contents, index. In Holmes.

Has historical reviews, parliamentary and judicial information, statistics; information on Indian tribes, physical characteristics of land, forestry and fishing industries, trade, finance, etc.

B.C. ARCHIVES

## 1286 Great Britain. Foreign Office

Correspondence with the United States' government respecting the seal fisheries in Behring Sea. Presented to both Houses of Parliament by command of Her Majesty, September 1897. London, Printed by Harrison and Sons [1897]

viii, 130 p. 34 cm. ([Great Britain. Parliament. Command papers] C. 8662) At head of title: United States, no. 4 (1897)

B.C. ARCHIVES

## 1287 Guide to the Klondike ...

Guide to the Klondike and the Yukon gold fields in Alaska and Northwest Territories; containing history of the discovery, routes of travel, necessary outfit, general and useful information, large map, corrected up to date from latest official surveys. Seattle, Published by Lowman & Hanford Stationery and Printing Co., 1897.

115 p. illus. 20 cm. Map lacking in copy examined.

B.C. ARCHIVES

## 1288 Harris, Josiah

Direct route through the North-west Territories of Canada to the Pacific Ocean; the chartered Hudson's Bay & Pacific railway route. London, Spottiswoode & Co., 1897.

66 p. fold. map. 26 cm.

A compilation of evidence shows the advantage of a route through Hudson's Straits to the prairies and the Pacific.

B.C. ARCHIVES

## 1289 Hattie Brown Gold Mining Comp'y

Hattie Brown Gold Mining Comp'y, Trail Creek Division, West Kootenay mining district, British Columbia ... Spokane [The Shaw-Borden Co., 1897]

16 p. plan. 18 cm. At head of text: Description of property and expert's report ...

B.C. ARCHIVES

## 1290 Hill-Tout, C[harles]
1859?-1944

Notes on the cosmogony and history of the Squamish Indians of British Columbia. Ottawa, J. Durie & Son, 1897.

85-90 p. 26 cm. Cover title. From: The Royal Society of Canada. *Proceedings and transactions.* ser. 2, v. 3, sec. 2, 1897-8.

B.C. ARCHIVES

## 1291 Hodges, L[awrence] K[aye]
EDITOR 1857-1938

Mining in the Pacific Northwest; a complete review of mineral resources of Washington and British Columbia. Seattle, Wash., The Post-Intelligencer, 1897.

192 p. illus., 28 maps (part fold.) 23 cm. The Table of Contents and indexes are bound among advertisements at end of volume and are not included in paging.

B.C. ARCHIVES

## 1292 Jackson Mines Limited

Description, maps and reports of the Jackson Mines, limited liability, incorporated under the laws of the province of British Columbia. [Kaslo, B.C., Kootenaian Power Print, 1897]

12 p. 2 maps (1 fold., 1 double) 22 cm. Cover title.

B.C. ARCHIVES

## 1293 James, Fred

The Klondike gold fields, and how to get there. London, New York, George Routledge & Sons, 1897.

88 p. map. 19 cm.

B.C. ARCHIVES

## 1294 Kingsmill, Harold
D. 1945

First history of Rossland, B.C., with sketches of some of its prominent citizens, firms and corporations. Rossland, Studen & Perine [1897?]

24 p. 30 cm. Cover title. Contents: A history of Rossland and the Trail Creek district, by Harold Kingsmill. — Business and biographical sketches: many old pioneers; some late arrivals, and all men, firms and corporations of ability and standing.

### 1295 Kitamaat Mission

Rules; Kitamaat home, 1897-8. [Kitamat, 1897]

[3] p. (folder) 17 cm. Caption title. Signed in print: Rev. G. H. Raley, principal; Miss Long, matron; Mr. Anderson, teacher.

Probably printed on Rev. George H. Raley's press.

### 1296 The Kootenay Mining Protective Association

Constitution and by-laws. Kaslo, B.C., Kootenaian Power Printing House, 1897.

6 p. 16 cm. Cover title.

### 1297 Law Society of British Columbia

The rules of the Law Society of British Columbia, taking effect on the 4th day of October 1897, and the Legal Professions Act, 1895. Victoria, The Colonist Printing and Publishing Co., 1897.

82 p. 23 cm.

Also see entries 830 and 990.

### 1298 Lugrin, Charles H[enry]
COMPILER 1846-1917

Yukon gold fields; map showing routes from Victoria, B.C., to the various mining camps on the Yukon River and its branches; mining regulations of the Dominion government, and forms of application, together with table of distances, extracts from Mr. Ogilvie's reports, and other information. Victoria, Published by Chas. H. Lugrin, 1897.

32 p. (incl. advertisements) fold. map. 23 cm. Cover title. Colophon: Printed by The Colonist Printing and Publishing Co.

Another edition, published in Vancouver by A. E. Goodman, had title: *Klondyke gold fields, Yukon district; map of routes from Vancouver . . .* The text is the same except for the last section entitled "Transportation and outfitting."

### 1299 McCullagh, James B[enjamin]
1854-1921

Nisg̱a primer. Part I: spelling and reading. Anspelsqum šim algiuḵ. For use in the day-school at Aiyansh Mission, Naas River, British Columbia. London, Society for Promoting Christian Knowledge, 1897.

32 p. 18 cm. Text in the Niska dialect of the Tsimshian language.

### 1300 McMillan, A. J.

The mineral resources of British Columbia and the Yukon; a lecture delivered at the Imperial Institute, London, on December 6th, 1897. [London, Printed by Cassell & Company, 1897?]

20 p. 19 cm. Cover title.

### 1301 Morice, [Adrian Gabriel]
1859-1938

Au pays de l'ours noir; chez les sauvages de la Colombie Britannique; récit d'un missionaire. Ouvrage enrichi d'une carte, de 5 photogravures et de 26 gravures par l'auteur. Paris, Delhomme et Briguet, 1897.

viii, 305 p. illus., map. 26 cm.

Concerned with the social life and customs of the Athapaskan Indians — chiefly the Chilcotins, Sekanis and Babines (Carrier Indians) — and with the travels of Father Morice among them.

### 1302 Munro, W[illiam] F.

Diary of the Christie party's trip to the Pacific coast. Toronto, C. M. Ellis [1897]

70 p. 21 cm.

About 20 pages relate to British Columbia.

Second edition, revised and enlarged: 1897. 87 p.

### 1303 Ogilvie, William
1846-1912

Lecture on the Klondike mining district, delivered at Victoria, British Columbia, November 5th, 1897. Victoria, Printed by Richard Wolfenden, 1897.

14 p. 27 cm. Reprinted from the Victoria *Colonist* 6 November 1897. In Holmes.

A revised and amplified version of the lecture appeared under title: *Lecture on the Yukon gold fields (Canada), delivered at Victoria, B.C.* (Victoria, "The Colonist" Presses, 1897). In 32 pages and illustrated. Not in Holmes.

**1304    Patterson, Marion**
PLAINTIFF

In the Supreme Court of British Columbia, before McColl, J., and a special jury; between Marion Patterson, the administratrix of the goods and chattels of James T. Patterson, deceased, plaintiff, and the municipal corporation of the city of Victoria, defendants. Reprint of the evidence of the experts Messrs. Warner and Lockwood, as reported by the official stenographer.    Victoria, The Colonist Printing and Publishing Co., 1897.

72 p., 193-320 1.    28 cm.

An action in respect to the collapse of Point Ellice Bridge.

B.C. ARCHIVES

**1305    Perkins, W. H. S.**
COMPILER

The gold mines of the Yukon and Clondyke; where they are, what to take, how to get there . . . A lot of useful information for the prospective miner, from authentic sources.    Victoria, Printed by Greenwood, Smith & Randolph [n.d.]

28 p. (incl. advertisements)    21 cm.    Cover title.

B.C. ARCHIVES

**1306    Phillipps-Wolley, [Sir] Clive [Oldnall Long]**
1854-1918

One of the broken brigade.    London, Smith, Elder & Co., 1897.

279 p.    20 cm.

Fiction. Part 1, which takes up nearly half the book, tells of a young Englishman who came to the Shawnigan Lake area as one of the numerous "remittance" men. The book is mainly a discussion of this social phenomenon.

B.C. ARCHIVES

**1307    Reco Mining and Milling Company, Limited**

First report. [Compiled by J. M. Harris]    Sandon, B.C. [1897]

64 p.    illus. (1 fold.) diagr., 3 plans.    22 cm.    On cover: Silver mining in the Reco.

B.C. ARCHIVES

**1308    Rome vs. Ruthven**

Rome vs. Ruthven.    [Victoria? 1897]

53 p.    22 cm.

Relates to events brought about by an attack on the Roman Catholic church made by Victor M. Ruthven. During 1897 Ruthven, who claimed he was an ex-priest, was acquitted in Victoria of charges involving criminal libel, breach of the peace, and distribution of obscene literature. The work was either written by Ruthven or a supporter.

B.C. ARCHIVES

**1309    Rossland, B.C., business directory . . .**

Rossland, B.C., business directory, 1897. [Rossland, Kootenay Publishing Co., 1897]

[17] p. (incl. advertisements)    19 cm.    Cover title.

B.C. ARCHIVES

**1310    Royal Gold Mining Company**

Gold fields of British Columbia and the state of Washington; Trail Creek district, B.C., and Colville Indian Reservation, Wash., the centre of great mineral wealth; the Royal Gold Mining Company's properties described.    [n.p., 1897?]

15 p. (incl. cover)    map (on back cover)    15 cm. Cover title.

B.C. ARCHIVES

**1311    Royal Gold Mining Company**

Report on a part of Royal Gold Mining Co's property.    [Rossland, 1897]

4 p. (folder)    14 cm.    Caption title.

A prospectus.

B.C. ARCHIVES

**1312    St. Barbe, Charles**
D. 1929

First history of Nelson, B.C.; with sketches of some of its prominent citizens, firms and corporations.    [Nelson] C. A. Rohrabacher & Son [1897?]

24 p.    30 cm.    Cover title. A history of Nelson and West Kootenay: p. [1]-8. Business and biographical sketches: p. 11-24.

B.C. ARCHIVES

**1313    Sarel, C. Wentworth**

The Yukon route via Kamloops and Cariboo; not an experimental route, but one that has been tried with success—feed plenty, provisions sure, by C. Wentworth Sarel, editor of the Kamloops Standard. [n.p., n.d.]

Sheet.    43 x 16 cm.

VANCOUVER PUBLIC LIBRARY

## 1314    "The Standard" map . . .

"The Standard" map showing the proposed route from Spokane to Alaska via Kamloops, Cariboo, and Cassiar, with explanatory notes. Published under authority of the government of the province of British Columbia.    Kamloops, The Kamloops Printing and Publishing Co., 1897.

[28] p. (p. [15]-[28] advertisements) fold. map. 23 cm.    Cover title: The inland route to the Yukon.

The route outlined is the overland route to the Klondike via Kamloops, Quesnel, Hazelton, and the Stikine River to Teslin Lake. The description of the route past Teslin Lake is notably vague.

B.C. ARCHIVES

## 1315    Takahashi, K. T.

The anti-Japanese petition; an appeal in protest against a threatened persecution, by K. T. Takahashi, a Japanese-Canadian.    Montreal, Gazette Printing Company, 1897.

16 p. (incl. cover)    Cover title.

Written to condemn a petition which "prays, in substance, that a new law be enacted to alter the present statutory provisions of Canada for naturalization as far as concerns the Japanese immigrants . . ."—p. 3. The author accused the petitioners of trying to monopolize the British Columbia labour market.

BIBLIOTHÈQUE SAINT-SULPICE

## 1316    Thompson, D'Arcy W[entworth]
### 1860-1948

Report by Professor D'Arcy Thompson on his mission to Behring Sea in 1896, dated March 4, 1897. Presented to both Houses of Parliament by command of Her Majesty, May 1897.    London, Printed by Harrison and Sons [1897]

39 p. col. diagr., tables. 34 cm. ([Great Britain. Parliament. Command papers] C. 8426) At head of title: United States, no. 3 (1897)

B.C. ARCHIVES

## 1317    Tuttle, C[harles] R[ichard]
### B. 1848

The golden North; a vast country of inexhaustible gold fields, and a land of illimitable cereal and stock raising capabilities. Illustrated with maps and engravings.    Chicago, Rand, McNally & Co., 1897.

x, [5]-307 p. 20 cm.    Engravings and maps wanting in copy examined.

Includes chapters on the Skeena River country, the Peace-Liard-Pelly river route to the Klondike, the Alaska boundary, and the resources of British Columbia.

B.C. ARCHIVES

## 1318    United States

Fur-seal arbitration. In the matter of the claims of Great Britain against the United States of America before the Bering Sea Claims Commission. Argument for the United States in reply. Washington, Government Printing Office, 1897.

iv, 496, iv p. 23 cm.    Counsel for the United States: Don M. Dickinson, Robert Lansing, and C. B. Warren. Not seen.

LIBRARY OF CONGRESS

## 1319    Vancouver. Public Library

The official catalogue of the books contained in the Free Library, Vancouver, B.C. By order of the Board.    Vancouver, Budget Presses, 1897.

27 [i.e. 72] p. 23 cm.    Last page has numbering transposed.

Catalogues were also published in 1899 (supplement, 1901?) and in 1904 (first supplement, 1906? and second supplement, 1907).

VANCOUVER PUBLIC LIBRARY

## 1320    The Vancouver routes . . .

The Vancouver routes to the Yukon; Vancouver City the best point of departure for the Yukon. [Vancouver, "News-Advertiser," printers, n.d]

32 p. 22 cm.    Caption title. On cover: To the land of gold; don't forget that Vancouver, B.C., the terminus of the Canadian Pacific Railway, is the base of supplies . . .

B.C. ARCHIVES

## 1321    Vancouver, Victoria, and Eastern Railway and Navigation Company

Vancouver, Victoria and Eastern Railway and Navigation Company.    [Vancouver, The Independent Printing and Publishing Co., 1897]

11 p. map. 22 cm.    Cover title.

Written to support the views of promoters seeking a bill to incorporate the company.

B.C. ARCHIVES

## 1322    Venning, R[obert] N[orris]
### B. 1854

The Behring sea question, embracing the fur sealing industry of the North Pacific Ocean, 1896. Ottawa, Government Printing Bureau, 1897.

71 p. tables. 25 cm.    At head of title: From Report of the Department of Marine and Fisheries, 1896.

Gives seal-catch statistics for 1896 as well as a review of the season's events in relation to the controversy.

B.C. ARCHIVES

**1323    Victoria (city)**
APPELLANT

In the Supreme Court of B.C., on appeal to the full court, between the corporation of the city of Victoria (defendant) appellant, and Martha Maria Lang, administratrix of the estate and effects of John Lang, deceased (plaintiff) respondent. Appeal of the defendant corporation from the judgment of the Hon. Mr. Justice McColl. Appeal book. C. Dubois Mason, solicitor for the appellants (defendants); D. G. Macdonell, solicitor for the respondent (plaintiff)    [n.p., 1897]

12 1.    28 cm.

B.C. ARCHIVES

**1324    Western recreation**

Western recreation.    v. 1-?; April 1897-? Victoria, Vancouver Recreation Publishing Co.

v.    illus.    26 cm.    monthly.

Includes notes on game laws, hunting and fishing, boating, chess, gardening, and such sports as rowing, soccer and tennis.

B.C. ARCHIVES

**1325    Agricultural and Trades Association of Okanagan Mission Valley**

A short history of Kelowna and its surroundings in the province of British Columbia, Dominion of Canada.    Victoria and Vancouver, the Province Publishing Co., 1898.

14 p.    illus., plate.    22 cm.    Cover title: Kelowna and its surroundings . . .

NATIONAL LIBRARY

**1326    Alaskan-Canadian Boundary Commission**

Joint report of the United States and British commissioners on the Alaskan-Canadian boundary. December 31, 1895.    Washington, Government Printing Office, 1898.

15 p.    24 cm.    William Ward Duffield, American commissioner; William Frederick King, British commissioner.

Also in: Canada. Sessional papers, 1896, no. 74 (entry 1187).

B.C. ARCHIVES

**1327    Auzias [de] Turenne, Raymond**
B. 1861

Voyage au pays des mines d'or, le Klondike. Paris, Calmann Lévy, 1898.

318 p.    illus., port., fold. maps, diagrs.    19 cm.

The author briefly comments on Vancouver merchants.

Also: 1899.    Third edition: 1899.

UNIVERSITY OF WASHINGTON LIBRARY

**1328    Baskerville, C[harles] G[ardiner]**

"Abba, Nigwaud" . . . Gením gamzín gígíengwuk'l gan'l anluzabukím Gaud. 'Le dames Rev. C. G. Baskerville. 'Le šim aigiuk̲dis Rev. J. B. McCullagh. Šibookst, A'l Ganzabim sawinsk.    Aiyansh Mission, Nass River, B.C., 1898.

72 p.    20 cm.    Not seen.

LIBRARY OF CONGRESS

**1329    Bible. New Testament. Acts. Haida**

The Acts of the Apostles in Haida. [Translated by the Rev. John Henry Keen]    London, British and Foreign Bible Society, 1898.

145 p.    16 cm.

B.C. ARCHIVES

**1330    Bible. New Testament. Epistles. Tsimshian**

The epistles of St. Paul the Apostle to the Galatians, Ephesians, Philippians, Colossians, Thessalonians, Timothy, Titus, and Philemon; the general epistles of Sts. James, Peter, John and Jude. Translated into the Zimshian [by William Ridley] London, Society for Promoting Christian Knowledge, 1898.

79 p.    18 cm.

B.C. ARCHIVES

**1331    [Bradley, George B.]**

The Klondike-Peace gold fields. Compiled from Canadian government reports.    Ottawa, 1898.

16 p.    24 cm.    Cover title. At head of title: Preliminary edition. Author from copyright information.

On the Findlay, Omineca, Peace, Liard, and Yukon gold deposits and their accessibility.

CANADIAN ARCHIVES

**1332    British Columbia Gold Property Company**

Prospectus for 1898.    [Victoria, H. P. McDowell, printer, 1898]

16 p.    22 cm.    Caption title. On cover: British Columbia Gold Property Company, limited liability. Head office: Victoria.

B.C. ARCHIVES

**1333  Brownlee's indexed map . . .**

Brownlee's indexed map of British Columbia; also map of Yukon gold fields.    [Vancouver, Published by J. H. Brownlee, 1898]

27, [5] p. (incl. advertisements)    2 col. fold. maps. 22 x 11 cm.    Cover title. On cover: Evans & Hastings, printers.

The maps show various routes to the Klondike.

B.C. ARCHIVES

**1334  Calgary route . . .**

Calgary route to the Klondyke gold fields; description of routes; miners' and prospectors' outfitting guide.    [Calgary, 1898]

10 p.    15 cm.    Cover title.    Charles W. Smith in *Pacific Northwest americana* (1950) attributes this work to J. B. Caldwell.

Gives distances for the Peace-Liard route.

B.C. ARCHIVES

**1335  Canada. Parliament. Senate. Special Committee upon Opening up Direct Communication between the Railway System of Canada and the Navigable Waters of the Yukon**

[Third] report. Printed by order of Parliament. Ottawa, Printed by S. E. Dawson, 1898.

134 p.    tables.    25 cm.    (Parliament, 1897-98. Senate. Journals. Appendix no. 5)    Cover title. Running title: Routes to the Yukon. Chairman: C. A. Boulton.

B.C. ARCHIVES

**1336  Canadian Development Co.**

San Francisco, Portland, Seattle, Tacoma, Victoria, Vancouver, to Atlin Lake and Dawson City (via Skagway and Lake Bennett) and all intermediate points on the Lewis and Yukon Rivers. Victoria [n.d.]

[8] p. fold. map.    21 cm.    Cover title: Rail and water route to Atlin Lake, B.C., and the Klondike gold fields . . .    At head of cover title: The Canadian Development Co.

NATIONAL LIBRARY

**1337  Canadian Pacific Navigation Company, Limited**

Memorandum and articles of association of the Canadian Pacific Navigation Company (Limited) incorporated under the Companies' Ordinance, 1869.    Victoria, Eugene P. Miller, 1898.

31 p.    22 cm.

The company was an amalgamation of several shipping interests, including those of the Hudson's Bay Company, R. P. Rithet, and John Irving. It was taken over by the C.P.R. in 1901.

B.C. ARCHIVES

**1338  Chung, Chuck**

An answer to Mr. Maxwell's statements on the Chinese question [by Chung Chuck and Goon Sun. Vancouver? 1898]

44 p., 10 l.    22 cm.    Cover title. At head of title: To the Dominion House of Commons. Text in English and Chinese. Chinese text on last ten leaves. Includes text of George R. Maxwell's speech and article.

CANADIAN ARCHIVES

**1339  Clark, Horace F[letcher]**
D. 1928

Miners' manual, United States, Alaska, the Klondike; containing annotated manual of procedure; statutes and regulations; mining regulations of the Northwest Territory, British Columbia and Yukon district; glossary of mining terms, and information regarding Alaska and the Klondike [by] Horace F. Clark, Charles C. Heltman, and Charles F. Consaul.    Chicago, Callaghan & Company, 1898.

404 p.    diagrs., fold. map.    16 cm.

A few references to British Columbia.

LIBRARY OF PARLIAMENT

**1340  Colter, Hattie E.**

In the heart of the hills; or, The little preacher of the Pacific slope.    Edinburgh, Oliphant, Anderson & Ferrier, 1898.

203 p.    3 plates.    19 cm.

Fiction. A young lady comes as a missionary to the Cariboo country and through her ministrations has a great influence on the community.

B.C. ARCHIVES

**1341  Dorsey, George Amos**
1868-1931

A cruise among Haida and Tlingit villages about Dixon's Entrance [from a lecture.    New York, D. Appleton and Company, c1898]

15 p. illus.    24 cm.    Cover title. Reprinted from *Appleton's popular science monthly*, v. 27, June 1898.

The object of the journey was to collect material for the Field Columbian Museum, Chicago.

B.C. ARCHIVES

**1342    Dyer, E. Jerome**

The routes and mineral resources of north western Canada. Published under the auspices of the Incorporated London Chamber of Mines (with which are affiliated the Australasian and Canadian Chambers of Mines, London)    London, George Philip & Son, 1898.

xx, 268 p.    2 fold. maps.    22 cm.    List of authorities consulted . . . : p. v-x.

Dyer wrote this extensive work on the Klondike with its description of the routes to the gold fields "from the point of view of a resident in England." — p. iii.

A cheaper edition appeared with title: *The gold fields of Canada and how to reach them; being an account of the routes and mineral resources of north-western Canada.*

B.C. ARCHIVES

**1343    Facts for Klondyke . . .**

Facts for Klondyke and Alaska seekers; experience of some of the most noted miners, Joe Ladue, Jas. McMann (Jimmy, the Diver) Clarence Berry, Alex Orr, and C. J. Mullins; authentic accounts of different trails, boat-building, etc. . . .    [n.p.] The Yukon and Alaska Publishing Co. [n.d.]

64 p. (incl. advertisements)    illus.    15 cm.    Cover title. Colophon: Victoria, G.S.R. Co. Print.

B.C. ARCHIVES

**1344    [Fraser, Agnes]**
B. 1859

British Columbia for settlers; its mines, trade and agriculture, by Frances MacNab [pseud.] London, Chapman and Hall, 1898.

369 p.    3 fold. maps.    20 cm.

Includes one chapter on the Chinese.

B.C. ARCHIVES

**1345    Fullager, L. H.**

The E. & N. and the land grant.    [Victoria, 1898]

19 p.    22 cm.    Caption title.

Calls for the management of the land grant by the provincial government.

B.C. PROVINCIAL LIBRARY

**1346    Gold dust . . .**

Gold dust; how to find it and how to mine it; an elementary treatise on the methods and appliances used by miners on the frontier, with other useful information.    Vancouver, Thomson Stationery Co., c1898.

43, 21 p. (incl. advertisements)    15 cm.    Cover title.

B.C. ARCHIVES

**1347    Goldseeker**
PSEUDONYM

Hints to intending Klondikers, by Goldseeker [pseud.    Kamloops, Kamloops Publishing Company] 1898.

28 p.    22 cm.    Cover title: Hints for intending Klondikers. On t. p.: Kamloops Standard Job Dept.

LIBRARY OF PARLIAMENT

**1348    [Gordon, Charles William]**
1860-1937

Black rock; a tale of the Selkirks, by Ralph Connor [pseud.]    Toronto, The Westminster Co., 1898.

vi, 327 p.    19 cm.

Also: New York, Fleming H. Revell Company, 1899. With an introduction by Professor George Adam Smith.    Also: 1900. 322 p.    Also: Toronto, McClelland and Stewart, n.d. 322 p.    Also: Chicago, M. A. Donohue & Company, n.d. 224 p.

B.C. ARCHIVES

**1349    Great Britain. Foreign Office**

Joint statement of conclusion signed by the British, Canadian, and United States' delegates respecting the fur-seal herd frequenting the Pribyloff Islands in Behring Sea. Presented to both Houses of Parliament by command of Her Majesty, January 1898.    London, Printed by Harrison and Sons [1898]

5 p.    34 cm.    ([Great Britain. Parliament. Command papers] C. 8703) At head of title: United States, no. 2 (1893)

B.C. ARCHIVES

**1350    Habel, Jean**
1845?-1902

The North Fork Valley of the Wapta (British Columbia)    [n.p., 1898]

[328]-336 p.    plates, map.    24 cm.    Cover title. Reprinted from *Appalachia*, v. 8, 1898.

An exploration account.

B.C. ARCHIVES

**1351    Hall, Richard [and others]**
1853-1918

To Her Most Gracious Majesty the Queen, the humble petition of Richard Hall, William John Goepel, Ferdinand Henry Siewerd, Caesar Doring, respecting the arrest of the British schooner "Araunah," her officers and crew by Russia in 1888. Tupper, Peters & Potts, solicitors for the petitioners, Victoria, B.C.    [Victoria, 1898?]

17 1.    35 cm.    Cover title.

B.C. ARCHIVES

**1352   Henley, G. F.**

Guide to the Yukon Klondike mines; full information of outfit, climate, Dawson City; with notes on alluvial and metalliferous prospecting; routes described in detail; report of Wm. Ogilvie, F.R.G.S., and diary of the late Archbishop Seghers (murdered on the Yukon)   [Victoria, Vancouver, Province Publishing Co., 1898]

71 p. (advertisements, p. 64-71)   1 illus.   21 cm.

B.C. ARCHIVES

**1353   Hill-Tout, Charles**
1858?-1944

Oceanic origin of the Kwakiutl-Nootka and Salish stocks of British Columbia and fundamental unity of same; with additional notes on the Déné. [n.p.] 1898.

187-231 p.   25 cm.   Cover title. From: The Royal Society of Canada. *Proceedings and transactions.* ser. 2, v. 4, sec. 2, 1898-9.

B.C. ARCHIVES

**1354   How to get to the Klondyke . . .**

How to get to the Klondyke; the safest, best and cheapest route to Yukon gold fields is via the Regina, Prince Albert, Green Lake and Fort McMurray water route.   Prince Albert, Sask., 1898.

29 p.   illus., 2 fold. maps.   22 cm.   Cover title: Yukon via Prince Albert.

Discusses the Liard River route (p. 13-20).

CANADIAN ARCHIVES

**1355   Hudson's Bay Company**

History of the Hudson's Bay Company; the oldest trading corporation in the world; its relation to the development of the great Northwest and the gold discoveries of California, British Columbia and Klondike.   [Chicago, John F. Higgins] 1898.

101 p.   illus., plate, map.   24 cm.   Preface signed: W. M. Pindell. Map shows Hudson's Bay Company posts.

MANITOBA PROVINCIAL LIBRARY

**1356   Jennings, W[illiam] T[yndale]**
1846-1906

Report . . . on routes to the Yukon. Printed by order of Parliament.   Ottawa, Printed by S. E. Dawson, 1898.

28 p.   tables.   25 cm.   (Canada. Sessional papers, 1898, no. 30)   Cover title.

An interim report to Clifford Sifton, Minister of the Interior, concerning the possibility of a highway or railway route between the Stikine River and Teslin Lake, and railway routes from Chilkat Pass to the Yukon River, from Dyea via Chilkoot Pass and Tagish Lake to Hootalinqua River, from Skagway via White Pass and Tagish Lake to the Hootalinqua River, and a route via Taku Inlet and the Nakina River to Teslin Lake.

There was also another edition of 34 pages with additional material and maps.

B.C. ARCHIVES

**1357   Jesup North Pacific Expedition**

Publications of the Jesup North Pacific Expedition. Edited by Franz Boas.   New York, American Museum of Natural History, 1898-1930.

11 v. in 30.   illus., plates, maps.   35 cm. (American Museum of Natural History. Memoirs) Contents: v. 1, pt. 1. Facial paintings of the Indians of northern British Columbia, by Franz Boas. — v. 1, pt. 2. Mythology of the Bella Coola Indians, by Franz Boas. — v. 1, pt. 3. Archaeology of Lytton, by H. I. Smith. — v. 1, pt. 4. The Thompson Indians . . . by James Teit. — v. 1, pt. 5. Basketry designs of the Salish Indians, by Livingston Farrand. — v. 1, pt. 6. Archaeology of the Thompson River region, by H. I. Smith. — v. 2, pt. 1. Traditions of the Chilcotin Indians, by Livingston Farrand. — v. 2, pt. 2. Cairns of British Columbia and Washington, by Harlan I. Smith and Gerard Fowke. — v. 2, pt. 3. Traditions of the Quinault Indians, by Livingston Farrand. — v. 2, pt. 4. Shell heaps of the lower Fraser River, by Harlan I. Smith. — v. 2, pt. 5. The Lillooet Indians, by James Teit. — v. 2, pt. 6. Archaeology of Puget Sound, by Harlan I. Smith. — v. 2, pt. 7. The Shuswap, by James Teit. — v. 3, pts. 1-3. Kwakiutl texts, by Franz Boas and George Hunt. — v. 4, pt. 1. The decorative art of the Amur tribes, by Berthold Laufer. — v. 5, pt. 1. The Haida of Queen Charlotte Islands, by John R. Swanton. — v. 5, pt. 2. The Kwakiutl of Vancouver Island, by Franz Boas. — v. 6, pt. 1. Religion and myths of the Koryak, by W. Jochelson. — v. 6, pt. 2. Material culture and social organization of the Koryak, by W. Jochelson. — v. 7, pts. 1-3. The Chukchee [*sic*] by W. Bogoras. — v. 8, pt. 1. Chuckchee mythology, by W. Bogoras. — v. 8, pt. 2. Mythology of the Thompson Indians, by James Teit. — v. 8, pt. 3. The Eskimo of Siberia, by W. Bogoras. — v. 9, pts. 1-3. The Yukaghir and the Yukaghirized Tungus, by W. Jochelson. — v. 10, pt. 1. Kwakiutl texts — second series, by Franz Boas and George Hunt. — v. 10, pt. 2. Haida texts—Masset dialect, by John R. Swanton. — v. 12, pt. 1. Craniology of the North Pacific coast, by Bruno Oetteking.

The object of the expedition was to study early migrations between Asia and North America.

B.C. ARCHIVES

**1358   Klondyke mining laws . . .**

Klondyke mining laws; the Canadian gold fields; how to get there; where to purchase supplies. [n.p.] Graphic Publishing Company [n.d.]

31 p. (incl. advertisements)   15 cm.   Cover title. Colophon: Victoria, G. S. R. Co., printers.

B.C. ARCHIVES

**1359    Kootenay Curling Association**

Constitution.    [Revelstoke] Revelstoke Herald
Presses [1898]

14 p.    fold. diagr.    17 cm.    Cover title.

**1360    The Kootenay guide . . .**

The Kootenay guide; a guide to the mining camps
of British Columbia and Klondike.    Rossland,
B.C., and Calgary, Alta., Young & Luxton, 1898.

78 p.    maps.    16 cm.    Cover title. On cover: No. 11,
April 1898.

Includes descriptions of routes to the Klondike.

**1361    Kootenay mining standard**

Kootenay mining standard.    v. 1-?; October
1898-?    Rossland, The Standard Publishing Co.

v.    illus.    30 cm.    monthly. Only issue for July
1899 found.

The July 1899 issue, a special annual, gives
descriptions of mining activities, local
communities, etc.

**1362    Lake Bennett and Klondike
           Steam Navigation Company,
           Limited**

[Prospectus.    London? 1898]

3, [1] p. (folder)    map (on unattached sheet.
26 x 38 cm.)    43 cm.    Map has title: Sketch map
shewing advantages of the Lake Bennett route. The
registered office is given as being in England.

**1363    [Le Jeune, Jean-Marie Raphael]**
           1855-1930

Chinook and shorthand rudiments, with which the
Chinook jargon and the Wawa shorthand can be
mastered without a teacher in a few hours, by the
editor of the "Kamloops Wawa."
Kamloops, 1898.

15 p. (incl. cover)    15 cm.    Cover title.

See entry 1652 for supplement.

**1364    Memorial . . .**

Memorial of the owners of sealing schooners
respecting regulations restricting their business.
Victoria, Tupper, Peters & Potts [1898]

4 l.    34 cm.    Cover title.

A petition.

**1365    Moberly, Walter**
           COMPILER    1832-1915

Eight routes to the Klondyke; with tables of
distances, cost of outfits, map of routes, and other
information. Compiled and edited by Walter
Moberly.    Winnipeg, The Colonist Printing &
Publishing Co. [1898]

56 p. (incl. advertisements)    fold. map.    23 cm.

**1366    Na-na-kwa . . .**

Na-na-kwa; or, Dawn on the Northwest Coast.
v. 1-31; January 1898—May 1907.    Kitamaat,
B.C., Rev. George H. Raley.

31 v.    22 cm.    quarterly.

Until 1905 the *Na-na-kwa*, a Methodist missionary
paper, was printed on a small hand press. It was mainly
distributed to the Indians of Kitamat and neighbouring
villages.

**1367    Nation**

Nation.    v. 1, no. 1-20; March–July 1898.
Victoria.

1 v.    weekly.    Microfilm copy examined.

Has short notes and articles on world and local
B.C. events.

**1368    Ogilvie, William**
           COMPILER    1846-1912

The Klondike official guide; Canada's great gold
field, the Yukon district; with numerous maps and
illustrations, and regulations governing placer
mining. Published by authority of the Department
of the Interior of the Dominion of Canada.
Toronto, Hunter, Rose Co., 1898.

153 p.    illus., ports., maps (2 fold.) diagrs.    26 cm.

Includes a discussion of the routes to the Yukon.

Also: 1898. 152 p.    French edition: Toronto,
Hunter, Rose Co., 1898.    Two American editions:
Buffalo, Matthews-Northrup, 1898.

**1369    Petition . . .**

Petition of the masters, mates, hunters and seamen
of various sealing schooners for protection of their
industry.    Victoria, Tupper, Peters & Potts [1898]

5 l.    34 cm.    Cover title. Signed: Chas. Campbell,
master, and fifty-nine others. On l. [3]: Appendix to
memorial of the masters, mates, hunters, and seamen
on British sealing vessels, presented in the month of
November 1898.

**1370 Pocket dictionary . . .**

Pocket dictionary of the Chinook jargon, the Indian trading language of Alaska, the Northwest Territory, and the northern Pacific coast. San Francisco, Downing & Clarke, 1898.

32 p. 14 cm. Contents: pt. 1. Chinook-English. — pt. 2. English-Chinook. Contains the Lord's Prayer in Chinook (with interlinear translation).

B.C. ARCHIVES

**1371 Price, Julius M[endes]**
D. 1924

From Euston to Klondike; the narrative of a journey through British Columbia and the North-west Territory in the summer of 1898. With map and illustrations from sketches by the author, and photographs. London, Sampson, Low, Marston & Company, 1898.

xvi, 301 p. illus., plates, fold. map. 19 cm.

In the first few chapters the author describes his travels in the Kootenay district and his outfitting in Vancouver.

B.C. ARCHIVES

**1372 Public works policy . . .**

Public works policy, outlined by the Premier in his speech on the second reading of the Public Works Loan Act by which $5,000,000 will be spent in assisting railway development—The Mackenzie & Mann contract. [Victoria, 1898]

7 p. 22 cm. Caption title. Reprinted from the Victoria *Colonist*, 7 May 1898.

Includes a speech made by John Herbert Turner (p. 4-7)

B.C. ARCHIVES

**1373 Re memorial . . .**

Re memorial respecting the seizure of S. S. "Coquitlam"; declarations in support of following claims: Thomas Earle, William Munsie, Hall, Goepel & Co'y, The Pacific Sealing Co'y, Limited, Cereno L. Kelley, E. B. Marvin & Co'y, George Collins, Richard Hall, on acct. of charterers. Victoria, Tupper, Peters & Potts [1898]

21 l. 34 cm. Cover title.

DEPARTMENT OF FISHERIES LIBRARY, OTTAWA

**1374 Rinfret, Raoul**

Le Yukon et son or. Montreal, Imprimerie du "Cultivateur" [1898]

89 p. (incl. advertisements) illus. 18 cm.

Includes a discussion of the various routes to the Yukon.

B.C. ARCHIVES

**1375 Rossland. Board of Trade**

Rossland in 1898. Toronto, Grip Printing and Publishing Company, 1898.

36, [4] p. illus., plates, ports., tables. 31 cm.

Relates to the development of mining activities; includes a speech by Lord Aberdeen.

B.C. ARCHIVES

**1376 Rossland Miners' Union No. 38, Western Federation of Miners**

Constitution and by-laws . . . adopted at Rossland, British Columbia, Oct. 22, 1896 and Nov. 23, 1898. Rossland, Stunden & Perine [1898?]

16 p. 15 cm.

B.C. ARCHIVES

**1377 Shaughnessy, Tho[ma]s G[eorge Shaughnessy]**
1ST BARON 1853-1923

Memorandum on the Kettle River Railway Bill now before Parliament. Montreal, 1898.

3 p. (folder) 29 cm. Caption title. Dated: 14 April 1898.

A request that the charter for the railway not be granted.

SHORTT COLLECTION

**1378 Sifton, [Sir] Clifford**
1861-1929

Speech on the Canadian Yukon Railway. House of Commons, Ottawa, 15th and 16th February, 1898. Ottawa, Government Printing Bureau, 1898.

36 p. 25 cm.

B.C. ARCHIVES

**1379 Smith, Harlan I[ngersoll]**
1872-1940

The natural history museums of British Columbia. [n.p., 1898?]

4 p. (folder) 25 cm. Caption title. Reprinted from *Science*, v. 8, new ser., 4 November 1898, p. 619-620.

B.C. ARCHIVES

**1380 [Swartout, Melvin]**
D. 1904

A short cathechism [*sic*] and hymnal, adapted to the use of the Indians in the language of the Ahts, Barclay [Barkley] Sound, Vancouver Island, B.C. Vancouver, Trythall & Son [n.d.]

20 p. 17 cm. Text in a dialect of the Nootka language.

B.C. ARCHIVES

**1381   Tacoma. Port Orchard Navigation Co.**

Stikine River route to the Klondike; shortest, safest, quickest, and best.   [Tacoma?] Van Duzen, printer, 1898.

12 p.   map.   24 cm.   Cover title.   Not seen.

LIBRARY OF CONGRESS

**1382   Tate, Cha[rle]s M[ontgomery]**
TRANSLATOR   1852-1933

Indian Methodist hymn-book. Staylim-paypa ta Methodist-ts'hayilth. Hymns used on the Fraser Indian mission of the Methodist Church, B.C. Conference; to which are appended hymns in Chinook, and the Lord's Prayer and Ten Commandments. Translated by Rev's. Thos. Crosby, Chas. M. Tate, and Wm. H. Barraclough, B.A., missionaries.   Chilliwack, B.C., Compiled and printed by Rev. W. H. Barraclough, 1898.

[2], 48, [2] p.   13 cm.   Translated mainly by Charles Montgomery Tate. On verso of t.p.: The following hymns are in the Chilliway-uk dialect of the language of the Alkomaylum nation of Indians, who live along the Fraser River, from Yale to the Coast, and on Vancouver Island, at Cowichan and Nanaimo.

B.C. ARCHIVES

**1383   Teit, James [Alexander]**
1864-1922

Traditions of the Thompson River Indians of British Columbia. Collected and annotated by James Teit. With an introduction by Franz Boas. Boston, Published for the American Folk-Lore Society by Houghton, Mifflin and Company, 1898.

viii, 137 p.   25 cm.   (Memoirs of the American Folk-Lore Society, v. 6)

B.C. ARCHIVES

**1384   Thompson, D'Arcy W[entworth]**
1860-1948

Despatch from Professor D'Arcy Thompson, forwarding a report on his mission to Behring Sea in 1897. (In continuation of "United States no. 3 (1897)") Presented to both Houses of Parliament by command of Her Majesty, January 1898.   London, Printed by Harrison and Sons [1898]

15 p.   tables.   34 cm.   ([Great Britain. Parliament. Command papers] C. 8702) At head of title: United States, no. 1 (1898)

B.C. ARCHIVES

**1385   Turner, J[ohn] H[erbert]**
1834-1923

The Premier's manifesto; an open letter to the electors of British Columbia in which the whole

policy of the government is reviewed.   [n.p., 1898]

19 p.   22 cm.   Caption title.

VANCOUVER PUBLIC LIBRARY

**1386   Tylor, Edward B[urnett]**
1832-1917

Totem-post from the Haida village of Masset. Two British Columbian house-posts with totemic carvings. Remarks on totemism. Three papers by Edward B. Tylor.   London, Harrison and Sons, 1898.

133-148 p.   2 plates.   29 cm.   Cover title. Reprinted from the *Journal of the Anthropoligical Institute,* August-November, 1898.

B.C. ARCHIVES

**1387   United States. Commissioners on the Alaska boundary**

Views of the United States' commissioners on the Alaska boundary, as defined by the treaty of 1825. (Communicated by General Foster to the members of the International Joint High Commission assembled at Quebec, August 1898) [Quebec? 1898]

109 p.   33 cm.   General Foster's memorandum: p. 1-7.   Not seen.

Accompanied by six appendices (p. 8-109) consisting of documents relating to the Alaska boundary and the history of the Northwest Coast.

YALE WESTERN AMERICANA CATALOGUE

**1388   United States. Library of Congress. Division of Maps**

Alaska and the northwest part of North America, 1588-1898; maps in the Library of Congress, by P. Lee Phillips.   Washington, Government Printing Office, 1898.

119 p.   24 cm.

B.C. ARCHIVES

**1389   United States. Treasury Department**

Regulations governing the entry and transportation of merchandise destined for the Klondike region and northwest territory of British Columbia via the United States subports of Juneau, Dyea, and Skagway, or other customs ports in Alaska.   Washington [Government Printing Office] 1898.

3 p.   26 cm.   (Department circular, no. 23. Division of Customs)   Not seen.

LIBRARY OF CONGRESS

**1390 United States. Treasury Department. Commission on Fur-seal Investigations**

The fur seals and fur-seal islands of the North Pacific Ocean, by David Starr Jordan, commissioner in charge of fur-seal investigations of 1896-97. With the following official associations: Leonhard Stejneger and Frederic A. Lucas, of the U.S. National Museum; Jefferson F. Moser, in command of the U.S. Fish Commission steamer Albatross; Charles H. Townsend, of the U.S. Fish Commission; George A. Clark, secretary and stenographer; Joseph Murray, special agent. With special papers by other contributors. Washington, Government Printing Office, 1898-99.

4 v. illus., plates, maps (part fold.) diagrs. *and* atlas of 14 fold. charts. 28 cm. Binder's title: Report of the fur-seal investigations, 1896-1897.

B.C. ARCHIVES

**1391 United States. Treasury Department. Special Agents Division**

Seal and salmon fisheries and general resources of Alaska. Washington, Government Printing Office, 1898.

4 v. illus., plates (part col., part fold.) ports., maps (part fold.) charts. 24 cm. ([United States] 55th Cong., 1st sess. House. Doc. no. 92, pts. 1-4)

Contains correspondence between the State and Treasury departments on the Bering Sea question, 1895-6.

B.C. ARCHIVES

**1392 Vancouver. Ordinances, etc.**

By-laws of the city of Vancouver. 1886+ Vancouver, 1898+

v. 21 cm. Various printers. Consolidations bound in B.C. Provincial Library for 1898 and 1902 with t.p. added.

B.C. PROVINCIAL LIBRARY

**1393 Venning R[obert] N[orris]**
B. 1854

The Behring Sea question, embracing the fur sealing industry of the North Pacific Ocean, 1897. Ottawa, Government Printing Bureau, 1898.

43 p. tables. 25 cm. At head of title: From Report of the Department of Marine and Fisheries, 1897.

Covers the season's seal-catch and events effecting the industry.

CANADIAN ARCHIVES

**1394 Victoria (city)**
APPELLANT

In the Privy Council, on appeal from the Supreme Court of British Columbia, between the corporation of the city of Victoria, appellants, and Martha Maria Lang (administratrix of the estate and effects of John Lang, deceased) respondent. Case for the appellants. Case for the respondents. Record of proceedings. Exhibit book. [London, 1898]

18, 15, 259, v, 41 p. diagrs. (part fold.) tables. 27 cm. Cover title. At head of title: No. 56 of 1898.

Action in respect to the collapse of the Point Ellice Bridge.

B.C. ARCHIVES

**1395 Victoria Sealers' Association**

Memorial of Canadian sealers respecting their interests, and the Quebec International Conference, 1898. [Victoria, 1898?]

18 l. 35 cm. Cover title.

A petition to the Governor-General. The copy examined has a record in manuscript of those sealers who signed it, together with the names of their vessels.

B.C. ARCHIVES

**1396 Victoria Wharf and Warehouse Company, Limited**

Memorandum and articles of association . . [Victoria, 1898]

16 p. 34 cm. At head of title: The Companies' Act, 1897; company limited by shares.

B.C. ARCHIVES

**1397 White, Trumbull**
1868-1941

Pictorial history of our war with Spain for Cuba's freedom; a thrilling account of the land and naval operations of American soldiers and sailors in our war with Spain, and the heroic struggles of Cuban patriots against Spanish tyranny . . . Vancouver J. M. MacGregor Publishing Co. [c1898]

560 p. plates, ports. 25 cm.

B.C. PROVINCIAL LIBRARY

**1398 Wyman, Gilbert**
COMPILER

Public land and mining laws of Alaska, the Northwest Territory, and the province of British Columbia. This work contains a careful compilation of all the mining laws, and all the public land laws now in force, of Alaska, of the Northwest Territory, and of the province of British Columbia. The United States mining laws and regulations are also inserted in full. Complete in one volume.   Fruitvale, Cal., G. Wyman, 1898.

776 p.   map.   16 cm.

1399   The Yukon territory . . .

The Yukon territory; the narrative of W. H. Dall, leader of the expedition to Alaska in 1866-1868; the narrative of an exploration made in 1887 in the Yukon district by George M. Dawson, D.S., F.G.S.; extracts from the report of an exploration made in 1896-1897 by Wm. Ogilvie, D.L.S., F.R.G.S.; introduction by F. Mortimer Trimmer. London, Downey & Co., 1898.

xiv, 438 p.   illus., plates, fold. map (in pocket) 25 cm.   Part 2: Extracts from the report on an exploration made in 1887 in the Yukon territory, N.W.T., and adjacent northern portion of British Columbia, by George M. Dawson.

1400   All Hallows' . . .

All Hallows' in the West.   v. 1-3; 1899-1901. Yale, All Hallows' School.

3 v. in 1.   22 cm.   triannual.   No index.

Contains pupil summaries of the work of the All Hallows' community in the private school for girls and the Indian mission school.

1401   Associated Boards of Trade of Eastern British Columbia

Proceedings of the . . . annual convention. 1899-1949?   Nelson, Nelson Daily News.

v.   14, 23 cm.   Title varies slightly. Conventions held in various cities. The first proceedings were printed by W. H. Jones in Rossland. Local boards of trade superseded the associated board, possibly in 1950.

1402   Bible. New Testament. John. Haida

The Gospel according to Saint John in Haida. [Translated by the Rev. John Henry Keen] London, Printed for the British and Foreign Bible Society, 1899.

116 p.   16 cm.

1403   Bible. New Testament. Luke. Haida

The Gospel according to Saint Luke in Haida. [Translated by the Rev. J. H. Keen]   London, British and American Bible Society, 1899.

156 p.   16 cm.

1404   Bindloss, Harold
       1866-1946

A wide dominion.   London, T. Fisher Unwin, 1899.

293 p.   19 cm.   (Overseas library, no. 7)

Mostly concerned with the author's experiences while he was working and travelling in British Columbia.

1405   British Columbia. Board of Trade

Kettle River Valley railway; report of a meeting of the British Columbia Board of Trade, held at Victoria on the 22nd & 23rd March, 1899. [n.p., 1899]

19 p.   21 cm.   Cover title. On cover: Reprinted from the Victoria "Colonist."

The meeting resolved: "That this Board of Trade urge upon the Dominion government the necessity of granting a charter to the Kettle River Railway . . ." — p. 19.

1406   British Columbia Amateur Lacrosse Association

Constitution and rules . . . adopted March 22nd, 1890, revised April 8th, 1899.   Vancouver, Evans & Hastings, 1899.

29 p.   table.   14 cm.

1407   The Caledonia interchange

The Caledonia interchange.   September 1899-? Aiyansh Mission, Naas River, B.C., James Benjamin McCullagh.

v.   illus.   25 cm.   occasional. Issue no. 5, 1900, examined. There were issues of the paper in September 1899 and Easter 1900 according to the note on p. 20.

Includes an address by the Bishop of Caledonia and several important articles on the Indian potlatch and its associated controversy.

**1408 Canada**

Memorandum on the boundary between Canada and Alaska showing the position of the Canadian government in respect thereto, 1899. [Ottawa? 1899]

129 p. fold. map. 33 cm. At head of p. 3: Confidential. Appendices: p. [37]-122.

CANADIAN ARCHIVES

**1409 Canada. Department of the Interior**

Descriptive atlas of western Canada, showing maps of the provinces of Manitoba and British Columbia and districts of Assiniboia, Alberta and Saskatchewan; also of the world and the Dominion of Canada. Issued by authority of Hon. Clifford Sifton, Minister of the Interior. Ottawa, 1899.

10 p. 5 col. maps (part double) 36 cm. Cover title. Not seen.

Also: Ottawa, 1900? 13 p. German edition under title: *Beschreibender Atlas des westlichen Canada . . .*

NATIONAL LIBRARY

**1410 Canada. Parliament. House of Commons**

Documents relating to the recent disallowance of certain statutes passed by the legislature of British Columbia. Printed by order of Parliament. Ottawa, Printed by S. E. Dawson, 1899.

32 p. 24 cm. (Canada. Sessional paper, 1899, no. 110)

The disallowed acts contained a clause attaching a penalty of five dollars a day for each Chinese and Japanese person employed in the construction or operation of undertakings authorized by legislation passed in the 1898 session.

B.C. ARCHIVES

**1411 Canada. Department of the Secretary of State**

Correspondence and papers in reference to Stanley Park and Deadman's Island, British Columbia. Ottawa, Printed by S. E. Dawson, 1899.

44 p. 25 cm. (Canada. Sessional papers, 1899, no. 68A)

Concerns the question of whether the park and island were federally or provincially owned.

B.C. ARCHIVES

**1412 Canadian Pacific Railway Company**

Banff in the Canadian Rockies and the glaciers of the Selkirks, reached by the Canadian Pacific Railway. [n.p.] 1899.

[14] p. (incl. cover; folds to provide 26 columns) illus., maps. 22 cm. Cover title.

NATIONAL LIBRARY

**1413 Church of England. Book of Common Prayer. Selections. Haida**

Portions of the Book of Common Prayer in Haida. Translated by the Rev. J. H. Keen. London, Society for Promoting Christian Knowledge, 1899.

39 p. 17 cm.

B.C. ARCHIVES

**1414 Cliffe, C[harles]**
1842-1931

The Slocan district, British Columbia; its resources and opportunities for investment. Sandon, B.C. [1899]

87 p. illus. 15 x 23 cm. Cover title. Mines of the Slocan; their location by towns: p. 9-72.

Gives a synopsis of the activity at various mines.

U.B.C. SPECIAL COLLECTIONS

**1415 Curle, J[ames] H[erbert]**
1870-1942

The gold mines of the world; containing concise and practical advice for investors, gathered from a personal inspection of the mines of the Transvaal, India, West Australia, Queensland, New Zealand, British Columbia, and Rhodesia. London, Waterlow and Sons, 1899.

317 p. fold. front., plates, plans (part. col.) 25 cm. Not seen. Second edition in B.C. Archives examined.

Second edition: 1902. Third edition: 1905.

LIBRARY OF CONGRESS

**1416 Deans, James**
1827-1905

Tales from the totems of the Hidery. Collected by James Deans; edited by Oscar Lovell Triggs. Chicago, 1899.

96 p. plates. 25 cm. (Archives of the International Folk-Lore Assciation, v. 2)

On the customs and legends of the Haida Indians.

B.C. ARCHIVES

**1417 Durieu, [Pierre]-Paul**
1830-1899

Chinook Bible history, by the Rt. Rev. Paul Durien [sic] O.M.I. Kamloops, 1899.

112 p. 2 ports. 18 cm. Chinook jargon, transcribed into Duployan shorthand by Jean-Marie Le Jeune.

B.C. ARCHIVES

**1418    Ford, Charles T.**

From coast to coast; a farmer's ramble through Canada, and the Canadian Pacific Railway system. Exeter, Printed by Bearne Brothers, 1899.

34 p.    plates (1 fold.)    17 cm.

About one-third of the pamphlet relates to British Columbia. The author was a member of the Royal Agricultural Society.

**1419    Garland, Hamlin**
     1860-1940

The trail of the goldseekers; a record of travel in prose and verse.    New York, Macmillan, 1899.

viii, 264 p.    20 cm.

An interesting account by an American novelist of his journey through the interior of British Columbia to Teslin Lake in the Yukon.

Also: 1906.

**1420    Gordon, Granville Armyne**
     LORD    1856-1907

Nootka; a tale of Vancouver Island. With twelve full page illustrations and map.    London, Sands and Company, 1899.

vi, 245 p.    plates, map.    20 cm.

Fiction. A tale of adventure on a trip from Victoria to Nootka Sound in the 1890's.

**1421    Gowen, Herbert H[enry]**
     B. 1864

Church work in British Columbia; being a memoir of the episcopate of Acton Windeyer Sillitoe, D.D., D.C.L., first Bishop of New Westminster. London, Longmans, Green, and Company, 1899.

xxv, 232 p.    plates, ports.    19 cm.

A record of the Bishop's activities in his large diocese, based on his diaries and those of his wife, with numerous extracts from letters. The work reflects to some degree the social and economic life of the province in the 1880's.

**1422    Grant, George Monro**
     EDITOR    1835-1902

Our picturesque northern neighbor; historical and descriptive sketches of the scenery and life in and around Toronto, along the Canadian shore of Lake Huron, in the Northwest Territories, and in British Columbia. Illustrated by wood-engravings from original drawings by W. T. Smedley, F. B. Schell, A. B. Frost, L. R. O'Brien, F. Hopkinson Smith,

and others.    Chicago, Alexander Belford & Co., 1899.

280 p.    illus.    31 cm.    Includes: British Columbia, by Principal Grant [p. 263-280]

**1423    Great Britain. Colonial Office**

Canada. Memorandum on the boundary between Canada and Alaska, showing the contention of the Canadian government in respect thereto, 1899. With appendices.    [London, 1899]

150, xii p.    fold. map.    33 cm.    (North American, no. 187)    At head of title: Printed for the use of the Colonial Office; confidential. Dated: October 1899. Index: p. [i]-xii.

**1424    Great Britain. Colonial Office**

Colonial Office correspondence, 1898 and 1899. [London, 1899]

8 p.    33 cm.

Confidential correspondence with the Canadian government respecting the Alaska boundary negotiations.

**1425    Great Britain. Foreign Office**

Certain correspondence of the Foreign Office and of the Hudson's Bay Company. Copied from original documents, London, 1898 [by Otto Klotz] Department of the Interior, Office of the Chief Astronomer, November 1899.    Ottawa, Government Printing Bureau, 1899.

5 pts. in 1 v.    3 fold. maps (in pocket)    25 cm. Contents: pts. 1-2. Hudson's Bay Company correspondence [1823-1849] — pt. 3. Foreign Office correspondence, international boundary, 49th parallel, British Columbia, 1858-1864. — pt. 4. Foreign Office correspondence, international boundary, 49th parallel, 1869-1870. — pt. 5. Foreign Office correspondence, north-west coast America-Alaska.

The documents contained in this work have a strange history. Both the American and British manuscript copies of the records of the international survey of the forty-ninth parallel, together with the final report of 7 May 1869, were lost for nearly thirty years. By chance Otto Klotz uncovered them in some boxes at the Royal Observatory at Greenwich in 1898 (see Otto Klotz's *The history of the forty-ninth parallel survey* . . . (entry 1635)).

**1426    Great Britain. Foreign Office**

Correspondence respecting the proceedings of the joint commission for the settlement of questions pending between the United States and Canada . . . [London, 1899-1901]

3 pts. in 1 v.   33 cm.   Parts 2-3 have title: Further correspondence . . .   At head of title: Printed for the use of the Foreign Office [date] confidential [number related to Foreign Office confidential document, and part number]   Binder's title on cover: Foreign Office confidential series; correspondence relating to the proceedings of the International Joint High Commission, Quebec and Washington, 1898-9; part[s] . . .

Series has index in Vancouver Public Library (designated in catalogue as v. 2) with title: *Joint High Commission, 1898-9; Foreign Office confidential series; correspondence relating to the proceedings of the International Joint High Commission, Quebec & Washington, 1898-9; part[s]* . . .   In xxxiii p. At head of title: Confidential. Running title: Index.

Relates to the Alaskan boundary question.

VANCOUVER PUBLIC LIBRARY

### 1427   Hanford, C[ornelius] H[olgate]
1849-1926

Boundary disputes with our northern neighbors, settled and unsettled; annual address before the Washington pioneers, June 7, 1899.   Seattle, Lowman & Hanford Stationery and Printing Co. [1899]

20 p.   22 cm.

On the San Juan and Alaska boundary disputes.

UNIVERSITY OF WASHINGTON LIBRARY

### 1428   High handed proceedings . . .

High handed proceedings on Vancouver's Island; or, How settlers were evicted in 1895; Samuel Waddington in possession 25 years, David Hoggan in possession 13 years, others for a shorter period; evidence and facts as to why existing rights of agricultural settlers could not heretofore be enforced against the Esquimalt and Nanaimo Railway Company.   [Victoria? 1899]

41, vi p.   23 cm.   Cover title.

B.C. ARCHIVES

### 1429   Kamloops and district mining gazette

Kamloops and district mining gazette; a monthly journal devoted to the mining interests of the district of North Yale, British Columbia. January 1899—March, 1900?   Kamloops, W. W. Clarke & F. E. Young.

v.   25 cm.   monthly.   Latest copy examined, which was located in the University of British Columbia Library, was no. 15 for March 1900.

B.C. ARCHIVES

### 1430   Kaslo. Board of Trade

Kaslo, British Columbia, the mineral metropolis of the world.   Kaslo, Board of Trade [1899?]

64, [33] p.   illus., ports.   15 x 21 cm.

TORONTO PUBLIC LIBRARY

### 1431   A Kwāgūtl translation . . .

A Kwāgūtl translation of hymns as sung in the C.M.S. missions on the north of Vancouver Island. London, Society for Promoting Christian Knowledge, 1899.

30 p.   17 cm.   Probably translated by Alfred James Hall.

Also: London, 1916. 46 p. Appendix: p. [31]-46.
Also: London, 1935. 46 p. Appendix: p. [31]-46.

B.C. ARCHIVES

### 1432   Lobel, Loicq de

Le Klondyke, l'Alaska, le Yukon, et les îles Aléoutiennes.   Paris, Société Française d'Editions d'Art, 1899.

40 p.   22 cm.   Cover title. Reprinted from the *Bulletin de la Société de Géographie.*

Includes a description of a trip up the Stikine River.

B.C. ARCHIVES

### 1433   McCullagh, J[ames] B[enjamin]
1854-1921

The Indian potlatch [substance of a paper read before C.M.S. annual conference at Metlakatla, B.C., 1899.   Toronto, Woman's Missionary Society of the Methodist Church, 1899?]

20 p.   20 cm.   Cover title.

B.C. ARCHIVES

### 1434   Martin, [Archer Evans Stringer]
1865-1941

Chart of the judges of the supreme courts of Vancouver Island and British Columbia. Victoria, The Law Society of British Columbia, 1899.

Sheet.   52 x 44 cm. fold. to 22 x 13 cm.

"Compiled and presented by the Hon. Mr. Justice Martin to the Law Society of British Columbia, and ordered by the Benchers (2nd October, 1899), to be published with the Law Reports."

B.C. ARCHIVES

**1435  Merriam, John C[ampbell]**
1869-1945

The fauna of the Sooke beds of Vancouver Island.
With one plate.    Issued March 6, 1899.    San
Francisco, The Academy, 1899.

175-180 p.    plate.    25 cm.    (Proceedings of the
California Academy of Science. 3d series. Geology.
v. 1, no. 6)    Issued in single cover with v. 1, no. 5.
Not seen.

LIBRARY OF CONGRESS


**1436  Mills, David**
1831-1903

The Canadian view of the Alaskan boundary
dispute, as stated by Hon. David Mills, Minister
of Justice, in an interview with the correspondent
of the Chicago Tribune on the 14th of August
1899.    Ottawa, Government Printing
Bureau, 1899.

23 p.    18 cm.

B.C. ARCHIVES


**1437  Mining exchange . . .**

Mining exchange and engineering news.    v. 1-19,
no. 9;1899—September 1917.    Vancouver, The
B.C. Mining Exchange.

19 v.    illus.    31 cm.    monthly.    No index. Title
varies: v. 1—v. 8, no. 7 (1899—July 1906) as
*British Columbia mining exchange and investor's
guide;* v. 8, no. 8—v. 10, no. 3 (August 1906—
March 1908) as *British Columbia mining exchange.*

Contains financial reports, descriptions of mining
towns and prospects, stock advertisements, and
relevant editorial quotations from newspapers.

B.C. ARCHIVES


**1438  Moore, E. K.**

Alaska; predicted times of slack water at Seymour
Narrows, Discovery Passage, B.C., and at Sergius
Narrows, Perit Straight, Alaska, from May to
December, 1899.    Washington, Government
Printing Office, 1899.

145-150 p.    tables.    30 cm.    (United States Coast
and Geodetic Survey. Bulletin no. 39)    Not seen.

BANCROFT LIBRARY CATALOGUE


**1439  Native Sons of British Columbia**

Constitution and by-laws . . . adopted March 8th,
1899.    Victoria, Smith & Randolph,
printers [1899?]

22 p.    15 cm.

B.C. ARCHIVES


**1440  New Westminster. Public Library.**

An appeal for the public library, New Westminster,
B.C.    [New Westminster] Columbian
Print [1899?]

[3] p. (folder)    20 cm.    Cover title.

U.B.C. SPECIAL COLLECTIONS


**1441  Ontario and Slocan Mines
Development Company, Limited**

The Canadian Group, owned and operated by the
Ontario and Slocan Mines Development Co.,
Limited.    [Silverton, B.C., 1899?]

20 p.    facsims., 3 plans.    23 cm.    Cover title.

A prospectus for the company "owning and operating
The Canadian Group of Mines, located near Sandon,
British Columbia."

B.C. ARCHIVES


**1442  Pacific and Arctic Railway and
Navigation Company**

White Pass & Yukon route; Pacific & Arctic
Railway and Navigation Co., British Columbia
Yukon Railway Co.; general information
regarding the Atlin gold fields, Yukon & Klondike
mining districts.    Seattle, Wash., 1899.

map.    43 x 39 cm. fold. to 22 x 10 cm.

NATIONAL LIBRARY


**1443  Rathbun, Richard**
1852-1918

A review of the fisheries in the contiguous waters
of the state of Washington and British Columbia.
Washington, Government Printing Office, 1899.

251-350 p.    plates.    23 cm.    (United States
Commission of Fish and Fisheries. Doc. 423)    At
head of title: U.S. Commission of Fish and Fisheries;
George M. Bowers, commissioner. From the Report
of commissioner, 1899.    Not seen.

LIBRARY OF CONGRESS


**1444  Roberts, S[ydney] A.**

Azimuths of the North Pole star for 1899 and 1900.
Lat. 48° N. to lat. 54° N.    [Victoria? 1899]

[5] p.    22 cm.

LIBRARY OF PARLIAMENT


**1445  Roper, Edward**

A claim on Klondyke; a romance of the arctic El
Dorado. With illustrations.    Edinburgh, William
Blackwood and Sons, 1899.

312 p.   plates.   19 cm.   (Blackwood's colonial library)

Fiction. In 1896 two men set out from Victoria for the Klondike via the White Pass route.

B.C. ARCHIVES

## 1446   [Smith, Harlan Ingersoll]
### 1872-1940

Archaeological investigations of the North Pacific coast of America.   [New York, 1899]

10 p.   24 cm.   Caption title. Reprinted from *Science,* new ser., v. 9, 14 April 1899, p. 535-539.

Report of investigations which were made in British Columbia in connection with the Jesup Expedition.

B.C. ARCHIVES

## 1447   Smith, Harlan I[ngersoll]
### 1872-1940

Stone hammers or pestles of the north-west coast of America.   [n.p., 1899]

363-368 p.   illus.   25 cm.   Caption title. Reprinted from the *American anthropologist,* new ser., v. 1, April 1899.

Some of the artifacts described were found in British Columbia.

B.C. ARCHIVES

## 1448   Stock, Eugene
### 1836-1928

The history of the Church Missionary Society; its environment, its men and its work.   London, Church Missionary Society, 1899-1916.

4 v.   illus., ports., fold. maps.   23 cm.   The last volume is supplementary.

The Church of England missions in British Columbia are mentioned in the last three volumes.

B.C. ARCHIVES

## 1449   United States. Treasury Department

Regulations governing vessels employed in fur-seal fishing during the season of 1899.   Washington, Government Printing Office, 1899.

7 p. (incl. cover)   23 cm.   Cover title.

Includes the regulations of the Paris Tribunal of Arbitration, which were applicable to British vessels.

B.C. ARCHIVES

## 1450   United States. Treaties, etc.

Great Britain—Alaskan boundary. Modus vivendi between the United States of America and the United Kingdom of Great Britain and Ireland,

fixing a provisional boundary line between the territory of Alaska and the Dominion of Canada about the head of Lynn Canal. Concluded by exchange of notes October 20, 1899, by John Hay, Secretary of State of the United States, and Reginald Tover, chargé d'affaires of Her Britannic Majesty at Washington.   [Washington? 1899]

2 p.   fold. map.   25 cm.   Caption title. Map prepared in the office of the U.S. Coast and Geodetic Survey.   Not seen.

LIBRARY OF CONGRESS

## 1451   Vaux, George
### 1863-1927

Additional observations on glaciers in British Columbia, by George and William S. Vaux.   [Philadelphia, 1899]

501-511 p.   25 cm.   Cover title. Reprinted from: Academy of Natural Sciences of Philadelphia. *Proceedings.* December 1899.

GLENBOW FOUNDATION LIBRARY

## 1452   Venning, Robert Norris
### B. 1854

The Behring Sea question, embracing the fur sealing industry of the North Pacific Ocean, 1898. Ottawa, Government Printing Bureau, 1899.

11 p.   24 cm.   At head of title: From Report of the Department of Marine and Fisheries, 1898. Not seen.

CANADIAN ARCHIVES

## 1453   Victoria. St. Barnabas' Anglican Church

Half-yearly letter.   no. 1-39/40; June 1899—Christmas 1918.   Victoria.

40 no.   illus.   21-23 cm.   semiannual. On microfilm.

B.C. ARCHIVES

## 1454   Western Canada Press Association

An editorial outing. June 13th to 30th, 1899. [Winnipeg, Man., The Stovel Company, printers, 1899?]

39 p.   plates, ports.   23 cm.   Cover title.

An amplified itinerary of a group tour which included visits to places in British Columbia.

B.C. ARCHIVES

## 1455   The Western recorder

The Western recorder.   April 1899—November 1946.   Victoria, Western Recorder Printing and Publishing Co.

47 v. illus. 30, 35cm. monthly. Title varies: v. 1, no. 1—v. 25, no. 10 (April 1899—May 1925) as *Western Methodist recorder;* v. 1, no. 1—v. 22, no. 5 (June 1925—November 1946) under the auspices of the United Church. No index.

Earlier numbers carry occasional biographies and notices of early Methodist missionary work.

B.C. ARCHIVES

## 1456    Adney, [Edwin] Tappan
### 1868-1950

The Klondike stampede, by Tappan Adney, special correspondent of "Harper's weekly" in the Klondike.    New York, Harper & Brothers, 1900.

xii, 470 p.    illus., plates (part fold.) 2 maps (1 double) facsims.    21 cm.

Includes several pages on outfitting in Victoria.

B.C. ARCHIVES

## 1457    Art work . . .

Art work on British Columbia, Canada; published in twelve parts [with text by R. E. Gosnell.    n.p.] William H. Carre, 1900.

20, [1] 1.    illus., 81 plates.    36 cm.

The plates are from contemporary photographs; the text is limited to a brief historical résumé.

B.C. ARCHIVES

## 1458    Baillie-Grohman, W[illiam] A[dolph]
### 1851-1921

Fifteen years' sport and life in the hunting-grounds of western America and British Columbia. With a chapter by Mrs. W. A. Baillie-Grohman. Illustrated by seventy-seven photographs, including the best trophies of North America big game killed by English and American sportsmen. With table of measurements and notes. With three specially prepared maps of the northwest coast of the United States, British Columbia, and the Kootenay district. London, Horace Cox, 1900.

xii, 403 p.    illus., plates, ports., 3 fold. maps (in pocket)    25 cm.

About half the book is on hunting, but in the rest, Baillie-Grohman relates his experiences as an enterprising pioneer in the Kootenay mining area, including the story of his ill-fated canal project at Columbia Lake.

Second edition: London, Horace Cox, 1907.

B.C. ARCHIVES

## 1459    Baker, Marcus
### 1849-1903

Survey of the northwestern boundary of the United States, 1857-1861.    Washington, Government Printing Office, 1900.

78, xi p.    maps, tables.    23 cm.    (United States. Department of the Interior. Geological Survey. Bulletin no. 174. 56th Cong., 1st sess. House. Doc. no. 748)    Sources of information: p. 9-13.

A history of the establishment, surveying, and marking of the northwestern land boundary. It includes as Appendix B the report of progress made on 12 November 1859 by John G. Parke, chief astronomer and surveyor (appeared as: United States. 36th Cong., 1st sess. Senate. Ex. doc. no. 16) ; and, as Appendix C, a letter from Archibald Campbell, a northwestern boundary commissioner, which summarizes the history of the survey (from: United States. 40th Cong., 3d sess. House. Ex. doc. no. 86).

B.C. ARCHIVES

## 1460    Begg, Alexander
### 1825-1905

Review of the Alaskan boundary question. Victoria, T. R. Cusack, printer [1900?]

32 p.    22 cm.    Cover title. Reprinted from the *British Columbia mining record,* June, July, and August, 1900.

The text is not the same as in entry 1481.

B.C. ARCHIVES

## 1461    Boas, Franz
### 1858-1942

Introduction to Traditions of the Thompson River Indians of British Columbia.    [n.p., 1900?]

18 p.    25 cm.    Cover title. Reprinted from: American Folk-Lore Society. *Memoirs.* v. 6.

The author of *Traditions of the Thompson River Indians* is J. A. Teit (entry 1383).

U.B.C. SPECIAL COLLECTIONS

## 1462    Boas, Franz
### 1858-1942

Sketch of the Kwakiutl language.    [n.p., 1900]

708-721 p.    26 cm.    Cover title. Reprinted from the *American anthropologist,* new ser., v. 2, October-December, 1900.

Report of investigations undertaken while the author was on the Jesup expedition.

B.C. ARCHIVES

## 1463    Brabant, A[ugustin] Joseph
### 1845-1912

Vancouver Island and its missions, 1874-1900; reminiscences of the Rev. A. J. Brabant.    [New York, Messenger of the Sacred Heart Press, 1900]

89 p.    illus.    25 cm.    Cover title.

On missionary work among the Nootka Indians.

B.C. ARCHIVES

**1464    Gardiner, A. Paul**

The house of Cariboo and other tales from Arcadia. Illustrated by Robert A. Graef.    New York, A. P. Gardiner, publisher, 1900.

218 p.    illus.    19 cm.    Chapter 3: On the way to the gold fields. — Chapter 4: Into the Cariboo Mountains. — Chapter 7: In the mining camp. — Chapter 12: Barbara in the Chilcoten Valley.

Fiction. Brief sketches.

B.C. ARCHIVES

**1465    Gregory, Charles Noble**
1851-1932

The Alaskan boundary question.    [London, 1900]

7 p.    23 cm.    Cover title. Reprinted from the *Law magazine and review* of London, February 1900.

B.C. ARCHIVES

**1466    Haldane, J[ohn] W[ilton] C[unninghame]**

3800 miles across Canada.    London, Simpkin, Marshall, Hamilton, Kent, & Co., 1900.

xxiii, 344 p.    illus., fold. map.    19 cm.

The author made his trip in 1898 to gather economic information. About one-hundred pages are on British Columbia.

Enlarged edition: 1908. xxiii, 344, 23 p.

B.C. ARCHIVES

**1467    Hanford, C[ornelius] H[olgate]**
1849-1926

San Juan dispute, by C. H. Hanford, judge of the United States Circuit Court, Ninth Judicial Circuit, District of Washington.    Seattle, Published by Dilettante Publishing Co., 1900.

15 p.    port.    19 cm.    (Dilettante booklet series, no. 1)    Cover title.

Discusses the leading personalities involved in the San Juan dispute and its settlement.

UNIVERSITY OF WASHINGTON LIBRARY

**1468    Herring, Frances E[lizabeth (Clarke)]**
1851-1916

Canadian camp life.    London, T. Fisher Unwin, 1900.

247 p.    plates, ports.    20 cm.

About the author's family life on the British Columbia coast.

Second edition: London, Griffiths, 1913. 188 p.

B.C. ARCHIVES

**1469    Hodgins, Thomas**
1828-1910

British and American diplomacy affecting Canada, 1782-1899: a chapter of Canadian history.    Toronto, The Publishers' Syndicate Limited, 1900.

102 p.    maps.    21 cm.

Contains twenty pages on the adjustment of the Alaskan boundary.

B.C. ARCHIVES

**1470    Jesup North Pacific Expedition**

Ethnographical album of the North Pacific coasts of America and Asia. Jesup North Pacific Expedition. Part I.    New York, American Museum of Natural History, 1900.

5 1.    28 plates.    28 x 36 cm.    No more published.

VANCOUVER PUBLIC LIBRARY

**1471    Kennedy, Sir William Robert**
1838-1916

Hurrah for the life of a sailor! Fifty years in the Royal Navy . . . With illustrations.    Edinburgh, Blackwood and Sons, 1900.

xiv, 356 p.    Not seen.    Private information as to contents.

Pages 193-196 relate to hunting on Vancouver Island and the mainland.

Also: London, Eveleigh Nash, 1910.

BRITISH MUSEUM CATALOGUE

**1472    Oregon historical quarterly**

Oregon historical quarterly.    v. 1 + March 1900+    Portland, Ore., Oregon Historical Society.

v.    illus., maps, plates (part fold.)    24 cm.    Title varies: v. 1-26 (March 1900—June 1926) as *Quarterly of the Oregon Historical Society*. Supersedes the society's *Sources of the history of Oregon*. Indexed in *International index*. Table of contents for each issue; index for annual bound volumes. A cumulative index for v. 1-40 (1900-1939) was published in 1941. Cumulative index for v. 41-60 in process.

B.C. ARCHIVES

**1473    Osborn, E[dward] B[olland]**
D. 1938

Greater Canada; the past, present, and future of the Canadian North-west.    London, Chatto & Windus, 1900.

243 p.    fold. map.    20 cm.

The two chapters on British Columbia are mostly concerned with a review of mining developments.

Also: New York, Wessels, 1900.

B.C. ARCHIVES

**1474 Phillipps-Wolley, Sir C[live Oldnall Long]**
1854-1918

The chicamon stone.　London, George Bell & Sons, 1900.

[v], 295 p.　19 cm.　(Bell's Indian and colonial library)

Fiction. The story is that of a prospector in the Stikine River area and northern British Columbia in the 1890's. The "boss" is supposedly a characterization of the author's friend, Warburton Pike.

B.C. ARCHIVES

**1475 Phoenix pioneer . . .**

Phoenix pioneer and boundary mining journal. v. 1—? 1900?—?　Phoenix, B.C.

v.　illus.　30 cm.

Includes historical articles on the development of mining activity in the Boundary mining district.

B.C. ARCHIVES

**1476 Pickett, La Salle (Corbell)**
1848-1931

Pickett and his men. Second edition.　Atlanta, The Foote & Davies Company, 1900 [c1899]

xiii, 439 p.　ports.　22 cm.

Pages 99-125 relate to Pickett's role in the San Juan Island dispute.

Also: Philadelphia, 1913.

B.C. ARCHIVES

**1477 Ridley, William**
BISHOP OF CALEDONIA　1836-1911

Not myth but miracle.　London, Seeley and Co., 1900.

63 p.　21 cm.

Poetry. Describes the conversion to Christianity of some Indians living near the mouth of the Skeena River.

B.C. ARCHIVES

**1478 Sproat, Gilbert Malcolm**
1834-1913

"Mr. Jones, and the fribble" (polite for ass); a new year's excursion among the politicians.　[n.p.] Published by the author [1900?]

38 p.　22 cm.　Cover title.

A criticism of the handling of civil servants under the Semlin government and, in particular, of the treatment received in 1899 by the author's son, Alexander Sproat.

B.C. ARCHIVES

**1479 Vaux, William S.**
1872-1908

The Canadian Pacific Railway from Laggan to Revelstoke, B.C.　Philadelphia, Engineers' Club of Philadelphia, 1900.

64-86 p.　illus., map, diagrs.　25 cm.　On t.p.: Authorized separate from the copyrighted Proceedings of the Engineers' Club of Philadelphia, v. 17, no. 2, May 1900.

LIBRARY OF PARLIAMENT

**1480 Wilcox, Walter Dwight**
1869-1949

The Rockies of Canada; a revised and enlarged edition of "Camping in the Canadian Rockies." With more than 400 photogravure.　New York, G. P. Putnam's Sons, 1900.

ix, 309 p.　plates, port., 3 maps (2 in pocket) 25 cm.

Also: 1903.　Third edition: 1916.

Also see entry 1250.

B.C. ARCHIVES

**1481 Begg, Alexander**
1825-1905

Review of the Alaska boundary question. [n.p., 1901]

[30]-40, [86]-96 p.　25 cm.　Caption Title. Reprinted from the *Scottish geographical magazine*, February 1901.

The text is not the same as in entry 1460.

B.C. ARCHIVES

**1482 Begg, Alexander**
1825-1905

A sketch of the successful missionary work of William Duncan amongst the Indian tribes in northern British Columbia, from 1858 to 1901. Victoria, 1901.

31 p.　23 cm.　Cover title.

B.C. ARCHIVES

**1483 British Columbia. Porcupine District Commission**

Porcupine-Chilkat districts; report under the Porcupine District Commission Act, 1900, by the Honourable Archer Martin, special commissioner, with observations on the P. and C. districts. Victoria, Printed by Richard Wolfenden, 1901.

13 p.　27 cm.

Concerns the validity of land titles and mining claims in a disputed boundary area.

B.C. ARCHIVES

**1484     Gosnell, R. E[dward]**
1860-1931

Compiled from the Year book of British Columbia and manual of provincial information, to which is added a chapter containing much special information respecting the Canadian Yukon and northern territory generally.     Victoria, 1897 [i.e. 1901]

215 p.   illus., plates (1 fold.) ports., maps, fold. diagr., tables.   25 cm.   Cover title: The year book of British Columbia; compendium, 1897-1901.

The contents are the same as entry 1284 to page [105].

B.C. ARCHIVES


**1485     Henshaw, Julia W[ilmotte] (Henderson)**
1869-1937

Why not sweetheart? By Julia W. Henshaw (Julian Durham)   Toronto, George N. Morang & Company, 1901.

viii, 246 p.   19 cm.

A romance dealing with travels and observations in the Kootenays during the time of the Klondike gold rush.

B.C. ARCHIVES


**1486     Victoria. Ordinances, etc.**

By-laws of the corporation of the city of Victoria to March 1901; revised, amended and consolidated, including a table of by-laws passed since the city's incorporation, and a reprint of loan by-laws and by-laws of a private character.   Victoria, Municipal Council, 1901.

A-O, lvii, 468 p.   26 cm.   Index: p. 431-468.

B.C. ARCHIVES


**1487     Balch, Thomas Willing**
1866-1927

The Alasko-Canadian frontier.   Philadelphia, Allen, Lane and Scott, 1902.

45 p.   maps.   27 cm.   Reprinted from the *Journal of the Franklin Institute* of Philadelphia for March 1902.

An historical review of British acknowledgments of the boundary line since 1825 presented to show the weaknesses of the British claim to territory. Copies of the reprint were sent to all members of the United States Fifty-seventh Congress. Also see entry 1499.

Second edition: 1902.

B.C. ARCHIVES


**1488     Begg, Alexander**
1825-1905

Statement of facts regarding the Alaska boundary question. Compiled for the government of British Columbia.   Victoria, Printed by Richard Wolfenden, 1902.

1381-1402 p.   map.   27 cm.   (British Columbia. Sessional papers, 1902)   Dated on p. 1381: 5 August 1901. Not found in Holmes.

A summary.

B.C. ARCHIVES


**1489     Canada**

Canadian correspondence . . .   [n.p., 1902?]

4 pts. in 1 v.   maps.   33 cm.   Parts [2]-[4] have title pages. Contents: [pt. 1] Canadian correspondence, 1872 to 1878 [caption title] 143 p. — [pt. 2] Canadian correspondence, February 1886 to February 1896. 56 p. — [pt. 3[ Canadian correspondence, 1896 to 1902. 66 p. — [pt. 4] Canadian correspondence, 141st meridian. 31 p.

Relates to the Alaska boundary question. Part 4 includes a letter from George Mercer Dawson, dated 17 September 1892, which is headed "Memorandum on papers connected with the Canada-Alaska boundary question" (p. 31).

VANCOUVER PUBLIC LIBRARY


**1490     Canada. Royal Commission on Chinese and Japanese Immigration.**

Report. Printed by order of Parliament.   Ottawa, Printed by S. E. Dawson, 1902.

xiv, 430 p.   25 cm.   (Canada. Sessional papers, 1902, no. 54)   Chairman: R. C. Clute.

B.C. ARCHIVES


**1491     Gibbs, Miffin Wistar**
1823-1915

Shadow and light; an autobiography with reminiscences of the last and the present century. With an introduction by Booker T. Washington. Washington, D.C., 1902.

xv, 372 p.   ports.   20 cm.

The author, an educated negro and an ardent civil rights worker, came to British Columbia in 1858 with a stock of goods for the Fraser River gold miners. He left Victoria in 1869 after achieving some prominence in local affairs. In five chapters (p. 59-106) he describes these years in British Columbia from 1858-1869.

B.C. ARCHIVES

**1492    Smith, Harlan Ingersoll**
1872-1940

The archaeology of the southern interior of British Columbia.    [n.p., n.d.]

7 p.    25 cm.    Caption title.

A summary of work done for the Jesup Expedition, fully reported in the memoirs of the American Museum of Natural History, v. 1, pts. 3 and 6 (not pts. 3 and 6 of v. 2 as given in the second paragraph of this paper).

B.C. ARCHIVES

**1493    Victoria Firemen's Relief Association**

The Fire Department; coronation souvenir. Victoria, Press of Thos. R. Cusack [1902]

1 v. (various paging; incl. advertisements)    illus., ports.    17 x 27 cm.

Includes a brief article on the history of the Victoria Fire Department.

B.C. ARCHIVES

**1494    Alaskan Boundary Tribunal**

Decision of the Alaskan Boundary Tribunal under the treaty of January 24, 1903, between the United States and Great Britain.    [Washington? 1903]

3 p.    fold. map.    34 cm.    Caption title. Not seen.

BANCROFT LIBRARY CATALOGUE

**1495    Alaskan Boundary Tribunal**

Maps relating to the Alaskan boundary. [n.p., n.d.]

41 maps.    63 x 92 cm.    Cover title.

Includes early Russian and British maps.

B.C. ARCHIVES

**1496    Alaskan Boundary Tribunal**

[Proceedings] before the tribunal convened at London under the provisions of the treaty between the United States of America and Great Britain, concluded January 24, 1903.    Washington, Government Printing Office, 1903.

3 v.    2 plates, map, facsims.    24 cm.    and atlas in 2 v.    46 cm.    Contents: v. 1. The argument of the United States. — v. 2. The case of the United States. — v. 3. The counter case of the United States. — Atlas: v. 1. Accompanying the case of the United States. — v. 2. Accompanying the counter case of the United States.

Also provides a good, though unorganized source of information for the early history of the northern part of the Northwest Coast.

B.C. ARCHIVES

**1497    Alaskan Boundary Tribunal**

Proceedings of the Alaskan Boundary Tribunal convened at London under the treaty between the United States of America and Great Britain, concluded at Washington, January 24, 1903, for the settlement of questions between the two countries with respect to the boundary line between the territory of Alaska and the British possessions in North America.    Washington, Government Printing Office, 1903-1904.

7 v.    plates, maps, diagrs. (1 fold.) facsims.    24 cm. and atlas in 3 v.    49 cm.    ([United States] 58th Cong., 2d sess. Senate. Doc no. 162)    Binder's titles v. 1: Report of the agent of the United States [John W. Foster]; protocols, decision, and opinions . . . case of the United States. — v. 2. Appendix to the case of the United States. — v. 3. Case of Great Britain, and appendix. — v. 4. Counter case of the United States, and appendix; counter case of Great Britain, and appendix. — v. 5. Printed argument of the United States; printed argument of Great Britain; correspondence since the treaty of January 24, 1903; extracts from British Parliamentary papers, 1904. — v. 6. Minutes of proceedings at London; oral argument of Sir Robert Finlay, David J. Watson. — v. 7. Minutes of proceedings at London; oral argument of Christopher Robinson, Hannis Taylor, Sir Edward Carson, Jacob M. Dickinson.

B.C. ARCHIVES

**1498    Alaskan Boundary Tribunal**

Protocols, oral arguments, with index, award of the tribunal, and opinions of its members, September 3 to October 20, 1903.    London, Harrison and Sons, 1903.

xvii, 978 p.    34 cm.    At head of title: Alaska Boundary Tribunal.

B.C. ARCHIVES

**1499    Balch, Thomas Willing**
1866-1927

The Alaska frontier.    Philadelphia, Allen, Lane and Scott, 1903.

xv, 198 p.    maps.    28 cm.

Deals with the history of the Alaska boundary question. Much of *The Alasko-Canadian frontier* (entry 1487) is incorporated in this work, which was sent to members of the United States Senate.

B.C. ARCHIVES

**1500    Begg, Alexander**
1825-1905

To the honourables the commissioners of the Alaskan Boundary Tribunal. [A letter together with an interpretation of a portion of the Anglo-Russian Treaty of 1825.    n.p., 1903]

8 p.    22 cm.    Title from letter on p. [1] which is dated from London, 14 September 1903.

B.C. ARCHIVES

## 1501 Davidson, George
1825-1911

The Alaska boundary.   San Francisco, Alaska Packers' Association, 1903.

235 p.   port., 2 fold. maps, facsims,   27 cm.

Makes use of quoted sources and documents to support the American claim to territory.

B.C. ARCHIVES


## 1502 Foster, John Watson
1836-1917

The Alaskan boundary.   [Washington, Government Printing Office, 1903]

17 p.   25 cm.   ([United States] 58th Cong., spec. sess. Senate. Doc. no. 2)   Caption title. Appeared in the *National geographic magazine* for November 1899.   Not seen.

YALE WESTERN AMERICANA CATALOGUE


## 1503 Great Britain

Alaska boundary. Appendix to British case. Index. [London? 1903?]

39 p.   34 cm.   At head of title: Confidential. Probably issued by the Foreign Office.   Not seen.

YALE WESTERN AMERICANA CATALOGUE


## 1504 Great Britain

Boundary between the Dominion of Canada and the territory of Alaska. Appendix to the case of His Majesty's government before the Alaska Boundary Tribunal . . .   London, McCorquodale & Co., 1903.

xi, 313 p.   34 cm.   *and* atlas of 37 maps (part fold.) 78 cm.   Atlas has title: British case Alaska boundary; atlas; appendix vol. II.

B.C. ARCHIVES


## 1505 Great Britain

Boundary between the Dominion of Canada and the territory of Alaska. Appendix to the counter-case of His Majesty's government before the Alaska Boundary Tribunal . . .   London, McCorquodale & Co., 1903.

iv, 100 p.   33 cm.   *and* atlas of 150 illus. on 38 leaves.   51 x 64 cm.   Atlas has title: British counter case; Alaska boundary; album of photographic views depicting the mountain boundary of the lisière; appendix vol. II (London, Waterlow & Sons)

B.C. ARCHIVES


## 1506 Great Britain

Boundary between the Dominion of Canada and the territory of Alaska. Argument presented on the part of the government of His Britannic Majesty to the tribunal constituted under Article I of the convention signed at Washington, January 24, 1903, between His Britannic Majesty and the United States of America.   London, Printed at the Foreign Office, by Harrison and Sons, 1903.

ii, 127 p.   34 cm.

B.C. ARCHIVES


## 1507 Great Britain

Boundary between the Dominion of Canada and the territory of Alaska. Case presented on the part of the government of His Britannic Majesty to the tribunal constituted under Article I of the convention signed at Washington, January 24, 1903, between His Britannic Majesty and the United States of America.   London, Printed at the Foreign Office, by Harrison and Sons, 1903.

105 p.   34 cm.

B.C. ARCHIVES


## 1508 Great Britain

Boundary between the Dominion of Canada and the territory of Alaska. Counter-case presented on the part of the government of His Britannic Majesty to the tribunal constituted under Article I of the convention signed at Washington, January 24, 1903, between His Britannic Majesty and the United States of America.   London, Printed at the Foreign Office, by Harrison and Sons, 1903.

81 p.   33 cm.

B.C. ARCHIVES


## 1509 Great Britain

Russian monuments, storehouses, customs. [London, 1903?]

25 p.   33 cm.

A Foreign Office or Colonial Office document comprised of correspondence from 1897 relating to the Alaska boundary question, and, specifically, to observed markers of Russian origin, and to the jurisdiction of Canadian customs.

VANCOUVER PUBLIC LIBRARY


## 1510 Great Britain. Foreign Office

Alaska boundary. Various documents bearing on the question of the Alaska boundary, printed for convenience of reference.   London, Printed by McCorquodale & Co., 1903.

3 v.   34 cm.   At head of title: Confidential. Vols. 2-3 have title: Alaska boundary; memorandum for

counsel no. II[-III] various documents . . .   Vol. 2 has imprint: London, Printed at the Foreign Office by Harrison and Sons.

B.C. ARCHIVES

## 1511   Great Britain. Foreign Office

Alaska Boundary Tribunal. Case of the United States, with appendix; index.   London, Printed at the Foreign Office by Harrison and Sons, 1903.

68 p.   34 cm.   At head of title: Confidential.

An index compiled for use of the Foreign Office.

VANCOUVER PUBLIC LIBRARY

## 1512   Hodgins, Thomas
### 1828-1910

The Alaska-Canada boundary dispute, under the Anglo-Russian treaty of 1825, the Russian-American Alaska treaty of 1867, and the Anglo-American conventions of 1892, 1894, and 1897; an historical and legal review. Second edition. Toronto, Wm. Tyrrell and Co., 1903.

26 p.   map.   26 cm.

B.C. ARCHIVES

## 1513   Johnson, George
### EDITOR   1837-1911

The all red line; the annals and aims of the Pacific cable project.   Ottawa, James Hope & Sons, 1903.

486 p.   map, facsims.   19 cm.   Bibliography: p. 10-44.

A good introduction to the subject.

B.C. ARCHIVES

## 1514   Martin, Archer [Evans Stringer]
### 1865-1941

Reports of mining cases decided by the courts of British Columbia and the courts of appeal therefrom to the 1st of October, 1902. With an appendix of mining statutes from 1853 to 1902; and a glossary of mining terms.   Toronto, Carswell Company, 1903.

2 v.   26 cm.

B.C. ARCHIVES

## 1515   Parker, Richard Wayne

The Alaska boundary question, by Richard Wayne Parker, member of the House of Representatives. New York, The North American Review Publishing Co. [c1903]

[16] p. (incl. cover)   23 cm.   Cover title. Reprinted from the *North American review*, June 1903.

B.C. ARCHIVES

## 1516   Piolet, J[ean]-B[aptiste]
### EDITOR   1855-1930

Les missions catholiques françaises au xixe siècle, publiées sous la direction du Père J.-B. Piolet, S.J., avec la collaboration de toutes les sociétés de missions. Tome VI: Missions d'Amérique.   Paris, Armand Colin, 1903.

520 p.   illus., ports.   28 cm.   At head of title: La France au dehors.

Chapter 4 relates to British Columbia.

B.C. ARCHIVES

## 1517   Pocock, [Henry] Roger [Ashwell]
### 1865-1941

Following the frontier.   New York, McClure, Phillips & Co., 1903.

338 p.   20 cm.

Fiction. A journalist recounts his experiences in the 1880's and '90's as a missionary amongst the Skeena River tribes, as a prospector in the Kootenays, and as an organizer of an expedition to take horses from the Ashcroft area to the Klondike.

B.C. ARCHIVES

## 1518   Ridley, William
### BISHOP OF CALEDONIA   1836-1911

Snapshots from the North Pacific; letters written by Bishop Ridley of Caledonia. Edited by Alice J. Janvrin.   London, Church Missionary Society, 1903.

viii, 192 p.   illus., ports., map.   19 cm.

Description of visits to the Church of England missions along the northern coast and on the Nass, Skeena, and Stikine rivers from 1879 to 1900.

Second edition: London, 1904. viii, 192 p.

B.C. ARCHIVES

## 1519   Stutfield, Hugh E[dward] M[illington]
### 1858-1929

Climbs & explorations in the Canadian Rockies, by Hugh E. M. Stutfield and J. Norman Collie. With maps and illustrations.   London, Longmans, Green, 1903.

xii, 342 p.   plates, 2 maps (1 fold.)   23 cm.

Except for one historical chapter, the book is comprised of the author's accounts of his climbs and travels in the Rockies from 1897.

B.C. ARCHIVES

**1520   United States**

Alaskan Boundary Tribunal. The argument of the United States before the tribunal convened at London under the provisions of the treaty between the United States of America and Great Britain, concluded January 24, 1903.   Washington, Government Printing Office, 1903.

vi, 3-204, 18 p.   24 cm.

B.C. ARCHIVES

**1521   United States**

Alaskan Boundary Tribunal. The case of the United States before the tribunal convened at London under the provisions of the treaty between the United States of America and Great Britain, concluded January 24, 1903. [With appendix] Washington, Government Printing Office, 1903.

2 v. in 1.   2 facsims.   24 cm.   *and* atlas of 25 maps. 45 cm.   The atlas is supplemented by: *Atlas accompanying the counter case of the United States.*

For British index see entry 1511.

B.C. ARCHIVES

**1522   United States**

Alaskan Boundary Tribunal. The counter case of the United States before the tribunal convened at London under the provisions of the treaty between the United States of America and Great Britain, concluded January 24, 1903. [With appendix] Washington, Government Printing Office, 1903.

2 v. in l.   2 plates.   24 cm.   *and* atlas.   45 cm. The atlas consists of maps numbered 26-47. It supplements: *Atlas accompanying the case of the United States.*

B.C. ARCHIVES

**1523   Balch, Edwin Swift**
EDITOR   1856-1927

Letters and papers relating to the Alaska frontier. Philadelphia, Press of Allen, Lane and Scott, 1904.

viii, 134 p.   28 cm.

Deals with the boundary question.

B.C. ARCHIVES

**1524   Canada. Parliament. House of Commons**

Correspondence respecting the Alaska boundary, together with the award of the Alaska Boundary Tribunal. Printed by order of Parliament. Ottawa, Printed by S. E. Dawson, 1904.

108 p.   25 cm.   (Canada. Sessional papers, 1904, no. 46a)

B.C. ARCHIVES

**1525   Canada's Alaskan dismemberment . . .**

Canada's Alaskan dismemberment; an analytical examination of the fallacies underlying the tribunal award.   Niagara-on-the-Lake, Ont., Printed by Charles Thonger, 1904.

76 p.   21 cm.   Cover title.

B.C. ARCHIVES

**1526   Davis, G[eorge] T[hompson] B[rown]**
1873-

Metlakahtla; a true narrative of the red man. Chicago, the Ram's Horn Company, 1904.

128 p.   illus., ports.   18 cm.

The story of the missionary work of William Duncan.

B.C. ARCHIVES

**1527   Dickinson, J[acob] M[cGavock]**
1851-1928

The Alaskan boundary case; a paper read by J. M. Dickinson before the American Bar Association at the Twenty-seventh Annual Meeting, St. Louis, Missouri, September 26, 1904.   [n.p., n.d.]

32 p.   23 cm.   Cover title. Reprinted from: American Bar Association. *Transactions.*

B.C. ARCHIVES

**1528   Great Britain. Foreign Office**

Correspondence respecting the Alaska boundary. Presented to both Houses of Parliament by command of His Majesty, January 1904. London, Harrison and Sons [1904]

88 p.   33 cm.   ([Great Britain. Parliament. Command papers] Cd. 1877) At head of title: United States, no. 1 (1904)   Has map bound in (see entry below)

VANCOUVER PUBLIC LIBRARY

**1529   Great Britain. Foreign Office**

Map to accompany correspondence respecting the Alaska boundary ("United States, no. 1 (1904)") Presented to both Houses of Parliament by command of His Majesty, February 1904. London, Harrison and Sons [1904]

map.   59 x 90 cm. fold. to 30 x 20 cm.   ([Great Britain. Parliament. Command papers] Cd. 1878) At head of title: United States, no. 2 (1904)   Map has title: Southeastern Alaska and part of British Columbia shewing award of Alaska Boundary Tribunal, Oct. 20th, 1903.

VANCOUVER PUBLIC LIBRARY

**1530**   Herring, Frances E[lizabeth (Clarke)]
1851-1916

In the pathless West, with soldiers, pioneers, miners, and savages.   London, Unwin, 1904.

xiii, 240 p.   plates, 2 ports.   20 cm.

A book of tales.

**1531**   Higgins, D[avid] W[illiams]
1834-1917

The mystic spring and other tales of western life. Toronto, William Briggs, 1904.

407 p.   plates, port.   20 cm.

Fiction. A good idea of the social life of early British Columbia is given in this collection of tales written by an early settler.

New and revised edition: New York, Broadway Publishing Co., 1908. ii, 312 p.

**1532**   Hodgins, Thomas
1828-1910

The Alaska Boundary Tribunal and international law; a review of the decisions.   Toronto, The Carswell Company, 1904.

24 p.   maps.   22 cm.   Cover title. Reprinted from the *Canadian law times*.

**1533**   Morice, A[drian] G[abriel]
1859-1938

Du Lac Stuart à l'océan Pacifique.   Neuchatel, Paul Attinger, 1904.

51 p.   illus., fold. map.   24 cm.   Reprinted from the *Bulletin de la Société Neuchâteloise de Géographie,* v. 15, 1905.

Comprised of remarks on the topography and previous mapping of the region and of notes from the author's journal, which was written during an exploring expedition in September and October of 1899. The map is entitled, "Carte des sources et du bassin supérieur de la Nétchakhoh (Canada)."

**1534**   Morice, A[drian] G[abriel]
1859-1938

The history of the northern interior of British Columbia, formerly New Caledonia (1660-1880) Toronto, William Briggs, 1904.

xi, 349 p.   plates, ports, fold. map.   23 cm.

Presents details of fur-trading days, life at the Hudson's Bay trading posts, the story of the gold-rushes, the work of missionaries (especially on the Babine and Skeena rivers), as well as information on Indian life.

Second edition: Toronto, 1904.   Third edition: Toronto, 1905. xii, 368 p.   English edition: London, John Lane, The Bodley Head, 1906.   At head of title of English and third editions: Primitive tribes and pioneer traders.

**1535**   Prosche, Charles
B. 1820

Reminiscences of Washington Territory; scenes, incidents and reflections of the pioneer period on Puget Sound.   Seattle, 1904.

128 p.   plates, port.   23 cm.

The work mentions the Fraser River gold rush and the San Juan controversy.

**1536**   Church Missionary Society

Among the Indians of the far West; a service of song. The narrative by the Right Rev. Bishop Ridley, D.D. (late of Caledonia) Arranged by the Rev. W. J. L. Sheppard, M.A. (Centenary Secretary, C.M.S.)   London, Church Missionary Society, 1905.

32 p.   22 cm.   Cover title. Includes music. On cover: re-issue, 1905.

Probably first published in 1899.

**1537**   Church Missionary Society

The British Columbia mission.   London, Church Missionary Society, 1905.

20 p.   illus., maps.   19 cm.   At head of title: Missions of the Church Missionary Society. On verso of front cover: This short account of the British Columbia mission was first published by the C.M. Association in Melbourne in 1904 . . .

Presents historical background of the early missions.

**1538**   Higgins, D[avid] W[illiams]
1834-1917

The passing of a race and more tales of western life. Toronto, William Briggs, 1905.

304 p.   plates.   20 cm.

Fiction. The author states in the Preface that these "reminiscent stories are all founded upon actual occurrences" and that the "stories of the occult . . . are left to the judgment of wiser heads than mine."

1539   The Inland Sentinel (Kamloops)

1880-1905, the land of heart's desire. The Inland Sentinel quarter century commemorative number. Kamlops, 1905.

71 p. (incl. advertisements)   illus., ports.   30 cm.

History and description of the Kamloops area.

B.C. ARCHIVES


1540   Jackson, J. A.

Bella Bella transformed.   [Toronto, Woman's Missionary Society of the Methodist Church, n.d.]

12 p.   13 cm.   (Our work, no. 1)   Caption title.

B.C. ARCHIVES


1541   Jobson, Anthony

Sketches of pioneering in the Rocky Mountains, British Columbia.   West Hartlepool [Eng.] B.T. Ord, 1905.

38 p.   plates.   18 cm.

Reminiscences of the author's life in the 1860's.

B.C. ARCHIVES


1542   Lynn-Browne, A. H.
COMPILER

The pioneer steamer Beaver, the first steamer on the Pacific Ocean; a brief but concise history of this most interesting craft.   Vancouver, Bailey Bros. [ca. 1905]

[3] p. (folder)   20 cm.   Cover title.

B.C. ARCHIVES


1543   Meeker, Ezra
1830-1928

Pioneer reminiscences of Puget Sound; the tragedy of Leschi; an account of the coming of the first Americans and the establishment of their institutions ...   Seattle, Lowman & Hanford, 1905.

xx, 554 p.   plates, ports., fold. facsims.   24 cm.
Chapter 21: The Fraser River stampede [p. 162-170]

B.C. ARCHIVES


1544   A Native Indian colony

A native Indian colony [Metlakahtla.   n.p., n.d.]

32 p.   illus. (on cover)   22 cm.   Caption title.

A history of William Duncan's accomplishments.

GLENBOW FOUNDATION LIBRARY


1545   Outram, [Sir] James
1864-1925

In the heart of the Canadian Rockies. With maps and illustrations.   New York, Macmillan, 1905.

xii, 466 p.   illus., plates, maps (1 fold.)   23 cm.

Contains references to climbs and achievements of various travellers in the Rockies.

Also: Toronto, Macmillan, 1906.   Also: New York, Macmillan, 1923.

B.C. ARCHIVES


1546   Rossland. Board of Trade

A brief history of Rossland, British Columbia, presented to the member of the American Institute of Mining Engineers on the occasion of their visit to Rossland, June 28, '95 [i.e. 1905.   Rossland, 1905]

[8] p.   tables.   21 cm.   Cover title.

B.C. ARCHIVES


1547   Sands, Harold [Percy]
1873-

The dashing Sally Duel and other stories.   New York, Broadway Publishing Company [1905]

143 p.   20 cm.

Fiction. Covers Barkerville in the gold rush era, Kaslo in its early days, and San Juan Island during the boundary dispute.

B.C. ARCHIVES


1548   Wheeler, A[rthur] O[liver]
1860-1945

The Selkirk Range.   Ottawa [Published by the Department of the Interior] 1905.

xvii, 459 p.   plates, ports., diagr., profile and atlas of 9 fold. plates, 4 fold. maps, fold. profile.   25 cm.

Part 1 of the book is an account of a topographical survey of a portion of the Selkirk Mountains adjacent to the Canadian Pacific Railway line. Parts 2-4 cover exploration, previous surveys, and mountaineering in the area.

B.C. ARCHIVES


1549   Crosby, Thomas
1840-1914

David Sallosalton.   [Toronto, Department of Missionary Literature of the Methodist Church, 1906?]

62 p.   illus., ports.   17 cm.   Cover title.

The story of an Indian boy, a worker for the Methodist coast missions, who died in 1873 at the age of nineteen.

B.C. ARCHIVES

**1550    Gosnell, R. E[dward]**
1860-1931

A history o[f] British Columbia. Compiled by the Lewis Publishing Co. [n.p.] Hill Binding Co., 1906.

x, 783 p.    plates, 83 ports.    28 cm.

Chiefly biographical sketches.

B.C. ARCHIVES

**1551    Grinnell, George Bird**
1849-1938

Jack, the young canoeman; an eastern boy's voyage in a Chinook canoe by George Bird Grinnell. Illustrated by Edwin Willard Deming and by half-tone engravings of photographs.    New York, Frederick A. Stokes Company [1906]

286 p.    plates.    20 cm.

Juvenile fiction. Canoeing along the B.C. coast in the 1880's enables a youth to learn much of natural history and Indian customs.

B.C. ARCHIVES

**1552    Lawson, Maria**
1852-1945

A history and geography of British Columbia for use in public schools. History, by Maria Lawson; geography, by Rosalind Watson Young.    Toronto, W. J. Gage & Company [1906]

148 p.    illus., maps.    20 cm.    (Gage's 20th Century series)

Also: Toronto, Educational Book Co., 1913. 156 p. (Dominion series).

B.C. ARCHIVES

**1553    Pacific Northwest quarterly**

Pacific Northwest quarterly.    v. 1 + October 1906+    Seattle, University of Washington.

v.    illus., maps.    23, 27 cm.    Title varies: v. 1-26, no. 4 (1906—October 1935) as *Washington historical quarterly*. Suspended October 1908—April 1912. Cumulative indexes in v. 10 and v. 20. Cumulative indexes issued in 1935 and separately in 1957 (v. 45-47, 1954-56) and 1964. See: Earle Connette, compiler, *Pacific Northwest quarterly index* (Hamden, Conn., The Shoe String Press, 1964) which covers v. 1-53. Indexed as *Washington historical quarterly* in *International index*.

Has scholarly articles, bibliographies and book reviews of importance to early British Columbia.

B.C. ARCHIVES

**1554    [Brown], Dazie M. (Stromstadt)**

Metlakahtla, by Dazie M. Stromstadt.    Seattle, The Homer M. Hill Pub. Co., 1907.

19 p.    17 cm.

Written in praise of William Duncan.

B.C. ARCHIVES

**1555    Church Missionary Society**

Outline histories of C.M.S. missions. Vol. III. London, Church Missionary Society, 1907.

159 p.    maps.    19 cm.    (At head of title: Handbooks for workers)

Chapter 10 deals with British Columbia missions and their establishment.

B.C. ARCHIVES

**1556    Crosby, Thomas**
1840-1914

Among the An-ko-me-nums, or Flathead tribes of Indians of the Pacific coast.    Toronto, William Briggs, 1907.

243 p.    illus., plates, ports.    20 cm.

An autobiographical account of the author's first twelve years (from 1862 to September 1873) as a Methodist missionary among the Cowichan and Nanaimo Indians.

B.C. ARCHIVES

**1557    Freemasons. British Columbia. Grand Lodge**

Proceedings of the convention to organize the M.W. Grand Lodge of Ancient, Free and Accepted Masons of British Columbia, held at the Masonic Hall, city of Victoria, October 21st, 5871 and of the First Grand Communication held December 26th and 27th, A. L., 5871; with an appendix containing the constitution, general regulations and list of lodges holding of the Grand Lodge of British Columbia.    Victoria, Printed at the Daily Standard Office, 1872; reprint by the Columbia Company Ltd., 1907.

45 p.    23 cm.

B.C. ARCHIVES

**1558    Johnson, John**
B. 1860

Childhood, travel, and British Columbia. [Abertillery, Monmouthshire, P. Wilson Raffan & Co., 1907?]

349 p.    plates, ports.    19 cm.

Autobiography.

B.C. ARCHIVES

**1559    Lyons, Herbert H.**
COMPILER AND PUBLISHER

6th Regiment, the Duke of Connaught's Own
Rifles.    Vancouver [Evans & Hastings] 1907.

[48] p.    plates, ports., group ports.    24 x 31 cm.
At head of title: Souvenir edition.

The seven pages of text are on early B.C.
military history.

B.C. ARCHIVES


**1560    Tate, C[harles] M[ontgomery]**
1852-1933

Our Indian missions in British Columbia.
[Toronto, The Methodist Young People's Forward
Movement, 1907?]

16 p.    2 ports. (1 on cover) double map.    23 cm.

Comprised of brief historical sketches of missions to
about 1900.

B.C. ARCHIVES


**1561    Tucker, L[ewis] Norman**
1852-1935?

Western Canada.    Toronto, Musson Book
Company [1907]

xii, 164 p.    plates, ports., fold. map.    17 cm.
(Handbook of English church expansion, no. 2)

One lengthy chapter relates to Church of England
missions in British Columbia.

B.C. ARCHIVES


**1562    Wade, Mark S[weeten]**
1858-1929

The Thompson country; being notes on the history
of southern British Columbia, and particularly of
the city of Kamloops, formerly Fort Thompson.
Kamloops, Inland Sentinel Print, 1907.

136 p.    plates, ports.    21 cm.    Addenda (2 p.)
inserted at end.

B.C. ARCHIVES


**1563    British Columbia Curling
Association**

Manual, 1907-8, of the British Columbia (formerly
Kootenay) Curling Association in affiliation with
the Royal Caledonian Curling Club.    [Rossland,
Press of the Rossland Miner, 1908?]

161 p.    illus., plates, ports.    Written and compiled
by W. J. Nelson.

Has considerable information on the development of
curling in British Columbia.

VANCOUVER PUBLIC LIBRARY


**1564    Canadian Press Association**

A history of Canadian journalism in the several
portions of the Dominion; with a sketch of the
Canadian Press Association, 1859-1908. Edited by
a committee of the association.    Toronto [Murray
Printing Company] 1908.

xv, 242 p.    ports.    25 cm.

Contains a chapter on British Columbia newspapers
by R. E. Gosnell.

B.C. ARCHIVES


**1565    Coats, Robert Hamilton**
1874-

Sir James Douglas, by Robert Hamilton Coats and
R. E. Gosnell. Edition de luxe.    Toronto, Morang
& Co., 1908.

369 p.    port.    24 cm.    (The makers of Canada.
Edited by D. C. Scott, P. Edgar, and W. D. Le Sueur)

Really a history of Vancouver Island and British
Columbia before amalgamation and during Douglas'
tenure as governor, with special emphasis on the
Cariboo gold excitement of 1858-62.

Also: Canadian Club edition (Toronto, Morang &
Co., 1910).    Also: 1912. (Parkman edition, v. 20).
Also: London, Oxford University Press, 1926.

B.C. ARCHIVES


**1566    Cody, H[iram] A[lfred]**
1872-1948

An apostle of the North; memoirs of the Right
Reverend William Carpenter Bompas, D.D., first
Bishop of Athabasca, 1874-1884, first Bishop of
Mackenzie River, 1884-1891, first Bishop of
Selkirk (Yukon) 1891-1906. With an introduction
by the Most Rev. S. P. Matheson.    London, Seeley
& Co., 1908.

385 p.    plates, ports., map.    23 cm.

A short chapter on Bishop Bompas' journey from
Dunvegan to Metlahkatla and his visits to the Queen
Charlotte Islands and the Nass River, which he
undertook in the fall and winter of 1877-8. He was
requested to visit Metlahkatla by Bishop Hills who
wished him to use his influence with William Duncan.

Also: Toronto, Musson Book Co., 1908.    Also: New
York, E. P. Dutton and Co., 1908.    Also: London,
Seeley & Co., 1910.    Also: London, Seeley, Service
& Co., 1913.    Also: New York, E. P. Dutton and
Co., 1913.

B.C. ARCHIVES

**1567    Freemasons. Vancouver. Knights Templars. Columbia Preceptory No. 34**

Annual report and historical sketch of Columbia Preceptory No. 34, G.R.C., Vancouver, B.C., May 14, 1908.   [Vancouver, Bolam & Hornett, 1908]

25 p.   2 ports., 1 group port.   19 cm.

B.C. ARCHIVES

**1568    [Graves, Samuel H.]**

On the "White Pass" pay-roll, by the President of the White Pass & Yukon route.    Chicago [The Lakeside Press] 1908.

258 p.   plates.   21 cm.

Concerns the building and early operation of the White Pass & Yukon Railway.

B.C. ARCHIVES

**1569    Marsh, E[dith] L[ouise]**

Where the buffalo roamed; the story of western Canada told for the young. With introduction by R. G. MacBeth; with illustrations from paintings by Paul Kane, and from photographs and drawings. Toronto, William Briggs, 1908.

242 p.   plates, port.   20 cm.   Chapter 13: Early days in British Columbia.

Second edition: Toronto, Macmillan, 1923.

B.C. ARCHIVES

**1570    Moberly, Walter**
1832-1915

Early history of Canadian Pacific Railway. Vancouver, Art, Historical and Scientific Association [1908]

15 p.   port.   23 cm.   Cover title. Caption title: Early history of C.P.R. road.

B.C. ARCHIVES

**1571    Platt, Harriet Louise**

The story of the years; a history of the Woman's Missionary Society of the Methodist Church, Canada, 1881-1906. Vol. I: Canada. Second edition.   Toronto, The Woman's Missionary Society [c1908]

154 p.   plates.   19 cm.

Several chapters relate to early British Columbia Methodist centres.

B.C. ARCHIVES

**1572    Vernon. Methodist Church**

Souvenir of the fifteenth anniversary of Vernon Methodist Church, November 29th and 30th, 1908. [Vernon, 1908?]

8 l.   illus., ports.   15 x 23 cm.   At head of title: 1893-1908.

An account of early Methodism in Vernon.

B.C. ARCHIVES

**1573    Arctander, John W[illiam]**
1849-1920

The apostle of Alaska; the story of William Duncan of Metlakahtla.    New York, Fleming H. Revell Company [c1909]

395 p.   plates, ports., map.   22 cm.

A partisan account of Duncan's missionary work and of his dispute with the Church Missionary Society.

Second edition: 1909.

B.C. ARCHIVES

**1574    DeWolf-Smith, W[illiam] A[ndrew]**
1861-1947

Address . . . on the occasion of the celebration of the fiftieth anniversary of the introduction of Freemasonry into the province of British Columbia. Victoria, B.C., 14th December, 1909. [Victoria? 1909?]

15 p.   23 cm.   Caption title.

An organizational history of lodges prior to 1886.

Also in: Freemasons. British Columbia. Grand Lodge. *Proceedings*. 1911. Appendix no. 2, p. i-xv.

B.C. ARCHIVES

**1575    Mercier, [Anne]**

Father Pat; a hero of the far West, by Mrs. Jerome Mercier. With a preface by the Right Rev. John Dart.    Gloucester, Minchin & Gibbs, 1909.

109 p.   plates, port.   19 cm.

A life of Henry Irwin, containing quotations from his letters and diaries.

B.C. ARCHIVES

**1576    Moresby, John**
1830-1922

Two admirals: Admiral of the Fleet Sir Fairfax Moresby (1786-1877) and his son, John Moresby; a record of life and service in the British navy for a hundred years.   London, John Murray, 1909.

xii, 419 p.   plates, ports., 2 maps.   23 cm.

Twenty pages relate to John Moresby's service as a lieutenant on board H.M.S. "Thetis" in Vancouver Island waters over the period from May 1852 to January 1853.

Also: London, Methuen, 1913. 343 p.

B.C. ARCHIVES

### 1577  [Sheepshanks, John]
BISHOP OF NORWICH  1834-1912

A bishop in the rough. Edited by the Rev. D. Wallace Duthie, with a preface by the Right Rev. the Lord Bishop of Norwich.   London, Smith, Elder & Co., 1909.

xxxvii, 386 p.   plates, ports.   22 cm.

Compiled and edited from the journals of John Sheepshanks, who was rector of Holy Trinity Church, New Westminster, from 1859 to 1867. Nearly half the book is concerned with Sheepshanks' activities during these years.

B.C. ARCHIVES

### 1578  Walbran, John T[homas]
1848-1913

British Columbia coast names, 1592-1906; to which are added a few names in adjacent United States territory; their origin and history. Ottawa, Government Printing Bureau, 1909.

546 p.   plates, ports., fold. map.   24 cm.   Binder's title: British Columbia place names.

Despite the binder's title, place-names in the interior of the province are not included.

B.C. ARCHIVES

### 1579  Watson, Sir Charles M[oore]
1844-1916

The life of Major-General Sir Charles William Wilson, Royal Engineers.   London, John Murray, 1909.

xv, 419 p.   plates, ports., 5 fold. maps.   23 cm.

Has a chapter on the North American Boundary Commission with which Sir Charles Wilson served as secretary and transport officer.

B.C. ARCHIVES

### 1580  Crosby, [Elizabeth]

Our work; how the Gospel came to Fort Simpson, by Mrs. Thomas Crosby.   [Toronto, The Woman's Missionary Society of the Methodist Church, Canada, n.d.]

8 p.   13 cm.   Caption title.

B.C. ARCHIVES

### 1581  Ellison, W[illiam] G[eorge] H[ollingworth]
1857-1929

The settlers of Vancouver Island; a story for emigrants.   [London, Arthur Chilver, 1910?]

154 p.   plates.   21 cm.   The log of an old sailor, by Captain Alexander Wybrow: p. 124-154.

Based on actual incidents and characters, the story centers around the activities of four youths in the 1890's.

Two editions are listed in Smith.

B.C. ARCHIVES

### 1582  Howay, Frederic W[illiam]
1867-1943

The work of the Royal Engineers in British Columbia, 1858 to 1863, by His Honour Frederick W. Howay, Judge of the County Court of Westminster; being an address before the Art, Historical and Scientific Association of Vancouver on 9th February 1909.   Victoria, Printed by Richard Wolfenden, 1910.

17 p.   plates (1 col.) ports.   32 cm.

B.C. ARCHIVES

### 1583  Morice, A[drian] G[abriel]
1859-1938

History of the Catholic church in western Canada, from Lake Superior to the Pacific (1659-1895) Toronto, Musson Book Co., 1910.

2 v.   plates, ports., 2 fold. maps, facsims. (part fold.) 24 cm.

Much of this valuable history refers to the development of the church west of the Rocky Mountains. It includes local historical information as well as extensive biographical details of numerous people.

For the French edition see entry 1600.

B.C. ARCHIVES

### 1584  Secretan, [James Henry Edward]
1854-1926

Out West, by Secretan.   Ottawa, The Esdale Press Limited, 1910.

206 p.   plates, ports.   18 cm.

Fiction. Contains a section entitled "The British Columbia" (p. 175-197) which gives brief stories of pioneer days in the Cariboo.

B.C. ARCHIVES

**1585 Strang, Herbert**
PSEUDONYM EDITOR

Adventures in the far West; Canada's story. London, Henry Frowde & Hodder & Stoughton [1910?]

160 p. col. plates, map. 20 cm. (Romance of the world) Herbert Strang was the pseudonym of George Herbert Ely and C. J. L'Estrange. It sometimes also encompassed a third writer.

A book for young readers which includes excerpts from the writings of Kinahan Cornwallis, Charles Barrett-Lennard, and Viscount Milton and Walter Butler Cheadle.

B.C. ARCHIVES

**1586 Tate, [Caroline Sarah (Knott)]**
1850-1930

Early days at Coqualeetza [by Mrs. Charles Montgomery Tate. Toronto, The Woman's Missionary Society, n.d.]

[8] p. (folder) illus. 15 cm.

A history of a Methodist Indian school at Sardis, near Chilliwack.

B.C. ARCHIVES

**1587 Vancouver. School Board**

Educational institutions of Vancouver; their progress from incorporation to the present time. Vancouver City schools. Vancouver, 1910.

[44] p. (incl. advertisements) illus., ports. 32 cm.

B.C. ARCHIVES

**1588 Bryce, George**
1844-1931

The Scotsman in Canada. Western Canada; including Manitoba, Saskatchewan, Alberta, British Columbia, and portions of old Rupert's Land and the Indian Territories. Toronto, The Musson Book Company [1911]

439 p. ports. 23 cm. (Scotsman in Canada, v. 2)

B.C. ARCHIVES

**1589 Coleman, A[rthur] P[hilemon]**
1852-1939

Canadian Rockies; new and old trails. With 3 maps and 41 illustrations. Toronto, Henry Frowde, 1911.

383 p. plates, 3 maps (2 fold.) 23 cm.

An account of the author's various journeys in the Rockies from 1884 to 1908.

Also: London, Unwin, 1911. Also: New York, Scribner, 1911. Also: Toronto, Henry Frowde, 1912.

B.C. ARCHIVES

**1590 Strahorn, Carrie Adell**

Fifteen thousand miles by stage; a woman's unique experience during thirty years of path finding and pioneering from Missouri to the Pacific, and from Alaska to Mexico. With 350 illustrations from drawings by Charles M. Russell and others, and from photographs. New York, G. P. Putnam's Sons, 1911.

xxv, 673 p. illus., col. plates, port. 24 cm.

Has one chapter on the author's canoe trip in 1893 on Harrison Lake and the Lillooet River.

Second edition: 1915.

B.C. ARCHIVES

**1591 Victoria. First Presbyterian Church**

Jubilee of the introduction of Presbyterianism into British Columbia and the organization of the First Presbyterian Church, Victoria, B.C. 1861-1911. Victoria, 1911.

19 p. illus., ports., group ports. 18 cm. At head of title: Souvenir.

B.C. ARCHIVES

**1592 Who's who in western Canada...**

Who's who in western Canada; a biographical dictionary of notable living men and women of western Canada. Edited by C. W. Parker. [Vancouver?] Canadian Press Association, 1911-12.

2 v. ports. 19 cm.

Only these two volumes were published under this title.

B.C. ARCHIVES

**1593 Baker, J[ohn] C[lapp]**
1828-1912

Baptist history of the North Pacific coast; with special reference to western Washington, British Columbia, and Alaska. Philadelphia, American Baptist Publication Society [1912]

xxiii, 472 p. plates, ports. 23 cm.

Presents Baptist history in British Columbia from 1874.

B.C. ARCHIVES

**1594 Bate, Mark**
1837-1927

History of the bastion. Nanaimo, Post No. 3, Native Sons of B.C. [n.d.]

[11] p. illus. 15 cm.

Also: [4] p. n.d.

B.C. ARCHIVES

## 1595 Boam, Henry J.
COMPILER

British Columbia; its history, people, commerce, industries, and resources. Edited by Ashley G. Brown.    London, Sells Ltd., 1912.

495 p.    illus., ports., fold. map.    31 cm.

An extensively illustrated collection of articles, chiefly depicting the economic life of the province.

B.C. ARCHIVES

## 1596 Canada. Treaties, etc.

Indian treaties and surrenders from 1680 to 1890. Ottawa, Printed by C. H. Parmelee, 1912.

3 v. in 2.    fold. facsims. (maps and plans)    26 cm.

B.C. ARCHIVES

## 1597 Dawson, E[dwin] C[ollas]
D. 1925

Missionary heroines in many lands; true stories of the intrepid bravery and patient endurance of missionaries in their encounters with uncivilised man, wild beasts, and the forces of nature in many parts of the world.    London, Seeley, Service & Co., 1912.

168 p.    plates.    20 cm.    Chapter 6: Mrs. Ridley among the redskins.

B.C. ARCHIVES

## 1598 The Days of old . . .

The days of old and days of gold in British Columbia; a few reminiscences of the early gold mining days. Kamloops centenary celebration, 1912.    [Victoria, Printed by W. H. Cullin, 1912]

15 p.    plates.    26 cm.    Cover title.

B.C. ARCHIVES

## 1599 Fawcett, Edgar
1847-1923

Some reminiscences of old Victoria.    Toronto, William Briggs, 1912.

294 p.    plates, ports.    20 cm.

The author came to Victoria in 1859.

B.C. ARCHIVES

## 1600 Morice, A[drian] G[abriel]
1859-1938

Histoire de l'église catholique dans l'Ouest canadien du Lac Supérieur au Pacifique (1659-1905)    Winnipeg, West Canada Pub. Co., 1912.

3 v.    plates, ports., fold. map, facsims. (1 fold.) 22 cm.    Bibliographie: p. [413]-425.

Nouvelle édition: Saint-Boniface, Man., 1915. 3 v. Also: Montreal, Granger Frères, 1921-1923. 4v. (for the period 1659-1915).    Also: Winnipeg, 1928. For the English edition see entry 1583.

B.C. ARCHIVES

## 1601 Tollemache, Stratford [Haliday Robert Louis]
1864-1937

Reminiscences of the Yukon.    Toronto, William Briggs, 1912.

x, 316 p.    plates, diagrs.    23 cm.

Contains a description of the author's 1898 trip to the Klondike via the Stikine River, Telegraph Creek, and Teslin Lake.

B.C. ARCHIVES

## 1602 Canada. Geographic Board

Handbook of Indians of Canada. Published as an Appendix to the Tenth report of the Geographic Board of Canada, reprinted by permission of Mr. F. W. Hodge, ethnologist-in-charge, from Handbook of American Indians north of Mexico, published as Bulletin 30, Bureau of American Ethnology, and edited by Frederick Webb Hodge. Reprinted under the direction of James White, secretary, Commission of Conservation.    Ottawa, Printed by C. H. Parmelee, 1913.

viii, 632 p.    fold. maps.    25 cm.    (Canada. Sessional papers, no. 21a, 1912)    Bibliography: p. 550-593.

Primarily a listing of Indian proper names from the writings of explorers, settlers, and scholars. Although changes have occurred in the concept and spelling of the listed words since 1913, it is a valuable guide to current terms as synonymous or nearly synonymous words are grouped together. References are given to the sources of cited words.

B.C. ARCHIVES

## 1603 Dunn, A[lexander]
B. 1843

Experiences in Langley and memoirs of prominent pioneers.    New Westminster, Printed by Jackson Printing Company, 1913.

100 p.    25 cm.    Cover title: Presbyterianism in British Columbia. Contents: Experiences in Langley [p. 1-18] — Memoirs of prominent pioneers [p. 19-26] — Presbyterianism in British Columbia [p. 61-100]

Another edition of 62 pages appeared in 1913 without the section entitled, "Presbyterianism in British Columbia."

B.C. ARCHIVES

**1604    Ewart, John S[kirving]**
1849-1933

British protection; Behring Sea seizures.   Ottawa, Thorburn & Abbott [1913]

59-112 p.   23 cm.   (Kingdom papers, no. 13)
Cover title.

B.C. ARCHIVES

**1605    Herring, Frances Elizabeth (Clarke)**
1851-1916

Nan and other pioneer women of the West. London, Francis Griffiths, 1913.

171 p.   plates, port.   20 cm.

Fiction. This collection of tales yields valuable insights into the hardships and problems of the pioneer women of the 1860's.

B.C. ARCHIVES

**1606    Ogilvie, William**
1846-1912

Early days on the Yukon and the story of its gold finds.   London, John Lane, The Bodley Head; Toronto, Bell & Cockburn, 1913.

xii, 306 p.   plates, ports.   20 cm.

Includes a chapter on the history of the Alaska boundary difficulties.

Also: Ottawa, Thorburn & Abbot, 1913.

B.C. ARCHIVES

**1607    Scholefield, E[thelbert] O[laf] S[tuart]**
1875-1919

A history of British Columbia; part one, being a survey of events from the earliest times down to the union of the crown colony of British Columbia with the Dominion of Canada [by] E. O. S. Scholefield; part two, being a history, mainly political and economic, of the province since confederation up to the present time [by] R. E. Gosnell.   Vancouver and Victoria, British Columbia Historical Association, 1913.

210, 226, vi p.   284 ports.   33 cm.   Half title, and title of three portrait sections of unnumbered plates: Sixty years of progress, British Columbia. Binder's title: British Columbia, sixty years of progress. Portraits accompanied by guard sheets with descriptive letterpress. Chapter headings of pt. 1: Early Pacific explorations. — Russian explorations and establishments. — Later Spanish and English voyages. — Later Spanish and English voyages (continued). — The Nootka affair.—Capt. George Vancouver. — Overland expeditions. — The era of the fur trader. — The Oregon boundary. — Changing headquarters. — Governor Blanshard's plight. —

Representative government established. — The awakening of Victoria. — The founding of British Columbia. — Fraser River in 1858. — Gold in Cariboo. — The two colonies, 1859 to 1864. — Union and confederation. Chapter headings of pt. 2: At the time of confederation. — Political conditions and early legislation. — Federal and other matters. — The Edgar incident. — The Carnarvon terms. — The dry dock and financial muddle. — Lord Dufferin's visit. — The story of the C.P.R. — The Dunsmuirs. — The Settlement Act. — A settled state of affairs. — A period of transition. — Stable government and prosperity. — Railway and industrial development. — Economic phases of the province. — The history of Kamloops (by M. S. Wade, M.D.) — Development of the Okanagan (by J. A. MacKelvie) — The Advisory Board.

B.C. ARCHIVES

**1608    Trimble, William J[oseph]**
1871-

The Indian policy of the colony of British Columbia in comparison with that of adjacent American territories.   [n.p., 1913?]

11 p.   26 cm.   Cover title. Reprinted from: Mississippi Valley Historical Association. *Proceedings.* v. 6.

B.C. ARCHIVES

**1609    Vancouver. St. Andrew's Church**

St. Andrew's Church (Presbyterian) Vancouver, British Columbia; twenty-fifth anniversary, 1883-1913. Rev. R. J. Wilson, M.A., moderator of session.   Vancouver, White & Bindon Limited, printers [1913]

26 p.   illus., ports.   24 cm.

Includes an historical sketch.

B.C. ARCHIVES

**1610    British Columbia . . .**

British Columbia; pictorial and biographical. Winnipeg, S. J. Clarke Publishing Co., 1914.

2 v.   298 ports.   32 cm.

Chiefly contemporary information.

B.C. ARCHIVES

**1611    Crosby, Thomas**
1840-1914

Up and down the North Pacific coast by canoe and mission ship.   Toronto, the Missionary Society of the Methodist Church, the Young People's Forward Movement Department [1914]

xiv, 403 p.   plates, ports.   20 cm.

On Methodist Indian missionary activities from 1871.

B.C. ARCHIVES

**1612 Herring, Frances E[lizabeth (Clarke)]**
1851-1916

The gold miners; a sequel to The pathless West. With a preface by Judge F. W. Howay. London, Francis Griffiths, 1914.

120 p. plates, port. 20 cm.

Fiction. This novel gives an excellent picture of life in the Cariboo gold rush era.

B.C. ARCHIVES

**1613 Longstaff, F[rederick] V[ictor]**
1879-1961

History and topography of Okanagan for the active militia in camp, May 1914. [Vernon, The Vernon News Press, 1914]

[13] p. 16 cm.

B.C. ARCHIVES

**1614 Macdonald, W[illiam] J[ohn]**
1829-1916

A pioneer, 1851. [Victoria? 1914]

30 p. 23 cm. Cover title.

Although the author was active in public affairs for many years, these reminiscences are mainly concerned with his private life.

B.C. ARCHIVES

**1615 Robinson, Noel**
1881?-1966

Blazing the trail through the Rockies; the story of Walter Moberly and his share in the making of Vancouver, by Noel Robinson, and the old man himself. [Vancouver] News-Advertiser [1914]

117 p. illus., ports. 24 cm. Includes chapters: Founding of New Westminster. — Building the Cariboo Road.

Largely the quoted recollections of Walter Moberly.

B.C. ARCHIVES

**1616 Scholefield, E[thelbert] O[laf] S[tuart]**
1875-1919

British Columbia, from the earliest times to the present, by E. O. S. Scholefield [and F. W. Howay] Vancouver, S. J. Clarke Publishing Company [1914]

4 v. plates, ports., maps, facsims. 27 cm. List of authorities: v. 1, p. xv-xlvi. Vols. 1-2 are historical (v. 1 by E. O. S. Scholefield; v. 2 by F. W. Howay) Vols. 3-4 are biographical. Chapter headings of v. 1: Prehistoric Northwest America. — Apocryphal voyages. — Spanish explorations. — Russian explorations. — Captain James Cook. — The maritime fur traders. — The Nootka Sound controversy. — Captain George Vancouver. — Sir Alexander Mackenzie. — Simon Fraser. — New Caledonia. — The Hudson's Bay Company. — The Oregon question. — The founding of Victoria. — The colony of Vancouver Island. — Representative government. — Vancouver Island in transformation. — The native races of British Columbia. — Medical. — The educational system of British Columbia. — Banks and banking. Chapter headings of v. 2: First news of gold; Queen Charlotte Islands excitement. — Governor Douglas and the miners; the Indian troubles, 1858; early mining. — Laying the foundations. — The Royal Engineers. — The advance of Cariboo. — The roads and trails to Cariboo. — The disbanding of the Royal Engineers. — The express. — A Sketch of Vancouver Island events from 1858 to 1864; list of officers of both colonies. — The Legislative Council and separate governors. — The Bute Inlet massacre and the Chilcotin War, 1864-1866. — Governor Kennedy and his troubles. — The union of British Columbia and Vancouver Island, 1866. — The Kootenay and the Big Bend excitements, 1864-1866. — Sketch of Legislative Council and legislation, 1866-1870. — Mining generally from 1866 including Omineca and Cassiar. — Confederation. — The San Juan difficulty. — Politics and general events, 1871 to 1875. — The railway difficulty of the Carnarvon terms. — Railway matters from the Carnarvon terms to Lord Dufferin's visit. — The Elliott government; the Walkem government; the secession resolution, 1878, and the Canadian Pacific Railway construction. — The graving dock; the last days of Walkem government; Beaven government; first years of Smithe government. — The Canadian Pacific Railway and how it was built. — The extension of the C.P.R. to Vancouver. — Politics and general events from 1883 to 1892. — The sealing industry and the fur seal arbitration. — The Kootenay mines; Nelson; Slocan; Granby; hydraulic in Cariboo; the railway development in Kootenay. — The Theodore Davie, Turner, Semlin, Martin, and Dunsmuir governments; Atlin. — The Pacific cable; the Prior government; the M'Bride government; "Better terms"; general events, 1902-1913. — The Alaska boundary dispute. — Chinese and Japanese immigration. — The Crow's Nest Pass and Nicola coal fields; salmon canning industry. — The beginnings of various agricultural sections on the mainland. — Missions and missionaries. — Early missions and missionaries (continued). — Bench and bar. Appendices, v. 1-2, contain documents and other source material.

B.C. ARCHIVES

**1617 Shortt, Adam**
EDITOR 1859-1931

Canada and its provinces; a history of the Canadian people and their institutions, by one hundred associates. Adam Shortt, and Arthur G. Doughty, general editors. Volume 21: [The Pacific province] Authors' edition. Toronto, Printed by T. & A. Constable at the Edinburgh University Press for the Publishers' Association of Canada Limited, 1914.

xii, 346 p. plates, ports. 29 cm. Contents: British Columbia in the Dominion; introduction, by Sir Richard McBride. — The period of exploration, by T. G. Marquis. — Colonial history, 1849-1871, by R. E. Gosnell. — Political history, 1871-1913, by

F. W. Howay. — Economic history, by C. H. Lugrin. — Indian tribes of the Interior, by J. A. Teit. — Indian tribes of the Coast, by E. Sapir.

Also: Toronto, Glasgow, Book & Co.

## 1618    Trimble, William J[oseph]
### 1871-

The mining advance into the inland empire; a comparative study of the beginnings of the mining industry in Idaho and Montana, eastern Washington and Oregon, and the southern interior of British Columbia, and of institutions and laws based upon that industry.    Madison, Wisc., 1914.

254 p.    map.    23 cm.    (University of Wisconsin. Bulletin, no. 638. History series, v. 3, no. 2)    A selected bibliography: p. 248-254. University of Wisconsin thesis.

A history of the economic and social consequences of gold discoveries, which also includes the study of law enforcement at the gold fields.

## 1619    Tupper, Sir Charles
### BARONET    1821-1915

Political reminiscences of the Right Honourable Sir Charles Tupper, Bart. . . . Transcribed and edited by the late W. A. Harkin. With a biographical sketch and an appendix.    London, Constable & Company, 1914.

xix, 302 p.    plates, ports., facsim.    23 cm. Appendix: Sir Charles Tupper's five-hour speech on the railway policy of the Mackenzie government [p. 199-296]

One chapter on British Columbia and confederation; another on Tupper's railway policy.

## 1620    Wade, F[rederick] C[oate]
### 1860-1924

Treaties affecting the North Pacific coast; read by F. C. Wade, K.C., before Sixth Annual Conference, Association of Canadian Clubs, Vancouver, August 4, 1914.    [Vancouver, Saturday Sunset Presses, 1914?]

19 p.    18 cm.

## 1621    Walkem, William W[ymond]
### 1850-1919

Stories of early British Columbia. Illustrated by S. P. Judge.    Vancouver, News-Advertiser, 1914.

287 p.    illus., port.    24 cm.

Reminiscences of early pioneers.

## 1622    Burpee, Lawrence J[ohnstone]
### 1873-1946

Sandford Fleming, empire builder.    London, Humphrey Milford, Oxford University Press, 1915.

288 p.    plates, ports., fold. facsim.    23 cm. Bibliography: p. 279-284.

## 1623    Collison, W[illiam] H[enry]
### 1847-1922

In the wake of the war canoe; a stirring record of forty years' successful labour, peril & adventure amongst the savage Indian tribes of the Pacific coast, and the piratical head-hunting Haidas of the Queen Charlotte Islands, B.C. With an introduction by the Lord Bishop of Derry. Toronto, Musson Book Company [n.d.]

351 p.    plates, map.    31 cm.

An account by a Church of England missionary of his early work in the Queen Charlotte Islands and along the Skeena River.

Also: London, Seeley, Service & Co., 1915.    Also: New York, E. P. Dutton, 1916.

## 1624    Muir, John
### 1838-1914

Travels in Alaska. [Prepared for publication by Marion Randall Parsons]    Boston, Houghton Mifflin Company, 1915.

ix, 326 p.    plates.    22 cm.

In part of the book the author, a mountaineer, describes a trip made in 1879 to the Cassiar district via the Stikine River.

Large-paper edition: 1915.    Also published in 1917 and 1930.

## 1625    Steele, [Sir] Samuel Benfield
### 1849-1919

Forty years in Canada; reminiscences of the great North-west with some account of his service in South Africa, by Colonel S. B. Steele, late of the N.W.M. Police and the S. African Constabulary. Edited by Mollie Glen Niblett, with an introduction by J. G. Colmer.    Toronto, McClelland, Goodchild & Stewart, 1915.

xvii, 428 p.    plates, ports.,    22 cm.

The author, one of the original members of the North-West Mounted Police, was appointed to take charge of a detachment detailed for duty along the C.P.R. construction line in British Columbia. He was also responsible for building a post in the Kootenays in 1887, and was later in command of the Force in the Yukon and British Columbia during the Klondike gold rush. The book briefly covers these activities.

Also: New York, Dodd, Mead & Company, 1915.
Also: London, Herbert Jenkins, 1915. Also:
Toronto, McClelland, Goodchild, Stewart, 1918.

B.C. ARCHIVES

### 1626    Laut, Agnes C[hristina]
1871-1936

The Cariboo Trail; a chronicle of the gold-fields
of British Columbia.    Toronto, Glasgow, Brook
& Company, 1916.

viii, 115 p.    plates (1 col.) ports., fold. map.    18 cm.
(Chronicles of Canada, v. 23)    Bibliographical
note: p. 110-111.

Includes two chapters on the Overlanders of 1862.

Also printed in 1920 and 1922.

B.C. ARCHIVES

### 1627    Morris, [C.] Keith
1879-

The story of the Canadian Pacific Railway.
London, William Stevens Limited, 1916.

154 p.    plates, port.    19 cm.

A popular rendering, covering mountain surveys,
subsequent construction, the railway's significance, and
its cost.

Also: 1923. 122 p.    Also: 1927. 181 p.

B.C. ARCHIVES

### 1628    Nelson. St. Paul's Presbyterian
Church

Twenty-fifth anniversary, November 5-12, 1916;
special services, brief historical sketch, present
organization.    [Nelson, W. H. Jones, printer,
1916]

[8] p.    20 cm.    Cover title.

B.C. ARCHIVES

### 1629    Smyth, Eleanor C[aroline
(Hill)]
1831-1926

An octogenarian's reminiscences.    [Letchworth,
Herts., Letchworth Printers Ltd., 1916?]

131 p.    21 cm.

The author was living on Vancouver Island in
the 1860's.

B.C. ARCHIVES

### 1630    Stephens, L[orenzo] Dow

Life sketches of a Jayhawker of '49; actual
experiences of a pioneer told by himself in his
own way.    [San Jose, Cal., Printed by Nolta
Brothers] 1916.

68 p.    plates, ports.    24 cm.

Mentions the Cariboo gold rush, which the author
joined in 1862.

B.C. ARCHIVES

### 1631    Victoria. St. Andrew's Church

To commemorate the fiftieth anniversary, St.
Andrew's Church, Victoria, B.C., 1866-1916.
[n.p., 1916]

12 p.    illus., ports.    19 cm.    Cover title.

Historical sketch. Also see entries 1698 and 1816.

B.C. ARCHIVES

### 1632    Baird, George M. P.

The story of Barney May, pioneer.    Pittsburgh,
Aldine Press, 1917.

61 p.    plates, ports.    26 cm.

One chapter about Barney May's life in the Cariboo
in the early 1860's.

B.C. ARCHIVES

### 1633    Gould, S[ydney]
1869-1938

Inasmuch; sketches of the beginnings of the
Church of England in Canada in relation to the
Indian and Eskimo races, by S. Gould, General
Secretary of the Missionary Society of the Church
of England in Canada.    Toronto, 1917.

xiv, 285 p.    front., maps.    20 cm.    (Handbook,
no. 1)    Bibliography: p.[283]-285.

One chapter on British Columbia missions.

B.C. ARCHIVES

### 1634    Klotz, Otto [Julius]
1852-1923

The forty-ninth parallel.    [n.p., 1917]

9 p.    23 cm.    Cover title. Reprinted from the
*University magazine*, October 1917.

A history of events centering on the forty-ninth
parallel west of the Rocky Mountains.

U.B.C. SPECIAL COLLECTIONS

### 1635    Klotz, Otto [Julius]
1852-1923

The history of the forty-ninth parallel survey west
of the Rocky Mountains.    New York, American
Geographical Society [1917]

382-387 p.    map.    26 cm.    Cover title. Reprinted
from the *Geographical review*, v. 3, May 1917.

Relates to the disappearance until 1898 of all copies
of the Northwest Boundary Commission's final report,
dated 7 May 1869.

B.C. ARCHIVES

**1636    Long, Elizabeth Emsley**

How the light came to Kitamaat, by Elizabeth Emsley Long, with additions by the Rev. Thomas Crosby.    Toronto, The Woman's Missionary Society of the Methodist Church, Canada, 1917.

26 p.    19 cm.

**1637    Splawn, A[ndrew] J[ackson]**
1845-1917

Ka-mi-akin, the last hero of the Yakimas. [Portland, Ore., Press of Kilham Stationery & Printing Co., c1917]

436 p.    illus., ports.    24 cm.

The author was a pioneer cattle drover of the Pacific Northwest. The book relates in part to cattle drives in the 1860's from the Willamette, Umpqua and Rogue river valleys to the mines of eastern British Columbia.

Also: Portland, Binfords & Mort for the Oregon Historical Society, 1944. xv, 500 p.

**1638    Gosnell, R. E[dward]**
1860-1931

The story of confederation, with postscript on Quebec situation.    [Victoria, c1918]

156 p.    illus., ports., facsim.    23 cm.

British Columbia is treated at length.

**1639    MacBeth, R[oderick] [George]**
1858-1934

The romance of western Canada.    Toronto, William Briggs, 1918.

xii, 309 p.    ports., facsim.    21 cm.

Includes a chapter on the history of British Columbia.

Second edition: Toronto, Ryerson Press, 1920.

**1640    Maclean, John**
1851-1928

Vanguards of Canada.    Toronto, The Missionary Society of the Methodist Church, the Young People's Forward Movement Department [c1918]

x, 262 p.    plates, ports., fold. map.    20 cm.

A chapter on the work of Thomas Crosby.

**1641    Palmer, Howard**
1883-1944

Early explorations in British Columbia for the Canadian Pacific Railway.    [Philadelphia, 1918]

17 p.    plates, fold. map.    25 cm.    Reprinted from: Geographical Society of Philadelphia. *Bulletin.* v. 16, July 1918, p. 75-91.

**1642    Sisters of St. Ann (Victoria)**

A chaplet of years: St. Ann's Academy to the pupils past and present of the Sisters of St. Ann, Victoria, B.C., 1858-1918.    [Victoria, Colonist Printing and Publishing Co., 1918]

106 p.    illus., ports.    27 cm.

An informal history with reminiscences.

**1643    Vancouver Island. House of Assembly**

House of Assembly correspondence book, August 12th, 1856, to July 6th, 1859. Printed by authority of the Legislative Assembly.    Victoria, Printed by William H. Cullin, 1918.

62 p.    25 cm.    (British Columbia. Provincial Archives. Memoir no. 4)

**1644    Vancouver Island. House of Assembly**

Minutes of the House of Assembly of Vancouver Island, August 12th, 1856, to September 25th, 1858. Printed by authority of the Legislative Assembly.    Victoria, Printed by William H. Cullin, 1918.

78 p.    25 cm.    (British Columbia. Provincial Archives. Memoir no. 3)

**1645    Vancouver Island. Legislative Council**

Minutes of the Council of Vancouver Island, commencing August 30th, 1851, and terminating with the prorogation of the House of Assembly, February 6th, 1861. Printed by the authority of the Legislative Assembly.    Victoria, Printed by William H. Cullin, 1918.

93 p.    25 cm.    (British Columbia. Provincial Archives. Memoir no. 2)

**1646    Langley. St. Andrew's Presbyterian Church**

St. Andrew's Presbyterian Church, Langley Fort, B.C.; Thirty-fourth anniversary, 1885-1919. [Vancouver, A. H. Timms, printer, 1919]

8 p.    illus., ports.    26 cm.

An historical sketch.

B.C. ARCHIVES

**1647    McCullagh, J[ames] B[enjamin]**
1854-1921

Red Indians I have known. Illustrations by H. E. Payne.    London, Church Missionary Society [1919?]

47 p.    illus.    22 cm.

Concerns the Tsimshian Indians.

B.C. ARCHIVES

**1648    Warren, G[ordon] B.**

The last West and Paolo's Virginia.    [Vancouver, Evans & Hastings, printers, 1919]

45 p.    plates.    19 cm.    Includes: A raid on the seal rookeries.

Fiction. "A raid on the seal rookeries" relates the manner in which Captain Hansen on his schooner "Adele" captured seals in the area of Pribilof Island. The "Adele," an actual ship, was totally wrecked off the Queen Charlotte Islands on 8 April 1891. The account of the foundering and details of the ship are recorded in the Victoria *Colonist* 13 May 1891, page 3.

B.C. ARCHIVES

**1649    Heyden, Joseph van der**

Life and letters of Father Brabant, a Flemish missionary hero.    Louvain, Printed by J. Wouters-Ickx [1920]

249 p.    plates, ports.    25 cm.

Father Augustin Joseph Brabant arrived in Victoria in 1869. He established the Hesquiat Mission, Barkley Sound, where he remained for thirty-five years. In 1908 he became the apostolic administrator of Victoria Diocese.

B.C. ARCHIVES

**1650    Ross, Victor [Harold]**
1878-1934

A history of the Canadian Bank of Commerce, with an account of the other banks which now form part of its organization.    Toronto, Oxford University Press, 1920.

2 v.    plates, ports., maps, diagrs., facsims., tables. 25 cm.

The Bank of British Columbia was founded in 1862 and amalgamated with the Canadian Bank of Commerce in 1901. Volume 1, Chapter 5 (p. 251-350), covers the history of the former bank in detail. Appendices 8-11 of Volume 1 enumerate provincial gold production, gold shipments, etc.

B.C. ARCHIVES

**1651    Freemasons. Nanaimo. Ashlar Lodge No. 3**

History of Ashlar Lodge No. 3, G.R.B.C., 1865-1921.    [n.p., n.d.]

26 p.    port.    15 cm.    At head of text: The history of early Masonry in Nanaimo and area from 1865 and particularly of Ashlar Lodge No. 3, G.R.B.C.

B.C. ARCHIVES

**1652    Le Jeune, Jean-Marie [Raphael]**
1855-1930

[Chinook jargon.    Kamloops, 1921]

14 l.    35 cm.    Mimeographed.

Gives a history of the jargon, some early Chinook publications, and lessons in Chinook. Pages 10-14 form a supplement to *Chinook and shorthand rudiments* (entry 1363). No Duployan shorthand appears in the publication.

B.C. ARCHIVES

**1653    Lefevre, L[ily] A[lice (Cooke)]**
D. 1938

A garden by the sea and other poems.    London, Arthur L. Humphreys, 1921.

129 p.    19 cm.    Contents in part: Eagle Pass. — Hail and farewell!

Poetry. "Eagle Pass" tells how the pass was discovered. In "Hail and Farewell!" the wrecked steamship "Beaver" ponders its fate and relives its past.

Also: Toronto, McClelland and Stewart, 1922.

B.C. ARCHIVES

**1654    O'Donnell, A. M.**

A brief history and souvenir booklet of Knox Presbyterian Church, Trail, British Columbia, 1896-1921.    [Trail, Trail News, 1921]

19 p.    illus., ports., group ports.    24 cm.

B.C. ARCHIVES

**1655    Palmer, Howard**
1883-1944

A climber's guide to the Rocky Mountains of Canada, by Howard Palmer and J. Monroe Thorington. First Edition.    New York, Published for the American Alpine Club by the Knickerbocker Press, 1921.

xvii, 183 p. front., maps (part. fold.) 17 cm. List of authorities: p. xiii. Principal maps of the Canadian Rockies: p. xiv-xv.

A list of approximately four hundred and fifty named peaks above nine thousand feet in elevation, with the names of climbers making first ascents, the dates of first ascents, and the climbers' routes when known.

Also: 1921. Second edition: Philadelphia, American Alpine Club, 1930. xv, 244 p. Third edition: Philadelphia, American Alpine Club, 1940-43. xviii, 307 p.

B.C. ARCHIVES

1656     Smith, Charles W[esley]
         COMPILER     1877-1956

Pacific Northwest americana; a checklist of books and pamphlets relating to the history of the Pacific Northwest. Edition 2, revised and enlarged. New York, The Wilson Company; London, Grafton & Company, 1921.

xi, 329 p.   27 cm.

The first edition was published in 1909 by the Washington State Library under title: *Check-list of books and pamphlets relating to the history of the Pacific Northwest to be found in representative libraries of that region.* In 191 pages. The third edition, revised and extended by Isabel Mayhew, was published by the Oregon Historical Society in 1950. In 381 pages.

B.C. ARCHIVES

1657     Macoun, John
         1831-1920

Autobiography of John Macoun, M.A., Canadian explorer and naturalist, assistant director and naturalist to the Geological Survey of Canada, 1831-1920. With an introduction by Ernest Thompson Seton. A memorial volume.   [Ottawa] The Ottawa Field-Naturalists' Club, 1922.

x, 305 p.   plates, ports.   24 cm.

Includes accounts of explorations undertaken in British Columbia for the Canadian Pacific Railway and of subsequent western trips made by Macoun for the purpose of studying and collecting fauna and flora.

B.C. ARCHIVES

1658     Macoun, John
         1831-1920

The Cariboo journal of John Macoun. [With an introduction by] J. Monroe Thorington. [n.p., 1922?]

[51]-61 p.   25 cm.   Cover title. Reprinted from: Geographical Society of Philadelphia. *Bulletin.* v. 28.

The diary of a journey over the Cariboo Road from north of Quesnel to New Westminster, written by John Macoun after he had left one of Sandford Fleming's exploring parties of 1872.

B.C. ARCHIVES

1659     New Westminster. St. Andrew's Presbyterian Church

St. Andrew's Presbyterian Church; a historical sketch.   [New Westminster, Jackson Printing Company, Ltd., 1922?]

16 p.   illus., ports.   25 cm.

B.C. ARCHIVES

1660     Sillitoe, Violet E. [ (Pelly) ]
         D. 1934

Early days in British Columbia, by Violet E. Sillitoe, wife of the first Bishop of New Westminster. With a foreword by the Bishop of New Westminster.   [Vancouver, Evans & Hastings, printers, 1922]

36 p.   illus., ports.   17 cm.

Includes some account of the work of Bishop Acton Windeyer Sillitoe.

B.C. ARCHIVES

1661     Trail. Methodist Church

Souvenir of the twenty-fifth anniversary of the Methodist Church, Trail, B.C., March 12th and 13th, 1922.   [n.p., 1922]

21 p. (incl. advertisements)   illus., ports.   24 cm.

Includes a short history of the church.

B.C. ARCHIVES

1662     Victoria. First Presbyterian Church

Historical sketch, 1862-1922; First Presbyterian Church, Victoria, B.C., Rev. W. G. Wilson, M.A., D.D., minister.   [Victoria, The Waterson Press, 1922?]

11 p.   19 cm.   Cover title.

B.C. ARCHIVES

1663     Bergman, Hans
         1869-1926

British Columbia och dess svenska innebyggare; historia, topografi, klimat, resurser, biografi. Victoria [Published by the author] 1923.

314 p.   illus., 5 col. plates, ports.   24 cm.

Has fifty pages of general history and a few biographical sketches of Swedes who arrived in the province before the turn of the century.

B.C. ARCHIVES

## 1664 Brown, W. R.

St. Andrew's Presbyterian Church, Merritt, B.C. Souvenir book, marking the thirteenth anniversary of the opening of the church [with] a short history of the church in the Nicola Valley, and sketch of the valley and the city of Merritt.   [Merritt] 1923.

36 p. (incl. advertisements)   illus., ports.   16 x 22 cm.   Cover title.

Mostly concerned with the early history of the Presbyterian, Anglican, and Catholic churches in the Nicola Valley.

B.C. ARCHIVES

## 1665 Gilson, W. R.

Up-hill in Canada and South California. Montreal, Printed by Adj. Menard, 1923.

86 p.   Not seen.

"Personal narrative full of the 'homey' flavor of the old days, from the 'fifties onward in the British Columbia gold fields, Oregon and California." — Eberstadt, cat. 132, item 294.

EBERSTADT

## 1666 Innis, Harold A[dams]
### 1894-1952

A history of the Canadian Pacific Railway. London, P. S. King & Son Ltd.; Toronto, McClelland and Stewart Ltd., 1923.

viii, 365 p. tables. 22 cm. Bibliography: p. 325-337. Extensive footnotes.

An economic study. The Introduction (p. 1-74) summarizes British Columbia's position with regard to the railway's completion. The footnotes in the Introduction have extensive notes on references to communications between Canada and the Pacific.

B.C. ARCHIVES

## 1667 Kirk, H[arry] B.

Obituary; James Hector.   Wellington, N.Z., W. A. G. Skinner, 1923.

ix-xii p.   port.   25 cm.   Cover title. Reprinted from the *Transactions of the New Zealand Institute,* v. 54, 1923.

B.C. ARCHIVES

## 1668 Moeran, J[oseph] W[illiam] W[right]

McCullagh of Aiyansh.   London, Marshall Brothers Limited [1923]

232 p.   plates, ports., map.   19 cm.

The story of the Church of England mission at Aiyansh on the Nass River and the work of its missionary, James McCullagh, among the Tsimshian Indians.

Second edition: London, 1923?

B.C. ARCHIVES

## 1669 Sillitoe, Violet E. [ (Pelly) ]
### D. 1934

Pioneer days in British Columbia; reminiscences by Violet E. Sillitoe [wife of the first Bishop of New Westminster.   Vancouver, Evans & Hastings, printers, 1923?]

32 p.   illus., port., group ports.   17 cm.

Mostly reminiscences, personal in content, which cover the duration of Bishop Acton Windeyer Sillitoe's episcopate from 1879 to 1894.

B.C. ARCHIVES

## 1670 Day, Patience
### D. 1934

Pioneer days, Provincial Royal Jubilee Hospital. Victoria [Colonist Presses, 1924]

20 p.   illus., ports., group port.   25 cm.

Concerned with events in the 1850's and '60's.

B.C. ARCHIVES

## 1671 Houghton, Frank
### 1897-

A western Delilah.   London, Hodder and Stoughton Limited [n.d.]

298 p.   19 cm.

This romance takes place in Fort Steele and the Kootenay area in its heyday.

B.C. ARCHIVES

## 1672 MacBeth, R[oderick] G[eorge]
### 1858-1934

The romance of the Canadian Pacific Railway. Toronto, Ryerson Press [1924]

263 p.   plates, ports.   22 cm.

Primarily concerned with the building of the railway in British Columbia.

Second edition: 1926.   Revised edition: 1931.

B.C. ARCHIVES

## 1673 McKellar, Hugh
### COMPILER 1842-1934

Presbyterian pioneer missionaries in Manitoba, Saskatchewan, Alberta, and British Columbia. Toronto, Murray Printing Company, 1924.

249 p.   illus., ports.   22 cm.   Cover title: Presbyterian pioneer ministers.

Contains articles and letters written for the compiler by numerous missionaries, together with extracts from books and periodicals.

B.C. ARCHIVES

## 1674   Robson, Ebenezer
### 1835-1911

How Methodism came to British Columbia. [Toronto, The Methodist Young People's Forward Movement for Missions, 1924?]

31 p.   illus., ports., double map.   23 cm.

B.C. ARCHIVES

## 1675   Secretan, J[ames] H[enry] E[dward]
### 1854-1926

Canada's great highway, from the first stake to the last spike.   London, John Lane, The Bodley Head; Ottawa, Thorburn and Abbott [1924]

252 p.   plates, ports.   19 cm.

Reminiscences which include the author's account of his experiences while surveying in British Columbia for the C.P.R.

B.C. ARCHIVES

## 1676   Trotter, Reginald George
### 1888-1951

Canadian federation, its orgins and achievement; a study in nation building.   Toronto, J. M. Dent & Sons Limited, 1924.

xiv, 348 p.   fold. map.   21 cm.   Bibliographic notes at end of chapters. Bibliography: p. 321-332.

Has several relevant chapters pertaining to the Hudson's Bay Company and the territory west of the Rockies, and to communications to the Pacific. One chapter relates in part to Edward Watkin's Atlantic and Pacific Transit and Telegraph Company.

B.C. ARCHIVES

## 1677   Davis, E. A.
### EDITOR

Commemorative review of the Methodist, Presbyterian and Congregational churches in British Columbia; a retrospect of the work and personalities of the churches in British Columbia up to the time of their union into the United Church, together with a prophetic forecast for the future.   Vancouver, Compiled and published by Joseph Lee, 1925.

xxxii, 380 p.   plates, ports.   19 cm.

Includes historical sketches of numerous churches.

B.C. ARCHIVES

## 1678   Drumheller, "Uncle Dan"
### 1840-1925

"Uncle Dan" Drumheller tells thrills of western trails in 1854, by "Uncle Dan" Drumheller. Spokane, Wash., Inland-American Printing Company, 1925.

xi, 131 p.   ports.   20 cm.   Not seen.

According to Soliday (pt. 2, item 364), this work includes an account of gold mining in British Columbia.

LIBRARY OF CONGRESS

## 1679   Harrison, Charles

Ancient warriors of the North Pacific: the Haidas; their laws, customs and legends, with some historical account of the Queen Charlotte Islands. London, H. F. & G. Witherby, 1925.

222 p.   plates, fold. map.   23 cm.

A description of what the author saw and heard during forty years residence among the Haidas.

B.C. ARCHIVES

## 1680   Mouat, A[lexander] N[aysmith]
### 1863-1950

History of British Columbia coast service. [Victoria, 1925]

2, [1] p. (folder)   23 cm.   Caption title. Reprinted from the Victoria *Times,* 19 February 1925.

An account of the shipping interests of the Canadian Pacific Navigation Company and the company's transfer to the Canadian Pacific Railway Company in 1901.

B.C. ARCHIVES

## 1681   Okanagan Historical Society (Vernon)

Report.   no. 1+ 1925+   Vernon, B.C.

v.   illus.   20, 23 cm.   annual.   Name varies: early years as *Okanagan Historical and Natural History Society.* No index. Table of contents.

B.C. ARCHIVES

## 1682   Pearce, William
### 1848-1930

William Pearce manuscript.   [Edited by J. A. Jaffary.   Edmonton, Alta., 1925]

2 v. (190 1.)   *and* photographic supplement.   28 cm. Mimeographed. Spiral binding.

Mostly concerned with the prairie provinces, but there is some mention of early postal and rail communication in British Columbia.

B.C. ARCHIVES

**1683    Stephenson, [Annie]**

One hundred years of Canadian Methodist missions, 1824-1924, by Mrs. Frederick C. Stephenson. In two volumes. Volume 1.    Toronto, The Missionary Society of the Methodist Church, The Young People's Forward Movement [c1925]

2 v.    maps (on lining papers)    20 cm.    Vol. 2 not seen.

Has five chapters on the establishment of B.C. Indian Methodist missions.

**1684    Teichmann, Emil**
1845-1924

A journey to Alaska in the year 1868; being a diary of the late Emil Teichmann. Edited with an introduction by his son Oskar. With a foreword by Ernest Gruening.    Kensington, Privately printed at the Cayme Press, 1925.

272 p.    illus., 2 ports.    21 cm.

After Alaska had been purchased by the United States, the author made a trip to Alaska to protect the interests of a firm of London fur merchants. In about a third of the book he describes his travels in B.C. coastal waters.

Also: New York, Argosy-Antiquarian Ltd., 1963.

**1685    Vancouver. Richmond Presbyterian Church**

An historical sketch of Richmond Presbyterian Church in Marpole, B.C., 1861-1925.    [n.p.] Prepared by the Session, and published by its authority, 1925.

37 p.    illus., ports.    24 cm.

**1686    Art, Historical and Scientific Association of Vancouver**

Museum and art notes.    v. 1-[10]; 1926-52.

10 v.    illus.    23 cm.    quarterly (irregular)    Vol. 1-8, 1926-35. Suspended between October 1935 and August 1949. Vol. 1-2, September 1949—April 1952. Title varies: v. 1-3 (1926-28) as *Museum notes*. Table of contents.

Short articles deal with such diverse topics as Vancouver's cultural life, early B.C. postage stamps, pioneer ranching, transportation, B.C. Indians, etc.

**1687    Burpee, Lawrence J[ohnstone]**
1873-1946

On the old Athabasca Trail.    Toronto, Ryerson Press [1926]
259 p.    plates.    22 cm.    Bibliographical note: p. 250-253.

The account of early travellers on the Athabasca Trail, for many years the main route across the Rockies.

Also: New York, Stokes, 1926.

**1688    Esquimalt. St. Paul's Royal Naval Station and Garrison Church**

Diamond jubilee historical sketch, 1866-1926; St. Paul's Royal Naval Station and Garrison Church. [Prepared by Rev. Frederic Colbourne Chapman] Esquimalt [1926?]

16 p.    illus.    23 cm.

**1689    Faris, John T[homson]**
1871-1949

The romance of the boundaries.    New York, Harper & Brothers, 1926.

xvi, 331 p.    plates, maps (1 on lining paper)    23 cm. Bibliography: p. 312-318.

A popular account which has references to B.C. boundary problems. It also includes a few pages on the building of the White Pass and Yukon Railway (p. 142-146).

**1690    Howay, Frederic W[illiam]**
1867-1943

The early history of the Fraser River mines. Victoria, Printed by Charles F. Banfield, 1926.

xvii, 126 p.    plates, ports.    25 cm.    (British Columbia. Provincial Archives. Memoir no. 6)

Comprised of correspondence. "The letters that are in this volume consist of a part of the correspondence of Richard Hicks from October, 1858, to May, 1859; of Chartres Brew, the Chief Inspector of Police and Assistant Chief Gold Commissioner, from November, 1858, to April, 1859; of Judge Begbie from January, 1859, to March, 1859; together with a few scattered but illuminating documents. The selection, however, has been carefully made with a view of showing the men, and the life of the time, the difficulties of maintaining order and collecting revenue, and generally the conditions prevailing in the Colony of British Columbia — that is, on the Fraser River — when it was in its swaddling-clothes." — p. xii

**1691**  MacInnes, T[h]om[as Robert Edward]
1867-1951

Chinook days. [With] nine drawings by J. Howard Smith, two by John Innes.  [Vancouver, Sun Publishing Co., 1926]
206 p.  illus.  16 cm.

A souvenir book for the opening of Grouse Mountain Highway and resort, which includes historical sketches, legends, and poetry.

Also: 193–.

B.C. ARCHIVES

**1692**  McKelvie, B[ruce] A[listair]
1889-1960

Early history of the province of British Columbia. London, Toronto, J. M. Dent & Sons Ltd., 1926.

ix, 118 p.  illus., port.  19 cm.

A history, from exploration days to 1886, designed as an outline to serve in the absence of a suitable textbook.

B.C. ARCHIVES

**1693**  McKelvie, B[ruce] A[listair]
1889-1960

Huldowget; a story of the North Pacific coast. Toronto, J. M. Dent and Sons Ltd., 1926.

ix, 221 p.  20 cm.

Fiction. The author's Foreword states "an effort has been made to picture some of the trials and tribulations, the dangers and disappointments of a missioner and his wife . . ."

B.C. ARCHIVES

**1694**  Moser, Cha[rle]s
COMPILER  1874-

Reminiscences of the west coast of Vancouver Island.  [Victoria, Printed by Acme Press, 1926]

192 p.  illus., ports.  21 cm.

A reprinting of Augustin Brabant's *Vancouver Island and its missions, 1874-1900* (p. 9-131), together with documents and historical notes, including excerpts from the journal of Bishop John Nicholas Lemmens and a biographical sketch of Father Peter Nicolaye.

B.C. ARCHIVES

**1695**  Pacific Northwest libraries . . .

Pacific Northwest libraries; history of their early development in Washington, Oregon and British Columbia. Papers prepared for the Seventeenth Annual Conference of the Pacific Northwest Library Association, 1926, contributing to the fiftieth anniversary of the founding of the American Library Association . . .  Seattle, Wash., University of Washington Press, 1926.

40 p.  23 cm.  Reprinted from the *Washington historical quarterly*, v. 17, October 1926, p. 243-279.

B.C. ARCHIVES

**1696**  Reid, R[obie] L[ewis]
1866-1945

The Assay Office and the proposed mint at New Westminster; a chapter in the history of the Fraser River mines. Printed by authority of the Legislative Assembly.  Victoria, Printed by Charles F. Banfield, 1926.

101 p.  plates (1 fold.) ports.  25 cm.  (British Columbia. Provincial Archives. Memoir no. 7)

Based mainly on newspaper accounts, government documents, and on the letters of Francis Claudet, assayer, Captain William Gosset, treasurer of the colony of British Columbia, and of the Colonial Secretary, this book is an account of the difficulties which arose because of the lack of a circulating medium. It also reveals the rivalry between Victoria and New Westminster, and the antagonism between Governor Douglas and Gosset.

B.C. ARCHIVES

**1697**  Robinson, J[ohn] M[oore]
1855-1934

The transition of the Okanagan.  [n.p., 1926?]

4 p. (folder)  31 cm.  Caption title.

An outline of the author's part in the beginnings of fruit farming in the Okanagan.

B.C. ARCHIVES

**1698**  Victoria. St. Andrew's Church

To commemorate the sixtieth anniversary, St. Andrew's Church, Victoria, B.C., 1866-1926.  [n.p., 1926]

16 p.  illus., ports.  19 cm.  Cover title.

Except for information on the last decade of the church's history, the contents are the same as in entry 1631.

B.C. ARCHIVES

**1699**  Anstey, Arthur
D. 1951

The romance of British Columbia.  Toronto, W. J. Gage & Co., 1927.

6, 216 p.  illus., ports., maps.  20 cm.

There were at least four editions of this school history text. Also see entry 1975.

B.C. ARCHIVES

**1700**    Kidd, Thomas
1846-1930

History of Lulu Island, and occasional poems. [Vancouver] Wrigley Printing Company, 1927.

247 p.   port., facsim.   18 cm.   Occasional poem: p. 187-247.

Most of Lulu Island is in the Richmond Municipality. The book includes biographical sketches.

B.C. ARCHIVES

**1701**    McKelvie, B[ruce] A[listair]
1889-1960

The Black Canyon; a story of '58.   London, J. M. Dent & Sons Ltd., 1927.

ix, 173 p.   plates.   20 cm.

Juvenile fiction. This story is based on historic events in 1858 at Fort Yale when a "war" was waged between Indians and white men. Contemporary notes by Dr. Wymond M. Walkem and information from Mark Bate were employed by the author.

Also: Toronto, Dent, 1927.

B.C. ARCHIVES

**1702**    Nelson, Denys
1876-1929

Fort Langley, 1827-1927; a century of settlement in the valley of the lower Fraser River. [Vancouver, Evans & Hastings] 1927.

31 p.   illus., ports.   24 cm.   On cover: Issued by the Art, Historical and Scientific Association of Vancouver, B.C.

Reprinted in 1947 by the Art, Historical and Scientific Association of Vancouver.

B.C. ARCHIVES

**1703**    Sage, Walter N[oble]
1888-1963

The annexationist movement in British Columbia. Ottawa, Printed for the Royal Society of Canada, 1927.

97-110 p.   25 cm.   Cover title. From: Royal Society of Canada. *Proceedings and transactions.* ser. 3, v. 21, sec. 2, 1927.

On events prior to 1871.

VANCOUVER PUBLIC LIBRARY

**1704**    Vancouver. Confederation Celebration Committee

Canada's diamond jubilee of confederation, 1867-1927.   Vancouver [1927]

64 p.   illus., port.   23 x 31 cm.

Includes brief histories of the provinces and of Vancouver.

B.C. ARCHIVES

**1705**    Wallace, J[ames] N[evin]
1871-1941

The passes of the Rocky Mountains along the Alberta boundary.   Calgary, The Historical Society of Calgary, 1927.

8 p.   25 cm.   Cover title.

A brief history of travel through the passes.

B.C. ARCHIVES

**1706**    Deaville, Alfred Stanley
1891-1948

The colonial postal systems and postage stamps of Vancouver Island and British Columbia, 1849-1871; a sketch of the origin and early development of the postal service on the Pacific seaboard of British North America. Printed by authority of the Legislative Assembly.   Victoria, Printed by Charles F. Banfield, 1928.

210 p.   illus., plates, ports., facsims., tables.   25 cm. (British Columbia. Provincial Archives. Memoir, no. 8)

B.C. ARCHIVES

**1707**    Gould, L[auretta] B[ernard]
1854-1936

History of the Aged and Infirm Women's Home, Victoria, British Columbia, 1897-1928, by Mrs. I. A. Gould.   [Victoria, Printed by Charles F. Banfield, 1928]

16 p.   plates, ports.   23 cm.

B.C. ARCHIVES

**1708**    Howay, F[rederic] W[illiam]
1867-1943

British Columbia; the making of a province. Toronto, The Ryerson Press [c1928]

ix, 289 p.   illus., plates, map.   21 cm.   Partial list of sources: p. 274-283.

B.C. ARCHIVES

**1709**    Kennedy, Howard Angus
1861-1938

Origin of the Canadian Pacific Railway.   Toronto, Ryerson Press [c1928]

30 p.   illus.   19 cm.   (Ryerson Canadian history readers)   Cover title.

Designed for school use.

B.C. ARCHIVES

1710    Lugrin, N[an] de Bertrand
1877-1962

The pioneer women of Vancouver Island, 1843-1866. Edited by John Hosie.    Victoria, Women's Canadian Club of Victoria, 1928.

312 p.    illus., plates, ports., map (on lining papers)    23 cm.

B.C. ARCHIVES

1711    O'Hagan, Thomas
1855-1939

Father Morice.    Toronto, The Ryerson Press [c1928]

31 p.    port.    19 cm.    (The Ryerson Canadian history readers)    Cover title.

Designed for school use.

B.C. ARCHIVES

1712    Pringle, George C[harles]
F[raser]
1873-1949

In great waters; the story of the United Church marine missions.    [Toronto, Ryerson Press, 1928]

xiv, 178 p.    plates, ports., maps (1 on lining paper)    20 cm.

Relates exclusively to Pacific coast missions; contains historical background.

B.C. ARCHIVES

1713    Victoria. St. John's Church

1928 souvenir of St. John's Church, Victoria, British Columbia.    [Victoria, Acme Press, 1928]

35 p. (incl. advertisements)    illus., port.    23 cm.

Includes a brief history.

B.C. ARCHIVES

1714    Godwin, George [Stanley]
1889-

The eternal forest.    London, Philip Allan & Co. [1929]

318 p.    19 cm.    On verso of t.p. is stamped: Colonial edition.

Fiction. Concerns life in a small Fraser Valley town at the turn of the century.

B.C. ARCHIVES

1715    Howay, F[rederic] W[illiam]
EDITOR    1867-1943

Builders of the West; a book of heroes.    Toronto, Ryerson Press [c1929]

v, 251 p.    illus.    21 cm.

Intended for the young reader, this work includes sketches of prominent people in the colonial period and a chapter on Metlahkatla.

B.C. ARCHIVES

1716    McMurtrie, Douglas C[rawford]
1888-1944

The first printing in British Columbia.    Chicago, Privately printed, 1929.

22 p.    facsims. (1 fold., 1 double)    22 cm.

On the province's first newspapers, Governor James Douglas' proclamations, Chief Justice David Cameron's work on rules of practice, and Alfred Waddington's *Fraser mines vindicated*.

Also appeared with facsimilies in the *Printing review of Canada*, v. 4, February, and March 1929.

B.C. ARCHIVES

1717    The Metchosin Farmers' Institute

The Metchosin Farmers' Institute and its history. [n.p., n.d.]

[4] p. (folder)    22 cm.    Caption title. At head of title: Production; progress; prosperity. Published about 1929.

Includes a brief account of the establishment of the institute in 1897 and 1898.

B.C. ARCHIVES

1718    Moberly, Henry John

When fur was king, by Henry John Moberly in collaboration with William Bleasdell Cameron. London, Toronto, J. M. Dent & Sons, 1929.

xvii, 237 p.    plates, port., fold. map.    21 cm.

A small proportion of the book relates to the author's wanderings in British Columbia. Chapter 23 is headed "The Cariboo gold rush."

Also: New York, E. P. Dutton, 1929.

B.C. ARCHIVES

1719    Reid, R[obie] L[ewis]
1866-1945

British Columbia; a bibliographical sketch. [n.p., 1929?]

20-44 p.    25 cm.    Reprinted from: Bibliographical Society of America. *Papers.* v. 22, pt. 1. Bibliographic footnotes.

B.C. ARCHIVES

1720    Skinner, Constance Lindsay
1879?-1939

Red willows.    Toronto, McClelland & Stewart Ltd. [1929]

viii, 412 p.    19 cm.

Fiction. The scion of an English aristocratic family comes to the Cariboo at the time of the gold rush to make his fortune. Glimpses of Victoria in early days, the heterogeneous mixture of people in the Cariboo, the arrival of the fur fleet and the celebrations which followed, all give a background of the social history of the time. "Fragments of actual history have been included in the story." — introd.

American edition: New York, Coward-McCann, 1929.

B.C. ARCHIVES

1721    Blake, Moffitt & Towne
PUBLISHERS

Pioneers in paper; the story of Blake, Moffitt & Towne, published in commemoration of the organization's seventy-fifth anniversary, 1930. [San Francisco, c1930]

49 p.    illus., plates, ports., facsim.    25 cm.

Contains a brief outline of the founding of the Victoria *Gazette* by the J. W. Towne Company in 1858.

B.C. ARCHIVES

1722    Mackay, Charles Angus
1872-1930

Memoirs of the life of Charles Angus Mackay, by himself.    Victoria, The Colonist Presses, 1930.

50 p.    18 cm.    Cover title: Life of a British Columbia prospector.

In his youth the author was active in the trade union movement.

B.C. ARCHIVES

1723    Morice, A[drian] G[abriel]
1859-1938

First years in western Canada; being the abridged memoirs of Rev. A. G. Morice, O.M.I., by D. L. S. Toronto, The Ryerson Press, 1930.

x, 267 p.    1 illus., plates, ports.    21 cm.

B.C. ARCHIVES

1724    Sage, Walter Noble
1888-1963

Sir James Douglas.    Toronto, Ryerson Press [c1930]

30 p.    illus.    19 cm.    (The Ryerson Canadian history readers)    Cover title.    Not seen.

BANCROFT LIBRARY CATALOGUE

1725    Sage, Walter N[oble]
1888-1963

Sir James Douglas and British Columbia. [Toronto] University of Toronto Press, 1930.

398 p.    fold. map.    25 cm.    (University of Toronto studies: history and economics [v. 6, no. 1]) List of authorities: p. [355]-362.

B.C. ARCHIVES

1726    Cheadle, [Walter Butler]
1835-1910

Cheadle's journal of trip across Canada, 1862-1863. With introduction and notes by A. G. Doughty and Gustave Lanctot.    Ottawa, Graphic Publishers Limited, 1931.

311 p.    illus., fold. map.    20 cm.    (Half title: The Canada series. Edited by F. P. Grove. v. 1)

B.C. ARCHIVES

1727    Cheng, Tien[g]-fang
1899-

Oriental immigration in Canada.    Shanghai, Commercial Press Limited, 1931.

x, 306 p.    23 cm.    Bibliography: p. [293]-296. University of Toronto thesis.

B.C. ARCHIVES

1728    Jacobsen, [Johan] Adrian
B. 1853

Die weise Grenze; Abenteuer eines alten Geebären rund um dem Polarsreis, herausgegeben von Albrecht Janssen.    Leipzig, Z. U. Brodhaus, 1931.

159 p.    plates, map.    20 cm.

Pages 66-122 are based on Captain Jacobsen's experiences in British Columbia and Alaska in the early 1880's, and present a more popular account than in *Captain Jacobsen's Reise an der Nordwestküste Amerikas, 1881-1883* (entry 661).

B.C. ARCHIVES

1729    McMurtrie, Douglas C[rawford]
1888-1944

The earliest British Columbia imprint.    Chicago, Privately printed, 1931.

11 p.    facsim.    22 cm.

Relates to James Douglas' proclamation of 25 August 1858 (entry 80).

B.C. ARCHIVES

1730    Mary Theodore, Sister
1856-1951

Pioneer nuns of British Columbia; Sisters of St. Ann.    Victoria [Printed by the Colonist Printing & Publishing Co.] 1931.

146 p.    plates, ports.    24 cm.

Biographies of Sister Mary of the Conception, Sister Mary Lumena, Sister Mary Bonsecours, Sister Mary Clement, and Mother Mary Anne of Jesus.

B.C. ARCHIVES

## 1731   Perry, M[artha] Eugenie
### 1881-1958

The girl in the silk dress and other stories. [Victoria, The author, 1931]

144 p.   20 cm.   Contents in part: Treasure of Leach River.

Fiction. A search for buried treasure in the days of the Leech River gold rush.

B.C. ARCHIVES

## 1732   Taylor, James Patton
### B. 1844

Pioneer life in California and British Columbia, dedicated to the Society of California Pioneers of San Francisco, by James P. Taylor . . .   [San Francisco?] 1931.

19 p.   23 cm.   Cover title.   Not seen.

BANCROFT LIBRARY CATALOGUE

## 1733   Victoria. Gordon Head School

Gordon Head School, 1891-1931. [Victoria, 1931?]

19, [3] 1.   28 cm.   Cover title.   Mimeographed.

A history.

B.C. ARCHIVES

## 1734   Wade, Mark Sweeten
### 1858-1929

The Overlanders of '62. Edited by John Hosie. Printed by authority of the Legislative Assembly. Victoria, Printed by Charles F. Banfield, 1931.

xiii, 174 p.   plates, ports.   25 cm.   (British Columbia. Provincial Archives. Memoir no. 9) Biographical and other notes: p. 158-174.

Largely based on five diaries, this book describes the passage of some one hundred and fifty people from the East, across the Rockies, to the Cariboo. It also briefly mentions other overland journeys to the Pacific during the period.

B.C. ARCHIVES

## 1735   Gellatly, Dorothy (Hewlett)
### 1856-1944

A bit of Okanagan history. Pen sketches by E. H. Emmens.   Kelowna, Kelowna Printing Company, 1932.

80 p.   illus.   22 cm.

Centennial (revised) edition: Kelowna, Printed by Orchard City Press & Calendar Co., 1958. 133 p.

B.C. ARCHIVES

## 1736   Hamilton, James H[erbert]
### 1879-1964

Western shores; narratives of the Pacific coast, by Capt. Kettle [pseud.]   Vancouver, Progress Publishing Company, 1932.

218 p.   plates.   21 cm.

Comprised of "many happenings of strange, romantic or peculiar character . . ." — fwd.

Also: 1933.

B.C. ARCHIVES

## 1737   Hazard, Joseph T[aylor]
### 1879-

Snow sentinels of the Pacific Northwest.   Seattle, Lowman & Hanford Co., 1932.

249 p.   plates.   24 cm.

Two chapters on the history and geography of the Mount Garibaldi region.

B.C. ARCHIVES

## 1738   Monro, A[lexander] S[tewart]
### 1872-1932

The medical history of British Columbia. [n.p., 1932?]

48 p.   illus., ports.   29 cm.   Reprinted from the *Canadian Medical Association journal*, v. 25-27, September 1931—August 1932.

Includes biographical information on some of the first doctors to practice in the province.

B.C. ARCHIVES

## 1739   Pacific historical review

Pacific historical review.   v. 1+ March 1932+ [n.p.] American Historical Association, Pacific Coast Branch.

v.   illus.   26 cm.   quarterly.   Indexed in *International index*. Table of contents.

B.C. ARCHIVES

## 1740   Reid, R[obie] L[ewis]
### 1866-1945

Alfred Waddington.   Ottawa, Printed for the Royal Society of Canada, 1932.

13-27 p.   25 cm.   Cover title. From: Royal Society of Canada. *Proceedings and transactions.* ser. 3, v. 26, sec. 2, 1932.

Primarily on Waddington's endeavours in the 1860's for the construction of a wagon road from the head of Bute Inlet to the interior gold fields and his scheme for a transcontinental railway.

B.C. ARCHIVES

**1741    Sage, Walter Noble**
1888-1963

The critical period of British Columbia history, 1866-1871.   [Glendale, California, 1932]

425-443 p.   26 cm.   Bibliographic footnotes. Reprinted from the *Pacific historical review*, v. 1, December 1932.   Not seen.

BANCROFT LIBRARY CATALOGUE

**1742    Day, J. Friend**
1887-1957

Our church in British Columbia.   Toronto, The Church of England in Canada, 1933.

16 p.   illus., ports.   23 cm.   (Our church in Canada, 5)   Cover title. At head of title: The restoration fund.

Mostly on events before 1900.

B.C. ARCHIVES

**1743    Duncan, Kenneth [Forrest]**
1881-1952

History of Cowichan.   [n.p., 1933?]

7 p.   31 cm.   Caption title. Read before the British Columbia Historical Association in Victoria, 9 June 1933, and before the Cowichan Historical Society, 15 June 1933.

Relates to the Cowichan Valley and district.

B.C. ARCHIVES

**1744    Morice, A[drian] G[abriel]**
1859-1938

Souvenirs d'un missionaire en Colombie Britannique.   Winnipeg, 1933.

374 p.   illus., facsims.   23 cm.   First written for the *Liberté* of Winnipeg.

B.C. ARCHIVES

**1745    Oliphant, J[ames] Orin**
1894-

The cattle trade on Puget Sound, 1858-1890. [n.p. 1933]

129-149 p.   26 cm.   Cover title. Reprinted from the *Agricultural history*, v. 7, July 1933.

Traces the development of trade in cattle and cattle products from Oregon and Washington to British Columbia.

B.C. ARCHIVES

**1746    Parson, C[harles] H[erbert]**
1867-1939

A short history of Mountain Lodge No. 11, A.F. & A.M., G.R.B.C., A.L. 5886-A.L. 5932.   [Golden, B.C., Golden Star Job Print, 1933?]

[12] p.   16 x 8 cm.   Cover title.

B.C. ARCHIVES

**1747    Pierce, William Henry**
1856-1948

From potlatch to pulpit; being the autobiography of the Rev. William Henry Pierce, native missionary to the Indian tribes of the northwest coast of British Columbia. Edited by Rev. J. P. Hicks.   Vancouver, The Vancouver Bindery Limited, 1933.

176 p.   illus., port.   20 cm.

Includes information on the Bella Coola and Tsimshian Indians.

B.C. ARCHIVES

**1748    Spinks, William Ward**
1851-1937

Tales of the British Columbia frontier. Illustrated by Edith MacLaren.   Toronto, Ryerson Press [c1933]

ix, 134 p.   illus., ports., map.   21 cm.

A recounting by the author of various happenings between 1884 and 1900 in which he participated or which were told to him.

B.C. ARCHIVES

**1749    Duncan, Eric**
1858-1944

Fifty-seven years in the Comox Valley. Courtenay, B.C., The Comox Argus Co., 1934.

61 p.   port.   20 cm.

B.C. ARCHIVES

**1750    Marshall, J. T.**

The development of public health in British Columbia.   [n.p., 1934]

359-368 p.   26 cm.   Reprinted from the *Canadian public health journal*, v. 25, 1934.

B.C. ARCHIVES

**1751    Parizeau, Henri Delpé**
1877-1954

The development of hydrography on the Pacific coast of Canada since the earliest discoveries. [Toronto] University of Toronto Press, 1934.

1259-1265 p. map, diagr. 24 cm. Cover title. Reprinted from: Pacific Science Association. *Proceedings of the Fifth Science Congress.* v. 2.

B.C. ARCHIVES

## 1752    Vancouver Club of Printing House Craftsmen

A brief historical account of the romance of British Columbia. [Vancouver] 1934.

93 p. illus., 3 plates (2 col.) map (on lining papers) 24 cm.

Includes a chapter on the introduction of printing into the province.

B.C. ARCHIVES

## 1753    Carroll, H[arry]
COMPILER    B. 1851

History of Nanaimo pioneers. Sponsored by the Nanaimo Pioneer Society. Nanaimo, Herald Presses, 1935.

71 p. ports. 16 cm.

Brief biographical notes on approximately one hundred and fifty early settlers.

B.C. ARCHIVES

## 1754    Chaldecott, F[rancis] M[illar]
1863-1949

Jericho and golf in the early days in Vancouver, 1892-1905. [n.p., 1935]

16 p. (incl. cover) illus. 21 cm.

B.C. ARCHIVES

## 1755    Fairbairn, A[rchibald] M[acdonald] D[uff]
1883-

Plays of the Pacific coast: Ebb-tide, The tragedy of Tanoo, A Pacific coast tragedy, The war drums of Skedans. Toronto, Samuel French (Canada) Limited, c1935.

111 p. plate, diagr. 19 cm. (Canadian playwright series)

Drama. The second play relates to the effect of the smallpox epidemic of 1863 on the Haida village of Tanoo in the Queen Charlotte Islands.

B.C. ARCHIVES

## 1756    Gibbon, John Murray
1875-1952

Steel of empire; the romantic history of the Canadian Pacific, the Northwest Passage today. Toronto, McClelland & Stewart [c1935]

423 p. illus., 43 plates (part col.) ports. (part col.) maps (part fold.; 1 on lining papers) facsims. 24 cm. Bibliography: p. [409]-411.

Also appeared under title: *The romantic history of the Canadian Pacific;* half title: Steel of empire (Toronto, McClelland & Stewart, 1935; New York, Tudor Publishing Co., 1937).

B.C. ARCHIVES

## 1757    Gosnell, R. [Edward]
1860-1931

The story of Hatley Park, residence of the late Hon. James Dunsmuir and Mrs. Dunsmuir of pioneer Vancouver Island family. Abridged from "Sixty years of progress," by the late R. W. [*sic*] Gosnell. [Victoria, Printed by Diggon-Hibben Ltd., n.d.]

[8] p. 21 cm. Caption title. Abridged from the portrait section of E. O. S. Scholefield's *A history of British Columbia.*

An account of the lives of James and Robert Dunsmuir, with only a brief reference to Hatley Park.

B.C. ARCHIVES

## 1758    Halliday, W[illiam] M[ay]
1866-1957

Potlatch and totem; and the recollections of an Indian agent. Illustrated from 30 original photographs by the author. London, J. M. Dent & Sons Ltd. [1935]

xvi, 240 p. plates. 23 cm.

Includes accounts of the customs of the Kwakiutl Indians during the late 1890's.

B.C. ARCHIVES

## 1759    Laing, Lionel Hassell
1905-

An unauthorized Admiralty court in British Columbia. Seattle, University of Washington Press, 1935.

8 p. (incl. cover) 26 cm. Cover title. Reprinted from the *Washington historical quarterly,* v. 26, 1935, p. 10-15.

Concerns the first Court of Vice-Admiralty which Sir James Douglas established in 1854 without authority from the Lords of the Admiralty.

B.C. ARCHIVES

## 1760    Murray, Margaret (L[ally])
1887-

St. Mary's of Lillooet; being a short record of the Anglican Church at the historic town of Lillooet, British Columbia, built in 1860. [Lillooet, The Bridge River-Lillooet News, 1935]

[8] p. (incl. cover) illus. 23 cm. Cover title.

B.C. ARCHIVES

**1761  New Westminster. St. Mary the Virgin**

70th anniversary of St. Mary the Virgin, Sapperton. Rev. Frank Plaskett, M.A., rector. [New Westminster, The Columbian Co., printers, 1935?]

32 p. (incl. advertisements)  illus., ports.  23 cm.

An historical sketch.

B.C. ARCHIVES

**1762  Steele, Harwood [Elmes Robert]**
1897-

Policing the Arctic; the story of the conquest of the Arctic by the Royal Canadian (formerly North-West) Mounted Police.  Toronto, Ryerson Press [1935]

390 p.  plates.  24 cm.

Briefly mentions police duties in British Columbia in connection with the Klondike gold discoveries, including an account of J. D. Moodie's journey.

Also: London, Jarrolds, 1936.

B.C. ARCHIVES

**1763  Sullivan, [Edward] Alan**
1868-1947

The Great Divide; a romance of the Canadian Pacific Railway.  Toronto, The Macmillan Company of Canada, 1935.

417 p.  21 cm.

The locale is the area around Yale and the story is "an attempt to recapture something of that period when . . . Sir John A. Macdonald's government in Ottawa embarked on the greatest railway ever conceived." — fwd.

B.C. ARCHIVES

**1764  Thomas, Edward Harper**

Chinook; a history and dictionary of the Northwest Coast trade jargon, the centuries-old trade language of the Indians of the Pacific; a history of its origin and its adoption and use by the traders, trappers, pioneers and early settlers of the Northwest Coast.  Portland, Oregon, Metropolitan Press, 1935.

179 p.  port. (on lining papers)  21 cm.  Books on the jargon: p. [48]-59.

B.C. ARCHIVES

**1765  Daniels, C[harles] H.**

A narrative history of the Terminal City Club Limited . . . established 1893, incorporated 1899; constitution and house rules; roster of membership. Vancouver, The 1936 Board of Directors, 1936.

110 p.  illus.  23 cm.

B.C. ARCHIVES

**1766  Duncan, Nora M. [(Dann)]**
1881-1946

The heroine of Moodyville; an epic of Burrard Inlet, 1883.  [n.p., 1936]

[4] p. (folder)  port.  26 cm.  Cover title. On p. [4]: Printed by kind permission of "Chatelaine."

The poem tells of the bravery of Mrs. John Peabody Patterson who, with a Squamish Indian, risked her life in crossing Burrard Inlet during a storm to nurse the wife of the lighthouse keeper at Point Atkinson.

B.C. ARCHIVES

**1767  Halminen, Matti**

Sointula; Kalevan Kansan ja Kanadan suomalaisten historiaa.  [Helsingissä] Kustantaja Mikko Ampuja, 1936.

143 p.  illus., ports.  20 cm.  Text in Finnish.

The story of the establishment and development of the Finnish colony of Sointula on Malcolm Island by one of its founders.  Also see entry 1993.

B.C. ARCHIVES

**1768  Quiett, Glenn Chesney**
1895-1936

Pay dirt; a panorama of American gold-rushes. New York, London, D. Appleton-Century Company, 1936.

xxv, 506 p.  illus., plates, ports., maps.  23 cm. Bibliography: p. 483-489. Chapter 8: Gold in British Columbia; the Fraser River and the Cariboo [p. 192-212]

B.C. ARCHIVES

**1769  Vancouver Club (Vancouver)**

Historical notes; constitution and house rules, list of members, amended to 31st May 1936. [Vancouver, The Clarke & Stuart Co., 1936]

64 p.  16 cm.

B.C. ARCHIVES

**1770  Veteran Steamboatmen's Association of the West**

11th Annual Reunion . . . to be held at Bonneville, Sunday, June 28, 1936.  [n.p., 1936]

[8] p. (incl. cover)  illus.  22 cm.  Cover title. Includes: The old steamer Beaver [by Capt. Frank J. Smith]

B.C. ARCHIVES

1771　Andrews, Clarence L[eroy]
1862-1948

Wrangell and the gold of the Cassiar; a tale of fur and gold in Alaska.　Seattle, Luke Tinker, c1937.

60 p.　illus., map.　22 cm.

On historical events to 1898 connected with the Stikine River.

B.C. ARCHIVES


1772　Bennett, William
1881-1949

Builders of British Columbia. With a foreword by Malcolm Bruce.　[Vancouver, Broadway Printers, 1937]

159 p.　illus., ports.　20 cm.

Traces the position of the working class and the development of unionism. The author was a member of the Communist Party of Canada.

B.C. ARCHIVES


1773　British Columbia historical quarterly

British Columbia historical quarterly.　v. 1+ January 1937+　Victoria, British Columbia Historical Association.

v.　illus.　25 cm.　Supersedes the association's *Annual report and proceedings.* Table of contents, index in each volume. Indexed in *Canadian index.* Last number appeared in 1958.

B.C. ARCHIVES


1774　Callahan, James Morton
B. 1864

American foreign policy in Canadian relations. New York, The Macmillan Company, 1937.

x, 576 p.　maps.　23 cm.　References at end of chapters.

Chapters on the Oregon question, the Bering Sea controversy, and the Alaska boundary settlement.

B.C. ARCHIVES


1775　Duncan, Eric
1858-1944

From Shetland to Vancouver Island; recollections of seventy-five years.　Edinburgh, Oliver and Boyd, 1937.

277 p.　port.　20 cm.

Reminiscences of pioneer days in the Comox district.

Third edition (enlarged): 1939. 304 p.

B.C. ARCHIVES


1776　Harvey, A[thelstan] G[eorge]
1884-1950

The mystery of Mount Robson.　[Victoria, 1937]

[207]-226 p.　plate.　25 cm.　Reprinted from the *British Columbia historical quarterly,* v. 1, 1937.

The title refers to the naming of Mount Robson.

B.C. ARCHIVES


1777　Kamloops. High School. Junior Historical Club

Kamloops, 1812-1937; a history.　Compiled and illustrated by the Junior Historical Club of the Kamloops High School under the direction of Mr. F. H. Johnson.　[Kamloops, 1937]

v, 102 p.　illus., fold. maps.　22 cm. Mimeographed. Bibliography: p. 99-100.

B.C. ARCHIVES


1778　Stott, William
1880-1955

The story of St. Andrew's United Church, North Vancouver, 1865-1937.　[North Vancouver, North Shore Press Limited, 1937?]

34 p.　illus., ports.　18 x 27 cm.　Cover title.

B.C. ARCHIVES


1779　Victoria. First United Church

Seventy-fifth anniversary, First United Church, Victoria, B.C., 1862-1937.　[Victoria, Colonist Presses, 1937?]

12 p.　ports.　24 cm.　Cover title.

An historical sketch.

B.C. ARCHIVES


1780　Alexander, John B.
COMPILER

Fifty years of Cascade Lodge, 1888-1938. [n.p., 1938?]

74 p.　plates, ports.　24 cm.

A history of a Masonic lodge in Vancouver.

B.C. ARCHIVES


1781　Anthony, Nina

An epic; with apologies to Longfellow. [n.p., n.d.]

sheet.　illus.　25 x 31 cm.　Negative offprint examined.

Records in verse of important incidents in the history of Squamish from 1874.

B.C. ARCHIVES

**1782    Banwell, Selwyn**
1880-

A frontier judge; British justice in the earliest days of farthest West.    Toronto, Rous & Mann Limited, 1938.

[6] 11-30 p.    port.    23 cm.

On the career of Judge Matthew Baillie Begbie.

Also appeared as an offprint from the *Canadian bar review*, v. 16, 1938, p. 550-565.

B.C. ARCHIVES

**1783    Bartley, George**
COMPILER   D. 1943

An outline history of Typographical Union No. 226, Vancouver, B.C., 1887-1938.    [Vancouver, Vancouver Typographical Union No. 226, 1938?]

64 p.    group ports.    23 cm.

B.C. ARCHIVES

**1784    Canada. Department of Transport**

A statutory history of the steam and electric railways of Canada, 1836-1937, with other data relevant to the operations of the Department of Transport. Compiled by Robert Dorman. Ottawa, 1938.

765 p.    26 cm.

Includes tables of cash and land subsidies.

B.C. ARCHIVES

**1785    Canada. Royal Commission on Dominion-Provincial Relations**

Report [and appendix]    Ottawa, 1938-40.

21 v.    tables.    30 cm. (v. 1 of appendix: 36 x 39 cm.)    At head of title of v. 1 of Report: . . . Public accounts inquiry. Chairman: Joseph Sirois. Report in 3 v. (printed in 1940) Appendix 1-[8] in 18 v. (printed in 1938-39) Appendix 1 includes appendix A-H, J-K.

Volume 2 includes a short history of the persistent claims of British Columbia for special subsidies and considerations from the federal government. Appendix 2, "British North America at Confederation," by Donald G. Creighton, is useful in assessing British Columbia's role in and contributions to the confederation movement. Scattered information, generally in the form of statistical tables, is found throughout the report and its appendices.

UNIVERSITY OF VICTORIA LIBRARY

**1786    Futcher, Winnifred M. (Hall)**
EDITOR

The great north road to the Cariboo. Illustrations from early photographs.    [Vancouver] Roy Wrigley Printing & Publishing Co., c1938.

113 p.    illus., plates, fold. map.    21 cm. Bibliography: p. 113.

History and description of the Cariboo.

B.C. ARCHIVES

**1787    Lamb, W[illiam] Kaye**
1904-

Early lumbering on Vancouver Island, 1844-1866. [Victoria, 1938]

[31]-53, [95]-121 p.    tables.    25 cm.    Cover title. Contents: pt. 1. 1844-1855. — pt. 2. 1855-1866. Reprinted from the *British Columbia historical quarterly*, v. 2, 1938.

B.C. ARCHIVES

**1788    McInnis, Alex[ander] P[atrick]**
1868-1946

Chronicles of the Cariboo, number one; being a true story of the first discovery of gold in the Cariboo district on the Horsefly River by Peter C. Dunlevey [*sic*] Written by Alex. P. McInnes [*sic*] Lillooet, Lillooet Publishers Limited, c1938.

iii, 27 p.    illus.    26 cm.    On cover: Dunlevy's discovery of gold on the Horsefly.

The story was told to the author in his youth by Dunlevy.

B.C. PROVINCIAL LIBRARY

**1789    Shiels, Archi[bald] W[illiamson]**
1878-

San Juan Islands; the Cronstadt of the Pacific, by Archie Shiels.    Juneau, Empire Printing Company, 1938.

275 p.    map.    24 cm.

Traces the San Juan boundary dispute and arbitration by the use of quoted material—letters, government documents, and extracts from periodicals, including newspapers.

B.C. ARCHIVES

**1790    Smyth, Fred J[oseph]**
1872-1949

Tales of the Kootenays. With historical sketches by the author and others.    Cranbrook, B.C., Printed in the office of The Courier, 1938.

205 p.    illus., ports.    22 cm.

Second edition with revision: 1942.

B.C. ARCHIVES

**1791    Trelawney-Ansell, E[dward] C[larence]**

I followed gold.    London, Peter Davies [1938]

320 p.    21 cm.

Has a few pages on the author's prospecting activities in British Columbia in 1896.

Also: New York, Le Furman, c1939.

## 1792    Victoria. Belmont United Church

Through the years, 1891-1938; Belmont United Church, Belmont Ave., and Pembroke St., Victoria, B.C. [Victoria? 1938]

22 p.    illus., ports.    23 cm.    Foreword signed in print: W. B. Wellwood, W. F. Emery, committee.

## 1793    Allan, Marjorie
### COMPILER

Christ Church Cathedral, 1889-1939. A short history compiled by Miss Marjorie Allan with the assistance of Major J. S. Matthews [and others. Vancouver, Printed by University Press, 1939?]

30 p.    illus., ports.    23 cm.

Revised edition: Vancouver, Price Printing Ltd., 1959? 36 p. Has added notes.

## 1794    McLaurin, C[olin] C[ampbell]
### 1854-1941?

Pioneering in western Canada; a story of the Baptists.    Calgary, Published by the author, 1939.

401 p.    plates, ports.    23 cm.    Errata slip.

A chapter on Baptist beginnings in British Columbia.

## 1795    Mary Theodore, Sister
### 1856-1951

Heralds of Christ, the King; missionary record of the North Pacific, 1837-1878.    New York, P. J. Kenedy & Sons, 1939.

xiv, 273 p.    plates, ports.    25 cm.

Contains information on the establishment of Roman Catholic missions in British Columbia.

## 1796    Morton, Arthur S[ilver]
### 1870-1945

A history of the Canadian West to 1870-71; being a history of Rupert's Land (The Hudson's Bay Company's territory) and of the North-west Territory (including the Pacific slope)    London, Thomas Nelson & Sons Ltd. [1939]

xiv, 987 p.    12 maps (part fold.)    24 cm.    Errata slip. Brief biographical notes: p. 933-942.

The book includes one chapter on the Pacific colonies as well as some information on British Columbia's entry into confederation.

## 1797    Ormsby, Margaret A[nchoretta]
### 1909-

The history of agriculture in British Columbia. [n.p., 1939]

61-72 p.    25 cm.    Caption title. Reprinted from *Scientific agriculture*, September 1939.

## 1798    Royal Engineers' Old Comrades Association (Vancouver)

The Royal Engineers; a record of their part in building British Columbia.    Vancouver [1939?]

27 p. (incl. advertisements)    illus., ports.    30 cm.

## 1799    Shippee, Lester Burrell
### 1879-1944

Canadian-American relations, 1849-1874.    New Haven, Yale University Press; Toronto, The Ryerson Press, 1939.

xi, 514 p.    maps (1 fold.; 1 on lining papers)    25 cm.    (The relations of Canada and the United States, a series of studies prepared under the direction of the Carnegie Endowment for International Peace, Division of Economics and History)    Extensive footnotes. Manuscript materials: p. 479-480. Chapter 11: The San Juan water boundary [p. 240-261]

## 1800    Vancouver. St. Paul's Church

St. Paul's Church, Vancouver, British Columbia; golden jubilee, 1889-1939.    [Vancouver, Wrigley Printing Co., 1939?]

31 p.    illus., plates, ports.    24 cm.    Cover title. At head of title: Pro Deo et Ecclesia.

## 1801    Canada. Army. 5th (B.C.) Coast Brigade, R.C.A.

History and tradition; a spur to esprit de corps. Victoria [Colonist Presses] 1940.

22 p.    16 cm.    Cover title.

**1802    Horton, Edward W.**

Sharon United Church golden jubilee anniversary (1890-1940) Sunday, February 25th, 1940, Murrayville, British Columbia.    [Langley, Langley Advance, 1940]

15 p.    illus., port.    25 cm.

B.C. ARCHIVES


**1803    Lamb, W[illiam] Kaye**
1904-

"Empress to the Orient."    [Victoria, 1940?]

29-50, 79-110 p.    plates, diagr., tables.    25 cm. Cover title. Reprinted from the *British Columbia historical quarterly*, v. 4, January, and April 1940.

An account of the original "Empress" liners and a history of the trans-Pacific service to 1913.

B.C. ARCHIVES


**1804    Morrell, W[illiam] P[arker]**
1899-

The gold rushes.    London, Adam and Charles Black, 1940.

xi, 426 p.    maps (part fold.)    23 cm.    (The pioneer histories. Edited by V. T. Harlow, and J. A. Williamson)    Contains a section entitled: Fraser River and Cariboo [p. 119-135]

B.C. ARCHIVES


**1805    Munday, W[alter] A[lfred] Don**
1888-1950

"Stanley Smith's travels" in the Coast Mountains, 1893.    [n.p.] 1940.

159-168 p.    plate.    23 cm.    Cover title. Reprinted from the *Canadian alpine journal*, v. 27, 1940.

The purpose of Stanley Smith's trip was to search for two men who were lost while making their way from Squamish to Chilcotin.

B.C. ARCHIVES


**1806    The Pacific Coast Fire Insurance Company**

Our fifty years, 1890-1940; the romantic story of Vancouver from pioneer days, and a brief history of our company during the last half century. Vancouver [Printed by Rose, Cowan & Latta Limited, c1940]

22 p.    plates, ports.    26 cm.    On t.p.: A brochure

B.C. ARCHIVES


**1807    Sage, Walter Noble**
1888-1963

John Foster McCreight, the first premier of British Columbia.    Ottawa, Printed for the Royal Society of Canada, 1940.

173-185 p.    25 cm.    Cover title. Reprinted from: Royal Society of Canada. *Proceedings and transactions*. ser. 3, v. 34, sec. 2, 1940.

B.C. ARCHIVES


**1808    Waites, K[enneth] A[rthur]**
EDITOR

The first fifty years; Vancouver high schools, 1890-1940.    [Vancouver, 1940?]

160 p.    illus., ports., map, facsims.    24 cm.

Also: 1942?    Also: 1943.

B.C. ARCHIVES


**1809    British Columbia District Telegraph & Delivery Co., Limited**

1891-1941, fifty years of service; a brief history of our company with reproductions of early Vancouver, from original sources. Vancouver [1941?]

[20] p. (incl. plates)    illus., 2 plates, ports., facsims.    25 cm.

B.C. ARCHIVES


**1810    Carrothers, W[illiam] A[lexander]**
1889-1951

The British Columbia fisheries. With a foreword by H. A. Innis.    Toronto, The University of Toronto Press, 1941.

xv, 136 p.    tables.    24 cm.    [Political economy series, no. 10]    Chapter 2: The fisheries to 1900 [p. 5-16]

Throughout the book, there is considerable statistical information for the pre-1900 period.

UNIVERSITY OF WASHINGTON LIBRARY


**1811    Ford, Clellan S[tearns]**
1909-

Smoke from their fires; the life of a Kwakiutl chief. New Haven, Published for the Institute of Human Relations by Yale University Press, 1941.

248 p.    3 plates (part col.) port., map.    24 cm.

The life of Charles Nowell as told to an anthropologist. Nowell was born at Fort Rupert in 1870.

B.C. ARCHIVES

**1812    Ireland, Willard E[rnest]**
1914-

Early flour-mills in British Columbia, by Willard E. Ireland and F. W. Laing.    [Victoria, 1941]

89-109, 191-214 p.    table.    25 cm.    Contents: pt. 1. Vancouver Island and the lower mainland, by Willard E. Ireland. — pt. 2. The upper country, by F. W. Laing. Reprinted from the *British Columbia historical quarterly*, v. 5, 1941.

Traces the development of the flour-milling industry up to the end of the colonial period in 1871.

B.C. ARCHIVES


**1813    Morris, Wilfred H.**

Captain William Oliver, a fisher of men; a biographical sketch.    Trujillo, Peru, Casa Evangélica de Publicaciones [c1941]

117 p.    port.    20 cm.

Most of the book is comprised of an account by Captain Oliver of his Methodist missionary work along the B.C. coast.

B.C. ARCHIVES


**1814    Munday, W[alter] A[lfred] Don**
1888-1950

Early explorations in the Coast Mountains. [n.p.] 1941.

65-80 p.    plates, port.    23 cm.    Cover title. Reprinted from the *Canadian alpine journal*, v. 28, 1941.

Concerns William Downie's exploring expeditions during the years 1858-61, with comments upon passages from Downie's *Hunting for Gold*.

B.C. ARCHIVES


**1815    Pharmaceutical Association of the Province of British Columbia**

50 years of progress in pharmacy, 1891 to 1941; golden jubilee souvenir.    [Vancouver, The Western Druggist, 1941]

80 p. (incl. advertisements)    illus., ports.    30 cm. Cover title.

B.C. ARCHIVES


**1816    Victoria. St. Andrew's Church**

St. Andrew's Church, Victoria, B.C., commemorating the seventy-fifth anniversary, 1866-1941.    [Victoria, The Colonist Presses, 1941]

16 p.    illus., ports.    18 cm.

An historical sketch with the same early historical information as is contained in entries 1631 and 1816.

B.C. ARCHIVES


**1817    Woods, J[ohn] J[ex]**
1895-

History and development of the Agassiz-Harrison Valley.    [Agassiz, B.C., Printed by the Agassiz-Harrison Advance, 1941]

68 p.    illus.    23 cm.

The second edition was published in 1958 under title: *The Agassiz-Harrison Valley; history and development* (Sidney, B.C., Published for the Kent Centennial Committee by the Peninsula Printing Co.). In 113 pages.

B.C. ARCHIVES


**1818    Woodsworth, Charles J[ames]**
1909-

Canada and the Orient; a study in international relations. Issued under the auspices of the Canadian Institute of International Affairs.    Toronto, Macmillan, 1941.

xii, 321 p.    tables.    23 cm.    Bibliography: p. 308-313.

Two extensive chapters on early Chinese and Japanese immigration.

B.C. ARCHIVES


**1819    Angus, H[enry] F[orbes]**
EDITOR    1891-

British Columbia and the United States; the North Pacific slope from fur trade to aviation, by F. W. Howay, W. N. Sage, and H. F. Angus.    Toronto, Ryerson Press, 1942.

xv, 408 p.    maps (1 on lining papers)    25 cm. (The relations of Canada and the United States, a series of studies prepared under the direction of the Carnegie Endowment for International Peace, Division of Economics and History)    Bibliographic footnotes.

Includes chapters on the settlement of British Columbia (1849-62), confederation, the San Juan boundary question (1845-72), railway building (1871-1915), American mining advances (1864-1910), lumbering and fishing (1860-1913), fur seals, the Klondike, and the Alaska boundary.

B.C. ARCHIVES


**1820    Carr, Emily**
1871-1945

The book of Small.    Toronto, London, Oxford University Press, 1942.

viii, 245 p.    port.    24 cm.    Contents: [pt. 1] The book of Small. — [pt. 2] A little town and a little girl.

Reminiscences of the author's childhood in Victoria.

Both parts were published separately in 1952 (copyrighted in 1951) with forewords by Ira Dilworth in the "Clark Irwin Canadian classics" series:

*The book of Small* (with the chapter "A cup of tea" from the second part), and *A little town and a little girl* (without the chapter "A cup of tea").

## 1821    Grimm, Ferdinand
### 1806-1895

Northwest water boundary; report of the experts summoned by the German Emperor as arbitrator under Articles 34-42 of the Treaty of Washington of May 8, 1871, preliminary to his award dated October 21, 1872. Edited, with a translation by [David] Hunter Miller.    Seattle, The University of Washington, 1942.

vii, 75 p.    map.    26 cm.    (University of Washington publications in the social sciences, v. 13, no. 1, p. 1-75. January, 1942)    On p. iv: By the courtesy of the German Foreign Office, a photostatic copy of the report of the experts was furnished to the Department of State in the summer of 1938, with permission to publish the text; it is that report (of eighty-five manuscript pages) which is now for the first time printed, with translation. . . . the report dated September 30, 1872, and signed by Dr. Grimm (pp. 2-29), is followed (pp. 30-67) by the divergent opinion of Dr. Goldschmidt, of September 10, to which is appended a brief account by Dr. Grimm, dated September 26, of conferences of the experts (pp. 68-69); finally (pp. 70-73) come observations by Dr. Grimm of the date of the report, on the opinion of Dr. Goldschmidt. Professor Kiepert concurred throughout with Dr. Grimm; and the view of Dr. Grimm and Professor Kiepert were adopted by the German Emperor in his award. Citations of law books by Dr. Goldschmidt: p. 75.

## 1822    Longstaff, F[rederick] V[ictor]
### 1879-1961

Esquimalt naval base; a history of its work and its defences.    [Vancouver, The Clarke & Stuart Co., c1942]

189 p.    plates.    22 cm.

## 1823    Rome, David
### 1910-

The first two years; a record of the Jewish pioneers on Canada's Pacific coast, 1858-1860.    Montreal, H. M. Caiserman, 1942.

120 p.    21 cm.

## 1824    Vancouver. St. Giles United Church

Golden jubilee anniversary, 1892-1942; St. Giles United Church, formerly Mt. Pleasant Presbyterian Church, Vancouver, British Columbia. [Vancouver, 1942]

48 p.    illus., ports.    24 cm.    Cover title.

## 1825    Celista. Celista School

Celista pioneers.    [Kamloops, Kamloops Sentinel Ltd., 1943]

16 p.    illus., group ports.    24 cm.    Cover title.

## 1826    Fraser, Donald A[ndrew]
### 1875-1948

Centenary; a collection of verses, arranged in celebration of the one hundredth birthday of the city of Victoria, B.C., 1843-1943.    [Victoria, The author, 1943?]

38 p.    24 cm.

The poems include descriptions of James Douglas and Richard Blanshard.

Second edition, revised: 1945. 39 p.

## 1827    Melrose, Robert
### 1828?-1898

The diary of Robert Melrose. Edited with an introduction and notes by W. Kaye Lamb. [Victoria, 1943?]

119-134, 199-218, 283-295 p.    25 cm.    Cover title. Reprinted from the *British Columbia historical quarterly*, v. 7, April, July, and October 1943.

A brief chronology of events on Vancouver Island from August 1852 to July 1857 with emphasis on shipping movements. During the period of the diary, Robert Melrose was assigned to Craigflower Farm as a labourer of the Puget Sound Agricultural Company.

## 1828    Miller, [David] Hunter
### 1875-1934

San Juan archipelago; study of the joint occupation of San Juan Island.    [Bellow Falls, Vermont, Printed at the Wyndham Press, c1943]

203 p.    fold. map.    26 cm.    Relevant papers: p. [10]-11. In pref.: This monograph . . . is substantially my draft of notes on Joint occupation of San Juan Island, for inclusion in Volume 8 of Treaties and other international acts of the United States of America . . .

An extensively documented work, accenting the years 1846-69.

**1829 Swanson, Robert E.**

Rhymes of a lumberjack; a second book of verse concerning the trials and tribulations, lives and ways of the loggers living and working in the great Northwest of America. Illustrated by Bert Bushell. Toronto, Thomas Allen Limited, 1943.

94 p.   illus. (1 double)   20 cm.   Contents in part: The wrecking of the "Beaver." — A logger's dictionary [p. 83-94]

The poem is also included in the author's *Complete poems* which appeared in 1946. This volume was comprised of separately printed works published between 1942-5.

B.C. ARCHIVES

**1830 Crimont, Joseph Raphael**
B. 1858

Sketch of the martyrdom of Archbishop Charles John Seghers.   [Victoria, Printed by Diggon-Hibben Limited, 1944?]

30 p.   illus., ports.   23 cm.   On cover: Victoria fides.

B.C. ARCHIVES

**1831 Grant, Rena V[ictoria]**

The Chinook jargon, past and present. [n.p., 1944]

259-276 p.   26 cm.   Caption title. Reprinted from the *California folklore quarterly*, v. 2, October 1944.

B.C. ARCHIVES

**1832 Lamb, W[illia]m Kaye**
COMPILER   1904-

A bibliography of the printed writings of Frederic William Howay. Compiled, with a biographical introduction, by W. Kaye Lamb.   [Victoria, 1944]

27-51 p.   25 cm.   Cover title. Reprinted from the *British Columbia historical quarterly*, v. 8, January 1944.

VANCOUVER PUBLIC LIBRARY

**1833 Robinson, Noel**
1881?-1966

History of the Art, Historical and Scientific Association, Vancouver's first cultural association. [Vancouver, Art, Historical and Scientific Association, 1944]

20 p. (incl. cover)   ports.   23 cm.

B.C. ARCHIVES

**1834 Vancouver. St. Paul's Hospital**

"Counting the years unto the year of jubilee," Leviticus xxv:x; commemorating the fiftieth anniversary of St. Paul's Hospital, 1894-1944, Vancouver, British Columbia.   [Vancouver, 1944]

85 p.   illus., ports.   31 cm.

Has a small section on the hospital's founding.

B.C. ARCHIVES

**1835 Andrew, F[rederick] W[illiam]**
1879-1957

The story of Summerland.   Penticton, The Penticton Herald [1945]

55 p.   map.   23 cm.

B.C. ARCHIVES

**1836 British Columbia digest**

British Columbia digest.   v. 1+ January 1945+ Quesnel, Cariboo Digest Ltd.

v.   illus.   25 cm.   bi-monthly.   Title varies: 1945-46 as *Cariboo digest;* 1946—spring 1948 as *Cariboo and northern B.C. digest;* summer 1948—June 1951 as *Cariboo and Northwest digest;* July 1951—December 1960 as *Northwest digest;* v. 17, no. 1 (January 1961+) as *British Columbia digest.* Not indexed.

Popularly written articles on pioneer days, with special emphasis on the history of the Cariboo.

B.C. ARCHIVES

**1837 Goodfellow, Florence [Eliza Margaret Askin (Agassiz)]**
1854-1940

Memories of pioneer life in British Columbia. Wenatchee, Washington, 1945.

43 p.   group port.   22 cm.

Written in the early thirties, the work covers the years 1862-76.

B.C. ARCHIVES

**1838 Graham, Clara [Lucy (Drake)]**
1860?-1957

Fur and gold in the Kootenays.   [Vancouver, Wrigley Printing Co., c1945]

xiii, 206 p.   illus., ports., map.   21 cm. References: p. 205-206.

B.C. ARCHIVES

**1839 Grant, Rena V[ictoria]**

Chinook jargon.   [n.p., 1945]

225-233 p.   26 cm.   Cover title. Reprinted from the *International journal of American linguistics,* v. 11, October 1945.

A paper on syntax and grammar which includes some historical information.

B.C. ARCHIVES

## 1840 Greater America . . .

Greater America; essays in honor of Herbert Eugene Bolton. [Edited by Dr. Adele Ogden and Professor Engel Sluiter]   Berkeley and Los Angeles, University of California Press, 1945.

ix, 723 p.   port., maps (part fold.)   23 cm. Bibliographic notes at end of each essay.

Includes an essay by Donald Curtis Davidson entitled "The Alaskan-Canadian boundary."

B.C. ARCHIVES

## 1841 Hacking, Norman R.

"Steamboat 'round the bend."   [Victoria, Printed by Charles F. Banfield, 1945]

26 p.   plate.   25 cm.   Cover title. Caption title: "Steamboat 'round the bend": American steamers on the Fraser River in 1858. Reprinted from the *British Columbia historical quarterly,* v. 8, October 1944.

B.C. ARCHIVES

## 1842 Holmes, Marjorie C[olquhoun]
### COMPILER

Royal commissions and commissions of inquiry under the "Public Inquiries Act" in British Columbia, 1872-1942; a checklist.   [Victoria, King's printer, 1945]

68 p.   25 cm.

Includes entries for manuscripts.

UNIVERSITY OF VICTORIA LIBRARY

## 1843 Kirksey, C[harles] W[alter Poston]

A parish history of Grande Prairie and Shuswap. [n.p., 1945?]

32 p.   23 cm.   Cover title.

The name of Grande Prairie was changed to Westwold in 1926.

B.C. ARCHIVES

## 1844 Roddan, Andrew
### 1883-1948

The church in the modern city; the story of three score years of practical Christian service, 1885-1945, by Rev. Andrew Roddan, First United Church, Vancouver, B.C.   [Vancouver, Dunsmuir Printing Co., 1945?]

61 p.   illus., ports.   23 cm.

Includes a few pages on the early Methodist, Congregationalist, and Presbyterian congregations in Vancouver.

B.C. ARCHIVES

## 1845 Vancouver. City Archives

Linking the Atlantic to the Pacific; ocean to ocean. Montreal greets Vancouver 23rd May 1887. [Vancouver, Wrigley Printing Co., 1945]

34, [1] p.   illus., ports., map (on inside cover) 23 cm.   Cover title. The all red route around the world, 1492-1887 [by James Skitt Matthews]; p. 25-[35]

Published on the occasion of the presentation to the city of Vancouver of the first locomotive to bring a through passenger train from Montreal to Vancouver, the work contains addresses and observations made when this first train reached Vancouver in 1887.

B.C. ARCHIVES

## 1846 Atlantic Mutual Insurance Company

Pioneer of the Pacific.   [n.p., Printed by William E. Rudge's Sons, 1946]

11 p.   illus.   18 cm.   (Cargoes, no. 23)   Cover title.

The story of the steamer "Beaver."

B.C. ARCHIVES

## 1847 Canada. Army. British Columbia Regiment

A short history of the British Columbia regiment, the "Dukes."   [n.p., n.d.]

[8] p.   16 cm.

Offers little historical information.

Second edition: 1953. 11 p.

B.C. ARCHIVES

## 1848 Cousland, P. A. C[lyde]

Early medicine of Vancouver Island.   [n.p., 1946]

13 p.   21 cm.   Cover title. Reprinted from the *Canadian Medical Association journal,* v. 55, 1946, p. 393-398.

Concerns the years 1778-1871; mentions early hospitals.

B.C. ARCHIVES

## 1849 Grant, Rena V[ictoria]

Alphonse Pinart and the Chinook jargon. [n.p., 1946]

277-297 p.   26 cm.   Caption title. Reprinted from the *California folklore quarterly,* v. 5, July 1946.

Concerns Pinart's manuscript "Dictionnaire du jargon tchinouk" (1849), the vocabulary of which is reproduced.

B.C. ARCHIVES

## 1850    Hacking, Norman R.

"Steamboating on the Fraser in the 'Sixties."
[Victoria, Printed by Charles F. Banfield, 1946]

41 p.   plates, facsim.   25 cm.   Cover title.
Appendix: Fraser River steamers, 1859-1870.
Reprinted from the *British Columbia historical
quarterly*, v. 10, 1946, p. 1-41.

B.C. ARCHIVES

## 1851    Hood, Robert Allison
1880-1958

Ballads of the Pacific Northwest; its discovery and
settlement.   Toronto, The Ryerson press [1946]

xii, 170 p.   illus. (1 col.)   21 cm.   Contents in
part: Cariboo days. — The rape of the boot. —
Walter Moberly. — Cariboo Cameron's pledge. —
Moriturus. — The camels on the Cariboo Road.

Poetry. "The rape of the boot" describes an incident
during Walter Moberly's exploration of the Fraser
canyon. The reflections of the last of the Cariboo
Road camels are given in "Moriturus." Both
poems also appear in the author's *Vignettes of
Vancouver* (1954), the latter poem under the title
"The last camel."

Reprinted in 1947.

B.C. ARCHIVES

## 1852    MacDermot, J[ohn] H[enry]
1883-

J. S. Helmcken, M.R.C.P. (Lond.), L.S.A.
[n.p., 1946]

13 p.   21 cm.   Caption title. Reprinted from the
*Canadian Medical Association journal*, v. 55, 1946,
p. 166-171.

A biographical sketch.

B.C. ARCHIVES

## 1853    Martin, Fredericka [I.]

The hunting of the silver fleece; epic of the fur seal.
New York, Greenberg [c1946]

xxiii, 328 p.   plates, port.   21 cm.   Reference
list: p. 309-319.

B.C. ARCHIVES

## 1854    Mary Dorothea, Sister

The tenth decade; a dramatic pageant
commemorating the one hundredth anniversary of
the founding of the Diocese of Victoria by Sister
Mary Dorothea, Sister of Saint Ann.   [Victoria,
Jacobus, 1946]

1 v.   illus., port., map.   23 cm.   On t.p.: . . . given
at the Royal Theatre, Victoria, B.C., July 31, 1946.

This pageant, with musical background, pays
"tribute to the builders of Catholicity of the Pacific
Coast of Canada and Alaska." — introd.

B.C. ARCHIVES

## 1855    [Nesbitt, James Knight]
1908-

A message to the people of St. John's Church,
Victoria, B.C.   [Victoria, Printed by Diggon-
Hibben Limited, 1946]

[9] p.   illus.   29 cm.   Cover title. At head of text:
St. John's of Victoria; past history, present activities,
future hopes.

B.C. ARCHIVES

## 1856    New Denver. Elementary School

New Denver, Eldorado of the past, by pupils of
Grade VII and VIII of the New Denver Elementary
School.   [Rossland, The Miner, 1946]

[19] p.   illus.   23 cm.   Cover title.

Republished by the New Denver Centennial
Committee in 1958.

B.C. ARCHIVES

## 1857    Runnalls, F[rank] E.

A history of Prince George. With a foreword by
Harry G. Perry.   [Vancouver, Wrigley Printing
Company] c1946.

xiv, 197 p.   illus., ports., maps, plans.   21 cm.
List of books consulted: p. 185-187.

B.C. ARCHIVES

## 1858    Sullivan, [Edward] Alan
1868-1947

Cariboo Road.   Toronto, Thomas Nelson and
Sons Limited [1946]

311 p.   21 cm.

Fiction. In 1862 a family travels from California to
the Cariboo. Much of the novel is based on historic
incidents and characters in the Cariboo in the days
of Judge Begbie and Billy Barker.

B.C. ARCHIVES

## 1859    Thorington, J[ames] Monroe
1894-

The Purcell Range of British Columbia.   New
York, The American Alpine Club, 1946.

152 p.   illus., plates, maps (1 in pocket)   24 cm.
Bibliography: p. 142-145.

Besides the author's accounts of his mapping and
exploring trips in the summers of 1928-33, the book
includes three chapters on the region's early fur
traders, surveyors, prospectors, and mountain
climbers. It also has some information on early
voyaging on the upper Columbia River.

B.C. ARCHIVES

1860 Walter, Margaret (Shaw)

Early days among the Gulf Islands of British Columbia. [Victoria, Printed by Diggon-Hibben Ltd., 1946]

67 p. 20 cm.

Comprised of the author's reminiscences and extracts from published sources.

Second edition: Victoria, Hebden Printing Co., 1958? 67 p. plates.

B.C. ARCHIVES

1861 Abraham, Dorothy [E.]

Romantic Vancouver Island; Victoria yesterday and today. Cover designed and donated by Bettie Dunnell. [Victoria, Acme Press, 1947]

118 p. illus., map. 23 cm.

Second edition: Victoria, Diggon-Hibben, 1949.
Third edition: Victoria, Diggon-Hibben, 1953.
Fourth edition: Victoria, Acme-Buckle Printing, 1964.

B.C. ARCHIVES

1862 Bone, P[eter] Turner
1859-1947?

When the steel went through; reminiscences of a railroad pioneer. Toronto, MacMillan, 1947.

180 p. plates, port., facsim. 22 cm.

Three chapters (p. 69-119) cover the author's life as an engineer in the C.P.R.'s Mountain Division, 1884-6.

B.C. ARCHIVES

1863 Carmichael, W[illiam] M.

These sixty years, 1887-1947; being the story of First Baptist Church, Vancouver, B.C. [Vancouver, Capitol Printers Ltd., 1947]

55 p. plates, ports. 20 cm. On t.p.: Diamond jubilee celebration.

B.C. ARCHIVES

1864 Chase, W[illiam] H[enry]
1874-

Reminiscences of Captain Billie Moore. Kansas City, Missouri, Burton Publishing Company [c1947]

236 p. port. 21 cm.

William Moore (1854-1945) navigated some of the great rivers of the Northwest, including the Fraser, Stikine, Nass, and Skeena.

B.C. ARCHIVES

1865 Doe, Ernest
COMPILER

History of Salmon Arm, 1885-1912. [Salmon Arm, B.C., Printed by the Salmon Arm Observer, 1947]

83 p. illus., ports. 23 cm.

Includes biographical information.

B.C. ARCHIVES

1866 Faessler, Carl
1895-1957

Cross-index to the maps and illustrations of the Geological Survey and the Mines Branch (Bureau of Mines) of Canada, 1843-1946 (incl.) Quebec, Laval University, 1947.

524 p. 28 cm. Mimeographed. Author and subject index: p. 119-522.

Supplement (1946-56): 1956.

B.C. ARCHIVES

1867 Green, George
1872-1955

History of Burnaby and vicinity. [North Vancouver, Printed by Schoemaker, McLean & Veitch, 1947]

233 p. illus., ports., plans. 23 cm.

B.C. ARCHIVES

1868 Hacking, Norman R.

British Columbia steamship days, 1870-1883. [Victoria, Printed by Don McDiarmid, 1947]

69-111 p. plates. 25 cm. Cover title. Appendix contains steamer statistics. Reprinted from the *British Columbia historical quarterly,* v. 11, April 1947.

Relates to the steamboats which navigated Burrard Inlet and the Fraser, Stikine, and Thompson rivers.

B.C. ARCHIVES

1869 Kaslo. Kaslo Elementary School

The early history of Kaslo; a booklet compiled by Grades III and IV pupils of Kaslo School, 1947. [Rossland, Printed by The Rossland Miner, 1947]

[24] p. illus., ports. 23 cm. Cover title.

B.C. ARCHIVES

1870 Kidd, Honor M.

Pioneer doctor, John Sebastian Helmcken. [n.p., 1947?]

419-461 p. illus., ports., map, facsim. 26 cm. Caption title. At head of title: The William Osler medal essay. Reprinted from the *Bulletin of the history of Medicine,* v. 21, July-August 1947. Includes short bibliography.

A biographical account.

## 1871 McKelvie, B[ruce] A[listair]
### 1889-1960

Fort Langley; outpost of Empire. Frontispiece by George H. Southwell, decorations by C. P. Connorton. [Vancouver] Vancouver Daily Province, 1947.

ix, 98 p. illus., maps (on lining papers) 27 cm. Authorities consulted: p. 96-98.

Mostly concerned with fur-trade days.

Reprinted in 1957 by Thomas Nelson and Sons, Toronto.

## 1872 Moir, George T[homas]
### 1871-1955

Sinners and saints; a true story of early days in the farthest West, by an old timer, written and told by himself. [Victoria, Printed by G. L. Wooding, n.d.]

165 p. plates, ports. 22 cm. Mimeographed and offset. Probably written in 1947.

## 1873 Nelson. Nelson Jubilee Committee

Nelson, British Columbia, golden jubilee, 1897-1947; souvenir programme, "fifty years of progress." [Nelson, Printed by the Nelson Daily News, 1947]

28 p. (incl. advertisements) illus., ports. 28 cm.

Includes: "History of Nelson, British Columbia," by Ruth Haslam.

## 1874 Robinson, Leigh Burpee

Esquimalt, "place of shoaling water." Illustrated by B. Digby Robinson. Victoria, Quality Press, printers, 1947.

128 p. illus. 23 cm. Authorities consulted: p. 127-128.

Primarily concerned with the history of Esquimalt during the early days of settlement until about 1870. It has a chapter on the British naval vessels in the harbour during this period.

Second edition: 1948.

## 1875 Scott, Robert C[lyde]
### 1880?-1960

My Captain Oliver; a story of two missionaries on the British Columbia coast. Toronto, The United Church of Canada [c1947]

xiv, 200 p. plates, ports., maps (on lining paper) 20 cm.

Relates in part to the period in which the Methodist mission boat "Glad Tidings," captained by William Oliver, operated in coastal waters. One of the main sources of information was the log of the mission boat which was begun in 1884.

## 1876 Alcock, F[rederick] J[ames]
### 1888-

A century in the history of the geological survey of Canada. Ottawa, Cloutier, 1948.

vii, 94 p. illus. 23 cm. (Canada. National Museum. Special contribution, 47-1)

A short, illustrated history of geological survey work, which includes chapters on A. R. Selwyn and G. M. Dawson.

## 1877 Barnes, Harry D[unford]
### 1869-1952

Early history of Hedley Camp. [Victoria, Printed by Don McDiarmid, 1948]

103-125 p. 25 cm. Cover title. Reprinted from the *British Columbia historical quarterly,* v. 12, 1948.

History of a gold-mining town in the Similkameen Valley.

Also in: Okanagan Historical Society. *Twelfth report.* v. 4, 1948, p. 67-88.

## 1878 Buckland, F[rank] M[organ]
### 1873-1953

Ogopogo's vigil; a history of Kelowna and district. [n.p., c1948]

111 l. illus., maps. 28 cm. Mimeographed.

A history of the Okanagan Lake district from exploration days to 1905.

## 1879 Holliday, C[harles] W[illiam]
### 1870-1955

The valley of youth. Caldwell, Idaho, Caxton Printers, 1948.

357 p. plates (1 col.) map (on lining papers) 25 cm.

The author's reminiscences of life in the Okanagan during the 1890's.

**1880    Hopper, Alfred E[dward]**
1870-

Composite cargo; a unique collection of poems and prose pieces, covering many years of experience and thinking.    [Ottawa] Tower Books, 1948.

43 p.    illus.    23 cm.    Contents in part: S.S. Beaver. — The prospector. — Some recollections of '98.

B.C. ARCHIVES


**1881    Longstaff, F[rederick] V[ictor]**
1879-1961

Historical notes on Glacier House.    [n.p., n.d.]

[4] p. (folder)    23 cm.    Caption title.

A longer article with the same title appeared in the *Canadian alpine journal,* v. 31, 1948, p. 195-200.

B.C. ARCHIVES


**1882    McCowan, Dan[iel]**
1882-1956

Hill-top tales.    Illustrated from photographs by the author and others.    Toronto, Macmillan, 1948.

xi, 266 p.    plates, ports.    23 cm.    A short bibliography: p. 259-260.

Includes information on the explorers and pioneers of the Rockies.

B.C. ARCHIVES


**1883    McDonald, (Mrs.) J.R.**

Baptist missions in western Canada, 1873-1948, by Mrs. J. R. McDonald.    Edmonton, The Baptist Union of Western Canada, 1948.

59 p.    illus., ports., fold. map.    23 cm.    Sources of information: p. [5]

B.C. ARCHIVES


**1884    MacEwan, [John Walter] Grant**
1902-

The sodbusters.    Toronto, Thomas Nelson & Sons [1948]

240 p.    col. front., illus., ports.    22 cm.

Includes biographical sketches of Joseph Greaves, Thomas Ellis, Norman Lee, and Clement Cornwall.

B.C. ARCHIVES


**1885    Maiden, Cecil**

Lighted journey; the story of the B.C. Electric. [Vancouver, The Public Information Department, British Columbia Electric Company, c1948]

170 p.    plates, ports.    24 cm.

B.C. ARCHIVES


**1886    Matthews, J[ames] S[kitt]**
1878-

The naming and opening of Stanley Park, 27 September 1888, and appointment of first Park Commission; a tribute from the citizens of Vancouver to the sixty-seven park commissioners who have served in that capacity during the years 1888 to 1948.    Vancouver, City Archives, 1948.

11 p. (incl. cover)    23 cm.    Cover title.

An address delivered to the Board of Park commissioners, 27 September 1948.

B.C. ARCHIVES


**1887    Pettit, Sydney G[eorge]**
1907-

Matthew Baillie Begbie.    [Victoria, Printed by Don McDiarmid, 1948]

1-14, 113-148, 187-210, 273-294 p.    port.    25 cm. Cover title. Reprinted from the *British Columbia historical quarterly,* v. 11, January, April, July, and October 1947.

B.C. ARCHIVES


**1888    Rickard, T[homas] A[rthur]**
1864-1953

Historic backgrounds of British Columbia. Vancouver, Printed for the author by the Wrigley Printing Company Limited [c1948]

xiii, 358 p.    plates, ports., maps.    21 cm.

One chapter is concerned with the period after settlement.

B.C. ARCHIVES


**1889    Souvenir book . . .**

Souvenir book; centenary of the Diocese of Victoria, British Columbia.    Nanaimo, Printed by the Acme Press Ltd. [n.d.]

150 p.    illus., ports.    23 x 31 cm.    Cover title. Centenary souvenir issue of the *Torch,* v. 7, no. 9.

Includes short biographical and historical sketches.

B.C. ARCHIVES


**1890    Cavers, Anne S.**

Our school of nursing, 1899 to 1949. [Vancouver, Printed by Ward & Phillips Ltd., 1949]

89 p.    illus., ports., tables.    26 cm.

A brief history of the School of Nursing of the Vancouver General Hospital.

B.C. ARCHIVES

**1891   Hatch, Melville H[arrison]**
1898-

A century of entomology in the Pacific Northwest. Seattle, University of Washington Press, 1949.

v, 42 p.   ports.   24 cm.   Literature cited: p. 29-40.

B.C. ARCHIVES

**1892   McKelvie, B[ruce] A[listair]**
1889-1960

Tales of conflict. Illustrations by C. P. Connorton. [Vancouver] The Vancouver Daily Province, 1949.

viii, 99 p.   illus.   27 cm.

Accounts of violence between Indians and Europeans during the early days of exploration and settlement in the province.

B.C. ARCHIVES

**1893   Maple Ridge. St. John the Divine**

St. John the Divine, Maple Ridge, B.C.; 90th anniversary, 1859-1949.   [n.p., 1949]

[13] 1.   28 cm.   Cover title. Mimeographed.

Primarily concerned with events prior to 1900.

U.B.C. SPECIAL COLLECTIONS

**1894   Nanaimo's jubilee ...**

Nanaimo's jubilee, May 21st-May 24th; Nanaimo, B.C., 75 years a city, 1874-1949; 100 years of coal, 1849-1949.   [Nanaimo, Filmer's Ltd., 1949]

36 p.   illus., ports.   21 cm.   Cover title.

Comprised of historical sketches.

B.C. ARCHIVES

**1895   North Vancouver. St. John the Evangelist**

Church of St. John the Evangelist, North Vancouver, B.C.; 50 anniversary, 1899-1949. [n.p., 1949?]

16 p.   illus.   16 cm.

B.C. ARCHIVES

**1896   Rossland ...**

Rossland, the golden city; a story of the first half-century of progress and development in the Trail Creek area of West Kootenay. Edited by Lance H. Whittaker.   Rossland, Rossland Miner Limited, 1949.

107 p.   illus., ports.   26 cm.

Includes biographical information.

B.C. ARCHIVES

**1897   Codere, Helen**

Fighting with property; a study of Kwakiutl potlatching and warfare, 1792-1930. With tribal and linguistic map of Vancouver Island and adjacent territory, drawn and compiled by Vincent F. Kotschar.   New York, J. J. Augustin [pref. 1950]

viii, 136 p.   illus., maps (1 fold., laid in)   25 cm. (Monographs of the American Ethnological Society, 18)   Bibliography: p. 130-135.

B.C. ARCHIVES

**1898   Diocese of Caledonia ...**

Diocese of Caledonia, 1879-1950 ...   [Prince Rupert, Dibb Printing Co., 1950?]

15 p.   illus., port., map.   17 x 23 cm.   Cover title.

Brief historical sketch of the Church of England diocese.

VANCOUVER PUBLIC LIBRARY

**1899   Haggen, R[upert] W[illiams]**
1887-1962

Historical sketch of Cariboo Lodge No. 4, A. F. & A. M., Barkerville, B.C.   New Westminster, Jackson Printing Co. [n.d.]

7 p. (incl. cover)   plate.   23 cm.   Cover title.

A history to 1900.

B.C. ARCHIVES

**1900   Holmes, Marjorie C[olquhoun]**

Publications of the government of British Columbia, 1871-1947; being a complete revision and enlargement of Publications of the government of British Columbia, 1871-1937, by Sydney Weston.   [Victoria, King's printer, 1950]

254 p.   25 cm.

UNIVERSITY OF VICTORIA LIBRARY

**1901   Hutchison, [William] Bruce**
1901-

The Fraser. Illustrated by Richard Bennett.   New York, Toronto, Rinehart [c1950]

368 p.   illus., double map.   21 cm.   (Rivers of America)   Bibliography: p. 351-355.

On the role of the Fraser River in B.C.'s history.

Also: Toronto, Clarke, Irwin & Co., 1950.

B.C. ARCHIVES

**1902   Lyons, C[hester] P[eter]**
1915-

Milestones on the mighty Fraser.   Toronto, Vancouver, J. M. Dent & Sons [c1950] xxxvi, 157 p.   illus., plates, ports., maps (incl. 2 on lining papers)   22 cm.

A tourist guidebook, with historical information, covering the area between Vancouver and Kamloops.

Revised edition: Vancouver, Wrigley Printing Company, 1956. xxii, 130 p.

B.C. ARCHIVES

1903   MacEwan, [John Walter] Grant
1902-

Agriculture on parade; the story of the fairs and exhibitions of western Canada.   Toronto, Thomas Nelson & Sons [c1950]

200 p.   plates, ports.   21 cm.

Has a little information on early B.C. fairs.

B.C. PROVINCIAL LIBRARY

1904   Marie-Jean-de-Pathmos, Sister

Les Soeurs de Sainte-Anne; un siècle d'histoire. Tome I; 1850-1900.   Lachine [Que.] Les Soeurs de Sainte-Anne, 1950.

640 p.   plates, ports., maps.   23 cm.   Bibliographie: p. [603]-610. Notes-références: p. [463]-601.

A chapter on the order's missionary work in the province.

B.C. ARCHIVES

1905   Thompson, James

"Know your diocese"; a brief review of the history of the Diocese of New Westminster, prepared by the Venerable James Thompson, archdeacon of the diocese. G. A. missionary study project for 1950. [n.p., 1950?]

13 l.   28 cm.   Cover title. Mimeographed.

U.B.C. SPECIAL COLLECTIONS

1906   Walker, Theodora Spencer

From log cabin to a streamlined school; the story of 57 years of education on Quadra Island. [n.p., 1950]

sheet.   44 x 28 cm.

B.C. ARCHIVES

1907   Adams, W. Claude

History of papermaking in the Pacific Northwest. Portland, Binfords & Mort [n.d.]

67 p.   map, table.   23 cm.   Reprinted from the *Oregon historical quarterly*, v. 52, 1951, p. 21-37, 83-100, 154-185.

B.C. ARCHIVES

1908   Corporation of British Columbia Land Surveyors

Report of proceedings of the Forty-Sixth Annual General Meeting. January 11th and 12th, 1951, at Victoria.   [Victoria, 1951]

66 p.   port.   23 cm.   Appendix F: Pioneer surveyors of Vancouver Island, by Willard E. Ireland [p. 47-51]

B.C. ARCHIVES

1909   Johnson, K[ate (Simpson)]

Pioneer days of Nakusp and the Arrow lakes. Nakusp, B.C., c1951.

146 p.   illus., ports.   23 cm.

Reprinted with additions: 1964. 240 p.

B.C. ARCHIVES

1910   Longstaff, Frederick V[ictor]
1879-1961

Christ Church Cathedral, Victoria, B.C.; a short history.   [Victoria] The author, 1951.

23 p.   plates, group ports.   22 cm.   Published for private circulation only. Addenda slip mounted on p. 18.

B.C. ARCHIVES

1911   Nelson. First Presbyterian Church

Sixtieth anniversary of the First Presbyterian Church, 1891-1951, Sunday, September 16th, 1951, Nelson, British Columbia.   [n.p., 1951]

[8] p. (incl. cover)   23 cm.

An historical sketch.

B.C. ARCHIVES

1912   Pharmaceutical Association of the Province of British Columbia

Pharmacy through 60 years in British Columbia; diamond jubilee souvenir, 1891-1951. [Vancouver, The Western Druggist, 1951]

84 p.   illus., ports., group ports.   29 cm.   Cover title.

B.C. ARCHIVES

1913   Trail. Trail Golden Jubilee Society

Trail, B.C.; a half century, 1901-1951.   [Trail, Printed by Trail Times Limited, 1951]

48 p.   illus., ports.   22 cm.

A history which begins with the fur-trade days.

B.C. ARCHIVES

**1914 Vancouver. City Archives**

The dedication of Stanley Park, 1889.
Vancouver [1951]

16 p. (incl. cover)   illus., facsim.   20 cm.   Cover title. Includes: historical address by City Archivist (Major [James] Matthews)

B.C. ARCHIVES

**1915 Victoria. Victoria High School**

75th anniversary; Victoria High School, Victoria, B.C., June 1 and 2, 1951.   [Victoria, The Acme Press Ltd., 1951]

[16] p. (incl. cover)   illus., ports.   23 cm.   Cover title.

Includes a brief history by Willard E. Ireland.

B.C. ARCHIVES

**1916 Wetherell, June [Pat]**
1909-

The glorious three.   New York, E. P. Dutton & Co., 1951.

320 p.   21 cm.

Although the setting of this novel is Bellingham Bay, Washington Territory, during 1853-9, the book mentions the Fraser River gold rush and refers to Victoria and to anti-British feeling amongst American settlers.

Also published in a paperback edition: New York, Popular Library, 1952. 352 p.

B.C. ARCHIVES

**1917 Williams, C. E. H.**

Parish history of St. Mary's Anglican Church, Lillooet.   [n.p.] 1951.

sheet.   26 x 46 cm.   Information in 2 columns; designed to fold.

A chronological record and list of incumbents.

VANCOUVER PUBLIC LIBRARY

**1918 The Consolidated Mining and Smelting Company of Canada Limited**

Trail's golden jubilee old timers, 1901 to 1951. [Trail, 1952]

38 p.   ports., group ports.   22 cm.   Cover title.

Contains brief biographical notes on pioneers who lived in Trail before 1901.

B.C. ARCHIVES

**1919 Fripp, Robert M.**

Capilano Creek, discovery of source, 1890. Vancouver, City Archives, 1952.

26 p. (incl. cover)   illus., map (on inside cover) 23 cm.   Cover title.

B.C. ARCHIVES

**1920 Ganges, Saltspring Island. St. Mark's Church**

St. Mark's Church, Parish of Salt Spring Island. [Ganges, B.C., 1952]

12 p.   illus., ports.   23 cm.   At head of title: Diamond jubilee, 1892-1952. Sheet attached following p. 12 with title: *St. Mary's Church, Fulford Harbour, 1894-1954.*

B.C. ARCHIVES

**1921 Green, George**
1872-1955

Outline of Burnaby history. Jubilee number, 1952. [Vancouver, Wrigley Printing Company, 1952]

26 p.   ports.   23 cm.

B.C. ARCHIVES

**1922 Hill, Hazel A. E.**

Tales of the Alberni Valley.   [Edmonton, Printed by the Hamly Press Ltd., 1952]

48 p.   illus., group port., map (on back cover) 23 cm.

An historical treatment.

B.C. ARCHIVES

**1923 Longstaff, F[rederick] V[ictor]**
1879-1961

A history of H.M.C.S. Naden, 1862-1952. Victoria, Published by the author, 1952.

15 l.   28 cm.   Cover title. Mimeographed.

A second edition of 68 pages was published in 1957 under title: *H.M.C.S. Naden naval barracks; a history of its work, senior officers, and ships.*

B.C. ARCHIVES

**1924 MacGregor, James G[rierson]**
1905-

The land of Twelve Foot Davis; a history of the Peace River country.   Edmonton, The Institute of Applied Art, Ltd., c1952.

395 p.   illus., maps, plans, tables.   23 cm.

An account of the fur traders, travellers, scientists, surveyors, missionaries, trappers, prospectors, and settlers who passed through, or pioneered, the country of the Peace between Hudson's Hope and Lesser Slave Lake, and north to Fort Vermilion. The title refers to a pioneer prospector and trader.

Second edition: 1952.

B.C. ARCHIVES

## 1925 Vancouver. City Archives

The pioneers of Burrard Inlet, Granville, Hastings, Moodyville, North Arm, Fraser River, 1886; our city is their monument. An appreciation by the Board of Park Commissioners upon the 66th anniversary of the incorporation of Vancouver as a city, 6th April 1886.   Vancouver, 1952.

15 p. (incl. cover)   illus.   23 cm.   Cover title. Published on the occasion of a dinner for all pioneers of Vancouver resident here in 1886 or earlier.

Includes: "Captain Edward Stamp; historical remarks by Bruce A. McKelvie" and a list of 190 pioneers.

B.C. ARCHIVES

## 1926 Vernon. Diamond Jubilee Committee

Vernon, British Columbia; diamond jubilee, 1892-1952.   [Vernon, The Vernon News Ltd., 1952]

104 p. (incl. advertisements)   illus., group ports. 24 cm.   Cover title.

Includes short historical articles.

B.C. ARCHIVES

## 1927 Wild, Roland Gibson
### 1903-

Nine o'clock gun. With foreword by W. A. McAdam.   London, Cassell and Company Ltd., 1952.

223 p.   20 cm.

This romantic novel traces the development of Vancouver from 1885 to World War II. It is a "skilful blend of fact and fiction" with "some entertaining pieces of authentic history." — frwd.

B.C. ARCHIVES

## 1928 Fraser, Geo[rge] J.
### 1872-1958

The story of Osoyoos, September 1811 to December 1952.   [Penticton, Penticton Herald, 1953]

212 p.   illus., ports.   23 cm.

Includes biographical sketches.

B.C. ARCHIVES

## 1929 Hendy, Albert E[dward]
### 1905-

St. Paul's Church, Nanaimo, B.C.; a brief history since its foundation, 1859-1952.   [n.p.] 1953.

36 p.   illus.   24 cm.   Cover title.

B.C. ARCHIVES

## 1930 Kaslo. Historical Committee

History of Kaslo. Kaslo diamond jubilee, 1893-1953.   [Kaslo, 1953]

64 p. (incl. advertisements)   illus., ports.   24 cm. Cover title: 1893-1953; sixtieth anniversary; Kaslo, British Columbia, diamond jubilee.

Primarily concerned with events before 1900.

B.C. ARCHIVES

## 1931 Murdock, George Peter
### 1897-

Ethnographic bibliography of North America. Second edition.   New Haven, Human Relations Area Files, 1953.

xvi, 239 p.   map.   28 cm.   (Behavior science bibliographies)

Entries for books and articles are arranged by tribal groups. A large section deals with those of British Columbia.

Third edition: 1960. xxiii, 393 p. maps.

B.C. PROVINCIAL LIBRARY

## 1932 Royal Oak. St. Michael and All Angels' Church

St. Michael and All Angels' Church, West Saanich Road, Royal Oak, Vancouver Island, British Columbia, 1883 to 1953.   [Victoria, 1953]

20 p.   illus.   22 cm.

History of an Anglican church.

Supplement of three mimeographed pages. n.d.

B.C. ARCHIVES

## 1933 Sangster, J[ames] Lewis
### 1891-

75 years of service; a history of Olivet Baptist Church, 1878-1953.   New Westminster, Olivet Board of Management, 1953.

77 p.   plates, ports.   23 cm.

U.B.C. SPECIAL COLLECTIONS

## 1934 Andrews, G[erald] S[medley]
### 1903-

Surveys and mapping in British Columbia resources development.   [Victoria, 1954]

33 p. fold. map. 25 cm. Reprinted from: British Columbia Natural Resources Conference. *Transactions of the Seventh Conference.* 1954.

Includes a brief outline of survey work from the days of the fur trade to present times.

B.C. ARCHIVES

## 1935 Banks, C[harles] A[rthur]
### 1885-1961

British Columbia and Sir James Douglas, K.C.B. (1803-1877) New York, Montreal, The Newcomen Society, 1954.

28 p. illus. 23 cm. The Newcomen address delivered in New York, 17 October 1952.

B.C. ARCHIVES

## 1936 British Columbia Historical Association. Vancouver Section

Historic Yale, British Columbia. [Vancouver] c1954.

32 p. illus., ports., facsims. 22 cm. Erratum slip.

B.C. ARCHIVES

## 1937 Brown, Harrison
### 1893-

Admirals, adventurers and able seamen; forgotten stories about places on our British Columbia coast and how they got their names. [Illustrations by Jack Grundle. Vancouver, The Keystone Press Ltd. 1954]

30 p. illus., map. 22 cm.

B.C. ARCHIVES

## 1938 Camsell, Charles
### 1876-1958

Son of the North. Toronto, The Ryerson Press [c1954]

xii, 244 p. plates, ports., maps. 23 cm.

Includes an account of the author's activities in the Cassiar district in the late 1890's.

B.C. ARCHIVES

## 1939 Great Britain. Laws, statutes, etc.

Proclamation providing for the government of British Columbia, 19th November 1858 [by His Excellency James Douglas; and: An Act to provide for the government of British Columbia, 2nd August 1858. Vancouver, Grant-Mann Printing Division, 1954]

[6] p. 30 cm. Cover title. On verso of cover: Reprinted from the original proclamation in the Howay-Reid Collection, University of British Columbia Library, for Friends of the Library.

B.C. ARCHIVES

## 1940 Gulick, [Grover C.]
### 1916-

A thousand for the Cariboo, by Bill Gulick. Boston, Houghton, Mifflin Company, 1954.

197 p. map. 21 cm.

Fiction. Describes the long cattle drive from The Dalles in Oregon to booming Barkerville in 1862.

B.C. ARCHIVES

## 1941 Hacking, Norman [R.]

Steamboat days on the upper Columbia and upper Kootenay. [Victoria, Printed by Don McDiarmid, 1954]

51 p. plates, map., facsim. 25 cm. Cover title. Appendix contains statistics on river steamers. Reprinted from the *British Columbia historical quarterly,* v. 16, January-April 1952.

B.C. ARCHIVES

## 1942 Hood, Robert Allison
### 1880-1958

Vignettes of Vancouver. With illustrations by Harry E. White. Vancouver, Education Services Ltd. [1954]

ix, 84 p. illus. 21 cm. Cover title: Vignettes of Vancouver and some vagrant verses.

Contains "The last camel" which appears in his *Ballads of the Pacific Northwest* under the title "Moriturus" (see entry 1851).

B.C. ARCHIVES

## 1943 Metlakatla, Alaska. William Duncan Memorial Church (Undenominational)

A short story of the Metlakatla Christian mission. [Metlakatla, Alaska, Co-trustees of the William Duncan Trust, c1954]

32 p. (incl. cover) illus., ports. 22 cm. Cover title.

B.C. ARCHIVES

## 1944 Myers, T[homas] R[athmell]
### 1884-1961

90 years of public utility service on Vancouver Island, 1860-1950; a history of the B.C. Electric. [Victoria, British Columbia Electric Railway Co., 1954]

359, xxi p. plates, ports., tables. 28 cm. Not for sale.

B.C. ARCHIVES

1945     Nicholson, Norman Leon
1919-

The boundaries of Canada, its provinces and territories.    Ottawa, Edmond Cloutier, 1954.

ix, 142 p.    plates, maps.    (Canada. Department of Mines and Technical Surveys. Geographical Branch. Memoir 2)    References: p. 124-130.

Includes a brief discussion of the evolution of B.C. boundaries.

B.C. ARCHIVES

1946     Reid, J[ohn] H[otchkiss] Stewart
1909-

Mountains, men & rivers; British Columbia in legend and story.    Toronto, Ryerson Press [1954]

x, 229 p.    plates, map (on lining papers)    21 cm. Notes on sources: p. 227-229.

Primarily concerned with the fur-trading era and the colonial period.

B.C. ARCHIVES

1947     Women's Institute. Canada. Westwold Women's Institute, B.C.

Saga of Westwold [by Mrs. H. Wessel, Mrs. L. Jones, and Mrs. L. Ness.    Westwold, 1954]

12 p.    23 cm.    Cover title.

A history of Westwold, a community thirty miles southeast of Kamloops which was formerly called Grande Prairie.

B.C. ARCHIVES

1948     Audain, James [Guy Payne]
1903-

From coalmine to castle; the story of the Dunsmuirs of Vancouver Island.    New York, Pageant Press [c1955]

213 p.    plates.    24 cm.

In consequence of legal action, publication was withdrawn.

B.C. ARCHIVES

1949     Borthwick, D[avid]
1920-

Settlement in British Columbia.    [Victoria, 1955]

12 p.    25 cm.    Cover title. Reprinted from: British Columbia Natural Resources Conference. *Transactions of the Eighth Conference*. 1955.

A history.

B.C. ARCHIVES

1950     Dufferin [and Ava, Frederick Temple Hamilton-Temple-Blackwood]
1ST MARQUIS OF    1826-1902

Dufferin-Carnarvon correspondence, 1874-1878. Edited by C. W. de Kiewiet [and] F. H. Underhill. Toronto, Champlain Society, 1955.

lvi, 442, xii p.    2 ports., fold. map.    25 cm.    (The publications of the Champlain Society, 33) Biographical notes on chief persons mentioned: p. 411-431.

Contains numerous comments on the Pacific railway question.

B.C. ARCHIVES

1951     Flucke, A[rchibald] F[rederick]
1913-

A history of mining in British Columbia. [Victoria, Provincial Archives, 1955]

19 l.    36 cm.    Cover title. Mimeographed.

A survey of mining development with the emphasis on the period before 1900.

Also printed in: British Columbia Natural Resources Conference. *Transactions of the Eighth Conference*. 1955, p. 6-26.

B.C. ARCHIVES

1952     McKelvie, B[ruce] A[listair]
1889-1960

Pageant of B.C.; glimpses into the romantic development of Canada's far western province. [Toronto] Thomas Nelson & Sons [1955]

263 p.    plates (part col.) ports.    23 cm.

One hundred and six historical sketches of events prior to 1900 which first appeared in serial form in the Vancouver *Province* between February 1953 and March 1955.

Second edition: 1957.

B.C. ARCHIVES

1953     MacNutt, W[illiam] Stewart
1908-

Days of Lorne; from the private papers of the Marquis of Lorne, 1878-1883, in the possession of the Duke of Argyll at Inveraray Castle, Scotland. Fredericton, N.B., Brunswick Press [1955]

x, 262 p.    plates, ports.    23 cm.    At head of title: Impressions of a governor-general. Bibliographic note: p. 259. Chapter 5: The conciliation of British Columbia [p. 100-124]

UNIVERSITY OF VICTORIA LIBRARY

**1954    Newell, Gordon R.**

S O S North Pacific; tales of shipwrecks off the Washington, British Columbia, and Alaska coasts. Portland, Ore., Binfords & Mort [c1955]

xii, 216 p.    illus., plates, ports., map (on lining papers)    23 cm.

B.C. ARCHIVES

**1955    [Sovereign, Arthur Henry]**
BISHOP    1881-1966

A tree grows in Vernon; the history of All Saints' Parish, Vernon, B.C. The diamond jubilee, 1893-1953.    [Vernon, 1955]

36 p.    illus., ports.    23 cm.    Cover title.

B.C. ARCHIVES

**1956    Stephen, [Irene Simmons (Phelan)]**
1902-

Winged canoes at Nootka and other stories of the Evergreen Coast, by Pamela Stephen [pseud.] Illustrations by Annora Brown.    Toronto, J. M. Dent & Sons [1955]

x, 227 p.    illus.    21 cm.

A collection of 24 short stories.

VICTORIA PUBLIC LIBRARY

**1957    Vancouver. City Archives**

Pioneers of Vancouver "before the train"; our city is their monument. An appreciation by the citizens of Vancouver on the 69th anniversary of the incorporation of Vancouver as a city, April 6th, 1886.    Vancouver [1955]

18 p. (incl. front cover)    illus., port., group port. 23 cm.    Cover title. Published on the occasion of a dinner for all pioneers of Vancouver resident before the arrival of the first passenger train. Includes: The story of Maddams Ranch [by James Matthews]

B.C. ARCHIVES

**1958    Victoria. Craigflower School**

Craigflower School, 1855-1955.    [Victoria, 1955]

[16] p. (incl. cover)    illus., ports.    24 cm.    Cover title. History of Craigflower School: p. [5]-[7]

B.C. ARCHIVES

**1959    Wilson, Neill C[ompton]**
EDITOR    1889-

Deep roots; the history of Blake, Moffitt & Towne, pioneers in paper since 1855. With decorations by Mallette Dean.    San Francisco, Privately printed, 1955.

112 p.    illus., plates, ports., facsims.    26 cm. Adventures in British Columbia: p. [19]-24.

James Towne published the province's first newspaper, the Victoria *Gazette*.

B.C. ARCHIVES

**1960    Alaska sportsman**

Blood on the arctic snow, and seventeen other true tales of far north adventure from the Alaska sportsman. Compiled and edited by B. G. Olson and Mike Miller.    Seattle, Superior Publishing Company [c1956]

279 p.    22 cm.

Three chapters relate to an account by E. L. Cole of the hardships of the Edmonton Trail. Cole and his party planned to travel the Nelson, Liard and Pelly rivers to the Klondike, but winter overtook them on the banks of the Liard. After relief arrived in the spring, Cole travelled down the Dease and Stikine rivers with forty other men, the remnants of those who had tried this route to the gold fields.

B.C. ARCHIVES

**1961    Andrews, Ralph W[arren]**
1897-

Glory days of logging.    Seattle, Superior Publishing Company [c1956]

176 p.    illus., ports.    28 cm.

A photographic record with some early pictures of B.C. logging.

B.C. ARCHIVES

**1962    Bissley, P[aul] L.**

A history of the Union Club of British Columbia. [Victoria, Printed by Colonist Printing, 1956]

43 p.    illus., port.    23 cm.    Cover title: The Union Club of British Columbia.

The Union Club was founded in 1897.

B.C. ARCHIVES

**1963    British Columbia. Natural Resources Conference. 1956**

British Columbia; atlas of resources. Editors: J. D. Chapman and D. B. Turner. Cartographic editors: A. L. Farley and R. I. Ruggles.    [Vancouver, Smith Lithograph Co. for the British Columbia Natural Resources Conference] 1956.

92 p.    illus., maps (part col.) diagrs. (part col.) tables.    44 x 56 cm.

Includes historical maps.

B.C. ARCHIVES

**1964    Canada. Navy. Esquimalt Naval Establishment**

Extracts from the "Esquimalt Naval Establishment records," 1862-1881 [by Cadet A. S. Troubetzkoy. Esquimalt, 1956]

[6], 22 p.   28 cm.   Cover title. Mimeographed.

Seventeen letters chosen to serve as an example of the collection of more than 450 letters in the archives of the Naval Museum, Esquimalt.

VANCOUVER PUBLIC LIBRARY

**1965    Colvile, Eden**

London correspondence inward, 1849-1852. Edited by E. E. Rich, assisted by A. M. Johnson. With an introduction by W. L. Morton.    London, Hudson's Bay Record Society, 1956.

cxv, 300 p.   illus.   25 cm.   (The publications of the Hudson's Bay Record Society, 19)    Binder's title: Eden Colvile's letters, 1849-52. Selected bibliography: p. 273-279.

Eden Colvile spent the winter of 1849-50 at Fort Victoria, and in journeying south of the border and along the coast to the north. Several of the letters are concerned with this period.

B.C. ARCHIVES

**1966    Dixon, Les B.**

The birth of the lumber industry in British Columbia.   [Vancouver, 1956]

24 p.   illus., ports., tables.   29 cm.   Cover title. Reprinted from eleven issues of the *British Columbia lumberman,* v. 39-40, November 1955 to September 1956.

Traces the development of the industry during the colonial period.

B.C. ARCHIVES

**1967    Freuchen, Peter**
1886-1957

The legend of Daniel Williams.    New York, Julian Messner [1956]

256 p.   22 cm.

Fiction. Williams, a bible-toting Negro and ex-slave, arrived in the Peace River country in the 1870's and worked for the Hudson's Bay Company in Dunvegan and Fort St. John. His career ended abruptly in March of 1880 when he was hanged for murder.

B.C. ARCHIVES

**1968    Glover, G[eorge] H[enry Wilson]**
1881-

History of the United Church of Canada, North and South Saanich areas.   [Sidney, B.C., The Review, 1956]

35 p.   illus., plates, ports.   23 cm.

B.C. ARCHIVES

**1969    Holbrook, Stewart H[all]**
1893-

The Columbia. Illustrated by Ernest Richardson. New York, Toronto, Rinehart and Co. [c1956]

393 p.   illus., maps.   21 cm.    (Rivers of America) Bibliography: p. 377-381.

In part relates to steamboating on the upper Columbia and the consequences of the building of the C.P.R. to water transportation.

B.C. ARCHIVES

**1970    Innis, Mary [(Quayle)]**
1899-

Travellers west. Illustrated by Illingworth Kerr. Toronto, Clarke, Irwin, 1956.

ix, 339 p.   illus., map (on lining papers)   21 cm.

On the journeys of James Carnegie, Earl of Southesk, Milton and Cheadle, George Monro Grant, and Sandford Fleming.

B.C. ARCHIVES

**1971    Knox, Olive [Elsie (Robinson)]**

The young surveyor.    Toronto, The Ryerson Press [1956]

164 p.   fold. map.   21 cm.

Juvenile fiction. In 1874-5 a young man accompanies Edward Warrel Jarvis on a C.P.R. exploratory survey from Kamloops to Tête Jaune Cache and an instrumental survey along the Fraser River to Fort George. The story was created from Jarvis' diary and field books.

B.C. ARCHIVES

**1972    Musk, George**

A short history and fleet list of the Canadian Pacific ocean steamships, 1891-1956, by George Musk in association with the World Ship Society. London [1956]

32 p.   illus., col. front.   22 cm.   Cover title: Canadian Pacific, 1891-1956.

Enlarged edition covering years 1891-1961: London, 1961. 40 p.

B.C. ARCHIVES

**1973    Nesbitt, James K[night]**
1908-

Album of Victoria old homes and families. Illustrations from Provincial Archives.    Victoria, Hebden Printing Co., 1956.

63 p.   illus., ports.   23 cm.

B.C. ARCHIVES

**1974    Peel, Bruce Braden**
1916-

A bibliography of the prairie provinces to 1953. [Toronto] University of Toronto Press [1956]

xix, 680 p.    26 cm.

Supplement: 1963. 130 p.

B.C. ARCHIVES

**1975    Anstey, Arthur**
D. 1951

British Columbia; a short history, by Arthur Anstey and Neil Sutherland. Illustrated by Huntley Brown. Toronto, W. J. Gage Limited [1957]

v, 55 p.    illus., maps.    25 cm.

A revision by Neil Sutherland of Arthur Anstey's original work (see entry 1699).

B.C. ARCHIVES

**1976    British Columbia. Centennial Committee**

Ethnic groups in British Columbia; a selected bibliography based on check-list material in the Provincial Library and Archives. [Compiled by Dorothy Blakey Smith]    Victoria, The British Columbia Centennial Committee, 1957.

64 l.    29 cm.    Mimeographed.

A selected list of entries for books, articles, newspapers, and unpublished material dealing with ethnic groups, other than Indians, during the period 1858-1956.

B.C. ARCHIVES

**1977    British Columbia . . .**

British Columbia official centennial record, 1858-1958; a century of progress.    [Vancouver, Evergreen Press, c1957]

174 p.    illus. (part col.) ports., maps (on lining papers)    26 cm.

Extensively illustrated.

Revised edition: 1957. A cheaper edition (minus p. 1-16) has title: *British Columbia, story with pictures.*

B.C. ARCHIVES

**1978    Galbraith, John S[emple]**
1916-

The Hudson's Bay Company as an Imperial factor, 1821-1869.    [Toronto] University of Toronto Press, 1957.

viii, 500 p.    maps (incl. 1 in pocket)    24 cm.
Notes: p. [431]-477. Bibliography: p. [480]-487.

Chapter 14: Company control of Vancouver Island, 1847-1865.

Chapter 14 gives a valuable summary of a subject seldom treated in its entirety.

B.C. ARCHIVES

**1979    Hamilton, Reuben**

Mount Pleasant early days; memories of Reuben Hamilton, pioneer 1890.    Vancouver, City Archives, 1957.

64 p.    illus., ports., group ports., facsims.    23 cm.

B.C. ARCHIVES

**1980    Harris, Christie Lucy (Irwin)**
1907-

Cariboo Trail.    Toronto, Longmans, Green & Co. [1957]

188 p.    21 cm.

Juvenile fiction. Christie Harris, a journalist who spent her early days in the Cariboo, describes a difficult wagon journey from Red River to the Cariboo in 1862.

B.C. ARCHIVES

**1981    Hickman, Mary**

Early history of East Chilliwack.    [London, Eng., Printed by Witherby & Co., n.d.]

105 p.    illus., ports.    21 cm.    Probably written in 1957.

Chiefly biographical sketches.

B.C. ARCHIVES

**1982    Kohlstedt, Edward Delor**

William Duncan, founder and developer of Alaska's Metlakatla Christian mission. [Metlakatla, Alaska, Board of Co-Trustees of the William Duncan Trust, c1957]

iv, 82 p.    illus., ports.    22 cm.

B.C. ARCHIVES

**1983    Lane, Myrtle E[liza (Mack)]**
1891-1967

Land of shining mountains; British Columbia in legend and story, by Myrtle E. Lane, Margaret G. Steer, Mary Carr Wright. Illustrations by Dick A. G. van den Hoogen.    Toronto, Vancouver, J. M. Dent & Sons [1957]

viii, 354 p.    illus. (part col.) col. plate, maps. 23 cm.

A book designed for the young reader.

B.C. ARCHIVES

**1984 Large, R[ichard] Geddes**
1901-

The Skeena, river of destiny. Vancouver, Mitchell Press [c1957]

ix, 180 p. plates, map (on lining paper) 23 cm. Bibliography: 173-177.

A history.

Second edition: Vancouver, Mitchell Press, 1958.

B.C. ARCHIVES

**1985 Lyons, C[hester] P[eter]**
1915-

Milestones in Ogopogo Land; in which the many wonders of the land of Ogopogo and sunshine are revealed. [Vancouver, Printed by the Evergreen Press, c1957]

xv, 215 p. illus., 7 maps (1 fold.; 1 on lining papers) 22 cm.

A tourist guidebook on the Okanagan with historical information.

B.C. ARCHIVES

**1986 McGivern, J. S.**
1908-

The Royal Engineers in British Columbia. Camp Chilliwack [R.C.E. Museum, Royal Canadian School of Military Engineering] 1957.

x, 24 p. illus., plates, ports. 25 cm. Mimeographed. On p. [ix]: The text of this publication was delivered by Captain McGivern over radio station CHWK in May 1957 . . .

B.C. ARCHIVES

**1987 McKenzie, Poppy**

The story of citizenship in British Columbia (from 1858 to confederation); a dramatization for Citizenship Day, July 1st, 1958. Script by Poppy McKenzie, research by A. J. Arnold. Victoria, Published by the British Columbia Centennial Committee, in co-operation with the B.C. Provincial Archives [1957?]

[2], 40 l. 28 cm. Cover title. Mimeographed.

"This is a documentary script based on events in B.C. history surrounding the introduction of the first naturalization laws . . . commissioned by the B.C. Centennial Committee at the suggestion of the Ethnic Groups and Provincial Organizations Sub-Committee."

B.C. ARCHIVES

**1988 Morse, J[ohn] J[esse]**
1906-

Kamloops, the inland capital; a condensed history. [Kamloops] Kamloops Museum Association for the Kamloops Centennial Committee [1957]

40 p. illus., maps, coat of arms. 23 cm. Not seen.

B.C. ARCHIVES

**1989 Powley, [Ellen Frances Gladys (Adams)]**
COMPILER 1884-1966

Early days of Winfield, B.C. Compiled by Mrs. W. R. Powley. [Winfield, Winfield Women's Institute, 1957]

30 p. illus., port., map. 23 cm.

B.C. ARCHIVES

**1990 Ramsey, Bruce**
1924-

The saga of mining in British Columbia. Prepared for C. M. Oliver & Company Limited. [Vancouver, 1957]

40 p. illus., map. 24 cm.

Outlines the history of gold, coal, copper, and silver-lead discoveries.

U.B.C. SPECIAL COLLECTIONS

**1991 Abdill, George B.**

This was railroading. Seattle, Superior Publishing Company [c1958]

192 p. illus. 28 cm.

An extensively illustrated work which includes a chapter on the early days of B.C. railways and a section on the White Pass and Yukon Railway.

B.C. ARCHIVES

**1992 Affleck, Edward Lloyd**
1924-

Sternwheelers, sandbars and switchbacks; a chronicle of steam transportation in southeastern British Columbia. Vancouver, c1958.

iii, 65 l. plate, map. 28 cm. Mimeographed.

The Appendix lists steamers which operated on the Columbia River waterways north of the international boundary.

B.C. ARCHIVES

**1993**    Anderson, Aili [Sophia]
1906-

History of Sointula.    [Sointula, B.C., Sointula Centennial Committee, 1958]

16 p.   illus.   26 cm.   Cover title.

Includes a summary of events which led to the establishment of the Finnish settlement of Sointula on Malcolm Island. The summary is based on Matti Halminen's history (see entry 1763).

B.C. ARCHIVES

**1994**    [Beckwith, Margaret Alice (Dunn)]
1898-

The Craigflower schoolhouse.    [Victoria, 1958]

16 p.   illus., ports., table.   23 cm.   Cover title. Printed under the auspices of the Board of Trustees of the Old Craigflower Schoolhouse.

A brief history of the school which was opened in 1855.

B.C. ARCHIVES

**1995**    Belsham, Alice [Ada (Carroll)]
COMPILER   1922-

History of Fort Fraser. Compiled by Alice Belsham and J. Philip Myers.    [Fort Fraser, B.C., Fort Fraser Centennial Committee, 1958]

11 p.   illus., ports., 2 maps.   20 cm.   Cover title.

B.C. ARCHIVES

**1996**    Berton, Pierre [Francis deMarigny]
1920-

Klondike; the life and death of the last great gold rush.    Toronto, McClelland & Stewart, 1958.

viii, 457, xix p.   maps.   22 cm.   A note on sources: p. 439-445. Bibliography: p. 446-457.

A well-documented account of the various aspects of the gold rush which includes coverage of the routes to the Klondike. The bibliography is a valuable source of references.

American edition (New York, Knopf, 1958) has title: *Klondike fever, the life and death of the last great gold rush.*    German edition (Munchen, P. List Verlag, 1960) has title: *Abenteuer Alaska; die grosse Jagd nach Gold und Glück.*

B.C. ARCHIVES

**1997**    The Boundary Historical Society (Grand Forks)

Report.   1958+   Grand Forks, B.C.

v.   illus., maps (part fold.)   22 cm.   annual. Table of contents.

Includes reminiscences and necrology.

B.C. ARCHIVES

**1998**    Burnaby Historical Society

Prize winning essays on Burnaby history. Burnaby high schools centennial essay contest, 1958, sponsored by Burnaby Historical Society, Burnaby Centennial Committee [and] Burnaby School Board.    [Burnaby, B.C., 1958]

[23] l.   36 cm.   Cover title.   Mimeographed.

B.C. ARCHIVES

**1999**    Calhoun, [Samuel] Henry
1877-1961

Fifty years ago at Tappen.    [Tappen, B.C., 1958]

9 l.   36 cm.   Caption title. Mimeographed. First appeared in the *Salmon Arm Observer.*

Reminiscences which relate in part to events before 1900 in the Shuswap Lake area.

B.C. ARCHIVES

**2000**    Carroll, Campbell

Three Bar; the story of Douglas Lake. Vancouver, Mitchell Press, 1958.

111 p.   plates, ports., 2 maps (1 on lining papers) tables.   28 cm.

The history of Douglas Lake Cattle Co., Ltd., formed in 1886.

B.C. ARCHIVES

**2001**    Christie, Ja[me]s R.
1877-

The story of Okanagan Falls, by Jas. R. Christie and Isabel Christie MacNaughton.    [Okanagan Falls] Okanagan Falls Centennial Committee [1958]

44 p. (incl. cover)   illus., group port.   23 cm.

Includes information on the first settlers in the area.

B.C. ARCHIVES

**2002**    Cleasby, Henry Standley
1868-1959

The Nicola Valley in review.    Merritt, Merritt Herald Ltd. [1958]

48 p.   illus., port.   20 cm.   Cover title. On cover: Volume one.

A history of the area between the Fraser Canyon and Forksdale (now Merritt).

B.C. ARCHIVES

**2003    The Convention of Baptist Churches of British Columbia**

The Convention of Baptist Churches of British Columbia, 1862-1958.    [A publication for the] B.C. Centennial year, 1858-1958. [Vancouver, 1958]

[20] p. (incl. cover)    illus., ports.    22 x 29 cm. Cover title.

Includes historical notes.

B.C. ARCHIVES

**2004    Conway, Alan**

Welsh gold miners in British Columbia during the 1860's.    Aberystwyth, 1958.

[375]-389 p.    26 cm.    Cover title. Reprinted from the *National Library of Wales journal*, v. 10, 1958.

Comprised mainly of letters from Welshmen prospecting in the Cariboo. The letters first appeared in various newspapers of the day.

An expanded version of this article appeared in the *British Columbia historical quarterly*, v. 21, 1957-8, p. 51-74.

B.C. ARCHIVES

**2005    Corbitt, H[arry] W[ellington]**
1889-

The history of Kaleden.    [Kaleden, B.C.] Kaleden Centennial Committee [1958]

61 p.    illus., port., group ports. (part fold.) map. 24 cm.

Chiefly concerned with post-1900 events in a community south of Penticton. Includes biographical sketches.

B.C. ARCHIVES

**2006    [Corner, Raymond Westley]**
1894-

Glenmore, the apple valley.    [Kelowna] Glenmore Centennial Committee, 1958.

57 p.    illus., ports., map.    23 cm.    Cover title.

A history of the Glenmore and Okanagan districts.

B.C. ARCHIVES

**2007    Cottingham, Mollie E.**

A century of public education in British Columbia; paper given at the First Annual Meeting of the Canadian College of Teachers, August 11, 1958. [Vancouver, 1958]

22, [2] 1.    28 cm.    Cover title. Mimeographed. Bibliography: 1. [23]-[24]

B.C. ARCHIVES

**2008    Coutts, M[arjorie] E[llen]**
EDITOR    1914-

Dawson Creek, past and present; an historical sketch.    [Dawson Creek] Dawson Creek Historical Society [1958]

115 p.    illus., map (on cover) tables.    28 cm. Cover title: Dawson Creek and district. At head of cover title: British Columbia centennial, 1958. Bibliography: p. 115.

Contains some information on fur trade days and early explorers and travellers, but mostly concerned with the early years of settlement before 1900.

B.C. ARCHIVES

**2009    Crown Zellerbach Canada Limited. Richmond Division**

A history of the municipality of Richmond. [Richmond, 1958]

28 p.    illus., port., double map.    21 cm.

The municipality consists of Lulu Island, Sea Island, Mitchell Island, and several other smaller islands situated in the mouth of the Fraser.

B.C. ARCHIVES

**2010    Duncan, Frances [Imogene]**
1926-

The Sayward-Kelsey Bay saga.    [Courtenay, B.C., Printed by Argus Publishing Co. for Sayward-Kelsey Bay Centennial Committee, 1958]

51 p.    illus., ports.    22 cm.    Cover title: Eighty-eight years at Sayward-Kelsey Bay, Port Neville, Hardwicke Island.

B.C. ARCHIVES

**2011    Elliott, Gordon R[aymond]**
1920-

Quesnel; commercial centre of the Cariboo gold rush.    Quesnel, Cariboo Historical Society, Quesnel Branch, 1958.

vii, 190, viii p.    plates, ports., maps, facsims.    23 cm. Bibliography: p. 189-190.

"This book is not a chronological history of Quesnel, but is an attempt to indicate why the hamlet at the junction of the rivers appeared, and why it developed, and why it prospered while others flourished and then decayed." — pref.

B.C. ARCHIVES

**2012    Farrington, Lawrence**

H.M.S. Beaver charts the seas, 1863-1870; Pacific naval surveys.    [n.p., 1958]

11 p.    33 cm.    Cover title. Mimeographed.

B.C. ARCHIVES

**2013    Gabriel, Theresa**

Vernon, British Columbia; a brief history. [Vernon] Published by the Vernon Centennial Committee with the assistance of the Vernon Branch of the Okanagan Historical Society, 1958.

63 p.    illus., ports, map.    23 cm.

B.C. ARCHIVES

**2014    Galloway, [Hazel Frances (Dempsey)]**
COMPILER    1921-

A history of the Cedar, Bright, Cranberry and Oyster districts on Vancouver Island, B.C. [Compiled by Mrs. Allan Galloway and Robert Strachan.    Ladysmith, Cedar Centennial Committee, 1958]

26 l.    illus. (on cover)    27 cm.    Cover title. Mimeographed.

B.C. ARCHIVES

**2015    Golden. Centennial Committee. Historical Branch**

Golden memories of the town where the turbulent Kicking Horse meets the mighty Columbia. [Golden, B.C., The Committee, 1958]

91 l.    illus., ports.    33 cm.    Cover title. Mimeographed. Spiral binding.

Chiefly biographical sketches.

B.C. ARCHIVES

**2016    Goodfellow, John [Christie]**
1890-

The story of Similkameen. Vol. 1. [Princeton, B.C., 1958]

88 p.    ports., map.    19 cm.    Cover title. First published in weekly instalments in the *Similkameen Spotlight*.

B.C. ARCHIVES

**2017    Great Britain. Public Record Office**

The early history of British Columbia, proclaimed a crown colony in 1858. An exhibition of documents at the Public Record Office, July 1958. [London, Her Majesty's Stationery Office, 1958]

16 p.    25 cm.

A catalogue of forty-five documents, mostly original correspondence and maps of the British Colonial and Foreign Offices.

B.C. ARCHIVES

**2018    Griffin, Harold [John Michael]**
1912-

British Columbia; the people's early story. Vancouver, Tribune Publishing Company [1958]

95 p.    16 cm.

A socialist's view of some political events to about 1920, written to show the origins of socialist principles and labour action.

B.C. ARCHIVES

**2019    Harker, Douglas E[dward]**
1911-

The city and the store.    [Vancouver, Woodward Stores, 1958]

[29] p.    col. illus., col. ports.    28 cm.

The first Woodward's store was opened in 1892.

B.C. ARCHIVES

**2020    Healey, Elizabeth**
COMPILER    1912-

History of Alert Bay and district.    [Alert Bay, B.C., Centennial Committee, 1958]

101 p.    illus., map (on inside cover)    23 cm. Cover title.

B.C. ARCHIVES

**2021    Johnson, Patricia M[ary]**
1913-

A short history of Nanaimo.    Nanaimo, Nanaimo British Columbia Centennial Committee, c1958.

55 p.    illus., port.    23 cm.    References: p. 55.

B.C. ARCHIVES

**2022    Johnson, Wellwood R[obert]**
1887-

Legend of Langley; an account of the early history of Fort Langley and an intimate story of the lives of some, but not all, of the early pioneers of the district of Langley.    [Langley] Langley Centennial Committee, 1958.

vi, 183 p.    illus., ports., tables.    23 cm.

B.C. ARCHIVES

**2023    Kitwanga. Superior School**

Gitwangag 1858 to Kitwanga 1958.    [Kitwanga, 1958]

[33] l.    illus.    31 cm.    Cover title: 100 years, B.C. Mimeographed.

Kitwanga is located at the junction of the Skeena and Kitwancool rivers.

B.C. ARCHIVES

**2024    Lindsay, F[rederick] W[illiam]**
1903-

The Cariboo story, published in B.C.'s centennial year. With pen and ink illistrations [sic] by Gwen Lewis.    [Quesnel, Printed by the Quesnel Advertiser, 1958]

52 p.    illus., ports., maps.    24 cm.

" . . . a compilation of extracts from original diaries of the miners and stories that have been told by those miners or by men who knew them." — p. [4]

**2025    Logan, Harry T[remaine]**
1887-

Tuum est; a history of the University of British Columbia. With a foreword by N. A. M. Mackenzie.    Vancouver, University of British Columbia, 1958.

xii, 268 p.    plates, ports., facsims., plans, tables. 28 cm.    Errata slips mounted on p. 65 and 268.

**2026    Ludditt, [Al]fred [William]**
1907-

Gold in the Cariboo.    Vancouver, Evergreen Press [1958]

[6], 40 p.    illus., map.    16 cm.    Compiled for the Wells-Barkerville Centennial Committee. Bibliography: p. [4]

A historical guide to the gold fields which includes descriptions of early gold-mining days.

**2027    Lyons, C[hester] P[eter]**
1915-

Milestones on Vancouver Island; the story of this "Island to the West," its past and its present. [Illustrated by Edward Goodall.    Vancouver, Printed by Evergreen Press, 1958]

viii, 314 p.    illus., ports., maps (on lining papers) diagr.    21 cm.

A tourist guidebook with historical information.

**2028    Mather, Barry**
1909-

New Westminster, the royal city, by Barry Mather and Margaret McDonald.    [Vancouver] J. M. Dent & Sons, and the Corporation of the City of New Westminster [1958]

xxvii, 192 p.    plates, ports., maps (1 on lining papers) 23 cm.    Bibliographic notes: p. 191-192.

A history with emphasis on the colonial period.

**2029    Matsqui-Sumas-Abbotsford Centennial Society**

Where trails meet; Sumas, Abbotsford, Matsqui. [n.p., 1958]

62 p.    illus., maps.    24 cm.    Cover title.

History of early pioneer days in the Fraser Valley.

**2030    Monk, H[arry] A[lbert] J[ervis]**
1913-

A history of Coquitlam and Fraser Mills, 1858-1958 [by] H. A. J. Monk and John Stewart. [New Westminster, District of Coquitlam-Fraser Mills Centennial Commission, 1958]

76 p.    illus., maps (1 on inside cover)    23 cm.

**2031    Murphy, Herbert H[alliday]**
1881-1964

Royal Jubilee Hospital, Victoria, B.C., 1858-1958. The Royal Hospital, 1858-1890; the Provincial Royal Jubilee Hospital, 1890-1938; the Royal Jubilee Hospital, 1938-1958.    Victoria, Hebden Printing Co., Ltd. [1958?]

vii, 160 p.    plates, ports. diagrs., facsim., tables. 23 cm.

**2032    Nicholls, M[argaret Alexandria]**
1915-

A history of Nanoose Bay. Compiled by M. A. Nicholls for the Nanoose Centennial Committee. [Nanoose Bay, B.C., 1958]

[54] l.    plates, ports., tables.    28 cm. Mimeographed.

Includes biographical sketches.

**2033    O'Hagan, Howard**
1902-

Wilderness men.    Garden City, N.Y., Doubleday & Company, 1958.

263 p.    22 cm.

A book of adventure and crime stories of which several are of B.C. interest, including one about the Cowichan Indian, Tzouhalem.

**2034** O'Neill, [William John]
1882-1964

Time and place; stories of northern British Columbia. Stories of the West Coast, Skeena River, Bulkley Valley, Douglas Channel, and old and new Kitimat, by Wiggs O'Neil [*sic*] Sperry Cline, Gordon Robinson, and Stanley Rough. [Prince Rupert, Daily News Ltd., 1958]

53 p. 23 cm. Cover title. Selections from "Time and place," a newspaper column that first appeared in various B.C. newspapers in 1955.

B.C. ARCHIVES

**2035** Oppenheimer Bros. and Company (Vancouver)

From the beginning. [Vancouver, 1958]

[18] p. illus. (part col.) ports. 29 cm. Cover title. On cover: 1858-1958; British Columbia, Canada.

Briefly mentions the early days of the company. Oppenheimer Bros. are food brokers.

B.C. ARCHIVES

**2036** Ormsby, Margaret A[nchoretta]
1909-

British Columbia; a history. [Toronto] The Macmillans in Canada, 1958.

x, 558 p. illus., plates (part col.) ports., maps. 25 cm. Bibliography: p. 527-534. Prepared in co-operation with the British Columbia Centennial Committee. Chapter headings: Approach from the sea. — Approach from the mountains. — Outpost of commercial empire. — Outpost of Empire. — Colony on the seaboard. — The gold colony. — Jewel in Queen Victoria's diadem. — Maritime union. — Canada on the Pacific. — The spoilt child of confederation. — The great potlatch. — "The People's Dick." — Splendor sine occasu. — "Honest John" and the Liberals. — Work and wages. — By sea and land we prosper.

Reprinted in 1959 with corrections.

B.C. ARCHIVES

**2037** Pearson, John
1900-

Land of the Peace Arch. Cloverdale, B.C., Surrey Centennial Committee [1958]

xii, 159 p. plates, ports., maps (1 on lining papers) 23 cm.

A history of the municipal district of Surrey, which includes biographical sketches of pioneers.

B.C. ARCHIVES

**2039** [Porter, Lancelot]
1882-

Burton, British Columbia: "Our days before yesterday," as told by Bob Hewatson [pseud.] to Mrs. H. D. McCormack. [Burton, Burton Centennial Committee, 1958]

31 p. illus., ports. 24 cm. At head of title: Centennial of British Columbia; B.C. 1858-1958. Cover title: Burton Centennial, 1858-1958.

B.C. ARCHIVES

**2040** Ramsey, Bruce
1924-

A history of the German-Canadians in British Columbia. [Winnipeg, Printed by] National Publishers, 1958.

v, 69 p. illus., ports. 23 cm. On cover: The contribution of the Vancouver Alpen Club towards British Columbia's centennial year.

B.C. ARCHIVES

**2041** Rendall, [Evalina] Belle
1889-

Healing waters; history of Harrison Hot Springs and Port Douglas area. [Harrison Hot Springs, B.C., The author, 1958]

34 p. illus., ports., map, plan. 24 cm.

B.C. ARCHIVES

**2042** Revelstoke Ski Club

The Revelstoke Ski Club centennial tournament of champions. Historical review of Revelstoke, presented by the merchants and city of Revelstoke. [Revelstoke, 1958]

35, 5 p. illus., ports., tables. 23 cm.

B.C. ARCHIVES

**2043** Rich, E[dwin] E[rnest]
1904-

The history of the Hudson's Bay Company, 1670-1870. With a foreword by the Rt. Hon. Sir Winston Churchill. London, Hudson's Bay Record Society, 1958-59.

2v. ports. (part col.) maps (incl. 4 on lining papers) 25 cm. (The publications of the Hudson's Bay Record Society, v. 21-22) Books for reference at end of each chapter. Contents: v. 1. 1670-1763. — v. 2. 1763-1870.

In Volume 2 one chapter deals with the company on Vancouver Island during the early days of settlement.

Also: Toronto, McClelland and Stewart, 1960. 3 v. Contents: v. 1. 1670-1763. — v. 2. 1763-1820. — v. 3. 1821-1870.

B.C. ARCHIVES

**2044 Rogers, Mary Isabella (Angus)**
EDITOR

B.C. sugar. [Vancouver, British Columbia Sugar Refining Co., 1958]

87 p. illus., ports. 24 cm. Cover title: B.C. Sugar Refinery. Not for sale.

The history of the company from its founding in 1889.

B.C. ARCHIVES

**2045 Rossland Historical Museum Association**

Historical guide map and story of the city of Rossland, British Columbia. Rossland, 1958.

[6] p. (folder) maps. 28 cm.

Revised and reprinted in 1962.

B.C. ARCHIVES

**2046 Rutland. Centennial Committee**

History of the district of Rutland, British Columbia, 1858-1958. Kelowna, Printed by the Orchard City Press & Calendar Co., 1958.

127 p. illus., ports., map, facsims. 22 cm.

B.C. ARCHIVES

**2047 Sederberg, Lilian [Margaret]**
1926-

The serpent's tail. [Malakwa, B.C.] Malakwa Centennial Committee [1958]

15 p. illus. 24 cm. Cover title.

A history of Eagle Valley, including the settlements of Craigellachie, Malakwa, and Taft. Most of the information pertains to the period after 1900.

B.C. ARCHIVES

**2048 Sisters of St. Ann (Victoria)**

The sisters of St. Ann in British Columbia, Yukon, and Alaska, 1858-1958. [Victoria, 1958]

100 p. illus., ports. 29 cm.

A popular publication commemorating one hundred years in the diocese.

B.C. ARCHIVES

**2049 Squamish. Centennial Committee**

A centennial commentary upon the early days of Squamish, British Columbia. [Squamish, 1958]

[32] p. illus., ports., maps. 14 x 21 cm. Cover title.

B.C. ARCHIVES

**2050 Taylor, Gordon [deRupe]**
1923-

Delta's century of progress. Cloverdale, Kerfoot-Holmes Printing Ltd. [1958]

96 p. illus., ports., map (on inside cover) facsim. 23 cm. Sponsored by the Delta Centennial Committee. References: p. 95-96.

B.C. ARCHIVES

**2051 [Terry, George]**
COMPILER

History and legends of the Chilcotin. [Prepared by the community clubs of Alexis Creek, Big Creek, Hanceville, Riske Creek, and Meldrum Creek. Williams Lake, B.C., Cariboo Press Ltd., 1958]

48 p. 22 cm. Cover title.

Chiefly comprised of biographical information.

B.C. ARCHIVES

**2052 Trail. Centennial Committee. Old Timers Sub-Committee**

Centennial oldtimers party, sponsored by Local 480 Trail & District Smelter Workers' Union, Mine Mill Union Centre, Trail, December 18th, 1958. [Trail, 1958]

33 p. 23 cm. Cover title. Mimeographed.

Comprised of biographical notes.

B.C. ARCHIVES

**2053 Turnbull, W[illiam] H[enry]**
1884-

One hundred years of beekeeping in British Columbia, 1858-1958. [Vernon, British Columbia Honey Producers' Association, 1958]

137 p. illus., ports. 24 cm.

B.C. ARCHIVES

**2054 Upton, Primrose [(Walker)]**
1915-

The history of Okanagan Mission; a centennial retrospect. Okanagan Mission, Okanagan Mission Centennial Committee, 1958.

81 p. illus., ports., group ports., maps (1 fold) 23 cm.

The history of a community near Kelowna which contains biographical information on the area's early residents.

B.C. ARCHIVES

2055    Vallance, J[ames] D[unlop]
1903-

Untrodden ways; dedicated to the pioneers of British Columbia.    Victoria, Published for the author by Hebden Printing Co. [1958?]

150 p.    illus., ports.    25 cm.

The text is based on an unorganized collection of drawings and photographs depicting events before the First World War.

B.C. ARCHIVES


2056    Vancouver. General Hospital. Public Relations Department

The VGH story from 1886.    [Vancouver, 1958?]

[32] p.    illus.    11 x 15 cm.

Also: 1961.

B.C. ARCHIVES


2057    Vancouver historical journal

Vancouver historical journal.    January 1958+ Vancouver, Archives Society of Vancouver.

v.    illus.    23 cm.    annual.    Compiled by Major J. S. Matthews.

Has articles on early Vancouver and areas in the lower mainland.

B.C. ARCHIVES


2058    Walton, Avis [Carroll (Gray)]
EDITOR

About Victoria and Vancouver Island. [Illustrated by Peggy Walton Packard] Vol. 2 [i.e. second edition]    Victoria, New Neighbour Services, 1958.

212 p.    illus., ports., maps (1 fold.) tables.    19 cm.

A guide book with historical notes.

Third edition: 1959.

B.C. ARCHIVES


2059    Watters, Reginald Eyre
EDITOR    1912-

British Columbia; a centennial anthology. Toronto, McClelland and Stewart, 1958.

xvi, 576 p.    illus., plates (part col.) ports. (part col.) maps (incl. 2 on lining papers) facsims.    24 cm.

Includes fiction and nonfiction.

B.C. ARCHIVES


2060    Wild, Roland [Gibson]
1903-

Amor De Cosmos. Foreword by Hon. W. A. C. Bennett, premier of British Columbia.    Toronto, Ryerson Press [1958]

xi, 146 p.    2 plates, port., facsim.    22 cm.

A biography.

B.C. ARCHIVES


2061    Women's Institute. Canada. Fruitvale Women's Institute, B.C.

History of Beaver Valley & Pend d'Oreille districts.    [Fruitvale, 1958]

[16] p.    illus., ports.    23 cm.    Cover title.

B.C. ARCHIVES


2062    Bowes, G[ordon] E[merson]
COMPILER    1914-

Eye-witness accounts from the first exploration in 1793 down to 1959 of the Peace River district of British Columbia, including the Finlay and Parsnip river basins. Together with several historical and descriptive narratives, maps, a bibliography and an index.    Vancouver, Western Development and Power, 1959.

188 p.    front., maps (1 fold.) fold. facsim.    28 cm. On t.p.: For private use and study only and not for public circulation or sale.

B.C. ARCHIVES


2063    British Columbia Railway Historical Association (Victoria)

Bulletin.    1959+    Victoria.

v.    illus.    29 cm.    Mimeographed. The original name of the association was the Vancouver Island Railway Historical Association, and the first bulletin was published by it. The present association was incorporated in 1961.

Contains some information on early railways and city transportation systems.

B.C. ARCHIVES


2064    Finney, Gertrude E[lva] (Bridgeman)
1892-

Stormy winter. Decorations by Don Lambo.    New York, Longmans, Green and Co., 1959.

viii, 246 p.    21 cm.

Fiction. The Puget Sound area during the San Juan boundary dispute is the scene of this historical novel.

B.C. ARCHIVES

2065 Frémont, Donatien
1881-

Les Français dans l'Ouest canadien. Winnipeg, Editions de la Liberté, 1959.

162 p. maps. 26 cm. Bibliographic notes at end of chapters.

B.C. ARCHIVES

2066 Gamble, William G[eorge]
1877-

A history of the early days of Freemasonry in British Columbia. Victoria, Centennial Committee, Grand Lodge of British Columbia, A.F. & A.M., 1959.

39 p. 22 cm. On p. [1]: This short account is based on the first chapters of his [the author's] great work, *A history of Freemasonry in British Columbia* . . .

B.C. ARCHIVES

2067 Goult, B[arrie] H[oward] E[amer]
1903-

"This mine house . . ."; a paper commemorating the 100th anniversary of Freemasonry in British Columbia, March 19, 1859-March 19, 1959. (The early days of the craft in Vancouver's Island and British Columbia, 1859-1871) [Victoria, 1959]

[vi] 13 p. 28 cm. Cover title. Mimeographed. Bibliography: p. [v]

B.C. ARCHIVES

2068 Hamilton, J[ames] H[erbert]
1879-1964

The "All-Red Route," 1893-1953; a history of the trans-Pacific mail service between British Columbia, Australia, and New Zealand. [Victoria, Printed by Don McDiarmid, 1959]

129 p. plates, ports., table. 24 cm. Cover title. Reprinted from the *British Columbia historical quarterly*, v. 20, 1956, p. 1-126.

B.C. ARCHIVES

2069 Lawrence, J[oseph] C[ollins]
1918-

The south-west coast of Vancouver Island from Metchosin to Bamfield, including Sooke, Otter, River Jordan, and Port Renfrew. [Sooke, 1959]

73, [1] p. plates, ports., map. 24 cm. Cover title: A brief history of Sooke district. Published under the sponsorship of the Sooke and North Sooke Women's Institute. Bibliography: p. [74]

B.C. ARCHIVES

2070 Lee, Norman
1862-1939

The journal of Norman Lee, 1898, which is the account of a cattle-drive from the Chilcotin country to Teslin Lake by the Telegraph Trail. Prepared for publication by Gordon R. Elliott. Vancouver, [Private press of] Robert and Felicity Reid, 1959.

x, 58 p. illus., fold. map, facsims. 25 cm.

Appeared in 1960 with a foreword by Eileen Laurie under title: *Klondike cattle drive; the journal of Norman Lee* (Vancouver, Mitchell Press).

B.C. ARCHIVES

2071 [Nielsen, Jean]
1922-

Choose this day [by] Hannah Sarver [pseud.] New York, Funk & Wagnalls Company [1959]

245 p. illus. 22 cm.

Juvenile fiction. Fort St. James, Victoria, and London are the settings of this novel in which a young girl of sixteen meets Queen Victoria. The story begins in 1849.

B.C. ARCHIVES

2072 Norcross, Elizabeth Blanche
1920-

The warm land. Duncan, B.C., Published by the author [1959]

xi, 112 p. plates, group port., map, tables. 23 cm.

A history of the Cowichan Valley, Vancouver Island, with biographical sketches.

B.C. ARCHIVES

2073 Ostos, Quoron

Skulamagee; a story of early Vancouver. Boston, The Christopher Publishing House [1959]

254 p. 21 cm.

Fiction. The setting is a Fraser River logging camp about 1889.

B.C. ARCHIVES

2074 Peake, Frank A[lexander]
1913-

The Anglican Church in British Columbia. Vancouver, Mitchell Press, 1959.

208 p. illus., plates, ports., map (on lining papers) facsim., table. 23 cm. Bibliography: p. 197-199. Bibliographic notes at end of chapters.

A general, popular history.

B.C. ARCHIVES

**2075 Pearson, Leslie T[rayer] H[olt]**
1906-1965

The memoirs of a cathedral; a century of Christian activity, 1859-1959. New Westminster, Holy Trinity Cathedral [1959]

71 p. illus., ports. 24 cm.

B.C. ARCHIVES

**2076 Spry, Irene M[ary (Biss)]**

Captain John Palliser and the exploration of western Canada. [London, Printed by William Clowes and Sons, 1959]

[149]-184 p. plates, ports., maps (1 fold.) 25 cm. Cover title. References: p. 170-184. Reprinted from the *Geographical journal*, v. 125, pt. 2, 1959.

Outlines the background to Palliser's expedition and the later ramifications of his exploration. The references (and notes) are a valuable aid to further inquiry.

B.C. ARCHIVES

**2077 Stewart, John**
1887-

Early days at Fraser Mills, B.C., from 1889 to 1912. [n.p., n.d.]

29 l. 29 cm. Caption title. Mimeographed.

A chronological record of lumbering at Fraser Mills.

B.C. ARCHIVES

**2078 Tutt, [Nellie (Hereron)]**
COMPILER 1895-

The history of Ellison district, 1858-1958. Compiled by Mrs. D. Tutt. [Kelowna] Published by the Ellison Centennial Committee, 1959.

116 p. illus., ports., maps (1 on inside front cover) 23 cm.

Includes biographical sketches.

B.C. ARCHIVES

**2079 Vancouver. Chinese United Church**

A hundred years of Christian Chinese work in British Columbia, 1859-1959. [n.p., 1959]

12 p. illus., ports. 27 cm. Cover title.

B.C. ARCHIVES

**2080 Veitch, D.**

The Royal Engineers and British Columbia. [n.p., n.d.]

106-107 p. illus., port., map. 25 cm. Reprinted from the *Royal Engineers journal*, v. 72, June 1959.

B.C. ARCHIVES

**2081 Victoria. Metropolitan United Church**

Metropolitan United Church, Victoria, B.C., 1859-1959. [Victoria, Printed by Hebden Printing Co., 1959]

14 p. illus., ports. 28 cm. Cover title.

Has four pages on early Methodist activity in Victoria.

B.C. ARCHIVES

**2082 Virgin, Victor E[rnest]**
1892-1964

History of North and South Saanich pioneers and district. Victoria, Saanich Pioneer Society [1959]

79 p. plates. 22 cm.

Contains biographical sketches under a section entitled "Pioneers" (p. 13-52).

B.C. ARCHIVES

**2083 Williams, J. Rae**

The story of a church; Queen's Avenue United Church, New Westminster, B.C., 1859-1959. [New Westminster, 1959]

32 p. illus., ports. 24 cm. Cover title: One hundred years, 1859-1959; a historical sketch . . .

Also outlines the history of Columbian Methodist College and other churches in New Westminster.

B.C. ARCHIVES

**2084 Akademîa Nauk SSSR. Trudy Instituta Etnografii**

Amerikanskiĭ etnograficheskiĭ sbornik. Moscow, Akademia Nauk SSSR, 1960. [Otvetstevennye redaktory: Îu. P. Averkieva]

202 p. illus., maps (2 fold.) 27 cm. (Trudy Instituta Ethnografii. Novaîa serîa, tom 58)

A work on the social organization of the Northwest Coast Indians, which includes a section (p. 5-126) on the families and potlatches of the Tlingit, Haida, and Tsimshian Indians in the middle of the nineteenth century.

B.C. ARCHIVES

**2085 Canada. Department of Citizenship and Immigration. Indian Affairs Branch**

Indians of British Columbia; an historical review. Ottawa, 1960.

16 l. 26 cm. Bibliography: p. 16.

B.C. ARCHIVES

## 2086    Case, Victoria

Applesauce needs sugar. [Drawings by Reisie Lonette]    Garden City, N.Y., Doubleday & Company, 1960.

232 p.    illus.    22 cm.

Fiction. The story of a large family living on a twenty-acre farm near Victoria in the 1890's. Some of the text appeared previously in the *Saturday evening post*.

## 2087    Chinese Consolidated Benevolent Association (Victoria)

[Chinese Consolidated Benevolent Association, 1884-1959, and Chinese public school, 1899-1959.    Victoria, 1960?]

1 v. (unpaged)    illus., ports.    27 cm.    Text in Chinese. Foreword in English by S. H. Chan.

## 2088    Copland, [Sir] Douglas [Berry]
### EDITOR   1894-

Giblin, the scholar and the man; papers in memory of Lyndhurst Falkiner Giblin.    Melbourne, F. W. Cheshire [1960]

vii, 228 p.    port., map.    26 cm.

Includes a chapter by Charles Camsell on Giblin's activities in the Cassiar district during the winter of 1898-9.

## 2089    Cronin, Kay

Cross in the wilderness.    Vancouver, Mitchell Press [c1960]

xxiii, 255 p.    plates, ports., map (on lining papers) 23 cm.    Bibliography: p. 246-249.

Stories highlighting the outstanding personalities and events in the history of the pioneer Oblate Fathers in British Columbia.

## 2090    Downs, Art[hur George]
### 1924-

Wagon road north; the story of the Cariboo gold rush in historical photos.    [Quesnel, Northwest Digest Ltd., 1960]

76, [4] p.    illus., ports., maps (1 double)    28 cm.

## 2091    [Forbes, George]

The history of St. Peter's Parish (Oblate Fathers) New Westminster, B.C., 1860-1960.    [New Westminster, Columbian Co., printers, 1960?]

48 p.    illus., plates, ports., group ports. (1 fold.) 26 cm.    Cover title: St. Peter's, New Westminster, 100th anniversary.

## 2092    Hardy, W[illiam] G[eorge]
### 1896-

From sea unto sea; Canada—1850-1910: the road to nationhood.    Garden City, N.Y., Doubleday, 1960.

528 p.    maps (1 on lining papers)    22 cm. [Canadian history series, v. 4]    Bibliography: p. [501]-504.

## 2093    Hayes, John F[rancis]
### 1904-

Quest in the Cariboo. Illustrated by Fred Finley. Vancouver, The Copp Clark Publishing Co. [1960]

240 p.    illus., maps (on lining papers)    21 cm. Bibliography: p. 239-240.

Juvenile fiction. In 1860 a young boy leaves Victoria to journey to the Cariboo in search of his brother whose gold claim was northeast of Williams Lake.

## 2094    Lamb, W[illiam] Kaye
### 1904-

Sawney's letters, or Cariboo rhymes, from 1864 to 1868. Texts by W. Kaye Lamb and Michael R. Booth.    [Vancouver, British Columbia Library Quarterly, 1960]

[12] p. (incl. cover)    24 cm.    (Early British Columbia imprints, no. 2)    Cover title.

## 2095    Large, R[ichard] G[eddes]
### 1901-

Prince Rupert, a gateway to Alaska.    Vancouver, Mitchell Press Limited, 1960.

210 p.    illus., ports.    29 cm.

On highlights of the city's history.

## 2096    Nesbitt, James K[night]
### 1908-

Early days of the Victoria Gas Company; our 100th year, 1860-1960. Illustrations [by] Mary Ellen Morgan.    [Victoria, Public Information Department, B.C. Electric Company, 1960]

23 p.    illus.    21 cm.    Cover title.

2097 New Westminster. Centennial
Committee

New Westminster, the royal city; a century of
history. [New Westminster, 1960]

[20] p. illus., ports. 21 cm. Cover title.
Includes: "New Westminster, the royal city; the first
100 years," by Willard E. Ireland.

B.C. ARCHIVES

2098 O'Neill, [William John]
1882-1964

Steamboat days on the Skeena River, British
Columbia, by Wiggs O'Neill. [Edited by Stan
Rough. Kitimat, B.C., Printed by Northern
Sentinel Press, 1960]

35 p. 21 cm.

B.C. ARCHIVES

2099 O'Neill, [William John]
1882-1964

Whitewater men of the Skeena, by Wiggs O'Neill.
[Edited by Stan Rough. Kitimat, B.C., 1960]

28 p. port. (on cover) 23 cm.

Stories of Skeena River steamboat days.

B.C. ARCHIVES

2100 Pearson, John
1900-

Land of the royal Kwantlen; "A history of North
Surrey, B.C.," by John Pearson and J. M. Reitz.
[North Surrey, North Surrey Athletic Association,
1960]

27 p. 24 cm. Cover title.

B.C. ARCHIVES

2101 Phair, A[rthur] W[illiam]
A[rmitt]
1880-

Outline history of Lillooet, British Columbia,
county of Cariboo. [Lillooet, The author, 1960]

[4] p. illus. (on covers) 22 cm. Caption title.
Title of illustration on cover: Hunters return from
hunter's paradise.

B.C. ARCHIVES

2102 Shier, Morley
1888-

Early days of dynamite plants in British Columbia.
[n.p., 1960]

16 p. 36 cm. Caption title. Mimeographed.

The story of nine dynamite plants operating in the
province from 1879 to present times.

VANCOUVER PUBLIC LIBRARY

2103 Stackhouse, Cyril
1886-

The churches of St. John the Divine, Derby
(1859)—Yale (1860) in the crown colony of
British Columbia, and their first rector, the
Reverend William Burton Crickmer, M.A.
(Oxon.) With illustrations from photographs
and drawings from the scrap-book of the Rev.
W. B. Crickmer. [Vancouver, Archives Society
of Vancouver, 1960]

32 p. illus., ports., map, facsims., tables. 23 cm.
Cover title: William Burton Crickmer, pioneer of the
crown colony of British Columbia. Reprinted from
the *Vancouver historical journal*, no. 2, 1959,
p. 77-104.

B.C. ARCHIVES

2104 Tanghe, Raymond
COMPILER 1898-

Bibliography of Canadian bibliographies.
Toronto, Published in association with the
Bibliographic Society of Canada by University of
Toronto Press, 1960.

206 p. 24 cm. Added t.p. in French. Index of
compilers and compilations: p. [183]-196. Author
index: p. [197]-203. Index of subjects: p. [204]-206.

Supplement, 1960 & 1961: Toronto, 1962.
Supplement, 1962 & 1963: Toronto, 1964.

UNIVERSITY OF VICTORIA LIBRARY

2105 Taylor, [Henry Edwin]
1889-

Powell River's first 50 years [by Harry Taylor.
Powell River, A. H. Alsgard, 1960]

1 v. (unpaged) illus., ports. 29 cm. Cover title.

B.C. ARCHIVES

2106 Texada Island Centennial
Committee

Texada. [Vananda, B.C.] 1960.

xii, 51 p. plates, ports., maps (incl. 1 on lining
papers) facsims. 24 cm. On slip mounted on t.p.:
Compiled under the direction of Mr. and Mrs. Cecil
May, historians for the committee.

B.C. ARCHIVES

2107 Booth, Michael R.

The beginnings of theatre in British Columbia.
[n.p., 1961]

[159]-168 p. 25 cm. Caption title. Reprinted from
*Queen's quarterly*, v. 68, 1961.

A history to 1898.

B.C. ARCHIVES

**2108  Clark, Henry W.**

Buck Choquette, stampeder.   [n.p., n.d.]

[vi], 152 p.  port.   28 cm.   Cover title. References: p. [iii]-[iv] Mimeographed. Spiral binding.

The story of a gold prospector, Alexander Choquette (1829-1898).

B.C. ARCHIVES

**2109  Freeman, Beatrice J. (Spalding)**
COMPILER

A gulf island patchwork; some early events on the islands of Galiano, Mayne, Saturna, North and South Pender.   Sidney, Published for the Gulf Islands Branch, B.C. Historical Association, by the Peninsula Printing Co. [1961?]

190 p.  illus., ports.   23 cm.

Comprised of short articles. It includes biographical information.

B.C. ARCHIVES

**2110  Freemasons. New Westminster. Union Lodge No. 9**

Union Lodge No. 9, A.F. & A.M., G.R.B.C.; souvenir programme and history.   [New Westminster, Jackson Printing Co., 1961]

25 p.   22 cm.   The first one hundred years, Union Lodge No. 9, A.F. & A.M., G.R.B.C., 1861-1961: p. 12-25. Xerox copy of cover and p. 12-25 seen.

VANCOUVER PUBLIC LIBRARY

**2111  Gest, Lillian**

History of Lake O'Hara in the Canadian Rockies at Hector, British Columbia, Canada. Philadelphia, Privately printed, 1961.

38 p.   23 cm.   Appendix A: Place names. Appendix B: First ascents. Bibliography: p. 37-38.

Primarily a history of mountaineering and exploration in the area.

B.C. ARCHIVES

**2112  McGregor, D[onald] A[nderson]**
1879-

Vancouver's early newspapers; an address to B.C. Historical Association, Vancouver Branch, by D. A. McGregor, February 23, 1961. [Vancouver, 1961]

24 l.   29 cm.   Cover title. Mimeographed.

VANCOUVER PUBLIC LIBRARY

**2113  McLarty, Stanley D.**

The story of Strathcona school.   [Vancouver] 1961.

85 p.  illus., group ports.   28 cm.   Cover title: Strathcona school, 1873-1961.

B.C. ARCHIVES

**2114  Morley, Alan P.**
1905-

Vancouver, from milltown to metropolis. Vancouver, Mitchell Press [c1961]

234 p.  plates, ports., maps.   24 cm.

A newspaperman's portrait of the city.

B.C. ARCHIVES

**2115  Ramsey, Bruce**
1924-

Barkerville; a guide in word and picture to the fabulous gold camp of the Cariboo.   Vancouver, Mitchell Press [1961]

iv, 92 p.  illus., ports., maps (on inside covers) 21 cm.

B.C. ARCHIVES

**2116  Rough, Stanley**
EDITOR

Along the totem trail; Port Essington to Hazelton, by Sperry Cline, Wiggs O'Neill, Mrs. E. N. Whitlow, Stan Rough.   [Kitimat, Printed by Northern Sentinel Press, c1961]

44 p.  illus. (on covers)   21 cm.   Cover title.

Stories of people and places along the banks of the Skeena River; primarily concerned with events after 1900.

B.C. ARCHIVES

**2117  Saanichton. Saint Stephen's Church**

Centenary of Saint Stephen's Church, 1862-1962 [by Muriel Watson.   Saanichton, B.C., 1961]

14 p.  illus.   25 cm.   Cover title: Saint Stephen's, 1862-1962.

B.C. ARCHIVES

**2118  Steffens, Sophia**
1886-

The land of Chief Nicola; poems, verses and historical reminiscences of the Nicola Valley. [n.p., 1961]

[24] p.  illus., ports.   24 cm.

B.C. ARCHIVES

2119  Turnbull, Elsie G[rant
      (Willard)]
      1903-

Trail, 1901-1961; 60 years of progress.
[Production editing by Craig Weir.   Trail, B.C.,
Trail Diamond Jubilee Committee, 1961]

61 p.   illus., ports., facsim., table.   23 cm.   Cover
title.

Relates in part to events before 1900.

B.C. ARCHIVES


2120  Vaulx, Bernard de

D'une mer à l'autre: les Oblats de Marie-
Immaculée au Canada, 1841-1961. Post-face de
Daniel-Rops.   [Lyon] Editions du Chalet [1961?]

220 p.   maps.   19 cm.   (L'Esprit et l'Eglise, v. 3)
Bibliographic notes at bottom of pages.

B.C. ARCHIVES


2121  Arnott, [Ida Janet (Gammage)]
      1906-

The burning bush in the sagebrush hills; a short
history of St. Andrews Presbyterian Church,
Kamloops, British Columbia, 1887-1962 [by]
Mrs. D. A. Arnott.   [North Kamloops, Overland
Press Ltd., 1962]

[20] p.   illus., ports.   20 cm.   Cover title.

B.C. ARCHIVES


2122  Ballon, H. C.

Sir James Hector, M.D., 1834-1907.   [n.p., 1962]

9 p.   illus., ports.   29 cm.   Cover title. Reprinted
from the *Canadian Medical Association journal,*
v. 87, 1962, p. 66-74.

B.C. ARCHIVES


2123  British Columbia Historical
      Association. Victoria Branch

Ross Bay Cemetery.   [Victoria? 1962?]

[5] p. (folder)   illus., map.   23 x 10 cm.

Includes a location key to the graves of over sixty
prominent Victoria pioneers.

B.C. ARCHIVES


2124  Daem, M[ary (Bannerman)]
      1914-

A history of early Revelstoke, by M. Daem and E.
E. Dickey.   Revelstoke [Printed by The Review]
1962.

13 p.   illus., map (on cover)   23 cm.

B.C. ARCHIVES


2125  Deutsch, Herman J[ulius]
      EDITOR

United States-Canada boundary in the Pacific
Northwest; surveying the 49th parallel, 1858-61.
Tacoma, Washington State Historical Society,
1962.

17 p.   illus., map.   27 cm.   (Pacific Northwest
historical pamphlet, no. 2)   Reprinted from the
*Pacific Northwest quarterly,* v. 53, 1962.

Mainly comprised of dispatches from Lt. Col. John
Summerfield Hawkins, Royal Engineers, dated 1860
and 1861.

U.B.C. SPECIAL COLLECTIONS


2126  Frith, Austin F[rancis]
      1919-

The lost stagecoach; a story of gold rush days on
the Cariboo Trail. [Drawings by Leo Rampen]
Toronto, W. J. Gage Limited [1962]

168 p.   illus., col. maps (on lining papers)   22 cm.
(Frontier books)

Juvenile fiction. A frontier coach driver relates
pioneer tales to two children.

B.C. ARCHIVES


2127  Greene, Ronald A[llen]
      1938-

Macdonald & Company, bankers, Victoria,
Vancouver Island, 1859-1864; a numismatic
study.   [Victoria, 1962]

[12] p.   facsims., tables.   21 cm.   Cover title.
References: cover, p. [3]

B.C. ARCHIVES


2128  Haig-Brown, Roderick
      [Langmere Haig]
      1908-

Fur and gold. Illustrated by Paul Duff.   Toronto,
Longmans Canada [1962]

ix, 131 p.   illus.   22 cm.   (Canadian pageant)

A story for the young reader based on the career of
Sir James Douglas.

B.C. ARCHIVES


2129  Hughes, Ben
      1882-

History of the Comox Valley.   [Nanaimo, Printed
by Evergreen Press (V.I.), 1962]

58 p.   ports.   23 cm.

Covers events up to the end of the Second World
War; includes twelve biographical sketches.

B.C. ARCHIVES

2130    Larson, Joan I.

From Cum Cloops 1812 to Kamloops 1962.
[Illustrated by the author.    Kamloops, 1962]

20 p.    illus., map (on cover)    22 cm.    Cover title.

B.C. ARCHIVES


2131    Lindsay, F[rederick] W[illiam]
        1903-

Cariboo yarns.    [Quesnel, 1962]

60 p.    illus., ports., map (on inside cover)    24 cm.

Stories of the gold rush days based on diaries and
reminiscences.

B.C. ARCHIVES


2132    MacEwan, [John Walter] Grant
        1902-

Blazing the old cattle trail. Illustrated by Wm. W.
Perehudoff.    Saskatoon, Modern Press [1962]

248 p.    illus.    23 cm.    [Prairie books]

Includes accounts of the cattle drives made by
Thaddeus Harper, Joseph Greaves, and Norman Lee,
and of the Hull brothers' horse drive.

B.C. ARCHIVES


2133    McLean, Frances
        1921-

Barkerville ballads.    Okanagan Centre [The
author] 1962

[25] p.    illus.    17 cm.

A collection of short poems describing Barkerville
characters of the gold rush period.

B.C. ARCHIVES


2134    Nicholson, George [Salier Willis]
        1887-

Vancouver Island's west coast, 1762-1962. With
illustrations, map, and list of shipwrecks.
[Victoria, Morriss Printing Company, 1962]

356 p.    illus., ports., maps (on lining-papers)
25 cm.

B.C. ARCHIVES


2135    Peterson, Lester Ray
        1917-

The Gibson's Landing story.    [Toronto, P.
Martin Books Canada, c1962]

viii, 121 p.    illus., plates, ports., maps.    26 cm.
On cover: An illustrated history of Gibson's Landing
and the "Sunshine Coast."

B.C. ARCHIVES


2136    Ramsey, Bruce
        1924-

P.G.E.; railway to the North.    Vancouver,
Mitchell Press [1962]

265 p.    illus., ports., map (on lining paper)    23 cm.

A history of the Pacific Great Eastern Railway which
includes considerable information on the various early
provincial railway schemes.

B.C. ARCHIVES


2137    Reinhart, Herman Francis
        1832-1889

The golden frontier; the recollections of Herman
Francis Reinhart, 1851-1869. Edited by Doyce B.
Nunis, Jr. Foreword by Nora B. Cunningham.
Austin, University of Texas Press [c1962]

353 p.    plates, port., maps.    24 cm.    (Personal
narratives of the West)    Bibliography: p. [311]-317.

Includes a chapter on Reinhart's hazardous overland
journey of 1858 to the Fraser River mines via Fort
Simcoe, Okanagan Lake, and Fort Thompson, and on
his prospecting activities. It offers an insight into the
American miners' lawlessness and their treatment of
Indians.

B.C. ARCHIVES


2138    Roberts, Eric A[rthur]
        1907-

Salt Spring saga.    Ganges, B.C., Driftwood
[c1962]

67 p.    plates, map.    23 cm.    Cover title: Salt
Spring saga; an exciting story of pioneer days. Errata
slip.

An account of the early settlement on Saltspring
Island.

B.C. ARCHIVES


2139    Rowland, C[harles] L[ouis]
        G[ordon]
        1920-

A memento of your visit to Barkerville; St.
Saviour's Church, Barkerville, B.C., built 1869.
[n.p., Observerprint, 1962]

[8] p. (incl. cover)    22 cm.    Cover title.

Relates to the work of James Reynard, vicar of the
church, 1863-71.

B.C. ARCHIVES


2140    Vancouver. City Archives

The founding of the Salvation Army, Vancouver,
as told by those who established it.    Vancouver,
City Archives, 1962.

43 p.    illus., ports., facsims.    23 cm.    Cover title.

B.C. ARCHIVES

## 2141 Victoria. First United Church

One hundred years, 1862-1962; First United Church, Victoria, British Columbia. Compiled by Centennial Committee of First United Church. [Victoria, Morriss Printing Company, 1962]

38 p. illus., ports. 28 cm.

A detailed history.

B.C. ARCHIVES

## 2142 Victoria. St. Joseph's Hospital

St. Joseph's Hospital, Victoria, British Columbia, 1875-1962. [Victoria, 1962]

[10] p. illus. 25 cm.

Two pages deal with a chronological listing of important events in the hospital's history.

B.C. ARCHIVES

## 2143 Victoria Centennial Celebration Society. 1962

Victoria, British Columbia, Canada; Centennial celebrations, 1862-1962. [Victoria, 1962]

[100] p. illus., ports. 28 cm. Cover title: Victoria historical review: 1862-1962, one hundred years of progress. Historical research, writing, and compilation by James K. Nesbitt.

Chiefly comprised of early newspaper excerpts; extensively illustrated from photographs.

B.C. ARCHIVES

## 2144 Bowes, Gordon E[merson]
### EDITOR 1914-

Peace River chronicles; eighty-one eye-witness accounts from the first exploration in 1793 of the Peace River region of British Columbia, including the Finlay and Parsnip river basins. Selected and edited by Gordon E. Bowes. Forty pages of illustrations; a bibliography, maps and an index. [Vancouver] Prescott Publishing Company [1963]

557 p. plates, ports., maps (1 fold. attached to back cover) 25 cm. Bibliography: p. 539-546.

B.C. ARCHIVES

## 2145 Bushby, Arthur Thomas
### 1835-1875

Journal, 1858-1859. Edited, with an introduction and notes, by Dorothy Blakey Smith. [Victoria, Printed by A. Sutton, 1963]

83-198 p. 24 cm. Reprinted from the *British Columbia historical quarterly*, v. 21, January-October 1957-8.

" ... it is also, in its frank and immediate comment on men and affairs in early British Columbia, a record of no inconsiderable value to the historian."—p. 83.

B.C. ARCHIVES

## 2146 Coombes, [Elizabeth Erna (Schneider)]
### 1901-

How gold came to Henry in a booming mining camp, by Mrs. A. P. Coombes. [Rossland] Printed by the Miner Printing Co., 1963.

45 p. illus., port. 23 cm.

Juvenile fiction. A young boy accompanies his father from Denver, Colorado, to Rossland in 1896, and learns much about life in a prosperous mining town.

B.C. ARCHIVES

## 2147 Florin, Lambert

Ghost town trails. Maps and drawings by David C. Mason, M.D. Seattle, Superior Publishing Company [c1963]

192 p. illus., maps. 28 cm. Acknowledgments and bibliography: p. 190.

Has information on the following former British Columbia settlements: Beaver Pass, Richfield, Barkerville, Cameronton, Stanley, Yale, Ashcroft Manor, Copper Mountain and Allenby, Granite Creek, Hedley, and Coalmont.

VANCOUVER PUBLIC LIBRARY

## 2148 Frontiers Unlimited

Frontier guide to the incredible Rogers Pass. [Calgary, Alta., 1963]

56 p. illus., port., map. 21 cm. (Frontier book, no. 8) References and sources: p. 56.

A history mainly concerned with railway events and construction.

B.C. ARCHIVES

## 2149 Frontiers Unlimited

The romantic Crow's Nest Pass. [Calgary, Alta., 1963]

48 p. illus., maps. 22 cm. (Frontier book, no. 5) Cover title.

A motorist's guide book with historical notes of the area between Cranbrook, B.C., and Fort Macleod, Alberta.

B.C. ARCHIVES

## 2150 Kiwanis Club of Nanaimo

Nanaimo Pioneer Cemetery. [Nanaimo, 1963?]

[4] p. 24 cm. Cover title. On p. [1]: Order of service for the Nanaimo Pioneer Cemetery; in memoriam; sponsored by Hub City Kiwanis Club.

Includes notes on Nanaimo's first cemetery by Patricia M. Johnson.

B.C. ARCHIVES

2151 Kootenay Lake General Hospital Society

Kootenay Lake General Hospital, since 1893. [Nelson, 1963]

51. 28 cm. Cover title. Mimeographed.

B.C. ARCHIVES

2152 Legg, Herbert
1891-

Customs services in western Canada, 1867-1925; a history. Creston, B.C., Creston Review Ltd., 1962 [i.e. 1963]

321 p. illus., ports., maps. 23 cm.

B.C. ARCHIVES

2153 Lindsay, F[rederick] W[illiam]
1903-

The outlaws. With pen and ink sketches by Florence Lindsay. [Quesnel, The author, 1963]

64 p. illus., ports., double map. 24 cm.

Biographical sketches of notorious B.C. criminals.

B.C. ARCHIVES

2154 MacMillan, Bloedel and Powell River Limited. Chemainus Division

A century of sawmilling. Chemainus, B.C., 1963.

[4] p. illus. 28 cm.

Traces the mill's history from its establishment by Thomas Askew in 1862 to its modern operation.

B.C. ARCHIVES

2155 Morse, J[ohn] J[esse]
1906-

Schools and scholars; a history of schools in Kamloops. [Kamloops, The author, 1963?]

14 p. 28 cm. Cover title. Mimeographed.

B.C. ARCHIVES

2156 Olsen, W[illiam] H[enry]
1914-

Water over the wheel. Illustrated by R. L. Ryan. [Chemainus, Chemainus Valley Historical Society, 1963]

169 p. illus., plates, ports., maps (1 fold.) 23 cm.

A history of Chemainus, Vancouver Island.

B.C. ARCHIVES

2157 Ramsey, Bruce
1924-

Ghost towns of British Columbia. Vancouver, Mitchell Press [c1963]

226 p. illus., maps. 24 cm.

Recounts the growth and decline of the mining towns.

B.C. ARCHIVES

2158 United States. National Archives

Preliminary inventory of the Sir Henry S. Wellcome papers in the Federal Records Center, Seattle, Washington. Record group 316. Compiled by Elmer W. Lindgard. Washington, National Archives, National Archives and Records Service, General Services Administration, 1963.

v, 13 p. 26 cm. (*Its* Publication no. 63-17. Preliminary inventory no. 150)

B.C. ARCHIVES

2159 Wells, Oliver N[elson]

A. C. Wells; a biography. [n.p.] 1963

9 l. 28 cm. Cover title. Mimeographed.

An account of Allen Casey Wells' farming activities which he began in 1865 in the Fraser Valley.

B.C. ARCHIVES

2160 Audain, James [Guy Payne]
1903-

Alex Dunsmuir's dilemma. Victoria, Sunnylane Publishing Company [c1964]

x, 133 p. plates, ports. 24 cm.

A popular account of the Dunsmuir family, with the accent on the private life of Alexander Dunsmuir (1854-1900).

B.C. ARCHIVES

2161 Brown, Robert Craig
1935-

Canada's national policy, 1883-1900; a study in Canadian-American relations. Princeton, New Jersey, Princeton University Press, 1964.

xi, 436 p. illus., map. 21 cm. Bibliography: p. 411-423.

Includes chapters on the Bering Sea dispute and the Alaska boundary question.

B.C. ARCHIVES

2162 Graham, Clara [Lucy (Drake)]
1860?-1957

This was the Kootenay. [Vancouver, Evergreen Press, 1964, c1963]

x, 270 p. illus., map. 21 cm. Some Kootenay place names: p. 265-269. References: p. 270.

B.C. ARCHIVES

2163 Hamilton, Walter R.
1872?-1964

The Yukon story; a sourdough's record of goldrush days and Yukon progress from the earliest times to the present day.    Vancouver, Mitchell Press Limited [c1964]

xiii, 261 p.    plates (1 col.) ports., maps (1 fold. col.) 24 cm.    Bibliography: p. [249]

Chief emphasis of the work is on events during the years 1897-1901. It includes several chapters on the routes to the Yukon. The author was one of the few men who reached the Yukon by travelling through the interior of British Columbia.

B.C. ARCHIVES

2164    Johnson, F[rancis] Henry
1908-

A history of public education in British Columbia. Vancouver, University of British Columbia, 1964.

viii, 279 p.    map, diagrs., tables.    24 cm.    A selected bibliography: p. 273-274.

B.C. ARCHIVES

2165    Lunny, W[illiam] J[ohn]
1930-

A history of St. Andrew's Comox District Church, 1864-1964.    [Courtenay, B.C., 1964]

18 p.    illus., ports.    22 cm.    Cover title: St. Andrew's, 1864-1964.

B.C. ARCHIVES

2166    McCabe, James O.

The San Juan water boundary question. [Toronto] University of Toronto Press [c1964]

163 p.    map.    26 cm.    (Canadian studies in history and government, no. 5)    Bibliography: p. [139]-144.

B.C. ARCHIVES

2167    [Morse, John Jesse]
1906-

The old saint; a biography of Mr. Captain Saint Paul, chief of the Shuswap Indians.    [Kamloops, The author, n.d.]

15 l.    28 cm.    Cover title. Mimeographed.

A biography of Jean Baptiste Lolo (1798-1868).

B.C. ARCHIVES

2168    Nesbitt, James K[night]
EDITOR    1908-

St. Louis College, Victoria, British Columbia,

Canada; centennial, 1864-1964.    [Victoria, 1964]

67 p.    illus., ports., group ports.    26 cm.

Includes historical information.

B.C. ARCHIVES

2169    Sprague, Marshall

The great gates; the story of the Rocky Mountain passes.    Boston, Toronto, Little, Brown and Company [c1964]

468 p.    plates, 2 maps.    22 cm.    A roster of passes: p. [371]-456. Notes: p. [323]-355. Sources: p. [356]-364.

A history of the utilization of the mountain passes, including those situated north of the 49th parallel. In the roster the passes of the Canadian Rockies and Selkirks are separately listed with notes on their location and name derivation.

VANCOUVER PUBLIC LIBRARY

2170    Spry, Irene M[ary (Biss)]

The Palliser expedition; an account of John Palliser's British North American expedition, 1857-1860.    Toronto, Macmillan Co. of Canada, 1963 [i.e. 1964]

vii, 310 p.    plates, ports., maps.    23 cm.

B.C. ARCHIVES

2171    Turnbull, Elsie G[rant (Willard)]
1903-

Topping's Trail.    Vancouver, Mitchell Press [c1964]

65 p.    plates, ports.    24 cm.

The story of Eugene Sayre Topping (1844-1917) and the early development of Trail.

B.C. ARCHIVES

2172    Victoria. Chamber of Commerce

100 years on forward thinking from 1863 to 1963. Victoria [1964]

25 p.    illus., ports.    28 cm.    Historian: James K. Nesbitt.

About one-half of the publication relates to events concerned with the Victoria Board of Trade prior to 1900.

B.C. ARCHIVES

2173    Washington (state) National Guard

Collection of official documents on the San Juan imbroglio, 1859-1872.    [n.p., 1964?]

[58] l.    27 cm.

B.C. ARCHIVES

# ABBREVIATIONS

| | | | | |
|---|---|---|---|---|
| acad. | academy | H.B.C. | Hudson's Bay Company |
| agric. | agricultural | hist. | historical, history |
| Am. | American | hon. | honorary |
| assoc. | association | incl. | including |
| asst. | assistant | inst. | institute |
| att.-gen. | attorney-general | jour. | journal |
| auth. | author | jt. | joint |
| b. | born | L. | Lake |
| B.C. | British Columbia | lt. | lieutenant |
| bp. | bishop | m. | married |
| Br. | Britain, British | nat. | national |
| Calif. | California | Ore. | Oregon |
| Camb. | Cambridge | p. | page |
| Can. | Canada, Canadian | pam. | pamphlet |
| cap. | caption | phil. | philosophical |
| chn. | chairman | pref. | preface |
| com. | commission, commissioner | *Proc. and trans.* | Proceedings and transactions |
| comp. | compiler | prof. | professor |
| corr. | correspondence | prov. | province, provincial |
| cov. | cover | pseud. | pseudonym |
| d. | died | pub. | publication(s), publisher |
| dau. | daughter | quart. | quarterly |
| dept. | department | R. | river |
| desc. | description | reg. | register |
| div. | division | rev. | review |
| doc. | document | roy. | royal |
| Dom. | Dominion | sc. | science |
| ed. | editor | sec. | secretary |
| Edin. | Edinburgh | soc. | society |
| fam. | family | supt. | superintendent |
| frwd. | foreword | t.p. | title page |
| Ft. | Fort | terr. | territory |
| gen. | general | trans. | translator |
| geog. | geographical, geography | U.B.C. | University of British Columbia |
| geol. | geological, geology | univ. | university |
| gov. | governor | v., vol., vols. | volume(s) |
| gov't | government | V.I. | Vancouver Island |
| H. of C. | House of Commons | y. | year(s) |
| H. of L. | House of Lords | | |

# INDEX

References in the Index are to entry numbers. Titles of publications are in italics and only appear if they are distinctive. Main entries, or what may be termed "item headings," which are either personal authors or corporate bodies, are in capitals. Subjects, joint authors, editors, translators, etc., are in roman type. Dates of publication appear in parentheses.

## Key to the sources for biographical notes

The authors' biographical notes were compiled from such varied sources as newspapers, book jackets, city directories, and the authors' books. A wealth of information was also found in the sources that are listed below together with their letter codes. In the Index the sources appear in parentheses immediately after the biographical notations.

| | |
|---|---|
| A | Allibone, Samuel Austin. A critical dictionary of English literature and British and American authors... London, J. B. Lippincott & Co., 1884-91. 5 v. (incl. supplements) |
| Am | American men of science; a biographical directory, edited by Jaques Cattell. 10th ed. Tempe, The Jaques Cattell Press, Inc., 1960-62. 5 v. Vols. 1-4, The physical and biological sciences; vol. 5, The social and behavioral sciences. |
| Apa | Appleton's cyclopaedia of American biography, edited by James Grant Wilson and John Fiske. New York, D. Appleton and Company, 1887-89. 6 v. |
| B | Biographical dictionary of well-known British Columbians, with a historical sketch by J. B. Kerr. Vancouver, Kerr & Begg, 1890. xxx, 326 p. |
| B.C. Cen. Com. | British Columbia Centennial Commission. The abbreviation refers to a series of brief biographies appearing in newspapers throughout the province during 1967 and released by the commission for the centennial of confederation in Canada. |
| Bi | Burpee, Lawrence Johnstone (editor). Index and dictionary of Canadian history. Toronto, Morang, 1911. 446 p. (The Makers of Canada series) |
| Bua | Burke, W. J. American authors and books, 1840 to the present day. By W. J. Burke and Will D. Howe, augmented and revised by Irving R. Weiss. New York, Crown Publishers Inc., 1963. 834 p. |
| Bup | Burke, Sir John Bernard. A genealogical and heraldic history of the peerage, baronetage and knightage... 8th ed. + London, Burke's Peerage Ltd., 1845+ Title varies slightly. |
| Cc | The Canadian parliamentary guide. Ottawa, Mortimer, 1862+ Originally called The Canadian parliamentary companion. Title, publisher, place of publication, and editor vary. |
| Cd | The Canadian who's who, with which is incorporated "Canadian men and women of the time"; a biographical dictionary of notable living men and women. Toronto, Trans-Canada Press, 1910+ Trienniel. Title, publisher, and place of publication vary. |
| Ch | Roberts, Charles G. D. (editor). A standard dictionary of Canadian biography; the Canadian who was who. Editors, Charles G. D. Roberts and Arthur L. Tunnell. Library edition. Toronto, Trans-Canada Press, 1934-38. 2 v. Cover title: The Canadian who was who. |
| Cn | Canadiana. Ottawa, National library of Canada, 1951+ |
| Co | Clergy list, with which is incorporated the clerical guide and ecclesiastical directory, 1882-1916... London, Kelly's Directories Ltd., 1882-1916. 7 v. (incomplete) |

233

| | |
|---|---|
| Cr | Crockford's clerical directory for 1868-   ; a reference book of the clergy of the Church of England and of other churches in communion with the See of Canterbury. London, Oxford University Press, 1868+ Title and publisher vary. Supplementary pages contain appointments, resignations, and obituaries. |
| Cy | A cyclopaedia of Canadian biography; being chiefly men of the time . . . edited by George Maclean Rose. Toronto, Rose Publishing Company, 1888. xvi, 816 p. (Rose's national biographical series) Cover title: Representative Canadians. |
| D | Debrett's peerage, baronetage, knightage and companionage, comprising . . .  London, Dean, 1904+ |
| DAB | Dictionary of American biography. Under the auspices of the American Council of Learned Societies. Edited by Allen Johnson. New York, Charles Scribner's Sons, 1928. 22 v. (incl. index vol. and 2 supplementary vols.) |
| DNB | Dictionary of national biography, edited by Leslie Stephen. London, Smith, Elder, & Co., 1885-1900. 70 v. (incl. a supplement of 3 v.; a second supplement of 3 v. covering 1912-50; and 4 v. with cumulated indexes to biographies contained in supplements 1901-50) |
| DNBc | The concise dictionary from the beginnings to 1911; being an epitome of the main work and its supplement to which is added an epitome of the supplement, 1901-1911, edited by Sir Sidney Lee. London, Oxford, 1925. 1456,   129 p. |
| EC | Encyclopedia Canadiana. Ottawa, The Canadiana Company Limited, a subsidiary of the Grolier Society of Canada Limited, 1965. 10 v. |
| Hy | Hyamson, Albert M. A dictionary of universal biography of all ages and of all peoples. 2d ed. London, Routledge & Kegan Paul Ltd., 1951. xii, 679 p. and 1 p. addenda. |
| K | Kelly's handbook to the titled, landed and official classes for 1901-  . London, Kelly's Directories, Limited, 1901+ |
| Ka | Kennedy, James. Dictionary of anonymous and pseudonymous English literature. (Samuel Halkett and John Laing) New and enlarged edition. Edinburgh, Oliver and Boyd, 1926. 9 v. (incl. index vol.; 2 supplements; an addenda to vols. 1-8) |
| Kua | Kunitz, Stanley J. American authors, 1600-1900; a biographical dictionary of American literature. Edited by Stanley J. Kunitz and Howard Haycraft. New York, The H. W. Wilson Company, 1938. 846 p. |
| Kun | Kunitz, Stanley J. Twentieth century authors; a biographical dictionary of modern literature. New York, The H. W. Wilson Company, 1942. 1577 p. First supplement: 1955. 1123 p. |
| Lu | Lugrin, N. de Bertrand. The pioneer women of Vancouver Island, 1843-1866, edited by John Hosie. Victoria, The Women's Canadian Club of Victoria, 1928. 312 p. |
| Me | The Macmillan Everyman's encyclopedia. 4th ed. New York, The Macmillan Company, 1959. 12 v. |
| Mo | Morgan, Henry James (editor). The Canadian men and women of the time; a hand-book of Canadian biography. 1st ed. Toronto, William Briggs, 1898. xii, 1117 p., 1 p. corrigenda. Second edition: 1912. xx, 1218 p. |

| | |
|---|---|
| Nc | The National cyclopaedia of American biography; being the history of the United States, as illustrated in the lives . . .  New York, James T. White and Company, 1892. 15 v. (incl. an index and conspectus vol., and 1 supplementary vol.) |
| Ncn | The New Century cyclopedia of names, edited by Clarence Barnhart, with the assistance of William D. Halsey, and others. New York, Appleton-Century-Crofts, 1954. 3 v. |
| O | Ormsby, Margaret A. British Columbia; a history. Toronto, The Macmillans in Canada, 1958. x, 558 p. |
| P | Peel, Bruce Braden. A bibliography of the prairie provinces to 1953. Toronto, University of Toronto Press, 1956. xix, 680 p. |
| Q | Qui êtes-vous? annuaire des contemporains, 1908. Paris, Libraire Ch. Delagrave, 1908. viii, 496 p. |
| S | Scholefield, Ethelbert Olaf Stuart. British Columbia, from the earliest times to the present. By E. O. S. Scholefield and F. W. Howay. Vancouver, The S. J. Clarke Publishing Company, 1914. 4 v. Vols. 1-2 are historical; vols. 3-4, biographical. |
| Sd | Scholefield, G. H. (editor). A dictionary of New Zealand biography. Wellington, Department of Internal Affairs, 1940? 2 v. |
| U | Universal pronouncing dictionary of biography and mythology. 4th ed. Philadelphia, J. B. Lippincott Company, 1915. 2550 p. Cover title: Lippincott's pronouncing biographical dictionary. |
| VF | Vertical file. The file is kept by the British Columbia Provincial Archives and is comprised of newspaper clippings, pamphlet material, etc. Biographical information on a particular person often extends to notes prepared by the Archives' staff and letters or notes from members of his family. |
| W | Walbran, John Thomas. British Columbia coast names, 1592-1906; to which are added a few names in adjacent United States territory; their origin and history . . .  Ottawa, Government Printing Bureau, 1909. 546 p. Cover title: British Columbia place names. |
| Wa | Wallace, W. Stewart. The dictionary of Canadian biography. Toronto, The Macmillan Company, 1945. 2 v. |
| Waa | Wallace, W. Stewart (compiler). A dictionary of North American authors deceased before 1950. Toronto, Ryerson, 1951. 525 p. |
| Wh | Who's who; an annual biographical dictionary with which is incorporated "Men and women of the time." London, Adam and Charles Black, 1897+ |
| Wha | Who's who among North American authors . . .  Los Angeles, Calif., Golden Syndicate Publishing Company, 1921+ From v. 2 (1925/26) published biennially. |
| Wha2 | Who's who and why; a biographical dictionary of notable men and women of western Canada, 1912-1921, edited by C. W. Parker. Vancouver, Canadian Press Association, Limited, 1912-21. 10 v. Title and publisher vary. |
| WhA | Who's who in America; a biographical dictionary of notable living men and women of the United States. A component volume of Who's who in American history. Chicago, The A. N. Marquis Company, 1899+ Biennial. |

| | |
|---|---|
| Whb | Who's who in British Columbia, 1931-1953; an illustrated record of British Columbia men and women of today. Victoria, S. M. Carter, 1930-53. 9 v. |
| Whc | Who's who in Canada, including the British possessions . . . an illustrated biographical record of men and women of the time. Toronto, International Press Limited, 1911+ Title, publisher, and place of publication vary. |
| Whj | Who's who in Canadian jewry, 1965. Compiled and prepared by the Canadian Jewish Literary Foundation for the Jewish Institute of Higher Research of the Central Rabbinical Seminary of Canada. Author and compiler, Dr. Eil Gottesman. Montreal, The Central Rabbinical Seminary of Canada, 1965. 525 p. |
| Whw | Who's who in western Canada; a biographical dictionary of notable living men and women of western Canada. Volume 1, 1911. Vancouver, Canadian Press Association, 1911. 390 p. |
| Ww | Who was who, 1897/1916—1951/60; a companion to Who's who containing the biographies of those who died during the decade(s) 1897-1960. London, Adam & Charles Black, 1920-61. 5 v. |
| Wwa | Who was who in America; a companion biographical reference work to Who's who in America . . . Chicago, The A. N. Marquis Company, 1942+ Sub-title varies. |
| Wwh | Who was who in America, historical volume, 1607-1896, a component volume of Who's who in American history; a compilation of sketches of individuals, both of the United States of America and other countries . . . to the year of continuation by Volume 1 of Who was who in America, 1897-1942. Chicago, The A. N. Marquis Company, 1963. 670 p. |

Almanacs: 204, 265, 892, 1147
*Along the totem trail,* 2116
*Alphonse Pinart and the Chinook jargon,* 1849
ALSTON, EDWARD GRAHAM (1832-1873). In
    1861 appointed reg.-gen. of V.I.; 1870 reg.-gen.
    of B.C.; 1871 first att.-gen. of B.C. (VF)   349.
    *See below*

Alston, Edward Graham: 372. *See above*

ALTA CALIFORNIA (SAN FRANCISCO): 55
*Am da malshk ga na damsh St. John; ligi, The Gospel
    according to St. John,* 807
*Am da malshk ga na damsh St. Luke; ligi, The Gospel
    according to St. Luke,* 736
*Am da malshk ga na damsh St. Mark; ligi, The Gospel
    according to St. Mark,* 737
*Am da malshk ga na damsh St. Matthew; ligi, The
    Gospel according to St. Matthew,* 676
*American foreign policy in Canadian relations,* 1774
American Museum of Natural History: memoirs of,
    1357
Americans in British Columbia: 99; in fiction, 1916
*America's wonderlands,* 1024
*Amerikanskiĭ etnagrofičeskiĭ sbornik,* 2084
*Amerika's Nordwest-Küste,* 627
*Amerika's Nordwest-Küste . . . Neue Folge,* 644
*Among the An-ko-me-nums, or Flathead tribes,* 1556
*Among the Indians of the far West; a service,* 1536
*Among the Selkirk glaciers,* 878
*Amor De Cosmos* (1958), 2060
Amur tribes: 1357
ANACONDA COMMERCIAL CLUB: 1253
ANACORTES PACKING COMPANY, LIMITED:
    1188
Ancient Order of Foresters, *see* Forester, Ancient
    Order of
Ancient Order of United Workmen, *see* United
    Workmen, Ancient Order of
*Ancient warriors of the North Pacific,* 1679
ANDERSON, AILI SOPHIA (1906-   ): 1993
ANDERSON, ALEXANDER CAULFIELD (1814-
    1884). Artist, agriculturist and auth. of
    descriptive pamphlets and essays on the province.
    Born in Calcutta, India; 1831 entered H.B.C.
    services in the Pacific fur trade, crossing overland
    through Yellowhead Pass and down the Columbia
    R.; explored most of New Caledonia and
    prepared maps and pamphlets; assisted in
    establishment of Ft. McLoughlin, and relocation
    of Ft. Simpson; 1846 when boundary line was
    fixed and H.B.C. was concerned over finding a
    new route to the Interior, Anderson pioneered
    the route which became the famous Brigade
    Trail to Interior, and took furs from Ft. Colville
    to Ft. Langley. (VF)   56, 388, 489, 625
ANDERSON, JAMES (1839?-1923?). Born in
    Scotland; went to Barkerville, 1863; entered into
    life of the community taking part in concerts and
    entertainment; 1866 he and a friend issued a
    weekly handwritten newspaper from which

extracts were read aloud; was a candidate for
    election to Cariboo Mining Board, 1866; a
    member of Cariboo Glee Club; showed a keen
    interest in Dramatic Club; pub. the *Sawney's
    letters* (in part) in the *Cariboo Sentinel* in
    summers of 1865, 1866; 1871 returned to fam.
    in Scotland and settled on fam. property in
    Fifeshire, later at Cupar. (VF; W. K. Lamb,
    *Sawney's letters, or Cariboo rhymes, from 1864
    to 1868*)   297. *See below*

Anderson, James: 2094; extracts from *Sawney's
    letters,* 1229. *See above*

Anderson-Henry, I.: 269

ANDREW, FREDERICK WILLIAM (1879-1957).
    Physician. Born in Penn.; educated Brooklyn,
    Toronto High, Harbord St. Collegiate, Normal
    School in 1897; 1898-1903 taught in Winnipeg;
    1903-7 Man. Medical School; 1908 went to
    Summerland to practise medicine; established a
    cottage hospital; 1914 first hospital was built;
    active in Red Cross, Masonic Lodge, Okanagan
    Hist. Soc. and in community affairs. (VF; S,
    v. 4, p. 1359; Okanagan Hist. Soc. *Report,* 1958,
    p. 7-8)   1835

ANDREWS, CLARENCE LEROY (1862-1948).
    Am. auth., historian, customs and gov't employee.
    In 1864 went to Ore. as a child and lived on a
    farm; 1883 went to Seattle as postal clerk;
    returned to Ore. to teach school; west as customs
    officer to Alaska and Yukon border during the
    Klondike gold rush; worked as a teacher with the
    School and Reindeer Service until 1929; 1936-47
    revived the publication *The Eskimo* to secure
    justice for natives of Alaska; contributed articles
    to many magazines, and wrote several books on
    Alaska. (*Pacific Northwest quart.,* v. 39, 1948,
    p. 248-250)   1771

ANDREWS, GERALD SMEDLEY (1903-   ).
    Aerial survey engineer. Went to Vancouver from
    Winnipeg; graduated from U.B.C. and Normal
    School; graduate in forestry at Univ. of Toronto;
    in charge of several surveys in B.C.; went to
    Oxford and Germany to study aerial surveying;
    instructor during World War II in military air
    photography; chief engineer of Aerial Survey
    Engineering Div. of B.C., and now director of
    Surveys and Mapping. (VF)   1934

ANDREWS, RALPH WARREN (1897-   ): 1961
*Angela College, Victoria* [prospectus], 346
Anglican Church, *see* Church of England
*The Anglican Church in British Columbia,* 2074
Anglo-Asian intercourse and monarchical settlement
    (cap. t.), 39
*Anglo-Asian intercourse via Great Britain,* 39
ANGUS, HENRY FORBES (1891-   ). Economist,
    lawyer, prof. at U.B.C.; member of roy. com.
    on Dominion-provincial relations, 1938-40;
    special asst. to Under-Secretary of State for

*hist. quart.*, and the Okanagan Hist. Soc. (VF; Okanagan Hist. Soc. *Report*. no. 16, 1952, p. 143-144)  1877

Barnett, George: comp., pub., 189

Barnston, John George: report of, 159

Barraclough, William: 1383

*The Barren Ground of northern Canada,* 998

BARRETT-LENNARD, CHARLES EDWARD: 157. *See below*

Barrett-Lennard, Charles Edward: 1585. *See above*

BARROWS, WILLIAM (1815-1891). Am. clergyman from Amherst College, Mass. (Waa) 643

BARTLEY, GEORGE (d. 1943). Printer and proof-reader. Born in London, Ont.; had extensive experience on newspapers in U.S. from Buffalo to Seattle; 1888 was listed as a new arrival in the Typographical Union, No. 226; 1893, on, was recording sec. for the union; later was on the executive for many years, represented the union in the Trades and Labor Congress, and was their delegate frequently; 1900-1905 published the labour paper *The Independent* in Vancouver; was the first sec. of the Trades and Labor Council, Vancouver, also pres. on two occasions; called "the grand old man of organized labor"; was one of the first linotype operators on the Vancouver *World,* also a member of the Typographical Union for 55 years; served on the Parks and the School Boards of Vancouver. (Van. *Sun,* 2 Jan. 1943, p. 28; from his *An outline history of Typographical Union No. 226*)  1783

BASKERVILLE, CHARLES GARDINER: 1328

*Basketry designs of the Salish Indians,* 1357

Bassarguine, Lt.: 298

BASTIAN, ADOLF (1826-1905). German traveller, ethnographer, and auth. Educated as a physician, but began his extensive travels around the world in 1851; became prof. of ethnology, and was administrator of the ethnological mus. in Berlin; added much to its ethnological collection; 1875-91 took journey to Oceania, Central and S. Am., Central Asia; his chief work was *The peoples of eastern asia,* 1866-71. (Me)  608. *See below*

Bastian, Adolf: 627, 644. *See above*

BATE, MARK (1837-1927). Mayor of Nanaimo, 1875-1927. Born in Birmingham; entered mercantile business; 1857 went to Victoria then Nanaimo to work for the H.B.C.; 1869 became manager of Vancouver Coal Mining and Land Co. in Nanaimo; 1873 first justice of the peace of the district; 1875-90 was mayor of Nanaimo (first), and again later; was active on school, library and hospital boards. (B; Vic. *Colonist,* 28 Aug. 1927, p. 1)  1594

Bates, Alfred: jt. auth., 731

BATES, EMILY KATHARINE (name spelled "Katharine" and "Catherine" on title pages). 732, 806

BATES, HENRY WALTER (1825-1892). Naturalist and explorer. Born in Leicester; 1848 sailed with Alfred Russel Wallace to Paraguay to collect specimens; spent 11 y. in S. Am.; went up the Amazon 1400 miles and discovered 8000 new species of insects. (Me)  321 (ed.)

BATTERTON, J. H.: 104

Baywater, J. W.: 15

BEADLE, CHARLES: 733

BEANLANDS, ARTHUR JOHN (1857-1917). Anglican clergyman, later canon. Born in Durham; graduated with B.A. 1876, M.A. 1891; 1881, became a deacon; 1883, a priest; 1884 went to Victoria to Christ Church Cathedral; 1905 m. Sophie Pemberton (later artist Sophie Deane-Drummond); 1909 resigned and returned to England; was one of the first directors of the Natural Hist. Soc. of B.C., and contributed articles to its *Proceedings.* (VF)  964, 1016

*Bear-hunting in the White Mountains,* 948

BEAUGRAND, HONORE (1849-1906). Journalist from Quebec. Went to Montreal Military School; joined Fr. army and went to Mexico; later to Europe for 2 y. travel; on newspapers in New Orleans, Boston, St. Louis, Montreal; 1879 founded *La Patrie;* sold *La Patrie* in 1897; 1885-7 mayor of Montreal; 1887 began *Daily News;* was founder and first pres. of the Montreal Folklore Soc.; contributed to magazines and wrote a novel. (Waa; Wa; Mo)  734, 735, 773

Beaven, Robert: budget debate, 1127

"Beaver" (ship): 1120, 1542, 1653, 1770, 1846, 2012; in poetry, 1880

Beaver Indian language: primer for, 350; text in, 568, 700

*Beaver Indian primer,* 350

Beaver Pass (town): 2147

Beaver Valley: history, 2061

BECKWITH, MARGARET ALICE (DUNN) (1898-  ). School teacher before her marriage; member of Victoria School Board; active in community affairs; 1948 elected pres. B.C. School Trustees Assoc.; a grand factor in Post No. 3., Native Daughters of B.C. (Vic. *Colonist,* 23 Sept. 1948, p. 23; 12 Mar. 1942, p. 13)  1994

Beekeeping: 2053

*Before the council,* 951

Begbie, Matthew Baillie (1819-1894). First chief justice of the province. A London barrister educated at Camb.; 1859 appointed judge; held circuit courts throughout B.C. and earned respect for fair treatment; 1870 was made chief justice of the united colonies of B.C. and V.I. (B.C. Cen. Com.; 0)  Judgments of, 451, 475, 610; pubs. on, 1621, 1782, 1887

Blackett, W. R.: 708

Blackwood, Frederick Temple Hamilton-Temple, *see* Dufferin and Ava, Frederick Temple Hamilton-Temple-Blackwood

BLAIKIE, WILLIAM GARDEN (1820-1899). Prof. of theology, Edin.; educated at Univ. of Aberdeen and at Edin.; 1842 ordained; joined Free Church of Scotland; moderator of General Assembly, 1892; ed. of *Free Church magazine,* 1849-53, and other magazines until 1883. (Ww, 1897-1916)   854

BLAKE, EDWARD (1833-1912). Lawyer, politician, an independent Liberal. Leader of Liberal Party of Canada, 1879-87; 1858 M.A. from Univ. of Toronto; 1867 elected to Ont. Legislative Assembly; leader of Opposition 1868-71; in 1872 resigned seat and premiership; 1873 a P.C.; 1875 appointed Minister of Justice; 1880 leader of Opposition. (P; Wa; Cc)   410, 561

BLAKE, MOFFITT & TOWNE, PUBLISHERS: 1721

BLAKE, WILLIAM PHIPPS (1826-1910). Am. geologist and mining engineer. One of the geologists of Pacific Railroad surveys; investigated mineral resources of N. Carolina; 1861-3 employed by Japanese gov't to organize their first school of science; 1863 returned to U.S. by way of Alaska, and explored the Stikine R. region; 1864 prof. mining and geology at College of Calif. (Berkeley); 1876 collected and installed gov't exhibits to illustrate U.S. mineral resources at Philadelphia Centennial Exposition (these formed the basis of the Nat. Museum's collection begun in 1879); made economic surveys in the West; was prof. and director of School of Mines at Univ. of Arizona. (DAB; Apa; Nc; A; WhA)   298

Blakey Smith, Dorothy, *see* Smith, Dorothy Blakey

BLAKISTON, THOMAS WRIGHT (1832-1891). Explorer interested in ornithology; 1858 accompanied the Palliser expedition in the Rockies; 1861 explored the upper Yang-tse-kiang; 1863-84 a merchant in Japan; d. in Calif. (Me)   82, 83. *See below*

Blakiston, Thomas Wright: report of, 120. *See above*

BLANCHET, FRANCIS NORBERT (1795-1883). Catholic missionary from French-Canada, later an archbishop. 1819 ordained a priest; 1838 went to B.C. as a missionary; 1845 consecrated Bishop of Ore.; 1850 became archbishop. (Wa; Waa)   32. *See below*

Blanchet, Francis Norbert: 380. *See above*

Blanshard, Richard (1817-1894): appointment as gov., 14; Br. gov't instructions to, 360; in poetry, 1826; *also see* Vancouver Island. Governor, 1849-1851 (Blanshard)

BLAVATSKY, HELENA PETROVNA (HAHN) (1831-1891). Travelled extensively in Asia, S. America, Africa, and India; 1858 returned to England and announced her initiation into esoteric Buddhism; 1875 founded the Theosophical Soc.; her secret powers were rejected by the London Psychical Research. (Me)   738

*Blazing the old cattle trail,* 2132
*Blazing the trail through the Rockies,* 1615
*Blood on the arctic snow,* 1960

BLOWITZ, HENRI GEORGES STEPHANE ADOLPHE OPPER DE (1825-1903). Austrian journalist and auth. Prof. of German in French universities to 1860; became involved in French politics; 1871 entered service of London *Times* which was kept informed through a direct wire. (Ww; London *Times,* 19 Jan. 1903, p. 10, 11)   1022

BOAM, HENRY J.: 1595 (comp.)

Board of Trade, *see* British Columbia. Board of Trade

BOAS, FRANZ (1858-1942). Anthropologist. Curator, Dept. Anthropology, Am. Mus. of Natural History, 1910-   ; 1888-96 carried on investigations in B.C. for Br. Assoc. for Advancement of Science; after 1897 worked for Smithsonian Inst.; directed operations and publications of Jessup North Pacific Expedition. (WhA; Wwh)   701, 702, 809, 810, 855, 913, 965, 1023, 1102, 1145, 1197, 1259, 1461, 1462. *See below*

Boas, Franz: auth., 677, 1159; ed., 1240, 1357. *See above*

Boats and boating, *see* Steamboats.

BODDAM-WHETHAM, JOHN WHETHAM (b. 1843): 449

BODDY, ALEXANDER ALFRED. English clergyman. (P)   1198

Bogoras, W., *see* Bogoraz, Vladimür Germanovich

Bogoraz, Vladimür Germanovich: 1357

Bolton, Herbert Eugene: 1840

BOMPAS, WILLIAM CARPENTER, bp. of Selkirk (1834-1906). Church of England clergyman; ordained in 1859; 1865-74 a missionary in Peace R. and Mackenzie R. areas; 1874 Bishop of Athabasca; later in 1884 Bishop of Mackenzie R. diocese; 1891 Bishop of Selkirk. (Waa; Wa; P; Ww; DNB)   350. *See below*

Bompas, William Carpenter, bp. of Selkirk: comp., 568; pub. on, 1566. *See above*

BONE, PETER TURNER (1859-1947?): 1862

BONNAUD, DOMINIQUE: 1260

BONNYCASTLE, SIR RICHARD HENRY (1791-1847). Lt.-col. in Royal Engineers; studied at the Royal Military Academy; served in the Am. campaign of 1812-4; in the Rebellion of 1837-9; a commanding engineer in Newfoundland; 1847 retired from service. (DNB)   3

*The book of Small,* 1820

BOOTH, MICHAEL R.: 2107. *See below*

Booth, Michael R.: jt. auth., 2094. *See above*

BORTHWICK, DAVID (1920-    ): 1949
Boscowitz, Joseph A.: 747
Botanical association: 182, 268, 269
Boulton, C. A.: report of, 1335
Boundaries: 1, 1425, 1620, 1689, 1945; of the colony
    of B.C., 201; *see* Alaskan boundary; Northwest
    Boundary Commission; *also see* San Juan Island
    and the establishment of a water boundary
*The boundaries of Canada,* 1945
*The boundary between the British and the Russian
    empires on the north-west coast of America,* 97
*Boundary between the Dominion of Canada and . . .
    Alaska. Appendix to the case,* 1504
*Boundary between the Dominion of Canada and . . .
    Alaska. Appendix to the counter-case,* 1505
*Boundary between the Dominion of Canada . . .
    Alaska. Argument presented,* 1506
*Boundary between the Dominion of Canada and . . .
    Alaska. Case presented . . . 1903,* 1507
*Boundary between the Dominion of Canada and . . .
    Alaska. Counter-case presented . . . 1903,* 1508
*Boundary disputes with our northern neighbors,* 1427
Boundary district: 1253, 1997
THE BOUNDARY HISTORICAL SOCIETY
    (GRAND FORKS): 1997
BOVEY, HENRY TAYLOR (1852-1912). English
    educator. Educated at Camb. Univ.; 1887
    became prof. in civil engineering at McGill;
    1888-1908 dean of Applied Science; 1908-1909
    rector of Imperial College of Science and
    Technology, London; auth. of many technical
    books. (Wa; Waa; Mo)   1146
Bower, Anthony: 254
Bowers, George M.: comp., 1443
BOWES, GORDON EMERSON (1914-    ). Born in
    Victoria; attended U.B.C.; is area development
    agent of B.C. Hydro and Power Authority,
    Vancouver; was pres. B.C. Hist. Assoc.,
    Vancouver, and a member of the council of the
    assoc. at time of publication of his anthology.
    (Advertising folder for book)   2062 (comp.),
    2144 (ed.)
Bowman, Amos: jt. auth., 731
BRABANT, AUGUSTIN JOSEPH (1845-1912).
    Belgian missionary. Ordained 1868, and came to
    B.C.; 1874 established an Indian mission at
    Hesquiat and remained there until 1908 when he
    was appointed apostolic administrator of the
    Diocese of Victoria. Name also appears as
    "Auguste" and "Augustus." (Waa; Wa; Joseph
    van der Heyden, *Life and Letters of Father
    Brabant*)   1463. *See below*
Brabant, Augustin Joseph: life of, 1649, 1694. *See
    above*
BRADLEY, GEORGE B.: 1331
*Bradstreet's reports,* 548
Brew, Chartres: 1690
BRIDGES, F. D. An Englishwoman who wrote an
    account of her travels around the world—Greece,

India, E. Indies, Japan, San Francisco to
    Portland, Victoria, Fraser R. to San Francisco,
    Utah, Colorado to Chicago.   628
*A brief account of the province of British Columbia,*
    625
*A brief description of the Boundary Creek district,*
    1253
*A brief historical account . . . of British Columbia,*
    1752
*A brief history and souvenir booklet of Knox
    Presbyterian . . . Trail,* 1654
*A brief history of Rossland,* 1546
*Brief sketches of C.M.S. missions,* 937
BRIGGS, HORACE: 811
Bright district (V.I.): 2014
*Britain redeemed and Canada preserved,* 20
Britannicus (pseud.), *see* McLeod, Malcolm
*British and American diplomacy affecting Canada,*
    1469
*British and American intercourse; letter,* 27
BRITISH AND AMERICAN JOINT COMMISSION
    FOR THE FINAL SETTLEMENT OF THE
    CLAIMS OF THE HUDSON'S BAY AND
    PUGET'S SOUND AGRICULTURAL
    COMPANIES: 245, 246, 247
BRITISH ASSOCIATION FOR THE
    ADVANCEMENT OF SCIENCE: 677, 1261
*The British colonist in North America,* 856
BRITISH COLUMBIA: 187
*British Columbia* (1871), 369
British Columbia (colony): bill to provide for gov't
    (1858), 70; Br. select committee (1857), 52;
    description of in the 1860's, 320, 364; gov't and
    Legislative Council of, 281; history, 1565, 1607,
    1690, 2036; history of establishment and
    administration, 731; journal of Arthur Thomas
    Bushby, 2145; papers relating to, 1103; *also see*
    Gold mines and mining; Union of Vancouver
    Island and British Columbia
BRITISH COLUMBIA. AGENT GENERAL IN
    LONDON: 411
BRITISH COLUMBIA. ASYLUM FOR THE
    INSANE (NEW WESTMINSTER): 678
BRITISH COLUMBIA. BOARD OF TRADE: 549,
    599, 774, 1199, 1262, 1405
British Columbia. Board of Trade: 603
BRITISH COLUMBIA. CENTENNIAL
    COMMITTEE: 1971
BRITISH COLUMBIA. CITIZENS: 370
BRITISH COLUMBIA. EXECUTIVE COUNCIL:
    679
BRITISH COLUMBIA. GOVERNOR, 1858-1864
    (Douglas): 188
BRITISH COLUMBIA. GOVERNOR, 1864-1869
    (Seymour): 280, 281
BRITISH COLUMBIA. IMMIGRATION BOARD:
    351
BRITISH COLUMBIA. LANDS AND WORKS
    DEPARTMENT: 266, 267, 299, 322, 323

Brown, Robert: and collecting of botanical specimens, 182, 268, 269; V.I. exploring expedition of 1864, 321. *See above*

BROWN, ROBERT CHRISTOPHER LUNDIN (d. 1876). A clergyman at St. Mary's Parsonage, Lillooet 1863-5. (British Columbia. Agent General in London. *British Columbia; information for emigrants* (1875), p. 4) 190, 354, 414

BROWN, ROBERT CRAIG (1935- ). Received his Ph.D. from Univ. of Toronto 1962. (B.C. Archives) 2161

BROWN, W. R. Minister of the United Church of Canada. Minister of St. Andrew's Presbyterian Church in Merritt in the 1920's; 1927 left Merritt; 1946 minister at St. Giles United Church, Vancouver, and at that time advocated church services in Stanley Park "Church under the Stars." (Van. *Province*, 11 Mar. 1946, p. 22) 1664

Brownlee, J. H.: Dominion land surveyor; Vancouver resident; published handbooks on B.C. 1333

*Brownlee's indexed map of British Columbia*, 1333

BRYCE, GEORGE (1844-1931). Presbyterian minister. Went to Winnipeg; founded Manitoba College; prof. at Univ. of Manitoba; auth. of books on Can. history. (Mo; P) 775, 1588

*Buck Choquette, stampeder*, 2108

BUCKLAND, FRANK MORGAN (1873-1953). Farmer, local historian. Born in Guelph, Ont.; family moved to Manitoba where he was educated; 1904 came to Kelowna; a partner in a cattle dealing business, sold it in 1911; had a cattle ranch at Penticton, then a fruit ranch at Rutland; active in community affairs—pres. of Board of Trade, a police com., and in hospital soc.; one of founders of the Okanagan Hist. Soc. in 1925. (VF; Vernon *News*, 24 Sept. 1953; Kelowna *Courier*, 17 Sept. 1953) 1878

Budget speech: 711

Budlong, F. L.: auth., 1167

BUEL, JAMES WILLIAM (1849-1920). Traveller, journalist, and auth. Taught school; went to Illinois Univ. to study law; 1870 made his way west to Kansas; published a newspaper; from 1878 onwards he wrote books as result of his travels; 1882 travelled in Russia and Siberia. (Nc; Wwa) 1024

*Builders of British Columbia*, 1772

*Builders of the West; a book of heroes*, 1715

BULKLEY, THOMAS A. Civil engineer trained in London. In 1872 became chief engineer of B.C. after experience in London and Bombay; 1874 com. of Police for the province; 1878-91 or later was senior resident engineer in Bombay. (Vic. *Colonist*, 25 Dec. 1874, p. 3; 2 Dec. 1891, p. 3; 26 Apr. 1892) 389

Bulkley Valley: 2034

BULL, WILLIAM KING (1811-1899). Auctioneer, storekeeper, public speaker. After 16 y. in Australia and a world tour, he began in Victoria as an auctioneer in 1864; prominent in community life; 1871 was in Olympia, Wash., for a year; 1883 became collector of revenue in Victoria electoral district and was returning officer; was also referred to as the "knight of the hammer." (VF) 645, 704 (appellant)

BURALL, W. T.: 917

Burnaby: history of, 1867, 1921, 1998

BURNABY HISTORICAL SOCIETY: 1998

*The burning bush in the sagebrush hills*, 2121

Burns, William: 392

BURPEE, LAWRENCE JOHNSTONE (1873-1946). Can. historian of note; co-ed. of *Index and dictionary of Canadian history*, and "Makers of Canada" series; librarian of Carnegie Library, Ottawa. (Mo; P) 1622, 1687

Burrard Inlet: 1864

Burton: history, 2039

*Burton, British Columbia*, 2039

BUSCHMANN, JOHANN KARL EDUARD, (1805-1880). German linguist, librarian. Travelled and studied languages, especially of Mexico, Malay, and Polynesia; collaborated with Humboldt brothers on their work on languages; 1862 published the fifth volume of *Kosmos;* wrote publications on native languages of areas he had visited. (Me) 43

BUSHBY, ARTHUR THOMAS (1835-1875). In 1858 came to B.C. from London; friend of James Douglas and Judge Matthew Begbie; was Begbie's secretary on first circuit in B.C. along Fraser and to the Cariboo; reg.-gen., also postmaster gen.; member of Legislative Council 1868-70; active in community affairs in New Westminster. (*B.C. hist. quart.*, v. 21, 1957-58, p. 83-198) 2145

Business: 618, 619, 635

BUSK, CHARLES WESTLY (1852-1934). Br. engineer of railroads. Graduate of Camb.; 1884 came to Canada, then travelled to Victoria via the Northern Pacific Railway; did engineering work on the E. & N. Railway between Chemainus and Nanaimo in 1885; established a practice in Victoria; engaged in surveying and engineering work on V.I. and in Nelson area; made survey of Fairview, in the lower area of Nelson, built the first wharf there; owned considerable property in the area, including the townsite of Balfour, where he retired on a fruit farm. (Vic. *Colonist*, 4 Apr. 1930; 31 Mar. 1934) 646

Bute Inlet and Esquimalt Route No. 6 (C.P.R.): 514

Bute Inlet massacre: 320, 1616

Bute Inlet route: 191,1740

BUTE INLET WAGON ROAD COMPANY, LIMITED: 191

BUTLER, SIR WILLIAM FRANCIS (1838-1910).
Auth. of several biographies and his
autobiography. Saw service in British army in
India and Africa; 1870 went to Red River and
Saskatchewan. (DNBc) 415, 562
BUTTERWORTH, HEZEKIAH (1839-1905). Asst.
ed. of *Youth's companion*, 1870-1894; wrote
juvenile books; travelled extensively. (Wwh)
860
*By ocean, prairie and peak*, 1198
*By the West to the East*, 683
*By track and trail; a journey through Canada*, 946
*Caesar Cascabel*, 901
CAINE, WILLIAM SPROSTON (1842-1903).
English politician and auth. Civil Lord of the
Admiralty in Gladstone administration; active in
temperance work and a mission church in
London. (Ww; DNB) 776
*Cairns of British Columbia and Washington*, 1357
Caldwell, J. B.: 1334
*The Caledonia interchange*, 1407
*The calendar . . . for the year of Our Lord, 1883*, 637
*Calgary route to the Klondyke gold fields*, 1334
CALHOUN, SAMUEL HENRY (1877-1961).
Farmer. Born in N.B.; went to New Westminster
as a boy in 1889; went to the Okanagan, settled in
Tappen; one of the sponsors of Farmers'
Exchange, Co-operative Granite Trading Assoc.,
Farmers' Inst., and Farmers' Telephone System.
(VF) 1999
*California and Alaska, and over the Canadian Pacific*,
906
CALLAHAN, JAMES MORTON (1864- ). Auth.
and prof. of history and political science at West
Virginia Univ.; 1902 became head of dept.; 1916
dean of the College of Arts and Sciences there.
(Me) 1774
Cameron, D. R.: 1045
Cameron, David: chief justice appointment, 200; and
. . . *rules of practice* 71, 1716; re V.I. courts,
71, 130
CAMERON, DONALD RODERICK (1834-1921).
Capt. in Royal Artillery; son-in-law of Sir
Charles Tupper; 1872-6 supt. of Br. section of
Br.-Am. boundary survey. (P) 705
CAMERON, MALCOLM COLIN (1832-1898).
Lt.-gov., N.W.T., 1898. In 1860 called to the bar;
practised in Goderich, Ont.; later became mayor;
1866-7 and 1896-8 in H. of C. (EC: Mo, 1898)
249
Cameron, William Bleasdell: jt. auth., 1718
Cameronton: 2147
*Camp-fires of a naturalist*, 1037
Campbell, Alexander (Minister of Justice): report of,
647
CAMPBELL, ARCHIBALD, bp. of London: 84
Campbell, Archibald: re northwest boundary, 315,
334, 1459

CAMPBELL, JOHN (1840-1904). A constant
contributor to the *Proceeding and transactions*
of the Roy. Soc. of Can. 1268
*Camping in the Canadian Rockies*, 1250
CAMSELL, CHARLES (1876-1958). Geologist, civil
servant. Born in N.W.T.; attended Univ. of
Manitoba, Queen's, Harvard, M.I.T.; 1900 asst.
on geol. sur. to Great Bear Lake and Coppermine
with Dr. J. Mackintosh Bell; 1904-20 in Geol.
Sur. Dept.; 1920-35 deputy minister of Mines;
1935-46 also com. of N.W.T.; founder and fellow
of Can. Geog. Soc.; and pres. 1929-41; 1921-36
member of N.R.C. (EC) 1938. *See below*
Camsell, Charles: 2088. *See above*
CANADA: 741, 777, 918, 1408, 1489
Canada: and the H.B.C., 65; interest in Pacific
territory, 47, 48
CANADA. DEPARTMENT OF AGRICULTURE:
629, 919
CANADA. ARMY. BRITISH COLUMBIA
REGIMENT: 1847
CANADA. ARMY. 5th (B.C.) COAST BRIGADE,
R.C.A.: 1801
CANADA. BRITISH COLUMBIA FISHERY
COMMISSION: 1025
CANADA. CANADIAN PACIFIC RAILWAY
ROYAL COMMISSION: 611
CANADA. DEPARTMENT OF CITIZENSHIP
AND IMMIGRATION: 2085
CANADA. DEPARTMENT OF CUSTOMS: 501
CANADA. EXECUTIVE PAPERS: 502
CANADA. GEOGRAPHIC BOARD: 1602
CANADA. GOVERNOR-GENERAL, 1854-1861
(Head): 47, 48
CANADA. GOVERNOR-GENERAL, 1861-1868
(Monck): 192
CANADA. GOVERNOR-GENERAL, 1868-1872
(Lisgar): 326, 375
CANADA. GOVERNOR-GENERAL, 1872-1878
(Dufferin): 416, 417, 418, 473
CANADA. DEPARTMENT OF THE INTERIOR:
681, 814, 861, 1026, 1202, 1269, 1409
Canada. Department of the Interior: 1356, 1368,
1425, 1548
CANADA. DEPARTMENT OF JUSTICE: 647,
1203
CANADA. LAWS, STATUTES, ETC.: 390, 419,
455, 612
Canada. Legislative Assembly: report of, re railway
to the Pacific (1852), 29
CANADA. DEPARTMENT OF MARINE AND
FISHERIES: 1004
Canada. Department of Marine and Fisheries: 1247,
1322, 1393, 1452
CANADA. NAVY. ESQUIMALT NAVAL
ESTABLISHMENT: 1964
CANADA. PARLIAMENT. HOUSE OF
COMMONS: 1410, 1524

opinion in B.C. (1876), 494; opinion of Br. press re B.C. (1877), 512; opinion re construction by gov't, 476; pam. on, 599; pam. on B.C., 723; pam. on Can. Rockies, 1412; pam. on excursion, 753; petition of Legislative Assembly re, 587, 596; pub. on its importance, 500; pubs. concerned with the route for, 400, 467, 514, 523, 530-534, 551, 555, 559, 566, 577, 578, 697; report of progress (1874), 459, 649; report of roy. com. (1882), 611; report on (1879), 556; report on prospects (1883?), 638; report on surveys (1872), 391; roy. com. and Sir Sandford Fleming, 616; Senate select committee on (1879), 550; and Sir Edward William Watkin, 767; speech of Joseph Tasse (1872), 402; speech to B.C. constituents on, 478; speeches in the H. of C., 530-535, 561, 570, 572, 583, 602, 621, 683; speeches in the Senate, 490, 600; surveying and exploration for route, 431, 466, 505, 564, 576, 1641, 1657, 1675; (in fiction) 798, 1971; surveying instructions (1871), 377; tender submitted by McDonald and Charlebois, 613, 617; tenders for, 565; trans-Pacific connections, 706; visit of Can. minister to B.C. in 1871, 398; *also see* Esquimalt and Nanaimo Railway; McLeod, Malcolm (pubs.); Pacific Scandal; Railway terminus of C.P.R.

*The Canadian Pacific Railway; address . . . 1888,* 789

*The Canadian Pacific Railway; an appeal to public opinion,* 697

*The Canadian Pacific Railway; contract . . .* 612

*The Canadian Pacific Railway (1873),* 422

*The Canadian Pacific Railway (1880?),* 566

*The Canadian Pacific Railway (1880),* 577

CANADIAN PACIFIC RAILWAY COMPANY: 377, 422, 474, 491, 523, 591, 649, 683, 706, **707,** 743, 967, 1271, 1272, 1273, 1412

*Canadian Pacific Railway from Emory's Bar,* 588

*The Canadian Pacific Railway from Laggan to Revelstoke,* 1479

*Canadian Pacific Railway routes; the Bute Inlet,* 514

Canadian Pacific Steamships, Ltd.: 1803, 1972

*The Canadian Pacific, the new highway to the East,* 743

*The Canadian Pacific, the new highway to the Orient,* 743

*Canadian pictures, drawn with pen and pencil,* 639

CANADIAN PRESS ASSOCIATION: 1564

*Canadian Rockies; new and old trails,* 1589

*The Canadian Rocky Mountains* [*with special reference*], 710

*Canadian savage folk,* 1228

*A Canadian tour; a reprint of letters,* 725

*The Canadian view of the Alaskan boundary dispute,* 1436

Canal de Haro: definition of boundary line through, 436; *also see* San Juan Island and the establishment of a water boundary.

CANESTRELLI, PHILIPPO (1839-1918). A Jesuit priest from Rome; 1878 came to Rocky Mountain Mission; assigned to Ft. Colville then to Kettle Falls; 1880-1 established land claims for church near Spokane Falls (later Gonzaga Univ. site); 1887-93 at St. Ignatius Mission, Mont., where he produced 13 works on languages of Indians and worked among Kootenai Indians. (Introd. of his *Kootenai grammar*) 968, 1108

*Capilano Creek, discovery of source, 1890,* 1919

THE CAPITAL LACROSSE CLUB (VICTORIA): 1204

*Captain Jacobsen's Reise,* 661

*Captain John Palliser and . . . western Canada,* 2071

Captain "Mac" (pseud.), *see* McAdam, J. T.

*Captain William Oliver . . . ,* 1813

*Cariboo; a true and correct narrative,* 206

Cariboo district: desc., 1274; desc. in the 1860's, 1632; desc. in the 1870's, 562; desc. in fiction, 1340, 1464, 1584, 1980, 2093; exploration (1863), 209; gold in, 1272; history, 1836, 1995, 2011, 2024, 2101, 2115; map, 363; pioneers of, 2051; in poetry, 1851; *also see* Cariboo gold fields

Cariboo gold fields: 160, 170, 173, 174, 206, 251, 257, 297, 709, 731, 1036, 1565, 1607, 1615, 1616, 1626, 1630, 1718, 1734, 1768, 1786, 1788, 1804, 2004, 2011, 2024, 2026, 2036, 2090, 2115, 2131; cattle drives, 1637; cattle for (fiction), 1940; in fiction, 1129, 1171, 1464, 1547, 1612, 1720, 1858, 1940, (juvenile) 2126; map and guide (1862), 164; Overlanders' journey to, 1229, 1626, 1734; in poetry, 2133

*The Cariboo journal of John Macoun,* 1658

CARIBOO QUARTZ MINING COMPANY, LIMITED: 524

Cariboo Road: 1658, 1786

*Cariboo Road,* 1858

*The Cariboo story,* 2024

*Cariboo, the newly discovered gold fields of British Columbia,* 160

*Cariboo Trail,* 1980

*The Cariboo Trail . . . ,* 1626

*Cariboo yarns,* 2131

CARMICHAEL, JAMES (1835-1908). Clergyman, auth., lecturer. Dean of Montreal, appointed 1883; was twice pres. of the Nat. Hist. Soc. of Montreal and also the Montreal Microscopical Soc.; active in community affairs. (Mo, 1898) 778

CARMICHAEL, WILLIAM M.: 1863

Carmichael-Smyth, Robert, *see* Smyth, Robert Stewart Carmichael

Carnarvon, Henry Howard Molyneux Herbert, 4th earl of (1831-1890). Politician. Educated at Eton and Oxford; succeeded to title in 1849; in the H. of L.; 1858 undersecretary of the colonies; 1867 introduced bill for federating the Can. provinces; 1878 resigned over Disraeli policy; 1885 made lord lt. of Ireland. (Me) Jt. auth., 1950; letters of, 502.

CARNARVON CLUB (VICTORIA): 492
Carnarvon terms: 480, 492, 545, 1607, 1616; *also see*
  Esquimalt and Nanaimo Railway
CARR, EMILY (1871-1945). B.C. writer and artist of
  note. Educated in Victoria, studied art in San
  Francisco, England, and France; taught art in
  Victoria; 1889-94 in San Francisco; 1898 visited
  Ucluelet and became interested in Indians and
  their crafts; 1899-1904 in Europe to study art;
  1907 visited Sitka and Yukon, met Wm.
  Newcombe; 1910 went to Paris to study the "New
  Art."; 1911-26 period of struggle to earn her
  livelihood as her paintings were not "accepted"
  as art except by some friends and Marius Barbeau
  who encouraged her to display her canvases,
  pottery, hooked rugs for an exhibition of West
  Coast art in the National Gallery; had many
  exhibitions in Paris, Amsterdam, London, etc.,
  during the next 10 y.; 1926 began writing with a
  course in Palmer Inst. of Authorship, Los
  Angeles. (VF; *Emily Carr, her paintings and
  sketches; the autobiography of Emily Carr,* with
  a foreword by Ira Dilworth (Toronto, Oxford
  University Press, 1946); Flora Hamilton Burns,
  "Emily Carr," in M. Q. Innis, *The clear spirit*
  (Toronto, Univ. of Toronto Press, 1966), p.
  221-241) 1820
Carrier Indian language: Catholic catechism, 922;
  in Déné syllabary, 950, 1124
Carrier Indians: 995, 1301
*Carrier reading-book,* 1124
*Carrier review,* 950
*Carrier sociology and mythology,* 995
CARROLL, CAMPBELL: 2000
CARROLL, HARRY (1851-    ). Coal miner for sixty
  years, of which fifty were in V.I. coal mines; pres.
  of the Nanaimo Pioneer Soc. (Van. *Sun,* 6 Mar.
  1939, p. 1) 1753 (comp.)
CARROTHERS, WILLIAM ALEXANDER (1889-
  1951). Economist. Born in Ireland; educated
  there and at the Univ. of Manitoba (1916), Edin.
  Univ., and London School of Economics (Ph.D.
  1921); in World War I; 1921-30 prof. of
  economics, Univ. of Saskatchewan; 1930-4 prof.
  of economics, U.B.C.; 1934-8 chn., Economic
  Council of B.C.; 1938-51 chn., Public Utilities
  Com. of B.C.; contributed to many economic
  journals and auth. of books, especially on B.C.
  economics. (Cd) 1810
Carson, Robert: plaintiff, 719
CARTER, JAMES COOLIDGE (1827-1905).
  Lawyer. Born in Lancaster, Mass.; 1850
  graduated from Harvard; 1853 admitted to N.Y.
  bar (common law was his interest); 1894-5 was
  pres. of Am. Bar Assoc.; was a founder of the
  National Municipal League; 1893 appeared as
  one of the counsels for U.S. before Bering Sea
  Tribunal of Arbitration. (DAB) 1027

Cartier, Sir George Etienne: report of, 326, re union
  with Canada, 373
CASE, VICTORIA: Am. newspaper woman
  interested in pioneer history of Oregon; early life
  was spent on V.I.; graduate of Univ. of Oregon;
  wrote many short stories and articles. (Book
  jacket) 2086
*The case of the Hudson's Bay Company,* 50
*Case presented on the part of the government of Her
  Britannic Majesty to the Tribunal . . . 1892,* 1043
Cassiar district: 894, 947, 1238, 1356, 1624, 1938,
  1960, 2070, 2088; gold mines, 894, 1036, 1283,
  1771
*Catalogue of books in the Free Public Library of
  Victoria City,* 902
*Catalogue of British Columbia minerals,* 790
*Catalogue of Corrig School, Victoria, B.C.,* 728
*Catalogue of John Weiler,* 606
*Catalogue of the library of the Law Society of British
  Columbia,* 991
*Catalogue of the Vancouver contribution,* 176
Catholic Church: attacks on 1308; re Diocese of
  Vancouver Island, 271, 1889; history in Nicola
  Valley, 1664; history of St. Peter's Parish, 2091;
  manual for sick room, 1152; missions of, 292,
  553, 760, 1190, 1301, 1463, 1516, 1534, 1583,
  1600, 1649, 1694, 1711, 1723, 1744, 1795,
  (drama) 1854, 1904, 2089; *also see* Seghers,
  John Charles; Sisters of St. Ann
CATHOLIC CHURCH. CATECHISMS.
  ATHAPASCA: 862
CATHOLIC CHURCH. CATECHISMS.
  CARRIER: 922
CATHOLIC CHURCH. CATECHISMS.
  SHUSWAP: 1028
CATHOLIC CHURCH. CATECHISMS.
  THOMPSON: 969
CATHOLIC CHURCH. LITURGY AND RITUAL:
  226, 923, 1029, 1205
CATHOLIC CHURCH. LITURGY AND RITUAL.
  ATHAPASKA: 863
CATHOLIC CHURCH. LITURGY AND RITUAL.
  LATIN: 864, 1206, 1207
CATHOLIC CHURCH. LITURGY AND RITUAL.
  OKANAGAN: 779, 1030
CATHOLIC CHURCH. LITURGY AND RITUAL.
  SHUSWAP: 970, 971
CATHOLIC CHURCH. LITURGY AND RITUAL.
  STALO: 924
CATHOLIC CHURCH. LITURGY AND RITUAL.
  THOMPSON: 972, 973
Catholic Church. Liturgy and ritual in Chinook
  jargon: 380
Cattle drives: 1637, 1940, 2070, 2132
Cattle trade: 1745, 2000
*The cattle trade on Puget Sound, 1858-1890,* 1745
CAVERS, ANNE S.: 1890
Cedar district (V.I.): history, 2014
*The celebrated Greer case,* 822

Antwerp, San Francisco; presented the collection to the B.C. Provincial Museum in 1894. (Vic. *Colonist,* 8 Apr. 1884, p. 3; 22 July 1894, p. 5)    614, 650, 685

Choir club: 1189

Chong, Wing: 704

*Choose this day,* 2071

Choquette, Alexander: 2108

Christ Church Cathedral (Vancouver): 1793

Christ Church Cathedral (Victoria): 1910

*Christ Church Cathedral, 1889-1939* (Vancouver), 1793

*Christ Church Cathedral, Victoria, B.C.,* 1910

CHRISTIE, JAMES R. (1877-    ): 2001

Christie party: 1302

*Chronicles of the Cariboo, number one,* 1788

Chu Lay: 704

Chuck, Chung: 1338

*The Chukchee* [sic], 1357

CHUNG, CHUCK: 1338

CHURCH, HERBERT E. (b.1868). Came to Canada from England in 1886 and was a short time in Ont.; settled near Calgary in 1888 farming at Sheep Creek; 1897 moved to B.C. (P)    815

Church, Richard: jt. auth., 815

*The church and the Indians,* 615

*The church in the modern city,* 1844

CHURCH MISSIONARY SOCIETY: 327, 378, 708, 1536, 1537, 1555

Church Missionary Society: 481, 579, 585, 754, 937, 1448, 1555; *also see* Metlahkatla; Duncan, William

Church of England: 1577, 1660, 1664, 1669, 1688, 1713, 1760, 1761, 1793, 1800, 1843, 1895, 1898, 1905, 1910, 1917, 1920, 1929, 1932, 1955, 2075, 2104, 2117, 2165; address of George Hills, 202; bishops of, 1234; church reserve, 250; Cridge controversy, 451, 457; ecclesiastical appointments (1859), 87; High Church practices, 488; history in B.C., 2074; hymns, 1431; in Lillooet (1870), 354; missions of, 264, 462, 481, 579, 585, 657, 937, 1062, 1169, 1198, 1400, 1421, 1448, (poetry) 1477, 1482, 1518, 1536, 1537, 1561, 1566, 1575, 1597, 1623, 1633, 1668, 1742, 2074; New Westminster diocesan gazette, 651; orphans' home, 413, 1011; re synods, 463, 518; *also see* Church Missionary Society; Columbia Mission; Duncan, William; Metlahkatla; Reformed Episcopal Church; and names of missions.

CHURCH OF ENGLAND. BOOK OF COMMON PRAYER. SELECTIONS. HAIDA: 1413

CHURCH OF ENGLAND. BOOK OF COMMON PRAYER. SELECTIONS. KWAKIUTL: 925

CHURCH OF ENGLAND. BOOK OF COMMON PRAYER. SELECTIONS. NISKA: 865

CHURCH OF ENGLAND. BOOK OF COMMON PRAYER. SELECTIONS. THOMPSON: 567

CHURCH OF ENGLAND. BOOK OF COMMON PRAYER. SELECTIONS. TSIMSHIAN: 866, 974

CHURCH OF ENGLAND. LITURGY AND RITUAL. BEAVER: 568

CHURCH OF ENGLAND. LITURGY AND RITUAL. FORM OF CONSECRATION OF A NEW CHURCH: 106, 107, 867

CHURCH OF ENGLAND. LITURGY AND RITUAL. HAIDA: 1109

CHURCH OF ENGLAND. LITURGY AND RITUAL. SALISH: 1110

CHURCH OF ENGLAND. LITURGY AND RITUAL. SLAVE: 816

CHURCH OF ENGLAND. LITURGY AND RITUAL. THOMPSON: 525, 526, 552

CHURCH OF ENGLAND. LITURGY AND RITUAL. TSIMSHIAN: 1150, 1209

CHURCH OF ENGLAND. SYNODS. BRITISH COLUMBIA: 493

CHURCH OF ENGLAND IN CANADA. DIOCESES. BRITISH COLUMBIA: 975, 1031

CHURCH OF ENGLAND IN CANADA. DIOCESES. NEW WESTMINSTER: 632

Church of Our Lord (Victoria): 869

*Church of St. John the Evangelist,* 1895

*Church work in British Columbia,* 1421

Churches: benediction of, 1029; consecration of, 106, 250; laying of corner-stone (1860), 107, 867; Nelson, 1628; Vancouver, 1609; Vernon, 1572; Victoria, 279, 1453, 1591; *also see* under name of city or town, and under names of churches

*The churches of St. John the Divine,* 2103

CHURCHILL, J. D.: 270. *See below*

Churchill, J. D.: jt. auth., 203. *See above*

*The churchman's gazette,* 651

*(Circular) Canadian Pacific Railway,* 573

*Circular letter* (1889), 827

*Circular letter to the people of British Columbia,* 1210

Citizenship: 1987

*The city and the store,* 2019

*City of Vancouver, terminus,* 756

Civil servants: 1478

*Claim of Governor Douglas of Vancouver's Island,* 98

*A claim on Klondyke,* 1445

Clark, George Archibald: 1390

Clark, George M.: 611

CLARK, HENRY W.: 2108

CLARK, HORACE FLETCHER (d.1928): 1339

Clark, Truman Celah: defendant, 719

*Classified digest of the records of the Society for the Propagation of the Gospel in Foreign Parts,* 1169

CLAUDET, FRANCIS GEORGE (1837-1906). Assayer. Born in London; educated there and in Germany; 1859 came to B.C. as chief assayer under Capt. William Gosset, R. E.; 1861 Gov. Douglas sent him to San Francisco to obtain a plan for a mint; in charge of the mint at New

Westminster but only a few coins were struck and then project was abandoned; 1871 made asst. com. of Lands; also a coroner; stipendiary magistrate in 1872; 1873 returned to England. (VF, included form filled out by descendant; *Vic. Colonist,* 13 Mar. 1906)   379. *See below*

Claudet, Francis George: 169, 1696. *See above*

CLEASBY, HENRY STANDLEY (1868-1959). Rancher, local historian. Born in Durham; 1887 went to the Nicola Valley, took up ranching and stock-breeding; active in community affairs; chn. of School Board, on City Council, Board of Trade, Hospital Board, on executive of first exhibition assoc. of area; wrote articles on local history. (VF)   2002

CLIFFE, CHARLES (1842-1931). Newspaper ed. and owner of eight papers in Canada. Born in Lansdowne, Ont.; taught school from 1859-65; 1870 began newspaper work, later bought several papers in Ont. and Man.; 1897 went to Sandon, B.C., and was founder and publisher of its *Mining Review* to 1902 when it was destroyed by fire; 1902 went to Sault Ste. Marie and d. there. (VF)   1414

Climate: 73, 85, 177, 180, 185, 388, 625, 630, 956, 1271; *also see* Meteorological observations

*A climber's guide to the Rocky Mountains of Canada,* 1655

*Climbs and explorations in the Canadian Rockies,* 1519

Cline, Sperry: jt. auth., 2034

Clute, R. C.: chn. of com., 1490

Clutterbuck, Walter J.: jt. auth., 791

Coal: 62, 258, 259, 325, 731, 997, 1990

Coal company: 1276

Coal Mines Regulation Act, 1897: 1276

Coalmont: 2147

Coast Brigade, R. C. A.: 1801

Coast Mountains: 667, 1737, 1805, 1814

*The coast of British Columbia,* 952

*Coast route to the northern mines,* 159

Coast Salish Indian languages: bibliography of works in 1082; *also see* Halkomelen Indian language; Sechelt Indian language; Sliammon Indian dialect; Squamish Indian language; Stalo Indian dialect.

Coast Salish Indians: 1556; Snanaimuq tribe, 809; *also see* Cowichan Indians

COATS, ROBERT HAMILTON (1874-    ). Journalist and statistician; in 1902 asst. ed. *Labour gazette;* 1896-1902 statistician; 1915-42 Dom. statistician and controller of census; 1931-9 on Advisory Com. on statistics in League of Nations; statistical consultant of FAO; visiting prof. at Univ. of Toronto, Dept. of Political Economy. (Mo; EC)   1565

Cochrane, J. J.: 153, 155

CODERE HELEN: 1897

CODY, HIRAM ALFRED (1872-1948). Anglican clergyman and auth. Born in New Brunswick; graduate of King's College, Windsor; 1897-1904 rector at Greenwich, N.B.; 1904-1905 a travelling missionary in Yukon; 1905-10 rector at Christ Church at Whitehorse, Yukon; 1910-25 rector at St. James Church at St. John, N.B.; 1927 appointed archdeacon of St. John. (Ww)   1566

COFFIN, CHARLES CARLETON (1823-1896). Am. novelist and historian; Civil War correspondent who wrote under pen name "Carleton" for Boston *Journal;* travelled extensively in Europe and Asia; wrote books for boys; popular lecturer. (Waa; DNAA; DAB; Apa; NCA)   60

COGSWELL, OLIVER H. (1857-1940). Customs officer and school teacher. Born in Kings County, N.S., graduate of Acadia Univ. 1888; taught at Digby Academy; 1890 went to Victoria; taught in N. Saanich and Mt. Tolmie schools for eight years; 1898 entered Can. Customs; transferred to Ottawa, 1900; 1924 retired to Victoria. (Death notice, 20 July 1940)   1032

Coinage: 1696

Cole, E. L.: 1960

COLEMAN, ARTHUR PHILEMON (1852-1939). Geologist; 1901-1922 prof. Univ. of Toronto and dean of Arts, 1919-22; 1900 Fellow Roy. Soc. and its pres. 1921. (Wa; Cd)   1589

COLEMAN, EDMUND THOMAS (d. 1892?). Artist, alpinist. In 1849 exhibited at Roy. Acad.; 1863 went to Victoria; 1865 librarian of Mechanics Inst. "for some four years"; 1868 successfully climbed Mt. Baker and recorded his adventures in *Harper's;* 1869 explored passes through the Cascade Range to discover a practicable route for the Northern Pacific Railway; 1870 left for Puget Sound to organize a party for the ascent of Mt. Rainier, leaving from Olympia; returned to London 1870 or 1871 and did art work there. (*Wash. hist. quart.,* v. 23, 1932, p. 243; VF; *Vic. Colonist,* 29 June, 1870, p. 3)   303

*Collection of official documents . . . San Juan,* 2173

*A collection of the public general statutes,* 218

Collie, John Norman: 1519

Collins, George: 1373

COLLINS, JOSEPH EDMUND (1855-1892). Toronto journalist and auth. Newfoundlander; ed. of newspapers in N.B.; city ed. of Toronto *Globe;* auth. of fiction and some historical works. (P; Wa; Waa; *Dominion Annual Register* 1885; Cy)   633

COLLIS, SEPTIMA MARIA (LEVY) (1842-1917). Am. auth. Wife of Gen. C. H. T. Collis; wrote about countries visited and experiences she had. (Her book, *A woman's trip to Alaska*)   868

DAWSON, EDWIN COLLAS (d. 1925). Canon of
St. Mary's Cathedral and rector of St. Peter's,
Edin.; in 1872 received B.A. from Oxford; 1873
deacon, and 1874 priest; 1878-90 incumbent St.
Thomas's, Edin.; 1890-1921 rector of St. Peter's;
convener of Publications Committee of Foreign
Missions and ed. of their *Chronicle of Scottish
Episcopal Church;* member of every provincial
synod of the Scottish Church from 1890; wrote
books and magazine articles. (Wa)   1597

DAWSON, GEORGE MERCER (1849-1901).
Geologist with Geol. Survey of Canada on
exploratory surveys of West. Studied geol. and
palaeontology at Royal School of Mines, London;
1873-5 geologist and botanist to Northwest
Boundary Commission; 1875 appointed to staff
of Geol. Survey; 1883 asst. director, and 1895
director; 1892 one of the Br. com. in Bering
Sea arbitration. (EC; Wa; P)   503, 528, 529,
554, 569, 593, 710, 745, 746, 781, 782, 818, 819,
870, 871, 872, 927, 928. *See below*

Dawson, George Mercer: 671, 1399, 1876; re Alaska
boundary, 847, 1489; Br. com. for Bering Sea
Commission, 979, 1017, 1046; report of, 1045.
*See above*

Dawson Creek: history, 2008

*Dawson Creek, Past and Present,* 2008

Day, Charles Dewey: chn. of com., 420; memorial of,
253

DAY, J. FRIEND (1887-1957). Prof. at U.B.C. Born
in England and an accountant in the Co-
operative Soc. there; after World War I came to
Canada; graduate in political science, Univ. of
Toronto; went to the Univ. of Chicago, then
lectured at Univ. of Alberta; 1930-39 head of the
new Dept. of Commerce at U.B.C.; active in
politics and in 1949 was unsuccessful candidate
(Conservative) in Vancouver; later joined Social
Credit Party. (Van. *Province,* 15 July 1957, p.
21)   1742

DAY, PATIENCE (d. 1934). In 1891 went to
Victoria with her husband; active in women's
organizations; 1894 at inaugural meeting of Local
Council of Women, Victoria and V.I.; 1907-12
its pres. 1908-19; on prov. Board; 1909 was ed.
of special women's edition of Victoria *Colonist*
(6 Nov.) as prov. vice-pres. of Local Council;
1911 Women's Club formed and was elected chn.
of committee for its formation; active in I.O.D.E.
municipal chapter and Patriotic Service
Committee during World War I; Royal Jubilee
Hospital was one of her interests. (VF)   1670

*Daylight land,* 794

*Days of Lorne,* 1953

*The days of old and days of gold,* 1598

*Dayspring in the far West,* 481

*De l'Atlantique au Pacifique à travers le Canada,* 788

*De Montréal à Victoria par le transcontinental,* 735

*De Québec à Victoria,* 1083

Deadman's Island: 1411

DEANS, JAMES (1827-1905). Employee of H.B.C.
from 1853; studied the dialects of B.C. Indian
tribes and Indian customs and traditions; gave
many papers on geol. and botany; 1892 prepared
an anthropological exhibit for World's Fair in
Chicago, reproducing a Haida village. (VF)
1416

Dease River: 1238

DEAVILLE, ALFRED STANLEY (1891-1948).
Philatelist and Can. gov't employee; 1898 went to
Victoria from England; worked in the Victoria
Post Office for 20 y., then worked in Ottawa; was
supt. of Postage Stamps and Philately Div. at
time of his death; member of Roy. Philatelic Soc.
of London. (VF)   1706

*Debate in the Senate on the Canadian Pacific Railway,*
490

*Debate in the Senate on the resolutions respecting
British Columbia,* 376

*Debate on the subject of confederation with Canada,*
353

*Decision of the Alaskan Boundary Tribunal,* 1494

*[Declaration, constitution, list of officers]* of the
Confederate League, 304

*The decorative art of the Amur tribes,* 1357

*The decorative art . . . of the North Pacific coast,* 1259

DE COSMOS, AMOR (1825-1897). Politician,
newspaperman, photographer, miner. Born in
Windsor, N.S., of English Loyalist stock; in
Calif., he changed his name from William
Alexander Smith (authenticated by the Calif.
legislature); 1858 went to Victoria, founded the
*British Colonist,* advocated the end of H.B.C.
rule, worked towards the union of the colonies
of V.I. and B.C.; member of the V.I. Legislative
Assembly and the Legislative Council;
1872-4 premier of B.C.; 1872-82 M.P. for
Victoria; 1874 won a seat in the first federal
election in the prov.; advocated Canada's right
to negotiate her own trade treaties. (B.C. Cen.
Com.)   530, 531, 532, 533, 534, 535, 570, 571
(comp.), 572, 594, 595, 596. *See below*

De Cosmos, Amor: agent for sale of iron mines, 487;
pub. on, 2060. *See above*

*The dedication of Stanley Park, 1899,* 1914

*Deed poll, by the governor,* 383

Deed poll of Hudson's Bay Company: 752, 827

*Deep roots; the history of Blake, Moffit & Towne,*
1959

DEGROOT, HENRY (1815-1893). Born on a farm
in N.Y.; graduate of Union College, studied law,
admitted to practice in 1841; studied medicine;
wrote articles for N. Y. *Tribune* and was sent to
Calif. in 1848 to report on the gold rush; settled
there and identified himself with hydraulic
mining, and did field work for the state; during a
brief stay in B.C. he transported supplies to

mining camps in the Interior. (Waa; *Overland monthly*, v. 22, Sept. 1893, p. 261-263) 85

DeLobel, Loicq, *see* Lobel, Loicq de

Delta: history, 2050

*Delta's century of progress*, 2050

DELUGE ENGINE COMPANY NO. 1 (VICTORIA): 193

DEMERS, MODESTE, bp. (1809-1871). Roman Catholic bp. Born in Quebec, ordained a priest in 1836; 1839 sent to Ore.; 1847 made Bishop of V.I.; devoted much of this time to work among the Indians; built the first Catholic cathedral in B.C.; started a church school; founded a hospital; brought the Sisters of St. Ann to Victoria; established missions on the Mainland. (B.C. Cen. Com.) 271, 380. *See below*

Demers, Modeste, bp.: 1795 *See above*

Déné Indians, *see* Athapaskan Indians

Déné syllabary, *see* Shorthand

*Denkschrift über den Canal von Haro*, 404

Denominational schools: 597

de Rouge, Etienne: trans., 779

Description and travel: 57, 61, 73, 85, 103, 108, 122, 124, 138, 142, 157, 173, 174, 177, 178, 185, 190, 203, (1863) 205, 225, 239, 249, 251, 255, 260, 275, 289, 388, 397, 398, 399, 415, 423, 440, 489, 509, 558, 562, 592, 614, 619, 628, 630, 641, 642, 650, 653, 659, 667, 672, 685, 690, 716, 718, 733, 757, 759, 769, 775, 776, 780, 791, 794, 796, 800, 804, 808, 810, 852, 854, 860, 894, 899, 907, 915, 917, 946, 948, 956, 960, 998, 1000, 1014, 1016, 1033, 1083, 1118, 1149, 1153, 1168, 1174, 1177, 1198, 1211, 1225, 1226, 1238, 1260, 1271, 1284, 1302, 1317, 1404, 1419, 1422, 1454, 1466, 1471, 1484, 1590, 1728; in juvenile fiction, 2071; of B.C. coastal waters, 675, 692, 715, 758, 831, 853, 868, 985, 1684; *also see* Exploration; Guidebooks; Overland journeys; Surveying; and specific towns, cities, districts, and regions.

*Description, maps and reports of the Jackson Mines*, 1292

*Description of country tributary to the proposed Shuswap and Okanagan railway*, 783

*Description of the country between Lake Superior*, 491

*Descriptive atlas of western Canada*, 1409

*Despatch from Lord John Russell . . . respecting the San Juan water boundary . . . 1869*, 334

*Despatch from Professor D'Arcy Thompson*, 1384

*Despatch from Sir R. Morier . . . 1893*, 1057

*Despatches. (A letter dated 12 December 1865)*, 261

*Despatches and correspondences . . . transmitted to the House of Assembly in Governor Douglas' message*, 217

DEUTSCH, HERMAN JULIUS: 2125

De Vaulx, Barnard, *see* Vaulx, Bernard de

*The development of hydrography on the Pacific coast*, 1751

*The development of public health in British Columbia*, 1750

Devereux, Hyacinthe Daly, *see* Rux (pseud.)

DEWAR, JAMES CUMMING. A wealthy Scotsman of Vogrie, Edin. County; owner and captain of yacht *Nyanza* which took a party of tourists on a cruise around the world, arriving in Victoria, 16 Apr. 1889; after leaving Victoria, the yacht was lost at sea off the Caroline Is. in 1890, but no life was lost. (Vic. *Colonist*, 17 Apr. 1889, p. 4; 18 Apr. 1889, p. 4; 27 Nov. 1890, p. 5) 977

DEWDNEY, EDGAR (1835-1916). Civil engineer and administrator from England; 1859 came to B.C. as a surveyor; 1869 elected to legislature; 1872 to H. of C.; supported J. A. Macdonald in Pacific Scandal; 1879 appointed Indian com.; 1881 lt.-gov., N.W.T.; 1888-92 Minister of the Interior; 1892-7 lt.-gov. of B.C. (Wa; Mo; Bi) 478, 494, 555

DE WOLF-SMITH, WILLIAM ANDREW (1861-1947). Physician, musician. Born in N.B.; attended McGill 1884; member of College of Physicians and Surgeons in Que.; 1886 first to be registered in C.P.S. in B.C. by examination; one of first medical health officers in prov., appointed to New Westminster; medical officer for penitentiary; an authority on Masonic matters, grand sec. for 34 y.; an organist; manager of the old opera house in New Westminster and pres. of New Westminster Operatic Soc. (VF; *Can. med. jour.* May 1947, p. 585) 1574

D'HERBOMEZ, LOUIS JOSEPH (1822-1890). French priest of the Oblate Fathers; 1848 entered the order and took his vows; 1850 arrived in Canada; 1851 founded the St. Joseph mission among the Yakamas; 1858 sent to Esquimalt; 1860 founded the mission of Ste. Marie and opened a school there; 1864 his episcopal consecration; was first vicar-apostolic of B.C.; 1868 visited the tribes in the Interior of B.C.; established many missions and schools; his residence was at New Westminster. (*Oblate missions*, v. 1, p. 329-346; v. 4, p. 6-7, 25) 597. *See below*

D'Herbomez, Louis Joseph: consecration of, 226. *See above*

*Diamond jubilee historical sketch, 1866-1926*, 1688

*Diamond jubilee of . . . Queen Victoria . . . 1897*, 1277

*The diary of Robert Melrose*, 1827

*Diary of the Christie party's trip*, 1302

Dickey, Estelle E. (Jones): 2124

Dickinson, Don M.: 1318

DICKINSON, JACOB McGAVOCK (1851-1928). Am. lawyer of outstanding reputation, Secretary of War. Born in Columbus, Miss.; graduate of Univ. of Nashville; studied law at Columbia College, in Leipzig and Paris; 1874 called to the bar; 1899 moved to Chicago; specialist in railroad law; 1903 was one of counsels for U.S. for the Alaskan Boundary Tribunal; 1909-11 was Secretary of War; held office in many law societies, and participated in organizing in 1906 the Am. Soc. of International Law; was an ardent conservationist. (DAB) 1522

DOWNS, ARTHUR GEORGE (1924-    ): 2090
Drake, M. W. T.: 539
Drama: 1755, 1854, 1987
Draper, Thomas: comp., 802
*Drei Jahre in Amerika, 1859-1862*, 158
DRUMHELLER, "UNCLE DAN" (1840-1925):
    1678
*Du Lac Stuart à l'océan Pacifique*, 1533
DUCK, SIMEON (1834-1905). Wheelwright,
    politician. In 1859 arrived in Victoria from Ont.;
    1871 elected to B.C. legislature; favoured
    confederation; later was defeated; 1882 returned
    to legislature; 1885-6 Minister of Finance in
    Smythe cabinet. (VF)    711. *See below*
Duck Simeon: plaintiff, 1015. *See above*
DUFFERIN AND AVA, FREDERICK TEMPLE
    HAMILTON-TEMPLE-BLACKWOOD, 1st
    marquis of (1826-1902). Diplomat and
    administrator. 1872-8 third gov. gen. of Canada.
    (DNB)    495, 1950. *See below*
Dufferin and Ava, Frederick Temple Hamilton-
    Temple-Blackwood, 1st marquis of: history of
    his administration, 540, 545; visit to B.C., 508,
    513, 1607. *See above*
DUFFERIN AND AVA, HARIOT GEORGINA
    (HAMILTON) HAMILTON-TEMPLE-
    BLACKWOOD, marchioness of (d. 1936).
    Auth. of several journals giving vice-regal life in
    India, Canada, Russia, Turkey; m. marquis of
    Dufferin and Ava in 1862. (Ww; Bup)    929
*Dufferin-Carnarvon correspondence, 1874-1878*, 1950
Duffield, William Ward: com., 1187, 1326
Duke of Connaught's Own Rifles: 1559, 1847
Duncan, *see* Cowichan Valley district
DUNCAN, ERIC (1858-1944). A Scotsman from
    Shetland Islands who settled in Comox Valley;
    known for his eccentric and independent
    characteristics. (VF; and his autobiography
    *From Shetland to Vancouver Island*)    1213,
    1749, 1775
DUNCAN, FRANCES IMOGENE (1926-    ):
    2010
DUNCAN, KENNETH FORREST (1881-1952).
    Business man, son of William C. Duncan after
    whom Duncan was named; 1912 elected first
    mayor of Duncan; entered politics as an
    Independent, 1919-24; active in community
    affairs; member of Masonic order, Can. Legion,
    Can. Red Cross Soc., Cowichan Hist. Soc. (VF)
    1743
DUNCAN, NORA M. (DANN) (1881-1946). Poet
    of Irish extraction, from County Limerick. Father
    a clergyman in London, Ont.; educated at Bishop
    Strachan School, Toronto; m. in 1908 to Wallace
    Craig Duncan; later went to Vancouver and was
    active in the Vancouver Poetry Soc.; organized a
    radio programme "The Lyric West." (Van.
    *Province*, 1 June 1946, p. 16; Van. *Sun*, 1 June

1946, p. 16; pref. of her *Rainbow reveries* (North
    Vancouver, North Shore Press Ltd., n.d.))    1766
Duncan, William (1832-1918). Missionary. Born in
    Yorkshire, worked in a tannery and then was a
    commercial traveller; attended training school of
    Church Missionary Society in London; 1857
    arrived at Ft. Simpson; 1862 founded site of
    Metlahkatla, which became a prosperous village
    under his guidance; 1881-7 a struggle between
    the Indians there, the Missionary Society, the
    Church of England and the B.C. gov't led to
    the establishment of a new Metlahkatla on Am.
    terr. (VF)    369, 378, 754, 897, 1482, 1526,
    1544, 1573; *also see* Metlahkatla
Dundas, R. J.: journals of, 462
Dunlevy, Peter Curran: 1788
DUNN, ALEXANDER (1843-    ). Scottish
    Presbyterian minister; 1875 ordained in Victoria;
    his charge was New Westminster area from
    Burrard Inlet to Yale; 1905 retired. (VF)    1603
Dunsmuir family: 1757, 1948, 2160
Duployan shorthand, *see* Shorthand
Dupont, T. C.: corr. of, 501
Durham, John Henry: 747
DURIEU, PAUL, bp. (1830-1899). A French Jesuit
    missionary of the Oblates of Mary Immaculate;
    1849 entered the order in France; 1854 ordained
    a priest and went to Ore. soon afterward; 1875
    consecrated as a bishop at St. Mary's Mission;
    1890 appointed first Bishop of New Westminster.
    (Vic. *Colonist*, 28 Oct. 1875, p. 3; 2 June 1899)
    1417. *See below*
Durieu, Paul, bp.: 717, 924. *See above*
Duthie, David Wallace: ed., 1577
Duties, *see* Tarriffs
DYER, E. JEROME: 1342
*Dying for our country*, 232
Dynamite plants: 2102
Eagle Pass: 1163, 1653
Eagle Valley: 2047
EARDLEY-WILMOT, SYDNEY MAROW (1847-
    1929): 428 (ed.)
Earle, Thomas: 1373
*The earliest British Columbia imprint*, 1729
*Early days among the Gulf Islands*, 1860
*Early days at Coqualeetza*, 1586
*Early days at Fraser Mills, B.C., from 1889 to 1912*,
    2077
*Early days in British Columbia*, 1660
*Early days of dynamite plants in British Columbia*,
    2102
*Early days of the Victoria Gas Company*, 2096
*Early days of Winfield, B.C.*, 1989
*Early days on the Yukon*, 1606
*Early explorations in British Columbia for the
    Canadian Pacific Railway*, 1641
*Early explorations in the coast mountains*, 1814
*Early flour-mills in British Columbia*, 1812
*The early history of British Columbia . . . 1858*, 2017

U.S.A. and Switzerland and contributed articles to science pub. and gov't reports. (Cd; Am) 1866

FAIRBAIRN, ARCHIBALD MACDONALD DUFF (1883- ) Lawyer, secretary, artist, playwright, actor, garden designer. A S. African; graduate of Cape of Good Hope Univ. in 1906; degree in law 1910; in B.C. was registrar of Courts, Cranbrook, and Supreme Court Registry; 1926-43 was sec. of lt.-gov.; now living in Calif; has private exhibitions of water-colours. (VF)    1755

Fane, Francis: auth., 919

*Far out; rovings retold*, 562

FARIS, JOHN THOMSON (1871-1949). Clergyman and auth. in Ore.; 1908-28 assoc. ed. and ed. of Presbyterian Board of Publications; 1923-37 director editorial division, Board of Christian Education of Presbyterian Church in U.S.A.; 1937-49 free lance writer. (Wwa, v.2)    1689

Farming: in the Fraser Valley, 2159; life on an Okanagan farm, 1014; *also see* Agriculture; Ranching

Farrand, Livington: auth., 677, 1357

FARRINGTON, LAWRENCE: 2016

Farwell (town): 680

*Father Morice:* 1711

*Father Pat; hero of the far West,* 1575

*The fauna of the Sooke beds of Vancouver Island,* 1435

FAWCETT, EDGAR (1847-1923). In 1859 went to Victoria with parents; in upholstery business; 1871 one of founders of Pioneer's Soc.; 1882-1910 in Dom. Customs Office. (VF)    1599

Federal-provincial relations, *see* Canadian Pacific Railway

FEMALE AID ASSOCIATION (VICTORIA): 252

FERNON, THOMAS SARGENT: 537

FERY, JULES H. (1812- ): 164

Fiction: 798, 896, 901, 1002, 1126, 1129, 1132, 1171, 1172, 1176, 1306, 1348, 1420, 1445, 1464, 1474, 1517, 1531, 1538, 1547, 1551, 1584, 1603, 1612, 1648, 1671, 1693, 1714, 1720, 1731, 1763, 1967, 1971, 2058, 2064; juvenile 1701, 1980, 2071 2093, 2126; short stories, 1956; *also see* Drama; Poetry

FIELD, HENRY MARTYN (1822-1907). Am. Presbyterian minister, ed. and auth. During 1842-7 was pastor in St. Louis, then went abroad; 1854 became partner and later sole ed. of *The Evangelist* for 44 y.; 1875-6 made a circuit of the globe; 1882, and 1886-7 travelled extensively to Holy Land and Mediterranean and wrote books on countries visited. (Wwa, v.1)    1153

*Fifteen thousand miles by stage,* 1590

*Fifteen years' sport and life,* 1458

*Fifth Avenue to Alaska,* 668

*Fifty-seven years in the Comox valley,* 1749

*Fifty years ago at Tappen,* 1999

*Fifty years of Cascade Lodge,* 1780

*50 years of progress in Pharmacy,* 1815

*A fight with distances,* 770

*Fighting with property,* 1897

FILLEY & OGDEN: 1282 (comp.)

Finance: 731; regulations for B.C. accounts, 114

*Finances of the province of British Columbia,* 711

*The financial, professional . . . interests of Vancouver,* 954

FINANCIAL REFORM ASSOCIATION (LIVERPOOL): 49, 65

Financial Reform Association (Liverpool) : 49, 63, 65

*Financial statement and annual report of New Westminster,* 1236

FINCK, HENRY THEOPHILUS (1854-1926). Auth., music critic, and traveller. Graduate of Harvard in philosophy, psychology 1876; until 1881 studied in Europe and listened to music, wrote articles for *Nation, The World, Atlantic monthly;* 1881-1924 music critic for *Nation.* Theophilus is a translation of his middle name "Gottlob," which he adopted by preference. (DAB; Apa; Nc; WhA)    873

FINDLAY, ALEXANDER GEORGE (1812-1875). Geographer, hydrographer, and cartographer; 1858 in business of cartography and publishing; 1844 F.R.G.S. (DNB)    23, 713

FINDLAY, GEORGE JAMES (plaintiff): 747

Finlay River: 2144

FINLAYSON, RODERICK (1818-1892). H.B.C. employee. Went to Montreal in 1837; 1839 sent with Dr. John McLoughlin overland to Jasper House, down Columbia to Ft. Vancouver; 1840 sent by the "Beaver" to Ft. Simpson, Ft. Stickeen to Sitka; traded with Indians at Ft. Taco and later Ft. Stickeen; 1843 returned to help build Ft. Victoria and left in charge of it in 1844; 1849 accountant when James Douglas took over; 1850 made chief trader and in 1859 chief factor, 1851-63 served on Legislative Council of V.I.; 1862 left for Interior to superintend H.B.C. affairs; 1872 retired. (B.C. Cen. Com.; from his autobiography)    930

FINNEY, GERTRUDE ELVA (BRIDGEMAN) (1892- ). Am. auth. of historical fiction who does research for her facts; wife of a doctor in Spokane. (Book jacket)    2064

Finns: 1767, 1993

Fire Department, *see* Victoria Fire Department

*The Fire Department; coronation souvenir,* 1493

Fire fighting organizations: 125, 150, 186, 193, 231, 446; history of 1493

First Baptist Church (Vancouver): 1863

FIRST BRITISH COLUMBIA SOCIETY OF SPIRITUALISTS: 931

*First catechism in Shuswap,* 1028

*First catechism in Thompson language,* 969

*The first fifty years,* 1808

*First history of Nelson, B.C.,* 1312

*First history of Rossland,* 1294

detail. (Her book *British Columbia for settlers*) 1344

FRASER, DONALD ANDREW (1875-1948). Poet and school teacher. Born in Ont., son of a Presbyterian minister; educated in Ont. and Victoria; 1884 came to B.C.; 1891-5 insurance clerk; 1897-1901 school teacher at Sooke; 1901-36 teacher in Victoria; ed. of *Public school magazine* from 1918; on National Council of Can. Authors Assoc. (VF)   1826

FRASER, GEORGE J. (1872-1958). Okanagan businessman in canning and real estate; 1917-38 in fruit ranching in Osoyoos; formed Osoyoos Cooperative; active in community affairs and in Okanagan Hist. Soc. (VF)   1928

*The Fraser*, 1901

Fraser Mills: history of, 2030, 2077

*The Fraser mines vindicated*, 81

*Fraser mines vindicated:* pub. on, 1716

Fraser River: 1864, 1868, 1902; and exploration, 145, 209; history based on, 1901

Fraser River gold fields: 55-57, 59, 61, 62, 66, 67, 72, 75, 79, 81, 731, 1036, 1140, 1491, 1535, 1543, 1565, 1607, 1616, 1690, 1696, 1768, 1804, 1850; fiction, 1916, 2036, 2137; experiences of J. Sewall Reed, 232; gov't doc. of Minn., 124; report of Am. agent on, 99; *see also* Gold mines and mining

*The Frazer River thermometer*, 66

Fraser Valley: history, 1817, 2029, 2030, 2050, 2159; in fiction, 1714

Free trade: 263, 843

FREEMAN, BEATRICE J. (SPALDING): A native daughter of S. Pender Is. whose father, Arthur Reed Spalding, arrived there in 1886; an officer of the Gulf Islands branch of the B.C. Hist. Assoc. (Her book, *A gulf island patchwork*) 2109

Freemasonry: account of progress of (1871), 384; inauguration of hall in Victoria, 277; history of, 2066, 2067; lodge histories, 392, 1574; *also see under* Freemasons

Freemasons. Barkerville. Cariboo Lodge No. 4: 1899

FREEMASONS. BRITISH COLUMBIA. GRAND LODGE: 282, 307, 328, 392, 1039, 1557

Freemasons. Golden. Mountain Lodge No. 11: 1746

FREEMASONS. NANAIMO. ASHLAR LODGE No. 3: 1651

FREEMASONS. NEW WESTMINSTER. UNION LODGE NO. 9: 538, 2110

Freemasons. Vancouver. Cascade Lodge: 1780

FREEMASONS. VANCOUVER. KNIGHTS TEMPLARS. COLUMBIA PRECEPTORY No. 34: 1567

FREEMASONS. VANCOUVER. MOUNT HERMON LODGE No. 7: 784

FREEMASONS. VICTORIA: 112

FREEMASONS. VICTORIA. BRITISH COLUMBIA LODGE No. 5: 429

FREEMASONS. VICTORIA. VANCOUVER LODGE No. 421: 196

FREEMASONS. VICTORIA. VICTORIA-COLUMBIA LODGE No. 1: 1154

FREEMASONS. VICTORIA. VICTORIA LODGE No. 1: 430

FREEMASONS. VICTORIA. VICTORIA LODGE 783: 283

FREEMASONS. VICTORIA. VICTORIA LODGE No. 1085: 113

FREEPORT, ANDREW (pseud.): 50

FREMONT, DONATIEN (1881-   ). Newspaper ed. in Prince Albert, Winnipeg, and Montreal. A Frenchman who came to Canada 1918; auth. of several historical books on Can. history in Fr. language. (P; Cd, 1961-63)   2065

French Canadians: 2065

FREUCHEN, PETER (1886-1957). Am. correspondent for Danish paper *Politiken*; 1910-33 Arctic explorer; well-known lecturer. (Book jacket; Kun)   1967

FRIESACH, CARL (1821-1891). Austrian mathematician and lawyer. Received LL.D 1846; 1848-50 Capt. in Austrian army in Austro-Italian War; 1852 prof. of mathematics in nautical school in Trieste; 1856-61 travelled to England, the Americas, and South Seas; visited Fraser R. mines in 1858; 1867 became "Privat Docent" in Univ. of Graz Styria; 1870 chief of Observatory of Austria. (*Beaver*, v. 18, 1958, p. 36-39; *B.C. hist. quart.*, v. 5, p. 221-228)   479

FRIPP, ROBERT M.: 1919

FRITH, AUSTIN FRANCIS (1919-   ). School teacher. Born in Prince Albert, Sask.; moved to Vancouver where he secured degrees in Arts and Education; principal of Delta Secondary School. (Book jacket)   2126

*From Britain to British Columbia*, 759

*From coalmine to castle; the story of the Dunsmuirs*, 1948

*From coast to coast; a farmer's ramble*, 1418

*From Cum Cloops 1812 to Kamloops 1962*, 2130

*From Edinburgh to Vancouver's Island*, 666

*From Euston to Klondike*, 1371

*From log cabin to a streamlined school . . .*, 1906

*From Ontario to the Pacific by the C.P.R.*, 761

*From potlatch to Pulpit*, 1747

*From sea unto sea*, 2092

*From Shetland to Vancouver Island*, 1775

*From the Atlantic to the Pacific*, 387

*From the beginning*, 2035

*From Yellowstone Park to Alaska*, 897

Frontier and pioneer life, *see* Pioneer life; Missionary life

*Frontier guide to the incredible Rogers Pass*, 2148

*A frontier judge*, 1782

FRONTIERS UNLIMITED: 2148, 2149

Fruit exchange society: 1201

Fruit farming, *see* Agriculture

Fruit growers' association: 812, 858, 859

Fruitvale: history, 2061

FULLAGER, L. H.: 1345

*Fur and gold,* 2128

*Fur and gold in the Kootenays,* 1838

*Fur-seal arbitration. Argument of the United States . . . 1892,* 1089

*Fur-seal arbitration. In the matter of the claims of Great Britain,* 1318

*Fur-seal arbitration. Oral argument of James C. Carter,* 1027

*Fur seal arbitration. Proceedings of the Tribunal . . . at Paris,* 1144

*Fur-seal arbitration. The counter-case of the United States . . . 1892,* 1090

*Fur-seal, sea otter, and salmon fisheries. Acts . . . ,* 1243

*The fur seals and fur-seal islands,* 1390

*The fur-seal's tooth,* 1126

Furrer, Edward: comp., 1161

*Further correspondence respecting the Behring sea seal fisheries* (1891), 935

*Further correspondence respecting the Behring sea seal fisheries* (1891), 936

*Further correspondence respecting the Behring Sea seal fisheries* (1892), 982

*A further despatch relative to the proposed union of British Columbia and Vancouver Island* (1866), 273

*Further exposition of Sir Richard Broun's great scheme for direct Anglo-Asian intercourse,* 40

*Further papers relative to the union of British Columbia and Vancouver Island* (1867), 285

FUTCHER, WINNIFRED M. (HALL): 1786 (ed.)

GABRIEL, THERESA: 2013

GAIRDNER, GEORGE W.: 1283

*The Gairdner & Harrison . . . guide,* 1283

GALBRAITH, JOHN SEMPLE (1916-    ): 1978

Galiano Island: history, 1860, 2109

Galloway, Mrs. Allan, *see* Galloway, Hazel Frances (Dempsey)

GALLOWAY, HAZEL FRANCES (DEMPSEY) (1921-    ): 2014 (comp.)

GAMBLE, WILLIAM GEORGE (1877-    ). Masonic grand historian of the Grand Lodge of B.C. (t.p.) 2066. *See below*

Gamble, William George: as Freemason historian, 392. *See above*

GANGES, SALTSPRING ISLAND. ST. MARK'S CHURCH: 1920

*A garden by the sea and other poems,* 1653

GARDINER, A. PAUL: 1464

Gardner, G. Clinton: 341

Garibaldi region: 1737

GARLAND, HAMLIN (1860-1940). Am. novelist. Early life of poverty on farms in West; then moved to Boston; contributor to *Harper's weekly;* wrote novels showing need for political and economic reform as well as books about frontier life. (DAB; WhA)    1419

GARNER, CHARLES (1885-1905). English or Australian journalist who wrote under the pseud. "Stuart C. Cumberland." (P; listed in Ka, v. 5, p. 5, and its Index vol., p. 105)    748

Garrett, John; comp., 108

Garrioch, Alfred Campbell: trans., 700

Gas company: 720, 2096

Gas industry: 1944

Gastown, *see* Vancouver

Gazetteers: 826, 1232; for post offices (1872), 408; *also see* Place-names

*Gegenantwort der Vereinigten,* 405

GELLATLY, DOROTHY (HEWLETT) (1856-1944). Wife of a well-known nurseryman in Westbank; a local historian contributing articles to the reports of the Okanagan Hist. Soc. (VF) 1735

*Gemini and lesser lights,* 1172

*General instructions, tariff of charges,* 891

*General report on the country round Nanaimo,* 121

*General report on the Cowichan Valley* (1860), 135

*General statistics . . . suitability of Kamloops as a health resort,* 1161

*General testimonials in favour of . . . Sproat,* 329

Geographical names, *see* Place-names

*Geographical notes upon Russian America and the Stickeen River,* 298

Geography: 630

*The geography of the Tsimshian Indians,* 1281

Geological Survey: 1866, 1876

Geology: 790, 910, 1251; papers by George Mercer Dawson, 503, 528, 529, 554, 593, 710, 745, 781, 818, 819, 870, 871, 927

GEORGE, HENRY (1839-1897). Am. economist and auth. Learned the printing trade; 1858 came to Calif. and had many jobs; 1865 was a reporter on the San Francisco *Times;* 1879 his *Progress and poverty* was published; became known as an apostle of a new social creed; wrote for many magazines and papers on economic and political subjects; lived in poor circumstances all his life. (Me)    654

GEORGE, WILLIAM. A seaman who kept a diary of his third voyage in the sealing schooner "Umbrina" in 1895. 1155

Germans: 2040; *also see* Ethnic groups

GERRISH, THEODORE (1846-1923). Am. clergyman. Born in Maine and died in Tenn. (Waa)    715

GEST, LILLIAN: 2111

*Ghost town trails,* 2147

Ghost towns: 2147, 2157

*Ghost towns of British Columbia,* 2157

GIBBON, JOHN MURRAY (1875-1952). Writer and publicist. Educated at Aberdeen, Oxford, and Univ. of Gottingen; 1913-45 publicity agent for C.P.R.; staged folk-song festivals across

Canada; auth. of *Canadian mosaic*, fairy tales, a novel, poetry, historical writings; founder and first pres. of Can. Authors Assoc.; 1922 F.R.S.C.; 1949 Lorne Pierce Medal. (EC; P)   1756

GIBBS, GEORGE (1815-1873). Am. ethnologist. At Harvard 1834-8; 1848 went to Ore. and Wash.; devoted himself to study of languages and traditions of Indians; on northwest boundary survey as geologist; made a report on natural history and geology of area; retired to Wash., D.C., and worked with Smithsonian Inst. on Indian languages. (DAB)   197. *See below*

Gibbs, George; 341. *See above*

GIBBS, MIFFIN WISTAR (1823-1915). Lawyer, publisher, U.S. consul. Born in Philadelphia of negro parents; 1850 went overland to Calif.; an ardent civil rights worker, he protested disfranchisement in an article in the *Alta California*; published the *Mirror of the times*, the state's first periodical; 1858 came to B.C. and resided in Victoria; 1866 elected to Council; 1869 went to Florida; was U.S. consul to Madagascar, then settled in Little Rock, Arkansas and practised law; became a municipal judge. (His autobiography, *Shadow and light*)   1491

Giblin, Lyndhurst Falkiner: 2088

*Giblin, the scholar and the man*, 2088

*The Gibson's Landing story*, 2135

Gibson's Landing: history and pioneers of, 2135

GILL, JOHN KAYE (1851-1929): 655 (comp.). *See below*

Gill, John Kaye: 32. *See above*

*Gills' dictionary of Chinook jargon*, 655

Gilmour, H. B.: auth., 1167

Gilson, W. R.: 1665

*The girl in the silk dress and other stories*, 1731

*Gitwangag 1858 to Kitwanga 1958*, 2023

Glaciation: 554 ,781, 818, 871, 878, 1451

*Glaciation of British Columbia* (1889), 818

*Glaciation of British Columbia and adjacent regions*, 781

Glacier House: 1881

*A glance at British Columbia . . . in 1861*, 173

Glenmore district: history, 2006

*Glenmore, the apple valley*, 2006

*The glorious three*, 1916

*Glory days of logging*, 1961

GLOVER, GEORGE HENRY WILSON (1881-  ): 1968

GODWIN, GEORGE STANLEY (1889-  ): 1714

Goepel, William John: 1351

*Gold dust; how to find it and how to mine it*, 1346

Gold Field Act, 1859: 188

*The gold fields of British Columbia* (1862), 167

*Gold fields of British Columbia* (1897?), 1310

*Gold fields of the Yukon, and how to get there*, 1275

*Gold, gold, in Cariboo*, 1129

*Gold in Cariboo and Kootenay*, 1272

*Gold in the Cariboo*, 2026

*"Gold," its properties, modes of extraction, value, &c.*, 379

*The gold miners; a sequel to The pathless West*, 1612

Gold mines and mining: 85, 167-169, 171, 174, 177, 178, 180, 287, 391, 658, 709, 726, 731, 1274, 1310, 1311, 1317, 1346, 1355, 1415, 1419, 1598, 1665, 1678, 1791, 1990, 2108; in Cariboo (1868), 309; gov't rules and regulations (1863?), 188; history of, 1534; in Kootenays, 1837; map of gold regions, 163, 211, 363; pam. by Francis Claudet (1871), 379; prospectus, etc. for co., 504, 1141; in Queen Charlotte Islands (1853), 33, 34; statistics, 1650; Trail Creek, 1241, 1242; *also see* Atlin gold fields; Cariboo gold fields; Fraser River gold fields; The Klondike and British Columbia; Mining laws.

*The gold mines of the world*, 1415

*The Gold mines of the Yukon and Clondyke*, 1305

*The gold rushes*, 1804

Golden: history, 2015

GOLDEN. CENTENNIAL COMMITTEE. HISTORICAL BRANCH: 2015

*The golden frontier*, 2137

*Golden jubilee anniversary, 1892-1942*, 1824

*Golden memories of the town*, 2015

*The golden North*, 1317

*The golden state; a history*, 399

Goldschmidt, Levin: 1821

GOLDSEEKER (pseud.): 1347

*The gold-seeker's handbook*, 287

Golf: 1754

Good, John Booth (1833-1916). Clergyman and pioneer missionary to Indians. Born in England, trained as a teacher; 1854-6 at St. Augustine's College, Canterbury; came to Canada, at Pugwash for 2 y.; 1861-6 at Nanaimo, built a church on the reservation; then for next 20 y. was on the Mainland, establishing a mission at Lytton and Yale; 1883-1900 rector at Nanaimo; 1892 made an honorary canon of Christ Church Cathedral, Victoria. He was an able Greek, Hebrew, and Latin scholar and made a study of Indian languages and was convinced they were of Syrian derivation. He wrote the Smithsonian Inst. to urge them to send competent men to study the Indians. (VF)   369; trans., 526, 552, 567

GOOD TEMPLARS, INDEPENDENT ORDER OF. WASHINGTON TERRITORY AND BRITISH COLUMBIA. GRAND LODGE: 656

GOODFELLOW, FLORENCE ELIZA MARGARET ASKIN (AGASSIZ) (1854-1940). Wife of a bank manager in early times in B.C. Born in London, Ont.; 1862 went as a child with the family to the Yale area, where her father had a gov't position there and at Hope; her husband became manager of the Bank of British North America at Barkerville in the 1870's and was transferred to Victoria in 1879;

later he went to Portland and then to Seattle where she died. (VF; name as given to B.C. Archives by her sister, Constance) 1837

GOODFELLOW, JOHN CHRISTIE (1890- ). United Church minister, historian. In World War I; 1921 graduate of Westminster Hall Theological College; came to B.C., and was pastor at Port Moody, then asst. pastor at First Presbyterian Church, Victoria; 1927 went to Princeton where he has continued to live; interested in church and local history; contributed articles to the reports of the Okanagan Hist. Soc., *B.C. hist. quart.* (VF) 2016

Goodman, A. E.: pub., 1298

Goon Sun: 1338

GORDON, CHARLES WILLIAM (1860-1937). Presbyterian minister and novelist who wrote under pseud. of "Ralph Connor." Born in Glengarry County, Ont., worked as minister in mining and lumber camps in Kootenay and Alberta foothills in 1890-93; 1894-1937 was pastor of St. Stephen's Church, Winnipeg; moderator of Presbyterian Church of Canada in 1922. (Charles W. Gordon, *Postscript to adventure; the autobiography of Ralph Connor (Charles W. Gordon)*, ed. by J. King Gordon (London, Hodder and Stoughton, 1938); P; Wa; Mo, 1912) 1348

GORDON, DANIEL MINER (1845-1925). Presbyterian minister; principal of Queen's Univ.; active in university and church life from Winnipeg to Halifax. (P; Mo, 1912; Wa) 576

GORDON, GRANVILLE ARMYNE, lord (1856-1907). Son of the 10th Marquis of Huntly; heir-presumptive to his brother, the 11th Marquis of Huntly; auth. of three books. (K, 1901; Ww, 1897-1916) 1420

*Gordon Head School, 1891-1931,* 1733

GOSNELL, R. EDWARD (1860-1931). Teacher and journalist in Ont.; 1888 came to B.C.; 1893 became prov. librarian and sec., Bureau of Provincial Information; sec. to premier 1896-1901; 1908-10 first provincial archivist; various gov't positions until 1917; 1917-31 in Ottawa. Initial "R" was used to avoid confusion: it does not stand for a name. (*B.C. hist. quart.*, v. 21, 1957-8, p. 1-14; VF) 875, 934, 1284, 1285, 1484, 1550, 1638, 1752. *See below*

Gosnell, R. Edward: auth., 1457, 1607, 1617; jt. auth., 1565; on newspapers, 1564. *See above*

*The Gospel according to Saint John in Haida,* 1402

*The Gospel according to Saint Luke,* 1101

*The Gospel according to Saint Luke in Haida,* 1403

*The Gospel according to St. Mark* (Beaver), 700

*The Gospel according to St. Matthew* (in Kwakiutl), 609

*The Gospel in the far west Metlakatla,* 327

GOSSET, WILLIAM DRISCOLL. A capt. in the Royal Engineers (but not Col. Moody's detachment); civil servant in England and Ceylon; 1858 sent out by Sir Edward Bulwer-Lytton as treasurer of the colony of B.C.; 1859-60 was acting postmaster-gen. of B.C. and V.I.; then became treasurer of B.C. and moved to New Westminster; 1862 returned to England and resigned as treasurer of the colony in 1863; retired from Br. army in 1873 with rank of maj.-gen. (A. S. Deaville, *Colonial postal system and postage stamps* (Victoria, 1928), p. 56-65) 114, 140. *See below*

Gosset, William Driscoll: 1696. *See above*

GOUDIE, D. R.: 460

*Goudie's perpetual sleigh roads,* 460

Gould, Mrs. I. A., *see* Gould, Lauretta Bernard

GOULD, LAURETTA BERNARD (1854-1936). Born in P.E.I.; wife of Capt. Isaac Gould; one of the founders of Aged and Infirm Women's Home in Victoria. (VF) 1707

GOULD, SYDNEY (1869-1938). General sec. of Missionary Soc. of Church of England in Canada. (t.p.) 1633

GOULT, BARRIE HOWARD EAMER (1903- ). Newspaperman, arbitration officer of the Dept. of Labour, Victoria; educated in Vancouver; attended U.B.C.; in newspaper work at Nanaimo; 1938 appointed sec.-reg. of Dept. of Labour dealing with trade-unions and conciliation and arbitration disputes; chief exec. officer of Labour Relations Board. (Vic. *Times,* 24 Dec. 1937, p. 11; 19 Dec. 1959, p. 2) 2067

Government: act re B.C. (1863), 201; bill re B.C. (1858), 70; bill re B.C. (1870), 359; of B.C. (1867), 281; Br. gov't doc., 1939; Br. gov't doc. re appointments, 87; Br. gov't docs. re B.C. (1859-62), 86; finances, 114, 711, 731; history, 731, 1616, 2036; journals of Legislative Council, 224; on municipal reform, 961; office of Treasurer, V.I., 280; the Semlin g., 1478; of V.I., 200, 207, 216, 1643-1645; *also see* Representative government

*The government gazette* (of Vancouver Island), 242

*Government gazette—British Columbia,* 187

The Government gazette extraordinary (running title): 353

*Government gazette for the colonies of Vancouver Island and British Columbia,* 100

Government gazettes: 100, 187, 242

*Government of New Caledonia. A bill ... 1858,* 70

*Government policy reviewed ...,* 1114

Gowan, James: com., 420

GOWEN, HERBERT HENRY (b. 1864). Educator, churchman, writer. English clergyman educated at Canterbury; 1886 ordained in Honolulu and in charge of Chinese missions there for 4 y.; then rector of St. Nicholas at Great Yarmouth; went to New Westminster; then in Seattle for 48 y.; prof. of Oriental studies;

retired in 1944 and went to Mill Bay, B.C., in 1945; wrote extensively. (VF; WhA, 1940-41) 1421

GRAHAM, CLARA LUCY (DRAKE) (1860?-1957). Dau. of Mr. Justice M. W. Tyrwhitt-Drake; b. in Victoria and lived most of her life there. (VF)   1838, 2162

*The grain, grass, and gold fields of south-western Canada,* 1274

*A grammar of the Kwagiutl language,* 824

Grande Prairie, *see* Westwold

Granite Creek (town): 726, 2147

GRANT, GEORGE MONRO (1835-1902). A Nova Scotian educated at Pictou Academy and Glasgow Univ.; principal of Queen's Univ.; 1872 accompanied Sir Sandford Fleming on tour across Canada to inspect the location of the C.P.R.; wrote articles of general interest. (Mo, 1898; P; DNB, supp. 2; Cy)   431, 1422 (ed.). *See below*

Grant, George Monro: 1970. *See above*

GRANT, RENA VICTORIA: 1831, 1839, 1849

Granville, *see* Vancouver

Graphic Publishing Company: 1358

GRAVES, SAMUEL H. Pres. of the White Pass & Yukon Railway (t. p.)   1568

Gray, John Hamilton, judge: judgment of, 450, 475, 610; report on Chinese immigration, 682

GREAT BRITAIN: 393, 432, 433, 434, 435, 1040, 1041, 1042, 1043, 1044, 1045, 1503, 1504, 1505, 1506, 1507, 1508, 1509

Great Britain: claims of, 44, 45 (*also see* Bering Sea controversy); colonial development of B.C., 964; colonial interests of, 60, 312

GREAT BRITAIN. ADMIRALTY: 198

GREAT BRITAIN. BEHRING SEA COMMISSIONERS: 979, 1046

GREAT BRITAIN. COLONIAL LAND AND EMIGRATION COMMISSIONERS: 227, 394

GREAT BRITAIN. COLONIAL OFFICE: 7, 13, 33, 34, 35, 51, 67, 68, 69, 86, 87, 88, 199, 200, 228, 308, 330, 461, 496, 1423, 1424

Great Britain. Colonial Office: re Alaskan boundary (1886), 705

Great Britain. Command papers: 2398, entry 67; 2476, 2578, 2724, 2952, entry 86; 2507, entry 88; 3310, entry 230; 3667, entry 274; 3694, entry 273; 3852, entry 385; 4144, entry 333; 4144-1, entry 334; C. 690, entry 432; C. 691, entry 443; C. 692, entry 434; C. 693, entry 444; C. 694, entry 433; C. 695, entry 442; C. 696, entry 435; C. 735, entry 436; C. 911, entry 461; C. 1217, entry 480; C. 1548, entry 496; C. 6041, entry 876; C. 6131, entry 876; C. 6253, entry 936; C. 6368, entry 935; C. 6633, entry 983; C. 6634, entry 981; C. 6635, entry 982; C. 6918, entry 1041; C. 6920, entry 1042; C. 6921, entry 1040; C. 6922, entry 1051; C. 6949, entry 1087; C. 6950, entry 1088; C. 6951, entry 1086; C.

6952, entry 1055; C. 7028, entry 1056; C. 7029, entry 1057; C. 7107, entry 1018; C. 7161, entry 1054; C. 7713, entry 1157; C. 7836, entry 1156; C. 8101, entry 1216; C. 8662, entry 1286; C. 8703, entry 1349; Cd. 1877, entry 1528; Cd. 1878, entry 1529

GREAT BRITAIN. COMMISSIONERS FOR EMIGRATION: 89

GREAT BRITAIN. FOREGN OFFICE: 14, 90, 91, 115, 331-334, 749, 876, 877, 935, 936, 980-983, 1047-1057; 1156, 1157, 1286, 1349, 1425, 1426, 1510, 1511, 1528, 1529

Great Britain. Foreign Office: corr., 1425

Great Britain. House of Commons papers: 619 of 1848, entry 5; 103 of 1849, entry 13; 788-1 of 1853, entry 33; 788 of 1853, entry 34; 83 of 1852-3, entry 35; 229 of 1857, 2d. sess., entry 51; 99 of 1858, entry 68; 534 of 1858, entry 69; 146 of 1859, entry 87; 438 of 1863, entry 199; 507 of 1863, entry 200; 483 of 1868, entry 308; 390 of 1869, entry 330

GREAT BRITAIN. HYDROGRAPHIC OFFICE: 141, 229, 284, 557, 785

GREAT BRITAIN. LAWS, STATUTES, ETC.: 70, 201, 272, 359, 1939

GREAT BRITAIN. PARLIAMENT: 1, 273, 274, 285, 480

Great Britain. Parliament: statutes affecting B.C., 371

GREAT BRITAIN. PARLIAMENT. HOUSE OF COMMONS. SELECT COMMITTEE ON THE HUDSON'S BAY COMPANY: 52

GREAT BRITAIN. PRIVY COUNCIL: 71, 116, 360

Great Britain. Privy Council: 1394

GREAT BRITAIN. PUBLIC RECORD OFFICE: 2017

GREAT BRITAIN. TREATIES, ETC.: 2, 230, 395, 436, 1058, 1115, 1216

*Great Britain—Alaskan boundary. Modus vivendi . . . fixing a provisional boundary line between . . . Alaska and . . . Canada,* 1450

*Great Britain one empire,* 30

*Great commercial prize,* 60

*The Great Divide,* 1763

*The great Dominion; studies of Canada,* 1168

*The great gates,* 2169

*The great gold fields of Cariboo,* 170

*The great north road to the Cariboo,* 1786

GREAT NORTHERN RAILWAY COMPANY: 1217

*A great territorial road to British Columbia,* 195

*In great waters,* 1712

*Greater America; essays . . . ,* 1840

*Greater Canada,* 1443

Greaves, Joseph: 1884, 2132

Green, Ashdown H.: report re Columbia River exploration, 266

GREEN, GEORGE (1872-1955). Went to prairies in 1874 from Lincolnshire; 1904 went to Vancouver as a carpenter; on Municipal Council

273

in 1916; active in community affairs; pres. of
B.C. Hist. Soc. (Vancouver) ; ed. of *Museum
notes* and director of Art, Hist. and Scientific
Assoc. (VF)    1867, 1921

GREEN, WILLIAM SPOTSWOOD (1847-1919).
An Irish alpinist of considerable experience. In
1880's in Swiss Alps, N.Z. (Mt. Cook),
Selkirks; gov't inspector of Irish fisheries, 1889-
1914; "highly regarded as an explorer and
mountaineer, his survey of the Selkirks being
carried out at a time when no map, except that
of the railway itself, existed." (*Can. alpine jour.,*
v. 30, 1947, p. 106-111.)    878

GREENE, RONALD ALLEN (1938-  ): 2127

GREER, SAMUEL. Blacksmith residing at
Chilliwack; came to B.C. about 1869 and also
engaged in farming. (From his evidence in
court)    822

GREGORY, CHARLES NOBLE (1851-1932).
Lawyer, prof. and auth. Between 1872-94
practised law in Madison, Wisc., 1894-1901
associate dean and prof. of law, College of Law,
Univ. of Wisconsin; 1901-    dean of College
of Law, Univ. of Georgia; chn. of section on
legal education and a member of Executive
Committee and General Council of the Am.
Bar Assoc.; a member of the International Law
Assoc. (WhA, 1910-11)    1465

GRIFFIN, HAROLD JOHN MICHAEL (1912-  ):
2018

GRIMM, FERDINAND (1806-1895): 1821

GRINNELL, GEORGE BIRD (1849-1938).
Naturalist, explorer, historian, auth. of many
books, incl. fiction for boys. In 1870 graduated
from Yale; 1874-80 in Peabody Mus. of Yale
Univ.; took summer expeditions on exploring
parties to study natural history and Indians; 1895
on U.S. com. for cessation of part of Blackfeet
and Ft. Belknap Indian land; regarded as
authority on Indians of the Plains. (Waa; Nc;
Bua; Wwh, v. 1; Wwa, v. 1)    1551

Gruenwedel, Albert: jt. auth., 627

THE GUARDIAN ASSURANCE COMPANY OF
LONDON DEFENDANTS: 823

Guide and history of Salmon River & Cariboo mining
district (cov. t.), 174

*Guide to the Klondike and the Yukon gold fields,*
1287

*Guide to the province ... 1877-8,* 507

*Guide to the Yukon Klondike mines,* 1352

*Guide book for British Columbia, &c., by a
successful digger,* 168

*Guide book for British Columbia; the wonders of the
gold diggings,* 168

*The guide-book to Alaska and the Northwest Coast,*
1084

*Guide-book to the gold regions of Frazer River,* 72

Guidebooks: 168, 397; to British Columbia, 507, 885,

921, 1084, 1861, 1902, 1985; V.I., 2027, 2058,
2115; Kootenay district, 2149

*A gulf island patchwork,* 2109

Gulf Islands: history, 1860, 2109

GULICK, GROVER C. (1916-  ). Am. novelist born
in Missouri; brought up on a farm in Kansas;
moved to Oklahoma City and graduated from
Univ. of Oklahoma; lives in Walla Walla, Wash.
(Book jacket)    1940

Gun club: 958

*H.M.C.S. Naden naval barracks,* 1923

*H.M.S. Beaver charts the seas, 1863-1870,* 2012

HABEL, JEAN (1845?-1902). German alpinist,
member of German-Austrian Alpine Club; 1893
climbed Swiss Alps and the Andes in Chile-
Argentine area; 1896 paid his first visit to Canada
to Banff-Lake Louise area; 1897 set out from
Field to Yoho Valley to climb his "Hidden
Peak" (later it bore his name and then changed
to Mt. des Poilus) ; 1898 in Mexico and Europe;
1901 returned to explore Fortress L. area; was
the first to cross the Yoho Pass through the
valley to Glacier to discover peaks. (*Can. alpine
jour.,* v. 30, 1947, p. 58-62)    1350

HACKING, NORMAN R. Journalist, marine ed. of
Vancouver *Province;* contributed to *B.C. hist.
quart.* articles on steamboats; 1965 sailed with
three others in a small craft from Hawaii to
Vancouver. (Van. *Province 7* Aug. 1965, p. 5)
1841, 1850, 1868, 1941

*Hagaga,* 1059

HAGGEN, RUPERT WILLIAMS (1887-1962).
Civil and mining engineer, politician. Born in
New Zealand; came to B.C. 1901; 1911 land
surveyor; in Cariboo 1911-25; 1925-35 in
Vancouver; 1934 civil engineer; 1935 went to
Rossland in charge of mine development; 1949-
56 C.C.F. member of B.C. legislature; member
of several surveying and engineering associations.
(Cc, 1950; VF)    1899

*Haida grammar,* 1158

Haida Indian language: dictionary of, 162; grammar
of, 1158; philology of, 1268; vocabulary of, 965;
works in, 912, 1021, 1109, 1329, 1357, 1402,
1403, 1413

Haida Indians: 401, 470, 608, 657, 1261, 1268, 1341,
1357, 1386, 1416, 1623, 1679, 2084; play about,
1755

*The Haida of Queen Charlotte Islands,* 1357

*Haida texts—Masset dialect,* 1357

*The Haidah Indians of Queen Charlotte's Islands,* 470

*Die Haida's,* 608

HAIG-BROWN, RODERICK LANGMERE HAIG
(1908-  ). Auth., sportsman, conservationist;
has won many awards for his books; came to
Canada when 18 y. old; worked in lumber camps;
was trapper, logger and guide; settled in Campbell
R. where he is also a magistrate. (Book jacket)
2128

HALCOMBE, JOHN JOSEPH (d. 1909?) Anglican clergyman. 1856 B.A. (Cantab.); reader and librarian, Charterhouse; 1862-74 Balsham rector, Linton, Cambs. (Cr, 1896)  396, 462 (ed.)

HALDANE, JOHN WILTON CUNNINGHAME: 1466

HALE, HORATIO EMMONS (1817-1896). Anthropologist, ethnologist, philologist. New Hampshire-born; called to the bar in Chicago, 1855; 1856-96 in Clinton, Ont.; supervised Br. anthropological work in B.C. and the Northwest; contributed many articles to anthropological publications. (DNBc)  879. *See below*

Hale, Horatio: auth., 677. *See above*

*Half-yearly letter,* 1453

Halkomelem Indian dialect: 382

HALL, ALFRED JAMES (d. 1918). Anglican missionary at Alert Bay; 1877 went first to Metlahkatla; 1878 went to Alert Bay and made many changes in Indian life; compiled a dictionary of their language and translated Scripture passages; 1913 retired to England and held a country living at Twickenham, near Bristol. (Vic. *Times,* 30 May 1918)  824. *See below*

Hall, Alfred James: trans., 925, 1101, 1257, 1431. *See above*

HALL, EDWARD HEPPLE: 558

Hall, Goepel & Co'y: 1373

HALL, RICHARD (1853-1918). A businessman and politician. Born in Grass Valley, Calif.; educated in Victoria; was a purser on several coast steamers; was in dry-goods business with William Denny; 1882 was in wholesale coal trade and an agent of insurance companies; formed the firm of Hall, Goepel & Co., general business agents for British firms; 1888 associated as a member with Victoria Sealing Company, purchased schooner "Araunah," fitted it with an Indian crew, sailed for Copper Island, where she was seized by the Russian gov't; crew was sent to Siberia and by intervention of Br. ambassador at St. Petersburg were forwarded to Japan, then to Victoria; 1899 formed partnership with Walker in coal business; was active in politics, first as a Conservative until 1896, then a Liberal; 1898 elected to legislature, re-elected in 1900 and 1903; 1905 was a com. on an enquiry into B.C. fisheries; in municipal affairs he was on the School Board in 1890-1 and on City Council in 1908; a member of several fraternal organizations. (Vic. *Times,* 29 Mar. 1918) 1351. *See below*

Hall, Richard: 1373. *See above*

Hall, Sydney: illus., 639

HALLER, GRANVILLE OWEN (1820-1897): 1218

HALLIDAY, WILLIAM MAY (1866-1957). Teacher and Indian agent. 1873 went to New Westminster from Ont.; 1880 went to Victoria; taught in Comox, Yakima, and Alert Bay; 1894 appointed magistrate for Comox; 1906-1933 Indian agent. (VF)  1758

HALMINEN, MATTI: 1767

HAM, GEORGE HENRY (1847-1926). Journalist. Born in Trenton; 1865 journalist on Whitby *Chronicle;* 1875-91 on Winnipeg paper, then advertising manager of C.P.R.; press representative in Northwest Rebellion in 1885 and the threatened Indian uprising in 1886; on Winnipeg Council; school trustee. (Waa; Wa; Cd; Mo)  786

HAMILTON, JAMES HERBERT (1879-1964). A member of Vancouver consular corps; founder and ed. of *Harbour and shipping* for 25 y.; 1939-43 Pacific coast representative on the Canadian Shipping Board; one of the founders of the Vancouver Merchants Exchange and its manager 1920-43. (*B.C. hist. quart.,* v. 20, 1956, p. 140) 1736, 2068

HAMILTON, REUBEN: 1890 left Ont. for Vancouver with his Irish parents; worked for a grocery store as a delivery man. (VF)  1979

HAMILTON, WALTER R. (1872?-1964). Real estate agent and notary public and interested in civic affairs; of Irish-Huguenot extraction; born in Que., but grew up in Ont.; attended London Military School; went to Klondike 1898 for ten y.; went to Vancouver, was alderman, police com., and on Parks Board. (VF; Cn)  2163

Hamlin, J. B.: report of, 1245

Hanceville: 2051

*Hand-book almanac for the Pacific states,* 204

*Hand-book and map to the gold region of Frazer's and Thompson's rivers,* 56

Handbook of American Indians north of Mexico: 1602

*The handbook of British Columbia and emigrant's guide,* 169

*Handbook of Indians of Canada,* 1602

*Hand book of the Church of England missions,* 1062

*Handbook to British Columbia; a general guide,* 1060

*A hand-book to British Columbia and Vancouver Island,* 349

*Handbook to Canada; a guide for travellers,* 598

*Handbook to the new gold fields,* 57

HANFORD, CORNELIUS HOLGATE (1849-1926). Lawyer and judge. Born in Iowa but lived all his life on the Pacific coast; 1904 received an LL.D from Whitman College; 1875 admitted to the bar and practised in Seattle, Wash.; 1877 was member of Territorial Council; 1881-1912 was attorney and chief justice of Supreme Court of Wash. Terr. and Western District of Washington; resumed the practice of law. (Wwa, 1897-1942) 1427, 1467

Harbours: Esquimalt, 1822; regulations for, 1106; regulations for New Westminster, 634;

regulations for Victoria and Esquimalt, 80; *also see* Naval stations

Hardwicke Island: 2010

HARDY, WILLIAM GEORGE (1896- ). Prof., Univ. of Alberta. Born in Ont. 3 Feb. 1896; attended Univ. of Toronto, and Univ. of Chicago; 1918-20 lecturer, Univ. of Toronto; 1920 appointed to Univ. of Alberta; 1933 appointed head of Classics Dept.; pres. of Can. Authors Assoc. 1950-52; chn. of Humanities Assoc., Alta.; writer of novels, serials, short stories. (Whc, 1958-59)   2092

Hare, Alexander: accused, 581

HARKER, DOUGLAS EDWARD (1911- ): 2019

Harkin, William A: ed., 1619

HARLAN, JOHN MARSHALL (1833-1911). Jurist. Born in Kentucky; studied law at Lexington; 1853 admitted to the bar; 1858 elected judge of county court; served as a col. in the Civil War; 1863-7 att.-gen. of Kentucky; 1871 and 1875 ran for governorship of Kentucky, but was defeated; 1877 appointed an associate judge in Supreme Court; 1889-1910 lectured on constitutional law at Columbian Univ.; 1892 appointed as an Am. representative in the arbitration of the Bering Sea controversy. (DAB)   1061

HARNETT, LEGH: 309

Harney, William Selby: corr. re San Juan Island, 126, 128, 129

HARNEY, WILLIAM SELBY (1800-1889). Am. gen. Educated in Tennessee; 1818 in the army, took part in many battles with Indians; 1858 in charge of the Ore. Dept. of army; visited Victoria in 1859; his seizure of the Island of San Juan caused an international situation; 1860 recalled from Ore.; 1861 commanded Dept. of the West; 1863 retired as maj.-gen.; (L. U. Reavis, *Life and military services of General William Selby Harney* (Saint Louis, Bryan, Brand & Co. 1878))   92

Harper, Thaddeus: 2132

HARRIS, CHRISTIE LUCY (IRWIN) (1907- ). Journalist and C.B.C. radio script-writer for school broadcasts; grew up in Cloverdale and Cariboo; was Women's Editor for Abbotsford *News;* writes novels, children's books, Indian legends, drama; 1964 received a Canada Council grant for research on Charles Edenshaw, a Haida carver. (VF; book jacket)   1980

Harris, John Morgan: comp., 1307

HARRIS, JOSIAH. A promoter of the Hudson Bay and Pacific Railway; resident of England. (P) 1219, 1288

Harrison, A. G.: jt. auth., 1283

HARRISON, CARTER HENRY (1825-1893). Am. politician. 1879-93 mayor of Chicago, lawyer, congressman; 1887-8 took a voyage around world. (Waa; DAB; Apa; Nc)   825

HARRISON, CHARLES: 657, 1158, 1679. *See below*

Harrison, Charles: trans., 912, 1021. *See above*

Harrison Hot Springs: history, 2041

Harrison Lake district: 145, 842, 1590

Harrison River: exploration of (1861), 145

HART, ALBERT BUSHNELL (1854-1943). University prof. Graduate of Harvard Univ. and Freiburg Univ.; prolific writer on Am. history. (Wwh, v. 3)   984 (ed.)

HARVEY, ARTHUR (1834-1905). Classical scholar, scientist in astronomical and magnetic studies, pioneer in statistical enquiry. Chief statistical clerk in Auditor-General's office 1862; 1867-70 founder and ed. of *Yearbook and almanac of British North America,* predecessor of *Canada year book.* (Mo; Ec)   286 (comp.)

HARVEY ATHELSTAN GEORGE (1884-1950): 1776

Haslam, Ruth: auth., 1873

Hastings, *see* Vancouver

HATCH, MELVILLE HARRISON (1898- ). Professor of zoology at Univ. of Washington. Am. *Physical and Biological Sciences,* 10th ed.) 1891

Hatley Park: 1757

*Hattie Brown Gold Mining Comp'y:* 1289

Hawkins, John Summerland: 2125

HAY, JAMES: 687

HAYDEN, ISAAC J. (plaintiff): 750

HAYES, JOHN FRANCIS (1904- ). Auth., commercial artist, director; educated in Ft. William and Winnipeg; resident of Toronto; diversified career, studied writing, commercial art; his books for children have won many awards; director of Southam Printing Co. (P; book jacket)   2093

HAYNES, WILLIAM (1835-1920). Bandsman on H.M.S. "Phoebe," one of the ships in the Flying Squadron, which visited Esquimalt in 1871. Born Sevenoaks, Kent; 1859 came to B.C. on clipper ship "Thames City" as bandmaster of the Royal Engineers; went with the corps to Sapperton where he remained until 1864; was bandmaster of Volunteers in early days of the Victoria Rifles and 5th Regiment; bandmaster of the band which went on the steamer *Yosemite* with the excursion party to Port Moody for the arrival there of the first C.P.R. trans-continental passenger train on 4 July 1886; a member of a Masonic lodge from 1866. (VF)   382

HAZARD, JOSEPH TAYLOR (1879- ): 1737

HAZLITT, WILLIAM CAREW (1834-1913). Bibliographer and man of letters; wrote on history of Venetian Republic; interested in old books entirely in later years and compiled extensive bibliographies. (DNB, 1912-21, supp.) 73, 170

HEADLAND, EMILY: 937

HEALEY, ELIZABETH (1912- ): 2020 (comp.)

*Healing waters . . . Harrison Hot Springs . . .*, 2041
*Health seekers', tourists' and sportsmen's guide*, 650
HEBREW LADIES ASSOCIATION (VICTORIA):
1220
Hector, Sir James: pub. on, 1667, 2122
Hedley: 2147
Hedley Camp: 1877
Helmcken, John Sebastian: pub. on, 1852, 1870
Heltman, Charles C.: jt. auth., 1339
*Henderson's British Columbia gazetteer*, 826; *also see*
624
*Henderson's Vancouver city directory*, 787
*Henderson's Victoria directory*, 880
HENDY, ALBERT EDWARD (1905-  ). Anglican
clergyman. In 1937 was asst. priest Christ Church
Cathedral, Victoria; a naval chaplain during
World War II; 1953 appointed archdeacon of
Comox; rector at St. Paul's Church, Nanaimo;
1963 rector of St. Richard's Church at Gordon
Head. (Vic. *Times*, 17 July 1939, p. 13; 23 July
1953, p. 3; 21 Oct. 1963, p. 2)   1929
HENLEY, G. F.: 1352
HENSHAW, JULIA WILMOTTE (HENDERSON)
(1869-1937). Journalist, novelist, botanist; auth.
of books on flora of Rockies. Born in Shropshire;
went to Vancouver 1890; active in musical and
other clubs in Vancouver; 1914-18 active in war
work in England; one of the original members of
Alpine Club of Canada 1906. (*Can. alpine jour.*,
v. 25, 1937, p. 128-131; VF; Wa; Wha; Www)
1485
*Heralds of Christ the King*, 1795
*The heroine of Moodyville*, 1766
HERRING, FRANCES ELIZABETH (CLARKE)
(1851-1916). Teacher, auth., newspaper
correspondent. In 1876 went to Fort Langley as
a teacher; married; her husband established
only wholesale drug store on the Mainland in
1877; was associate ed. of *Commonwealth* and
correspondent for Toronto *Globe;* active in
equal rights for women movement. (VF)   1468,
1530, 1605, 1612
Hesquiat Mission: 1649, 1694
Hewatson, Bob (pseud.), *see* Porter, Lancelot
HEWSON, M. BUTT. Civil engineer; gained honorary
military rank of gen. for services to Am. railways
in the mid-West. (P)   559, 577
HEYDEN, JOSEPH VAN DER: 1649
Hibben & Carswell: pub. of Indian language
dictionary, 162
Hibben (T. N.) & Co.: pub. of Chinook dictionary,
381; guide to the province, 507
HICKMAN, MARY. Grand-dau. of a pioneer of
Chilliwack area, Joseph Brannick; her mother
was the first school teacher there. (VF)   1981
Hicks, John Peak: ed., 1747
Hicks, Richard: 1690
Higgins, D. W.: 729

HIGGINS, DAVID WILLIAMS (1834-1917).
Auth., ed., journalist. Born in Halifax, brought
up in Brooklyn; 1852 went to Calif., founded the
*Morning Call;* 1858 went to the Fraser R. gold
rush; 1860 joined staff of *Colonist;* 1862 founded
*Daily Chronicle;* 1862-86 publisher and ed. of
*Colonist;* 1890 speaker of Assembly and M.L.A.
to 1900; defended responsible gov't and was an
anti-annexationist; 1906-7 ed. of Vancouver
*World.* (VF; EC)   751, 1531, 1538
Higgins, William: defendant, 766
*High handed proceedings on Vancouver's Island*,
1428
High schools, *see* Schools
HILL, HAZEL A. E.: 1922
*Hill-top tales*, 1882
HILL-TOUT, CHARLES (1858?-1944). A
distinguished anthropologist. Born in England;
an Oxford graduate; came to B.C. in 1880's; 1895
Roy. Soc. published his monograph on
archaeology of B.C. which led to extensive
investigations later by Jessup and others; a
specialist on Indians of B.C. and was interested in
totemism; 1900 made Corresponding Fellow of
Roy. Anthropological Inst. of Great Britain and
Ireland; 1908 made Fellow of Am. Ethnological
Soc.; 1911 vice-pres., Archeological Inst. of Am.
(Can. Dept.). (*B.C. magazine,* Mar. 1913, p.
144-147; Mo, 1912)   1159, 1290, 1353. *See
below*
Hill-Tout, Charles: 1261. *See above*
HILLS, GEORGE, bp. of Columbia (1816-1895).
Anglican clergyman. Born at Egthorne, near
Dover; ordained 1840; vicar of Greater
Yarmouth, for 11 y.; 1859 consecrated Bishop of
Columbia in Westminster Abbey; 1860-92 in
Victoria Diocese which at first included all of
B.C. until 1879 when the dioceses of New
Westminster and Caledonia were formed; erected
the "iron church," later the first cathedral which
was burned, then another cathedral; built a girls'
school and other new churches in the outlying
areas; died at Parham vicarage, Suffolk, England.
(VF; B.C. Cen. Com.)   93, 117, 142, 202
463. *See below*
Hills, George: appeal for funds, 109; Cridge
controversy, 451, 457; information on, 1234;
journals of 138, 142; letters from, 108;
"Occasional paper" controversy, 117, 123.
*See above*
HIND, HENRY YOULE (1823-1908). Geologist on
exploratory expedition to the Red River and
Assiniboine-Saskatchewan in 1857-8; travelled
and explored in Labrador-Newfoundland area
and mapped the cod banks of the Atlantic coast;
published extensively. (P; Mo, 1898)   171
*Hints to intending Klondikers*, 1347
*Histoire d'un contrat*, 617
*Histoire de l'église catholique dans l'Ouest*, 1600

12; charter of grant of V.I., etc., 13; claim of chief factors, etc., 994; claims of, 44, 45, 215, 230, 240, 245-247, 253; colonization of V.I., 7-9, 11, 12; deed poll, 752; deed poll regulations, 827; docs. and corr. of, 1425; and Edward Watkin, 511; and the Fraser River gold rush, 55; history, 1355, 1496, 1497, 1534, 1616, 1676, 2043; history of the establishment of the V.I. colony, 731; history on V.I. (1847-1865), 1978; and Indians, 42; and lands, 217, 261, 262, 767; mentioned in gov't doc. of Minnesota, 124; property in Wash. Terr., 41; rights and duties of officers, 383; rights and privileges of, 1045; and shipping, 1120, 1337; and V.I., 35, 930, 1965

*Hudson's Bay Company and Sir Edward Watkin,* 511

The Hudson's Bay Company and the late government: 65

*The Hudson's Bay Company as an Imperial factor,* 1978

*Hudson's Bay Company. Copies of correspondence . . . in consequence of the report of the select committee . . . 1858,* 68

*The Hudson's Bay Company versus Magna Charta,* 49

*The Hudson's Bay Company; what is it?* 233

HUGHES, BEN (1882-   ). Newspaper publisher Born in Derbyshire; newspaper apprenticeship in England; went to U.S. then to Cobalt, Ont.; founded the *Northern Miner;* after World War I went to V.I., published the *West Coast Advocate,* then bought the Courtenay *Argus;* sold it in 1955 to his employees; active in the community; interested in the history of the area. (VF)   2129

HUGHES, THOMAS (1818-1883); 287

*Huldowget; a story of the North Pacific coast,* 1693

HULEATT, HUGH. An English clergyman who visited America in 1889. (P)   828

HULOT, ETIENNE GABRIEL JOSEPH, baron (1857-1918). French lawyer, political scientist, and auth.; sec.-gen. of the Geog. Soc. (Q, 1908) 788

*A hundred years of Christian Chinese work,* 2079

Hunt, George: jt. auth. 1357

Hunting: 424, 667, 796, 799, 800, 840, 842, 898, 899, 948, 1037, 1238, 1324, 1458, 1471; advertisement for, 1258; animals of B.C., 1128; game protective association, 958

*Hunting for gold,* 1036

*The hunting of the silver fleece,* 1853

Huntington, Lucius Seth: report on charges of, 420; *also see* Pacific Scandal

*Hurrah for the life of a sailor!,* 1471

HUSDELL, G. D.: 203 (comp.)

Hutchinson, G.: tenant-farmer delegate, 919

HUTCHISON, WILLIAM BRUCE (1901-   ). Auth., journalist. From 1925-   B.C. reporter at Ottawa; 1944-50 assoc. ed. Winnipeg *Free Press;* 1950-63 ed. Victoria *Times;* contributor to magazines and newspapers; 1961 first winner of award for distinguished journalism in

Commonwealth by Roy. Soc. of Arts, London. (Cd, 1961-63)   1901

*Hyack Engine Company No. 1 (New Westminster):* 231

*The Hydah mission, Queen Charlotte Islands,* 657

Hydrography: 1751; *also see* Pilot guides

*Hymns in the Chinook jargon language (1878),* 536

*Hymns in the Tenni or Slavi language,* 881

*I followed gold,* 1791

*I smemeies, i nkaumen i snkuenzin l okenakan nkolkoeltens,* 779

*Illustrated British Columbia,* 659

*Illustrated travels; a record,* 321

Immigration, *see* Emigration and immigration

*Imperial Atlantic and Pacific railway,* 21

*Imperial blue books . . . relating to Canada,* 1

*Impression of a tenderfoot,* 899

IMRAY, JAMES FREDERICK (1829?-1891). British publisher.   36, 310

*In memory of Sir James Douglas, K.C.B.,* 510

*In memory of Sir John* [sic] *Douglas,* 510

*In the heart of the Canadian Rockies,* 1545

*In the heart of the hills,* 1340

*In the pathless West,* 1530

*In the wake of the war canoe,* 1623

*Inasmuch; sketches of the beginnings of the Church of England in Canada,* 1633

*Inaugural address . . . in the Market Hall,* 1231

Incorporated London Chamber of Mines: 1342

Independent Order of Odd Fellows, *see* Odd Fellows, Independent Order of

*Index prepared by Mr. DeCosmos,* 594

*Indian bazaar,* 1116

*Indian fairy tales,* 1237

Indian languages: 1228; comparative vocabularies, 671; *also see* Beaver Indian language; Bella Coola Indian language; Carrier Indian language; Chinook jargon; Haida Indian language; Halkomelem Indian language; Kootenay Indian language; Kwakiutl Indian language; Lillooet Indian language; Niska Indian dialect; Nootka Indian language; Okanagon Indian language; Shuswap Indian language; Slave Indian language; Stalo Indian dialect; Tahltan Indian language; Thompson Indian language; Tlingit Indian language; Tsetsaut Indian language; Tsimshian Indian language; Wakashan Indian language

*Indian Methodist hymn-book,* 1382

*The Indian policy of . . . British Columbia,* 1608

*The Indian potlatch,* 1433

*Indian treaties and surrenders, from 1680 to 1890,* 1596

*Indianische sagen von der Nord-Pacifischen Küste Amerikas,* 1145

Indians: 24, 157, 177, 592, 639, 661, 677, 696, **731,** 868, 913, 1085, 1145, 1151, 1184, 1228, 1237, 1446, 1447, 1534, 1583, 1600, 1616, 1617, 1728, 1892, 2085; art of, 470, 627, 644, 855, 1240, 1259, 1357; artifacts 857; bibliography of, 1931;

Br. gov't docs. re (1859-62), 86; census of (in 1849), 13; conversion of, 414; criticism of Indian land policy, 835; deed of land to Samuel Greer, 822; drama with Indian theme, 1755; education of, 695; ethnological survey, 1261; and fed. act (1874), 455; in fiction, 1551; fishing, 486; near Fort Simpson, 95; and the Hudson's Bay Company, 42; in Hudson's Bay Company territory (1857), 53; of northern B.C., 746; notes on (1874), 466; of Pacific states (in 5 v.), 472; in poetry, 485; policy of B.C. colonial gov't, 1608; potlatch, 1433; prehistoric man in B.C., 1159; reference book, primarily of proper names, 1602; report of Israel Wood Powell (1873), 421; report on reserves (1878), 544; of Simpson district, 883; study of early migrations of, 1357; treaties, reservations, land transfers, etc., 1596; of V.I., 311, 313; warfare among (1869), 323; *also see* Athapaskan Indians; Bella Coola Indians; Coast Salish Indians; Haida Indians; Kwakiutl Indians; Lillooet Indians; Nootka Indians; Swuswap Indians; Thompson Indians; Tlingit Indians; Tsimshian Indians; *also see* Baptists; Church of England; Catholic Church; Methodist Church; Presbyterian Church *under* missions; *also see* Jesup North American Expedition

*Indians of British Columbia: an historical review,* 2085

Industrial association: 1077

*Industrial exhibition* (1861), 143

*Industrial exhibition; circular* (1861), 140

Industry: 639, 659, 731, 875, 1285; dynamite plants, 2102; in Vancouver, 795

*Information respecting the Yukon district,* 1269

INGALL, ELFRIC DREW (1858-1944). Chief of Mining Div., Geol. Survey of Can. 1117

INGERSOLL, ERNEST (1852-1946). Am. naturalist. Born in Monroe; ed. of C.P.R. immigration literature; lecturer in zoology at Univ. of Chicago; wrote on popular scientific subjects. (Waa; Nc; Bua; WhA; Wha; P) 753. *See below*

Ingersoll, Ernest: auth., 921. *See above*

*The inland passage; a journal of a trip to Alaska,* 831

THE INLAND SENTINEL (KAMLOOPS): 1539

Inland Tlingit Indians, *see* Tlingit Indians

INNIS, HAROLD ADAMS (1894-1952). Economist and historian. Born in Ont.; attended McMaster, Univ. of Toronto and Univ. Chicago; 1920-52 in Dept. of Political Science at Univ. of Toronto; 1937 appointed head; 1947 dean of School of Graduate Studies; 1934 F.R.S.C. and society's pres. 1946. (Wa; Cd, 1949-51) 1666

INNIS, MARY QUAYLE (1899- ). Auth. of economic histories, a novel, short stories and magazine articles. In 1955 appointed dean of Women, University College, Univ. of Toronto. (Cd, 1961-63) 1970

*Instructions from the engineer . . . ,* 474

*Instructions pour naviguer,* 445

*Instructions to Mr. Blanchard* [sic], 360

Interior Salish Indian languages: bibliography of works in 1082; *also see* Lillooet Indian language; Okanagon Indian language; Shuswap Indian language; Stalo Indian dialect; Thompson Indian language

Interior Salish Indians, *see* Lillooet Indians; Salish Indians; Thompson Indians

*International bimetallism,* 1096

INTERNATIONAL COAST SEAMEN AND SEALERS' UNION OF BRITISH COLUMBIA: 986

*An international idiom,* 879

*Introduction to Traditions . . . Thompson River Indians,* 1461

IRELAND, WILLARD ERNEST (1914- ). Provincial archivist and librarian of B.C. Born in Vancouver; graduated from U.B.C. n 1933; 1935 M.A. from Univ. of Toronto; 1937 did research in London; 1937-40 teacher at Burnaby High School; 1940 appointed provincial archivist, 1942-5 was in the R.C.A.F.; 1946 became provincial archivist and librarian; active in historical and library associations; ed. of the *B.C. hist. quart.* (VF) 1812. *See below*

Ireland, Willard E.: 1908, 1915, 2097. *See above*

Irving, John: 1337

Irwin, Henry ("Father Pat"): pub. on, 1575

*Island Mountain Mine, Cariboo district,* 709

*Island of San Juan. Letter from the secretary of State . . . relative to the occupation,* 127

*Island of San Juan. Message from the President . . .* 293

[*Island railway papers, 1872-1881*], 595

Israel, Joseph, *see* Benjamin, Israel Joseph

IVES, WILLIAM BULLOCK: Politician, industrialist, lawyer. Born in Lower Canada; educated at Compton Acad.; 1867 called to Quebec bar; practised law in Sherbrooke; active in railway and industrial development; 1878-99 in Can. H. of C.; 1892-4 pres. of Council; 1894-6 Minister of Trade and Commerce. (EC; Cc, 1885) 660

J., M. E., *see* Johnson, M. E.: 481

*J. S. Helmcken,* 1852

*Jack, the young canoeman,* 1551

JACKSON, J. A.: 1540

JACKSON, SHELDON (1834-1909). Presbyterian missionary for southern and western U.S. working from Denver, Col. In 1877 visited Alaska and was its first ordained minister; chief interest was in education and welfare of Alaskan natives; 1892 was responsible for introducing the reindeer to Alaska to prevent starvation of natives. (John Eaton, "Sheldon Jackson, Alaska's apostle and pioneer," *The review of reviews,* June 1896, p. 691-696) 579

JACKSON MINES LIMITED: 1292

Kitimat: 2034

Kitwanga: history of, 2023

KITWANGA. SUPERIOR SCHOOL: 2023

KIWANIS CLUB OF NANAIMO: 2150

*Klatsassan, and other reminiscences of missionary life,* 414

KLAUCKE, M. F.: 288

The Klondike and British Columbia: 1252, 1262, 1263, 1266, 1273-1275, 1283, 1284, 1287, 1293, 1298, 1303, 1305, 1313, 1314, 1317, 1320, 1327, 1331, 1333-1335, 1339, 1343, 1347, 1352, 1354, 1358, 1359, 1362, 1365, 1368, 1371, 1374, 1381, 1399, 1432, 1456, 1601, 1819, 1872, 1960, 2070; and customs on goods, 1389; in fiction, 1445, 1517; and the North-West Mounted Police, 1625, 1762

*Klondike cattle drive,* 2070

*Klondike fever,* 1996

*The Klondike goldfields, and how to get there,* 1293

*The Klondike official guide,* 1368

*The Klondike-Peace gold fields,* 1331

Klondike Publishing Co.: 1347

*The Klondike stampede,* 1456

*Klondike; the life and death of the last great gold rush,* 1996

*Klondyke, Cassiar, Omineca, and Cariboo gold fields* (cov. t.), 1262

*Klondyke gold fields, Yukon district; map of routes,* 1298

*Le Klondyke, L'Alaska, Le Yukon,* 1432

*Klondyke mining laws; the Canadian gold fields,* 1358

*Klondyke; the Yukon . . . mines, and how to reach them,* 1263

KLOTZ, OTTO JULIUS (1852-1923). Astronomer, civil engineer. Born in Preston, Ont.; attended Toronto Univ. to study medicine and engineering; 1879-1908 entered Dom. gov't service in the Topographical Surveys Branch; 1886 made an accurate survey of C.P.R. through the Rockies and Selkirks; determined altitudes and named many peaks; 1893-4 in Alaska on boundary survey; determined longitude of Pacific islands between Vancouver and Australia; 1908 appointed asst. chief astronomer; first pres. of Assoc. of Dom. Land Surveyors; 1908 elected pres., Roy. Astronomical Soc. of Can.; was a fellow of the Am. Assoc. for Advancement of Sc.; member of many scientific associations; 1917 appointed director, Dom. Observatory, Ottawa, (Mo, 1912) 1634, 1635. *See below*

Klotz, Otto Julius: re Alaska, 1045; re forty-ninth parallel, 1425. *See above*

KNEVETT, J. S.: 509

KNIGHT, WILLIAM HENRY (1835-1925). Am. writer. Compiler of Bancroft's *Handbook* and also of maps of the Pacific states, 1862-4; 1864-9 in Bancroft's publishing dept.; 1870-96 went into business; a writer and lecturer on astronomy and scientific subjects; pres. of S. Calif. Acad. of Sciences, 1894-7 and 1899-1902; 1905 an editorial writer on Los Angeles *Times.* (Wwh, v. 1.) 204 (ed.)

Knights of Pythias: history of, 1167

KNIGHTS OF PYTHIAS. BRITISH COLUMBIA. GRAND LODGE: 1063

KNIGHTS OF PYTHIAS. COMOX. COMOX LODGE No. 5: 829

KNIGHTS OF PYTHIAS. VICTORIA. FAR WEST LODGE No. 1: 988

KNIGHTS OF PYTHIAS. VICTORIA. SUNSET LODGE No. 10: 1064

KNIPE, C.: 311

*"Know your diocese" . . . New Westminster,* 1905

KNOX, OLIVE ELSIE (ROBINSON): Auth., resident of Winnipeg. Born in Ont.; graduate of Univ. of Manitoba; lived in U.S., Sask., Man. (Book jacket; Cd, 1949-51) 1971

Knox Presbyterian Church (Trail): 1654

Koch, George A.: jt. auth., 709

KOHLSTEDT, EDWARD DELOR: Methodist minister in Wisconsin. 1922-7 pres. of Dakota Wesleyan Univ.; chn. of interdenominational Board for Christian Work in Santo Domingo and Home Missions Council of North America; exec. sec. of National Missions Div. of Methodist Board of Missions; 1936-53 was one of trustees of trust fund set up by the will of William Duncan to aid Metlakatla Christian Mission; 1944 retired. (Frwd. of *William Duncan . . .*) 1982

*The Kootenai country,* 1217

*A Kootenai grammar,* 1108

*The Kootenay country of British Columbia,* 976

KOOTENAY CURLING ASSOCIATION: 1359

Kootenay Curling Association: 1200, *also see* British Columbia Curling Association

Kootenay district: 680, 791, 976, 1217, 1274, 1289, 1312, 1360, 1361, 1371, 1458; and Baillie-Grohman, 640, 699, 772; Boards of Trade, 1401; in fiction, 1485, 1517, 1671, 2146; guidebook for, 2149; history of, 1546, 1790, 1838, 1896, 1909, 1930, 1969, 1997, 2039, 2042, 2045, 2047, 2162; mining in, 1143, 1170, 1280, 1375

*The Kootenay guide,* 1360

Kootenay Indian language: grammar of, 1108; catechism in, 968

*Kootenay Lake General Hospital, since 1893,* 2151

KOOTENAY LAKE GENERAL HOSPITAL SOCIETY: 2151

Kootenay Lake Syndicate: 640

*The Kootenay mines; a sketch,* 1170

THE KOOTENAY MINING PROTECTIVE ASSOCIATION: 1296

*Kootenay mining standard,* 1361

Kootenay Syndicate (Limited): 699

*The Kootenay valleys and the Kootenay district in British Columbia,* 772

*The Kootenay valleys in Kootenay district,* 699

Koryak tribe: 1357
Kotschar, Vincent F.: 1897
KRAUSE, AUREL (1848-1908): 688
Krause, Eduard: auth., 627, 644
Kuper Island: 1860
KURTZ, JOHN (1832?-1891). Cigar manufacturer,
mining operator. Born in Philadelphia; began as a
druggist's apprentice; 1849 went to Calif. where
he was in the tobacco business; organizer of the
state militia and the fire dept., on the vigilance
committee of 1856; 1858 went to the Fraser R.
area; 1861 organizer and sec. of Yale Steamboat
Co.; went to the Cariboo and organized the Lane
and Kurtz Mining Co.; 1881 started a cigar
factory in Victoria. (VF)   790
*A Kwāgūtl translation of hymns . . . , 1431*
*A Kwāgūtl version of portions of the Book of*
*Common Prayer, 925*
Kwakiutl Indian language: bibliography of, 1130;
grammar of, 824; notes on, 1462; vocabulary of,
782, 1023; works in, 609, 925, 1101, 1257, 1357,
1431
Kwakiutl Indians: 782, 1197, 1352, 1357, 1758, 1811,
1897
*The Kwakiutl of Vancouver Island, 1357*
*Kwakiutl texts, 1357*
Labour movement: history of, 2018; steamshipmen's
association, 1069; and unions 986, 1376, 1722,
1772, 1783
Lacrosse association: 1204, 1406
La Hache (lake): 184
Laing, Frederick William: 1812
Laing, J. W.: testimonials for, 1249
LAING, LIONEL HASSELL (1905-   ). Prof. of
political science. Born in Nelson, B.C.; educated
in Revelstoke and Victoria; graduated from
U.B.C. 1929; M.A., Clark Univ. 1930; Ph.D.,
Harvard 1935; 1935-42 asst. prof. of government
at College William and Mary; 1942-   assoc.
prof. and prof. of political science, Univ. of
Michigan; membership in several pol. sc.
associations including Hansard Soc.; jt. auth. of
*Canada and the law of the nations* (1939),
*Source book of European government* (1950),
*British elections studies* (1951). (*Who's who in
American education*, v. 22, 1965; personal
information)   1759
THE LAKE BENNETT AND KLONDIKE STEAM
NAVIGATION COMPANY, LIMITED: 1362
Lake O'Hara: history of, 2111
LAMB, WILLIAM KAYE (1904-   ). Dominion
archivist, historian. Born in New Westminster;
1927 B.A. from U.B.C.; M.A. in 1930; 1928-9
and 1930-2 at Sorbonne; 1933 Ph.D. from Univ.
of London; 1934-40 B.C. provincial librarian and
archivist; 1940 head librarian at U.B.C. and
later Dominion archivist; membership in
historical and library associations. (Cd, 1948)
1787, 1803, 1832 (comp.), 2094. *See below*

Lamb, William Kaye: ed., 1827. *See above*
Lambert, T. W.: 1161
Lanctot, Gustave: jt. ed., 1726
*The land laws of British Columbia, 412*
*The land of Chief Nicola . . . , 2118*
*A land of gold! Trail Creek, B.C., 1241*
*Land of shining Mountains, 1983*
*The land of the muskeg, 1177*
*Land of the Okanagan, British Columbia, 934*
*Land of the Peace Arch, 2037*
*Land of the royal Kwantlen, 2100*
*The land of Twelve Foot Davis, 1924*
Land surveyors' association: 911
Land tenure: statutes concerning, 411; on V.I.
(1858), 69
Lands: Baillie-Grohman reclamation and settlement
scheme, 640, 699, 772; and the C.P.R., 590, 647,
814; criticism of Indian land policy, 835; deeded
by Indians, 822; Dom. lands within the C.P.R.
railway belt, 681, 861, 1026 and the Esquimalt
& Nanaimo Railway, 1215, 1270, 1345, 1428;
and the Hudson's Bay Company, 767; and
settlement in B.C., 1949; subsidies re railways,
1784; public lands, 86, 217, 243, 244, 261, 262;
validity of title in disputed boundary area, 1483
*Lands of plenty, 558*
Landsberg, F.: 857
LANE, CHARLES C. Mining engineer. Co-owner
and general agent of Lane & Kurtz Mining Co.,
active in the Omineca district in 1870's; 1872
elected a member of Am. Inst. of Mining
Engineers. (Vic. *Colonist*, 13 July 1872, p. 3)
437
LANE, MYRTLE ELIZA (MACK) (1891-1967).
Author, novelist. Born in Donald, B.C.; resident
of Victoria for 46 y.; long standing member of
the Can. Authors Assoc., and P.E.O. sisterhood.
(Vic. *Times*, 10 Mar. 1967)   1983
Lang, John: 1323, 1394
Lang, Martha Maria: 1323, 1394
LANGELIER, SIR FRANCOIS CHARLES
STANISLAS (1838-1915). Lawyer, politician,
lt.-gov. of Quebec. 1860 LL.B. from Laval Univ.;
1861 called to bar; 1873-5, 1878-81 in provincial
legislature, Que.; 1884-7, 1887-8 member of H.
of C.; 1898 appointed judge of Superior Court of
Que.; 1906-11 acting chief justice of Superior
Court of Quebec; 1911-15 lt.-gov. of Que.; 1911
given title; 1909 made member of Roy. Soc. of
Can.; auth. of several legal treatises. (Wa; Mo;
Cy; Cc; P)   599
LANGEVIN, SIR HECTOR LOUIS (1826-1906).
Lawyer, politician; a Father of Confederation.
Born in Quebec City; 1850 called to Que. bar;
1857-67 in Legislative Assembly of United
Canada; sol.-gen. for Lower Canada 1864-6, and
postmaster-gen. 1866-7; a delegate to conferences
on confederation; 1867-9 sec. of state; 1867-73

Min. of Public Works; 1878-9 again postmaster-gen.; 1879-91 Min. of Public Works. (EC; DNB) 398. *See below*

Langevin, Sir Hector Louis: speech of, 583. *See above*

Langford, Edward Edwards: 200, 207

LANGLEY, ALFRED JOHN (1820-1896). Businessman. Born in Lichfield, Staffordshire; went to Digby, N.S., then to N.Y.; 1849 went to San Francisco and founded a drug firm; 1858 arrived in Victoria and established a wholesale drug firm; was a member of the Legislative Council; 1862 sent to London as com. for the colony during the exhibition; for his services he was offered a knighthood but declined; m. in England and returned to Victoria in 1863; 1872-8 was on the Provincial Board of Education; an advocate of free non-sectarian schools. (Vic. *Colonist,* 10 Apr. 1896, p. 5, 8; 11 Apr. 1896, p. 5)   173

Langley: history and pioneers of, 2022, 1702, 1871

LANGLEY. ST. ANDREW'S PRESBYTERIAN CHURCH: 1646

Langley. Sharon United Church: 1802

LANGLEY AGRICULTURAL ASSOCIATION: 989

LANSDOWNE, HENRY CHARLES KEITH PETTY-FITZMAURICE, 5th marquis of (1845-1927). Gov.-gen. of Canada, 1883-8. Educated at Eton and Balliol College, Oxford; 1866 succeeded to peerage; 1868-72 one of the lords of the Treasury; 1872-4 under-sec. for India; 1883-8 gov.-gen. of Canada; 1888-93 gov.-gen. of India; 1895-1916 in Br. cabinet; 1895 made Knight of Garter; 1917 chancellor of Order of St. Michael and St. George; received D.C.L., Oxford. (Wa; Ww, 1928-1940; P)   716

LARGE, RICHARD GEDDES (1901-   ). Doctor of medicine. Born in Bella Bella, B.C.; Univ. of Toronto medical school graduated 1923; practised in Hazelton, Port Simpson and in Prince Rupert; contributed to medical journals; interested in history of the area and active in community affairs; F.A.C.S.; was pres. of Mus. of Northern B.C. and on the committee for the care and upkeep of totem poles in Prince Rupert Park. (Book jacket of his *The Skeena;* VF; Cd; *Who's who in B.C.,* 1947-48)   1984, 2095

LARSON, JOAN I.: 2130

*The last West and Paolo's Virginia,* 1648

*Later prehistoric man in British Columbia,* 1159

*Latest mining laws of British Columbia,* 1282

LATHAM, ROBERT GORDON (1812-1888). Ethnologist and philologist. In 1841 his well-known textbook on English language published; 1870 revised Dr. Johnson's dictionary; 1852 became director of ethnological dept. of Crystal Palace. (DNBc)   24

Latin: hymns, etc. in Duployan shorthand, 864, 1205-1207; prayer in roman characters, 863

*Latin manual,* 864

*Latin manual; or hymns and chants,* 1205

Laufer, Berthold: 1357

LAUT, AGNES CHRISTINA (1871-1936). Prolific writer on historical subjects, especially on western Canada. Born in Ont.; Univ. of Manitoba graduate; editorial writer and correspondent for Am., Can., and Br. papers and magazines; spent summers in Rockies and Selkirks. (Ww, v. 1)   1626

Law enforcement: at the gold fields, 1618, 1690

LAW SOCIETY OF BRITISH COLUMBIA: 336, 830, 990, 1297

Law Society of British Columbia: 1434

LAW SOCIETY OF BRITISH COLUMBIA. LIBRARY: 991

*Law Society of British Columbia; acts . . . 1892,* 990

Laws: Pacific coast collection laws, 539; plea for revised medical legislation, 905; *also see* Acts; British Columbia. Laws, statutes, etc.; Canada. Laws, statutes, etc.; Great Britain. Laws, statutes, etc.; Vancouver Island. Laws, statutes, etc.

*The laws of British Columbia,* 372

*The laws of British Columbia, consisting of the acts . . . ,* 58

LAWRENCE, JOSEPH COLLINS (1918-   ): 2069

LAWSON, MARIA (1852-1945). Teacher and newspaperwoman in Victoria. In 1890 came from P.E.I. with family; taught until 1907; 1906-34 worked on Victoria *Colonist;* active in women's groups in community. (VF)   1552

Lay, Chu: 704

Lecture delivered at the Imperial Institute . . . new British route to the Pacific . . . (1896), 1219

*Lecture delivered . . . to Young Men's Mutual Improvement Association,* 249

*Lecture on British Columbia and Vancouver's Island, delivered . . . 1863,* 205

*Lecture on the Klondike mining district . . . 1897,* 1303

*A lecture on the subject of "current events,"* 645

*Lecture on the Yukon gold fields,* 1303

LEE, NORMAN (1862-1939). Cattle rancher and freight handler. Born in Westmoreland; educated at Hartford House; 1882 came to B.C.; eventually settling in Chilcotin area; traded with Indians, hauled freight from Ashcroft by way of Gang Ranch. (VF, letters of his sisters; Grant MacEwan, *The Sodbusters*)   2070

Lee, Norman: 1884, 2132

Leech River: in fiction, 1731

Leechtown: history of, 2069

LEES, JAMES ARTHUR (b.1852): 791

LEFEVRE, LILY ALICE (COOKE) (d.1938). Poet. Born in Kingston, Ont.; contributor to Montreal and Vancouver papers; some of her lyrics have been set to music; d. in Vancouver (Waa; Wa; Wha2)   1163, 1653

*Legal Professions Act of British Columbia,* 830

Church, Vancouver, 1915-32. (P; Wa; VF) 1639, 1672

MCCABE, JAMES O.: 2166

MCCAIN, CHARLES W. (1867-1933). Born in Colborne, Ont; 1888 went to Vancouver; made souvenir canes, etc., from oak and teak from the wreck of the *Beaver*. (VF) 1120 (comp.)

MCCLELLAN, ROLANDER GUY: 399

McCormack, Mrs. H. D.: 2039

M'Cormick, S. J.: pub., 32, 655

MCCOWAN, DAN (1882-1956). Naturalist, auth., lecturer; fellow of Zoological Soc. of England; worked occasionally for the C.P.R.; lived in Banff for 26 y. and explored area: accompanied the royal tour in 1939 from Banff to Revelstoke to explain the natural history of the Rockies. (VF) 1882

McCreight, John Foster: 610, 1807

MCCULLAGH, JAMES BENJAMIN (1854-1921). Methodist missionary to Indians on Nass R. at Aiyansh. Born in County Down; in the army until 1883, decided to be a lay missionary and attended a training college; 1883 came to B.C. and went from Victoria to Metlahkatla, Ft. Simpson, and then to the Nass R.; learned the Indian language. (J. W. W. Moeran, *McCullagh of Aiyansh*) 1067, 1299, 1433, 1647. *See below*

McCullagh, James Benjamin: 865, 1059, 1150, 1328; pub. on, 1668. *See above*

*McCullagh of Aiyansh*, 1668

MACDERMOT, JOHN HENRY (1883- ). Physician and surgeon. Born in Jamaica; educated to end of secondary school there, then went to McGill Univ. in 1901; interned in Montreal General Hospital in 1905; 1906-7 at Britannia then on the Columbia Coast Mission ship as doctor; 1909-58 practised in Vancouver as a general practitioner; 1916-7 pres., Vancouver Medical Assoc.; 1926-7 pres., B.C. Medical Assoc.; life member of College of Physicians and Surgeons (B.C.); ed. of B.C. medical journal. (His own notes in B.C. Archives) 1852

MCDONALD, ARCHIBALD (1790-1853). Fur-trader of H.B.C.; was in Selkirk colony; 1826-8 chief trader at Kamloops, then at Ft. Langley, 1828-33; at Ft. Colville in Columbia R. area, 1836-43; 1844 retired from H.B.C. and moved to Montreal then Ottawa; made no less than 15 trips across continent during 1812-45 and kept accurate journals; was interested in topography and agriculture. (*Wash. hist. quart.*, v. 9, 1918, p. 93-102, and v. 16, 1925, p. 186-197) 400

MACDONALD, DUNCAN GEORGE FORBES (1823?-1884). Agricultural engineer. Member of gov't survey staff and one of the commissioners appointed to adjust Northwest boundary line. (DNB) 177, 205

MCDONALD, MRS. J. R.: 1883

Macdonald, Sir John A. (prime minister): 633

McDonald, Margaret: jt. auth., 2028

McDonald, Ranald [*sic*]: report of, 159

MACDONALD, WILLIAM JOHN (1829-1916). In 1851 went to V.I. from Scotland in service of H.B.C.; left it in a few y. to enter business; 1859-66 in Legislative Assembly of V.I.; 1866-71 on Legislative Council of B.C.; 1871-1915 in Senate; was mayor of Victoria twice. (Wa; Mo, 1912; Cd, 1910; Cc; B.C. Cen. Com.) 1614. *See below*

Macdonald, William John: visit to Metlahkatla, 615, 620. *See above*

McDonald and Charlebois: 613, 617

*Macdonald & Company, bankers . . . 1859-1864*, 2127

MACDONELL, ALLAN. Toronto railway promoter in the 1850's. (P) 25, 74

Macdougall, Alan: 662

McDougall, William: report of, 326

MACEWAN, JOHN WALTER GRANT (1902- ). 1946-51 dean of Agriculture, Univ. of Manitoba; 1952 gen.-manager, Council of Can. Beef Producers, Western Section; 1953-8 alderman, Calgary; 1955-9 member of Alberta legislature; lt.-gov. of Alberta. (P; book jackets) 1884, 1903, 2132

MACFIE, MATTHEW: An English clergyman. Came to B.C. in 1859; collected much information on V.I. and the Mainland and used this on a lecture tour through Canada, N.S., N.B., Great Britain in 1864; 1870 resigned as pastor of Congregational Church, Moseley Road, Birmingham, and withdrew from the ministry. (VF; Vic. *Colonist*, 29 June 1870, p. 3) 255

MCGIVERN, J. S. (1908- ): 1986

MCGREGOR, DONALD ANDERSON (1879- ). Chief editorial writer for Vancouver *Province*. Arrived in Vancouver in 1910; past pres. B.C. Hist. Assoc. (*B.C. hist. quart.*, v. 10, 1946, p. 174, and v. 17, 1953, p. 256) 2112

MACGREGOR, JAMES GRIERSON (1905- ). Auth., historian, engineering manager. Born 1905 in Scotland, but brought up in rural Alberta; 1926 graduate of Univ. of Alberta; pres. Hist. Soc. of Alberta; gen.-manager of Canadian Utilities, Ltd. (P) 1924

McInnes, Alexander Patrick, *see* McInnis, Alexander Patrick

MACINNES, DONALD (1824-1900). Merchant, politician, senator. Born in Scotland; came to Canada in 1840 with his family; pres. of Bank of Hamilton, Canada Cotton Co., and South Saskatchewan Valley Railway Co., and a director of Canada Life; chn. of roy. com. to enquire into civil service of Canada 1860; 1881 became a senator. (Cc, 1898-99) 832

MACINNES, THOMAS ROBERT EDWARD (1867-1951). Lawyer. Born in Ont., went to New Westminster 1874; graduate of Univ. of Toronto, Osgoode Hall; 1893 called to the B.C. bar; sec.

of Bering Sea Claims Com., and on Salmon Fisheries Com. 1901; investigated anti-Oriental riots in B.C.; in China 1916-22; auth. of several books incl. poetry. (VF) 1691

MCINNES, WILLIAM WALLACE BURNS (1871-1954). Lawyer and magistrate. Born in Ont., went to New Westminster as a boy in 1874; 1893 admitted to the bar; elected to H. of C. for Nanaimo 1896; 1900 in B.C. legislature; 1903 Minister of Education; 1905-1908 com. for Yukon; 1944 police magistrate in Vancouver. (VF) 1227

MCINNIS, ALEXANDER PATRICK (1868-1946). Born in Barkerville, son of one of the first group of gold miners in Cariboo gold fields; acquired a ranch on Beatty Creek; operated as a dairy farmer; later went into cattle raising; retired to Marguerite, B.C., where he was postmaster for a time; familiarly known as "Sandy." (VF) 1788

MACKAY, CHARLES ANGUS (1872-1930). Coal miner, prospector, mining broker. Came to Canada from Scotland in 1890; worked in C.P.R. in Kootenays; in Cumberland coal mines; prospector in E. Kootenays; went to Victoria 1917 as a mining broker; located oil shale land in Saskatchewan. (VF) 1722

McKeivers, Charles: 214

MCKELLAR, HUGH (1842?-1934). Presbyterian minister. In 1852 came to Canada from Argyllshire; educated in Sarnia and at Knox College, Toronto; 1874 went to Man. then Sask., and Ont.; 1905 went to Foothills Mission near Priddis, Alta.; retired in 1912. (VF) 1673 (comp.)

MCKELVIE, BRUCE ALISTAIR (1889-1960). Newspaperman, historian. Born in Vancouver; 1913 became a reporter for Vancouver *Province;* in B.C. legislative press gallery for 30 y.; on several newspapers; became managing-ed. of Victoria *Colonist;* director of information for B.C.; wrote books and pamphlets on history and resources of B.C. (VF) 1692, 1693, 1701, 1871, 1892, 1952. *See below*

McKelvie, Bruce Alistair: 1925. *See above*

MacKelvie, J. A.: history of Okanagan, 1607

*McKenney's Pacific coast directory,* 290

MACKENZIE, HENRY: 118

Mackenzie & Mann contract: 1372

McKenzie, K.: report of, 154

MCKENZIE, POPPY: 1987

MacLachlan, Charles: jt. auth., 841

MCLARTY, STANLEY D.: 2113

MCLAURIN, COLIN CAMPBELL (1854-1941?). Baptist minister from Ont., serving on the prairies, 1897-1901; 1907-24 asst. supt., and supt. of missions, Peace River area. (Cd, 1936-37; P) 1794

MCLEAN, ALLAN (accused): 581

McLean, Archibald: accused, 581

McLean, Charles: accused, 581

MCLEAN, FRANCES (1921- ): 2133

MACLEAN, JOHN (1851-1928). Methodist missionary in Sask., Man., N.W.T. Active member of Am. Folklore Soc. and Am. Assoc. for Advancement of Sc.; frequent lecturer on Indian tribes of Canada. (Mo, 1912; P) 1228, 1640

MCLELAN, ARCHIBALD WOODBURY (1824-1890). Lt.-gov. of Nova Scotia, 1888-90. Educated at Mt. Allison Academy, N.B.; lumber merchant and ship-builder; 1858-67 M.L.A.; 1867-9 M.P.; 1869-81 senator; 1881-8 an M.P. again; Minister Fisheries, Finance, and postmaster-gen.; at first opposed Nova Scotia's entry into confederation. (Wa; Cy; Cc) 600

MCLEOD, MALCOLM (1821-1899). Publicist. Born in Hudson's Bay Terr.; son of factor, John McLeod; educated in Edin.; studied law in Montreal; called to bar, 1845; 1874-6 district judge in Ont. and practising barrister; wrote under pen name "Britannicus." (Waa: P; Wa) 467, 482, 483, 498, 582, 833, 994. *See below*

McLeod, Malcolm: ed., 400. *See above*

MACMANUS, ROBERT H. (1840-1897). Journalist. In early life a soldier in 1st Life Guards; went to Wellington for newspaper work until 1894 when he was appointed postmaster at Northfield; lived in B.C. several years before his death; wrote for the Victoria *Times* under the pseud. "The Town Major." His letters attracted attention. (Vic. *Colonist,* 14 Feb. 1897, p. 5) 885

MACMASTER, SIR DONALD (1846-1922). Lawyer, born in Upper Canada. Degree in civil law from McGill; 1871 called to Que. bar; 1879-82 M.L.A. in Ont.; 1882-6 in H. of C.; 1905 went to England to specialize in appeals before Judicial Committee of Privy Council; 1910-18 in Br. H. of C. (Wa; Ww, 1916-28; Ch; Cc; Mo, 1912) 1121

MCMILLAN, A. J. Agent for Manitoba in Liverpool; 1896 claimed to have had 14 y. acquaintance with Manitoba. (P) 1300

MACMILLAN, BLOEDEL AND POWELL RIVER LIMITED: 2154

MCMURTRIE, DOUGLAS CRAWFORD (1888-1944). Typographer. Born in N. J.; attended M.I.T. 1906-1907; member of many typographical assoc.; auth. of books on printing and printers. (Wwh, v. 2) 1716, 1729

MacNab, Frances (pseud.), *see* Fraser, Agnes

MCNAMARA, JAMES (plaintiff): 1068

MacNaughton, Isabel Christie: jt. auth., 2001

MCNAUGHTON, MARGARET (PEEBLES). Auth. and journalist; second wife of Archibald McNaughton, one of the "Overlanders" of 1862. Born in Scotland; went to New Westminster in 1888; m. in 1890; wrote for the press on history of B.C.; elected a lady associate of the Roy. Inst. of London; active in philanthropic work. (P; S) 1229

M'Neil, W. F.: auth., 1167

MACNUTT, WILLIAM STEWART (1908- ): 1953

MACOUN, JOHN (1831-1920). Botanist. In 1850 came to Canada from Ireland to farm; learned botany and geology; 1868 appointed prof. of botany and geology at Albert College, Belleville; 1872 was on Sandford Fleming's expedition to Pacific; 1879 appointed explorer for Can. gov't in Northwest Terr.; 1882 botanist for Geol. Survey of Can.; 1885 made director and naturalist of Survey Dept.; charter member of Roy. Soc. of Can. (Wa; EC; Mo, 1912; Waa)   1657, 1658

MCPHILLIPS, ALBERT EDWARD (1861-1938). Lawyer, politician. Attended Manitoba College; 1882 called to Man. bar; 1885 in Saskatchewan Rebellion; 1891 moved to B.C.; 1898-1903 and 1907-13 in B.C. legislature; 1913 judge of Court of Appeal. (P; Cc, 1898; Whc; Wha2; VF) 1230

MAIDEN, CECIL: 1885

Mail service, *see* Postal service

Maill, Edward: com., 611

MAINLAND STEAMSHIPMEN'S PROTECTIVE AND BENEVOLENT ASSOCIATION OF BRITISH COLUMBIA: 1069

*Making a start in Canada*, 815

Malakwa: history of, 2047

Malcolm Island: 1993

Mallandaine, Edward (1827-1905). Architect publisher. First architect to practice in B.C.; first night school instructor in B.C.; first publisher of a city directory in B.C. (VF)   111; headmaster, 132; pub., 739

*The Manitoba question*, 1230

*Manners and customs of the Indians of Simpson*, 883

*Manual and prize list of the . . . annual bonspiel*, 1200

*Manual, 1907-8*, 1563

*Manual of devotion in the Beaver Indian dialect*, 568

*Manual of provincial information*, 1285

*Map & guide to Cariboo and Frazer River gold mines*, 164

*Map and guide to the Cariboo gold mines*, 164

*Map and information . . . New Westminster*, 834

*Map of the Cariboo and Omineca gold fields*, 363

*Map of the gold regions in British Columbia*, 163

*Map to accompany correspondence respective the Alaska boundary . . . 1904*, 1529

MAPLE RIDGE. ST. JOHN THE DIVINE: 1893

*Maps relating to the Alaskan boundary*, 1495

MARIE-JEAN-DE-PATHMOS, SISTER: 1904

*The marine mammals of the north-western coast*, 469

Marine history: 1185

MARK, WILLIAM: 206

Marquis, Thomas Guthrie: 1617

MARSH, EDITH LOUISE. Ontario writer of children's books. (P)   1569

MARSHALL, J. T.: 1750

MARTIN, ARCHER EVANS STRINGER (1865-1941). Lawyer, and chief justice of B.C. 1937. Born in Hamilton; called to bar 1887; 1898 made a puisne judge of Supreme Court; and deputy judge in Admiralty for B.C.; 1900 special com. to settle mining disputes on Canadian-Alaskan border; 1902 appointed judge in Admiralty for B.C. (Cd, 1911; VF; P)   1434, 1514

MARTIN, FREDERICKA I.: 1853

MARTIN, ROBERT MONTGOMERY (1803?-1868). English student of colonial problems; historical writer and statistician; travelled in many of the British colonies; wrote books on them between 1830-60. (DNB)   8

MARTLEY, JOHN (1859-1896). Capt. in the Crimean War; 1862 came to B.C.; farmed on his property "The Grange," 25 miles from Lillooet; was a justice of the peace; possessed marked legal attainments; was A.D.C. to the Marquis of Lorne when he visited the province in 1882. (Vic. *Colonist*, 28 Oct. 1896)   719, 1122

*A marvellous experience*, 1080

Marvin (E. B.) & Co'y: 1373

Mary Anne of Jesus, Sister: 1730

Mary Bonsecours, Sister: 1730

Mary Clement, Sister: 1730

MARY DOROTHEA, SISTER: A Sister of St. Ann; provincial superior in Victoria; 1953 superior of St. Ann's Academy, New Westminster. (*St. Ann's journal*, July 1953, p. 9)   1854

Mary Lumena, Sister: 1730

Mary Mildred, Sister: trans., 1190

Mary of the Conception, Sister: 1730

MARY THEODORE, SISTER (1856-1951). A Sister of Saint Ann. Born in Oswego, N.Y., as "Victoria Pinault"; 1871 entered sisterhood in Lachine where she met Bishop Demers, who inspired her with the need for missionary sisters on V.I.; 1878 arrived in Victoria, served in Duncan, Nanaimo, Juneau, and Vancouver; church history in B.C. was her chief interest upon retirement. (VF; her *Heralds of Christ the King*)   1730, 1795

MASON, GEORGE (1829-1893). Anglican clergyman. Graduate of Oriel College; 1853 ordained; 1862-7 at Hawaiian mission; 1873 came to B.C. to join Bishop Hills; 1873-4 in New Westminster; 1875-9 in Nanaimo; 1878 appointed dean of Christ Church Cathedral; 1881 returned to England; appointed to Long Cross, near London. (VF; B.C. hist. quart., v. 15, 1951, p. 47-70)   484, 485, 510

Masset: 585

*The mate of the Vancouver*, 1002

*Material culture and social organization of the Koryak*, 1357

MATHER, BARRY (1909- ). Newspaperman, politican. Born in Alberta; educated in Vancouver; 1962 elected to H. of C. (Cc, 1965) 2028

Matsqui: history, 2029

MATSQUI-SUMAS-ABBOTSFORD CENTENNIAL SOCIETY: 2029

*Matthew Baillie Begbie*, 1887

MATTHEWS, JAMES SKITT (1878- ). Archivist, Vancouver City. 1886. *See below*

Matthews, James Skitt: 1845, 1957, 2057. *See above*

MAXWELL, GEORGE R.: 1231

Maxwell, George R.: speech of, 1338

May, Barney, *see* May, Baruch

May, Baruch: pub. on, 1632

May, Cecil (Mr. and Mrs.): 2106

Mayhew, Isabel: 1656

MAYNE, RICHARD CHARLES (1835-1892). A naval officer on vessels "Plumper" 1857-60, and "Hecate" 1861. Educated at Eton; in Baltic campaign and the Crimea; 1849 first visit to V.I.; 1858 toured gold rush areas of Interior, prepared maps of Fraser R. and Thompson R. areas; explored a route for a wagon road from Nanaimo to Alberni Canal; 1862 was one of three com. to accompany specimens of Island minerals, timber and produce to London International Exhibition; 1863 his articles on V.I. appeared in the *Illustrated London News;* after survey of V.I. and West Coast he went to Australia and N.Z.; 1866 in command of ship *Nassau* for survey of Straits of Magellan; M.P. for Pembroke Boroughs. (W; VF; *Beaver,* outfit 289, autumn 1958, p. 12-17; B.C. Cen. Com.) 145, 146, 178, 179

Mayne Island: history of, 2109

*A mechanic's tour around the world,* 718

*Medical directory,* 886

Medical history: 1616, 1738, 1848; *also see* Public health

*The medical history of British Columbia,* 1738

Medical legislation: 905

MEEKER, EZRA (1830-1928). Pioneer. Born near Huntsville, Ohio; d. in Seattle; 1852 crossed over Oregon Trail by ox-team; 1906 returned with ox-team to Wash.; farmed in Wash. for 50 y.; pres. of Pioneers of Am.; wrote several books on early days in the West. (Waa; DAB; Nc; Bua; WhA; Wwa, 1897-1942) 1543

*Mélanges; trois conférences,* 773

Meldrum Creek: 2051

MELROSE, ROBERT (1828-1898). Arrived from Scotland with his wife in 1853 to work as a labourer on Craigflower Farm. (*B.C. hist. quart.,* v. 7, 1943, p. 118 f) 1822

*A memento of your visit to Barkerville,* 2139

*The memoirs of a cathedral,* 2075

*Memoirs of a professional lady nurse,* 440

*Memoirs of the life of Charles Angus Mackay,* 1722

*Memorandum addressed to the Honourable the minister* (1880), 574

*Memorandum on "A report of a committee",* 596

*Memorandum on Indian reserves,* 544

*Memorandum on the boundary between Canada and Alaska . . . 1899,* 1408

*Memorandum on the Kettle River Railway,* 1377

*Memorandum respecting the Island of San Juan,* 91

*Memorandum; the trans-Pacific connections,* 706

[*Memorial and statement of claims of the Hudson's Bay company upon the United States*], 245

[*Memorial, and statement of claims of the Puget Sound Agricultural Company upon the United States*], 246

*Memorial in connection with the Omineca road petition,* 370

*Memorial of Canadian sealers . . . 1898,* 1395

*Memorial of Marshall G. Moore,* 348

*Memorial of the Legislature of Oregon praying for the extinguishment of the Indian title . . . 1851,* 26

*Memorial of the owners of sealing schooners,* 1364

*Memorial of the people of Red River,* 212

*Memorial on the Canal de Haro as the boundary line* (Berlin, 1872?), 404

*Memorial to the government and Parliament,* 833

*The memorials of the Hudson Bay Company and the Puget Sound Agricultural Company to the commissioners . . . 1863,* 253

*Memories of pioneer life in British Columbia,* 1837

Menzies, D.: auth., 1167

Merchandise list: 60

*Merchant's agency red book,* 1232

MERCIER, ANNE. English writer. 1575

Mercier, Mrs. Jerome, *see* Mercier, Anne

MERRIAM, JOHN CAMPBELL (1869-1945). Palaeontologist, educator, administrator. Born in Hopkinton, Iowa; attended Columbia, Princeton, Yale; Ph.D., Munich Univ.; instructor, prof. and dean of faculties at Univ. of California from 1894; 1919 chn., National Research Council; 1920-38 pres., Carnegie Inst., Washington; 1928- regent, Smithsonian Inst.; member of many scientific and learned societies; prolific writer in his field. (Waa; Bua; WhA; Wha; Wwa, v. 2) 1233, 1435

Merritt: history of, 2002

*Mesozoic volcanic rocks of British Columbia,* 503

*Message from His Excellency Governor Kennedy, C.B., to the Legislative Assembly . . . 1865,* 262

*Message from the President of the United States, in response to Senate resolution of January 8, 1895,* 1178

*Message from the President of the United States, transmitting a convention . . . 1892,* 1008

*Message from the President of the United States, transmitting a report of the Sec. of State relative to the frontier line between Alaska and British Columbia,* 727

Mining laws: 188, 236, 298, 437, 1242, 1278, 1282, 1358, 1368, 1398; B.C. case decisions, 1514

*The mining laws of British Columbia . . . ,* 437

Mining protective association: 1296

Minesota. Legislature: report by James Wicks Taylor, 124

MINNESOTA. LEGISLATURE. HOUSE. SELECT COMMITTEE ON OVERLAND ROUTE TO BRITISH OREGON: 75

MINNIE (SHIP): 1123

Mints: 1696

*Minute of council . . . re China-Japan mail,* 774

*Minutes . . . being an account of the re-organization,* 519

*Minutes of a preliminary meeting of the delegates,* 305

*Minutes of evidence* [re liquor traffic], 1107

*Minutes of evidence taken before the select committee,* 550

*Minutes of proceedings of a Select Committee of the House of Assembly,* 243

*Minutes of the Council of Vancouver Island August 30th, 1851, and terminating . . . 1861,* 1645

*Minutes of the House of Assembly August 12th, 1856, to September 25th, 1858,* 1644

[*Miscellaneous hymns*], 1067

Misinchinka River: 1177

*Missa de requiem,* 1207

*Missionary heroines in many lands,* 1597

Missionary life: 414, 462, 1198, 1301, 1421, 1463, 1518, 1556, 1575, 1597, 1623, 1647, 1649, 1744, 1747; in fiction, 1340, 1517, 1693

Missions: college proposed for V.I. (1853), 38; *also see* Baptists; Catholic Church; Church of England; Methodist Church; Presbyterian Church *under* missions; *also see* Church Missionary Society; Columbia Mission; *also see* specific missions, i.e. Metlahkatla, etc.

*Les missions catholiques françaises au xix<sup>e</sup> siècle,* 1516

*"Mr. Jones, and the fribble",* 1478

*. . . Mr. Mason submitted the following report,* 46

*Mr. Sumner, for the Committee on Foreign Relations,* 240

MOBERLY, HENRY JOHN (1835-1931). Fur trader. Born in Penetanguishene, Upper Canada; d. in Sask. (Waa; Wa)    1718

MOBERLY, WALTER (1832-1915). Engineer and surveyor. Trained as engineer in Toronto; came to B.C. in 1858 to discover overland route and explore Fraser R. area; assisted Col. Moody in founding Queensborough, later New Westminster; made surveys of Fraser R. and Thompson R.; 1861 became engaged on the building of a section of the Cariboo Road up the Fraser upon which he had reported to Gov. Douglas as a possible route; 1864-5 member of Legislative Council for Cariboo West; 1865-7 surveyor-gen. for B.C.; 4 y. in U.S. exploring and railway building; returned to B.C. in 1871 as engineer in charge of railway surveys from

Shuswap Lake to Rocky Mountains; d. in Vancouver in comparative poverty. (*B.C. hist. quart.,* v. 21, 1957-58, p. 83; B.C. Cen. Com.) 689, 1365 (comp.), 1570. *See below*

Moberly, Walter: re Columbia River exploration, 266, 322; surveys of, 459. *See above*

MOCKRIDGE, CHARLES HENRY (1844-1913). Anglican clergyman; ed. of *Canadian churchman magazine and missionary news;* rector of churches in Ont., N.S., and the U.S. (Mo 1912) 1234

*Model farming a science,* 724

MOERAN, JOSEPH WILLIAM WRIGHT: 1668

Mogg, H. Herbert: 560

MOHR, N.: 664

MOHUN, EDWARD (1838-1927). Civil engineer. Responsible for many engineering projects of the B.C. prov. gov't; planned Victoria's sewerage system and received a silver medal when a paper on this was read at a meeting of the Can. Soc. of Civil Engineers 1897; wrote to newspapers on the water supply and sewage during 1901-1908. (Vic. *Times,* 29 Dec. 1928, p. 7; B.C. Archives news index)    793, 1235

MOIR, GEORGE THOMAS (1871-1955). Railwayman. Left Scotland as a boy for Stratford, Ont.; worked on Great Northern and later C.P.R.; stationed at Slocan, Sandon, Rossland, Grand Forks, Trail, and Cranbrook, 1910-37; alderman in 1922 and active in Y.M.C.A. and United Church. (VF)    1872

MONK, HARRY ALBERT JERVIS (1913-    ): 2030

*Monographie des Déné-Dindjié,* 499

MONRO, ALEXANDER STEWART (1872-1932). Surgeon in Vancouver. Born in Perthshire; educated in Toronto and Winnipeg; 1896 graduated from Univ. of Manitoba; surgeon for C.P.R. at Kamloops 1896-8; from 1898 surgeon in Vancouver; pres. of medical associations; F.R.C.S. (S; VF)    1738

*Mgr. Seghers, l'apôtre de l'Alaska,* 1190

MONTEAGLE OF BRANDON, THOMAS SPRING RICE, 1st baron (1790-1866). Politician. Born in Limerick; 1820-39 member of Br. Parliament and responsible for many reforms in Irish administration; 1835-9 chancellor of exchequer; 1839 elected to peerage and retired from public life; was a trustee of National Gallery; member of Senate of Univ. of London, and of Queen's University in Ireland; F.R.S., F.G.S. (DNB)    9

Moodie, John Douglas: 1762

Moodyville Saw Mill Co.: 610

MOORE, E. K.: 1438

Moore, Marshall F.: memorial of, 348

Moore, William ("Billie"): 1864

Moresby, Sir Fairfax (admiral): 1576

MORESBY, JOHN: Admiral of the Fleet and son of Sir Fairfax Moresby (1786-1877). (t.p.)    1576

MORGAN, JOHN TYLER: Lawyer, Am. senator. Educated in Tennessee and Alabama; 1845 admitted to bar; lived in Selma from 1855; had law practice there; 1861 member of the state secession convention; 1863 took part in military campaigns; 1876 elected to the Senate; 1892 served with Justice Harlan in the Bering Sea fisheries dispute and voted against Great Britain. He was a strong expansionist, fought for social and anti-trust legislation, believed strongly in state rights. (DAB)    1070

MORICE, ADRIAN GABRIEL (1859-1938). French missionary, anthropologist, linguist, historian. In 1879 entered order of Oblates of Mary Immaculate and sent to B.C. 1880; 1882 sent to work among the Chilcotins; 1885 at Ft. St. James where he worked out his Déné syllabery and produced works on his printing press. (*B.C. hist. quart.*, v. 21, 1957-58, p. 1-14) 888-890, 995, 1124, 1125, 1301, 1533, 1534, 1583, 1600, 1723, 1744. *See below*

Morice, Adrian Gabriel: auth., etc., 950; pub. on (for school use), 1711; trans., 862, 863, 922. *See above*

MORISON, JOHN HOPKINS (1808-1896): 232

MORLEY, ALAN P. (1905-   ). Newspaperman. Born and educated in Vancouver; 1917 went to Penticton High School; spent a year at U.B.C.; was a reporter for the Vancouver *Sun;* worked on newspapers in eastern Canada, Mich., Calif., Texas. (Book jacket)    2114

*The morning and evening prayers* [in Thompson] (1878), 525

MORRELL, WILLIAM PARKER (1899-   ): 1804

MORRIS, ALEXANDER (1826-1889). Politician. Born in Perth, Ont.; M.L.A. and cabinet minister in Manitoba; chief justice of Queen's Bench (Man.) 1872; 1872-7 lt.-gov. of Man. and N.W.T.; negotiated Indian treaties in N.W.T.; attended Univ. Glasgow, McGill Univ.; 1851 called to bar of Upper and Lower Canada; 1861-72 in Legislative Assembly of Canada; advocate of confederation; 1869-72 Minister of Inland Revenue; 1872 appointed chief justice of Court of Queen's Bench; 1872-7 lt.-gov. of Man. and N.W.T.; 1878-86 in Legislative Assembly of Ont. (Waa; P; Wa; Cy)    94, 665

MORRIS, C. KEITH (1879-   ). English auth.; wrote extensively on Canada. (P)    1622

MORRIS, W. J. Resident of Perth, Ont.; interested in the development of the West. (P)    836

MORRIS, WILFRED H.: 1813

MORSE, JOHN JESSE (1906-   ). One of the originators of the Kamloops Mus. Assoc. about 1936; was its pres. for many years; retired from the position in 1966. (Kamloops *Sentinel,* 25 Oct. 1966, p. 3; VF)    1988, 2155, 2167

MORTON, ARTHUR SILVER (1870-1945). First provincial archivist of Saskatchewan 1941-5; wrote many books and articles on early history of West; received Tyrell Gold Medal from Roy. Soc. of Can.; prof. of history and librarian in Univ. of Saskatchewan 1914-40. (P; *Beaver,* Mar. 1945, p. 46-47; Roy. Soc. of Can. *Proc. and trans.* 3d ser., 1945, v. 39, Appendix B, p. 99-102)    1796

MOSER, CHARLES (1874-   ). Benedictine priest stationed at Clayoquot in 1900; 1910 relieved Father A. J. Brabant at Hesquiat Mission; active in work among Indians; built many churches; was shipping master in sealing days, and also postmaster, telegraph agent; 1930 left his charge and went to headquarters of the Order in Mt. Angel, Ore. (VF)    1694

Moser, Jefferson F.: 1390

MOUAT, ALEXANDER NAYSMITH (1863-1950). Comptroller-gen. of B.C. Born in Edin.; went to western Canada in 1882 and served for 20 y. with the H.B.C. as chief inspector; 1913 became auditor of Edmonton and in 1915 was its first comptroller; 1916 went to B.C. as comptroller-gen.; 1929 retired. (VF)    1680

*Mount Pleasant early days,* 1979

Mt. Pleasant Presbyterian Church (Vancouver): 1824

*Mountain and prairie,* 576

Mountaineering: 1519, 1545, 1548, 1589, 1655, 1859, 2111

*Mountains, men & rivers,* 1946

MUIR, JOHN (1838-1914). Geologist, explorer, naturalist. Born in Dunbar, Scotland; graduate of Univ. of Wisconsin; discoverer of Muir Glacier, Alaska. (WhA, 1910-11; Wwa, v. 1) 1624

MUNDAY, WALTER ALFRED DON (1888-1950). Alpinist, auth. of books on mountaineering and flora. Born in Manitoba; went to B.C. and joined newly formed mountaineering club; 1912-14 leader of parties to climb ranges between Vancouver and Garibaldi area; saw service in World War I; 1921 joined Alpine Club of Can.; climbed many mountains, including Mt. Robson, Mt. Arrowsmith, Mt. Waddington. (*Can. alpine jour.,* v. 34, 1951, p. 146-152)    1805, 1814

*Municipal voters list . . . 1895,* 1181

MUNRO, WILLIAM F. An agent for C.P.R. and Canadian North West Land Company in Glasgow. The latter was formed for settlement of village farm colonies within the railway belt of the N.W.T. (his *Emigration made easy; or How to settle on the prairie* (Glasgow, Macrone & Co., 1883))    1302

MUNROE, KIRK (1850-1930). Am. auth. of many books, mostly for boys. Born in Wisconsin; educated there and at Harvard Engineering School; 1867-8 assisted in exploring routes for Santa Fe and North Pacific Railways; 1879-82 first ed. of Harpers' "Round Table." (Wwa, v. 1) 1126

Munsie, William: 1373
Murder: iniquity of charges, 134
MURDOCK, GEORGE PETER (1897-    ): 1931
MURPHY, HERBERT HALLIDAY (1881-1964).
      Doctor and radiologist. Born in Antrin, Ont;
      McGill Univ. graduate; 1912 went to Kamloops
      after postgraduate work; 1917 began diagnostic
      radiology; 1931-51 director of Dept. of Radiology
      of Royal Jubilee Hospital, Victoria. (VF)    2031
Murray, Joseph: 1245, 1390
MURRAY, MARGARET (LALLY) (1887-    ).
      Newspaperwoman. Born in Kansas; m. George
      Murray, a newspaperman and later an M.P.;
      co-owner of newspapers in Lillooet and Peace
      River area; active in political life of her husband;
      founded 8 weekly newspapers in B.C.; familiarly
      known as "Ma" Murray. (Van. *Province,* 1 Aug.
      1964, p. 4)    1760
MURRAY, WILLIAM HENRY HARRISON (1840-
      1904). Clergyman, political and social scientist.
      Born in Connecticut; Yale Univ. graduate 1862;
      clergyman in N.Y. and Conn. area for 15 y.;
      studied English commercial methods, trade
      relations, land system, social and political forces;
      made a study of resources of N. Am. (From his
      *Daylight land*)    794
Murrayville, *see* Langley
*Museum and art notes,* 1686
Museums: 1379
Musgrave, Sir Anthony (1828-1888): appointment
      as gov. of B.C., 331; instructions to, 332
Music: 1029; choir club, 1189; society, 604
MUSK, GEORGE: 1972
*My Canadian journal, 1872-8,* 929
*My captain Oliver; a story of two missionaries,* 1875
*My log; a journal of . . . the Flying Squadron,* 382
*My policy for the construction of the Canada Pacific
      railway as a government work,* 476
MYERS, THOMAS RATHMELL (1884-1961).
      Clerk and publicist. Born in England, went to
      Vancouver; 1908 clerk timekeeper for B.C.
      Electric Co.; 1916-49 publicity supervisor and
      first ed. of the company's *Buzzer* which he edited
      for 34 y.; well-known in musical circles in
      Vancouver as an organist. (VF)    1944
*The mystery of Mount Robson,* 1776
*The mystic spring and other tales,* 1531
*Mythology of the Bella Coola Indians,* 1357
*Mythology of the Thompson Indians,* 1357
Naden, *see* Esquimalt
Nakusp: history, 1909
Names, geographical, *see* Place-names
*The naming and opening of Stanley Park . . . 1888,*
      1886
*Nan and other pioneer women of the West,* 1605
Nanaimo: 692, 731; the bastion at, 1594; history of,
      1894, 2021, 2150; pioneer days, 1948; pioneers
      of, 1753
Nanaimo district: exploration, 121, 179

*Nanaimo Pioneer Cemetery,* 2150
NANAIMO POULTRY SOCIETY LIMITED: 1165
*Nanaimo's jubilee . . . 1849-1949,* 1894
*Na-na-kwa; or, Dawn,* 1366
Nanoose Bay: history, 2032
*A narrative history of the Terminal City Club,* 1765
Nass River: 1864
*Nation,* 1367
*A native Indian colony,* 1544
*The native races of North America,* 1184
*The native races of the Pacific states,* 472
NATIVE SONS OF BRITISH COLUMBIA: 1439
Natural history: 275, 942, 1037, 1071, 1093, 1657; in
      fiction, 1551; museums for, 1379; trees, 569;
      *also see* Birds; Entomology; Fish; Zoology
*The natural history museums of British Columbia,*
      1379
NATURAL HISTORY SOCIETY OF BRITISH
      COLUMBIA: 942, 1071
Natural resources: 73, 166, 177, 178, 185, 255, 388,
      309, 447, 592, 625, 630, 659, 762, 837, 841, 851,
      875, 1016, 1105, 1271, 1813; utilization of, 1819
*Natural resources of . . . Trail Creek,* 1175
*The naturalist in Vancouver Island and British
      Columbia,* 275
NAVAL CLUB (ESQUIMALT): 291
Naval stations: orders for, 198; *also see* Esquimalt
Navigation: 1438; *also see* Pilot guides
*The necessity of reform,* 101
Nechako River: in fiction, 1176
Negroes: 1491; in fiction, 1967
Neklakapamuk language, *see* Thompson Indian
      language
NELSON, DENYS (1876-1929): 1702
NELSON, JOSEPH. Englishman who wrote
      pamphlets on railways and Canada. (P)    233,
      511, 1072
Nelson, W. J.: comp., 1563
Nelson: history, 1873; history with biographical
      sketches, 1312
NELSON. FIRST PRESBYTERIAN CHURCH:
      1911
NELSON. NELSON JUBILEE COMMITTEE:
      1873
NELSON. ST. PAUL'S PRESBYTERIAN
      CHURCH: 1628
*Nelson & Fort Sheppard Railway Co. vs. Jerry et al*
      (case), 1212
*Nelson . . . golden jubilee . . . 1897-1947,* 1873
Nemos, William: jt. auth., 731
NESBITT, JAMES KNIGHT (1908-    ).
      Newspaperman, free lance writer, local historian
      of Victoria. Irish ancestry; grandparents arrived
      in Victoria in 1850; educated in Victoria; 1927
      joined Victoria *Times* as a reporter; 1936-45
      legislative reporter; worked for Vancouver *News-
      Herald;* has held office in B.C. Hist. Soc. and
      Craigdarroch Castle Soc. (VF)    1855, 1973,
      2096, 2168 (ed). *See below*

P., M.: 721

"Pacific" (ship): 484

PACIFIC AND ARCTIC RAILWAY AND
   NAVIGATION COMPANY: 1442

Pacific cable: 1513, 1616

*Pacific coast business directory*, 290

*Pacific coast; coast pilot of Alaska*, 342

*Pacific coast; coast pilot of California*, 343

*Pacific coast collection laws*, 539

THE PACIFIC COAST FIRE INSURANCE
   COMPANY: 1806

*The Pacific coast scenic tour*, 873

*P.G.E.; railway to the North*, 2136

*Pacific harbour light*, 959

*Pacific historical review*, 1739

*Pacific Northwest americana*, 1656

*Pacific Northwest libraries; history*, 1695

*Pacific Northwest quarterly*, 1553

*The Pacific Northwest; some facts*, 780

*The Pacific province*, 1617

THE PACIFIC RAILWAY . . .: 583

*The Pacific railway; Britannicus' letters*, 482

*Pacific railway, Canada*, 483

*Pacific railway; extra tax for it, not necessary*, 498

*Pacific railway route, British Columbia* (1879?), 555

*Pacific railway routes, Canada*, 467

*The Pacific railway scandal; an address*, 439

*The Pacific railway; speech delivered during the
   debate* (1881), 602

*Pacific railway, speech delivered in the House of
   Commons* [by Amor De Cosmos] (1880), 572

*Pacific Railway; speech delivered in the House of
   Commons* [by Edward Blake] (1880), 601

*The Pacific railway; speeches delivered by Hon. Sir
   Charles Tupper*, 583

Pacific Scandal: 410, 417, 418, 420, 439, 441, 448;
   Br. gov't corr. (1874), 461, 465

Pacific Sealing Co'y: 1373

Pacific squadron: station regulations, 198

Pacific Transit and Telegraph Company: 1676

*Le Pacifique: historique de la question*, 599

*Pageant of B.C.*, 1952

*Pages from a seaman's log*, 944

Paleontology: 1233, 1435

PALLISER, JOHN (1807-1887). English geographer
   and explorer; in command of Br. gov't expedition
   exploring Br. N. Am. during 1857-60. (Wa; P;
   DNB)   96, 120, 208

Palliser expedition: 82, 96, 120, 136, 208, 2076, 2170

*The Palliser expedition . . . 1857-1860*, 2170

PALMER, HENRY SPENCER (1838-1893).
   Engineer, surveyor, astronomer, mathematician,
   auth. Born in India; 1856 gazetted a lt. in Royal
   Engineers, engaged in many engineering and
   surveying tasks in B.C.; 1858 came to B.C. with
   Col. R. C. Moody; 1863 surveyed and supervised
   construction of a part of the Cariboo Road. (B.C.
   Cen. Com.)   209, 210. *See below*

Palmer, Henry Spencer: asst. ed., 194; on North
   Bentinck Arm route, 459. *See above*

PALMER, HENRY THOMAS: 1080

PALMER, HOWARD (1883-1944). Mountaineer.
   Born in Norwich, Conn; 1905 graduate of Yale
   Univ.; 1908 LL.B. from Harvard; pioneer
   explorer of Selkirk Mts.; 1907-15 studied
   glaciation; 1916-27 visited remote sections of
   Rocky Mountains; organized Mt. Logan
   expedition in 1925; 1930-33 ed. of *Am. alpine
   jour.*; F.R.G.S. (Wwa, 1943-1950; Waa; WhA;
   Wha; Bua)   1641, 1655

PALMER, WILLIAM HARRY: A signalman on
   H.M.S. *Warspite* who wrote an account of the
   voyage from Chatham to Victoria from Feb. 1890
   to Aug. 1891. (His book, *Pages from a seaman's
   log*)   944

PANTON, JAMES HOYES (1847-1898). Educator.
   Born in Scotland; attended Univ. of Toronto,
   M.A. 1878; 1878-98 on staff of Ont. Agric.
   College except for year 1883-4 which was spent
   in Winnipeg; contributed papers to *Trans.* of the
   Literary and Scientific Soc. of Man. (Wa; Mo,
   1898)   690

Papermills: 1907

*Papers and communications read before the Natural
   History Society of British Columbia*, 942

*Papers in connection with crown lands in British
   Columbia*, 217

*Papers* [re British and American Joint Commission for
   the Final Settlement of the Claims of the
   Hudson's Bay and Puget's Sound Agricultural
   Companies]   247

*Papers relating to Behring Sea fisheries* (1887), 763

*Papers relating to the Treaty of Washington*, 406

*Papers relative to the Hudson's Bay Company's charter
   and licence of trade . . . 1859*, 88

*Papers relative to the proposed union of British
   Columbia and Vancouver Island* (1866), 274

*The Paris Belle Mine*, 1212

*A parish history of Grande Prairie and Shuswap*, 1843

*Parish history of St. Mary's Anglican Church*, 1917

PARIZEAU, HENRI DELPE (1877-1954): 1751

PARK, JOSEPH (1828-1877): 236

Parke, John G.: 1459

PARKER, RICHARD WAYNE: 1515

"Parliamentum" (pseud.), *see* Hodgins, Thomas

PARRISH, H. E.: 997

Parsnip River: 2144

PARSON, CHARLES HERBERT (1867-1939).
   Postmaster at Golden, B.C., for 20 y.; lived there
   for 45 y. working for a lumber company and in
   his brother's store. (Van. *Province*, 5 Apr. 1939,
   p. 9)   1746

Parsons, Marion Randall: ed., 1624

PARSONS, ROBERT MANN: 183, 184, 211

Parsons, W. H.: auth. of poem, 303

PASCOE, CHARLES FREDERICK (1854-   ):
   1169 (comp.)

Pettipiece, Richard Parmater: comp., 1279

PETTIT, SYDNEY GEORGE (1907- ). Head of Dept. of History, Univ. of Victoria. 1887

PHAIR, ARTHUR WILLIAM ARMITT (1880- ). Prospector, mine owner, storekeeper, coroner. Born in Lillooet; son of a teacher; educated in Victoria; amateur botanist and mineralogist. (VF) 2101

PHARMACEUTICAL ASSOCIATION OF THE PROVINCE OF BRITISH COLUMBIA: 945, 1815, 1912

*Pharmacy through 60 years in British Columbia,* 1912

Phillipps, George: com., 372

PHILLIPPS-WOLLEY, SIR CLIVE OLDNALL LONG (1854-1918). Writer, game hunter, lawyer. In 1876 inherited title and assumed name "Wolley"; 1884 called to bar from Middle Temple; Br. consul in Russia; 1886 came to B.C. on game hunting expedition; settled in Victoria; F.R.S.C. 1913; knighted 1915. (EC; Ww; K, 1917) 667, 796, 893, 1128, 1129, 1306, 1474

PHILLIPS, WALTER SHELLEY (1867-1940). Artist, auth. with pseud. of "El Comancho"; adopted by the Sioux Indians; wrote several books for young people on Indians. (Bua; Waa; Bua) 1237

*Phoenix pioneer and boundary mining journal,* 1475

*Physical characteristics of the Indians,* 913

Physicians: 886, 1738, 1852, 1870

PICKEN, M.: 756 (comp.)

PICKETT, MRS. LA SALLE (CORBELL) (1848-1931). Second wife of George Edward Pickett, a Confederate soldier and later a maj.-gen.; a writer of negro dialect stories during the period 1879-1917. (Bua; DAB) 1476

*Pickett and his men,* 1476

*Pictorial history of our war with Spain,* 1397

*Picturesque Alaska,* 853

PIERCE, J. H.: 894

PIERCE, WILLIAM HENRY (1856-1948). Indian Methodist missionary. Born in Ft. Rupert; had Scottish father, mother was from Ft. Simpson tribe: brought up at Ft. Simpson; under Rev. Thomas Crosby's influence became a missionary to Indians along the coastal areas from Naas R. to Bella Coola; understood problems of natives in adjusting to modern living. (VF) 1747

PIERREPONT, EDWARD WILLOUGHBY (1860-1885). Diplomat. In 1882 left Oxford Univ.; 1883 accompanied his father, Judge Edwards Pierrepont, to Pacific coast and Alaska; 1884 F.R.G.S.; appointed sec. of legation at Rome and later made chargé d'affaires. (Waa; Apa) 668

PIKE, WARBURTON MAYER (1861-1915). Englishman who travelled extensively; recognized as an authority on natural history, especially that of B.C.; big game hunter. In 1882 went to U.S.; in 1885 bought property on Saturna Island, B.C.; 1889-92 and 1896 on expeditions to Arctic, Yukon and Bering Sea; 1898-1915 interests were in transportation and trading in the Cassiar area; mining was another interest. (VF; *Beaver,* v. 6, 1925, p. 24-25) 998, 1238. *See below*

Pike, Warburton: characterization of, 1474. *See above*

PILLING, JAMES CONSTANTINE (1846-1895). Am. ethnologist. During 1875-80 accompanied a Rocky Mt. survey party led by John W. Powell; collected items on Indian life; studied their language; named chief of U.S. Geol. Survey and chief clerk of Ethnological Bureau; 1892-5 worked on specialized bibliographies relating to Indians. (Nen; DAB; Waa; Apa; Nc) 999, 1081, 1082, 1130

Pilot guides: 23, 36, 141, 229, 284, 342, 343, 445, 557, 713, 785, 952

Pilotage: 1106

*Pilotage by-laws for . . . Yale and New Westminster . . . 1894,* 1106

*Pilote de île Vancouver,* 284

PINART, ALPHONSE LOUIS (1852-1911): 486

Pindell, W. M.; 1355

Pine River: 1177

Pine River Pass: 530

PIOLET, JEAN-BAPTISTE (1855-1930): 1516 (ed.)

*Pioneer days in British Columbia,* 1669

*Pioneer days of Nakusp and the Arrow lakes,* 1909

*Pioneer days, Provincial Royal Jubilee Hospital,* 1670

*Pioneer Doctor John Sebastian Helmcken,* 1870

*A pioneer, 1851,* 1614

Pioneer life: 1404, 1458, 1468, 1530, 1535, 1541, 1558, 1569, 1581, 1614, 1621, 1629, 1632, 1669, 1722, 1732, 1748, 1837, 1872, 1879, 1882, 1884, 2131, 2132, 2137, 2145; in fiction, 1531, 1538, 1584, 1603, 2086; in poetry, 1766

*Pioneer life in California and British Columbia,* 1732

*Pioneer nuns of British Columbia,* 1730

*Pioneer of the Pacific,* 1846

*Pioneer reminiscences of Puget Sound,* 1543

Pioneer societies: 740, 1136, 1186

*The pioneer steamer Beaver,* 1542

*The pioneer women of Vancouver Island,* 1710

*Pioneering in western Canada; a story of the Baptists,* 1794

*Pioneers in paper,* 1721

*The pioneers of Burrard Inlet, Granville,* 1925

Pioneers of Vancouver "before the train", 1957

Pitt, Robert: auth., 919

Place-names: 1148, 1937; Indian names, 1602; of the Kootenay district, 2162; origin and history of coastal, 1578; of Rocky and Selkirk Mts., 2169; of Rocky Mts., 1655

Plaskett, Francis: 1766

Plaskett, Frank, *see* Plaskett, Francis

PLATT, HARRIET LOUISE: 1571

*Plays of the Pacific coast,* 1755

Plumb, John B.: speech of, 583

correspondent in Greek-Turkey war 1897, and in Boer War; F.R.G.S. 1898. (P; DAB)    1000

*Rambles in the North-West,* 690

RAMSEY, BRUCE (1924-    ). Journalist, newspaper librarian for Vancouver *Province.* Born in Nakusp, educated in West Vancouver; did radio broadcasts on various areas of B.C.; writes historical articles for newspapers; a past-pres., B.C. Hist. Assoc., Vancouver Branch. (Book jacket of his *P.G.E.; railway to the North*) 1990, 2040, 2115, 2136, 2157

Ranching: 2000; juvenile fiction about, 893

RAND & LIPSETT: 669

*Rapport conjoint des commissaires . . . pour definer la ligne frontière . . . 1896,* 1187

RATHBUN, RICHARD (1852-1918). Zoologist and museum curator. Born in Buffalo, N.Y.; 1871 entered Cornell Univ.; 1874-5 asst. in zoology in Boston Soc. of Natural Hist.; acquired knowledge of marine life as a voluntary asst. with U.S. Fish Com. along New England coast; 1880-1914 was curator of marine invertebrates in Nat. Mus. and later in the Smithsonian Inst.; 1891 prepared case of U.S. on sealing at Paris Tribunal of Arbitration; Am. rep. on the jt. com. with Gr. Br. to study the condition of fisheries in the boundary waters between U.S. and Canada; supervised construction of Nat. Mus. of Natural Hist. building; held offices in many scientific societies and wrote numerous publications, particularly on marine biology. (DNB; Wwa, 1918-19)    1443

RATTRAY, ALEXANDER: 185

RATTRAY, WILLIAM JORDAN (1835-1883). Journalist from London. In 1848 came to Canada from Scotland; obtained Univ. of Toronto degree in philosophy; 1872-8 wrote for the *Canadian monthly;* on Toronto *Mail,* writing on religious, political, and social topics. (Waa; Wa; pref. to v. 4 of *The Scot in British North America*)    584

RAWLINGS, THOMAS. Merchant who lived in Am. for several years prior to 1863. (P)    237, 260

Ray, R. C.: comp., 952

RAYMOND & WHITCOMB COMPANY: 1001

*Raymond's vacation excursions,* 1001

*Re Memorial respecting . . . S.S. "Coquitlam,"* 1373

*The re-annexation of British Columbia,* 357

Real estate: 817

Real estate brokers: 669

*Reasons for not joining "Synod"; a letter,* 518

*Réception officielle à Paris du Tribunal . . . de Bering,* 1019

RECO MINING AND MILLING COMPANY, LIMITED: 1307

*[Record of oral testimony . . . at Victoria]* 1194

*Records of the convention; arguments . . . British and American,* 1195

*Red Indians I have known,* 1647

*"The Red River Rebellion": the cause,* 355

RED RIVER SETTLEMENT. CITIZENS: 212

*Red willows,* 1720

REECE, WILLIAM SHELDON: 238

Reed, J. Sewall: 232

Reed, S. B.: 649

*Reflections from sunny memories of a tour,* 1149

Reformed Episcopal Church: 869

*Les régions nouvelles,* 312

*Regulations for the disposal of Dominion lands within the railway belt in . . . British Columbia, 1885,* 681

*Regulations for the disposal of Dominion lands within the railway belt in . . . British Columbia, approved . . . 1887, and amended . . . 1889,* 814

*Regulations for the survey, administration, disposal and management of the Dominion lands . . . within the . . . railway belt . . . in . . . British Columbia, 1890,* 861

*Regulations for the survey, administration, disposal . . . of the Dominion lands . . . in . . . British Columbia,* 1026

*Regulations governing the entry . . . of merchandise,* 1389

*Regulations governing vessels employed in fur-seal fishing during the season of 1899,* 1449

*Regulations of the Victoria Fire Department,* 186

REID, JOHN HOTCHKISS STEWART (1909-    ). Teacher, journalist in Vancouver, Seattle, Portland, San Francisco. Born in Scotland; educated in New Westminster; attended U.B.C. and Univ. of Toronto; did research in B.C. history; prof. of history and chn., Dept. of History at United College, Winnipeg. (Book jacket)    1946

REID, ROBIE LEWIS (1866-1945). Lawyer and historian. Built up an outstanding library of 9000 books, 4000 pamphlets on B.C., Klondike, Yukon, and Maritimes which he bequeathed to U.B.C.; member of B.C. Hist. Assoc. from its organization in 1922; launched the *B.C. hist. quart.* (VF; Roy. Soc. of Can. *Proc. and trans.* 3d ser., v. 39, 1945, p. 109-110)    1696, 1719, 1740. *See below*

Reid, Robie L.: Freemason historian, 392. *See above*

"Reindeer" (ship): 497

REINHART, HERMAN FRANCIS (1832-1889). Miner, prospector, sawmill owner, in bakery and saloon business, farmer (but principally a prospector). In 1851 travelled Oregon Trail to Calif.; 1851-69 in Calif., Oreg., Wash., and B.C. in search of gold. (Book jacket)    2137

"Reise in den Nordwestgegenden Nord-Amerika's," 158

Reitz, J. M.: jt. auth., 2100

*Religion and myths of the Koryak,* 1357

*Religion and rum,* 694

*Reminiscences of Captain Billie Moore,* 1864

*Reminiscences of the west coast of Vancouver Island,* 1694

*Reminiscences of the Yukon,* 1601

Richards, Alfred Bate: jt. auth., 20
Richards, George Henry: 141, 229, 284
Richardson, A. G.: 282, 307
Richfield: 2147
Richmond Municipality: 1700, 2009
Richmond Presbyterian Church (Vancouver): 1685
RICKARD, THOMAS ARTHUR (1864-1953).
    Mining engineer. Educated in Russia; attended
    Univ. of London, Royal School of Mines; 1885
    went to U.S.; travelled in U.S., Australia, New
    Zealand, France; ed. of several mining journals
    and auth. of books on mining and history; retired
    in Victoria; in B.C. Hist. Assoc. (Wha, 1946-47)
    1888
RIDLEY, WILLIAM, bp. of Caledonia (1836-1911).
    Anglican clergyman. Worked for Church
    Missionary Society at Metlahkatla and in 1879
    was consecrated first Bishop of Caledonia. (Mo,
    1898) 620, 1477, 1518. *See below*
Ridley, William: 1536; trans., 676, 736, 807, 866,
    1209, 1330. *See above*
Ridley, Mrs. William: 1597
RINFRET, RAOUL: 1374
Riske Creek: 2051
Rithet, Robert Paterson: 730, 1337
River Jordan (V.I.): history, 2069
Roads: 146, 1740; from Alberni to Nanaimo, 179;
    Bentinck Arm and Fraser River Road Company,
    159; from Bute Inlet, 191; *also see* Cariboo Road
Robb, S. R.: auth., 1167
ROBERTS, ERIC ARTHUR (1907- ); 2138
ROBERTS, MORLEY (1857-1942). An English
    auth. who travelled extensively. In 1884 in Texas
    and central states; then came to Canada, worked
    on construction of C.P.R.; lived in B.C., and then
    moved to San Francisco; 1927 returned to B.C.
    on a visit. (VF; his books *The western Avernus,
    On the old trail*) 757, 896, 1002
ROBERTS, SYDNEY A.: 1444
Robertson, W. A.: 729
Robinson, George: report of, 258, 259
Robinson, Gordon: jt. auth., 2034
ROBINSON, JOHN MOORE (1855-1934).
    Newspaper proprietor in Manitoba and in the
    Manitoba legislature 1887. Born in Ont.; settled
    in Man. 1879; ed. and publisher of papers in
    Brandon and Portage La Prairie; his first visit to
    B.C. in 1888 lead him to settle in the Okanagan in
    1897 and develop orchards; 1906 was the first
    reeve of Summerland; interested in community
    activities. (VF; Cc, 1887) 1697
ROBINSON, LEIGH BURPEE. Author. Left eastern
    Canada for B.C. about 1928; living in Victoria;
    has written articles for *Can. geog. jour.* and other
    magazines; m. Bertram Digby Robinson who did
    the illustrations for her book *Esquimalt*. (VF)
    1874
ROBINSON, NOEL (1881?-1966). Newspaperman,
    writer, historian. On British newspapers in

Brighton before going to Vancouver in 1908; did
    some farming in the southern boundary area; was
    columnist for the Vancouver *World, Star,* and
    *Province;* active in community affairs—City
    Mus., Little Theatre, B.C. Hist. Soc.; won the
    Good Citizen award in Vancouver; contributed
    articles to historical publications. (VF) 1615,
    1833
ROBSON, EBENEZER (1835-1911). Methodist
    missionary. Born in Perth, Ont.; lived in Sarnia;
    1856 entered ministry; ordained 1858; went to
    Victoria and was assigned to gold fields with
    headquarters at Hope where he established a
    school; 1860 transferred to Nanaimo, then to
    Yale while the Cariboo Road was being built;
    1864 went to New Westminster and served in
    Fraser Valley; moved to Pt. Simpson and to
    Vernon. (B.C. Cen. Com.) 1674
*A rock painting of the Thompson River Indians,* 1240
*The Rockies of Canada,* 1480
*The rocks and rivers of British Columbia,* 689
Rocks of British Columbia & Chile (cov. t.), 503
Rocky Mountains: 255, 256, 690, 710, 898, 1250,
    1350, 1454, 1480, 1519, 1589, 1655, 1687, 1705,
    1859, 1881, 1882, 2111; history of its passes,
    2169; *also see* Exploration; Surveying
RODDAN, ANDREW (1883-1948). Minister of
    United Church of Canada. Born in Hawick,
    Scotland; 1903 came to Canada; studied for the
    ministry at Manitoba Theological Inst.,
    Winnipeg; 1930 went to Vancouver to First
    United Church; interested in social welfare,
    especially amongst unemployed during the
    depression years; his sermons were broadcast on
    radio every Sunday for many years. (Vic.
    *Times,* 26 Apr. 1948, p. 12; Vic. *Colonist,* 27
    Apr. 1942, p. 5; Van. *Sun,* 26 Apr. 1948, p. 12)
    1844
ROGERS, MARY ISABELLA (ANGUS). Wife of
    the founder of the B.C. Sugar Refining Company,
    Limited. 2044 (ed.)
Rogers family: 2044
Rogers Pass: 2148
Rohrabacher (C. A.) & Son: pub., 1312
Roman Catholic Church, *see* Catholic Church
*The romance of British Columbia,* 1699
*The romance of the boundaries,* 1689
*The romance of the Canadian Pacific Railway,* 1672
*A romance of the Rockies,* 798
*The Romance of Western Canada,* 1639
*The romantic Crow's Nest Pass,* 2149
*The romantic history of the Canadian Pacific,* 423
*Romantic Vancouver Island,* 1861
ROME, DAVID (1910- ). Librarian and historian.
    Born in Russia; graduate of U.B.C.; attended
    Univ. of Washington, McGill Library School, and
    Univ. of Montreal; 1953 director of Jewish
    Public Library in Montreal. (Whj, 1965, p. 403)
    1823

*Rome vs. Ruthven,* 1308

ROPER, EDWARD. An Englishman who travelled across Canada; visited Vancouver in 1890; some of his original water-colours are in the Vancouver Public Library; F.R.G.S. (P; *B.C. hist. quart.,* v. 10, 1946, p. 169)   946, 1445

ROSS, VICTOR HAROLD (1878-1934). Journalist and industrialist. Educated in Ont.; financial ed. for Toronto *Globe;* 1917 joined Imperial Oil Co.; 1919 made a director, later a vice-pres. (Waa; Wa)   1650

Ross & Ceperley: pub., 764

*Ross Bay Cemetery,* 2123

ROSSI, LOUIS: 213

Rossland: 1294, 1375, 1546, 1896, 2045; in fiction, 2146

ROSSLAND. BOARD OF TRADE: 1375, 1546

*Rossland, B.C., business directory, 1897,* 1309

ROSSLAND HISTORICAL MUSEUM ASSOCIATION: 2045

*Rossland in 1898,* 1375

ROSSLAND MINERS' UNION No. 38, WESTERN FEDERATION OF MINERS: 1376

*Rossland, the golden city,* 1896

Rouge, Etienne de, *see* de Rouge, Etienne

ROUGH, STANLEY: 2116 (ed.)

Rough, Stanley: ed., 2098, 2099; jt. auth., 2034

*Roughing it after gold,* 947

ROUHARD, HIPPOLYTE: 312

*Round the globe, through greater Britain,* 895

*Round the world by doctors' orders,* 1112

*A rousing meeting,* 839

*Route in exploring a road from Albernie canal,* 179

*The routes and mineral resources of north western Canada,* 1342

ROUTHIER, SIR ADOLPHE BASILE (1839-1920). Jurist in Quebec; chief justice of Que.; administrator of gov't of Que. prov., 1904, 1905; wrote words of "O Canada." (Mo, 1912; P; Wa) 1083

ROWE, GEORGE: 239

ROWLAND, CHARLES LOUIS GORDON (1920-   ): 2139

ROYAL AGRICULTURAL AND INDUSTRIAL SOCIETY OF BRITISH COLUMBIA: 691

Royal Canadian Mounted Police: 1625, 1762

Royal commissions: of B.C., 1842; *also see* Canada. Royal Commission . . .

*Royal commissions and commissions of inquiry,* 1842

*The Royal Engineers; a record,* 1798

*The Royal Engineers and British Columbia,* 2080

*The Royal Engineers in British Columbia,* 1986

Royal Engineers in British Columbia: 86, 194, 1582, 1616, 1798, 1986, 2080

ROYAL ENGINEERS' OLD COMRADES ASSOCIATION. VANCOUVER: 1798

ROYAL GOLD MINING COMPANY: 1310, 1311

Royal Jubilee Hospital (Victoria): 1670, 2031; *also see* Victoria. Provincial Royal Jubilee Hospital; Victoria. Royal Hospital; Victoria. Royal Jubilee Hospital

*Royal Jubilee Hospital . . . 1858-1958,* 2031

ROYAL OAK. ST. MICHAEL AND ALL ANGELS' CHURCH: 1932

Rules and manner of proceedings of the Supreme Court (cap. t.), 71

*Rules and regulations for the guidance of employes* [sic], 712

*Rules and regulations for the management of the Public Library,* 235

*Rules and regulations . . . graving dock at Esquimalt,* 742

*Rules and regulations issued in conformity with the Gold Field Act,* 188

*Rules and regulations of the New Westminster Home Guards,* 276

*Rules and regulations subject to the provisions,* 752

*Rules for the government of the Royal Hospital,* 517

*Rules governing subscribers,* 1208

*Rules; Kitamaat home, 1897-8,* 1295

*The rules of practice and forms to be used in the Superior and Inferior Courts of Civil Justice,* 71

*Rules of the Naval Club . . . established 1867,* 291

RUNNALLS, FRANK E. A United Church minister; held several pastorates in B.C.; was pastor of Knox Church, Prince George, at the time of publishing his history. (Van. *Province,* 17 May 1945, p. 24)   1857

*Rural rhymes and the sheep thief,* 1213

*Russian monuments, storehouses, customs,* 1509

Rutgers, Lispenard (pseud.), *see* Smith, Henry Erskine

Ruthven, Victor M.: 1308

Rutland: history of, 2046

RUTLAND. CENTENNIAL COMMITTEE: 2046

RUX (pseud. of Capt. Hyacinthe Daly Devereux). (Ka, v. 5, p. 142)   947

S., D. L.: ed., 1723

S. W. Silver & Co.'s Canada (cov. t.), 598

Saanich Peninsula: history and pioneers of, 2082

SAANICHTON. SAINT STEPHEN'S CHURCH: 2117

*The saga of mining in British Columbia,* 1990

*Saga of Westwold,* 1947

SAGE, WALTER NOBLE (1888-1963). Educator. Born in London, Ont.; attended Univ. of Toronto and Oxford; 1918 appointed prof. of history, U.B.C.; wrote extensively on Canadian and B.C. history; 1933 F.R.H.S. (Whb, 1949-50; *Can. hist. rev.,* v. 45, 1964, p. 180-182)   1703, 1724, 1725, 1741, 1807

Sage, Walter Noble: 1819. *See above*

*Sailing directions for the west coast* (1853), 36

*Sailing directions for the west coast* (1868), 310

St. Andrew's Church (Victoria; Presbyterian): 316, 1631, 1698, 1816

*St. Andrew's Church* [of Victoria] *. . . 1866-1941,* 1816

speech in Senate, 361, speech on, 1427; study of joint occupation, 1828; Wash. Terr. corr., 348

*San Juan Island. Memorial . . . (1868),* 319

*San Juan Island; speech* of Hon. Jacob M. Howard, 361

*San Juan Island; the Cronstadt of the Pacific,* 1789

*The San Juan water boundary question,* 2166

*Sandford Fleming, empire builder,* 1622

SANDS, HAROLD PERCY (1873-  ): 1547

SANGSTER, JAMES LEWIS (1891-  ): 1933

SANSUM COPPER MINING COMPANY, LIMITED: 214

Sapir, Edward: auth., 1617

SAREL, C. WENTWORTH: 1313

Sarver, Hannah (pseud.), *see* Nielson, Jean

Saturna Island: history of, 2109

Sawmilling: 2154

*Sawney's letters* (1960), 2094

*Sawney's letters; or, Cariboo rhymes,* 297

*The Sayward-Kelsey Bay saga,* 2010

SCAIFE, ARTHUR HODGINS. English auth., poet, ed. During 1894-7 first ed. of Victoria *Province,* a literary publication issued weekly on local and world news, music, drama, markets, etc.; much of his literary work first appeared in the *Province* under the pseud. "Kim Bilir" and was published separately later; 1897 left for London to publish his synoptical charts of history; 1900 his volume of poems *The soliloquy of a shadow shape on a holiday from hades* was published in London. (Vic. *Colonist,* 26 Aug. 1900, p. 9; 28 Oct. 1896, p. 5; 8 Oct. 1897, p. 5; issues of Vic. *Province,* 1894-1897)   1132, 1171, 1172

SCAMMON, CHARLES MELVILLE (1825-1911). Naval officer. Born in Pittston, Maine; 1850 sailed to Calif.; engaged in whale fishing, discovered habitat of the gray whale in a bay on the Calif. coast.; 1861 com. of U.S. revenue cutter in San Francisco at the beginning of the Civil War; later was appointed capt. in Revenue Service. (Waa; Apa)   469

*Scenes and studies of savage life,* 313

*Scenes on Pacific shores,* 424

SCHOLEFIELD, ETHELBERT OLAF STUART (1875-1919). Librarian and archivist. Came to B.C. in 1887 (his father was an Anglican clergyman in New Westminster and later in Esquimalt); worked in the B.C. Provincial Library under R. E. Gosnell; 1898 became provincial librarian, and in 1910 became provincial archivist; he planned the B.C. Archives Memoirs and edited the first three. (*B.C. hist. quart.,* v. 21, 1957-8, p. 1-14)   1607, 1616

School of Nursing of the Vancouver General Hospital: 1890

Schools: appeal for, 622; calendar for, 637, 728; convent, 1642; in Kamloops, 2155; prospectus for, 131, 132, 346, 560, 1138, 1248; publication of, 744; in Vancouver, 1587, 1808, 2113; in Victoria, 1249, 1733, 1915, 1958, 1994

*Schools and scholars,* 2155

Schreiber, Collingwood: 588

SCHULENBURG, ALBRECHT CONON GRAF VON DER (1865-1902): 1133

Schwatka, Frederick: report of, 696

SCIDMORE, ELIZA RUHAMAH (1856-1928). Am. auth.; a foreign sec. for Nat. Geog. Soc.; wrote books and articles on Alaska, Japan, China, India. (Wha, 1910-11)   692, 1084

*The Scot in British North America,* 584

*Scotland and Scotsmen,* 654

Scots: 654, 1588; biographical information on, 584; society for, 1004

*The scotsman in Canada,* 1588

Scotson, William: auth., 919

SCOTT, ROBERT CLYDE (1880?-1960). United Church missionary along Pacific coast, skipper of the coastal mission boats. In 1913 came to B.C. from Ont.; 1914-19 at Howe Sound and Hazelton; 1919-25 undertook marine mission work at Cape Mudge, Queen Charlotte Is., Ocean Falls, Bamfield; 1934 principal of Coqualeetza Indian School. (VF)   1875

Sea Island: history of, 2009

*The sea of mountains; an account,* 513

*Seal and salmon fisheries and general resources of Alaska,* 1391

*The seal arbitration,* 1173

*The seal arbitration, 1893,* 1121

*Seal fisheries of Behring Sea. Message from the President of the United States transmitting a letter from the Secretary of State with accompanying papers,* 900

*Seal fisheries of the Behring Sea. Message from the President of the United States transmitting a letter from the Sec. of State submitting the official correspondence between the . . . United States and . . . Great Britain,* 953

Seal Fishery (North Pacific) Act, 1893: 1123

Sealers' association: 1395

*A sealer's journal,* 1155

Sealers' union: 986

Sealing: 979, 1245, 1616, 1819, 1853; Am. gov't doc. re regulations of the Paris Tribunal of Arbitration, 1449; Am. regulations for, 1178, 1243; Am.-Can. jt. statement of conclusions on 1898), 1349; Br. gov't doc., 1286; in fiction, 1128, 1648, 1720; re memorials, petitions, etc. of schooner owners, 1351, 1364, 1369, 1373, 1395; report by D'Arcy Thompson, 1316, 1384; report by Robert Venning on, 1137, 1247, 1322, 1393, 1452; reports of Am. investigation com. (1898-99), 1390; a sealer's journal, 1155; *also see* Bering Sea controversy

Sealing vessels: action re condemnation of, 1123

Seamen's union: 986

at Brown Univ.; 1910 at Univ. of Minnesota; member of several historical societies. (Wwa, v. 2) 1799

Shipping: 105, 1337, 1362, 1680, 1803, 1954; marine history, 1185; of V.I. (1852-7), 1827; *also see* Timetables

Ships: British naval vessels, 1874

Shipwrecks: 484, 1736, 1954, 2134; in marine history, 1185

*Shores and alps of Alaska,* 758

*A short cathechism* [sic] *and hymnal . . . Ahts,* 1380

*A short history and fleet list . . . Canadian Pacific,* 1972

*A short history of Kelowna and its surroundings,* 1325

*A short history of Mountain Lodge No. 11,* 1746

*A short history of Nanaimo,* 2021

*A short history of the British Columbia regiment, the "Dukes,"* 1847

*A short story of the Metlakatla Christian mission,* 1943

Shorthand: in Beaver Indian language, 568; Duployan primer in Chinook jargon, 992; Duployan reading book, 1066, 1223, 1224; elements of Duployan method, 939, 1119; works in Déné syllabary, 863, 888, 889, 950, 1124; works in Duployan s., 864, 923, 938, 969, 970-973, 987, 993, 1003, 1028-1030, 1065, 1196, 1205-1207, 1363, 1417

*Shorthand primer for the . . . language,* 940

SHORTT, ADAM (1859-1931). Economist, historian. Born near London, Ont.; 1883 graduated from Queen's Univ. (1884 M.A.); studied at Glasgow and Edin.; 1885 appointed asst. prof. of philosophy at Queen's; then prof. of political science in 1892; 1908-18 on Civil Service Com., Ottawa; appointed chn. Board of Historical Publications of the Public Archives; 1906 a F.R.S.C.; auth. and ed. of books on Can. economics and constitutional history. (Wa; Mo, 1912) 1617

SHOTBOLT, THOMAS (1842-1922). Chemist and druggist from Lincolnshire; 1862 came to B.C. and established his business in Victoria. (B; VF) 384

*Shushwap manual; or Prayers, hymns, and catechism,* 1205

*The Shuswap,* 1357

Shuswap and Okanagan Railway: 783

Shuswap Indian language: in Duployan shorthand, 970, 971, 993, 1028, 1205

Shuswap Indians: 928, 1357

Shuswap Lake: 266, 322

Shuswap Lake district: history of, 1999

Shuttleworth, J. K.: speech of, 175

Siberia: migrations from, 1357

*Sick room altar manual,* 1152

Siewerd, Ferdinand Henry: 1351

SIFTON, SIR CLIFFORD (1861-1929). Lawyer and politician. From 1882 lawyer in Manitoba; 1888-96 in Man. legislature; 1891-6 att.-gen. and Min. of Education; 1896-1905 federal Min. of Interior;

1911 withdrew; prosecuted a vigorous immigration policy; 1909-18 chn. of Can. Conservation Com. (Wa; Ww; Cc; Mo, 1912; Cy; 1919; P) 1378

Sillitoe, Acton Windeyer: 1234, 1421, 1660

SILLITOE, VIOLET E. (PELLY) (d. 1934). Wife of the first Bishop of New Westminster, Acton Windeyer Sillitoe. In 1880 went to New Westminster; travelled frequently with her husband to Cariboo, Okanagan, and Kootenays. (VF) 1660, 1669

Silver: 1990

*Silver mining in British Columbia,* 1117

Silver (S.W.) & Co.: pub., 598

Similkameen district: 726, 1036, 1037, 1877, 2016

Simmons, H.: tenant-farmer delegate, 919

Simpson, Sir George: canoe voyage of (in 1828), 400

*Single tax advocate,* 843

*Sinners and saints; a true story,* 1872

Sinnett, Charles: ed., 194

*Sir, I am instructed by the committee . . . to transmit . . . a copy of resolutions adopted,* 269

*Sir James Douglas* (1908), 1565

*Sir James Douglas* (c1930), 1724

*Sir James Douglas and British Columbia,* 1725

*Sir James Hector, M.D., 1834-1907,* 2122

*Sir, the following is a copy of a petition . . . western terminus . . . on Vancouver Island,* 386

THE SIR WILLIAM WALLACE BENEFIT SOCIETY: 1004

Sirois, Joseph: chn., 1785

*The sister dominions,* 1221

Sisters of St. Ann: 1642, 1770, 1904, 2048

SISTERS OF ST. ANN (VICTORIA): 1642, 2048

*The sisters of St. Ann . . . 1858-1958,* 2048

*6th Regiment, the Duke of Connaught's Own Rifles,* 1559

*Sixtieth anniversary of the First Presbyterian . . . ,* 1911

*The Siwash; their life, legends, and tales,* 1151

*Six ans en Amérique,* 213

Skeena River: 800, 836, 1317, 1864, 1984, 2034, 2098, 2099, 2116

*The Skeena, river of destiny,* 1984

*A sketch of an overland route to British Columbia,* 171

*Sketch of the Alaskan missions,* 760

*Sketch of the country between Jervis Inlet and Port Pemberton,* 146

*Sketch of the Kwakiutl language,* 1462

*Sketch of the martyrdom of Archbishop . . . Seghers,* 1830

*Sketch of the proposed line of overland railroad,* 347

*Sketch of the rise and progress of Metlahkatlah,* 306

*A sketch of the successful missionary work of William Duncan,* 1482

*Sketches of pioneering in the Rocky Mountains,* 1541

*Sketches of the life of Mgr. de Mazenod,* 553

SKEWTON, LADY LAVINIA (pseud.): 123

SKINNER, CONSTANCE LINDSAY (1879?-1939).
Novelist, historian, newspaper woman. Born at
Quesnel; both parents had literary background;
worked on newspapers in B.C., Los Angeles,
Chicago, and N.Y. (VF; Waa; Bua; WhA; Wha;
P) 1720

*Skulamagee; a story of early Vancouver*, 2073

Skwamish Indian language, *see* Squamish Indian
language

*Skwamish manual; or, Prayers, hymns and catechism*,
1205

SLADEN, DOUGLAS BROOKE WHEELTON
(1856-1947). Australian novelist, poet, critic.
Born in London; educated in Cheltenham and
Trinity College, Oxford; travelled extensively in
Australia, America, Japan, China and Italy;
1889 visited Vancouver. (P; Me; *B.C. hist. quart.*,
v. 10, 1946, p. 170) 1174

SLATER, JOHN B.: 1175

Slave Indian language: vocabulary of, 335; works in,
816, 881

*Slave Indians, Tenne [vocabulary]*, 335

*Slayamen manual; or, Prayers, hymns and catechisms*,
1205

Sliammon Indian dialect: in Duployan shorthand,
1205

SLIVERS (pseud): 1176

Slocan district: mining, 1307, 1414

*The Slocan district, British Columbia*, 1414

SLOUGH CREEK MINING COMPANY: 1005

Sluiter, Engel: jt. ed., 1840

Smallpox: 450

SMITH, CHARLES WESLEY (1877-1956).
Librarian. 1656 (comp.)

Smith, Donald Alexander, *see* Strathcona and Mount
Royal, Donald Alexander Smith, 1st baron of

Smith, Dorothy Blakey: comp., 1976; ed., 2145

Smith, Frank J.: 1770

SMITH, HARLAN INGERSOLL (1872-1940). Am.
archaeologist, graduate of Univ. of Michigan;
1891 on staff of Peabody Mus.; 1895-1911 at
Am. Mus. of Natural Hist.; 1911-20
archaeologist with Geol. Survey of Can.; 1920
archaeologist at Nat. Mus. of Can.; wrote
numerous reports and contributed to scientific
periodicals. (Wa; Cd, 1936-37) 1379, 1446,
1447, 1492

Smith, Harlan Ingersoll: 1357

SMITH, HENRY BADELEY: 844

SMITH, HENRY ERSKINE (1842-1932). Wrote
under the pseud. "Lispenard Rutgers." 1134

SMITH, J. GREGORY. Pres. of the Northern Pacific
Railroad in the 1860 period. (t.p.) 341

Smith, Marcus: C.P.R. survey report, 491; surveys of,
in 1872 and 1873, 459

*Smoke from their fires*, 1811

SMYTH, ELEANOR CAROLINE (HILL) (1831-
1926). Dau. of Sir Rowland Hill, postal reformer;
1861 came to B.C. as wife of Arthur Fellows;

remained for several years and then returned to
England. (Her book, *An octogenarian's
reminiscences*; Lu, p. 163 *f*) 1629

SMYTH, FRED JOSEPH (1872-1949). A newspaper
man (printer, publisher, and columnist well-
known in the Kootenays). Born in Quebec, but
brought up in the state of Washington; 1897
founded the *Moyie Leader*; 1911-28 returned to
Wash. state; 1928-1936 published Cranbrook
*Courier*; after the sale of the paper he continued
as a contributor. (VF) 1790

SMYTH, ROBERT STEWART CARMICHAEL
(1800?-1888). Maj. in the Royal Engineers;
commissioned in 1818; saw service principally in
eastern Canada; retired in 1849. (VF) 16, 17,
19

Snanaimuq (Indians): 809

*Snap, a legend of the Lone Mountain*, 893

*Snapshots from the North Pacific*, 1518

SNOW, WILLIAM PARKER (1817-1895).
Mariner, explorer, auth. In 1850 was purser,
doctor, and chief officer of the "Prince Albert"
on a search for Sir John Franklin; 1854 in
command of the S. Am. Missionary Society's
boat in Patagonia; compiled volumes of indexes
of arctic voyages; his manuscripts were purchased
by the Roy. Geog. Soc. after his death. (DNB)
77

*Snow sentinels of the Pacific Northwest*, 1737

*Social letter*, 670

*Social re-union . . . 1868*, 316

Society for the Prevention of Cruelty to Animals: 803

Society for the Propagation of the Gospel: pub. on,
1169

*The sodbusters*, 1884

*Les soeurs de Sainte-Anne*, 1904

*Sointula*, 1767

Sointula: 1767, 1993

Solicitors, *see* Law Society of British Columbia

*Some account of the Tahkaht Language*, 311

*Some reminiscences of old Victoria*, 1599

*Some startling facts*, 578

*Some thoughts and suggestions on municipal reform*,
961

Somenos district: surveying of (1859), 89

SOMERSET, HENRY CHARLES SOMERS
AUGUSTUS: 1177

SOMERSET, SUSAN MARGARET (McKINNON)
SAINT MAUR, duchess of. A lady of Grace of
the Order of St. John of Jerusalem in England;
1877 m. 15th Duke of Somerset, who had served
with the Red River expedition of 1870. (D) 899

SOMERVILLE, THOMAS (d. 1915). Presbyterian
minister. In 1865 arrived in Victoria as minister
of First Presbyterian Church; resigned 1866;
established St. Andrew's Presbyterian Church
in Victoria and was its pastor until he returned
to Scotland in 1870; was prominent Mason.
(VF) 277

Alaska and its mineral resources; 1897 returned to business. (DAB, v. 17)    1239

STACKHOUSE, CYRIL (1886-    ). Grandson of Rev. William Burton Crickmer, who was the first rector of St. John the Divine, Derby (1859), Yale (1860). (t.p.)    2103

Stalo Indian dialect: 924, 1205

*Stalo manual; or, Prayers, hymns and the catechism,* 1205

*Standard extra . . . removal of steel rails stopped,* 546

*"The Standard" map,* 1314

Stanley (town): 2147

Stanley Park: 1411, 1886, 1914

*"Stanley Smith's travels,"* 1805

STANNARD, M: 440

STANTON, STEPHEN BERRIEN (1864-    ): 1007

*Statement of facts . . . Alaska boundary question,* 1488

*Station regulations and port orders . . . Pacific, 1863,* 198

A statistical account of British Columbia, 286

Statutes: Br. statutes affecting B.C., 371; for colony of V.I., 218; colonies of V.I. and B.C., 372; *also see* British Columbia. Laws, statutes, etc.; Canada. Laws, statutes, etc.; Great Britain. Laws, statutes, etc.; Vancouver Island. Laws, statutes, etc.

*A statutory history of . . . railways,* 1784

*Steamboat days on the Skeena River,* 2098

*Steamboat days on the upper Columbia and . . . Kootenay,* 1941

*"Steamboat 'round the bend,"* 1841

*"Steamboating on the Fraser in the 'sixties,"* 1850

Steamboats: 1841, 1850, 1859, 1864, 1868, 1941, 1969, 1992, 2098, 2099

steamships: 774, 2068; *also see* Steamboats

*Steel of empire,* 1756

STEELE, HARWOOD ELMES ROBERT (1897-    ). Soldier, auth., journalist. Born at Ft. MacLeod; lived in England; was historian of one of the last Can. gov't arctic expeditions co-operating with R.C.M.P.; was a regular contributor to the Vancouver *Province* in the 1920's; 1965 visited Cranbrook area for special ceremonies to honour his father at Ft. Steele; now lives near Rugby, England. (VF; P)    1762

STEELE, SIR SAMUEL BENFIELD (1849-1919). First Mounted Police officer stationed in B.C. in 1898. Born in Orillia; attended Royal Military School; was in Fenian Raid, 1866; 1873 troop sgt.-maj. of newly formed R.N.W.P.; in several skirmishes with Indians on prairies; stationed in Kootenays; 1898-9 in White and Chilkoot passes and in Yukon; in the Boer War he commanded Strathcona's Horse (Royal Canadian) (Mo, 1912)    1625

Steer, Margaret G.: jt. auth., 1983

STEFFENS, SOPHIA (1886-    ). Nurse. Born in Liverpool; came to Canada with her parents in

1886; lived in Lytton; then in 1904 moved to Mamette L. in the Merritt area. (VF)    2118

Stejneger, Leonhard Hess: 1390

STEPHEN, IRENE SIMMONS (PHELAN) (1902-    ). Feature writer for magazines, newspapers, radio. Born in Ottawa and brought up in Vancouver; her "Story time" programme over radio was sponsored for three years by the B.C. Teachers' Federation; travelled widely in B.C., meeting pioneers to give atmosphere to her stories. (Book jacket)    1956

STEPHENS, LORENZO DOW: 1630

STEPHENSON, ANNIE: 1683

Stephenson, Mrs. Frederick, *see* Stephenson, Annie

*Sternwheelers, sandbars and switchbacks,* 1992

STEVENS, ISAAC INGALLS (1818-1862). Soldier, congressman, territorial gov. of Washington. From 1849-53 executive asst. on U.S. Coast Survey; director of exploration for northern route of Pacific Railway; made report in 1855; 1854-55 made treaties with Indians. (Wwh; Waa; Apa; Nc; DAB)    78. *See below*

Stevens, Isaac I.: aid from Gov. Douglas, 98; report of, 41. *See above*

STEVENS, ROBERT JULIUS (1824-1889). Consul of United States at Victoria for "British Columbia and its dependencies." Born in Newport, R.I.; went into gov't service; 1849 went to Calif.; in banking business; was supt. of mint at San Francisco; was a col. in Civil War; chief sec. of U.S. Congress and on committee on Appropriations; was later consul at Cyprus; 1884 appointed to consulate at Victoria. (Vic. *Colonist,* 27 Dec. 1889, p. 1)    670

Stevenson, Major: tenant-farmer delegate, 919

STEVENSON, EADY: 694

STEWART, GEORGE (1848-1906). Journalist. Born in N.Y.; d. in Que.; ed. of several publications; auth. of books on literary and historical themes; charter member of Roy. Soc. of Can.; F.R.G.S.; on International Literary Congress of Europe and only Can. member in 1879. (EC; Waa; Wa)    545

STEWART, JOHN (1887-    ): 2077

Stewart, John: jt. auth., 2030

Stickeen River, *see* Stikine River

Stikine River: 894, 1238, 1432, 1601, 1624, 1771, 1864, 1868; in fiction, 1474; Russian survey of (1868), 298

*Stikine River route to the Klondike,* 1381

Stlatliemoh language, *see* Lillooet Indian language

STOCK, EUGENE (1836-1928): 585, 1448 (supposed author)

*Stone hammers or pestles,* 1447

*Stories of early British Columbia,* 1621

*Stormy winter,* 2064

*The story of a church; Queen's Avenue United Church,* 2083

*The story of Barney May, pioneer,* 1632

*The story of citizenship in British Columbia*, 1987
*The story of confederation*, 1638
*The story of Hatley Park*, 1757
*The story of Metlakahtla*, 768
*The story of Okanagan falls*, 2001
*The story of Osoyoos, September 1811 to December 1952*, 1928
*The story of St. Andrew's United Church*, 1778
*The story of Similkameen*, 2016
*The story of Strathcona school*, 2113
*The story of Summerland*, 1835
*The story of the Canadian Pacific Railway*, 1627
*The story of the Pacific Scandal*, 441
*The story of the years*, 1571

STOTT, WILLIAM (1880-1953). Minister in the United Church of Canada. Born in Scotland; came to B.C. 1891; educated in New Westminster; 1900-1903 taught school in Port Moody and Surrey Centre; B.A. from Queen's; 1910 ordained and went to Quesnel until 1915; then 2 y. at Manitou, Man., and 12 y. at Armstrong, B.C.; 1930 called to St. Andrew's Church in New Westminster; 1950 retired. (VF) 1778

Strachan, Robert: jt. auth., 2014

STRAHORN, CARRIE ADELL: 1590

STRANG, HERBERT (pseud.). Pseud. of George Herbert Ely and C. J. L. 'Estrange. The pseud. sometimes also encompasses a third writer. 1585 (ed.)

*Stranger than fiction*, 396

STRATHCONA AND MOUNT ROYAL, DONALD ALEXANDER SMITH, 1st baron of (1820-1914). Businessman and politician. Born in Scotland; entered H.B.C.'s service at an early age; later became its gov.; was a special com. during first Riel Rebellion, 1869-70; 1870 was member of first Executive Council of N.W.T.; 1871-84 in Man. legislature and also M.P. in H. of C. to 1896; chancellor of McGill and of Aberdeen Univ.; director of many companies. (Ww, 1897-1916) 799 (plaintiff). *See below*

Strathcona and Mount Royal, Donald Alexander Smith, 1st baron of: defendant, 750. *See above*

Strathcona School (Vancouver): 2113

*Ein Streifzug durch den Nordwesten Amerikas*, 664

*The strength of Canadian Douglas Fir*, 1146

Strikes and lockouts: 1772

Stromstadt, Dazie M., see Brown, Dazie M. (Stromstadt)

STRONG, JAMES CLARK (b. 1826): 1085

Stuart River: 1177

STUTFIELD, HUGH EDWARD MILLINGTON (1858-1929): 1519

Submarine cable, *see* Pacific cable

Successful digger: 168

Suffrage: pam. on, 101

Sugar: 2044

*Suggestions on the inter-colonial railway*, 165

SULLIVAN, EDWARD ALAN (1868-1947). Auth., engineer. Native of Montreal; spent youth in far North; worked for C.P.R. for many years; lived in England and travelled on Continent; 1941 won gov.-gen. medal for *Three came to Ville Marie;* wrote under pseud. "Sinclair Murray." (P; EC; VF) 1763, 1858

Sumas: history of, 2029

*Summer suns in the far West*, 854

Summerland: history of, 1835

Sun, Goon: 1338

*The superficial geology of British Columbia and adjacent regions*, 593

*Supplemental charter* [of the Bank of British Columbia], 222

Supreme court, *see* British Columbia. Supreme Court; Canada Supreme Court.

Surrey (municipality): history and pioneers of, 2037; *also see* North Surrey

*Survey of boundary line between Alaska and British Columbia*, 1180

*Survey of the northwestern boundary of the United States*, 1459

Surveying: for C.P.R., 459, 874, 1627, 1641; C.P.R. instructions for (1871), 377; in fiction, 798, 1971; history of, 1934; of Nanaimo district (1860?), 121; pioneer surveyors of V.I., 1908; report on Cowichan Valley (1860), 135; in Selkirks, 878, 1548; of the Stikine River (1868), 298; of V.I., 89; Victoria to Fort Alexander, via North Bentinck Arm, 210

Surveyors' association: 911

*Surveys and mapping in British Columbia resources*, 1934

Sutherland, Neil: jt. auth., 1975

SWAN, JAMES GILCHRIST (1818-1900). Studied Indians and their language and contributed articles to Smithsonian Inst. In 1850 went to Calif. from Mass., then to the Northwest in 1852 as customs collector; was probate judge; 1883 sent by U.S. Nat. Mus., accompanied by James Deans, to Queen Charlotte Is. to collect specimens of natural history and objects of Indian manufacture; many of the specimens in his ethnological collection were described by A. P. Niblack in his work on the coast Indians of southern Alaska and northern British Columbia which appeared in the Nat. Mus. annual report for 1888. (Guy Allison, *Forgotten great man of Washington history, James G. Swan* (Longview, Longview Daily News c1951)) 54, 470

SWANSON, ROBERT E. Mechanical engineer, chief inspector of railways, writer. Born at East Wellington; worked as a machinist then studied engineering; invented a locomotive and a steamship whistle "Air Chimes"; the whistle on the centennial train (1967) giving the first notes of "O Canada" was his invention. (VF) 1829

Swanton, John Reed (1873-1958). Anthropologist and ethnologist. Doctorate from Harvard; interested in mythology, and linguistics; an associate of Franz Boas; was on staff of Smithsonian Inst. from 1900. (WhA)   1357

SWARTOUT, MELVIN (d. 1904). Presbyterian missionary amongst the Indians of the Barkley Sound area, V.I., learned their language. (VF)   1380

Swedes: 1663

Syllabic characters, *see* shorthand

SYNGE, MILLINGTON HENRY (1823-1907). An officer in the Royal Engineers at Bytown (Ottawa) in 1848; his interest was in the defense and development of Canada; auth. of several pamphlets on these subjects; was son of Sir Edward Synge, 2d bart. (Bup; Wa; P)   10, 30, 31, 149

*Synods; their constitution and objects,* 463

*Synopsis of the birds of Vancouver Island,* 301

*Table of distances [to forks of Thompson River],* 79

TACOMA. PORT ORCHARD NAVIGATION CO.: 1381

Taft: history of, 2047

Tagish Indian language: 746

Tahkaht Indian language: 311

Tahltan Indian language: vocabulary of, 746

TAKAHASHI, K. T.: 1315

*Tales from the totems of the Hidery,* 1416

*Tales of conflict,* 1892

*Tales of the Alberni Valley,* 1922

*Tales of the British Columbia frontier,* 1748

*Tales of the Kootenays,* 1790

TANGHE, RAYMOND (1898- ). Librarian. Born in France and educated there; 1924 graduated from Univ of Montreal; 1928 Ph.D. in economics; director, Maison des Etudiants Canadiens, Cité Internationale de l'Université de Paris; 1918-20 served in French army; asst. librarian, National Library of Canada; then national librarian. (Cd; 1964-66)   2104 (comp.)

TANNER, HENRY. Prof. at Inst. of Agric., London. In 1886 came to B.C. for the Dom. gov't with the task of interesting "persons of property" to emigrate from England; he had already reported on Ont. and the Northwest Territories for the gov't and believed that wealthy Englishmen would buy out Ont. farmers who would then settle in the West. (Vic. *Colonist,* 18 Sept. 1886, p. 3)   762

Tappen: history of, 1999

Tariffs: on fish and fish-oils, 496; *also see* Customs

TASSE, JOSEPH (1848-1895). Journalist, politician, historian. Born in Montreal; educated Bourget College, Rigaud, Lower Canada; 1869-72 assoc. ed. of *La Minerve* and later ed.; 1878-87 member of H. of C.; 1891-5 in Senate; charter member of Roy. Soc. of Can. (Waa; Wa; Cy; Cc)   402

TATE, CAROLINE SARAH (KNOTT) (1850-1930). Wife of Rev. Charles Montgomery Tate. Born in London; went as a child in 1862 to Hamilton, Ont.; 1877 came to B.C. for mission work at Port Simpson. (VF; Van. *Province,* 28 Feb. 1933)   1586

TATE, CHARLES MONTGOMERY (1852-1933). Methodist missionary born in Yorkshire. In 1870 came to B.C. and was influenced by the work of Thomas Crosby; 1879 ordained, and worked among Indians; founded a boarding school which later became Coqualeetza Indian Residential School at Sardis; advocate of better treatment for Indians. (VF)   845, 1382, 1560

TAYLOR, GORDON DE RUPE (1923- ): 2050

Taylor, Harry, *see* Taylor, Henry Edwin

TAYLOR, HENRY EDWIN (1889- ): 2105

TAYLOR, JAMES PATTON (1844- ): 1732

TAYLOR, JAMES WICKES (1819-1893). Am. consular officer. (Waa; DAB; Apa; A)   124

TEICHMANN, EMIL (1845-1924): 1684

TEIT, JAMES ALEXANDER (1864-1922). Anthropologist. Worked with Dr. Franz Boas; had considerable knowledge of Thompson Indians; worked for Anthropological Div. of the Nat. Mus. of Can. in the Thompson R. and Stikine R. areas. (Roy. Soc. of Can. *Proc. and trans.,* 3d ser., v. 39, 1945, p. 91)   1240, 1383

Teit, James: 1357, 1617

Telegraph, *see* Overland communication

Telegraph company: 1809

Telegraph Trail: 1238, 2070

*Telegraphic correspondence . . . seal fishing . . . 1892,* 983

Telephone companies: 586, 605, 891, 903, 1208

*Telephone exchange; rules, regulations,* 605

Temperance: 110, 694

Temperance organizations: 951, 962

*Ten years' wild sports in foreign lands,* 840

*Tenant-farmer delegates' visit to Canada in 1890,* 919

*Tenders for works on the Canadian Pacific Railway,* 565

Ténné, *see* Athapaskan Indians

Tennis club: 1012

*The tenth decade; a dramatic pageant,* 1854

Terminal City Club (Vancouver): 1765

Terms of union with Canada: 305, 473, 571, 596, 1950, 2036; league for preservation of, 454; *also see* Carnarvon terms

TERRY GEORGE: 2051 (comp.)

*Testimonials; Dr. W. F. Tolmie,* 385

*Testimonials for J. W. Laing,* 1249

*Texada,* 2106

*Texada Iron Mines, British Columbia,* 487

Texada Island: desc., 815; history of, 2106

TEXADA ISLAND CENTENNIAL COMMITTEE: 2106

Theatre: history of, 2107

Theatre company: 674

Waddington, Alfred: pub. on, 1740; report of, 191.
*See above*
Waddington Samuel: 1428
WADE, FREDERICK COATE (1860-1924).
Lawyer, editorial writer. Born in Bowmanville;
1882 graduate of Univ. of Toronto; 1886 called
to bar in Man.; 1897-1901 legal adviser to Yukon
Council; 1902 a K. C.; 1903 one of the counsels
for Br. on Alaskan Boundary Tribunal; 1918-24
agent gen. for B.C. in London. (P; Mo, 1912;
Wa; Waa)    1620
WADE, MARK SWEETEN (1858-1929). Physician,
historian, ed. Born in Sunderland, England;
graduate of Durham Univ.; studied medicine at
Anderson's College and Royal Infirmary; 1881
came to Canada; 1882 graduate of Fort Wayne
Medical College; did postgraduate work at Univ.
of Toronto; 1883 settled in Victoria, then
practised in Surrey and in Clinton 1885-9; 1889-
95 in Victoria as ophthalmic surgeon and medical
officer for B.C.; 1895-1929 in Kamloops; ed. of
*Inland Sentinel* 1898-1912. (P; Wa; VF)    905,
1562, 1734. *See below*
Wade, Mark Sweeten: history of Kamloops, 1607.
*See above*
*Wagon road north,* 2090
WAGSTAFF, JOHN (d. 1925?). Vicar of Christ
Church, Macclesfield. During 1868-83 curate and
vicar at churches in Westmoreland, Cumberland,
Durham; 1883-96 vicar of Christ Church,
Macclesfield and chaplain of the infirmary; 1896-
rector of Whittonstall, Ebchester,
Northumberland. (Co, 1882-1916; Cr, 1910-25)
960
*Wah-kee-nah and her people,* 1085
WAITES, KENNETH ARTHUR. Educated in
Victoria; at Victoria High School in the 1920's.
(Private information)    1808
Wakashan Indian languages: bibliography of, 1130
WALBRAN, JOHN THOMAS (1848-1913).
Educated at Ripon grammar school; 1881
became master mariner; 1888 came to B.C. as
chief officer of "Islander"; 1891 employed by
federal Dept. of Marine and Fisheries; concerned
with lighthouses, buoys, fisheries, etc., along B.C.
coast. (Wa; EC)    1578
WALKEM, GEORGE ANTHONY (1834-1908).
Lawyer, politician. Born in Ireland; 1847 his
father came to Canada as surveyor on staff of
Royal Engineers; educated in Montreal; attended
McGill Univ.; 1858 called to bar of Lower
Canada; 1861 called to bar of Upper Canada;
1862 went to Victoria; called to B.C. bar 1863;
1864-70 in Legislative Council for Cariboo East;
a strong advocate of confederation; 1871
elected to Legislative Assembly; 1872 chief com.
of Lands; 1872-4 att.-gen.; 1874 F.R.G.S.;
succeeded De Cosmos as premier, 1874-6; then
leader of Opposition; advocated the completion

of C.P.R.; 1878-82 again premier; 1882
appointed to Supreme Court of B.C.; 1903
retired. (EC; Cc, 1886)    766 (plaintiff). *See
below*
Walkem, George Anthony: 480; plaintiff, 751. *See
above*
WALKEM, WILLIAM WYMOND (1850-1919).
Auth., politician, physician. Received M.D. from
Queen's Univ. 1873; a medical health officer; a
coroner during Nanaimo mine disaster 1887;
M.L.A. for Nanaimo 1894. (VF; Wa; Cc, 1894)
1621
Walker, C. M.: report re Northwest Boundary
Commission, 334
Walker, Samuel: plaintiff, 607
WALKER, THEODORA SPENCER: 1906
WALKER, WALTER JAMES (b. 1852-    ).
Accountant, notary public, alderman. Born in
Halifax, England; attended Commercial College,
Rippendon; 1885 went to New Westminster;
1886 appointed city auditor; later established his
own accountancy and real estate firm; 1891
elected alderman; appointed to police com.; chn.
of Finance, Railway and Ferry Committee; chn.
of Board of School Trustees. (*British Columbia
directory, 1892,* p. 1145)    961
WALLACE, JAMES NEVIN (1870-1941). Surveyor
and historian. Graduate of Trinity College,
Dublin; 1895 came to Canada from Ireland;
1900 in charge of Alberta division for baseline
and meridian surveys; made survey for Sask.
border and was in charge of levelling operations
in the West 1912-24; 1925-32 in Ottawa;
returned to Alberta. (P; Wa)    1705
WALTER, MARGARET (SHAW): 1860
WALTON, AVIS CARROLL (GRAY): Born in
Winnipeg, dau. of former mayor, Charles Gray;
proprietor of an advertising agency in Victoria.
(Vic. *Times,* 16 May 1956)    2058 (ed.)
The Wanderer (pseud.), *see* Lord, John Keast
WARDMAN, GEORGE (b. 1838): 675
*The warm land,* 2072
WARREN, GORDON B.: 1648
"Warspite" (ship): 944
WASHINGTON (STATE) NATIONAL GUARD:
2173
WASHINGTON (TERRITORY) GOVERNOR,
1867-1869 (Moore): 348
WASHINGTON (TERRITORY) LEGISLATIVE
ASSEMBLY: 319
*Washington historical quarterly,* 1553
*Water over the wheel,* 2156
Water works: 844
Waterworks company: 955
WATKIN, SIR EDWARD WILLIAM (1819-1901).
Statesman; pres. of Grand Trunk Railway; an
M.P. in Br.; a director of several railways;
interested in the confederation of the B.N.A.
colonies and the construction of the

Intercolonial Railway; visited Canada in 1851, 1861, and 1875. (P; Mo, 1898) 767. *See below*

Watkin, Sir Edward William: 1676; and the H.B.C., 511. *See above*

Watson, Alexander, treasurer, V.I.: 280

WATSON, SIR CHARLES MOORE (1844-1916). Soldier, administrator. Educated at Trinity College, Dublin; 1866 in Royal Engineers; saw service in Egypt to 1886; 1886-91 gov.-gen., Red Sea littoral; 1891-1902 insp. of fortifications. (DNB) 1579

Watson, Muriel: auth., 2117

WATTERS, REGINALD EYRE (1912- ): 2059 (ed.)

*The Wawa shorthand first reading book*, 1223

*The Wawa shorthand instructor*, 1224

Wawa shorthand, *see* Shorthand *under* in Duployan shorthand

WEBB, WILLIAM SEWARD (1851-1926). Capitalist. Born in N.Y.; studied medicine in Europe 1871-2; pres. of several railway and transportation companies. (DNAA) 906

WEILER, JOHN (FIRM): 606

Weir, Craig: ed., 2119

*Die weise Grenze*, 1728

Welch, Andrew: 730

WELLCOME, SIR HENRY SOLOMON (1853?-1936). Manufacturing chemist and patron of science; interested in archaeology and Indians; engaged in a lengthy legal struggle on behalf of a dispossessed tribe from Ft. Simpson. (DNB) 768. *See below*

Wellcome, Sir Henry Solomon: papers of, 2158. *See above*

Wells, Allen Casey: 2159

WELLS, OLIVER: 135. *See below*

Wells, Oliver: report of V.I. survey, 89. *See above*

WELLS, OLIVER NELSON. A grandson of Allen Casey Wells, who came to B.C. in 1867 and established a large dairy farm in the Chilliwack area; operates part of the former farm; was named citizen of the year by Chilliwack Chamber of Commerce as a progressive farmer and a local historian. (Van. *Province*, 20 Feb. 1967, p. 8) 2159

Wellwood, W. B.: 1792

Welsh: 2004

*Welsh gold miners in British Columbia*, 2004

Wessel, Mrs. H.: 1947

"West Indian" (ship): 963

*The western Avernus*, 757

*Western Canada*, 1561

WESTERN CANADA PRESS ASSOCIATION: 1454

*A western Delilah*, 1671

*The Western Division of the Canadian Pacific Railway*, 662

Western Federation of Miners: 1376

*The western recorder*, 1455

*Western recreation*, 1324

*Western shores; narratives of the Pacific coast*, 1736

*Western wanderings; a record of travel*, 449

*Western world*, 907

WESTMINSTER CLUB: 1013

Weston, Sydney: 1900

Westwold (formerly Grand Prairie): history, 1843, 1947

WETHERELL, JUNE PAT (1909- ). Was born and grew up in Bellingham, Wash. (Book jacket) 1916

Whale-fishery: 469

WHEELER, ARTHUR OLIVER (1860-1945). Topographer, mountaineer, auth., lecturer. In 1876 came to Canada from Ireland; 1881 qualified as land surveyor and specialized in topographical work from 1885; made surveys in Crow's Nest Pass, Selkirks, Rockies, Alaska, Yukon and Coast Mts.; 1913-25 was B.C. com. on Alberta-B.C. boundary; 1906 founded Alpine Club of Canada and was pres. until 1910; F.R.G.S.; organized exhibits from Canada at the Congress of Alpinism. (EC; *Can. alpine jour.*, v. 21, 1944-5, p. 140-146) 1548

*When fur was king*, 1718

*When the steel went through*, 1862

*Where the buffalo roamed*, 1569

*Where trails meet; Sumas, Abbotsford, Matsqui*, 2029

White, James: 1602

*White Pass & Yukon route*, 1442

White Pass & Yukon Railway: 1568, 1689, 1991

WHITE, THOMAS (1830-1888). Born in Montreal; studied law; active in municipal affairs in Peterboro and Montreal; 1864 founded the Hamilton *Spectator;* 1869 was emigration agent of Can. gov't; 1870 assumed control of Montreal *Gazette;* 1878 elected to H. of C.; after the second Riel Rebellion reorganized the government of the N.W.T. (P; Wa; Cc, 1885) 447

White, Thomas: speech of, 583

WHITE, TRUMBULL (1868-1941). Am. ed. and explorer. City ed. of papers in Illinois, Indiana; 1903-1906 ed. of *Red book;* 1906-1909 ed. of *Appleton's magazine;* travelled extensively. (Waa; Bua; WhA; Ww, v. 1) 1397

WHITE, WILLIAM (1830-1912). Civil servant. Born in London; came to Canada in 1854; in Post Office Dept.; became its sec., then deputy minister of dept. (Waa; Wa; Mo, 1912) 408 (comp.)

WHITEAVES, JOSEPH FREDERICK (1835-1909). Palaeontologist. Born in Oxford; 1862 emigrated to Montreal; curator of the Mus. of Montreal Natural Hist. Soc.; 1876 appointed to staff of Geol. Survey of Can.; one of the original fellows of the Roy. Soc. of Can.; 1900 McGill conferred degree. (Waa; Wa; Mo, 1898) 1093

*Whitewater men of the Skeena*, 2099

Whitlow, Mrs. E. N.: jt. auth., 2116

Whittaker, Lance H.: 1896
*Who's who in western Canada,* 1592
*Why not sweetheart?,* 1485
WHYMPER, FREDERICK (b. 1838- ). Artist, traveller, explorer. In 1864 accompanied Robert Brown as artist on the exploring expedition on V.I. (W) 320
*A wide dominion,* 1404
*Wila yelth; gigiangwaklthum hialthukq,* 1150
WILCOX, WALTER DWIGHT (1869-1949). An honorary member of the Alpine Club of Canada; his record of first ascents in the Canadian Rockies numbered more than twenty. (*Can. alpine jour.,* v. 33, 1950, p. 130-133) 1250, 1480
WILD, ROLAND GIBSON (1903- ). Newspaperman, press correspondent, auth. Born in Yorkshire; newspaper man in England; war correspondent during Afghan revolution in late 1920's; during World War II was press chief of psychological warfare; 1947 came to Canada; 1954 made an around the world tour for newspaper and magazine reports. (Van. *Herald,* 27 Sept. 1955, p. 8) 1927, 2060
*The wild north land,* 415
*Wilderness men,* 2033
*William Duncan, founder,* 1982
*William Pearce manuscript,* 1682
WILLIAMS, C. E. H.: 1917
WILLIAMS, J. RAE: 2083
WILLIAMS, JOHN G. (b. 1824). Farmer, sailor, prospector. In 1841 left eastern Can. farm and went on a whaling ship to Azores and Australia; 1849 went to Calif. gold fields, Australia, Boston; returned to Calif.; went to Cariboo, prospected near Hope and then along the Thompson R.; returned to Boston; settled down in Charlestown and had his own business there. (His book, *The adventures of a seventeen-year-old lad*) 1140
Williams, Frederick: 587
Williams, Robert Taylor: comp., 624; pub., 739, 802
Williams Lake: 209, 2051
*The Williams' official British Columbia directory,* 624
*Williams' Vancouver & New Westminster cities directory,* 908
*Williams' Victoria and Nanaimo cities directory,* 909
Wilmot, Samuel: chn. fishery com., 1025
Wilson, Sir Charles William: book on, 1579
WILSON, EDWARD FRANCIS: An Anglican clergyman who was living on Galiano Is. at the time of the publication of his book; went to Galiano Is. in 1894. (Vic. *Colonist,* 27 Feb. 1895, p. 2) 1183 (comp.)
Wilson, Edward F.: 677
WILSON, F. A. Capt. in British army. (P) 20
WILSON, NEILL COMPTON (1889- ): 1959 (ed.)
WILSON, WILLIAM: 471
WILSON, WILLIAM: 851
Winfield: history, 1989

Wing Chong: 704
*Winged canoes at Nootka,* 1956
*The Winnipeg and North Pacific Railway,* 846
*A winter trip on the Canadian Pacific Railway,* 721
WISHART, ANDREW: 1094
WITHROW, WILLIAM HENRY (1839-1908). Methodist minister, auth., journalist. Born in Toronto; graduate of Univ. of Toronto; 1866-74 had various charges; 1874 ed. of *Canadian Methodist magazine;* 1884 F.R.S.C. (Mo, 1898) 852, 1184 (ed.)
Wolff, Martin: trans., 158
Wolley, Sir Clive Oldnall Long Phillipps, *see* Phillipps-Wolley, Sir Clive Oldnall Long
*A woman's trip to Alaska . . . 1890,* 868
WOMEN'S CHRISTIAN TEMPERANCE UNION OF BRITISH COLUMBIA: 962
WOMEN'S INSTITUTE. CANADA. FRUITVALE WOMEN'S INSTITUTE, B.C.: 2061
WOMEN'S INSTITUTE. CANADA. WESTWOLD WOMEN'S INSTITUTE, B.C.: 1947
Wood, Charles B.: letter of, 144
WOOD, EDMUND BURKE (1820-1882). Chief justice of Manitoba, 1874-82. In 1848 called to bar of Upper Canada; 1863-67 in Legislative Assembly; 1867-72 in H. of C. and in Legislative Assembly of Ont. as prov. treasurer; 1874-82 chief justice of Man. (Wa; P; *Dominion annual register,* 1882; Apa) 448
Wood, J. T.: tenant-farmer delegate, 919
WOODMAN, ABBY (JOHNSON) (b. 1828): 853
WOODS, CHARLES THOMAS (1825-1895). Anglican clergyman and headmaster. In 1860 came to B.C. to be headmaster of Boy's Collegiate School, Victoria, under Bishop Hills, officiating at St. John's Church and in Esquimalt and Saanich; 1868 made archdeacon of Diocese of B.C.; moved to Sapperton; rector of St. Mary's Church there and Holy Trinity Cathedral in New Westminster and was chaplain to the penitentiary and asylum. (VF) 488, 518
WOODS, JOHN JEX (1895- ). Supt. Saanichton Experimental Farm. Born in Vancouver; graduate of U.B.C. (M.S.A.); 1925-41 asst. supt. Agassiz Experimental Farm. (VF) 1817
WOODSWORTH, CHARLES JAMES (1909- ). Born in Winnipeg; son of James S. Woodsworth, founder of the C.C.F.; educated at College of Ottawa and at Aurora; 1932 B.A. from Univ. of Manitoba; 1939 Ph.D. London School of Economics; 1944-6 in research div. of Br. Ministry of Information at Singapore, New Delhi, Ceylon; 1948-55 on editorial staffs of Vancouver *Province,* Winnipeg *Tribune,* Ottawa *Citizen;* 1956 joined Dept. of External Affairs; member of Can. Inst. of International Affairs; 1960 on Can. com. to the International Truce Supervisory Commission in Vietnam; 1965 ambassador to S. Africa. (Cd, 1960, 1964-66) 1818

WOODWARD, HENRY: 1251
Woodward's stores: 2019
*Work in the colonies*, 264
*The work of the Royal Engineers in British Columbia*, 1582
WORKINGMEN'S PROTECTIVE ASSOCIATION (VICTORIA): 547
*Wrangell and the gold of the Cassiar*, 1771
WRIGHT, EDGAR WILSON (1863-1930): 1185 (ed.)
Wright, George Edwards: pub., 725
Wright, Mary Carr: jt. auth., 1983
WRIGLEY, HOWARD: 963
Wrigley, J.: 827
Wybrow, Alexander: 1581
WYMAN, GILBERT: 1398 (comp.)
Wyse, John. Ed. of *Queen Charlotte Islands* by Francis Poole; used the pseud. of "John W. Lyndon." 401
*Yakasinkinmiki*, 968
Yale: 731, 1701, 1936, 2147
Yale convention: 305
Yale district: 783
YALE LILLOOET DISTRICT PIONEER SOCIETY: 1186

*Year Book of British Columbia and manual of provincial information*, 1285
The year book of British Columbia; compendium (cov. t.), 1284
*A year in the great republic*, 732
*Yearbook and proceedings of the ... convention*, 962
*Yika qāyīlelas ... The Acts of the Apostles translated into ... Kwagutl*, 1257
Young, Charles Bedford: 214
Young, Rosalind Watson: 1552
*The young surveyor*, 1971
*The Yukaghir and the Yukaghirized Tungus*, 1357
Yukaghir tribe: 1357
Yukon and Alaska Publishing Co.: 1343
*Le Yukon et son or*, 1374
*Yukon gold fields; handbook of information*, 1273
*Yukon gold fields; map showing*, 1298
*The Yukon route via Kamloops*, 1313
*The Yukon story; a sourdough's record*, 2163
*The Yukon territory: the narrative of W. H. Dall*, 1399
*Zigzag journeys in the great Northwest*, 860
Zimshian Indian language, *see* Tsimshian Indian language
*A Zimshian version of portions of the Book of Common prayer*, 866
Zoology: 469; *also see* Birds; Fish

*Book design by E.W. Harrison*

*Printed on "Strathmore Impress" paper*

*Text in Linotype Times Roman Type*

*End sheet "British Columbia Government Buildings" courtesy*
*of British Columbia Provincial Archives*

*Printed and bound in Canada by Evergreen Press Limited, Vancouver, B.C.*

PRINTED IN CANADA